BIRMINGHAM
PALS

Best wishes

Terry Carter

DISCARDED

BIRMINGHAM
PALS

14th, 15th & 16th (Service) Battalions
of the Royal Warwickshire Regiment
A HISTORY OF THE THREE CITY BATTALIONS
RAISED IN BIRMINGHAM IN WORLD WAR ONE

TERRY CARTER

Pen & Sword Books Limited

Also available in the same series:

Accrington Pals: **The 11th (Service) Battalion (Accrington)**
The East Lancashire Regiment *by William Turner*
Barnsley Pals: **The 13th & 14th (Service) Battalions (Barnsley)**
The York & Lancaster Regiment *by Jon Cooksey*
Sheffield City: **The 12th (Service) Battalion (Sheffield)**
The York & Lancaster Regiment *by Paul Oldfield and Ralph Gibson*
Liverpool Pals: **A History of the 17th, 18th, 19th & 20th Service Battalions**
The King's (Liverpool Regiment) *by Graham Maddocks*
Leeds Pals: **A History of the 15th (Service) Battalion**
The Prince of Wales's Own (West Yorkshire Regiment) *by Laurie Milner*
Salford Pals: **A History of the 15th, 16th, 19th & 20th Battalions**
Lancashire Fusiliers *by Michael Stedman*
Manchester Pals: **The 16th, 17th, 18th, 19th, 20th, 21st, 22nd & 23rd**
Battalions of the Manchester Regiment *by Michael Stedman*
Tyneside Irish: **The 24th, 25th, 26th, 27th, 30th,**
Battalions of the Northumberland Fusiliers *by John D Sheen*

First published in Great Britain in 1997 by Pen & Sword Books Limited,
47 Church Street, Barnsley, South Yorkshire S70 2AS

Copyright © Terry Carter 1997

For up-to-date information on other titles produced under Pen & Sword
and Leo Cooper imprints, please telephone or write to:
Pen & Sword Books Ltd
FREEPOST
47 Church Street
Barnsley
South Yorkshire
S70 2BR
Telephone (24 hours): 01226 734555

ISBN 0-85052-547-0

British Library Cataloguing in Publication Data

Printed by Yorkshire Web
47 Church Street, Barnsley, South Yorkshire S70 2AS

Contents

Below: A Company, 2nd Birmingham Battalion (15th Royal Warwicks) on their final parade before embarkation to France. Codford Camp (Salisbury Plain), Friday 19 November 1915. The officers from left to right are: Captain P C Edwards DCM, Lieutenant C W Davis, Second Lieutenant A H Handford, Lieutenant I E Rubery, Lieutenant W L Hemus and Second Lieutenant E G Crisp

Foreword

EVERY POPPY DAY me and my brother would be called to Our Dad. He'd sit us down and open a 'baccy tin which contained medals, newspaper cuttings and a certificate of membership for the Old Contemptibles. That name fascinated us and each year Dad would tell us what it meant. He explained how a small number of British soldiers had been sent to France when war broke out in 1914, and how the Kaiser had boasted that he would sweep 'that contemptible little army into the sea'. With colly-wobbles in our tummies and with shivers running down our backs we listened as Dad described how those lads from Britain and Ireland had battled and held up the might of the German Army. Dad always finished by saying that after the war those men who survived decided to keep in touch and ironically called their association the Old Contemptibles.

My Grandad was an Old Contemptible and the medals in the tin were his. With the rest of the 2nd Battalion Coldstream Guards he was part of 4 (Guards) Brigade, 2nd Division, I Corps, British Expeditionary Force. He landed in France on 13 August and over the next few months was involved in heavy fighting from the Aisne to the First Battle of Ypres. We have his letters. Like most other soldiers, they were addressed to his Mum and invariably they ended with an appeal for news about the Villa and the Blues.

Grandad's war ended in the autumn of 1915 when he was badly wounded at Loos, up to that time the biggest battle in which the British Army had fought. By then the Birmingham City Battalions had landed in France. All volunteers, they had flocked to fight for King and Country and to defend 'little Belgium'. It is an easy thing now to dismiss their patriotism, their sense of duty, their commitment to their City's honour and their determination never to let down their pals. No-one should do so. They were brave, honourable men and their names shall live on thanks to the work of Terry Carter. We shall remember.

DR CARL CHINN
Community Historian
The University of Birmingham

Below: Neville Chamberlain (centre) Lord Mayor of Birmingham, William Bowater (stout gentleman in uniform, centre left) the Deputy Lord Mayor and the Bishop of Birmingham (dog collar) pictured with the officers of the 2nd Birmingham Battalion (15th Royal Warwicks) at Codford Camp, Friday 19 November 1915.

Prelude

The Last Days of Peace

'The visit of the British Fleet to Kiel is a good omen, it indicates a marked improvement in the relations between Great Britain and Germany, and on this score affords the liveliest satisfaction. A couple of years ago such an exchange of courtesies as these now taking place in the Baltic would have been impossible, and the fact that the Kaiser is evincing a keen personal interest at the visit, is in evidence of his anxiety to promote the new spirit of cordiality which has sprung up between the two nations. An optimistic correspondent declares that Mr Winston Churchill's policy is finding the warmest commendation on the other side of the North Sea, and with the German return Naval calls in the Autumn, Europe will be in the midst of a new era. We hope he correctly interprets the situation, for there is no reason why such keen European rivals as Germany and Great Britain should not be the Best of Friends.'

Birmingham Evening Despatch,
Thursday 25th June 1914

The editorial quoted above, concerned the visit to the British Warship, HMS *King George V*, by the Emperor of Germany, Kaiser Wilhelm II. He was met on the quarter-deck by Vice Admiral Sir George Warrender. Naval etiquette required that the Union flag should be flown at the masthead of the battleship, thus denoting that the most senior British Naval Officer was now aboard. The officer in question was in fact the Kaiser, he held the honorary rank of Admiral of the Fleet in the Royal Navy.

The *King George V*, was in a class of ships known as Dreadnoughts. In 1906 Great Britain led the world in sea power with the completion of HMS *Dreadnought*, the first super Battleship of its type. It had 300mm thick armour plate, ten 12 inch guns and was faster than any other ship in the world of a similar size. Subsequently all other ships in the Royal Navy that were built in this style were known as Dreadnoughts. It was the first time that the Kaiser had inspected such a ship. In an hour long visit he inspected the crew, toured the upper deck and signed his name in the ship's book. Before leaving he chatted to Sir George and fellow officers about his love of the sea and sailing, and gossiped about old acquaintances in London.

That evening, Sir George Warrender and all the officers of the British naval ships at Kiel were entertained aboard the German Flagship, *Friedrich der Grosse*. Earlier the crews of both British and German vessels held an athletic meet-

Below: British battleship of the Dreadnought Class, *King George V*. IWM Q39387

Above: Men of the 2nd Battalion the Royal Warwickshire Regiment go ashore at Scutari, Albania as part of the International peace keeping force in June 1914.

Right: The German Emperor with two of his admirals; Admiral von Tirpitz, Grand Naval Minister and Admiral von Holtzendorf, Commander-in-Chief of the German High Sea Fleet.

ing at the town's Municipal Sports Ground. Two football matches also took place.

The visit of the Royal Navy culminated with a special luncheon, given by the city of Kiel, on 27 June 1914. In a speech, the German Grand Admiral von Koesler said that, 'the German Navy would ever strive to model itself upon the example set by Nelson, and to work upon his principles.' He was pleased that the relations between the British and German 'Bluejackets' were the best imaginable.

The following day, Sunday 28 June, in the Bosnian capitol of Sarajevo, the heir to the Austrian throne, Archduke Franz Ferdinand, and his wife were murdered. They were shot by the seventeen year old student, Gavrilo Princip (who, incidently, was to die of tuberculosis in 1918, whilst in prison).

June 1914, also saw the formation of what was known as the 'International Force'. As a result of the Balkan Wars, Albania had received its independence from the Ottoman Empire in July 1913. Consequently, an internal conflict broke out between Albanians and Montenegrins. Similar to the present United Nations Protection Force, the Force was sent in to keep the peace. The Force con-

sisted of a battalion each from Italy and Austria: a detachment of French Infantry: two companies of German Marines: the band and two companies from the 2nd Battalion, the Royal Warwickshire Regiment.

The HQ of this peace-keeping force was in the town of Scutari, in a fortification known as the Citadel. In 1924 an unidentified 2nd Royal Warwicks Officer contributed the following to the regimental magazine, *The Antelope*, concerning the Battalion's involvement in this period of 'entente' so close to the outbreak of war:

'The country around Scutari is well wooded and water is plentiful. It was a very pleasant life, and the men got on well with the soldiers of other nationalities, carrying on their conversations in an unknown language as only a British soldier can do. They were most friendly with the French and Austrians, with whom we were stationed in some old Turkish barracks.

A considerable number of the German and Austrian NCOs spoke English well, and I was informed by a German that as a punishment for small offences they were given the task of English to learn.

A somewhat unusual sight was to see the flags of the five nations flying side by side on the Citadel.

The German officers took great interest in everthing we did, and as their mess was next door to ours they frequently came in to see us and asked numerous questions as to how we did things and about the army in general. As they had no band with them they asked if they might come route marching with us twice a week, which they were given permission so to do. When the band stopped playing their officers would give the word of command and they would begin to sing.

On Saturday July 4th (six days after the Archduke's assasination in Sarajevo), we received sudden orders to leave Scutari, being ordered to march thirty-five miles the following day and embark on a ship which would be waiting for us.

On hearing this, the German officers

Left: Flags of Great Britain and Germany flying together in 1914.

invited us to dinner that night, and gave us a very cheery time. They asked us why we were leaving so suddenly, but no mention was made of war. We had no knowledge of what had happened, but suspected that if war had not already been declared, it was about to be.'

In Birmingham, on Monday 29 June, the story of the assassination had made the headline news in the morning editions of the local press. Perhaps the more important news on this morning for the young men of the City was that the American Jack Johnson had retained the World Heavyweight Boxing title. Another item of interest may have been that work was soon to start on ground improvements to Aston Villa Football Club, thus

Left: German marines, part of the International Peace Keeping Force, goosestepping through the streets of Scutari, Albania, in the summer of 1914.

making it the best ground in the country. When completed the new ground capacity would be, by today's standards, a staggering 104,000 spectators. But, as the days rolled by, reports were published on possible repercussions from the assassination, 'war clouds on the horizon', was a typical headline. War was certainly not in the minds of these young men. It was now summer, cloth caps were being exchanged for straw-boaters. Thoughts were now focused on holidays, it was time for the seaside and girls.

Yet, a war was coming; a complex political sequence of events was now taking place across Europe. The explanation I am glad to say, is not the objective of this book. Within thirty-seven days of the assassination in Sarajevo, came the outbreak of the most destructive military conflict that Europe and the world was to experience so far. Backed up with the full commitment of modern industrial production and popular support of the general public and political powers of the time; for the Allies and central powers alike.

Akin to the rest of the United Kingdom, Birmingham responded admirably to the call of arms. The following four and a half years, the period of the Great War, cost Birmingham the lives of nearly 13,000 of her sons; with a further 36,000 suffering permanent disability from severe wounds.

Below: Corporation Street, Birmingham prior to the First World War. When developed it was hailed as the 'showpiece of the municipality.'

Chapter One

Birmingham

By 1914 Birmingham had been a City for twenty-five years. When the City boundaries were expanded in 1911, to include the suburbs of Aston, Erdington, Handsworth, Kings Norton and Northfield, the population had increased to 922,000. Birmingham had now become second only to London.

'City of 1001 trades', 'workshop of the world', 'toy shop of Europe' (toys being small iron-ware products) and 'best governed city in the world' were all expressions given to describe Birmingham over the years. Tradionally it is Birmingham's Industrial heritage that is remembered by historians, but by 1914, Birmingham was also established in products that delighted the palate: for example Bird's Custard, HP Sauce, Typhoo Tea and Cadbury's Chocolate. The City was now at its pinnacle of civic development. Corporation Street, the showpiece of the Municipality, was developed only a few years before, stretching from New Street Station to Gosta Green. Built in the style of a Parisian Boulevard, the street had replaced the inner city slum area which was a by-product of the City's growth brought on by the Industrial Revolution.

Yet, just over 800 years earlier, when the Domesday Book had been compiled during the reign of William the Conqueror, Birmingham was one of the poorest hamlets in the region. It consisted of nine families, two ploughs and sixteen oxen; and was worth the grand sum of twenty shillings! (Aston, the neighbouring hamlet was worth a fiver!)

Consider these facts about early Birmingham:

It was not a main religious centre such as York, Salisbury, Canterbury etc. It was not in a strategic position to warrant a stronghold which would evolve into a castle, such as Warwick, Kenilworth or Dudley. A fair portion of the land was infertile heathland, suitable only for grazing, the Winson Green area; another third of the land was used as a private hunting ground for the Lord of the Manor. It had no large navigable river in the vicinity. Birmingham had no natural resources, such as coal or iron ore.

In fact Birmingham was in the middle of nowhere! But, that nowhere happened to be approximately the middle of England; on a shallow ford across what is now known as the River Rea. With the emergence of county boundaries during

Above: Birmingham after 1911 expansion of its boundaries.

the 10th Century, the small hamlet of Birmingham, Boerma-Ing-Ham, which derives from its early Anglo-Saxon origins as the homestead of the Boerma family, was conveniently placed close to where lay the borders of Warwickshire, Worcestershire and Staffordshire. It became an ideal meeting place for the local farming community to sell their produce and livestock. Wool and leather were the main source of business in these early days. Therefore Birmingham's prosperity sprang from trade.

From the south, roads made their way from Coventry, Warwick, Stratford and Alcester; all converged at Deritend and the ford on the River Rea. This then formed the main road of the growing village. At the top of the hill, now the site of St Martin's Church and the Bull Ring the roads fanned out to Dudley, Halesowen, Lichfield, Stafford and Wolverhampton. Therefore the majority of passing trade for this part of the Midlands had to pass through Digbeth; truly an ideal site to set up shop.

The importance of how Birmingham was slowly developing and becoming more influential in the region was shown in 1155, when a Royal Charter was granted allowing a weekly market, the first in Warwickshire. Seeds were now being sowed for Birmingham's long established links with the iron industry. With the closeness of the coalfields of

South Staffordshire and the abundant supply of timber from the Forest of Arden, artisans such as blacksmiths, lorimers, nailmakers and blademakers were allowed to set up workshops in and around Digbeth to ply their wares.

Birmingham also had the knack of keeping it's nose out of other people's business. During the many years of turmoil, feuds and rebellion that beleaguered England in its history, Birmingham always remained neutral. Mind you, it is alleged that Birmingham supplied 15,000 swords for the Parliamentarians during the English Civil War, causing retribution from Prince Rupert, who, with a force of Royalist cavalry and foot soldiers, ransacked the town on Easter Monday, 3 April 1643.

The death of Oliver Cromwell (1658), saw the eventual restoration of Charles II to the English throne (1660). This saw a reversal in dress fashion from the colourless puritanical way of life that had exsisted in England after the Civil War. King Charles introduced from France the the fashion of wearing metallic ornaments such as buttons and buckles, and the 'smiths' of Birmingham were not slow in recognising that the production of these items was an industry in which they could outrival any other in the country.

During this period, Birmingham was slowly becoming a victim of its own success. As the town expanded, its exsistence relied on a continual flow of traffic in and out of the town, bringing in many tons of raw materials and fresh food daily. Then came the shipping out of the finished goods; all done by relays of slow and cumbersome ox-drawn waggons. This was probably a contributory factor to why Birmingham workers evolved into becoming skilled in the making of smaller and intricate metal products, for they were cheaper to transport. Another drawback with the ox-drawn waggons, was that in severe weather conditions it was possible for Birmingham to be isolated for days. Therefore, to further expand and grow into the City we know today, a cheaper and quicker type of transport was required urgently, and it came just in time.

Birmingham has no claim to the innovation of canals, or the honour of having the first canal. But in 1769, when the first ten miles of an intended twenty-two mile stretch of canal was opened from the coalfields of the Black Country (South Staffordshire) to a wharf in Easy Row (nowadays where Broad Street meets Paradise Circus), the price of coal dropped to half price. Soon other canals were cut and, during the next fifty years, Birmingham became the hub of the canal network throughout the entire country and through an intricate network of canals and locks, goods from the town were able to be transported to most of the major ports around the country.

Birmingham expanded along its canals as it was the ideal place to set up new business ventures. Small villages on the outskirts of the town were engulfed as new factories and workshops were built alongside the canals. As an example, over 120 workshops flourished in a two mile stretch of canal between Aston and Bordesley. The land in between was used to build poor quality housing for the multidude of immigrants from all parts of the country, that were now being attracted to seek work. Birmingham was seen as an 'El Dorado' fortunes were to be made; in many cases this was true, for many Birmingham firms that survive to this day have their roots in this boom time of 'canal mania'. For thousands of others, their dream ended with long hours and poor pay and their new homes were so shoddy and so close together that within a few years they had become slums. In a space of fifty years Birmingham's population had grown from 24,000 in 1750 to 73,000 in 1800, and from 4,000 houses to nearly 16,000.

Entrepreneurs of the brass trade were enticed along a section of canal running by Broad Street. Before the turn of the century, brass had become one of the town's major manufacturing products. The celebrated partnership of James Watt (a Scot) and Matthew Boulton (a Brummie) was formed in 1774 to improve the design of Newcomen's Steam Engine, designed for pumping water from mineshafts. By 1796 the famous Soho foundry was set up to manufacture Watt's historic rotary steam engine, which could be used to power all types of machines. A friend of Watt and Boulton, William Murdock (another Scot), had invented gas lighting and by 1802 the Soho Works can give Birmingham another claim to fame; 24 hour production using shift work! (To be accurate, the Soho Works were in the parish of Handsworth, which was still in Staffordshire.)

At this period of time the Birmingham jewellery and gun trades were still in their infancy. This was soon to change. First came the opening of the Birmingham Assay Office in 1773, thus making the 'Anchor' hallmark world known. Secondly, with the outbreak of the Napoleonic wars, Birmingham gunmakers made 65% of the rifles supplied to the British Army. The importance of the town's gun trade was shown when parliamentary sanction was given to build a gun barrel proof house. The Birmingham Proof House in Banbury Street was opened in 1814, and is still in business today

If the canal age helped to put Birmingham 'on the map' regarding the Industrial Revolution, then the next important step in the City's history, the railways, catapulted the town into the forefront of it. As with the canals, Birmingham has no claim to having the first railway in the country. The first attempt failed in 1824, when local canal proprietors managed to thwart a Bill being passed in Parliament to sanction a line from the town to Birkenhead. It took a further nine years for a Bill to be passed, but when the first line was opened from a temporary terminus at Vauxhall to Liverpool in 1837, there was no looking back. The following year the line to London was in operation; the capital was now only five hours away (the 1836 stagecoach service from Birmingham to London took on average thirteen hours). As with the canals, Birmingham soon became the hub of the country's railroad system. It become the most important rail junction and passenger crossroads in the country.

With railways expanding all over the country, new industries developed in Birmingham to provide various pieces of equipment, such as brass and iron tubes for steam engines, pressure gauges and valves etc. One of the most important business ventures that came to Birmingham was the Metropolitan Railway Waggon Works in Saltley, which opened in 1838. The new factory gave employment to 3,000 people, and rolling stock was built not only for the British Isles but for export around the world.

This new era of Birmingham's growth, starting with the railways in 1837, coincided with the crowning of the young Queen Victoria. Even though Birmingham was becoming the main industrial town in the midlands, it was still only a relatively small town. Its boundaries were not much bigger than the present day city centre. But within a year, a Charter of Incorporation was granted and four local parishes were absorbed into the new Borough of Birmingham; these being Edgbaston, Bordesley, Duddeston and Nechells. Birmingham for the first time had a Mayor, 16 Aldermen and 48 Councillors. At the first Council meeting it was decided to adopt a maxim for Birmingham, something that was appropriate for the future aspirations of the new borough. 'FORWARD' was selected, and a befitting choice too. With the onset of railways the British Isles had become considerably smaller. Travelling time was now cut down to hours instead of days. Migration from the remotest parts of the country was now achieved with ease. As the young Queen Victoria's reign flourished and her empire grew, so did Birmingham's population. There had always been a strong Welsh presence in Birmingham, which dated back to medieval days, when Welsh drovers brought cattle to market. By the mid 19th century there were enough Scottish in the town to warrant their own church. But by far the largest immigrant community by the middle of the 19th century was the Irish. But by now immigrants started to trickle in from various parts of Europe, from Italian street musicians to German and Swiss watchmakers.

Even though I have painted a pretty picture of the success of Birmingham's development, living conditions were pretty grim for the poorer working class of the Borough. For the first twenty years or so the Borough Council paid little attention to the welfare of its citizens. Records show that by 1850 nearly a quarter of a million people were living in an area of approximately 18 square miles. There was no proper sewerage system; water collected and stagnated; wells became polluted; there was negligible public health care; and no parks or public baths. Living conditions were deteriorating at an alarming rate. The worst type of houses were the back to back with a single downstairs room to live in. These were built around a courtyard that contained a communal wash-house and lavatories; no better than cess pits. In the worst slum areas these houses were damp, dilapidated and decaying. They

Above and Below: From the 18th Century the 6th Foot used Birmingham as its recruiting centre – thus began the connections with Brum and the Royal Warwickshire Regiment. Above is a private of the Grenadier Company, 1751 and below an officer of 1782.

were built so close together that no sunlight or ventilation penetrated the gloom. Smallpox and fevers were rife, with the death rate double that of the outlying districts. Interspersed amongst all this squalor there were nearly 7,000 workshops, with the best part of these being former private dwellings.

In a census held in 1851 it is interesting to note that the main industrial occupation in Birmingham was that of button-makers, with nearly 5,000. Coming a close second were brassfounders. But by far the largest occupation was that of domestic servant, of which nearly 9,000 were in the service of the new middle class society; the factory owners, business men etc who by now were leaving the unhealthy town and spreading out to the suburbs.

1851 was also the year that Birmingham Corporation took over complete control of sanitation with the formation of the Birmingham Public Works Committee. Slowly the environment began to improve. A notorious slum area of the town known as 'the froggery' had been demolished to make way for New Street Station which opened in 1854. This slow improvement into the living conditions of the working class coincided with the arrival in Birmingham of two men, who in a few years would mastermind Birmingham's revolution in municipal administration.

The first was George Dawson (born in 1821, the son of a London schoolmaster), who was a non-conformist minister and part-time teacher. He came to Birmingham in 1844 and devoted much time to municipal reform in the town. Dawson achieved very strong support over the years for his theory of the 'Civic Gospel', which in a 'nutshell' meant that the town council had a duty to provide its population with good municipal services and a healthy habitat in which to live.

The second was Joseph Chamberlain; who, has been described as the founding father of the future City of Birmingham. He came to Birmingham in 1854, aged eighteen, as a representative of his father's interests in the family wood-screw firm of Nettlefold and Chamberlain (forerunner of GKN) which was situated in Broad Street. Seeing at first hand the squalidness of the slums whilst travelling back and forth to his lodgings had a profound effect on young Joseph during his early years in the town. So much so, that he became a leading disciple in Dawson's 'Civic Gospel'. Having amassed a fortune, he retired before the age of forty, to give the whole of his dynamic energy to making Birmingham to what it has become to-day. He entered Birmingham political life in 1869 as a town councillor and soon became its most influential leader; becoming Mayor from 1873 to 1876.

It was during his Mayoralty that saw the earliest attempt at town planning in Birmingham. The Birmingham Improvement Scheme was an excellent example of slum clearance and re-housing combined with a better water supply for which Joseph Chamberlain was chiefly responsible. At the same time, the town's private gas companies were obtained by the Borough. Benefits were soon apparent; within nine years the Birmingham Gas Department had made nearly half a million pounds profit, which were then ploughed back into the town's coffers; whilst gas charges came down by 30%.

By the time that City status was achieved in 1889 Birmingham had obtained a higher quality in roads, sewers, water and gas supplies, and an improved standard of public health. There were also public facilities, unheard of a few years before, such as libraries, parks, baths and a transport system. Birmingham's fame and reputation was now spreading world wide. It was becoming the leading provincial City, second only to London.

After a stay in the City, a visiting American journalist proclaimed Birmingham as, and this is where I began this short history, 'the best governed city in the world'.

Birmingham's links with the Royal Warwickshire Regiment

There is now no Royal Warwickshire Regiment. In the modern streamlined British Army it has been amalgamated with other famous regiments to become the Royal Regiment of Fusiliers. But the Royal Warwickshire Regiment lives on; in the hearts of its many veterans and the families of those men who died in the service of their country. A further reminder of its traditions and history can be found at the Royal Warwickshire Regimental Museum in Warwick, one of the best in the country.

The Royal Warwickshire Regiment can trace its roots back to 1674, when a force of men from England, Ireland and Scotland were recruited to fight under the Dutch flag against the French. There were enough men to divide the force into four regiments i.e. one Scottish, one Irish and two English. Of the two English regiments it was the one known as Lillington's Regiment to which the Royal Warwickshire Regiment can trace its origins.

In those days, regiments were not known by numbers but by the surname of the commanding officer. With the quick turn round of senior officers, there may have been confusion concerning which regiment was which and commanded by who; this may have persuaded the government of the practicality of giving regiments distinguishing numbers corresponding to the date it was originally formed. Lillington's Regiment became known as the 6th Foot, although official sanction on regimental numbering was not secured until 1743.

Birmingham's first links with the 6th Foot began during the American War of Independence of 1776 to 1783. The regiment had spent four years stationed in the West Indies before being posted to New York in November 1776. But sickness and fevers had taken their toll upon the regiment. What

able men were left were drafted into other regiments, leaving a nucleus of men to return to Britain on a recruiting mission. During 1777 the 6th Foot was brought back to full strength with men from Bristol, Derby and Leicester. It was March 1778 when twelve companies of 6th Foot marched into Warwickshire for the very first time. Three companies were stationed at Warwick, three at Coventry, two at Stratford upon Avon and four came to Birmingham. After two months the regiment reformed and went into camp situated on Warley Common (which nowadays may be in the vicinity of the Hagley Road/Wolverhampton Road junction).

In 1782 a territorial system to aid recruiting was put into operation. This lead to regiments being given a county designation. Recruiting parties from the 6th Foot had used Birmingham regularly between 1778 and 1779. Perhaps the Commanding Officer was impressed with the quality of recruits from the town and surrounding area. Therefore the regiment opted for Warwickshire. From then on the regiment was known as the 6th Foot (1st Warwickshire).

Strange that it may seem, but until the Cardwell reforms of 1881 took effect, 1796 was the last time the regiment had any connection with the county of

Warwickshire! The regiment was continually on foreign service, only returning to Britain when its rank and file was so much depleted that it needed to recruit, before moving overseas again. Where did the 6th Foot (1st Warwickshire) recruit? Well, oddly enough, not Warwickshire. The majority of men who enlisted into the regiment came from the north of England, with a strong contingent from Ireland. Even when a second battalion of the 6th Foot was formed in 1804 (the object being to supply drafts to the 1st Battalion), the men were recruited in Liverpool!

After the downfall of Napoleon the second battalion was disbanded in 1815. It was raised again between the years 1846 to 1850, but took on a permanent place in the regiment's history when it was raised again in 1857. In Warwickshire? No, this time in Preston. Until 1870 these two battalions had no connection whatsoever with each other. Each battalion maintained its own depot, which was situated seemingly anywhere but Warwickshire.

Even though the regular battalions recruited elsewhere, the county of Warwickshire did not entirely lose its identification with the regiment. It was the conflict known as the 'Seven Years War'

Above: Shooting Team, 1st Battalion Royal Warwickshire Regiment at the turn of the century. The officer on the left, J F Elkington, was the Commanding Officer of the battalion when war broke out in August 1914. During the British retreat after the Battles of Mons and Le Cateau, Colonel Elkington and the CO of the Royal Dublin Fusiliers had in their charge remnants of their own battalions and stragglers of others. On reaching the town of St Quentin, the men were totally exhausted and needed a few hours' rest. The Mayor of the town fearful of a German bombardment, asked the two commanding officers to sign an agreement that they would surrender if the advancing Germans got too close for comfort. In return for food for their men, they agreed. After a few hours' rest the remnants of the two battalions resumed their march. Unfortunately, the powers that be got to hear of this incident and the two colonels were cashiered by court-martial. Elkington determined to recover his good name, enlisted as a Private in the French Foreign Legion and served heroically for eighteen months before being seriously wounded. In that time he had distinguished himself by winning the Médaille Militaire and the Croix de Guerre. For his gallant conduct his British Army rank and position were restored (though not with the Royal Warwicks) and he was awarded the DSO. *Dave Vaux collection.*

Above: Sergeant, 1811.

Below: Private, 1839.

Private, 1839

(fought against the French in the Caribbean) of 1756 to 1763 which lead in 1759 to the raising of a Militia force in each county; a second force for defence of the realm. It was to be a part-tme conscripted force. The men would receive basic training at annual camps during times of peace, but to be called up in times of national emergency. Each parish was expected to supply a quota of men. If not enough volunteers came forward, a ballot system was introduced. Parishes not fulfilling their quota were fined. It seems there was little problem in the raising of the Warwickshire Militia, each company within the battalion having local connections. The battalion served from June 1759 until December 1762. For part of its service the battalion guarded French prisoners on the south-coast. It was not uncommon for men serving in the Militia to volunteer for service with its regular army battalion; it was a good way of gathering recruits. In the ensuing years the Militia were embodied on several occasions. During the Napoleonic Wars of 1803 to 1815, Warwickshire raised two Militia battalions.

In regard to recruiting in Birmingham, during the early part of the 19th Century, it is probable that 'Brummies' wishing to enlist in the army would have no particular preference as to which regiment they served in. The deciding factor would be which regiment had recruiting officials in the vicinity at the time. There is also Birmingham's rapid expansion during the 19th Century to consider. Men who had spent their youth living in the outer suburbs of the growing town, which in some parts were either in Worcestershire or Staffordshire, may have considered to enlist in the county regiment of their birth, either the Worcestershire or South Staffordshire Regiments. To confirm this theory, at one time the Worcestershire Regiment drew on Birmingham so heavily that it was nicknamed 'The Brummagem Guards'.

During the latter half of the 19th Century reform of the British Army began to take place. The man responsible was Edward Cardwell, who was appointed Secretary for State for War in 1868. Until then, the Army was deemed to be made up of rogues, drunkards and vagabonds; army service as an alternative to prison and kept in order by a strict and brutal regime of branding and flogging. The majority of regiments were run by officers who thought breeding and gentlemanly pursuits more important than military training. In the reform of the British Army, Cardwell made his main priority the improvement of general training and thanks to the better standards of education during the 19th century, attracted a better quality of recruit to the army. Certainly, one way he achieved this was by introducing a six year short-service system instead of the minimum twelve years. He also abolished the system where officers could buy their commissions. They now had to prove themselves by passing an entrance exam.

Perhaps his main claim to fame was the scheme of dividing the country into sixty-six territorial districts. Each had two Regular Battalions; one to serve abroad, the other on home service. Each district was also required to have a varying number of reserve and part-time battalions (Militia and Volunteers). There would also be a recruit/basic training depot in each district. This would help stimulate local connections and entice more men of better quality to enlist. The Cardwell reforms took effect in 1881 and Budbrooke Barracks in Warwick became the basic training depot for the Royal Warwickshire Regiment. Here recruits from all parts of Warwickshire, including Birmingham, passed through before joining either the 1st or 2nd Regular Battalions.

Birmingham's Royal Warwickshire Territorials

After the Boer War, many people forecast that the next major conflict the world would see, would take place in Europe; with Germany being the main antagonist. With these forebodings in mind plus lessons learned during the Boer War, the Secretary of State for War, Richard Burdon Haldane, who came into office in 1905, introduced a new package of reforms enabling Britain to have a quality rather than quantity, efficiently organised and equipped expeditionary force, which could be transported promptly to where needed. One important development of these reforms was the formation of the Territorial Force.

Haldane's plan was to transform the existing Yeomanry, Militia and Volunteer units into a much larger and efficient Territorial force of 300,000 men, which would give Britain a second line fighting force of fourteen divisions comprising infantry, cavalry, artillery and medical units. This would be Britain's main defence in case of invasion (which at this time was thought very possible).

Prior to the formation of the Territorials, the Volunteer Regiments were affiliated with army cadet units within the grammar and public schools across Britain. One of Haldane's new schemes was the introduction of the Officer Training Corps (OTC) at universities with junior contingents formed from within the existing Army Cadet Force. The theory was that, within a few years, Britain would have a few thousand men competent to take a commission upon the oubreak of war.

The new Territorial Force came into being on April 1st, 1908. In many cases it was a straight forward change. Overnight a 'Volunteer' battalion was given a slight name change and a different number designation within the regiment. Each serving man was required to re-enlist and had to be attested and measured for his new khaki uniform. The majority of men did, but many 'old hands' chose not to continue and resigned.

How did this affect the Royal Warwickshire Regiment? From April 1st, 1908, the following bat-

talions now constituted the Regiment:-

1st and **2nd** Battalions: Regular Army battalions.

3rd (Special Reserve) and **4th** (Extra Reserve) Battalions: These were made up of time served regulars, who were put on the reserve list and called up for training yearly. In the event of war these battalions were for home service and to keep the two regular battalions up to fighting strength.

5th and **6th** Battalions: These were Birmingham's two new Territorial battalions, formed from the '1st Volunteer Battalion The Royal Warwickshire Regiment'. They were to train on different nights at the Drill Hall in Thorp Street.

7th Battalion: This was formed from the '2nd Volunteer Battalion The Royal Warwickshire Regiment' from Coventry.

8th Battalion: A new battalion raised in Aston Manor, Birmingham, around the nucleus of the two companies: the Teacher Training College Company (Saltley, B'ham) and the Dunlop Works Company which had formerly been attached to the 2nd Volunteer Battalion.

On the same day that the Territorial Force came

Above: Birmingham's Royal Warwickshire Territorials on parade in Victoria Square 23 April 1913. The statue of King Edward VII (sculptor: Albert Toft) was unveiled by HRH Princess Louise, Duchess of Argyle. It was removed from the Square in March 1950 and re-sited in Highgate Park.
Dave Vaux Collection

into being, April 1st 1908, the Birmingham Daily Post, published an article about events in Aston concerning the raising of the 8th Royal Warwicks on the previous night.

'To the sound of the rolling drums, the shrill call of the fife, and all the pomp and circumstance of military ceremonial, England's Volunteers passed out of action last night, and the new Territorial Army was born. So far as Aston was concerned (and the scene in the Victoria Hall was but typical of what was taking place throughout the length and breadth of the land) the occasion was honoured by the holding of one of the most remarkable meetings in the history of the borough. In the past, ere Birmingham's neighbour had attained municipal dignities, the patriotism of its inhabitants flowed over into the Volunteer battalions of the City and neighbourhood. Aston had no regiment it could call its own. Into its work-a-day world there entered little that brought colour and brightness and light to gleam through the grey background and point the way to higher aspirations. Public spirit, however, was but slumbering. No one who witnessed last night's scenes could doubt that this was so. The clarion call of the reveille which rang through the crowded hall to hail the birth of the Territorial Army fell not upon stony ground. So eagerly did men press forward to enrol their names that the officers charged with the duty of registration had a task of the utmost difficulty, and every indication pointed to the probability that Colonel Ludlow will soon have what he has much desired, a force, a thousand strong, of the best men Aston has to give the nation.'

'The audience was mainly one of men, and from the first it was easy to see they were men with a purpose. The attention they paid to the speeches showed they were already half converted, and whatever waverers there were must have been won over by the earnestness of General Raitt and Colonel Ludlow, judging by the eager hundreds who pressed forward when the Union Jack was unrolled.'

In part of his speech, General Raitt made the following comments:

'As for Aston itself, its chief claim to fame at present rested on football. To the outside world the name of the town was little more than something which gave the much more important word 'VILLA'. They should have something more to be proud of, the smartest battalion in the South Midland Division.'

During the early days of the new battalion, Aston Town Council allowed a fixed number of employees (fifty) who enlisted an extra week's holiday, with pay, for the men to attend annual camp. Back at Thorp Street, the transition from Volunteers to Territorials went well. The Birmingham Daily Post reported that nearly all the former volunteers had been attested to the new force. Dividing the one battalion to form two allowed many more recruits to enlist, and the Drill Hall was opened each night for this purpose. In fact, so many men from Birmingham's Jewellery Quarter came forward, that a Jewellers' Company was raised. In the 6th Royal Warwicks there was also formed the BSA Company.

The formation of the Officer Training Corps also concerned Birmingham, with the formation of two companies at Birmingham University. Meanwhile, King Edward's School in New Street, Handsworth Grammar and Solihull School formed units of the OTC Junior Division.

This was the state of play regarding Birmingham's military links until the outbreak of war, August 4th, 1914

Chapter Two

Birmingham: August 1914

EVE OF WAR. As the last days of July 1914 played out, a conflict, which for many years was considered probable, was about to occur. It had been a month since the assassination of the Archduke Franz Ferdinand and his wife in Sarajevo. Time for talking was now over. Europe and the world was on an irreversible path to war.

However, war or not, the August Bank Holiday (Monday, August 3rd) was nearing; Birmingham was about to go on holiday. Not only was there planned a mass evacuation of holiday-makers and day-trippers from the city but also starting the same Bank Holiday weekend was the annual camp in the vicinity of Rhyl of the Territorial Force's South Midland Division. The 5th, 6th, 7th and 8th Warwicks formed the 'Warwickshire Brigade'. With other units, such as Artillery, Army Service Corps, Royal Army Medical Corps and Royal Engineers, it was estimated by one Birmingham newspaper that around 10,000 Midland troops would be off to camp.

At this time, unlike the Regular Army, the Divisions and Brigades of the Territorials were not numbered but were named after the military district of the recruit catchment area. When the Territorial Force began to move overseas en masse, in May 1915, a numbering system was introduced; then the South Midland Division became the 48th (South Midland) Division.

The *Birmingham Daily Mail*, on Friday, 28 July, made the following comment:

'Though the weather during the past few days has not been exactly summer-like, and what with rain and cold, the spirits of the holiday-makers have been temporarily depressed, yet the approach of the August Bank Holiday, has awakened the holiday zest with a vengeance. Judging by the arrangements made by the various railway companies which serve Birmingham, the fullest possible scope is being provided for those who desire to go near or far; and all the popular resorts are brought within reach of the pockets of would-be holiday-makers.'

For example, the London and North-Western Railway Company, had the innovation to put on a special train for the North Wales coastal resorts, leaving from Birmingham New Street Station at

midnight, Saturday, 1 August. This was put on to suit the convenience of business people who could not get away until late at night. Ilfracombe was as popular with 'Brummies' as it is nowadays. But the journey then was more appealing than the tedious motor-way travelling of modern holiday-makers. Then, it was a train journey to Bristol, followed by a pleasant sea voyage along the North Devon coast by steam-ship. According to the *Birmingham Daily Mail*, the most popular resort

Above: This Brummie family enjoy the last days of peace at Blackpool in the hot summer of 1914. Holidays would never be the same again for many a family. The world was about to enter a period of unparalleled violence.

Above: A postcard of an unidentified family enjoying a day trip, nothing unusual in that except that the postmark is dated 4 August 1914.

of Evesham and the Peak district. For those who could only spare a few 'coppers' there was always the tram down the Bristol Road to the ever popular Lickey Hills.

For those Brummies who decided to stay in the city, the Summer of 1914, also saw the opening of Birmingham's new pleasure resort; the Fun Park in Aston Reservoir Grounds (later known as Salford Park, nowadays an oasis amid the concrete columns of 'Spaghetti Junction' and the Aston Express Way). Open daily from 2:30 to 10:30 pm, sixpence for adults and threepence for kids it was claimed to be the greatest outdoor entertainment ever presented. The park had a beautiful lake where motor-boats, pleasure craft and devices for cycling on water could be hired, all surrounded by sylvan scenery. Every Wednesday and Saturday evening the park also boasted 'the most gorgeous firework display in the Midlands'. On a specially-laid floor, dancing took place all day to 'the greatest aggregation of musical talent ever heard in the Midlands'. Twice a day the Full Band of the British ex-Guards performed. There were also numerous concerts, variety acts, trapeze artistes and side-shows. And if that was not enough there was 'Correa' the Indian Scout with Cowboys and Cowgirls of his Wild West Show; and 'Yukio Tani', the world famous Japanese exponent of ju-jitsu, was there to challenge all-comers. But, whatever the social background of these would be holiday-makers of 1914, they all had one thing in common: holidays would never be the same again for many a family, not only in Birmingham, but across the entire country. Sons, husbands, brothers, uncles and fathers would soon be off to enlist, many never to return.

for Birmingham folk of 1914 was the Cardigan Bay resort of Aberystwyth; there was even a special camping train from Snow Hill Station, exclusively for Boy Scouts, leaving on July 31st. At this time six or more children in a family was quite common and no doubt holidays for the working-class with large families were a very rare experience. This is probably why over the few days of the Bank Holiday weekend there were so many day-tripper trains on the timetable. There were trips to all the major seaside resorts around the British Isles: Blackpool, Bournemouth, Great Yarmouth and Weston-Super-Mare to name but a few. This weekend was the only chance in the year the working-class of Birmingham could escape from the hustle and bustle of city life and partake in a little bit of sea-breeze. Those 'Brummies' who chose not to venture far afield were also catered for with day-trips within the Midlands area, for example the Vale

August Bank Holiday

On Bank Holiday Monday, 3 August, the day before war was declared, the *Birmingham Daily Mail*, made the following comments:

Right: Blackpool – a popular choice for Birmingham day trippers during the August Bank Holiday of 1914.
Ray Frankel Archives

'Light hearted crowds left the inland towns of England on Saturday for the coast, there to learn (but possibly to remain in ignorance until to-day) of the grave turn which events have taken during their brief absence from the usual channels of information. The holiday spirit flowed freely during the week-end, but there may be a different story to tell to-day.'

'Realisation of the serious state of affairs in Europe was brought sharply home to intending Birmingham holiday-makers by the action of the Great Western Railway Company in cancelling excursion trains from Snow Hill Station. During last evening the officials received an intimation from head-quarters that holiday services would have to be cut down, and later, a notice was put up at the station announcing that there would be no bookings to-day for excursions. Last night only a limited number of trains were run. Apparently the company are desirous of having as much rolling stock as possible at their command in an emergency.

'The thousands of visitors who poured into Aberystwyth on Saturday, many hundreds of whom came from the midlands, bore testimony to the growing popularity of the town as a holiday resort. The weather was wretched, heavy rain pouring down just as the heavily-loaded trains arrived.

'Considering the extreme gravity of the situation in the Near East, the calmness of holiday-makers to Blackpool was remarkable. Twenty-three special trains from the midlands arrived on Sunday, and the record number of 123 were unfreighted on Saturday. Most of them packed, as Blackpool will be after receiving 100 more specials to-day. The weather has been changeable, sunshine and showers alternating. Most of Saturday was fine, and yesterday from early afternoon the sun shone brilliantly. Birmingham, Coventry, Walsall, Dudley, Leicester, Nottingham and North Staffordshire have sent more visitors than ever before. So dense was the crowd in the Central Station on Saturday that an official with a megaphone had to stand at the entrance on a box and shout out instructions.'

Birmingham's Territorials off to camp

Having mentioned the great exodus from the city, of day-trippers and holiday-makers on Saturday August 1st it was now the turn of Birmingham's Territorial Infantry, i.e. the 5th, 6th

and 8th Royal Warwicks. According to the newspapers, events in Europe were drawing to a head; war now seemed probable. In fact, by now German troops had already crossed the border into France without any declaration of War between the two countries. Once German troops entered Belgium, the process leading to Germany's declaration of war was set, despite desperate moves to avoid such a calamity. Regardless of all the war talk in the press, Birmingham's Territorials continued in their preparations to leave the following day (Sunday August 2nd). Amidst the crowds of friends, relatives and well-wishers lining the streets of Birmingham, the troops marched, accompanied by their bands and drums, to entrain at Snow Hill Station. The proposed camp of the Warwickshire Territorials was to be on the open ground between the railway line and the coastal road running from

Above: One wonders if 'Old Gipsy Sarah's Only Clever Daughter-inLaw' saw the Great War coming! Blackpool pre-1914.
Ray Frankel Archives

Below: Territorials of the Royal Warwicks leaving Thorp Street and marching through Birmingham, before entraining for their summer camp at Rhyl.

Above: A matter of hours before war was declared the Territorials throughout the country were recalled from their summer camps. Here elements of the 5th and 6th Royal Warwicks arrive back at Snow Hill Station.

Below: Bridge (Edmund Street) connecting the old and new Art Gallery extension completed in 1914.

Rhyl to Abergele. The Warwickshire Brigade reached Rhyl on Sunday afternoon and proceeded to settle into their allotted camping areas. All was quiet until 11 pm on Sunday evening, when news was brought to the various units that a 'Move Order' may be close at hand. It came at 2 am, Monday August 3rd, and as dawn was breaking the men had re-packed their equipment and were marching back to Rhyl Station. The 5th and 6th Royal Warwicks arrived back at Snow Hill at 10 am, just as many 'Brummie' day-trippers were milling around the station after discovering that their 'trips' had been cancelled. The 5th and 6th

Battalions returned to Thorp Street and the 8th their Drill Hall in Aston. With no further orders, the men were dismissed and sent home with the warning that they should be ready to return at a moment's notice.

Birmingham at War

German troops crossed onto Belgium soil, near the town of Verviers, fifteen miles south-east of Liège, during the early hours of 4 August. Honouring its treaty to protect Belgium's neutrality, Britain declared a state of war to exist between herself and Germany from 11 pm the same day.

Army and Navy Reservists were mobilised first and were soon followed by the Territorials. The concern in Birmingham was that there were at least 5,000 to 6,000 Reservists in the City and the mobilisation would make a very considerable demand on the police force, fire brigade, railway, tramway, postal and gas department employees (Birmingham Tram Way Department had over 500 men rejoin the colours). On Saturday, 1 August, the Reservists that comprised the 4th (Reserve) Battalion of the Royal Warwickshire Regiment were due back at Budbrooke Barracks after completing twenty-seven days' annual training at Parkhurst on the Isle of Wight. On reaching Budbrooke, orders were awaiting the battalion to return immediately to the Isle of Wight for coastal and railway guard duties. A special train from Warwick was chartered for the battalion the same evening, and amid enthusiastic scenes they returned. This must have caused much distress amongst wives and children, as the men were not given enough time to say goodbye before returning. One soldier told a representative of the *Warwickshire Advertiser* that 'all the battalion responded cheerfully to the call of duty, although some were disappointed at being unable to see relations and friends after their month's training, and were anxious about their civil employment'. Approximately 300 of these Reservists were drafted immediately into the 1st and 2nd Regular Battalions of the Regiment, bringing them up to fighting strength. One wonders, how many of these Reservists, who bid their families farewell in July, and expecting to be back home in a month, were killed fighting with the 1st Royal Warwicks at the Battles of Mons and Le Cateau, before the month of August had ended? One of those Reservists was No.9952 Private William Henry Farrell, from 3 back 118, Park Road, Hockley, who before attending the annual camp was employed at the Dunlop Rubber Company. Private Farrell was drafted into the 1st Royal Warwicks, and found himself in France on 22 August. The battalion reached Le Cateau on 24 August; the Battle of Mons had been fought the previous day. Under a series of heroic rear-guard actions the British Army had now begun to retreat, South, towards the River Marne.

Before the censors began to curb reports from the front, the *Birmingham Daily Mail* on 7

September, 1914, published the following account of Private Farrell's, concerning the first few hectic days of the BEF in France:

> 'The slaughter during these three days was terrible, the loss on the German side being far more severe than that of the Allies. The scene was rendered all the more horrible by the barbarous actions of the German Army. Every village they passed through they set on fire and it made the hearts of the Allied soldiers ache to see the Belgian and French people with their poor little children leaving their homes. The Germans have suffered already for it, and we shall make them suffer more for it before we have done with them. The French and Belgium people have been very good to us. They are good-natured people and though they could ill afford it, they gave us fruit and cigarettes.'

The newspaper article continued:

> 'After Farrell's two comrades had been shot, he himself received a bullet which fortunately struck him sideways, passing through his right shoulder. He lay on the battlefield for an hour before he was picked up and conveyed to hospital. There he found two or three hundred dead and dying soldiers. He had not been there long before the order came for all men who could walk to clear out at once, as the Germans were firing on the hospital, and Farrell had not been out an hour before it was completely blown up, and many officers and men must have perished.'

On recovery, Private Farrell did not go back to the Dunlop Rubber Company, he was sent back, this time to the 2nd Royal Warwicks. Whilst the battalion was entrenched in the vicinity of Le Maisnil, Private Farrell was killed in action on 13 February, 1915.

The hundred or so Reservists who worked for the well known Birmingham Brewery Mitchells and Butlers, of Cape Hill, had financial worries eased when the firm announced on August 4th that they would make up their army pay to their average weekly wage. It was also announced that the men's jobs would be kept open for them. Compared to London, where within hours of the declaration of war, hundreds of men were queuing at recruiting offices to enlist, Birmingham men took it fairly quietly at first. There were a few men who enlisted straight away, but it took a couple of days or so before the rush started. In the Birmingham Evening Despatch, published on August 5th, there was a very good piece concerning this matter, under the heading:

STREETS QUIET BUT CROWDS ANXIOUS

> 'Nothing approaching a mafficking spirit has yet spread itself abroad over the city of Birmingham. During the period of waiting a calm restraint of the fighting impulse is being exercised by the man in the street.

> 'He is, of course, interested in the trend of events and eagerly seizes on the latest piece of war news. Last night little clusters of people might have been seen scanning the newspapers under the glare of gas lamps, and quietly discussing the position.

> 'The notices announcing the mobilisation which had been published broadcast and exhibited on most of the public buildings in Birmingham, very quickly became the centre of attraction, and large crowds hastened to read them.

> 'Outside the Central Police Station a couple of raw-looking young men might have been carefully spelling out the message. After they had thoroughly digested it, one turned to the other and remarking, "then we'll recruit," shook hands heartily.

> 'It was remarkable what a large number of young fellows, and older ones too, who clustered around the notices, seemed directly to be affected. Youthful-looking Territorials, many who appeared not yet to have had their first shave, paraded the streets, and were visibly pleased to think that they might have an opportunity to show their mettle. Brisk and hustling scenes were noticed outside the recruiting office in Birmingham yesterday. Up to three o'clock a steady stream of able-bodied men, stimulated by a spirit of patriotism, called to make enquiries and offer their services. Most of them were young fellows, but older and experienced men made calls. Most classes were represented.

> 'Later in the evening, after the official notices of mobilisation had been posted, crowds of reservists invaded the offices to learn what they had to do, and the staff had a very busy time. Young men eagerly discussed the merits of the various branches of service which they intended to join.

> 'Yesterday there was not a heavy general rush to recruit, but a steady stream of men willing and eager to fight for their country if necessary.

> 'Here and there in the streets one would see a spruce young fellow snatching a brief conversation with a friend , and hurriedly explaining that he had to report himself at the barracks in the early hours of the morning, fully armed and prepared.'

Birmingham's Territorials

It was now time for the Territorials to be called up, or in the parlance of the time 'embodied'. At 5:30 pm on Tuesday, 4 August, orders were received to mobilise, and at once staffs of the 5th, 6th and 8th Royal Warwickshire Regiment got to

Right: Lieutenant-Colonel
Ernest Martineau,
Commanding Officer of
the 1/6 Royal
Warwickshire Regiment
and Mayor of Birmingham
in August 1914.
D Vaux Collection

work. The Drill Hall in Thorp Street, shared by the 5th and 6th Battalions, as might be imagined it was much too small for two fully equipped and up to strength battalions in which to parade in. Therefore the two Commanding Officers tossed a coin to see which battalion had the Drill Hall.

The CO of the 5th Warwicks was forty-seven year old, Lieutenant-Colonel A I Parkes, an iron-master and manufacturer, who was in partnership with his father, with works at Smethwick and Widnes. He had joined the 1st Warwickshire Volunteers as a subaltern in 1890. The CO of the 6th Warwicks was the fifty-three year old Lieutenant-Colonel Ernest Martineau: who was also the then Lord Mayor of Birmingham. Born in Beaufort Road, Edgbaston, his military career began when he joined the School Volunteer Corps at Rugby School; he then became Sergeant in a similar Corps whilst at Cambridge University. He

joined the 1st Warwickshire Volunteers as Captain in 1882. Lieutenant-Colonel Martineau first became actively associated with municipal affairs in 1901, when he became a member of the City Council for St Martin's Ward. He was unanimously elected Lord Mayor in 1912.

Lieutenant-Colonel Parkes of the 5th Warwicks lost the toss and had to make do with the railway goods yard in the locality of Holliday Street and Suffolk Street. Now that Lieutenant-Colonel Martineau was called up with the 6th Warwicks, it befell to Alderman William Bowater, as his Deputy, to take on the role of Lord Mayor of Birmingham. The following information was sent by the Chief Constable of Birmingham (C H Rafter) to Superintendents of Divisions, dated August 5th, 1914:

'The 5th Battalion Royal Warwickshire Regiment will leave Holliday Street in two sections, and march, one at 6 pm the other at 7 pm, via Suffolk Street, Paradise Street and Colmore Row into Snow Hill Station.

'The 6th Battalion Royal Warwickshire Regiment will march in two sections, one at 8 pm and the other at 9 pm, from Thorp Street and will proceed via Horsefair, John Bright Street, Hill Street and Colmore Row.'

Along with the 7th Royal Warwicks from Coventry (their Drill Hall was situated near to the Adelaide Bridge in Queen Victoria Road), the 5th, 6th and 8th Royal Warwicks from Birmingham and the other units of the South Midland Division were now moving to their coastal war-station in the vicinity of Weymouth and Portland. As the Birmingham contingent marched through the streets, it was a very different scene from that of the previous Sunday, when they were off to camp. The crowd lining the

streets this time was enormous, giving loud cheers, especially when soldiers passed by relatives and friends. But there was a serious significance to what might lie ahead: for this time the band, instead of marching ahead with their musical instruments, were now carrying stretchers.

Before continuing with the next phase of recruiting in Birmingham, I should just mention a small minority of soldiers, who over a period of time had deserted from the army, but now with the outbreak of war wished to rejoin their former Regiments and 'do their bit'. In relation to this, the Chief Constable of Birmingham circulated a copy of the following letter, received from the War Office, to all Police Stations on August 7th:

> *'His Majesty the King has been graciously pleased to approve of pardons being granted to soldiers who were in a state of desertion from the regular forces on the 5th August 1914, and who surrender themselves in the United Kingdom on or before the 4th September 1914, or at any station abroad where there are regular forces, on or before the 4 October 1914. They will forfeit all service prior to the date of surrender, but such service may be subsequently restored under the conditions laid down in the Kings Regulations for restoration of service forfeited under section 79 of the Army Act. Deserters who enlist between the 5th August, and the 4th October, both days inclusive, in any Colonial Corps which have been or may be placed at the disposal of the Imperial Government for the war will be granted a free pardon, and at the expiration of their service in such corps, will not be claimed for further service in the regular forces of the United Kingdom.*
>
> *They will, however, forfeit all service rendered in the regular forces of the United Kingdom prior to the date of such enlistment. The provisions of this order will not apply to men who have fraudulently or improperly enlisted.'*
>
> *Signed R H Braid,*
> *by command of the Army Council*

The Chief Constable further added, that deserters who give themselves up in Birmingham, should be taken to the recruiting office in James Watt Street, who would then send them on to their regiments.

'Your King and Country Need You': Kitchener's Call to Arms

Lord Kitchener, at the request of the Prime Minister (Asquith), assumed the duties of Secretary of State for War on 5 August. He was also the most popular choice of the British public. Before Kitchener had set foot in the War Office, a pre-war plan to form a British Expeditionary Force (the

BEF) was already in motion. The BEF, under the command of Sir John French, initially comprised of five Regular Army Divisions, the 1st, 2nd, 3rd, 5th and the Cavalry Division. These five Divisions landed on French soil between the 11th and 16th August. Within a few weeks it was further strengthened when the 4th and 6th Divisions were sent to France. During August and September, various regular battalions were called back from overseas stations to create the 7th Division, which when completed landed at Zeebrugge on 6 October. With regard to the Royal Warwickshire Regiment: the 1st Battalion was in the 10th Brigade of the 4th Division, and the 2nd Battalion was in the 22nd Brigade of the 7th Division. By 8 August, the best part of Birmingham's Reservists and Territorials had departed the City. The Reservists were now at their Regimental Depots or Naval Bases, whilst the Territorial Force began taking over Home defence duties from the departing Regular Army. The general consensus of opinion held by many at the time, was that the war would be 'over by Christmas'. Kitchener and a few others shared the view that the war would be a long drawn out affair lasting three or more years, and that Britain would require at least seventy Divisions in the Field. Therefore, on the very same day Lord Kitchener took over his duties as Secretary of State for War, he asked Parliament to sanction a further 500,000 men for the Army. On August 11th, 1914, Kitchener's recruiting campaign began in earnest, when the national and local press featured his 'CALL TO ARMS' proclamation, asking for the first 100,000 men to come forward.

Formation of Kitchener's New Army

The patriotic zeal that swept the country in the opening few weeks of the war, perhaps took Kitchener and the War Office off guard. There was no doubt that 500.000 men would come forward, but it took many by surprise as to how quickly men, of all social classes, volunteered to 'do their bit'. After Kitchener's first appeal in the press on 11 August, 100,000 had rushed to enlist within two weeks. To understand more of the problems this caused, the following extract is from a book, published in 1918, entitled *Raising and Training the New Armies* by Captain Basil Williams:

> *'Not only was our Army a small one before the war, but it had no arrangements for expansion. The recruits expected in any one year under the old system were about 30,000, and the recruiting machinery and personnel to secure even this number was barely adequate; in fact, less than a month before the beginning of the war, solemn conclaves were being held at the War Office to find means of improving the methods of obtaining these 30,000 in a*

Your King and Country Need You.

A CALL TO ARMS.

An addition of 100,000 men to his Majesty's Regular Army is immediately necessary in the present grave National Emergency.

Lord Kitchener is confident that this appeal will be at once responded to by all those who have the safety of our Empire at heart.

TERMS OF SERVICE.

General Service for a period of 3 years or until the war is concluded.

Age of Enlistment between 19 and 30.

HOW TO JOIN.

Full information can be obtained at any Post Office in the Kingdom or at any Military depot.

GOD SAVE THE KING!

Below: Lord Kitchener.

Above and Below:
Birmingham Municipal Technical School – the centre for recruiting in 1914.
John Marks Collection

year. Within four weeks of the declaration of war over 30,000 recruits were attested in one day. Naturally, machinery and personnel intended to deal with 30,000 recruits in a year broke down hopelessly when one day would bring in more that that number, especially since many of the most experienced recruiters were at once called to the front. But the crowds who came in were not deterred from their purpose by any breakdown of machinery, and the machinery itself was quickly adjusted to the needs of the time. The War Office, faced with difficulties for which it was not and could not have been prepared, showed no hesitation in accepting the offers of business-like civilians to supply the dearth of expert recruiters. Energetic Members of Parliament armed with a scrap of Lord Kitchener's handwriting rushed forth North, South, East and West of the Kingdom to take responsibility doing unheard-of things quite contrary to regulations. In one city of the Midlands the local Member of Parliament within twenty-four hours changed the recruiting office from a pokey back street to the Town Hall, engaged eight civilian doctors to help the one overworked medical officer to examine recruits, printed locally the sacred Army Forms for recruits, with their seventeen elaborate questions, and had the bath — to which, in the old leisurely days, each recruit had to submit — cut out of the programme. Mayors and Provosts hired or lent the largest halls they could in their own towns, improvised accommodation for the attested recruits, and organised the supply of food necessary during the hours, or even days, they had to be detained till they could be sent off to a depot, and beat up volunteers to supplement the regular recruiting clerks, who were snowed under by various forms, pay sheets, and other documents that required filling up.'

The Midlands city mentioned in the previous extract was Birmingham, and the MP was Leo Amery who held Birmingham South for the Conservative Party. The pokey back street was in fact James Watt Street Recruiting Office. To open up the Town Hall as a recruiting centre, Amery had the help of the Deputy Lord Mayor, Alderman W H Bowater, Colonel Ludlow, the well known Birmingham Territorial officer and many more of Birmingham's leading citizens. The sacred Army Forms, were in fact attestation forms, for which the Birmingham Daily Post printed 20,000 copies for him. Following on the heels of the Town Hall, the next large building used for recruiting in Birmingham was the Technical School in Suffolk Street. With no let up, every day the staffs had their hands full, dealing with the increasing numbers of men enlisting into all branches of the New Army. In this early part of the war, when every recruit was a volunteer, the Royal Warwickshire Regiment was the most popular choice with those 'Brummies' wishing to join an infantry regiment. The Kings Royal Rifle Corps, the Oxford and Bucks Light Infantry and the Duke of Cornwall's Light Infantry were also popular Regiments for Birmingham volunteers. With the boundary changes in 1911, Birmingham expanded into parts of Worcestershire and Staffordshire; I would imagine many Birmingham men also opted to enlist into the county regiment of their birth, i.e. the Worcestershire Regiment and the South Staffordshire Regiment.

One novelty that Birmingham Corporation, introduced during the August of 1914 was a mock up of a huge thermometer outside the Town Hall. The rising 'mercury' represented the daily recruiting level in the city (changed once a day with the help of Boy Scouts). Hopefully, each days recruiting figure bettered the previous one. As August drew to an end, the *Birmingham Daily Mail* claimed:

'No other town of the size in Great Britain can bear comparison with the results achieved here, not even London, which taking its vast population into consideration, has hardly done so well as the Midland metropolis.'

A proud boast indeed, but can it be substantiated? In the book *Birmingham and the Great War*, published in 1921, the following analysis of recruiting up to October 10th, 1914, was given:

'Warwickshire and the City of Birmingham constituted a record for Great Britain. The percentage was 3.35 for Birmingham on a population estimated at 850,947. The number of recruits was given as 28,521.'

Even with the opening of the Technical School, congestion did not ease at Birmingham's recruiting centres. Curzon Hall, in Suffolk Street, and Queen's College in Paradise Street were soon turned into annexes for the Technical School. New recruits were given their medicals in Curzon Hall and Queens College and attested in the Technical School. The *Birmingham Daily Mail*, on September 2nd, gives us a further insight into recruiting in the City:

'Recruiting sergeants are scouring the City, and invariably return with a dozen or two men who have responded to the appeal. When the men are examined and attested and all the formalities are complied with, they are separated into the particular arms of the service for which they have enlisted, and leave for the different stations at varying times. For instance, the Bucks and Oxford (sic) contingent would go together, the Rifle Brigade would leave by another train and the men destined for Budbrooke Barracks, Warwick would

march to Snow Hill and leave there at frequent intervals during the day. In fact there is hardly a train between Birmingham and Warwick which does not carry away batches of recruits, all in the best of spirits and accompanied by their women-folk.

Expansion of the Royal Warwickshire Regiment During August 1914

The volunteers for Kitchener's New Army signed on for three years or until the war was concluded; hence the name 'Service Battalions'. These newly raised battalions formed part of the existing British infantry regiments. They were to be distinguished from the Regular and Territorial battalions by the word 'Service' after the battalion number. If we use the Royal Warwickshire Regiment as an example, we already know that the 1st and 2nd were the Regular Battalions. Then there was the 3rd and 4th Reserve Battalions, followed by the 5th, 6th, 7th and 8th Territorial Battalions. A good proportion of men from Birmingham and Warwickshire who volunteered for the infantry in the opening weeks of the war were sent to the Royal Warwick's Depot at Budbrooke Barracks.

Without trying to get too involved, I should first explain that as the first 100,000 men of Kitchener's anticipated 500,000 strong New Army enlisted, the battalions were put into six newly created

Divisions, to form the first of five New Armies (the first new army was known as K1, the 2nd New Army, K2, the third K3 etc, etc). New battalions were created when an accumulation of new recruits, at various Regimental Depots reached approximately a thousand men. The following, is a brief description of how the battalion strength of Royal Warwickshire Regiment grew with the creation of the Kitchener Battalions during the first few hectic weeks of the war. They were largely made up of Birmingham men:

9th (Service) Battalion The Royal Warwickshire Regiment

Once enough men were recruited to create the 9th Battalion, they were sent to Tidworth (on the eastern edge of Salisbury Plain) to commence their training. The battalion became part of the 39th Infantry Brigade of the 13th (Western) Division (K1). By February 1915, the Division was concentrated at Blackdown near Farnborough. The Battalion entrained at Frimley Railway Station on the 17th and 18th June, 1915 to Avonmouth Docks. From here, the 13th Division sailed to Gallipoli, via Malta, Alexandria (Egypt) and Lemnos (Greek island). The 9th Warwicks landed at V Beach, Cape Helles during the early hours of 14 July, and within hours took over front line and support trenches in a position known as Essex Ravine. After a brief respite back at Lemnos the battalion returned, this time to Anzac Cove, on 3 August. For a few days, the 9th Warwicks were in Divisional Reserve. Then, on 8 August, an attack had pushed back the Turks

Above: Curzon Hall, Suffolk Street August/September 1914. *Dave Vaux Collection*

from their position on the ridge known as Koja Chemen. Here the 9th Warwicks dug in at Farm Gully and came under severe Turkish rifle and machine-gun fire. Early in the morning of 10 August, the Turks counter-attacked with devastating results for the battalion. With no close supports, it was found impossible to hold the line. The Turkish counter-attackers gained a foothold to the side of the 9th Warwicks, and their machine guns caused havoc amongst the ranks. A total of 333 officers and men became casualties; of these 96 were killed.

All these casualties were original men from that first rush of volunteers to enlist during the second week of the war. Perhaps, an idea of how many 'Brummies' enlisted into the 9th Royal Warwicks can be given if we look at the 92 other ranks that were killed on August 10th. We find that fifty-two of these men came from, or lived in, Birmingham on enlisting.

When the 9th Warwicks landed at Cape Helles on 14 July, 1915, the fighting strength amounted to 26 officers and 728 other ranks (4 Officers and 152 other ranks remained at a base depot in Lemnos). By 11 August, after the Turkish counter-attack, the fighting strength of the battalion was now Officers, nil, and 288 other ranks. After the Gallipoli campaign came to an end, the 13th Division moved on to Mesopotamia (Iraq), where it stayed for the rest of the war.

10th (Service) Battalion The Royal Warwickshire Regiment

The second thousand men sent to Budbrooke Barracks, during August 1914, became the 10th Battalion. Once raised this battalion like the 9th was sent to Tidworth, to become part of 57 Brigade of the 19th (Western) Division (K2). The 10th Warwicks landed in France on 17 July, 1915, and made for the La Bassée Front. During April, 1916, the 19th Division moved to the Somme battlefield and took a principal part in the taking of the village of La Boisselle. The 10th Warwicks and the 19th Division remained on the Western Front throughout the war. During 1918 the battalion suffered extremely heavy casualties.

11th (Service) Battalion The Royal Warwickshire Regiment

The third Service Battalion formed at Warwick was sent to the South Downs, near to Shoreham-by-Sea and Brighton. By September, 1914, the battalion had become surplus Army Troops attached to the 24th Division (K3). In March 1915, a 44th Division was created with the surplus Army Troops (11th Warwicks included) of the 24th Division. By April 1915, the War Office had decided that the 16th (Irish) Division (K2), due to a lack of equipment and arms, was falling behind in its training. Consequently, the 44th Division replaced the 16th Division in K2. To make matters more complicated, the 44th Division was then re-numbered to become the 37th Division; with the 11th Warwicks becoming part of 112 Infantry Brigade.

The Battalion landed in France on 30 July, 1915 and made its way to the northern reaches of the Somme Front. Hebuterne was the first destination, followed in September, by a move further north to Hannescamps. The battalion remained in this vicinity until June 1916. July 6th, 1916, saw the battalion and 112 Brigade temporarily attached to the 34th Division and on 15 July, the 11th Warwicks, took part in its first attack in front of the German fortified village of Pozières. Sadly for the Warwickshire men, they were met with heavy machine-gun fire, causing a total of 275 casualties. The Battalion and the Division remained on the Western Front throughout the remainder of the war.

12th and 13th Battalions The Royal Warwickshire Regiment

Those readers familiar with the history of the Royal Warwickshire Regiment, will know, that the 12th and 13th Battalions did not go abroad, but remained in the UK as Reserve Battalions. But, both battalions had their beginnings as Service Battalions during the rush to the colours in August and September of 1914. On formation, the two battalions were sent to the Isle of Wight to begin their training. Both the 12th and 13th Royal Warwicks formed part of the 'original' 97 Brigade of the 'original' 32nd Division (K4). In April, 1915, the six Divisions (30th to 35th) that made up Kitchener's fourth New Army (K4) were disbanded and regenerated into 18 Reserve Infantry Brigades. Thus, the 12th and 13th Royal Warwicks became known as 2nd Reserve Battalions of the 8th Reserve Infantry Brigade. These Brigades would now be used to keep the first three New Armies up to full strength.

To complicate matters even further, as a result of the re-titling of the 'original' Fourth Army, the Fifth New Army (37th to 42nd Divisions) now became the new Fourth Army and the Divisions renumbered 30th to 35th.

It is with the Fourth New Army, that our story of the Birmingham Pals begins. Before the story unfolds, it may be interesting to recollect other events happening or involving Birmingham during the opening weeks of the war.

Birmingham: August 1914

Military recruiting for fighting overseas was not the only form of spontaneous patriotic action taken during the opening few days of the war. For example, The *Birmingham Daily Mail* on 7 August reported that a certain Captain Huxley of Harborne had contacted the War Office offering to form a unit of motor-cyclists for special service with the regular forces. Men had ridden their motor-cycles to Birmingham from many parts of the country to become part of such a unit, and many more had sent telegrams offering their services. The War

Office had to instruct Captain Huxley to cease recruiting owing to the list being full.

Also in the same edition was a report concerning Mr Ernest Fowlkes (of Wellington Road, Edgbaston) who was the District Commissioner for Birmingham Boy Scouts. It concerned a short telegram he had sent to the Chief Scout, Sir Robert Baden-Powell:

> *'Can find about 1,000 Birmingham scouts for service at home or abroad, and am prepared to serve with them myself.'*

In the *Birmingham News* on Saturday, 8 August, there was a brief mention of a volunteer force being raised in south Birmingham not connected with the Territorial Force. Calling themselves 'The Warwickshire Horse', they offered their services en masse to the War Office. Sadly, no other mention of this unit appears in later editions of the paper.

On Saturday, 15 August, *The Birmingham Evening Despatch* published an official government press release concerning the raising and drilling of town guards. These were unofficial units and considered by the authorities as undesirable. 'It is considered that the unauthorised recruitment of men for military or police purposes may interfere with the great national response which is being made to Lord Kitchener's appeal.'

Yet the next item in the same column concerned the decision of a crowded meeting, held at the Birmingham Temperance Hall, to form a Civilian Volunteer Force in Birmingham! The Deputy Mayor (Alderman Bowater) presided over the meeting and said 'the meeting was called for the purpose of giving citizens an opportunity to do something for the defence of the Empire. Many citizens had volunteered for service abroad; many, from one cause or another, were unable to do that, but most felt the dissatisfaction of having to sit quietly at home doing nothing'. Application forms for the proposed unit could be obtained from Mr E G Freeman of Gillott Road, Edgbaston.

HMS *Birmingham*

One major story that hit the headlines in Birmingham during the second week of the war concerned the first Royal Naval ship named after the City, the light cruiser HMS *Birmingham*. The action took place in the North Sea on Sunday, 9 August when the British 1st Light Cruiser Squadron was attacked by a German submarine flotilla. All the submarines were submerged with only their periscopes showing. The Birmingham, steaming at full speed, fired one shot as the nearest submarine (U15) got within striking distance. That shot destroyed the periscope. The other German submarines turned round and sped off, but the U15 was now sailing blind. As the U15 slowly emerged from the sea, a second shot from the *Birmingham*, ripped the conning tower clean out of the upper structure; she sank like a stone.

The next day, Monday 10 August, the following

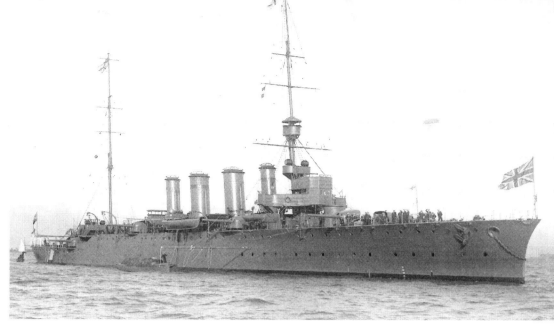

telegram was received by Alderman Bowater, in his capacity as Deputy Mayor, from the First Lord of the Admiralty:

> *'Birmingham will learn with pride that the first German Submarine destroyed in the war was sunk by HMS* Birmingham.*'*

One member of the crew was Able Seaman Pearson of Argyll Street, Nechells, who wrote about the action in a letter to his father:

> *'Well, dad, I will tell you all about it. It was on a Sunday morning, I had been on watch from 8 to 12, and was in my hammock. We were scouting about 100 miles from Germany, when an Able Seaman on watch sighted a periscope above the water. We opened fire at once. Then the Captain altered his course and dashed towards the submarine, which could not fire when broadside on.*
>
> *'Just imagine, I was sleeping, when all of a sudden I was awakened by about half-a-dozen guns going off and the sounding of*

Above and Below: The light cruiser HMS *Birmingham* which had the distinction of sinking the first German U-boat, the U-15, just four days after the declaration of war. The postcard below dramatises the action which took place in the North Sea.

IWM Q38334

the bugle. I turned out quicker than I have ever done in my life. I often laugh as I think of dashing along the upper-deck with one leg in my trousers and one out. Nearly everybody was the same; the Lieutenants came in their pyjamas.

'When the firing started the periscope got blown away, then she came to the top. All the guns were trained on her, and just before she was hit the second time, she switched on a small light, and a lieutenant came up in the conning tower. Just as he poked his head up a shell hit the tower and blew it and him to atoms. Then she sank. I felt a bit sorry for the crew, but if we had been a second later, we should have been up in the air. I thought it was 'good-bye Brum', but we were too busy loading to think much.

'It is the first action I have been in, but I hope it isn't the last. I am dying to get at the Germans, to blow them to atoms, for it makes my blood boil to read about the way they are serving brave men, I am itching to have a go at them.'

Southern General Hospital

Prior to the war, the HQ of the South Midland Division's Territorial Royal Army Medical Corps was the barracks in Great Brook Street. One of the departments was the 1st Southern General Hospital, which before the war had only a small 'management team'. Within seven days of the war starting, this small department had administered the transformation of Birmingham University into a 500 bed hospital; and according to the *Birmingham Daily Post* was: 'the best hospital of its kind in the country'.

Birmingham's Munitions Achievement

It goes without saying, that the 'City of 1001 trades', or'Workshop of the World', as Birmingham has often been described, became the nerve centre of the nation's munitions industry during the First World War. The following extract from *The Municipality and the Great War*, tells us that:

'Four hundred factories and works, diverted from peace-time activities, were equipped with special machinery and plant. Works, large and small, were enlarged. Over these there was a measure of official control, and buildings to accelerate the production and despatch of munitions were erected by the Government. In manufacturing methods, something like a revolution was brought about. Individualistic effort militated against the speeding up of economic production, and cautious-minded manufac-

turers, influenced by the pressing need for war equipment, took the wider view, and showed adaptability in meeting new and difficult problems. Large and rapid output, the thing that really mattered, was secured largely by the adoption of methods of standardisation and the utilisation of automatic and semi-automatic machinery.

'A Board of Management of the local Munitions Committee, composed of leading industrialists, acted in conjunction with works under direct Government control. An effective co-operative scheme was devised and the creation, in the City, of a national shell-factory ensured a pre-scribed output of shells of a specified type, as well as the additional production by engineering firms. Owing to the depletion of male labour in the factories many thousands of women and girls were employed.'

Birmingham Small Arms Company

During the Boer War the BSA factory in Armoury Road, Small Heath made the Lee Metford rifle which was used by the British Army. At one period of time production output peaked at 2,500 rifles per week. For the five years leading up to the First World War, Government orders ran to a paltry 7,000 a year. To keep in business the BSA had to rely heavily on orders for sporting and air rifles. At this time the BSA was also acknowledged through-out the world for the high standard of bicycle and motor-bicycle production. The company even dab-bled in the automotive industry by manufacturing a 13.9 horse power motor car, which was made at the BSA's Sparkbrook factory. Similar to many Birmingham factories during the August Bank Holiday week of 1914, the BSA Works were closed and the majority of the workforce were on holiday, with no thoughts of war. There were a handful of employees on site and these were occupied with the yearly stocktaking. As soon as war was declared, the management had expected contracts from the War office to come in thick and fast; which they duly did. The first contract came in within a few days of the war being declared. Rifles? Lewis-Guns? No. It was for 500 military bicycles! Fully assem-bled, lamps front and rear, carriers front and rear, bells, rifle clips and ready for riding in twenty-four hours! Special messengers and Boy Scouts were sent round to all the homes of the workforce, and gradually they began to drift in. Enough employees were found to complete the order and before the twenty-four hours were up 500 new bicycles were despatched and sent on their way via a special train.

It was on 10 August 1914, that the BSA received the anticipated War Office contract for the Lee-Enfield Short Pattern Mark III rifle, which at the time was the standard rifle for the British Army.

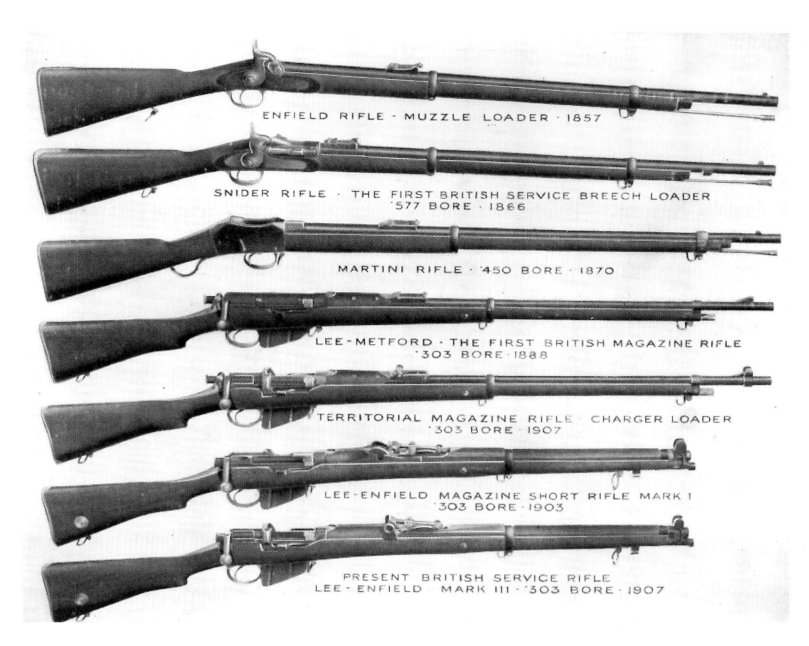

ENFIELD RIFLE · MUZZLE LOADER · 1857

SNIDER RIFLE · THE FIRST BRITISH SERVICE BREECH LOADER
·577 BORE · 1866

MARTINI RIFLE · ·450 BORE · 1870

LEE-METFORD · THE FIRST BRITISH MAGAZINE RIFLE
·303 BORE · 1888

TERRITORIAL MAGAZINE RIFLE · CHARGER LOADER
·303 BORE · 1907

LEE-ENFIELD MAGAZINE SHORT RIFLE MARK I
·303 BORE · 1903

PRESENT BRITISH SERVICE RIFLE
LEE - ENFIELD · MARK III · ·303 BORE · 1907

Until further notice the contract was for 3,000 per week. In stages over the following thirty months rifle production increased. Towards the end of 1916 rifle production peaked at 10,000 per week; which was then maintained for the rest of the war. Those who have never worked in a production engineering environment may think nothing of 10,000 rifles per week. With the new computerised machining methods of the modern world and enough machines this target would no doubt be easily achieved. But during the Great War, the mass production of rifles at the BSA was an immense accomplishment. To manufacture one rifle required 131 machined parts taking 1,505 various machin-

Above: Over a period of fifty years, the British Army's Service Rifle developed from a muzzle loader to the Short Lee-Enfield Mark 111 – the British Service Rifle of the First World War. They were used so proficiently by the British Expeditionary Force in August 1914, that German troops thought British Army battalions were equipped with large quantities of machine guns.

Left: Lewis Guns being tested at the BSA, Birmingham.

Above: Lee Enfield rifle production shop.

Below: As you can guess, a fold up bicycle, was not the ideal piece of kit once trench warfare became established.

Below right: Once war broke out, the BSA in Birmingham were contracted to supply the War Office with 500 military bicycles.

Automatic Machine Gun. Designed by an American, Colonel I N Lewis, BSA secured the sole manufacturing rights to make the machine gun. It was first shown to representatives of the Government in November 1913. The Lewis Gun was light enough, at 26 lbs (approx 12 kg), for a British soldier to fire off its forty-seven round magazine at the hip in six seconds. When attached to an aeroplane it was shown that the feeding mechanism operated perfectly at any angle. Within days of War being declared both the War Office and the Admiralty had placed contracts with the BSA. In August 1914, the Lewis Gun Department employed fifty workers and had machinery to manufacture twenty Lewis Guns per week. Within two-and-a-half years a new factory had been built on the Small Heath site and 10,000 machines had been installed. The fifty employees had increased to 5,000! Production reached a peak of 2,000 per week which was steadily maintained.

Meanwhile at the Birmingham firm of Kynochs at Witton production figures expanded and reached figures that before the war would be thought an impossible task. Very soon the firm was contracted to manufacture 25 MILLION rifle cartridges, 300,000 revolver cartridges, 500,000 cartridge clips, 110,000 brass cases for 18 pounder artillery guns and 300 tons of cordite (smokeless explosive) per week. These figures were successfully met and maintained. In 1918 the weekly production of rifle cartridges was raised to meet the demands caused by the German Spring offensive. At one stage production reached a staggering 29,750,000 cartridges per week!

ing operations. The majority of these required tolerances to within a thousandth or two of an inch (and in some instances there were parts with specifications where 'no tolerance is permissible' within the powers of measuring). This one rifle also required 1,205 different gauges to maintain the quality control throughout the manufacturing process; now multiply all that by 10,000!

A similar story can be told concerning the BSA's war output of the newly invented Lewis Air-Cooled

Chapter Three

Birmingham Pals: The Turn of the Middle Class

To the upper and middle class of Britain, the rank and file of the British Army was the domain of the working class and apart from a sprinkling of the better educated, this was true for the first rush of volunteers during August of 1914. In the book, *Kitchener's Army, From Citizen to Soldier*, published during the war, the following extract is taken:

> *'The average young man of Britain was wont to cheer enthusiastically stories of British heroism. He himself was immensely patriotic and honestly desired to serve his country as best he could. That he did not enlist was due not to his lack of patriotism, not to his failure to appreciate the extraordinary demands which were being made upon his country, but just from sheer failure to understand that he himself could be of any service in the ranks of the Army. Indeed, it would be fairer to reduce down the preliminary hesitation of the young men of England to a sense of modesty rather than to a desire to shirk.'*

These then, were the young non-manual workers, of the commercial districts of towns and cities across Britain. In the late 1980s a term was coined for these young men of the business class, 'yuppies' or 'hooray Henrys'; in 1914, for some reason they were known as 'knuts'. An incentive was needed for these 'knuts' to come forward en masse. It was during the last week of August, when reports from France began to circulate which

The Allied Troops Retire From Namur After A Great Battle.

DAILY SKETCH

BRITAIN'S BEST PICTURE PAPER

WHERE THE BRITISH SOLDIERS ARE FIGHTING : OFFICIAL REPORT OF A BATTLE THAT LASTED A WHOLE DAY.

BRITISH FORCE HELD THEIR GROUND

GERMAN ADVANCE IN THIS DIRECTION

GERMANS HAVE TAKEN NAMUR

Page 3.

DAILY SKETCH, THURSDAY, AUGUST 27, 1914.

HOW THE BRITISH LINE STOOD FIRM AGAINST SIX ATTACKS

THE BRITISH ARMY'S HARDEST TASK.

Retreat, Though Unbeaten, By Order Of Commander-in-Chief.

SIX ATTACKS REPELLED.

'Hecatomb Of German Corpses' After The Battle.

WARM FRENCH PRAISE.

Now Reinforced And Battle Line Rearranged.

These messages describe that part of the fighting in which the British troops were engaged—in which the British troops were engaged between Lille, the nearest great fortress to Dunkirk and Calais, and Maubeuge, on the French frontier, 50 miles farther from the sea. The British were in action for 36 hours.

PARIS, Wednesday.

Details received here of the fighting in Belgium leave no doubt that enormous losses were ... by both sides. ... British inflicted

LATEST WAR SITUATION AT A GLANCE.

The next great stroke in the land war is being prepared in deep silence. No official statement was issued yesterday morning or afternoon by the French War Ministry, usually so communicative.

The French were attacked in force on their southern frontier on Tuesday.

This attack was repulsed, and the enemy retired all along the line, says a British official message.

In other parts of the field the Germans are advancing slowly, and the deciding battles must now take place on French soil.

Isolated German attacks were reported yesterday at the following places in France :—

CONDÉ, 10 miles north of Valenciennes.
BOUCHAIN, near Cambrai, 20 miles within Northern French frontier.
Near VERDUN, 30 miles within Eastern frontier.
At DOUAI, between Lille and Cambrai. Lille is the nearest fortress inland from the North

The British troops have reluctantly fallen back with their French comrades.

They have not been beaten, and retreated "only at the express orders of the Commander-in-Chief and not under pressure from the enemy."

The British victoriously repelled six German attacks running.

After the failure of these assaults the ground was so thick with German bodies that the French colonial troops found it difficult to charge.

Owing to the extended front it is difficult to publish a complete British casualty list, Sir John French reports.

A German army corps has been surrounded by the Russians, who now occupy the whole of the eastern and southern parts of East Prussia.

Togoland, the German West African colony, has surrendered unconditionally to a British force.

TEETH NOT TO BAR RECRUIT

Emergency Army Age Limit M Be Raised To 40.

MR. ASQUITH'S STATEMENTS.

The Chancellor of the Exchequer, replying to Austen Chamberlain, in the Commons yesterday said he would make proposals the next day in connection with death duties arising out of the estates of soldiers on active service.

Mr. Asquith, replying to questions as to the desirability of compulsory service, said the answer was in the negative. (Cheers.)

The question of enlisting able-bodied men between 30 and 40 in the emergency army was a point that had not been lost sight of.

Mr. Asquith, replying to a question, said that Kitchener needed all the recruits he could get. It was a mistake to think that only 100,000 men were needed.

Mr. Tennant said instructions had been given to medical examiners of recruits that no recruit organically sound was to be refused on account of bad teeth unless this was the cause of malnutrition.

Mr. Herbert Samuel said the Government had decided that there was not sufficient reason to postpone the municipal elections. Local arrangements could be made to avoid party contests.

CHANCELLOR'S WARNING TO BANKS.

Mr. Lloyd George moved a resolution authorising the Treasury to borrow "in such manner as the thought fit" on the security of the Consolidated Funds.

With regard to the moratorium, the Chancellor said he had inquired of all trading and financial interests in the country. So far he had received 8,000 replies. Four thousand five hundred were in favour of bringing the moratorium to an end, and 3,500 of continuing it. He was trying to arrange a moratorium which would protect those interests which required it. ... a good deal depended on the banks. The Government

33

Above: Some of the first wounded from the Battle of Mons, safely back in Brighton.

Below: A *Daily Mirror* cartoon. An example of the mood of the nation during August 1914. Women of England had the ability to become Kitchener's recruiting sergeants.

perhaps influenced their thinking. On Tuesday, 25 August, the press published the news which the population had eagerly anticipated; the BEF's first encounter with the German Army. This had taken place the previous Sunday in the vicinity of the Belgian mining town of Mons. However the news was sparse and not very encouraging. The BEF, it was reported, had been in an all day and night fight. To make matters worse, forty or so miles fur-

"WHY DON'T YOU ENLIST?"

Every woman in England who has trained herself to do a woman's work should nag every man she has influence over to enlist, so long as Lord Kitchener calls for recruits. — (By Mr. W. K. Haselden.)

ther east, the Belgian fortress city of Namur, 'the gateway to France', had fallen to German forces. Consequently, to prevent being outflanked, the BEF, even though it had checked a much larger German force, had begun to retreat.

The following day, August 26th, the press reported at least 2,000 British losses and Lord Kitchener declared in the House of Lords, 'the war would demand considerable sacrifices from the people, and would strain the resources of the Empire.' The Prime Minister, Mr Asquith, told the House of Commons 'that the British troops were pressed hard by the enemy, who were shaken off', and it was not desirable to say more.

By now Belgian refugees were streaming to the coast for safety with stories of alleged atrocities by German troops, against the civil population. These worrying events of which the British public were now reading also coincided with the announcement that Kitchener's first 100,000 men had come forward and that the second 100,000 were just as urgent. Newspapers the length and breadth of Britain were now urging more and more young men to volunteer. On 27 August, under the headlines 'Woman's power to make New Armies', the *Daily Mirror* declared that women of England had the ability to become Kitchener's recruiting Sergeants. How? By denying their menfolk love, until they had enlisted! This was now the era of white feathers, which implied cowardice. Young men not wearing uniform or some kind of identification showing they belonged to a military unit, were handed white feathers by certain groups of women. Letters were published from elderly armchair critics, too old for war, but urging the young men of Britain to 'go forth and die a hero for King and country and not to stay at home a coward'.

With news breaking of the Battle of Mons and the subsequent retreat, this was now the much needed spur for the middle and upper classes. The following extracts from *Kitchener's Army, From Citizen to Soldier* explains all:

'It was this that stirred the imagination and roused the conscience of our young manhood. It is true that the incident was not a disaster; though on first inspection it bore a resemblance to such.

'This terrible news of defeated British soldiers straggling all over the countryside in France; of beaten units, the remnants of what had been great regiments, coming wearily into the little towns of the north of France, to tell their harrowing story to a shocked correspondent.'

The grave situation in France was to have the desired effect on recruiting in Britain. As August drew to an end, Recruiting Offices all over the country would soon be unable to cope with the flood of new volunteers. Regimental depots were full; they already had recruits sleeping in village halls, schools, farm buildings, tents and many households had offered to put up volunteers on a

temporary basis. Officers and senior NCOs were in short supply. Reserve stocks of uniforms, equipment and especially rifles were depleted. The War Office was in a dilemma. Kitchener needed these men signed up and attested whilst patriotic feelings were high, thousands more men were anticipated. Therefore a stopgap period was required for volunteers to be allotted a battalion and given rudimentary training until the War Office had the Officers and equipment to take over. Now was the time for civilian help.

Pals Battalion

During the last week of August and the beginning of September committees were formed in many large cities or towns, predominantly made up of leading citizens, industrialists, council officials and usually the officer in command of the local recruiting office. The object was to help ease the pressure off the War Office by raising battalions for Kitchener's New Army. A further incentive for recruiting was now introduced; these battalions were to be composed of men from the same social background or who lived in a particular district and shared the same occupations. These committees would provide food, billets, uniforms, kit and a basic military training programme until the War Office was ready to take them over. One of the first locally raised battalions became known as the Stockbroker's Battalion (10th Royal Fusiliers). A special recruiting office was opened on 21 August for men employed in the City district of London. A few days later an idea was put forward to attract

the 'better class' of young men in Bristol (12th Gloucesters). However, it was the Right Honourable the Earl of Derby who was credited with bringing public awareness of the locally raised battalions. He also originated the term 'Pals' for such battalions. This occurred during a meeting, held on the evening of 28 August, to discuss the possibility of Liverpool raising a battalion of non-manual workers (whose story is admirably told in the book *Liverpool Pals* by Graham Maddocks).

Birmingham cannot lay claim to the fame of being the first provincial city to raise a local battalion. It can claim that, of the approximately 150 locally raised Service Battalions that existed during the war, Birmingham's were recruited via the local newspaper; the *Birmingham Daily Post*.

Birth of the Birmingham Pals

On Friday morning, 28th August, after the latest appeal by Lord Kitchener, the Birmingham Daily Post published the following leading editorial, the last paragraph being the most significant:

'Lord Kitchener has appealed for 100,000 recruits as an instalment of a contemplated new army of 500,000. Relatively to other towns Birmingham has responded handsomely.

'But Birmingham can and ought to do much more. Lord Kitchener is asking for men aged between 19 and 30. At the last census, Birmingham with a total population of 840,000 had some 140,000 male inhabitants qualified by age to join the

Above: Some of the first wounded from the Battle of Mons, seen here at Moor Street Station, Birmingham on their way to the Southern General Hospital.
Birmingham Library services

35

new army. It is difficult to say how many of these have responded to the call of the state. Certain deductions have to be made for men over the age of 30 who are in the Regular Army, the Territorials, or the Navy. Probably there are about 5,000 Birmingham men in the Regular Army, about 7,000 in the Reserves, and about 5,500 in the Territorials. Apart from this about 7,000 men have been recruited since the war broke out.

'Roughly, then, it may be fair to estimate that Birmingham has contributed some 25,000 men to the defence of the national honour. Even if it be assumed, which it cannot, that all these are under 30 there would still remain 115,000 men eligible by age to join the colours. Of these, probably rather less than half, at least 50,000, are unmarried.

'What are these 50,000 men, nearly all without dependants, doing that they have not presented themselves for the service of their country? Have they realised that upon them rests the first responsibility; that whatever may be said of the duty of our married manhood there can be no question that patriotism insists that the unmarried shall offer themselves without thought or hesitation?

'A time may come when the country will demand instead of invite. We hope not, for it is infinitely preferable that we should fight for our national preservation under the stimulus of patriotism. For the present, at any rate, there is no compulsion, and every man can do his part with the abiding satisfaction of having acted voluntarily. We cannot but believe that such hesitation as at the present exists will be immediately dispelled the moment the full significance of the call is realised. Perhaps it would help to bring the young manhood of the city the better to recognise the privilege which is offered them of serving their King and country in an emergency if employers would co-operate to assure all their unmarried servants between the ages of 19 and 30 that if they go to the front their places will be reserved for them at the end of the war.

'Something might also be done if the authorities would facilitate the raising of a battalion of non-manual workers. Splendid material is available, and we do not doubt that such a battalion, if associated in some way with the name of the city, would fill rapidly. We think the suggestion, which has reached us from more than one quarter, is well worthy of consideration by the War Office.'

News concerning the possible raising of a non-man-ual workers battalion soon spread around Birmingham's commercial district, from managers down to clerks and council employees to shop assistants. By midday Friday, the offices of the *Birmingham Daily Post* in New Street, the *Birmingham Daily Mail* in Corporation Street and the Lord Mayor's Parlour at the Council House were inundated with prospective volunteers willing to offer their services. 'I didn't wait to shave or have breakfast but pelted the two miles to the city on my bicycle and reached the *Post* offices at ten minutes to eight', recalled the twenty year old Chartered Accountant, Cedric Pritchard Powell, of Chad Road, Edgbaston. Cedric, who in later years would represent the Edgbaston Ward on the Birmingham City Council, had tried to enlist in the first week of the war but had been turned down because he wore glasses. This time his youthful zeal was rewarded and he would be accepted into the new battalion.

During Friday afternoon, the Deputy Lord Mayor, Alderman William Henry Bowater having given the matter consideration consulted three of Birmingham's most senior Territorial officers, Lieutenant-Colonel Hart, Lieutenant-Colonel Ludlow and Lieutenant-Colonel Sir John Barnsley, as to the best method of raising a force of 1,000 men.

After the meeting Alderman Bowater told a *Post* representative 'that nothing definite had been decided upon, and the matter would receive further consideration. The suggestion is an excellent one, and there is no doubt that the requisite number would be forthcoming without delay'. He later spoke to a representative of the *Birmingham Evening Despatch*, in which he further expanded his views. 'There is,' explained Alderman Bowater, 'such a wide difference between the commissioned officers of the Army and the middle class youth that the latter, finding it impossible to obtain a commission, feels that there is nothing that he can do to serve his country in such a time of national crisis. Should such a battalion be formed, these fellows would find themselves among those of their own class.' Lieutenant-Colonel Ludlow further added that 'he agreed entirely with the proposal and that the class of which the men should be drawn would include school teachers, clerks, articled pupils, shop assistants, warehousemen, farmers, corporation officials and others.' He further added that, 'I quite think that many professions and trades would find their own special quota, and such institutions as the Birmingham University and Old Boys and large numbers from the Officers Training Corps would also form companies.'

Saturday 29 August, 1914

The local press had summed up the previous day's events, concerning the possibility of a Birmingham Battalion; which, as you can guess

BIRMINGHAM CITY BATTALION.

"FORWARD, BIRMINGHAM!"

BRITISH LOSSES.

FIRST RETURN OF CASUALTIES.

36 OFFICERS AND 127 MEN KILLED.

NEARLY 5,000 WOUNDED AND MISSING.

A communiqué from the Official Press Bureau, issued late last night, says:—

A report has been received from General Headquarters of the Expeditionary Force giving a return of the casualties of one of the cavalry brigades and of three of the divisions less one brigade. It shows the following numbers.—

	Officers.	Other ranks.
Killed	36	127
Wounded	57	629
Missing	95	4,183
	188	4,939

As regards the "other ranks," it is known that a considerable proportion of the missing were wounded men who had been sent down country, of whom particulars were not available at General Headquarters. The missing are those not accounted for, and may include unwounded prisoners and stragglers as well as casualties.

The return includes the names of officers only. The next of kin have been informed by telegram, and the names will be published to-morrow (Wednesday) evening.

It may take a little time yet to collect the information as to "other ranks," but their names also will be published when they have been received and their next of kin have been informed.

Further reports of casualties are expected with little delay.

DEATH OF THE HON. ARCHER WINDSOR-

---

motivated more people to put pen to paper. One in particular, published in the Birmingham Daily Mail, had this to say:

'To anyone who has seen the recruiting parades through the city during the last few days the question, 'Do we deserve to win?' surely has occurred. The recruits, with one or two exceptions, have been composed entirely of the so-called working classes, while the streets have been lined with young fellows wearing good clothes, looking superciliously on. Will these 'knuts' never realise that but for the men whom they refuse to mix with, they would have to learn to shout 'Hoch! Hoch!' and the flappers and barmaids, whom their life's work seems to be to fascinate, will be treated as the Belgian women have been treated by the Germans.'

Not all letters came from armchair critics, a couple were published from future recruits to the battalion. 'I notice that a battalion of clerks, etc, is being raised in Liverpool. Why not one in Birmingham? I know of many others who like myself would be only too willing to join'. So wrote a certain J E B Fairclough, who did enlist and survived the war to be the author of the book *The 1st Birmingham Battalion in the Great War*. Another, was from twenty-two year old Harry Gibbons of Highgate Road, Camp Hill, who had this to say:

'I think the suggestion made in your leading article last night that Birmingham should follow the example of Liverpool in raising a city battalion of non-manual workers, young professional men, and such like, is a most useful one. For myself, I cannot see where any serious objection could be made to such a battalion on the part of the War Office, and I believe, with you, that a sufficient number of young men would be almost immediately forthcoming in Birmingham. In this, the most serious period of our nation's history, snobbishness is quite out of all our minds. We young men feel that we ought to be 'up and doing,' each his level best in defence of our great Empire. At the same time there are those of us who would more gladly join such a company as this than any other at present in existence. I hope your suggestion will be acted upon.'

In less than two years after writing this letter, Private Harry Gibbons (No.705, C Coy, 2nd B'ham Battalion) was posted missing, presumed killed, after an unsuccessful attack upon German trenches.

War Office Acceptance

Alderman Bowater convened another meeting on Saturday morning. The outcome was that Birmingham should not only offer the men, but undertake the responsibility, in the name of the city, of equipping the force. Before announcing his decision, Alderman Bowater had also invited a number of Birmingham's prominent citizens to associate themselves with him in guaranteeing the sum necessary for this purpose, in anticipation of a satisfactory response from the War Office. During the course of Saturday morning the following telegram was sent to Lord Kitchener:

'In absence of Lord Mayor, who is on military duty, I offer on behalf of the city of Birmingham to raise and equip a battalion of young business men for service in His Majesty's Army, to be called the Birmingham Battalion. This is in addition to the ordinary recruits who have enlisted in this city to the number of nearly 8,000'.

W H Bowater, Deputy Mayor

To this telegram Lord Kitchener replied as follows on Saturday afternoon:

'The Battalion you offer would be most acceptable and a valuable addition to his Majesty's forces. I presume you mean a regular battalion on usual terms of service. If so, it might form a battalion of the Royal Warwickshire Regiment, to be designated the Birmingham Battalion, with a number.

Kitchener

Once confirmation was received from the War Office, The *Birmingham Daily Post* announced it would open a register for men desiring to join the new battalion. The reason for this was that before Alderman Bowater could proceed with enlistment, there were certain military formalities to be observed. Therefore the register was a time-saving measure and the motive of the *Post* was to place itself in a position to hand over to the authorities the makings of the battalion. Subsequently on Saturday afternoon, 29 August, the sister paper of the *Post*, the *Birmingham Daily Mail* announced that the *Daily Post* 'invites all who will be willing to join the new battalion, to send in their names and addresses. These will be entered in a register and published in the columns of the paper'. It was also reported that the *Daily Post* offices would stay open until 10 pm on Saturday evening and for a couple of hours on the following Sunday morning for the registration of names. After the office closed, at noon on Sunday, 352 men had registered in person over the weekend.

Remarkable Response

On Monday morning, 31 August, the *Birmingham Daily Post* published the first list of names and addresses of young men who had registered over the weekend. This, no doubt, was a further stimulus to recruiting to those still undecided when they saw names of friends, work colleagues and relations in the list. Another subtle ploy was aimed at those, still hesitant, in the evening edition of the *Birmingham Daily Mail*. No doubt, for some, a decision was made after reading the following article, in an adjacent column on the same page, by a *Mail* journalist writing under the pseudonym of 'Rally'. Under the heading 'THE TURN OF THE MIDDLE CLASS', it went as follows:

'I think you have hardly emphasised the growing opinion of the country as to the little part the better clad, better fed, and better educated class of Britain's single men

Below: Birmingham Council House 1914

have done to help.

'When one has visited various recruiting offices as the writer has done, and has seen that the cry "To Arms" is responded to mainly by the poorest of the poor – who after all, have the least to lose if our nation loses – one wonders when the middle class young men, the shopmen, accountants, bank clerks, etc., with those who are kept in idleness by fond parents, will come forward to prove the boast that the strength of Britain lies in the middle class.

'To the young single men of Britain, I say: "If you are without responsible ties, Enlist! or the nation brand you a coward!" To the women of Britain, I say: "Do not mate with a man who could enlist and would not; the world has no room for a future generation of cowards".

'If we lose our prestige only in this world-war it will not be the fault of those who went with big hearts and empty stomachs to enlist to fight for King and country. The blame will lie with the "knuts" of tennis, rugger, and soccer, and the pap-reared "knuts" of "bar"-dom. Is it not better to die as a Briton than live as a subject of a nation which, having beaten you, would say, "We should not have conquered the British if those who had most to lose had met us with the steel and fire as their poor did". Our Regular Army can beat, with equal numbers, anything in Europe. Our officers and men will die before surrender. The bottom dog and the top dog are fighting for us! Our Territorial and Auxiliary Forces are doing their duty. Our Reserves have responded to a man.

'Single men of the middle class, what are you doing?'

Second Birmingham Battalion Suggested

By Tuesday, 1 September, over twelve hundred names had been registered. Subsequently, on the same day, Alderman Bowater and Sir John Barnsley travelled to London and visited the War Office to inform the authorities that there was a distinct possibility of the city raising two battalions, and that both of them would be offered with equipment. Duly the authorities confirmed that a second battalion would be welcomed no less than the first.

Most of the volunteers were registering in person at the *Daily Post* offices rather than posting their applications to join. There was a continuous stream of applicants from 9 am to 10 pm, without a slack period in between. In one such queue, waiting to register, was seventeen year old Ted Francis, whose father was the licensee of the Glassmaker's Arms Public House in Granville Street. Some of the pub's regular clientele had seen Ted waiting his turn in the line, and soon his mother got to hear of it. On returning home Ted had to explain that he had put his name down on the Lord Mayor's list to join an elite unit of Birmingham men for Kitchener's New Army. His mother was suitably impressed until he told her they would become part of the Royal Warwickshire Regiment; and then 'she hit the roof'. 'They're full of thieves and vagabonds;' she claimed. But Ted had made his mind up and within a day or two Ted's elder brother Harry, a trainee accountant, would also register. Ted enlisted into the 2nd Birmingham Battalion and Harry into the 3rd Battalion. Soon after both battalions had commenced their training, Ted transferred to join Harry.

The *Daily Post* also reported that the 'applicants form splendid material for fighting. For the most part they are clean, well set-up, healthy looking young men, well educated and refined, intelligent and vigorous'. Many applicants, it was also reported, were from the working class, but their names were being passed onto the various other recruiting offices within the city. Furthermore, it was also announced that the 'Birmingham Battalion' was originally intended to be filled by Birmingham men only but, many middle-class young men from neighbouring towns were also anxious to join; these too, for the time being, were accepted and forwarded on to Alderman Bowater. There was one young man who, at the time, was living with his aunt and uncle in Yateley Road, Harborne. The person in question was seventeen year old Charles Carrington. Born in West Bromwich, he had spent most of his life in New Zealand, where his father was the Dean of Christchurch. Having aspirations to be a journalist he came over to Britain to finish off his education at Oxford University. At the start of war he had been living with relatives at Fleet near Aldershot, but when discussions about his future began taking place over his head, about whether he should return home or not, between relatives and his parents back in New Zealand, he decided to enlist and applied for a commission in The New Zealand Forces by means of the New Zealand High Commission in London. He was turned down because of his age. Consequently he moved up to Birmingham to live with more sympathetic relatives, namely his uncle Philip Carter who was a Captain in the Territorial 5th Battalion of the Royal Warwickshire Regiment who encouraged him to enlist. To ease the worries of his mother, he wrote the following on September 3rd:

'If I join the Birmingham City Battalion under the influence of the Lord Mayor, I don't think I'll do badly. Probably we'll never get further than guarding communications. With previous experience I may possibly get a commission.

'The editor of the Birmingham Gazette says that it would be hopeless to begin any profession, especially journalism, anywhere now, but that I would not be too old

to begin at twenty. The war won't last more than three years at the extreme outside. There is miles more opening here than in New Zealand. A reporter can get £100 a year to begin with, if he has any luck.'

Perhaps Carrington's opinions of how long the war would last and how the new battalion would be employed was shared by many other volunteers. This is probably why numerous men who had registered their names with the *Birmingham Daily Post*, during the first week of September, went elsewhere and enlisted into other regiments, hoping to get a speedier passage to the front line.One of these was Henry Ogle, of Church Green East, Redditch. He decided instead to enlist into the 7th Royal Warwicks. During his service he was awarded the Military Cross and finished the war as a captain. His Great War journals were published by Pen and Sword in 1993, in a book entitled *The Fateful Battle Line*.

Register Closes

The *Daily Post* register closed at 6 pm Saturday, 5 September, with a total of 4,500 names and addresses of young non-manual workers. Men possessing the necessary qualifications who had not registered could still present themselves at the special recruiting centre, soon to be announced. One young man was nineteen year old, and former pupil of George Dixon Grammar School, James Percy Eames who was an office boy in the City Treasurer's Department of the Council House. He was on holiday in North Wales when news of the formation of the City Battalions reached him. By then the lists had been closed. He cut short his holiday and sought the help of Mr Arthur Collins, the City Treasurer, the post James held himself from 1948 to 1960. Together they went to see the

Deputy Lord Mayor, Alderman Bowater. 'Who closed the list?' Alderman Bowater asked. 'You did', replied Mr Collins. 'Well if he passes his medical, I will re-open it for him' said the Deputy Mayor. The Medical Officer passed him fit in full view of Alderman Bowater. James would later recall, 'Twenty minutes of influence to get in and four-and-a-half years to get out!'

To clear up a point here, the list was not composed entirely of the middle-class. As the term suggests, 'non-manual worker' encompassed the whole range of the social classes of Birmingham, from office clerks or shop assistants with working class backgrounds, to solicitors, chartered accountants and the heirs of Birmingham's most distinguished and wealthy citizens.

When the complete register was entered into a computer database, the information acquired proved very interesting. For example, there were 160 sets of brothers; mostly twos but several sets of three and a sprinkling of four brothers from one household. A couple of homes even had both father and son registered. Another common occurrence was that many addresses had several men living there, all with different surnames. Perhaps these were lodging houses, or, possibly men who were not 'Brummies' but giving the address of a friend who was. The majority of homes on the register had a straight forward house number, but the social background of applicants was also in evidence by a certain few who had addresses such as 3 back 23 or 2 court 5 etc; whilst applicants at the top end of the social ladder could be identified by homes with no number, just a name, i.e., 'The Laurels', 'The Poplars' or 'The Cedars'. The years prior to the First World War, saw the rise of the suffragette movement, which brought one amusing house name to light, at an address in the aptly named Suffrage Street, Smethwick; the house was called 'Votingemin'. This was the home of Sydney Henry Lane who, five months after enlisting into the 1st Birmingham Battalion, took a commission into the Royal Garrison Artillery. Captain Lane was killed in action on 5 April, 1918, and is buried in Cabaret Rouge British Cemetery, France. Considering that the original intent was that the Birmingham Battalions were to be filled by Birmingham men, approximately 500 who registered did not live in the city. The best part of these lived in the regional towns surrounding Birmingham; even as far as Leamington Spa (40 men) and Stratford upon Avon (15 men). The largest group of non-Brummies (120) were men from Sutton Coldfield, which at the time was part of Staffordshire, whilst within the city boundary, Edgbaston and Handsworth yielded the most recruits, with just over 300 men each.

Companies of Chums

On the same Saturday the register closed (5 September), the press announced there was now the likelihood of a third Birmingham battalion in

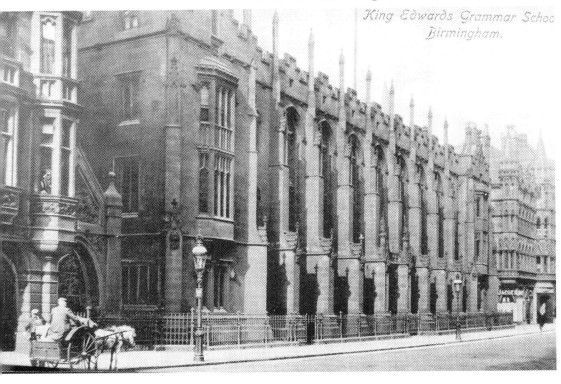

King Edwards Grammar School Birmingham.

the offing. But the most interesting item concerned the forming of companies of chums within the new battalions, which in fact helped me in the decision in the titling of this book. One frequent problem that I encountered during my research was that many relatives of those who enlisted into the Birmingham Battalions had not heard the term 'Birmingham Pals'. The *Birmingham Daily Post* had this to say:

> 'One of the primary objects for which these special battalions were promoted and the 'Daily Post' register opened was that young men should be enabled, as far as possible, to serve shoulder to shoulder with their friends and colleagues in civil life. They were intended to be not only Birmingham Battalions, but 'PALS' battalions, and the special facilities offered to particular groups, members of associations, and business colleagues to serve in the same companies, or even form their own companies where the numbers warrant it, will be largely taken advantage of.
>
> 'Representatives of such groups were invited to call yesterday at the Lord Mayor's Parlour at the Council House to hand in the names of their respective parties, and the response indicates how highly these facilities are appreciated.'

The dominant association behind many, recruits lay with the old boys of the King Edwards Schools of Birmingham, namely the High School in New Street, Aston, Camp Hill and Five Ways. Representatives of each school's old boys association called impromptu meetings inviting members who had put their name forward to attend. Lists of names were then forwarded onto the Lord Mayor's Parlour. In addition, there were groups of men from George Dixon's, The Central Secondary School and Handsworth Grammar. Other strong contingents of men came from St Peter's Teacher Training College at Saltley, Birmingham University Officer Training Corps, Birmingham Corporation officials and the General Electric Company at Witton. Companies for the new battalions were also envisaged to have a residential district connection, such as Edgbaston, Moseley, Handsworth, Erdington and Sutton Colfield.

Equipment Fund

On 29 August, when Alderman Bowater, had gained official sanction to raise a non-manual workers' battalion, he had invited a number of prominent citizens to associate themselves with him in guaranteeing the sum necessary for this purpose. An official fund had not been opened because it might have had an adverse effect with the city's collection for the Prince of Wales' National Relief Fund. Therefore to coincide with the opening of the *Daily Post* register, the local press began publishing daily lists of voluntary donations with the names of the firms or citizens and the amount sub-

scribed. Accordingly, as the register of volunteers multiplied, so did the equipment fund. When the register closed on Saturday evening, 5 September, the amount contributed to the equipment fund was approaching £14,000. The fund eventually rose to £17,000.

What was not appreciated, in the opening few days of recruiting, was that the War Office would allot a grant for the normal allowance of equipment, therefore the money provided could only be used to provide the Birmingham Battalions with better quality uniforms and certain articles not included in the official kit and accoutrements. For many cynics, who thought that a battalion of non-manual workers, would perhaps only be used for home defence, the words 'chocolate-box soldiers' had already sprung to mind.

Enlistment and Attestation

Lieutenant-Colonel Sir John Barnsley was given the honour of becoming the chief recruiting officer for the Birmingham Battalions. The appointment proved to be a most popular choice, for he had been well known for many years in local military circles, and to many others through his civilian occupation as head of one of Birmingham's leading building contractors. Sir John began his military experience as a junior subaltern in the 1st Volunteer Battalion of the Royal Warwickshire Regiment in 1883. With the formation of the Territorial Force in 1908 he subsequently became the first commanding officer of the 5th Royal Warwicks.

To ease the pressure from the various other recruiting offices within the city, it was decided to establish an alternative venue for the attestation of the Birmingham Battalions. The newly built extension of the Art Gallery in Great Charles Street was chosen and given the official title 'Special Recruiting Office No.11'. A fine choice indeed, except for one small oversight; the interior of the new extension had not been finished! Netherless, amid scaffolding and decorators and all the paraphernalia needed to embellish such a large building, the special recruiting office opened for business on Monday morning 7 September, 1914.

During the previous week, whilst the register was still open, the volunteers had begun to receive specially printed post-cards inviting them to attend the new recruiting station at a given day and time. Over the next three weeks or so 250 men daily were called for. Sir John Barnsley had as his chief of staff Captain Dimmock, and the attesting was done by a staff of stockbroker's clerks, under the direction of Mr Howard Todd. There were also a number of Boy Scouts on hand to guide the volunteers to the enlistment officer and medical staff through the network of passages, full of ladders, trestles and dust-sheets.

The first contingent of men to present themselves for enlistment were from the Council House and other municipal offices, and, fittingly, the

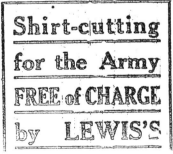

Deputy Lord Mayor, Alderman Bowater, swore them in. Directly after being accepted into the battalion, many of these men entered upon duties assisting the recruiting staff. The honour of being the first man attested into the 1st Birmingham Battalion, and given the service number '1' went to H Fleming, who worked in the Water Department at the Council House.

Of the first 250 summoned for the first day of recruiting, 236 turned up, and of these, 192 were accepted for service. The main cause for rejection was poor dental hygiene. These men were deferred until they had received some dental treatment, and then accepted. Small chest measurements, lack of height and hammer-toes were other reasons why many did not make it into the battalions. One new recruit was J E B Fairclough, who recalled this little anecdote about these early days:

'The physical standard set for the battalion was a very high one, but so keen were the volunteers to join the battalion that many dodges were resorted to, to overcome the medical examination. Great anxiety was felt by individuals as to whether they would pass the physical tests, and in one or two cases little whispers outside the door during the eyesight test enabled the volunteers to pass the examination, and it was not discovered till four years afterwards that two brothers had given their ages with only one month between the dates of their births.'

In charge of the medical examinations was Major Hall-Edwards, who had stated that men rejected as not being up to the 'City Battalion' physical standard would be accepted for other units in Kitchener's Army. Once attested the new recruits resumed their civilian employment until further orders. Some no doubt had already given their notice or resigned and according to one local newspaper, 'many of the men expressed their keenest disappointment that there should be any interval before entering upon military duties. They were anxious to go into camp at once.' Arrangements for training were being made as speedily as possible. Commanding Officers would have to be appointed, subordinate officers selected and instructors assigned; until this was done, the men would be paid sixpence (two-and-a-half pence, nowadays) per day until called up; then they would receive a private soldier's daily rate of one shilling and nine pence.

3rd Birmingham Battalion

Official War Office sanction to raise a third Birmingham Battalion was given on Monday, 14 September. This was also the day that the *Birmingham Daily Post* published the list of names of men accepted into the 1st Battalion, which had been completed the previous Friday (11

September). The 2nd Battalion came up to full strength on Saturday morning, 19 September, and its full list of names was published on Monday, 21 September.

As you can imagine, as soon as the 2nd Battalion was completed, all subsequent men then went into the 3rd Battalion. There now came a slight hiccup in the proceedings; there were approximately only 250 men remaining from the original list of 4,500 names to call upon for medicals and attestation. Apart from those who failed on health grounds, several hundreds of those who originally enrolled themselves into the battalions were too impatient to get on with their military training to wait for the 'City' Battalions, and had already joined other units. Therefore on the same day as the completed list of the 2nd Birmingham Battalion was published, the local press announced that there were still vacancies for the 3rd Battalion. Those wishing to apply were informed to make their way to the Art Gallery Extension between the hours of 9 am and 6 pm. Because of this slight set-back, the 3rd Battalion took a few days longer to be completed than the first two. However, the 3rd Birmingham Battalion was completed and the full list of names was published in the *Birmingham Daily Post* on Friday, 3 October.

One interesting item is to be found in the local press concerned the official classification of the three City Battalions during the early stages of their formation. On 14 September, the *Birmingham Daily Mail* reported that the 1st and 2nd Birmingham Battalions would be officially known as the 11th and 12th Royal Warwicks and, presumably, the 3rd City Battalion when raised would be the 13th Royal Warwicks. However, as mentioned in the previous chapter, the 11th, 12th and 13th Battalions of the Regiment were in the process of being formed from recruits being sent to Budbrooke Barracks. Clearly this was an example of the confusion caused in many quarters by the rapid expansion of the Royal Warwickshire Regiment, and perhaps many more regiments, during the opening weeks of the war.

Equipment Fund Committee

The committee appointed to deal with the question of the equipment regarding the three City Battalions met on Wednesday, 16 September. It was decided to advertise for tenders for supplying the battalions with clothing, boots, shirts, socks and for many other implements necessary in a large encampment. As regards the uniform, The committee was advised by a directive from the War Office, that khaki cloth was in short supply and that units of Kitchener's Army were to wear blue serge uniforms during their training. Apart from the Deputy Lord Mayor, Alderman Bowater, the rest of the Equipment Fund Committee comprised of: Mr F Dudley Docker, Colonel C J Hart, Alderman Neville Chamberlain, Captain Kenneth Davis, Mr Charles

Hyde, Mr A J Keen and Alderman Sir Hallewell Rogers, while R S Hilton of the Corporation Gas Department acted as Honorary Secretary. Once established, the future commanding officers of the three Birmingham Battalions would also assist in an advisory capacity.

Also on the agenda was the subject of training grounds for the three battalions. The two areas which found favour with the committee were Sutton Park, for two battalions, whilst the other would train at Castle Bromwich Playing Fields in the vicinity of the River Tame near Castle Vale housing estate.

As mentioned previously, with patriotic feelings running high, young men not in uniform or wearing some type of distinctive badge or emblem showing they were connected to a military unit, were liable to be given a mouthful of abuse or handed a white feather. Therefore it was decided that for an interim period, whilst uniforms were being made, an enamelled button-hole badge would be given to all recruits accepted into the City Battalions. However, because of the public mood prevailing at the time, the committee also decided to issue a badge bearing the inscription 'Volunteered for Birmingham Battalion' to those who had volunteered for service with the battalions but had been rejected on medical or other grounds. As a spokesman for the Equipment Fund Committee explained: 'It was hoped in this way to restrain thoughtless persons from reflecting on the patriotism of those who had done their duty.'

'The Pets of the City'

The first parade for the City Battalions was the Drill Hall, Thorp Street (HQ of the 5th and 6th Royal Warwicks) on Saturday afternoon, 19

September (this was the same day the 2nd Battalion came up to full strength and the beginning of recruitment for the 3rd Battalion). The aim of the parade was to issue the enamel button-hole badge to the men of the 1st and 2nd battalions and to put the men in the picture as to, what future lay in store for them, as regards training.

One of those who attended was J E B Fairclough, who later recalled:

The floor of the Drill Hall was filled with members of the First and Second City Battalions, full of enthusiasm, and feeling that a further step nearer the commencement of training days had been reached. It

Top: The New Art Gallery Extension on the corner of Great Charles Street and Congreve Street; or in military parlance "No.11 Recruiting Station."

Above: Example of the Postcards sent to all men who applied to join the Birmingham Battalions. This one was sent to Alan Thomas Furse who lived at School Road, Moseley.

43

Above: Thorp Street Drill Hall, Saturday 19 September 1914. The Deputy Lord Mayor, William Bowater, and his wife issuing button hole badges to members of the 1st and 2nd Birmingham Battalions, after their first parade. The bottom badge, is thought to be a prototype (see page 47) that turned up in the Jewellery Quarter a few years ago. Even though this badge was suggested, I believe they were never issued.
Birmingham Library Services
Bottom badge: Dave Seeney Collection

was a very eager crowd and opportunity was taken to look around and see what our future comrades would be like.'

Another young recruit, this time from the 2nd Birmingham Battalion, was Francis J Field, who hailed from Great Hampton near Evesham. This was only his third visit to the midlands metropolis; the other two were only fleeting visits.

'Here, in an excitement of chatter, unfamiliar commands and anxious, shuffling manoeuvres, we formed into long irregular lines to answer our first echoing roll-call. Most of the men were already grouped into sections, each from a famous firm, professional interest, "old school" boys, civil servants and so on. To me they were a thousand complete strangers..... but not for long.'

Standing on the upper balcony, overlooking the Drill Hall, Alderman Bowater, amid enthusiastic cheering, was first to speak. During his speech he described the City battalions as 'the pets of the city.' (Loud laughter and cheers.) 'They all knew, of course, that the pet of the family was usually the spoilt child.' ('Oh!') 'He was usually the worst of the flock.' ('Oh!') 'Birmingham wanted to see the men of the City Battalions the exception to the rule.' (Hear, hear.) 'The citizens were proud of

them. They knew the men did not want to be petted or coddled or have any fuss made of them. They wanted them to make a name for themselves by their own actions.' (Hear, hear.) 'They had not been invited to a picnic.' (Laughter.) 'They would know what sort of a 'picnic' it was in a few weeks time.' (Renewed laughter.) 'Whilst the city was quite sure their bravery and pluck and enthusiasm would be all that could be called for,' there was one other virtue that he wished to speak of for one moment – patience. For the next week or two their patience might be sorely tried. If their uniforms and arms and other items of their equipment were not ready as soon as they would like, if there was any hitch in the arrangements for their housing and training, he asked them to remember that half a million new troops for Lord Kitchener's New Army had been raised. 'Have a little patience if all does not at first go smoothly.' The Deputy Lord Mayor concluded, 'Your city looks to you to maintain the reputation of the Birmingham Battalions.'

Amid wholehearted scenes of cheering and applause, the 2,000 recruits sang, 'For he's a jolly good fellow.'

Next to speak was Sir John Barnsley, his first topic concerned the commanding officers for the 1st and 2nd Birmingham Battalions. Earlier in the week the War Office had notified Alderman

Bowater of the selection. Unfortunately, there was one slight problem, both of these men, Captain F A C Hamilton of the Scottish Rifles and Major T H F Price of the Duke of Cornwall's Light Infantry, were both serving in France. Consequently, the War Office asked Sir John Barnsley to take over temporary command of the 1st Birmingham Battalion, to organise its staff and get it out for training as quickly as possible. (More loud applause and cheering.) He also reported that an alternative commanding officer for the 2nd Battalion would be selected within a few days.

Sutton Park, Sir John informed them, had been selected for the training ground of the 1st Battalion, and the building known as the Crystal Palace would become the HQ of the battalion. Sir John had already been notified, by Mr Reay-Nadin, the Town Clerk of Sutton Coldfield, of nearly 800 offers from private house-holders offering their homes as billets. The decision about training grounds for the other two battalions would rest with the future commanding officers. Next, Sir John informed the men that the Equipment Fund Committee was placing contracts for two suits of uniform; both would be strictly of regulation pattern, one would be grey for working and the other blue, for walking out. However, for a short while, the men would continue to wear their own clothes, until the uniforms were made. When the meeting ended, Alderman Bowater and his wife presented the 'Birmingham Battalion' enamelled button-hole badge to the men as they filed out of the Drill Hall.

Second Battalion Command

A few days after the first parade at Thorp Street, the War Office informed Alderman Bowater that Captain George Smith, of the South Staffordshire Regiment, was to take temporary command of the 2nd Birmingham Battalion. Captain Smith was no stranger to the City, he lived at Wellington Road, Edgbaston and since the outbreak of the war had been the chief recruiting officer at the Technical School in Suffolk Street; where, between August 14 and 8 September, he enlisted 8,694 men into the services.

Captain Smith was forty-six years old and had joined the 1st Volunteer Battalion, The South Staffordshire Regiment as a private in 1885. He rapidly rose through the ranks and gained a commission. He took command of the South Staffs No.2 Service Company in South Africa in 1900 (by profession, Captain Smith was an architect and surveyor and a partner in the firm of Riley and Smith of Colmore Row). His first priority was to select the training area for his new battalion. Castle Bromwich Playing Fields, favoured in many quarters as the next choice to Sutton Park, had been rejected after a second inspection. The problem was that this section of the Tame Valley was liable to flood in winter. Two other locations suggested at the time were Weston-Super-Mare and Rhyl, but

after further consultation with the Sutton Coldfield Town Council, Sutton Park was considered big enough to take a second battalion. The Streetly side of the Park was suggested, in an area once used by early Volunteer battalions for camping purposes. However, probably because the billeting arrangements were more favourable, the area of the park close to the Boldmere and Wylde Green district was chosen; with the boathouse situated alongside Powells Pool as the new HQ of the 2nd Birmingham Battalion.

Sunday 4 October, 1914. 1st Birmingham Battalion Church Parade

As September drew to an end, the groundwork for the 1st Battalion had now been completed. The men were to commence training on Monday, 5 October. By this time, Sir John Barnsley had chosen a select band of 'Top Management' from the city, all with previous military experience of one form or another, to take up senior officer appointments within the battalion. Junior subalterns would be selected once training was under way. Major Charles Playfair had been appointed second in command. Formerly of the Royal Irish Rifles, Major Playfair was better known in Birmingham as the 'Proof Master' at the Birmingham Gun Barrel Proof House in Banbury Street.

Billets had been organised and basic military training was to be undertaken by time-expired ex-Regular senior NCO's who had come forward. Postcards had been sent to all the recruits, the first notifying each man of which company he was in, and the second, telling him of the assembly instructions for the battalion's commencement of training at Sutton Coldfield. It was now time for various Old Boys associations around Birmingham to hold farewell concerts in honour of their members who would soon be off training.

On the eve of moving to Sutton, a special valedictory parade and church service had been arranged for the 1st Birmingham Battalion to take place at St Martin's in the Bull Ring, the Parish Church of Birmingham, on Sunday afternoon, 4 October. Instructions were given for the new battalion to parade at Thorp Street at 2 pm; Private J E B Fairclough remembered that:

'The recruits assembled in the companies to which they had been posted, and platoons were made up. Before moving off, they were put through a short drill in making turns and forming fours by the instructors attached to the platoons. This drill finished, the order was given to move off, the band struck up (Birmingham Police Band), and in good style the battalions moved out into the streets to meet the critical eyes of the spectators who lined the route to St Martin's Church. It was the first opportunity the citizens of Birmingham

Above: Church Parade, 1st Birmingham Battalion, Sunday 1 October 1914. Leading the parade, and behind the Bass Drummer of the Birmingham City Police Band, is Sir John Barnsley, the temporary Commanding Officer. The three young men behind him are from left to right: Emile Jacot, William Ehrhardt and Thomas Barnsley.

Right: Postcard sent to William Henry Furse of School Road, Moseley (see page 191), informing him that he was now No.399 (on reverse of card) of B Company, 1st Birmingham Battalion.

had of seeing their own first battalion on parade, and appreciative remarks were passed on the physique and bearing of the new troops. A special service in a crowded church was held at which the address was given by the Bishop of Carlisle, a former Rector of Birmingham. A souvenir order of service was presented to each man, and on

this the battalion was described as the 11th Battalion.'

With reference to this parade, it is interesting to mention the three young men marching behind Sir John Barnsley (see illustration). I said previously that junior officers were to be selected once training commenced. However, these three young men, old boys of King Edward's School, had already

46

Lord Kitchener's Army.

SPECIAL RECRUITING OFFICE, No. 11,
COUNCIL HOUSE, BIRMINGHAM.

CITY OF BIRMINGHAM BATTALION.

It is notified for your information that you are a member of _B_ Company, No. _1_ Battalion of the above unit. If you wish to draw pay on account of the 3/- per day due, you should attend at the COUNCIL HOUSE (Margaret Street entrance), on _24th inst._ between the hours of ~~10.30~~ _11_ a.m. and 12.30 p.m.

You are to bring this card with you.

JOHN BARNSLEY, Lt.-Col.,
O.C. Recruiting Station.

been selected as subalterns to the new 1st Birmingham Battalion. The first of the three was Thomas Kenneth Barnsley, the son of Sir John Barnsley. After a few months with the 1st Birmingham Battalion, Thomas transferred to the 1st Battalion, Coldstream Guards. He was killed in action 31 July, 1917, and is buried in the Guards Cemetery, Canada Farm near Poperinghe, Belgium. The other two were an example of Birmingham's allure as an industrial magnet, for artisans from various parts of Europe who came over to start their own small business during the early part of the 19th Century. The first was Emile Jacot (whose family home was 'The Hill' in Perry Bar), his grand-parents came from Switzerland and the other was William Hereward Ehrhardt (Edgbaston) whose forebear's came from Germany; both of them had their roots in Birmingham's watchmaking trade.

WILLIAM HEREWARD EHRHARDT

I hope the reader will excuse my digression, here, and let me describe in a paragraph or two the interesting story of William Ehrhardt. By 1914 the Ehrhardt family business had expanded to the own-ership of the Mersey Chemical Works in Chester. By 1914, William's father, Ernest (an ex-pupil of King Edward's), was living in Heidleberg and was responsible for all the affairs relating to English and American Patents for the German company BASF. Until he was fourteen, William had been taught at Heidelberg College, which was founded by William's uncle (William Catty) and was an 'English School' for Heidelberg's international community. It was run on the same principles as an English public school. During July 1906, after Heidelberg, William continued his education in Birmingham at King Edward's School, New Street. After leaving King Edward's he went to Cambridge University to read Chemistry and Law with the intention of becoming a barrister specialising in Patents.

A few weeks prior to the war, William and the rest of his family were staying at his grandmother's house in Heidelberg. On 2 August, 1914, with war becoming imminent and certain, William's mother with six of her seven children took the decision to get out of Germany as soon as possible and made their way to the safety of Holland and from there back to Britain. Unfortunately, William's father, Dr Ernest Ehrhardt, was at his office in the town of Ludwigshafen and Mrs Ehrhardt was unable to con-tact him and tell him of her intentions. With the outbreak of war, William's father was placed under house arrest, probably due to his background in the chemical industry and his possible awareness of Germany's capability of producing Mustard Gas. One of Dr Ehrhardt's friends was the American Consul, who supplied him with an official looking but totally unofficial document with carefully selected wording so as not to cause a diplomatic incident if detected. It stated that it was 'not a pass-port', but, with the word 'passport' highly empha-

sised. It was good enough to allow William's father to cross the German border into Switzerland, and he reached Zurich on 23 September. By then, his son was now Second-Lieutenant William Ehrhardt of the 1st Birmingham Battalion. So confident of getting a commission within the battalion, he had already bought his uniform!

Who were these Birmingham Pals?

Before continuing with the formation of the three battalions, this, perhaps, is the ideal time to find out a little more of the background of some of the men who volunteered.

William Ehrhardt was not the only future mem-ber of the Birmingham Battalions, who was in Germany just before the war. There was also a cer-tain William Lynes of Grove Avenue, Moseley, whose family concern was known as Rainsford and Lynes and dealt in Hot Brass Stamping in Emily Street, Sparkbrook. William had been working in Germany for two years prior to the war starting. He had succeeded in getting back to Britain on the last boat to leave the German port of Hamburg. He eventually joined the 1st Birmingham Battalion (unfortunately, poor William was to see a bit more of Germany; he finished up a POW, after being commissioned in the 2/6th South Staffs).

Henry Yeandle was another young Brummie away from home which, by the way, was Acocks

Above: Scott Sunderland an actor from the Birmingham Repertory Theatre, became Private Sunderland, No.258, until being commissioned into the 2/8th Royal Warwicks in January 1915.
Birmingham Library Services

Below: Warwickshire County Cricketer and soon to become Private Percy Jeeves No.611, of C Company 2nd Birmingham Battalion.

Green. He had originally moved to Canada to become assistant manager in a Graphite Mine, but by the start of the war he was working in Brussels. He arrived back in his home town in time to enlist. Another was Harold Shaw, of Old Hill, Tettenhall near Wolverhampton, he happened to be on holiday from his job in Brazil at the outbreak of war, but rather than return he decided to enlist in the 1st Birmingham Battalion. After a few months training with the battalion he took a commission into the 1st Lincolns; sadly, he would never return to Brazil. An old boy of King Edward's Camp Hill and the Central Secondary School was Angus Macauley of Ivor Road, Sparkhill. Before enlisting into the 2nd Birmingham Battalion he was an aerographic artist and designer working in Paris. Apart from Thomas Barnsley, other notable heirs of Birmingham's leading citizens were the two sons of the former Lord Mayor of Birmingham, Alderman Henry James Sayer; they were Alfred and Leslie, of Belle Walk, Moseley. Both of them enlisted into the ranks of the 1st Birmingham Battalion, but after a few months they would take a commission into the 3rd City Battalion. There, they would meet up with twenty year old Basil Tangye, the son of Sir Lincoln Tangye the Chairman and Managing Director of Tangye's Ltd; whose Cornwall Works in Smethwick were renowned the world over for hydraulic lifting equipment. In fact, the position the future Sir Basil would himself hold.

The entertainment industry also provided a sprinkling of volunteers to the battalions. Two were well known actors from Birmingham's Repertory Theatre, Scott Sunderland and Foden Flint. The world of light entertainment gave up Will Kings, who was well known throughout the city, but would become known to radio listener's nation-wide forty years or so later, as one of the original cast of *The Archer's*. Though not in the entertainment business directly, Alfred Sorge, who worked at the Cost Office at the Dunlop Rubber Works, was the son of the Musical Director of Birmingham's Prince of Wales Theatre. There was also the brother of the world famous contralto Dame Clara Butt, who enlisted into the 1st Birmingham Battalion (L A K Butt who gave his address as Belize House, Soho Road, Handsworth; what his connections with Birmingham are I do not know). Her rendition of 'Land of Hope and Glory' would bring a lump to many a throat during the war years.

Birmingham's sporting community also provided a vast number of young men to the battalions. With the strong contingent of King Edward's School old boys amongst the volunteers, Rugby was by far the most popular sporting activity played and many fine club players from around the city found themselves in the new battalions. Warwickshire County Cricket Club supplied a handful of men to the 2nd Birmingham Battalion. Two men were actually born at the ground, they were Len and Sam Bates the sons of John, the groundsman. Both brothers were educated at Tindal Street Council

School in Balsall Heath. Sam the eldest (born 1890) made his debut for Warwickshire against Leicester in 1910, and made five professional appearances for the club. Prior to the war Sam Bates was on the groundstaff at Lords cricket ground. He was destined never to return. In 1916 Sam was declared as missing in action, presumed killed. His younger brother Len (born 1895), made his debut for Warwickshire against Sussex in 1913. His first professional appearance would come after the war, in 1919. By the time he retired in 1935, Len Bates would play 440 times for Warwickshire. Another, destined to become one of nearly 80,000 missing men on the Somme, was Percy Jeeves. A Yorkshire man by birth (his parents lived in Craven Street, Ravensthorpe near Dewsbury), Percy had been playing in the Birmingham League for Moseley before making his Warwickshire debut against Australia in 1912. Before enlisting into the 2nd Birmingham Battalion, Percy Jeeves had played forty-nine matches for Warwickshire. It was said Percy Jeeves was certain to be one of England's greatest cricketers, in fact the author P G Wodehouse was so impressed after seeing Percy play one afternoon, he decided to use Percy's name for the butler in his celebrated 'Bertie Wooster' novels.

Before enlisting, 'Tiger' Smith was Warwickshire's well established wicket-keeper and right-arm bowler. Born at Highgate in 1886 he made his Warwickshire debut in 1904 against South Africa. A cartilage injury during his training resulted in an early discharge from the 2nd Birmingham Battalion. Another Warwickshire player was Eric Crockford of Sutton Coldfield, he played twenty-one times for the club as an amateur, some of these as Captain. He would spend a year with the 1st Birmingham Battalion before being commissioned. After the war Crockford and Sons were a well known firm of solicitors of Bennett's Hill. Other Volunteers associated with Warwickshire were, Harry Austin, Eric Cross, the brothers Arthur and Gerald Curle, George Byrne applied but was not accepted (his brother Francis though, was accepted as an officer for the 3rd Birmingham Battalion), Verner Valentine Luckin, Percy Whitehouse and finally Alec Hastilow who would also become the future Chairman of Warwickshire County Cricket Club. Football players amongst the new recruits seemed to be very sparse indeed, though there must have been many amateur players from clubs around the city that had enlisted. Two names have surfaced though from the football world who are worth mentioning. The first was Harry Morris of St Oswald's Road, Small Heath, who enlisted in the 1st Birmingham Battalion. Harry, who played for Birmingham City Football Club of which his father was also a Director, would finish the war with a Military Medal for gallantry. To keep everybody happy, I had better mention Aston Villa, because their half-back from the 1905 English Cup winning side was J W Windmill, a schoolmaster from Brierly

Hill. Formerly a student at St Peter's Teacher Training College at Saltley, J W Windmill would soon become a platoon sergeant in the 3rd Birmingham Battalion. He would resume his career of teaching after the war with a Distinguished Conduct Medal to his credit.

As I mentioned earlier, the term non-manual worker covered the whole range of the social class structure of Birmingham. No doubt, with a deeper investigation, there would be found many manual workers who had made their way into the battalions. Apart, say, from a few hundred men of the 1st Birmingham Battalion and a sprinkling in the 2nd and 3rd battalions, who were from wealthy middle-class homes, it would be a fair assumption to make that the majority of men who made up the three City battalions came from working class backgrounds but who had shown more ability at Council School, consequently leading them on to a non-manual occupation. A good illustration of this, was a sixteen year old lad (from Metchley Lane, Harborne), by the name of Charles Edward Leatherland, who falsified his age to nineteen and enlisted into the 3rd City Battalion. After a distinguished career in journalism he was honoured with the title the Right Honourable Lord Leatherland OBE. He recalled his early years:

'In 1914 I was sixteen years old. We were a happy family, but faced every week with the hard task of making ends meet. So at the age of ten I had a newspaper round, bringing in half-a-crown a week. At eleven I went as a boot-boy in the house of the local JP. This involved cleaning half a dozen pairs of shoes, a dozen knives and forks and spoons, getting in half a dozen buckets of coal, stoking the central heating furnace and grooming a large collie dog who lived in what looked like a lion's cage. And then, rushing off two miles to reach school just before nine o'clock. There were similar tasks in the evening, and on Saturdays there was the lawn to roll for tennis, and the cleaning of over twenty windows.

'At twelve, I went back to newspaper delivering for a year or so. Whether that prepared me for a later forty years of hard work in journalism, I do not know (News Editor for the Daily Herald). It also left me free for several hours on Saturday, which enabled me to do two rounds caddying at Edgbaston Golf Club, at ninepence (4p) a round plus tips.

'There were in addition what Tax Inspectors would call 'other casual earnings'. I was a choirboy and had a good voice, so at Christmas time my brothers and I would set out on an extensive carol singing tour, with me leading the quartet on my violin. And in winter there were always a few shillings to be earned by snow sweeping. Then at thirteen my part-time activities jumped in status. I became errand boy to a local chemist. Not only did I deliver medicines to the district's invalids, but in the morning, before going to school, I had to sweep out the shop and scrub the marble doorstep. This should have been easy, but it was not. As soon as I made the step shining white, some of my more leisurely schoolfriends would scrape handfuls of mud from the gutter and deposit it neatly where I had been scrubbing. At lunchtime if there were no medicines to deliver, I was put to work weighing and wrapping quarter pounds of boric acid or Epsom salts. In the evening there were the drug bottles on the shelves to polish, crates of medicaments and cosmetics from the wholesale depot to unpack, and occasionally I had to hold an unwanted cat while the assistant put it to rest with a dose of prussic acid. Unpacking the crates often carried a bonus. Straw was used as a packing and I was able to sell this to a man near the shop who kept a dozen hens. This only brought in threepence, but was welcome.

'As I approached fourteen the chemist

suggested to my father that I should become apprenticed to the pharmaceutical profession, coupling experience gained in the shop with evening study at the Birmingham Technical College (Suffolk Street). But this involved paying a premium and drawing a small wage till I was qualified. The family financial circumstances made this impossible. It was the first of many frustrations.

'I was very happy at the local council elementary school (Station Road, Harborne). I had every reason to be. I was regarded as one of the bright boys of the top class; another of our group became a schoolmaster; another was Stanley Evans, who later became an MP (Labour, for Wednesbury) and attained notoriety by the onslaught on 'featherbed Farmers.' Like me, he later joined the army. At fourteen I left school and set about the task of becoming a full-time wage earner. There was no easy passage to secondary school in those days; that was reserved for boys whose fathers went to work (though they called it 'going to business') in dark suits and white collars.

'I had fitted myself for some kind of office work in several ways. At school I had been very quick at my work. At the end of an essay or arithmetic lesson, I found myself with twenty minutes or so to spare while many of the other boys were toiling on. So out came Pitman's Shorthand Manual from under the desk, and by the time I left school, I could write 140 words a minute. This later went up to over 200 at evening classes. I also, in a rather peculiar way, learned something about typewriting; enough to pass a test that a future employer set me. There was a typewriter shop near the chemist's, and in spare moments I would stand at the window, gaze at the typewriters there on show, and memorise the keyboards and the general mechanism of the machines. Then, outside the window, I would manipulate my fingers as though operating the machine. This may not be the way Typewriting Academies teach their pupils. But it worked.

'Finding a job then was no easier than it is today (1976). My first application was to Bellis and Morcom, the engineers, and although my Headmaster sent a letter saying I was one of his 'brightest boys' there was no response.

'Then I tried for employment at Cadbury's head office and was interviewed by one of the Cadbury brothers personally. Here I made a terrible mistake. I showed him three or four cuttings from the Birmingham Weekly Post, containing essays for which I had won the paper's periodical prizes. He cross-examined me ruthlessly as to whether the essays were all my own work. They were. But I could see he did not believe me. I did not get the job.

'However before I was fifteen, after a spell of shorthand-typing in the office of a golfing journal, I obtained a post as personal shorthand typist to the head of a department of the Birmingham Corporation. At last I had a feeling of confidence. But also disappointment, for whereas the appointment had been advertised at £275 a year, I was told that they had expected a man of twenty-six who had the necessary qualifications, and that £75 was the appropriate scale for that age, and that at fifteen my salary would be only £26 a year.

'I was very happy in this job and was told I was marked out for promotion. So I kept on with my evening classes, studying book-keeping, shorthand, typing and business methods. The promised promotion, incidentally, did not come till after the war, when a special costing department was set up and I was put in charge of it. But, when I was sixteen the war broke out, and in this year of 1914 I told my chief I intended to join the army. He said such a thing was impossible. I was too young. I insisted, however, and he agreed to see what was said by the alderman who was chairman of our committee (Lighting, Stables & Refuse Disposal Committee). So I was called in when the chairman paid his next visit. My chief told the alderman how ridiculous the whole idea was. But dear old bearded Alderman Lucas (head of what was then the Lucas, King of the Road, motor lamp company) saved me. He said: "I certainly would have refused to grant permission, but tomorrow night I am addressing a recruiting meeting in the Town Hall, and I cannot very well do that if I say no to you". I learned how closely balanced many of the problems of life can be. So off I went to the recruiting office. The Medical Officer ran his tape over me, looked rather hesitant, turned to the Medical Sergeant and said "He looks rather skinny for nineteen". But fortune came to my aid again. By what the newspapers would call a 'remarkable coincidence', I recognised the sergeant as the foreman at one of our Corporation depots. He rose to the occasion wonderfully. "That's so sir," he said. "But these ginger-headed lads soon fill out by the time they are twenty".

'So I was medically passed, and then

Left: Sixteen year old Charles Edward Leatherland, 3rd Birmingham Battalion; and **above** Lord Leatherland as he later became.
Clive Hereward

51

ACCOMMODATION
TO BE FURNISHED BY
KEEPER OF BILLETING HOUSE.

Every Householder providing Billets for N.C.O's. and Men,
shall supply meals, etc., as follows:—

(a). **For BREAKFAST.**—Six ounces of bread, one pint of tea with milk
and sugar, four ounces of bacon, or equivalent.

(b). **For HOT DINNER.**—One pound of meat previous to being dressed,
eight ounces of bread, eight ounces of potatoes or other vegetables,
and pudding.

(c). **For TEA.**—Six ounces of bread, one pint of tea with milk and sugar,
one ounce of butter.

(d). **For SUPPER.**—Bread and Cheese.

The usual times for meals will be as follows:

BREAKFAST ..	...	**8** a.m.
DINNER	... ...	**1** p.m.
TEA ...	... ...	**5** p.m.
SUPPER	... ...	**9-30** p.m.

(Signed) J. BARNSLEY, Lieut. Colonel,
Commanding 1st Birmingham Battalion.

SUTTON COLDFIELD,
2nd October, 1914.

*taken before the Colonel for the final for-
malities. Here again I was lucky. It turned
out that my father had served in his company in the army in India, many years
before.'*

Most certainly, all the hard work and dedication in
the pursuit of his clerical skills saved the life of
Charles Leatherland. After a short spell in the
trenches, with the 3rd City Battalion, his clerical
expertise was needed at Corps Headquarters. He
was made CQMS at eighteen, and by the time he
was demobilised in 1919, still only twenty years
old, he held the rank of Sergeant-Major with a
Meritorious Service Medal and a Mention in

Despatches in recognition of the proficient manner
in which he undertook these duties.

Apart from a few who had had a basic military
training with the school or University Officer
Training Corps, the bulk of these young men who
applied to join the Birmingham Battalions would
never have had any leaning towards military life
and a desire to kill another human being. Many
were ex-choir boys, Sunday School Teachers and
sons of the clergy. Others were involved in movements such as Boy Scouts or the Boys Brigade.
Compared to the youth of today's world, quite a few
of these volunteers would have lived quite sheltered
lives, a few, perhaps, even waited on hand and foot
by servants. Sunday afternoons would be the high-
light of the week, all the family gathering round the
piano to sing and afterwards play parlour games
such as charades. These then, were the young non-
manual workers of Birmingham, the majority being
church-going, non-swearing tee-totallers. Young
men, who would soon be meeting up with their new
instructors: tough, blasphemous ex-Regular NCO's
who had been called up from the Reserves. Picture
yourself as one of these young men, whom I have
just described, and imagine his thoughts and feelings, when in a few short weeks he would be learning the tactical use of the bayonet; with instructions
such as these:

*'To fire into an opponent's body is only
permissible when it is necessary to loosen
the bayonet which is fixed through a bone,
and cannot be withdrawn by physical
force.'*

*'Four of five inches is sufficient to inca-
pacitate, and allows for quick extraction.'*

*'When a bayonet enters the stomach it is
generally grasped in the death grip, and
hard to release.'*

*'In hand-to-hand fighting, the knee
brought up between the fork, the heel
stamped on the instep, the point of the bayonet cut down on the face, the butt used
horizontally on the jaw, should be thought
of and practised... These methods will only
temporarily disable an enemy, who must
be killed with the point of the bayonet.'*

NON-MANUAL WORKERS OF BIRMINGHAM;
WELCOME TO THE WAR

Below: The 1st
Birmingham Battalion,
Sutton Park, October
1914
*Birmingham Library
Services*

Chapter Four

Training Commences –'Berlin via Sutton'

Monday morning, 5 October, 1914, thirty-nine days after the first inkling of a possible Birmingham Battalion; the 1st Birmingham Battalion (and still thought to be the 11th Royal Warwicks) was now in a position to begin its first stage of preparation for active service. Rumours were still around of the eventual use of all three battalions. Would they be for coastal guard duties or maybe replacing Regular battalions from far flung corners of the British Empire?

Two special trains were assigned to leave New Street Station; the first containing A and B Coys at 08.50 am, with the second containing C and D Coys soon after; an advance party of forty-two men under the command of Captain Dimmock had made their way to Sutton the day before to get the Crystal Palace ship-shape. As departure time neared, a large crowd of spectators assembled to greet the departing men, but only relatives were allowed on to the platform; no doubt there were quite a few Birmingham business girls there hoping to catch a few minutes with their 'best boy'. The drive dividing New Street Station began to fill with nigh on 700 men wearing buttonhole badges and carrying suitcases (members of the battalion who lived in Erdington and Sutton Coldfield were ordered to make their own way to the park). One of those at New Street Station was Private J E B Fairclough, who later recalled:

'Looking round one began to realise dimly that we were saying 'goodbye' to our civilian life and entering on some new existence with promise of unknown adventure. We could not look far ahead for we had very little idea of what war entailed. Most of us had only very hazy memories of the Boer War and it was very difficult to imagine what this new life would mean.'

The enthusiasm of the men was apparent with sentiments such as 'Tipperary via Sutton Coldfield' and 'Berlin via Sutton' chalked upon the carriages. Lieutenant-Colonel Sir John Barnsley arrived in time to witness the departure, and after much hand-shaking and leave-taking the trains began to pull out. This was the signal for the barricades holding back the general public to be thrown open and to the accompaniment of a huge roar of cheers

and a flourish of hats and handkerchiefs the trains slowly chugged out of the station. As the last carriage of the second train slowly receded into the gloom of the tunnel, that took the track to Sutton, another chalked message could be seen clearly 'Right away to Berlin'.

Sutton Coldfield

After the two trains had left New Street Station, Sir John Barnsley and his entourage motored to Sutton Coldfield and made it in time to greet the trains as they pulled into Sutton Park Station. There was also a rousing welcome from Sutton people as the men detrained and made their way to the Town Gate entrance of Sutton Park. Here they formed up on open ground in front of the battalion's new Headquarters; the huge glass-domed former dance hall known as the Crystal Palace. In a letter home Arthur Guy Osborn (No.955, D Coy), a Schoolteacher from Kings Norton Council School, who lived at Beaumont Road, Bournville, had this to say:

'The scenes of parting and greeting at New Street and Sutton Park Stations, respectively, were marked by a strong note

Above: Crystal Palace used by 1st City Battalion as headquarters.

Below: Information sent to original volunteers of the 1st Birmingham Battalion prior to the move to Sutton Park.

ROYAL WARWICKSHIRE REGT. 1st. CITY OF B'HAM BATTALION.

The Battalion will assemble for training at Sutton Coldfield on Monday, Oct. 5th. A special train for A & B Companies will leave No. 4 Platform, New Street Station at 8.50 A.M. You will wear your badge, and show this card at Sutton Station.

On arrival at Sutton, you are to report yourself to your Co. Quartermaster Sgt. at the Headquarters, Crystal Palace, for your billiting instructions.

It will be necessary for you to bring private clothing until uniform is issued. To every man in possession of a good pair of boots, a suit of clothes and a good great coat, a grant of ten shillings will be made. Small necessaries, such as brush and comb, tooth brush and shaving tackle, should be brought.

JOHN BARNSLEY, Lt. Col.

Top right: each original volunteer to the 1st Birmingham Battalion was issued with a small booklet giving advice on military etiquette.
Dave Vaux Collection

of cheerfulness, even hilarity, and throughout all the early proceedings there was evident a quiet determination on the part of the great mass of the fellows, which promised well for the military future of the battalion.'

After a roll call was made by the four Company Sergeant Majors, the CO, Lieutenant-Colonel Sir John Barnsley, addressed the battalion. He reminded them that they were now regular soldiers and under military law. The honour of the city of Birmingham and of the 1st City Battalion was in their individual keeping. He asked them to be absolutely punctual on parade; they must turn up five minutes before time, and no excuse except that of sickness would be accepted for late attendance. Sir John also took the opportunity of acknowledging the kindness of the people of Sutton Coldfield in opening their homes for billeting purposes. They must not abuse the generosity of the people of Sutton, and must treat the men with civility and the women with perfect respect. He also reminded the men that they must be in their billets by 10 o'clock until 6 o'clock the next morning. He did not want to interfere with the life of Sutton or close the public-houses at an earlier hour than usual unless he was compelled to do so. In regard to the allotment of companies, Sir John explained that applications for transfers could be made before 15 October. A call to Old Edwardians to hold up their hands showed so many that they would make one complete company and overflow into another. The main business of the morning was next on the agenda, which was the allotting of billets. Once sorted the battalion was dismissed and the men went off to find their billets and have their first chance to taste their new hosts' cooking. The battalion had its first parade later in the afternoon. This took the form of basic squad drills. The first day ended at 1700, with a fair number of the battalion making their way back to Birmingham, and home. Training was to commence in earnest the following morning at 0700. A picture now comes to mind of a tearful mother waving her son goodbye from New Street Station, thinking she may never see him again; yet he turns up later for his supper!

Basic Military Training

Next morning, 6 October, at 0700 a bugle called the men to 'assembly'. Training had now begun in real earnest. Almost immediately a thousand men were in their places. The *Sutton News* reported

that there was hardly a late arrival though a few dozen found it necessary to sprint from the main entrance of the park to the drill ground. For the first hour the battalion undertook a stiff bout of 'Swedish Drill' or PT as we know it from school. An anonymous drill sergeant told a representative of the Sutton News that:

> *'Physical fitness is the basis of military training. Our aim is to get the men as 'hard as nails', so that when we start on long marches across rugged parts of the park few will fall out from exhaustion, sore feet and aching joints.'*

Perhaps this was the same sergeant known as 'streaky', who during these early morning sessions was apt to roar 'when I say jump, jump! and don't come down until I tell you!' Whilst another Drill Sergeant declared to a reporter with evident satisfaction that his squad was about the most willing and enthusiastic body of lads he had had for years. 'They're a bit ponderous – a few of them – but I'll make grasshoppers of them before I've finished with 'em.' The same routine was now to continue throughout the battalion's stay at Sutton Park. After breakfast the battalion would break up into small groups for training known as squad drill. Sections

of men would be dotted over fifty acres of grass-land on the Blade Mill Hill, the gorse covered high-lands in the direction of Hollyhurst and Keeper's Pool, and in the meadow Platt; marching, turning and saluting.

If the weather was wet, then there would be no 'Swedish Drill', and lectures would be given in the Crystal Palace.

Lord Mayor's Inspection

On Wednesday, 7 October, the Lord Mayor of Birmingham (Alderman Bowater) visited Sutton to inspect the 1st Birmingham Battalion. He was accompanied by senior officials of Sutton Coldfield Town Council and the CO of the 2nd Birmingham Battalion, Captain G H Smith. He had important news for the battalion; the War Office had promised 200 rifles for each battalion. Sadly, the bad news was that they were obsolete models, they could not be fired. They were to be used for drill purposes only. In turn, companies would become accustomed to the care and use of arms.

The War Office had also directed that huts should be built so that training might be conducted under stricter military conditions. That request, Alderman Bowater told the men, was in hand by the

Above: a section of men from the 1st Birmingham Battalion beginning the process to get themselves 'hard as nails'.

Below: 1st Birmingham Battalion, Sutton Park. One platoon can be seen shouldering the obsolete Long Lee-Enfield rifle (an example can be seen on page 31, third rifle up).

Above: At first glance this section of Birmingham Pals looks very disorientated. I think the photograph was taken just as the men were about to do a turn on the march.
Birmingham Library Services

authorities in Birmingham, and possibly huts might be ready by Christmas.

In the name of the battalion, Lieutenant-Colonel Sir John Barnsley, thanked Alderman Bowater for paying them a visit. Sir John announced that he was proposing to the War Office that the Lord Mayor be made Honorary Colonel of the 1st Birmingham Battalion. The news was received with much applause and a round of cheers for His Lordship. After the parade, the Lord Mayor, Sir John and Captain Smith toured the area in the vicinity of Powell's Pool, the future training ground of the 2nd Birmingham Battalion, who were due to commence training on Monday, 12 October.

First Week Over With

With the first week of training over, for the 1st Birmingham Battalion, the selection process for junior NCOs had begun. Even though many men of the eventual three Birmingham Battalions may have had some type of basic military training, i.e. the school cadet force or the Officer Training Corps, this was no guarantee in the selection of these posts. Those men wishing to be considered for promotion were allowed to take turn in giving orders during the daily sessions of squad drill. It was not unheard of either that senior NCOs with a wicked sense of humour, would place a young office boy in charge of a section of men who were

Right: Apart from their obsolete rifles, the men had by now received their second item of uniform, navy blue Field Service caps.
Birmingham Library Services

formerly solicitors, accountants and bank clerks. No doubt with the first week of training over, many men of the 1st Birmingham Battalion put pen to paper to express their thoughts and tribulations of their new surroundings and comrades. Luckily, two letters have survived from this period. The first was written by former teacher Private Arthur Guy Osborn (No.955, D Coy) on Saturday, October 10th:

'The enthusiasm, the hilarity, and the determination, after a week's 'gruelling', have been well maintained, and there has already sprung into existence a factor which will make even more than these towards the success of the 'Birmingham Boys' as soldiers of the King. This factor is the sense of comradeship between fellows in the same squad or same company, – the esprit de corps *which makes 'D' Company, or No.23 Squad, THE BEST – indeed the ONE AND ONLY – for the men in it. It leads to the most healthy desire to make one's squad or one's company excel, and leads to the passing round of the word "smarten up boys!" when, after more than three hours hard drill, the return to the parade ground is made.*

'This week we have had three 'Parades' daily:-

1. From 7 am to 7:50 am for physical exercises (many of which are stiff).

2. From 9:30 am to 12:45 pm.

3. from 2 pm to 4:45 pm.

The second and third parades are devoted to squad drill, but so rapid has been the progress that all squads have already had considerable practice in extended order drill (skirmishing) while

the BEST company... D Company, in which the majority of the teachers (including myself) are enrolled, has actually had two practices in company drill. D Company is fortunate in having a most splendidly efficient Sergeant-Major in Sergeant-Major Phillips (CSM J W Phillips, No.1084), who is perhaps the best officer in the whole battalion. With regards to myself, I am glad to say that I am standing the hard grind jolly well. My heart is in this business, and though I am not yet free from 'aches' I am beginning to feel most fit. Apparently, I am doing well. On Thursday I was called out with others to give a few commands to the fellows in my squad, i.e.

Above: Newly promoted NCO's were issued with another item of kit; a grey canvas brassard with black chevrons stencilled on. *Birmingham Library Services*

Below: A few men of C company, 10 Platoon of the 2nd Birmingham Battalion October/November 1914. *Birmingham Library Services*

Roll of No. 7 Platoon

No. 9 Section.

407	Sgt.	Hatwell, W. B.
940	L/Cpl.	Locker, A. C.
351	Pte.	Arnold, P. G.
507	,,	Barton, F. C. G.
530	,,	Chare, F.
331	,,	Dewbury, J. P.
223	,,	Elliott, H.
397	,,	Firkins, A. E.
165	,,	Grove, W. C.
376	,,	Hoskins, W. J.
444	,,	Marshall, F.
457	,,	Patterson, R. F.
477	,,	Powell, C. P.
19	,,	Summers, W. F.
265	,,	Wheatley, L. J. D.

20 fellows, for the whole of the first parade. In a week or so I am taking the Corporal's examination, so I may soon be "955 Cpl A G Osborn" (I say, I may). I am billeted with three chums: Jack Reeves (No.971, from Beaumont Road, Bournville), Wilfred Ward (from Featherstone Road, Kings Heath), and Arthur Bacon (No.852, from Birchwood Crescent, Moseley). Bacon is a singer of sentimental and comic songs, and is a real humorist at times. We all find ourselves very jolly and comfortable together; and spare time passes only too quickly. Our hosts are "doing us well". Mr C Jones, in whose house we are living, said to his wife: "The lads are doing their best for their country; let us do our best for them." And they are doing it right down well.

'So far we are without uniforms, but we are proud of the badge we all have to wear.'

The second letter concerning this early training period was written by Private Charles Carrington (No.247, B Coy). His letter was written to his parents back home in New Zealand, after the second week of training:

'I have now been in training 10 days and billeted on a worthy inhabitant of the name of Holloway (Edgehill Farm, Four Oaks), to whom the government pays 2/9 (14p) a day for giving me lodging and food to the extent of twenty-two ounces of meat, one and a half pounds of bread and indefinite quantities of tea, milk, butter, cheese, pudding and vegetables per diem. It sounds formidable but soon vanishes. Work begins with three quarters of an hour of Swedish Drill at seven o'clock and continues with morning and afternoon

parades for two and a half to three hours. At other times we are free, until ten o'clock, when every man must be in his billet.

'When I joined, I knew no one but an actor of the name Sunderland (Scott Sunderland, No.258, B Coy, from the Birmingham Repertory Theatre), whom aunt Alice and Mavis had fallen in love with and had introduced to me. (By the Bye he further introduced me to John Drinkwater, the poet.) I didn't inflict myself on Sunderland much but made friends with my billet companions. Two are clerks in municipal offices and one is a commercial traveller who is a good fellow but of no particular interest.

'Of the clerks, one is an ardent Rugby football player and a protégé of Fr Adderly and above all a very fast young person. The other is a teetotaller nonconformist and a Marxian Socialist, a long lean sandy haired person perpetually smoking. Incidentally he has about the worse table manners I know. All three talk, argue, quarrel and joke continually in a pronounced Birmingham accent.

Example:

"Will yer av anoother coop er tay, kid, Cus I will, any road yer know."

'Which takes some translating. It is a sample of teatime conversation. I am surprised to find what respectable people talk the Birmingham dialect.

'We have been doing only recruit drill until today when we went for a route march. The weather is breaking at last after a wonderful summer and it was damp and muddy. The heather is brown and the chestnuts and earlier trees are all gold and red while the gorse is still flowering. I only wish I could see it in Kent. I agree with Hilaire Belloc that the midlands are 'sodden and unkind'. The Forest of Arden and the wild sweep of land through Sutton Park beat anything in New Zealand but are heavy after the New Forest and the South Downs. Through the park we went and came back along the Lichfield Road, smoking, singing, whistling and here I make another diversion on the subject of marching songs. Our favourite seems to be the Marseillaise, whistled not sung. The inevitable Tipperary always appears. It has already become a popular tradition that the army eats and sleeps and marches and fights and dies singing about the "long long way to Tipperary". Then there are the latest ragtimes but the Marseillaise seems the most popular. I wish I knew La Brabanconne [the Belgian National Anthem]. Well coming back we attracted every servant girl and nursemaid for mile and had a great ovation, an old women rushed out of a shop with a box of Woodbine cigarettes and thrust them all on us. Another waved a huge Union Jack from an attic window. It was wonderful business. When we get our uniforms of blue, because they are short of khaki, there will be no holding us.

'Now about England. You mustn't worry, we are in great straits. Everything is going on exactly as before except for the unusual numbers of troops being drilled. Young

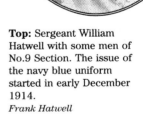

Top: Sergeant William Hatwell with some men of No.9 Section. The issue of the navy blue uniform started in early December 1914.
Frank Hatwell

Above: Once uniforms were issued, many buttonhole badges were turned into 'sweethearts jewellery'. An example can be seen in the necklace worn by Sergeant Hatwell's wife.
Frank Hatwell

men are rather scarce, Union Jacks are rather plentiful, Belgian and French refugees are common and motors generally have the Allies' flags for mascots. Otherwise there is nothing unusual.

'Birmingham is far the most patriotic town I have seen: it has raised 40,000 new recruits, but now there is very little to be seen. They had a huge thermometer on the Town Hall, which registered the number of recruits, and everything, motors, carts, buildings and hoardings had huge notices on them YOUR KING AND COUNTRY NEED YOU, A CALL TO ARMS, etc etc.'

(Before continuing, the reader may interested to know of the Midland connection to the song *It's a long way to Tipperary*. The composers were Jack Judge and Harry Williams. Williams came from the small village of Temple Balsall, which nowadays is sited along the B4101 midway between Knowle and Balsall Common; which is now part of the Solihull Metropolitan Borough. Williams died in 1924 aged fifty, and is buried in the family plot in Temple Balsall graveyard.)

After the second week of training an important change took place in the command of the 1st Birmingham Battalion. 'One remembers seeing a gentleman in civilian clothes, wearing a trilby hat tipped well over his eyes, and carrying a cane, critically examining our work, and many were the conjectures as to his identity.' It was in fact the new CO of the battalion Colonel George White Lewis, who took over from Sir John Barnsley on October 17th. Colonel Lewis, 'dug-out' from retirement, was a Boer War veteran of the Worcester Regiment.

2nd Birmingham Battalion Begin Training

On Saturday afternoon, 10 October, two days before the start of training in Sutton Park, the 2nd Birmingham Battalion (which was thought to be the 12th Royal Warwickshires) assembled in the quadrangle of the Birmingham General Hospital. 'A noteworthy feature of the battalion was the excellent physique of the men; they were all well over the average height, while a few exceeded 6 ft', was how one journalist reported. For a short period of time the battalion practised a few basic drill movements under the gaze of a growing number of bystanders in the vicinity of the hospital. At 3 pm, headed by The Birmingham Police Band, the battalion swung under the arched entrance into Steelhouse Lane and were at once greeted by loud and hearty cheering from the large crowd that had now gathered. Led by the CO, Captain G H Smith, who was riding a dappled grey horse, the men, all proudly wearing the button-hole badges, marched along the principal streets of Birmingham. Large crowds lined the route displaying tremendous enthusiasm as the 'city boys' filed past; and it goes without saying *It's a long way to Tipperary* was

the number one song as the battalion made its way to Edgbaston Park for a period of basic drill instruction.

The following day, Sunday 11 October, similar to the 1st Birmingham battalion, a week earlier, a special valedictory parade and church service was held for the 2nd Birmingham Battalion. The men assembled at the Drill Hall in Thorp Street. Once again headed by the Birmingham Police band the battalion marched around the city streets to the Parish Church of St Martin's in the Bull Ring. The service was conducted by Canon Willink, the Rector of Birmingham. A crowd of several thousand turned up at New Street Station the following morning, Monday 12 October, to cheer the battalion off. Again, similar to the 1st Birmingham's departure, many messages had been scrawled on the carriages of the two specials. One in particular, which to my mind may have been the first piece of work from 'Ricardo' (Private R B L Moore, No.1010, B Coy) the celebrated poet of the 2nd Birmingham Battalion whose efforts will be printed as our story takes its course. Alongside a grotesque cartoon drawing of the Kaiser's head was the following inscription:

Gaze on this mug on our carriage hung
The man with the eagle eye;
Little you dream how is neck will be wrung
By us in the near by-and-by.

On reaching Sutton, the majority of the men detrained at Wylde Green and proceeded directly to their billets. One of these was Harold Victor Drinkwater who was by now No.161, A Coy, formerly of John Street, Stratford upon Avon:

'On Wylde Green platform we were given instructions regarding our movements for the immediate future, and then we made off, some thousand fellows, in varying directions to find our billets. I was separated from my other Stratford fellows and joined in with a general throng going in the direction where the majority of billets appeared to lay, getting in conversation with a fellow here and there as I passed along comparing address's of billets eventually finding Drakeford (Private Harold Drakeford, No.160, A Coy) who was going to the same house as myself, together we made our way to Jockey Road and introduced ourselves to Mr and Mrs Blackband, our billet people.'

The first parade took place on Monday afternoon at 3 pm on the stretch of open land that slopes gently down to Powell's Pool. Parades would follow the same routine as those of the 1st Birmingham Battalion. In the *Birmingham Daily Post*, the following day, the battalion's first parade was reported:

'Without ceremony or speech-making, the work of converting the members of the 2nd 'City' Battalion into efficient soldiers began in Sutton Park yesterday. It was

Left: Birmingham General Hospital, Steelhouse Lane. The newly formed 2nd Birmingham Battalion paraded in the quadrangle prior to marching to Edgbaston Park on Saturday 10 October 1914.

really surprising how well they shaped. The clerk of a fortnight ago, whose life was as circumscribed as the red lines in his ledger, the young warehousemen with horizons perhaps even more limited, the 'knut' and the exquisitive, with thoughts hitherto concentrated upon the things that do not matter... these and many other types started their military careers yesterday in a way that showed what a wonderful change the words duty and discipline can effect. There were 1,070 of them, few of whom had probably had more than an hour's drill in their lives... some perhaps not even that. And yet before the last ray of feeble October sun had shimmered Powell's Pool and touched the yellow and brown leaves of the trees they had all given evidence of quick response to the words of command and of keen desire to acquit them creditably.'

One of those present in this first parade of the 2nd Birmingham battalion was Private Harold Victor Drinkwater (No.161). The following are his recollections after he had the chance to appraise his new comrades in arms:

Below: The temporary Commanding Officer of the 2nd Birmingham Battalion, Captain G H Smith, leading the battalion into Edgbaston Park, 10 October 1914.
Birmingham Library Services

'We were an extraordinary collection of fellows. Later on I found out the fellow next to me had never done a day's work in his life. He had had something in the nature of a valet to do it for him. He was barely seventeen. There were barristers, solicitors, land clerks, qualified engineers and men and boys who by their looks at least required some good square meals before they would ever be able to stand the conditions which we were beginning to understand existed in France. Regarding one of the latter, a boy of sixteen who gave his age as eighteen, so that he could join up, became our Lance Corporal.'

Headquarters of the 2nd Birmingham Battalion were allotted to the boatsheds that were situated alongside Powell's Pool whilst the nearby refreshment rooms was appropriated for use as the orderly room and storage purposes. For lecture and recreation periods the Boldmere Parish Rooms and the Brotherhood Hall were made available. Arrangements had also been made that NCO's and all future junior NCOs were made honorary members of the Boldmere and Wylde Green Conservative Club in Jockey Road.

Training began in earnest the following morning at 7 am. The one major change in the command structure had now taken place; the temporary CO, Captain G H Smith was now second in command. The new CO, allotted by the War Office had assumed command. He was Lieutenant-Colonel L J Andrews formerly of the 79th Carnatic Infantry (Indian Army).

First Casualty

The short military career of one young man, Private Frederick Thomas Griffiths (No.236, A Coy) was painfully cut short on Friday, 16 October. After only five days training Private Griffiths suffered a breakdown in health which resulted in his death from pulmonary tuberculosis on 25 October. Private Griffiths was thirty years of age, and by trade a jeweller. For the two years prior to the war he had been living with an uncle in Boldmere, Sutton Coldfield. For his short five days training he had been billeted in Jockey Road. According to

friends, he had not felt well since August, but having passed his medical for the 2nd Birmingham Battalion, it was put down to only a cold. The funeral cortege set off from his father's house in Gower Street, Lozells, and accompanied by many of his comrades from A Coy, the procession slowly made its way to Witton Cemetery, where Private Griffiths was laid to rest. It is interesting to note the confusion caused by the sudden expansion of the Royal Warwickshire Regiment during the first few weeks of the war. The late Private Griffiths is accredited as being a member of the 10th Royal Warwicks.

3rd Birmingham Battalion Mobilised

As previously stated, the 1st and 2nd Birmingham Battalions left the city in style; parades through Birmingham, Valedictory Services and a big send off at New Street Station. Sadly none of these honours were given to the 3rd 'City' Battalion. It was simply a case of 'report to Spring Hill College, Moseley, and here's your bus fare', so to speak. The Spring Hill Weselyan College (once the home of the Birmingham Botanical Gardens, but more well known in later years as Moseley Grammar School) was situated in the triangle of land formed by Wake Green Road, College Road and Springfield Road, Moseley. The buildings were commandeered by the military authorities during the middle of September, 1914; and under military parlance were renamed the Moseley Barracks. Their purpose was to reduce the congestion of new recruits at various other local depots such as Budbrooke in Warwick and Whittington near

Lichfield. Birmingham would now be able to equip, feed, house and provide basic training for approximately 800 recruits of Kitchener's New Army until they were ready to be drafted on to their prospective regimental depots. Colonel Ludlow, who had been the chief recruiting officer at the Birmingham Town Hall, was given command of the new depot, along with a staff of fifty to sixty NCOs who were mostly old soldiers; too old for active service. The old theatre of the College had been converted into a dining hall, and washing accommodation had been provided in what was once the greenhouse.

By the middle of October, with local authorities

Above: Brought out of retirement to Command the 3rd Birmingham Battalion, Colonel D F Lewis CB, of Salford Priors, Warwicks.
Dave Vaux Collection

raising New Army battalions across the country, congestion had eased at many depots, and therefore the Moseley Barracks were deemed an ideal training centre for the 3rd Birmingham Battalion. An interesting item transpired during my research: when the 3rd Birmingham Battalion came up to full strength on 6 October, the surplus names were passed on to Colonel Graham at Thorpe Street Drill Hall. At this period of time the Second Line Territorials were in the process of being raised, i.e. the 2/5th, 2/6th, 2/7th and 2/8th Battalions of the Royal Warwickshire Regiment. The result was that these battalions had one or two companies classed as 'non-manual'.

Colonel D F Lewis C.B. of Salford Priors (near Bideford on Avon, Warwickshire) was called out of retirement and appointed by the War Office to command the 3rd Battalion. An old boy of Oswestry Grammar School and former career soldier, the fifty-nine year old Colonel Lewis had entered Sandhurst in 1875, and first saw service with the 2nd Buffs (East Kent Regiment) in the Zulu War of 1879. On 12 October, Colonel Lewis moved into his temporary HQ, the Plough and Harrow Hotel (Hagley Road), whilst he made the necessary arrangements for the mobilisation of The 1,107 men that comprised the 3rd Birmingham Battalion. (31 officers, one warrant officer, 54 sergeants, 16 buglers and 1,005 rank and file.)

Eventually an advance party of 100 men of A Coy of the 3rd City Battalion moved into Moseley Barracks on Friday morning, 16 October. The plan was, that the remainder of the battalion would be called up in batches over the following few days. Apart from the few men who were selected for sentry duty, the others began their military career in a slightly different way than they imagined. A soldier's best friend is his rifle, as the saying goes, but in the case of the advance party, the soldiers best friend was a mop, bucket and broom.

'But one and all entered upon the necessary if somewhat irksome duties with splendid spirit', commented the *Birmingham Daily Mail*. 'When a man who has handled nothing more substantial than a golf club, suddenly found himself armed with a cleaning mop; a bank clerk was detailed for the novel occupation of 'washing up' and sundry soft handed 'Birminghams' were told off to perform that duty detested of all dignified gardeners, clearing the drives of fallen leaves.'

Mobilisation of the 3rd Birmingham Battalion took longer than anticipated as it was soon realised the barracks could not accommodate a whole battalion comfortably. After around 500 men of the battalion had been called up it became apparent that there was insufficient sleeping accommodation for the rest. Therefore billeting arrangements were hastily made with local Moseley residents. The officers, meanwhile, were billeted in a large empty residence near the barracks known as 'Windermere', whilst the CO, Colonel Lewis, continued to commute from the 'Plough and Harrow'. The battalion was fully mobilised by the first week of November.

November 1914; Training Difficulties

By November 1914, with winter rapidly approaching the opposing armies in France and Belgium had fought to a standstill. The British Regulars of the BEF had been bled dry in the slaughterhouse of what was known as the First Battle Of Ypres. Both sides were now 'digging in' and before long a trench system would run from the Belgian coast to the Swiss border. Now was the time for both sides to lick wounds, and count the costs of the first three months of war. In many British Regular battalions, there were only a handful of the original men who had arrived in France in August, still surviving. Reservists from the base depots were running out. A few Territorial Battalions had been drafted to Flanders, but the majority of men 'topping up' the BEF were now volunteers. They were not Kitchener's New Army men at present, but those men who volunteered through the Regular Army recruiting stations; and in doing so, many were in the front line within weeks rather than months.

Trench warfare had now begun in earnest. The world would have to wait almost another four long years for a war of movement to return. Until then the Western Front would become seemingly one long artillery duel. The infantry crouched in their trenches or sought cover in their dugouts, whilst each side tried to blow each other off the face of the earth. Men in the front line trenches, on both sides, had become night-owls; unseen by day, emerging at night either to put up barbed wire entanglements, dig new trenches, carry supplies or patrol No Man's Land.

As Kitchener's New Army began to expand the new battalions were allotted to divisions; a division, roughly 18,000 men, was the smallest self-contained formation in the British Army. The first six divisions became known as the First New Army, the second six became the Second New Army and the 3rd six the Third New Army. It was these first three New Armies that came under War Office control from the outset.

Hence, the first three New Armies had an advantage over the locally raised battalions (who would make up the Fourth and Fifth New Armies), in the fact that when formed into divisions they could concentrate on one training ground. Thus it was possible to secure uniformity in training and, with the need for every able man to be at the front, also economise on instructors. Another advantage the first three New Armies had was that the majority of battalions were allocated at least one or two experienced Regular Army officers with the knowledge of up-to-date training methods. All this helped the first three new Armies develop a very important quality of 'esprit de corps' very early on in their training. Consequently some of the locally raised battalions, the Birmingham Battalions included, were handicapped at the beginning by the men being scattered about in billets. Another disadvantage was that the senior officers and NCOs had learned their trade in colonial wars of years gone by, and were not familiar with the Field and Service Regulations that were issued in 1909. The issue of uniforms, arms and equipment was irregular and only available in small quantities for the first few months.

According to guide-lines laid down by the War Office, in ideal conditions, to turn a civilian into a soldier ready for the front, should take six months. But by now conditions were far from ideal. With difficulties regarding facilities, equipment, arms, experienced instructors etc, the majority of locally raised battalions would take at least a year.

Commissions, Transfers and Reserve Companies

Being non-manual workers, with various social backgrounds, the three Birmingham battalions, had a multitude of men suitable to be temporary officers in the New Army. From the very first week of training applications for commissions for various arms of the services were submitted from men of the three battalions. This did not cause much of a problem with the 2nd and 3rd Birmingham Battalions due to the fact that during their thirteen months' training period the 2nd Battalion had around 100 men commissioned and the 3rd Battalion about sixty. The main cause for concern was the 1st Birmingham Battalion. Around fifty men received commissions within the first three months, and there were around 350 more before the battalion went overseas. Overall 550 men gained commissions from the three battalions whilst in training, which reflects the high character of Birmingham's non-manual battalions. In fact hundreds more were certainly 'officer material', but were happy to stay in the ranks and keep the 'Pals' spirit alive. Using the Daily Orders of the 1st Birmingham Battalion as an example (and presuming they represent the affairs of the other two bat-

talions), we also find a number of men with specialist training transferred, some voluntarily and some not, to other units. For example, Alex Hastilow, a former chemistry student and volunteer to the 2nd Birmingham Battalion, had not long graduated from Birmingham University. He was transferred into the Royal Engineers and employed in perhaps an equally hazardous environment to that of the Western Front; the explosives laboratory at Kynochs (Birmingham munitions firm). A certain number of men would be discharged under King's Regulations, paragraph 392 (iii), 'Not being likely to become an efficient soldier'. This would be

Above: Second Lieutenant Hatwell is seen here with his wife when she visited him during his training at Salisbury Plain. More of William Hatwell's service life with the 1/8th Royal Warwicks can be found out in the book *Some Desperate Glory* by E G Vaughan. Around 400 men of the 1st Birmingham Battalion were commissioned prior to the battalion going to France. Sergeant William Hatwell (pictured on pages 62 & 63) was commissioned to the 1/8th Royal Warwicks on 26 June 1915.
Frank Hatwell

20

CHAPTER VI.

A REGIMENTAL "WHO'S WHO."

Before joining your Regiment it is as well to fix in your mind's eye the functions and the status of the various regimental dignitaries, for you will feel awkward if you find yourself saluting the band-master or treating the Colonel as a long-lost brother.

The Colonel, usually spoken of as "the C.O." (Commanding Officer); and spoken to as "Sir," is "IT," and must be treated accordingly. On Parade, you will treat him as you would the King (whose authority he represents), off parade as you would treat a rich uncle from whom you have expectations. Honour and obey him; perhaps you may even learn to love him— in time!

The Major, Second in Command is a modified "IT" and should be treated

21

accordingly. You may address him as "Major" when you get to know him better, but it's wiser to start with "Sir."

Other Majors who command squadrons in the Cavalry, batteries in the Artillery, No. I Double Company in the Infantry, etc., etc., should also be addressed as "Sir," until you feel entitled to do as the other officers do and call them "Major" when addressing them.

The Adjutant is your own particular scourge. He has been appointed for that purpose. He is the Colonel's right-hand man. The only way to become popular with the Adjutant is to learn your work and to do it well. The Adjutant transacts most of the official business of the unit on behalf of the Commanding Officer. When in doubt, ask the Adjutant; but don't ask him anything silly. He is a busy man.

A Captain. The Captain of your own particular battery, squadron, or

22

company stands "in loco parentis," and will probably prove your guide, philosopher and friend. He will stick up for you if you are worth it, and he will make things pretty hot for you if you are not.

The Senior Subaltern will be to you what the Senior Prefect is to the new boy at school. He is, by an unwritten law, entrusted with the ungrateful task of "licking into shape" each newly-joined subaltern. When he speaks to you seriously —which we hope will not be often —it is wise to listen and to take notice, for he has the power to convene that totally illegal assembly, a Subaltern's Court-Martial, and being jealous of the privilege he will do so if your general behaviour gives him any excuse.

The Junior Subaltern (yourself !) is a blot on the earth until he justifies his existence. He should assume the attitude of the new boy at school.

The Quartermaster looks after the clothing, equipment, housing and

23

feeding of the regiment. He usually has been promoted from the ranks, has all the regulations at his finger tips, but is just a little shy when mixing with the other officers.

The Sergeant-Major is a "Sir" by Officer, is addressed as "Sir" by the N.C.O.'s and men, and is an official to be conciliated by the new recruit officer. You will address him as "Sergeant-Major," he will give you all the respect to which an officer as such is entitled; but according to your capabilities he will contrive to show you exactly how much you are worthy of that respect. Do not attempt to put him in his place. He knows it better than you do. Incidentally, he knows

Your Orderly, soldier servant or batman, is the man told off to act as your valet. You should remember however that he is a soldier more than a servant and should be treated as such. No man, so it is said, is a hero to his own valet; but re-

24

member you must try and appear as one to your batman for your back-slidings will be duly re-counted by him to the men of your company. If you overwork him you should also overpay him.

BY THE SAME AUTHOR.

TACTICS
FOR COMPANY COMMANDERS
AND FIELD OFFICERS.

Price 2s. 6d.   In preparation.

Above: Example of tunic button issued to the 2nd Birmingham Battalion.

due to medical reasons and not because they were inept.

To combat this steady trickle of men leaving the battalions, it was decided to raise a 'Reserve' E Coy for each battalion, enabling them to be kept at full strength. When the battalions were eventually taken over by the War Office in June 1915, the three reserve companies amalgamated to form the 17th (Reserve) Battalion of the Royal Warwickshire Regiment.

14th, 15th and 16th (Service) Battalions

At some period during the early days of training, the three Birmingham Battalions were given their official classification. The 1st Birmingham Battalion officially became the 14th Royal Warwicks, the 2nd Battalion the 15th Royal Warwicks and 3rd 'City' Battalion the 16th Royal Warwicks. The surviving Daily Orders of the 1st Birmingham Battalion begin on 1 January, 1915 and the title 14th Royal Warwicks is used thereon.

Having mentioned earlier the misunderstanding in the Birmingham press concerning the 1st Birmingham Battalion being the 11th Royal Warwicks, there is no mention at all of the battalions receiving their official nomenclature. Therefore, throughout their training period I will still refer to them as the 1st, 2nd or 3rd Birmingham Battalions.

Uniforms

By December 1914, the majority of men had received their new 'Blue' uniform and were allowed to wear them on their Christmas leave. I say 'majority', because measurements were based on the medicals when the volunteers were attested. Then, the men were measured bare chested. Therefore nothing was allowed for items of clothing worn under the tunic i.e. vest, shirt and cardigan. Throw in the three good meals a day plus vigorous exer-

cise there is no wonder that many men found their tunics were very tight fitting indeed, and had to be re-measured.

During this early training period of Kitchener's New Army, many newly raised battalions had to make do with anything as regards uniforms and equipment. Countless photographs turn up in post-card fairs of these motley groups of men staring at the camera for posterity attired in their varied bits of obsolete uniforms and equipment. In fact, some northern Pals Battalions even wore their cloth caps as part of their uniform.

The Birmingham Pals were fortunate to have nearly £17,000 in the equipment fund which was used to enhance their Kitchener Blue uniform. First of all the uniforms were made to measure and were of a finer navy-blue serge cloth than issued to other battalions. I am fairly confident in saying that no other New Army battalions wore a red banded service hat like those issued to the Birmingham Battalions. To complement the hat, they wore trousers with a thin red welt down the seams. Looking closely at photographs we also find that for everyday wear along with puttees, they were issued with 'knickerbocker' type breeches; buttons can be seen around the knee area. Another interesting item not seen on other New Army troops was an apron of the same navy-blue cloth that was attached to the shoulder via the tunic buttons and epaulette. It seems the idea was to save wear and tear on the uniform whilst marching with a rifle. Special Royal Warwickshire cap badges were made bearing an extra scroll with the wording 1st, 2nd or 3rd Birmingham Battalion. Each battalion had its own shoulder titles and tunic buttons. For walking out, all original volunteers were issued with a silver topped swagger stick embellished with the City coat of arms and the name of the battalion. Concerning their uniforms, Private J E B Fairclough, of the 1st Birmingham Battalion, had this to say after the Christmas leave of 1914: 'When the battalion assembled again, it was learned that in many cases the red banded service

Right: Former staff of the Birmingham Reference Library who enlisted into D Coy's 15 Platoon of the 1st Birmingham Battalion.
From left to right:
Standing: 922 William W Howe, 925 Frank T Izzard.
Kneeling: 976 Thomas Riley, 3 Frederick J Patrick
Sitting: 874 George H Dyer, 873 Henry W Checketts, 7 Percy A Garner
Birmingham Library Services

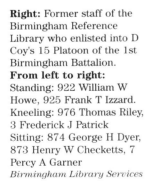

cap had received salutes and caused guards to be turned out.'

Once most of their uniform and items of equipment had been issued, Private Charles Carrington (No.247), of the 1st Birmingham Battalion, wrote the following in a letter home to his parents in New Zealand:

'The British Army is the most lavishly equipped in the world, and no unit is more lavishly clothed than this, whose supplies are augmented by a fund of £16,000 raised for us by the city of Birmingham. We have at present:-
1 blue uniform with breeches and blue putees
1 blue uniform with slacks
1 Khaki greatcoat
1 waterproof cape, like a cycling cape
2 good pairs of boots, one pair (full dress) better than any of my private ones
1 forage cap (blue and red)
1 glengarry cap
1 pair of canvass overalls
1 cardigan jacket
1 pair of mittens
3 shirts
4 pairs of socks
2 pairs of underpants
1 pair of khaki puttees
2 towels
1 housewife (I'd better explain, this is a sewing kit. TC)
1 holdall for shaving tackle, toothbrush etc, and a small allowance to buy them with
1 canvas kit bag.'

The basic harness that a solder strapped around his body, which carried his equipment and ammunition, was a strongly woven canvas material known as 'webbing'. Due to the sudden increase of the

armed forces, this piece of kit also became very scarce. The War office introduced a temporary leather harness known as the 1914 Pattern Leather Infantry Equipment. This can be easily identified due to the fact that the belt was done up with a large snake buckle. This was the equipment issued

Above: Three photographs showing the 3rd Birmingham Battalion at Moseley
Dave Vaux Collection

to the majority of New Army troops, including the Birmingham Battalions.

Christmas 1914

Only a small percentage of men from the three 'City' Battalions were on duty during the Christmas holiday. Those not having four days leave were given time off over the New Year celebrations instead. Prior to the Christmas vacation, each member of the 1st Birmingham Battalion received a two-ounce packet of tobacco the result of the generosity of Dame Clara Butt, the world renowned cantatrice, whose brother (L A K Butt, No.597), until being commissioned, was a humble private in D Coy. Those on duty, though, had little to complain about, their only duties would be semi-relaxed guard work, allowing plenty of time to participate in the home celebrations of the hosts with whom they were billeted. Writing home on December 23rd, 1914, Charles Carrington described events leading up to Christmas:

'On Monday when I woke it was snowing hard and the snow lay. Yesterday and today it froze hard and there is still a little snow and now the sun is out. We may get skating and snow on Xmas day. 85% of the Battalion left this morning for four days Xmas leave. The rest, including me, are having it at New Year instead. Last night in the Hall of the 'Crystal Palace', which is our headquarters, it was quite like the last day of term at school. They couldn't get anything done and 600 or 700 of us insisted on singing carols instead of attending to business, till they had to march us out into the snow to do anything.

'This Xmas in the right atmosphere is most thrilling. I've shovelled snow off the doorstep and sung carols on Route Marches, and been knocked out by a

snowball, and done everything that is done.'

The following verse, concerning the Christmas Guard, was written by Private R B L Moore of the 2nd Birmingham Battalion (No.1010), who was more widely known as 'Ricardo' the battalion poet:

THE SPECTRE OF POWELL'S POOL

It was Christmas Eve at Sutton,
And the snow lay deep and hard.
Most of us were on leave, sir,
But some of us were on guard.

They'd chosen the guard and piquet
From the men who were living near,
And we had no Christmas dinner
So we thought we'd have some beer.

We had 'soaked' thro'out the morning
Till at twelve we scarce could see,
And the Sergeant of the guard, sir,
Fell sick just after three.

So I up and said to him then, sir:
'Sarge, you're lookin' white,
Shall I go an' fetch a doctor?'
He said 'Hic, thash, hic, orright.'

So I put him to sleep in a corner,
and pinning his stripes on my arm,
I fetched up another gallon
From old George Fellowes's farm.

I'd just got back from the guard-room,
And the chaps gave a joyful shout,
When I heard a cry from the sentry,
'Guard-hic-Guard turn out!'

We straightened ourselves a bit, sir,
And put the beer out of sight;
Then, grabbing our rifles and bay'nits,
We dashed out into the night.

Above: In 1919 a book, edited by Alderman William Bowater, was published entitled the *Birmingham City Battalions Book of Honour*. The first 160 pages are concerned with the Birmingham Pals. The remaining 260 pages contain the Rolls of Honour of Birmingham firms and institutions; the result of the above appeal in the local Birmingham press at the beginning of the war.

Above right: Sergeant Ernest Braddock and Corporal Arthur Knight supervising 13 Platoon of D Coy 2nd Birmingham Battalion.
Arthur Knight

Below: Members of 12 Platoon, C coy of the 1st Birmingham Battalion. The trees of Westwood Coppice can be seen in the background. Seated left of the middle row, and pretending to play his shovel like a banjo, is Private Herbert Bayliss (No.505, from Handsworth New Road). Herbert was wounded during the Somme battles of 1916. On recovery he was commissioned to the Kings Liverpool Regiment.
Gordon Bayliss

And the sentry was standing there, sir,
With his rifle held at the 'charge,'
And his eyes standing out of his head, sir,
Like a lunatic at large.

I looked for the 'visiting rounds,' sir,
But nobody was in sight
Except for a spectral figure
That stood just out of the light.

We could not speak a word, sir,
For the fear was on us all,
And I gripped my rifle tighter

And prayed for a round of ball.
Then, from out of the darkness, A voice spoke all at once
'I've brought yer a case o'stout, sir,'
And the voice was the voice of Bunce.
I threw my rifle from me
And fell on his neck and wept;
Then we dragged him into the guard-room
And drank up the beer – and slept.

We woke with bad heads in the morning,
And each of us felt a fool
When we thought of the fright we'd had, sir,
At the spectre of Powell's Pool.

Above: Photographers found plenty of scope for their activities at Westwood Coppice. Excellent business was done during the 1st and 2nd Birmingham Battalions' training period at Sutton Park. The photographs sold as postcards and many survive to this day as souvenirs of happy training days. It was the done thing during lunch breaks to sneak out of the park for a few swift halves in the Parson and Clerk, situated on the Chester Road nearby.
Dave Vaux Collection

Left: Men of D Coy, 2nd Birmingham Battalion in the vicinity of the 'Gun Slade' Sutton Park.
Steve Farrant Collection

Private Charles Carrington of the 1st Birmingham Battalion visited relatives in London over the New Year period. Whilst there he visited the Pantomime at Drury Lane Theatre. The leading song was so good, he wrote it down for his parents (Before reading aloud, I suggest if the reader has false teeth, take them out! T.C.):

> 'Sister Susie's sewing shirts for soldiers
> Such skill at sewing shirts our shy young sister Susie shows

Some soldiers send epistles
Say they'd rather sleep in thistles
than the saucy soft short shirts for soldiers, sister Susie sews.'

Training: January to June, 1915

Until re-shuffles occurred in the Divisional numbering system on 27 April 1915, the three Birmingham Battalions (14th, 15th and 16th

Calthorpe Park, Saturday 13 March 1915. The 1st and 2nd Birmingham Battalions marched from Sutton Park via Erdington and Aston and were received with great enthusiasm by the crowds, lining the roads, en route. When all three battalions reached the park, sandwiches were provided by the Lord Mayor, and the beer courtesy of Mitchells & Butlers, the well known firm of Cape Hill Brewers.
The Royal Regiment of Fusiliers Museum (Royal Warwickshire)

Warwicks) and the 12th Gloucesters (Bristol) formed the 116th Brigade of the 39th (New Army) Division. At the beginning of the new year the CO of the 116th Brigade, Brigadier-General F W Evatt DSO, took up residence in Sutton Coldfield. He was said to be 'favourably impressed by the battalions who were engaged on advanced military work'. The next important event in the training period of the three City Battalions was an inspection by General Pitcairn Campbell (GOC, Southern Command) in Calthorpe Park, on Saturday afternoon, 13 March. Fortunately, the weather was fine, and as the three battalions made their way across the city, the streets were thronged with citizens who warmly welcomed the 'Boys in blue' as they marched to the park. There was no attempt at military manoeu-

This page: Three views of the inspection made by General Pitcairn Campbell (GOC Southern Command) and his entourage upon the 1st, 2nd and 3rd Birmingham Battalions at Calthorpe Park, Saturday 13 March 1915.

Pictured above, Alderman William Bowater, Lord Mayor of Birmingham, can be seen walking behind the General (with walking stick). To the left of Alderman Bowater is Captain Thomas Kenneth Barnsley of B Coy 1st Birmingham Battalion (see page 50), who would soon transfer to the Coldstream Guards.

The Royal Regiment of Fusiliers Museum (Royal Warwickshire)

vres; just a straightforward inspection by General Pitcairn Campbell. Also parading in Calthorpe Park were Territorials of the Royal Army Medical Corps from Great Brook Street Barracks. Once inspected, all those assembled marched back to Birmingham to pass a saluting base in Victoria Square. On the return march they were joined by the young Birmingham lads from the various Birmingham Grammar Schools' Cadet and Officer Training Corps companies. Also in the parade was the largest muster of Boy Scouts ever seen in Birmingham. It was estimated that there was nearly 5,000 Scouts from all districts of the city. The saluting base was a specially erected platform opposite the Queen Victoria statue and, at 3.30 pm, General Campbell and his staff, the Lord Mayor (W H Bowater) in his scarlet robes, Austen Chamberlain MP, and Neville Chamberlain and their wives took their places. Surrounding the base stood many of Birmingham's leading citizens. Everywhere was enthusiasm, and as the head of the long line of blue-uniformed men swung into the square a mighty cheer went up, and from the buildings surrounding Victoria Square flags and handkerchiefs fluttered from the people perched at the windows. In the *Picture World* newspaper published on Monday, March 15th, an anonymous 'Birmingham Pal' gave his impression of the days events:

'*Should we please? Would Birmingham be proud of us – proud of the battalions she has raised and christened? Or should we fail to realise expectations?*

'*These were the thoughts uppermost in the minds of most of us when we set out from Sutton Park on Saturday morning for Birmingham to undergo a far more critical inspection than the official one in Calthorpe Park – an inspection by our fellow citizens of civil life. We knew a kind reception awaited us; for Birmingham people, however critical, are always generous; but should we arouse real, genuine enthusiasm and not merely receive that faint kind of praise to which blame is preferable? Six months seems a long time, and people who know nothing of the Army are inclined to think that a Field Marshal's training could comfortably be accomplished within that period. Even as far back as September last I should not have credited what a lot of things a "Tommy" has to learn before he becomes efficient and the little he seems to be able to show for it.*

'*"M,m," soliloquises the casual observer, "they look all right and march well, but, after all, I'd back myself to march as well in less than six months." And such a person would not mean it unkindly. Still, I can assure readers of the Picture World that it has been no picnic at Sutton, but real hard gruelling work – harder, it must be confessed, than many anticipated.*

'*Even so, I would not have missed it for a lot. Parenthetically, I may remark that I dread the thought of having to return to the office stool and the desk, and the common round, after my brief hour of glorious life!*

'*Such, I say, were the thoughts with which my mind was occupied as we stepped along at an exhilarating pace, the keen morning air helping to whet our appetites and look forward to the luncheon hour in Calthorpe Park. I remember in pre-war days that I regarded myself as somewhat of a pedestrian if I walked to the office in the morning from my home – a matter of two miles and a half – and I should have laughed if anyone had proposed a tramp to Sutton. Saturday's journey was a mere ramble compared with some of our route marches, and it seemed that we were back again in the familiar streets of Birmingham in no time.*'

AN AFFECTIONATE GREETING

'*No longer was there any need to hesitate as to the warmth of the greeting which awaited us. There was no doubt about it that we passed the test all right – although, perhaps, I ought not to say it.*

Above: Victoria Square, Birmingham. Saturday afternoon, 13 March 1915.
Following the inspection at Calthorpe Park, Birmingham's three Pals Battalions marched via Five Ways and Broad Street to the saluting point in Victoria Square. All along the route the streets were crowded with cheering citizens. When the Birmingham Battalions reached Victoria Square Birmingham City Police Band played the Regimental march past 'The Warwickshire Lads and Lassies'.
Dave Vaux Collection

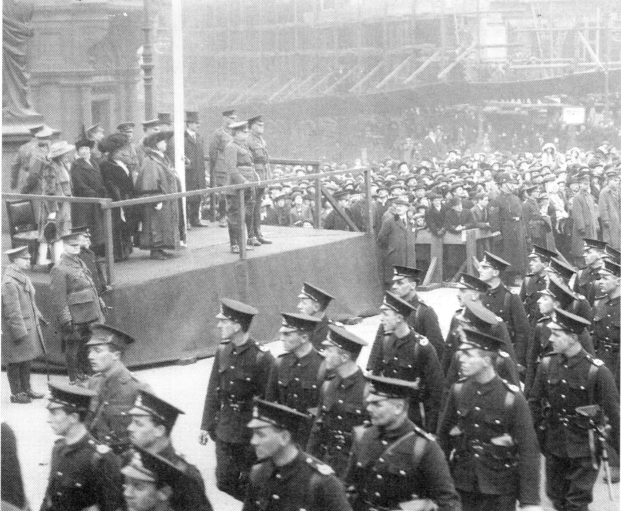

Left: Part of 7 Platoon, B Coy, 1st Birmingham Battalion, commanded by Second Lieutenant Emile Jacot (wearing khaki uniform, left hand side of photograph). During the march past it was clearly evident that the six months' training so far had converted a collection of individuals into three battalions of soldiers in which dwelt a magnificent esprit de corps.
Royal Regiment of Fusiliers Museum (Royal Warwickshire)

75

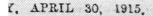

PUBLIC NOTICES.

G. R.

RECRUITING

Is again open for

BANTAM BATTALION

Height: Minimum 5 feet.
Maximum 5 feet 3 inches.

All Recruits will be sent to Bristol to join the 14th Battalion Gloucestershire Regiment (West of England).

Recruits are wanted in the 14th SERVICE BATTALION ROYAL WARWICKSHIRE REGIMENT (1st Birmingham). These used to be called non-manual workers.

This is an opportunity for young fellows of better standing and education to enlist, and be amongst their fellows.

APPLY

RECRUITING OFFICE,
STRATFORD-ON-AVON.

(Signed) T. H. BAIRNSFATHER,
Major,
Recruiting Officer.

NOTICE.
STRATFORD-ON-AVON.

Above: Recruiting advert from a Stratford upon Avon newspaper, 30 April 1915. The 1st Birmingham Battalion continually required new recruits during its training period to replace men being commissioned. The CO of the Stratford Recruiting Office, Major T H Bairnsfather, was the father of Captain Bruce Bairnsfather of the Royal Warwicks who created the famous 'Old Bill' cartoon character.
Gordon Rea Collection

Right: NCOs of 15 Platoon, D Coy of the 1st Birmingham Battalion. Only one NCO can be positively identified; standing second from the right is Sergeant John Eldridge, No.885, from Alfred Road, Sparkhill.
Dave Vaux Collection

Birmingham was obviously pleased, nay delighted, with our appearance, and if I was at all prone to such a habit I am afraid I should have blushed to the roots of my hair by reason of the many complimentary remarks about 'BIRMINGHAM'S OWN' which reached my ears. What a triumphal progress it was! Indeed I felt a kind of lump rising in my throat at the really affectionate welcome we received; the cheery greetings, the smiles of the old ladies, and yes, why hide it? The kisses which were thrown by the young ones. What crowds there were; I had never thought Birmingham contained such a lot of people. In and around the park there must have been getting on for a hundred thousand spectators.

'The inspection by Lieutenant-General W. Pitcairn Campbell C.B., the general officer commanding the Southern Command was timed for two o'clock, so that we had plenty of time to spare, seeing that Calthorpe Park was reached about noon. The 3rd Battalion came along from Moseley at about half past one and looked as smart and spruce as – why be modest? – as ourselves.

'The City Battalions were not the only troops present, however, there being units also of the North Midland Mounted Field Ambulance, 1st South Midland Brigade R.A.M.C., 3rd South Midland Brigade (second line), Royal Field Artillery, Transport and Supply Column, and the Southern Command Motor Wireless Signal Section, all of whom, being in khaki, served to throw into relief the blue-serge uniforms of our men, thus providing an object lesson as to the advantage of khaki from a screening point of view.

'In readiness for the inspection we were drawn up in a line of quarter column, and I can assure you it was a bit nippy standing there waiting for the General. He arrived at last, however, accompanied by the Lord Mayor, who, we were somewhat disappointed to find, was not in uniform, although he is the Honorary Colonel of the 1st Battalion.

A TEST OF STAMINA

'"'Tion!" rang out the order, and we stood rigid as the salute was given. Then the detailed inspection was commenced and carried out with such thoroughness that it occupied half-an-hour. I felt nearly frozen when the time came, at long last it seemed, to stand easy. Let those who regard soldiering as easy work try and remain rigid for half-an-hour in an exposed position; if he comes through the ordeal alive he may regard himself as being possessed of uncommonly fine stamina (before the end of the year, this unknown recruit would be manning trenches waist deep in cold liquid mud; then he would understand the meaning of 'uncommonly fine stamina'). We were anxious to be on the move again, and no one was sorry when the signal was given to move off to Victoria Square, where we had to pass the General at the saluting base. More crowds en route, more cheering, more complimentary remarks. The spectators lined the roadway more thickly than ever, I think, in Broad Street, where members of the King Edward School Officers Training Corps, large numbers of Boy Scouts, and the 1st Cadet Battalion of the Royal Warwickshire Regiment, fell in at our rear.

THE MARCH PAST

'Hitherto the drums and bugles had provided the only musical accompaniment to the tramp, tramp, tramp, but opposite the Prince of Wales Theatre the Police Band met us, and the lilting strands of the 'Warwickshire Lads and Lasses' filled us with renewed strength. The Lord Mayor, wearing his scarlet robe and gold chain of office, accompanied the General at the saluting base, as also did the Lady Mayoress, her daughter, Mr and Mrs Neville Chamberlain, and a number of officers. The march past occupied just over an hour, and at the close the united bands played the National Anthem.'

Lord Kitchener Visits Lichfield

After the parade in Birmingham, events began to move more quickly for the three battalions. The huts being erected in Sutton Park for the 1st and 2nd Birmingham Battalions were nearly finished, and would soon be ready for habitation. Meanwhile, with the limited training space at Moseley, it was decided that the 3rd Birmingham Battalion should move out to Malvern in Worcestershire. But first all three battalions were to participate in field training in the outer suburbs of the city. Two companies from each battalion were to spend two weeks field

Above: April 1915, D Coy's 15 Platoon of the 3rd Birmingham Battalion at Alcester.
Dave Vaux Collection

Below: Led by their Drums, the 2nd Birmingham Battalion arrive at Whittington Heath near Lichfield on Saturday 20 March 1915.
Birmingham Library Services

training in new surrounds with the other two companies moving out on their return. On 19 March, 1915, B Coy of the 1st Birmingham Battalion went to Coleshill, whilst C Coy went to Henley-in-Arden and trained amid the Beaudesert Hills. With no Daily Orders surviving for the 2nd and 3rd Battalions, I've had to search through old newspapers to find out that B Coy of the 2nd Birmingham Battalion were stationed in the village of Knowle for two weeks; the Knowle Institute becoming the Coy HQ. whilst C Coy stayed at Solihull. What of the 3rd Birmingham Battalion? D Coy stayed at Alcester over the Easter period and indulged in skirmishing work in the grounds of Ragley Hall. No mention is made of the other companies, so I assume they also trained in the same area.

According to Private Fairclough in the battalion history, prior to B Coy of the 1st Birmingham Battalion moving out to Coleshill, 'The girls of the village had been warned of the evils of talking to the brutal licentious soldiery billeted in their midst: but the charm of B Coy soon created an impression, and later on C Coy reaped the advantage of the good pioneer work done by B Coy'.

On Saturday 20 March, Lord Kitchener was to make a flying visit to Whittington Barracks near Lichfield. The purpose was to inspect the Reserve New Army battalions that were quartered there; namely the 14th Sherwood Foresters (Notts and Derby Regt.), 14th Manchesters, Army Service Corps units and men from the Royal Army Medical Corps.

To complete the line up at Lichfield the remaining companies of the 1st and 2nd Birmingham Battalions and their E (Reserve) Coys, were also invited to attend the parade. The two battalions began a three hour route march at Sutton Park at 10 am. Once in the vicinity of Whittington Heath they had a couple of hours' rest. Then, at 3pm, headed by their bugle bands, the 1st and 2nd Birmingham Battalions marched onto the bleak and breezy stretch of Whittington Heath and lined up behind the other New Army troops. Of course the City battalions stood out a mile with their dark blue uniforms and red banded service hats. As frequently happens in these cases, the battalions were lined up much too early. Kitchener did not arrive at Lichfield's Trent Valley Railway Station until 4.30 pm. He was met by Colonel Churchward who was in charge of the Army Record Office at the barracks. Lord Kitchener and his entourage then motored over to the Heath where he remained for roughly forty minutes only. However, in those forty minutes he had expressed himself at being pleased and satisfied with the serviceable appearance of the Birmingham Battalions.

The City Battalions' New Home

During the second week of April, 1915, the 1st and 2nd Birmingham Battalions began to move into their newly completed huts. The 1st Birmingham camp opposite the Crystal Palace whilst the 2nd Birmingham's hutment's were in the vicinity of Powell's Pool. Private J E B Fairclough remembered that:

'The huts were very comfortable and situated in picturesque surroundings. They had been well built and excellent recreation rooms had been provided. The baths were good, and after a route march in the warm spring weather there was a concerted rush for the shower baths. With a battalion in billets, it was not an easy matter to maintain the corporate spirit of the regiment, but this move into huts proved very beneficial, and very soon one realised that here at Sutton was a grown-up boarding school. The sections and platoons, which off parade had been

separated in billets, now messed and slept together: this was all to the good in producing a more homogeneous body. Life in the huts proved very pleasant; acquaintances ripened and closer contact was made with one's companions. Keen rivalry existed between companies and between various huts.

'The move into huts involved many changes in our daily routine. New bugle calls were heard and, at first, each call produced many arguments as to its meaning. Orderly duties and sundry fatigues added to the day's work and week-end guard mounting was an evil to be shunned when possible.'

Each battalion's rank and file were quartered in forty 60ft by 20ft huts, and those belonging to the 2nd Birmingham Battalion were all aptly named. For example one hut that overlooked the cook-house was known as 'OT-AZ-EL'. The one that over-looked the guard house was 'CLINK-IN-VIEW'. Others were named 'A-MEN', 'B-LIMIT', 'THE DEWDROP INN', 'SPIKANSPAN', 'STAN ZIE

Above: A group of men from 8 Platoon, B Coy, 1st Birmingham Battalion, photographed outside their hut in Sutton Park. Fifth from the right in the middle row, holding his pipe, William Furse of School Road, Moseley (see pages 190-191).
Dave Vaux Collection

Left: The 1st and 2nd Birmingham Battalions moved into their huts on 13 April 1915. They were very comfortable and situated in picturesque surroundings. Each battalion also had a Recreation Hut built, that could each seat around 400 men. The 1st Birmingham's was donated by Mr John Feeney and the 2nd Birmingham's was donated by the Birmingham Chamber of Commerce. Both were run by the YMCA and the facilities included a piano, reading and writing areas and two billiard tables.
Birmingham Library Services

Above: Typical hut interior. Life in the huts proved very pleasant and friendships ripened. Once the new style daily routine got under way, this period of training was likened to a grown up boarding school.
Birmingham Library Services

Far Right: Tented camp of the 3rd Birmingham Battalion, Malvern Common, April 1915.
Howard Stanley

Right: Private Charles Lodge, No.219, of 3 Platoon, A Coy, 2nd Birmingham Battalion who came from Durham Road, Sparkhill. He is outside the hut known as "Be Jovia." Which was a well known phrase known throughout the battalion frequently uttered by a senior NCO.
Steve Farrant Collection

Below: The 3rd Birmingham Battalion lined up at Malvern, having just detrained, Monday 17 April 1915.
Dave Vaux Collection

VILLA', 'BE-JOVIA', 'THE NUTSHELL', 'SOME HUT' and so on.

3rd Birmingham Battalion Move to Malvern

On Monday, 17 April 1915, the 3rd Birmingham Battalion marched from Moseley to Snow Hill Station for field training at Malvern. Moseley residents assembled in large numbers to give them a send off from the college. There were also large crowds at Snow Hill to greet the battalion and send

them on there way. Two special trains were laid on to take the battalion via the Great Western Railway route to Malvern Wells. To meet them was the Silver Band of the 13th Gloucesters (this battalion would serve as the Pioneer Battalion in the 39th Division) who were already camped on the upper part of Malvern Common in an area known as the Golf Links.

The 13th Gloucesters were camped on the fairway in front of the 17th green on high ground above the railway line (now dismantled), whilst the 3rd Birmingham's tented camp was below the line

and stretched out either side of the road leading from the station towards Hanley Castle. The 3rd Birmingham's camp also overflowed onto the golf links. The officers' mess tent stood on the 9th green.

Wensleydale

Without going into too much detail of who went where and why, it is suffice to say that on 27 April 1915 the War Office undertook a Divisional reorganisation. The 39th Division, to which the Birmingham Battalions belonged, was now renumbered the 32nd Division. This also brought about a change in the Brigade numbering system. The Birmingham Battalions along with the 12th Gloucesters now formed 95 Infantry Brigade. From May, 1915, the War Office began to take over the running of the 32nd Division. 96 and 97 Infantry

This page: Various views of the 3rd Birmingham Battalion at Malvern. **Top right:** Private Jim Randle (No.991, D Coy), in the centre, also acted as the company barber.
Above left and right: Dave Vaux, middle left and below: author's collection, below left; Steve Farrant

Left: The Drums and Bugles of the 3rd Birmingham Battalion at Malvern. Now wearing khaki, Sergeant I F Grigg (No.334) can be seen standing in the forefront. Another member of the band was Drummer H A R Tolkien (No.1020) whose brother J R R Tolkien would become famous for writing *Lord of the Rings*.

81

Top left: D Coy officers, 3rd Birmingham Battalion. Second Lieutenant Ian Hamilton can be identified standing, second from left. Seated is Second Lieutenant Thomas Pearman.
Mrs Gwyneth Pearman

Top right: Private S B Hopkins, No.680, C Coy, 1st Birmingham from Algernon Road, Ladywood.

Above right: Major A B Lovekin, Commanding Officer, C Coy, 3rd Birmingham Battalion.
John Leatherland

Above middle: 2nd Birmingham Battalion Sports day, June 1915.
Birmingham Library Services

Right: 1st Birmingham Battalion Sports Day, 4 June 1915.
The Royal Regiment of Fusiliers Museum (Royal Warwickshire)

Left: Officers' Donkey Derby, 2nd Birmingham Battalion.
Birmingham Library Services

Below: Some men of 10 Platoon, C Coy, 2nd Birmingham Battalion outside their hut known to all as "Some Hut," prior to moving to Wensleydale.
Mr Gannaway

Brigades were assembled first, doing so in the region of Catterick Army Camp in North Yorkshire. However, the new home for the twelve 'Pals' Battalions, that made up the three Infantry Brigades of the 32nd Division, was to be a huge tented camp in the grounds of Bolton Hall, situated near the village of Leyburn in Wensleydale.

Advance sections from all three Birmingham Battalions were sent ahead to make their prospective camps ready for occupation a few days or so before the main body of men left Sutton and Malvern. On Friday morning, 25 June, 1915, two special trains were laid on to transport the 1st Birmingham Battalion from Sutton Park Station to North Yorkshire. One local newspaper of the day reported that:

> *'Punctually to time the first train steamed out of the station at 08.50, loud*

Above: Second Lieutenant Ernest Hingeley, of South Grove, Erdington, leading 2 Platoon, of the 1st Birmingham Battalion's A Coy, onto the platform of Sutton Park Station, Friday 25 June 1915. On the right of the forward group is possibly Platoon Sergeant W G L Rice, No.836 of Hart Road Erdington.
The Royal Regiment of Fusiliers Museum (Royal Warwickshire)

Right: A well known photograph that appeared in the Birmingham local press when an article about the City in the Great War was featured. Therefore I am glad I can at last put the record straight and give the photograph the correct caption. The group looking towards the camera, belong to 13 Platoon, D Coy, 2nd Birmingham Battalion. It was taken on Saturday morning 26 June 1915. If you look closely the three men nearest the camera have their "Swagger Sticks" attached to their rifles.
Birmingham Library Services

Below: Group of 1st Birmingham Pals, Sutton Park Station.
The Royal Regiment of Fusiliers Museum (Royal Warwickshire)

cheers being raised by the spectators, and evoking deafening responses from the lads in blue who crowded the windows of the compartments on the platform side, to catch the last glance of their friends. The morning had been full of a quiet excitement and interest for the battalion. Reveille was sounded at five o'clock, and following the parade in the park, the men in full marching order and headed by their band, went by way of Upper Clifton Road to the Midland Railway Station. No time was lost in getting the men into the train, but the officers remained on the platform talking to their friends and comrades until a bugle sounded. Then they took their seats in the train, and it moved slowly off, the route evidently being by the way of Water Orton Junction on to the main north line.

'To a good many of the civilians on the platform the moment of departure was one of pathos, but all were very brave, especially the ladies who formed the greater part of the throng, and whatever may have been their inner thoughts they were hidden under sunny smiles and cheery adieux.

The Second Train

It had just turned 10.30 when the second train left; and again there was a huge crowd to bid the men goodbye. By this time, too, more of the wounded soldiers convalescing in the town had arrived on the station, and from none was the send-off accorded the City men more hearty than from these heroes of the trenches. A fatigue squad from the 2nd Battalion at Boldmere were also present, they having just brought up some of the limber wagons and baggage of that battalion. They promptly joined the merry crowd on the departure platform, and started singing in chorus 'Farewell, farewell, my own true love,' and other pieces of vocal sentiment. The train was in the charge of Major Fleming, and comprised men of 'B' Company and of the transport section, the latter in charge of Lieutenant Bore, whose chief NCO, Corporal Tuffley, was before the war a well known Master Haulier at Sutton, and who, before he enlisted, proved himself a very smart reserve police officer. In addition to the coaches for the men, there were horse-boxes and wagons loaded with limber wagons, ammunition carts, field cookers, harness, officers' furniture, motor-cycles etc. The kitbags were mostly on the first train. The men were in happy

Above: One of the trains taking the 1st Birmingham Battalion to Yorkshire, pulling out of Sutton Park Station on Friday 25 June 1915.
The Royal Regiment of Fusiliers (Royal Warwickshire)
Seeing all the friends, relations, sweethearts and former billeting hosts who came to bid the battalion farewell, reminds me of the well known World War One song:

Brother Bertie went away
To do his bit the other day
With a smile on his lips
and his Lieutenant pips
upon his shoulder bright and gay
As the train moved out he said
'Remember me to all the Birds!'
Then he wagged his paw
and went away to war
shouting out these pathetic words

'Good-bye-ee, good-bye-ee
Wipe a tear, baby dear from your
eye-ee
Tho' its hard to part I know,
I'll be tickled to death to go
Don't cry-ee, don't sigh-ee
There's a silver lining in the sky-ee
Bonsoir old thing
Cheerio chin chin!
Nah-poo! Toodle-oo!
Good-bye-ee.'

85

Above: Private Donald Brandon Cheshire, No.53, A Coy, 2 Platoon, 1st Birmingham Battalion (14th Royal Warwicks), from Holly Road, Edgbaston. The badge Donald is wearing on his right arm means that he is a member of the Company Scout section.

Below: The camp of the 32nd Division in the grounds of Bolton Hall, Wensleydale. A postcard sent by a Birmingham Pal back home. He marked with an arrow the part of the camp where the Birmingham Battalions had their tents. Penn Hill can be seen in the background.

humour, and seemed glad of the prospect of a change after nine months training in one camp. Parents, wives, sweethearts were present in great numbers to bid their menfolk 'God speed,' and whatever the feelings within might have been, there was nothing but smiling, happy faces to cheer the soldiers on their way; and when at last the train steamed out of the station the cheering was enthusiastic and prolonged. Various legends were to be observed chalked on the carriages; such as, 'Berlin, via Yorkshire'; 'Who said we should not leave Sutton?'; and so on.

The following morning, Saturday 26 June, at 05.45, the first of the two trains transporting the 2nd Birmingham Battalion, left Sutton Park Station. During this same period, the 3rd Birmingham Battalion left Malvern to join up with her sister battalions in Wensleydale. Prior to the move up to Wensleydale, men who had sufficient service in each battalion's E Coy were absorbed into the other four companies to bring them up to full strength. Then the remaining men in each battalion's reserve company amalgamated to form the 17th (Reserve) Battalion, Royal Warwicks. This new battalion moved into the huts vacated by the 1st Birmingham Battalion in Sutton Park.

The following battalions made up the infantry of the 32nd (New Army) Division, in June 1915:

95 BRIGADE

14th Royal Warwicks (1st Birmingham)
15th Royal Warwicks (2nd Birmingham)
16th Royal Warwicks (3rd Birmingham)
12th Gloucesters (raised by Citizens Recruiting Committee, Bristol)

96 BRIGADE

16th Northumberland Fusiliers (raised by Chamber of Commerce, Newcastle & Gateshead)
15th Lancashire Fusiliers (1st Salford Pals)
16th Lancashire Fusiliers (2nd Salford Pals)
19th Lancashire Fusiliers (3rd Salford Pals)

97 BRIGADE

11th Borders (raised by the Earl of Lonsdale at Penrith, Cumbria)
15th Highland Light Infantry (1st Glasgow, raised from Glasgow Tramways employees)
16th Highland Light Infantry (2nd Glasgow, raised from Glasgow Boys Brigade)
17th Highland Light Infantry (3rd Glasgow, raised by Glasgow Chamber of Commerce).

'Ard – Cruel Ard!'

Unfortunately there is very little information concerning the Birmingham Battalions' experiences in Wensleydale. Letters and diaries are scarce for this period of time. However, the 1st Birmingham Battalion's history, written after the war, contained the following reminiscences about life in North Yorkshire:

'Only the 14th and 15th Battalions (1st & 2nd Birmingham) *wore the blue uniform: the rest of the division was already in khaki* (the 3rd Birmingham Battalion was issued with khaki at Malvern). *Conditions of life were very different from our Sutton experiences, and we soon had a foretaste of a harder and more concentrated life. Sixteen men in a tent with full equipment and kitbags took some getting used to, and many were the recriminations passed at times when everyone was dashing round getting ready for parade. Men who were heavy footed and awkward proved a constant source of annoyance to their comrades. The surroundings were beautiful and the air was wonderfully bracing, and on the wide moors there was plenty of room for military schemes, but camp life in the early days at Wensley seemed ' 'ard – cruel 'ard! ' There was only a single line of rail to bring rations and other military requirements up to the camp, so that the sudden dumping of over 12,000 men in the midst of a peaceful and quiet dale meant a very heavy strain on the railway resources. Consequently rations were very meagre, and the canteen could do little to supplement them, but this matter, including the beer supply, occupied the very early attention of Colonel Lewis* (CO of 1st Birmingham Battalion), *and an improvement was soon effected.*

'The water supply was inadequate, and for washing purposes resort was made to a running stream in a small glade near the camp. For bathing we were able to use the River Ure at Wensley, and this was a very popular parade. Very shortly after our arrival we experienced severe rainstorms and large ditches had to be dug round tents and through the camp to take away the heavy rainfall, in fact the camp might

have served as a model for a Heath Robinson trench system. During periods of leisure, excursions were made to the many beauty spots near the camp, Bolton Castle, Aysgarth, Penn Hill, Redmire and Leyburn; these names bring back many happy recollections of pleasant hours spent amongst delightful people, in gorgeous country. Very often in the fine summer evenings, with the setting sun outlining the mountains of the Lake District, a magnificent panorama would be gained of the dale looking towards Aysgarth.'

As Private Fairclough explained, for the first couple of weeks or so, camp life at Wensleydale was a shock to the system for our 'sheet and blanket' soldiers of the 1st and 2nd Birmingham Battalions; the 3rd Birmingham Battalion having had two months camp experience at Malvern. Letters home to parents and loved ones back in the Midlands were soon full of moans and groans about their new environment. Of course, back home, their grievances were greatly exaggerated and very soon the Lord Mayor of Birmingham, Alderman Bowater, was inundated with complaints concerning the poor living conditions and unnecessary hardships that the Birmingham Battalions were now putting up with. To get to the bottom of these stories, the Lord Mayor in his capacity as Honorary Colonel of the 1st Birmingham Battalion decided to make investigations on the spot, and determined to visit the camp. On his return he spoke to a Birmingham Daily Post representative:

'I was especially on the alert to discover what justification there was for these rumours. All the men were in the camp, and I had an opportunity of seeing everyone; but the enquiries I made proved to me that the rumours were without foundation. I was, indeed, very pleased with the general appearance, the cheerfulness, and the energy of the men: they seemed to be in the best of health and condition, and I heard no serious complaint whatever.

'During the first two or three days, however, there had been some unavoidable discomfort which apparently gave rise to the subsequent rumours. Several thousand troops were moved to the camp practically simultaneously, and as it is served by only a single line of railway, the delivery of food supplies and camp equipment was protracted. The supply of drinking water was also limited, but the water was of good quality. In this connection, Alderman Bowater had been told that a guard was mounted over the water supply to prevent anyone from drinking it because it was poisoned. A sentry was posted there merely to see that the water was not wasted..

'Then it was alleged there were 200

cases of dysentry. As a matter of fact, there has not been a single case. During the first few days food supplies came in irregularly, and the absence of a regimental canteen or YMCA refreshment tent made things worse for the men, who had been in the habit of augmenting their War Office rations by purchases there.

'The change from comfortable huts at Sutton, where each man had a bedstead with palliasse, blankets, and in most cases, sheets, to the conditions in Yorkshire, where the men sleep twelve in a tent, with only a ground sheet and a blanket, was, of course, great; and it is not surprising some of the men in writing home spoke of their hardships. But I am certain they were not really grumbling; they only desired to let their friends know that at last they were serving under war conditions. Perhaps some of the men were like the Fat Boy in the Pickwick Papers, *and desired to make our flesh creep. At any rate, I am sure there was no real complaining after the first day or so, and I am assured by the Brigadier and the respective colonels that there has not been the slightest reluctance on the part of the men to carry out whatever duties they have been called upon to face. The three colonels are absolutely delighted with their men, and feel they have the privilege of commanding troops equal to any in the New Army.*

'The worst inconvenience the men have been called upon to suffer apparently has been through two or three severe thunderstorms, which nearly washed away both men and tents. Now, however, measures have been adopted to lessen even this discomfort, and the trenching of the camping ground has been so thorough that

Above: Aysgarth Falls, Wensleydale, a favourite haunt of Birmingham Pals when the days training was over.
Seated on the left is Private Herbert Bayliss, No.505, of the 2nd Birmingham Battalion, with his comrades from C Coy's 12 Platoon.
Gordon Bayliss

it looked like an irrigation system.

'The change from the Sutton huts to the tents was undoubtedly great, and for a few days things were more or less disorganised; but the men realise that the discomforts were unavoidable, and say the result has been only to harden them and make them more fit for active service. They certainly look in the best of spirits and health, and their officers feel certain they are equal to anything they may be called upon to do.

The city should be proud of them and feel satisfied things are going on as well as possible.'

Even though the Birmingham Battalions training period at Wensleydale lasted just over four weeks it was four weeks of incident and hard work which when looked back upon produced many happy memories. Whilst at Wensleydale the 1st and 2nd Birmingham Battalions were eventually kitted out with their khaki uniforms. For those acquainted with the book, *Birmingham City Battalions, Book of Honour* edited by Sir William Bowater in 1919, it was during this period that the platoon photographs reproduced in the book were taken.

Life at Wensleydale is also recalled in the poetry of 'Ricardo' of the 2nd Birmingham Battalion. The first poem concerns how now and again the water supply at Wensleydale used to fail which resulted in the men resorting to various methods to keep themselves and their eating and drinking utensils clean. The second poem is self explanatory:

THE MESS ORDERLY (WENSLEYDALE)
The mess-orderly came down like a wolf on the
    fold,
And his tunic was gleaming with gravy gone cold;
But the sheen on his dixie was glorious to see,
And his face beamed with pride as he showed it to
    me.
And I said to him: 'Fellow! Now what does this
    mean?
And how have you managed that dixie to clean?'
Then he told me, as water was hard to procure,
He'd cleaned it with earth mixed with grass and –
    er –manure.
So I cautioned him: 'Youngster, do you realise

The position you'll be in if somebody dies
From the germs in that dixie?' he answered me,
'Nay, the chaps would be glad to pass quietly away,
For they'd all of them know, as they went to their
    rest,
That no one in the future would care how they
    dressed;
That they needn't clean dixies but do as they
    pleased -
They'd die quite contented, their minds would be
    eased.'
So spake that young soldier, then onward he went,
And I said to myself as he entered his tent:
'It'd be quite a pleasure to die, I am sure,'
So I cleaned out my mess-tin with grass and – er –
    manure.

THE CANTEEN AT WENSLEY

'Do you know me? Ricardo the poet.
In the Bar of the Empire with you.
It's a miserable night, *mon ami,*
Ah, thanks, I don't mind if I do.

Hark to the wind how it whistles,
Up thro' the streets of the town;
It was just such a night, *mon ami,*
When the canteen at Wensley blew down.

Finish your drink. Have another?
And I will tell you a tale
Of a deed of true English courage –
'Waiter! Two glasses of ale.'

It was seven o'clock on the evening
Of a stormy July day,
We were standing round the beer bar
Spending our well-earned pay,

When somebody shouted 'Hook it!'
Outside we managed to crush,
Then we heard a rending of canvas
And the canteen came down with a rush.

Mon Dieu, shall I ever forget it?
The wind was blowing a gale
And the rain was pouring in torrents
On 'beautiful' Wensleydale.

Then out spake our brave Captain:
'What about the beer?'
'Will no one go and save it?'
'Oh, who will volunteer?'

My friend, it was just like magic,
The way they answered the shout –
It was 'Beer,' 'Volunteer;'
In a body the Warwicks stood out.

One man was then selected.
He crawled underneath the tent.
He didn't come back, so another

After him straightaway went.

We anxiously scann'd the canvas
Where we saw him disappear,
Then another, and yet another,
Crawled 'neath the tent – to the beer.

A fifth, a sixth, and a seventh,
Go the same way as the first,
An eighth, a ninth – it was splendid,
Mon Dieu, how these Warwickshires thirst.

A tenth, an eleventh, undaunted,
Step forward to meet their death
For the sake of that precious liquid
With which men change their breath.

Then out sprang a red-nosed giant
It was madness, but oh! How divine,
A typical Warwickshire soldier
Who could shift all the beer on the Rhine.
He crawled 'neath the marquee curtain
Into that wind-stricken hell,
Where beer and tobacco and chocolate

Were blended together well.

And he'd gone some fifteen seconds,
Whilst our hearts were gripp'd with fear,
When we noticed the canvas rising;
Mon Dieu! How those Warwicks did cheer.

He'd reached the rope in the centre,
Was pulling, whilst, very close
To the barrels behind the beer bar,
Eleven lay – comatose.

My eyes filled with tears, *mon ami*,
As I gazed on that dreadful scene,
Only those that have danced to their music
Can know what the beer barrels mean.

The canteen was righted, *mon ami*,
And the drinking again was begun,
By the courage of twelve Royal Warwicks
The road to the beer bar was won.

Hornsea

Even though it had been ten months since the Birmingham Battalions had been raised they were still handicapped by the shortage of rifles. Whilst at Wensleydale the Birmingham men still had their small supply of the obsolete 'Long' Lee-Enfield rifles which were used for drill purposes only. During the latter half of July, depending on how advanced their training had reached, the infantry battalions of the 32nd Division began to depart for various destinations. For example the Salford Pals Battalions were issued with their service rifles and undertook a two week proficiency course in Northumberland. Other battalions who were advanced in their training and had received their rifles moved south to their next Divisional training area on Salisbury Plain.

The Birmingham Battalions, however, were not issued with their rifles. On Wednesday 28 July, they left Wensleydale to spend one week at a tented camp, situated on a cliff-top overlooking the North Sea, two miles south of the North Yorkshire coastal resort of Hornsea. Here, for practice purposes, the men were temporarily issued with Short Magazine Lee-Enfield rifles; the main British infantry weapon of the Great War; or commonly known as the SMLE for short. Private J E B Fairclough of the 1st Birmingham Battalion later recalled that, 'Every available minute of daylight was utilised for firing, but when a company was not engaged on the range – either firing or marking – sea bathing was allowed.'

Fortunately, the week spent at Hornsea was blessed with fine weather, which made early morning parades and waiting around for turns on the ranges quite enjoyable and relaxing. Most evenings, off-duty 'Brummies' made their way to Hornsea and the nightly orchestral concerts in the Floral Hall were enthusiastically supported.

Above: Major Charles Playfair, Second in Command of the 1st Birmingham Battalion; and Proof Master of the Birmingham Gun Barrel Proof House in Banbury Street.

Codford Camp: Salisbury Plain

On Thursday 5 August, 1915, the three Birmingham Battalions left Hornsea and made a twelve hour train journey that ended in Wiltshire at Wylye Station, situated roughly ten miles north-west of Salisbury. Here then, at Codford Camp, near the village of Codford St Mary, on the southern edge of Salisbury Plain, the Birmingham Battalions began their last stage of training for active service.

Those Birmingham men who thought life at Wensleydale primitive were in for a bigger shock when they reached Codford. The former occupants of the huts, who had now departed for France, had left them and the cooking utensils in a filthy condition and much hard work was done to make them respectable again. Of course, concerning these conditions, 'Ricardo' of the 2nd Birmingham Battalion soon put pen to paper:

Sure a Corporation dust-cart overturn'd itself one
     day,
An' all its rotten contents near a Wiltshire village
     lay;
An' when headquarters saw it –
Sure it looked so wet an' damp –
That they said t'would make a lovely place for
     infantry to camp.
So they plastered it wid rat-traps,
That politely they called huts,
And the roads around were muddy
And all crumpled up in ruts.
An' they thought they'd call it Codford
(Wid the accent on the Cod)
An' there they put the Warwicks an' commended
     'em to God.

For a better description of life at Codford, we have to thank Private Fairclough of the 1st Birmingham Battalion:

'Manoeuvres were soon resumed, and much of the training centred round a big trench system, which had been commenced a considerable time before and then carried on by successive units. These trenches, dug in the white chalk so

prevalent there, were on the plain some two or three miles from the camp, and the battalion did its share of extending the trenches, and spent night and day tours in them. Big training schemes involving several divisions were participated in, and gradually the length and severity of operations were increased. Shortly after arrival at Codford five days leave was granted to the old members of the battalion and week-end leave was resumed. A special train for members of the three battalions left Wylye Station for Birmingham every Friday afternoon, and returned from Snow Hill late on Sunday evenings; (some readers may remember the famous clock in the booking hall of Snow Hill Station. This became the favourite spot for sweethearts to meet). The train was always very full, and many people came down to Snow Hill on Sunday evening to witness the departure of the train, which arrived at Wylye in the early hours of Monday morning. Sometimes those returning were informed that as the battalion was out on a training scheme, they would have a slack day, but more often orders were received that the leave party was to start right away and join the battalion in the trenches. After a long railway journey and a march up from Wylye, this seemed the last straw. Those unfortunates remaining in camp during the week-end consoled themselves by visits to Salisbury, Bath and other places near by. Salisbury was always full of troops, and on Saturday nights the theatre was packed. Codford was quite a busy little wartime village: its many wooden shacks gave it the

appearance of a country fair with the usual amusement and refreshment centres, and in addition to these, a music hall, known to the battalion as the 'Codford low-down,' provided light and varied fare for the evenings. This theatre was one of many dotted all over the plain and the artistes travelled by car from one theatre to the next. One cannot say that the turns were of a high order, but we were not over-critical; while occasionally a member of one of the battalions would be invited to give a show. So, although the training was heavy, there were compensations.'

Slowly, day by day, the training intensified at Codford. The battalions began to spend longer periods of time away from their huts. Apart from days and nights spent in the trenches open warfare schemes were practised many miles from the camp, which involved lengthy and strenuous route marches with nights spent sleeping in the open. Rumours throughout the Division were now rife of the date they would be leaving England, and their eventual destination. Writing to his sister Ethel, who lived in Little Green Lanes, Sutton Coldfield, Private John Ford (No.1064, B Coy) of the 2nd Birmingham

Above: The Guard Room of 2nd Birmingham Battalion's section of Codford Camp.

Below: The sentry with rifle is Private Frank Woolley, No.593, of C Coy, 2nd Birmingham Battalion who came from Second Avenue, Selly Park.
Mr F Woolley

Battalion, mentioned that the battalion would definitely leave Codford sometime between the 5th and 11th November; where he did not know. However, there were three rumours: France, Serbia, and the most likely one being Egypt for the winter and then the Balkans later on.

In another letter written from Codford, this time by Private Jim Randle (No.991, D Coy) to his girlfriend Ethel Hill who lived in Clissold Street, Hockley, mentioned that the song most of the battalion sang is 'Keep the home fires burning,' and that 'we are going to sing it when we leave for the Dardanelles.' (Dardanelles: another name for the Gallipoli campaign which had been under way since March 1915). Jim also informed Ethel to disregard the rumours that the Lord Mayor of Birmingham had sent a letter to the King requesting that battalion men with an engineering background be returned to work in the munitions factories and to keep the remainder for home service use only. In a later letter Jim tells Ethel that garrison duty in India was their probable destination and not to worry, he would be having his Christmas dinner in England. Subsequently, the outcome of all this hearsay inspired another ditty from the 2nd Birmingham Battalion's 'Ricardo':

TRAVELLINGITIS

OH! Oh! Always on the go,
We've got travellingitus on the brain;
From Birmingham we hail,
We've been to Wensleydale,
To Hornsea and Salisbury Plain.

OH! Oh! Always on the go,
We've got travellingitus on the brain;
We're going away
To Bombay,
Then we'll come back home again.

An indication that active service was nearing was when three new Commanding Officers were appointed by the War Office to take charge of the three battalions. Colonel L Murray took command of the 1st Birmingham Battalion. Colonel C Harding the 2nd Battalion and Colonel A C De Trafford the 3rd Battalion. Of Colonels Murray and De Trafford little is known but fortunately Colonel Colin Harding's memoirs were published in a book entitled *Far Bugles*. Without going too deeply, I thought the reader might be interested in the eventful background of the man who would take the 2nd Birmingham Battalion to France.

Colin Harding was a son of a gentleman farmer. His early home was Montacute Abbey, not far from Yeovil in Somerset. On the death of his father in 1893 it was revealed that neither he nor the rest of his family were as well off as first thought. Therefore armed only with a good public school education and the ability to ride well he left England in 1894, hoping to make his fortune in South Africa.

On reaching the Cape he made for the rough and ready shanty town of Bulewayo, which was then in Matabele Land. At this time Bulewayo was akin to the gold rush towns of the United States of America and those in Australia. He started work at the bottom, so to speak. His first job was that of a pit sawyer's mate; which meant he was in the pit! Soon afterwards he became a second rate bricklayer. Then his education helped him become Chief Clerk in a Bulewayo Solicitor's Office. Finding this life boring, with a friend, he decided on gold prospecting. During the Matabeleland rebellion of 1896 Colin Harding enlisted into the Umtali Volunteers which was a Colonial Frontier Force used to help suppress the rebellion.

His experiences during the rebellion helped him get a commission into the newly raised British South African Police Force; and he was given command of a Native Contingent. His exploits then centred around suppressing various rebellions during the formative years of Rhodesia, during which he became good friends with Cecil Rhodes and a certain Princess Radziwill. Harding also met up for the first time with a Lieutenant John Norton-Griffiths, who in later life would become MP for the Wednesbury Division of Birmingham. In 1902, Colin Harding escorted King Lewanika of Barotseland to London for the coronation of King Edward VII. During the years leading up to the First World War he was appointed Commissioner in the Northern Territories, which was the Gold Coast area of West Africa.

On 4 August, 1914, the day war was declared, Harding was on leave from Africa, and found out that his old friend, who was now Sir John Norton-Griffiths MP, was trying to get permission from the War Office to raise a Colonial Battalion made up of men who had seen service in the various outposts of the British Commonwealth. This unit eventually

A CITY BATTALION'S IMPRESSION OF SALISBURY PLAIN QUARTERS.
(Adapted from "The Pow-Wow, the organ of the Universities' and Public Schools' Brigade.)

became known as the 2nd King Edward's Horse and Colin Harding was given a commission as a Squadron Commander. The 2nd King Edward's Horse were brigaded with Canadian Cavalry regiments. Unfortunately, their horses were taken from them, the brigade took on an infantry role and went to France as part of the 1st Canadian Division in the spring of 1915. When the 2nd King Edward's Horse moved into the trenches at Festubert, Colin Harding was now a Major and second-in-command. After a period in the trench lines in Messines he decided to apply for a battalion of his own. Thus he was offered the command of the 2nd Birmingham Battalion.

Another strong sign that overseas service was not long coming occurred in the second week of October; the three Birmingham Battalions were issued with their service rifles. Thus began an intense period on the ranges. Even though 95 Brigade (1st, 2nd, 3rd Birmingham's and 12th Gloucesters) received their rifles approximately six weeks before they were due to go overseas, the shooting standard they achieved was remarkably high. Not only did 95 Brigade have the best shooting record in the 32nd Division, but were very nearly the best out of all the New Army Battalions. Of the 1st Birmingham Battalion, Captain George Lander Bryson's (from Barnt Green) C Coy won the cup for the best shooting company; whilst Private J D d'A Northwood (No.835, A Coy, an old boy of King Edward's High School, New Street) proved to be the best shot of the battalion. Subsequently the best shots became battalion snipers.

Preparations for France

Despite all rumours, the 32nd Division was destined to join the BEF in France,. Consequently, at the beginning of November 1915, the last concentrated period of training began. Live firing exercises in conjunction with the Divisional artillery firing

shrapnel had now begun. Meanwhile the men had been forewarned that on leaving camp for a route march they might suddenly be ordered to entrain for one of the channel ports. Consequently, on all route marches from now on the men had to carry every piece of kit they possessed; on route marches that by now were a thirty mile round trip from camp.

On Friday, 19 November, two days before the 32nd Division was due to embark to France, the Birmingham Battalions received a visit from the Lord Mayor of Birmingham, Neville Chamberlain, the ex-Lord Mayor and Honorary Colonel of the 1st Birmingham Battalion, Alderman William Bowater and the Bishop of Birmingham. In turn each battalion was addressed and the evening ended with the visiting party being the guests of honour at a dinner held in the Officers' Mess of the 1st Birmingham Battalion.

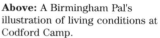

Above: A Birmingham Pal's illustration of living conditions at Codford Camp.

Above: The Silver Cup awarded to Captain G L Bryson's C Coy of the 1st Birmingham Battalion for being the 'Best Shooting Company.'
Dave Vaux Collection

Left: Friday 19 November, Codford Camp. Left to right: Alderman William Bowater (raiser of the Birmingham Pals and Honorary Colonel of the 1st Birmingham Battalion and Deputy Lord Mayor), Arthur Neville Chamberlain (Lord Mayor of Birmingham), Lieutenant W H Buxton (Acting Adjutant, 2nd Birmingham Battalion), Second Lieutenant Ernest Crisp (A Coy, 2nd Birmingham Battalion, and also the battalion Bombing Officer), and Major A W Woolley (CO of B Coy ,the 2nd Birmingham Battalion).
The Royal Regiment of Fusiliers Museum (Royal Warwickshire)

93

Above: Part of 4 Platoon, A Coy, 2nd Birmingham Battalion (15th Royal Warwicks) commanded by Lieutenant W L Hemus (extreme left of picture) being inspected by Neville Chamberlain and Honorary Colonel of the 1st Birmingham Pals, William Bowater. The officer on the right of the group is the CO of the 2nd Birmingham Battalion, Lieutenant-Colonel Colin Harding. The patch seen sewed to the side of the service hats is some type of Divisional/Brigade battlefield identification insignia. The men with their greatcoats buttoned in a similar style to French soldiers, are dressed in the same manner as they would adopt in the trenches in the very near future. Steel helmets were not issued until March 1916.
The Royal Regiment of Fusiliers Museum (Royal Warwickshire)

Right: Private Jim Randle, No.991, 3rd Birmingham Battalion.

During the last couple of weeks prior to leaving for France a few days home leave was granted for every man. Sadly, for many men this was their last visit home. On returning back to Codford there was time for that last letter, such as this example written by Private Jim Randle (No.991, D Coy, 3rd Birmingham) to his sweetheart Ethel Hill who lived in Clissold Street, Hockley:

> *Dear Ethel,*
> *I arrived here safe feeling tired. I wished I had spent a few extra hours in Brum as this was my last leave. When I got back the boys told me no more leave was going to be granted as we were moving Thursday.*
> *One thing, I feel downhearted not wishing my people good-bye and others, but still I hope to see them later when I've done my share. Now don't get downhearted, as most of us will return with smiling faces as usual.*
> *Well I will close now with much love.*
> *From the Boy*

Ethel never saw Jim again.

Chapter Five
14th, 15th & 16th Royal Warwicks: Birmingham Pals to France

Above: Captain Sir Basil Richard Gilzean Tangye, 2nd Baronet (created 1912), 16th Royal Warwicks (3rd Birmingham Battalion). Captain Tangye undertook the duties of 'Captain of the week' prior to the battalion moving overseas. In later life he became the Chairman and Managing Director of Tangyes Ltd (manufacturers of Hydraulic lifting equipment), Cornwall Works, Birmingham.
Colin Smith

An advance party from each battalion left Codford early on 20 November. This included all the transport, cooks, signallers and machine-gunners with their various pieces of equipment. The War Diary of the 15th Royal Warwick's tells us that the composition of the Transport consisted of sixty-four horses and mules, fifteen four-wheeled vehicles, four two-wheeled vehicles and 102 other ranks. Captain F D Todd was in charge assisted by Lieutenants R I Gough and F W Trott. The 14th's was under Captain T P Cooke and the 16th's under Major A W Clifford. No doubt the transport organisation off all the battalions would be standard. The parties entrained at Wylye Station, Codford for Southampton and sailed to Le Havre on the SS *Maiden*, which before the war was used for cattle transport. The crossing took 14 hours, an unusually long time, but for safety they sailed around the Channel Islands to avoid mine fields.

On the same day the three Birmingham Battalions were making their final preparations to leave the camp. Various details were to be left behind to clear up and hand over the camp to the Barrack Warden. In the history of the 14th Warwicks, Private J E B Fairclough tells us:

> *'2nd Lieutenant G F Bennett, who had only just come out of Salisbury Hospital and was not fit to proceed overseas with the battalion, was left behind in charge of the details to hand over the camp to the Barrack Warden, who tried to confiscate all the private property which had belonged to the battalion since Sutton days. This had been given to us by the citizens of Birmingham, and we were free to dispose of it as we liked. With the aid of Drum-Major A E Gould (No.1098), most of the stuff was sold to Salisbury tradesmen, and quietly carted away. Long and lengthy arguments took place concerning the battalion flag, which was kept flying till the last moment. The Barrack Warden wanted it, and 2nd Lieutenant Bennett wanted to keep it for the battalion. Somehow it disappeared during the last night and found its way to Minehead, where it remained during the war.'* (The flag can now be seen on the main staircase wall in the Royal

Warwickshire Regimental Museum, St John's House, Warwick.)

The 14th were to lose Major Fleming who was left behind, perhaps because of his age. He had been the popular CO of B Coy since the commencement of training. (Major Fleming had commanded the Service Company of the 1st Warwickshire Volunteers in South Africa in 1901.) Orders were given for the men of the 14th to breakfast at 10.30 pm (yes, breakfast!) and presumably the 16th also, as their train was leaving not long after the 14th's. After a short service with every man in full marching order wearing greatcoats and back packs bursting at the seams, they formed up on the open road running through the camp. One man of the 14th had his pack with rifle weighed, it just touched 70lbs (32 kg). Lieutenant Alan Furse (14th Royal Warwicks) made the following comment about the weight they all carried:

> *'Like all amateurs in this war we were carrying about twice as much as we really needed for use on the journey and it took us over a month to get out of this very tiring habit.'*

At midnight on the 20/21 November 1915, a freezing cold pitch black night, the first contingent of Birmingham Pals marched from Codford Camp to

Below: Leaflet issued to all members of Kitchener's New Army before going overseas.

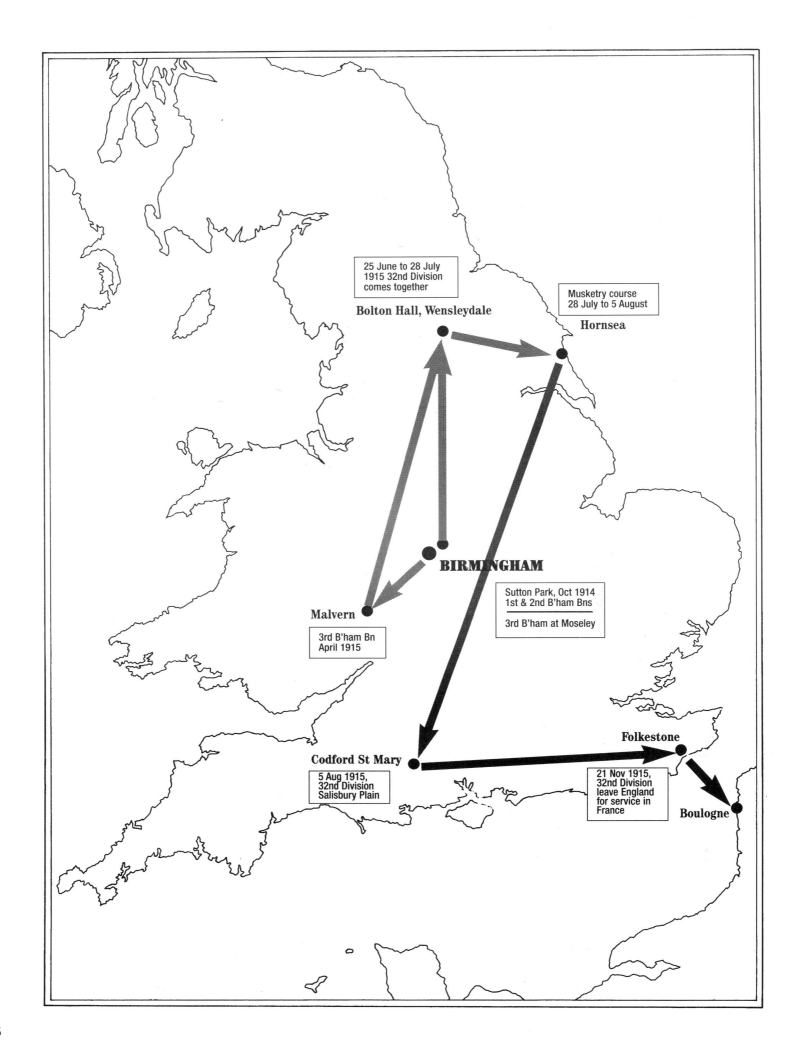

25 June to 28 July 1915 32nd Division comes together

Bolton Hall, Wensleydale

Musketry course 28 July to 5 August

Hornsea

BIRMINGHAM

Sutton Park, Oct 1914 1st & 2nd B'ham Bns

3rd B'ham at Moseley

Malvern

3rd B'ham Bn April 1915

Codford St Mary

5 Aug 1915, 32nd Division Salisbury Plain

Folkestone

21 Nov 1915, 32nd Division leave England for service in France

Boulogne

No.1. **CAPTAIN OF THE WEEK.** Captain B.R.G Tangye.
          Next for duty:-   Captain L.Hardy Smith.

No.2. **ORDERLY OFFICER** For tomorrow:- 2nd Lieut. B.T.Greenwood.
                        For Monday   :- 2nd Lieut. T.E.Pearman.
                        Next for duty:- 2nd Lieut. N.G.Yardley.

No.3. **ROUTINE.** For tomorrow:-
          REVEILLE   6.0 a.m.
          HOLY COMMUNION. 6.30 a.m. in Bde. Church Hut.(attendance voluntary)
          CHURCH PARADE.   7.15 a.m. (clean fatigue dress)
          BREAKFAST.   7.30 a.m.
          ROLL CALL (prior embarkation)
                    "C" & "D" Coys. & H.Q.Staff will parade at
          10 a.m. for roll call prior to embarkation. 16/111 Lance Sgt.
          Bromley will call the roll witnessed by 16/862 Sergt.Wheeler
          in accordance with K.R. 1504.
                    "A" & "B" Coys. will parade under Capt.G.Deakin,
          at 10.30 a.m. for roll call as above.
          RATIONS.   Rations for the day will be carried by each man,
                           water bottle filled with water.
          DRESS.   Full marching order - Waterproof sheet & blanket
                           rolled on top of valise.
          AMMUNITION.   O. C. Cos. have been issued with the requisite
          amount of ammunition. They will be held responsible that each
          man is in possession of 100 rounds.
          NOTES.   Companies will be formed up in line (Sergts. on
          right of Company) and will be told off in sections of 8.
                    O. C. Cos. will detail 1 N.C.O. or senior private
          to be in charge of each section, and he must take a nominal roll
          of his section.
                    O. C. Cos. will keep a roll of N.C.Os. and men
          in charge of sections.
                    All ranks are forbidden to throw out of trains
          any empty bottles. All Officers,&N.C.Os. must see that this
          order is strictly enforced.

No.4. **MESSAGE FROM HIS MAJESTY THE KING.** Div. Routine Order No. 564,
       dated 19th instant, is published for information:-
       "Officers, Non-Commissioned Officers, and Men of the 32nd Division,
       "on the eve of your departure for Active Service I send you my
       "heartfelt good wishes. It is a bitter disappointment to me,
       "owing to an unfortunate accident, I am unable to see the Division
       "on Parade before it leaves England; but I can assure you that my
       "thoughts are with you all. Your period of training has been long
       "and arduous, but the time has now come for you to prove on the
       "Field of Battle the results of your instruction. From the good
       "accounts that I have received of the Division, I am confident
       "that the high traditions of the British Army are safe in your
       "hands, and that with your comrades now in the Field you will
       "maintain the unceasing efforts necessary to bring this War to a
       "victorious ending.
       "   Goodbye and God-Speed.
       "   GEORGE. R.I.
       "To the above the following reply was sent.
       "Please convey to His Majesty the heartfelt thanks of all ranks
       "of the 32nd Division for his gracious message and their
       "determination to justify His expectations. The Division deeply
       "regrets the accident which has deprived it of the honour of a
       "visit from His Majesty, and humbly offers its best wishes for
       "His speedy and complete recovery."

Wylye Station. The train containing the 14th Royal Warwicks was to depart first at 00.20 am, followed by that of the 16th Royal Warwicks ten minutes later. Next stop, Folkstone. Meanwhile the 15th Royal Warwicks had a few more hours of rest before their turn later in the morning. Lieutenant-Colonel Colin Harding, the new CO of the battalion, recalled the battalion's last night on English soil:

'Leave had been given to the whole battalion, and to-night, the eve of our departure, they return in twos and threes from their respective homes, laden with delicacies bestowed upon them by affectionate parents and loving friends. The battalion is blessed by a devoted and tactful padre. He pays me a visit and asks permission to hold a short service in a hut adjoining my own. It is given, and as, preparatory to an early morning start, I retire to rest, I hear through my thin partitioned hut the final verse of "Abide with Me, fast falls the eventide," and with the rhythm of this wonderful hymn in my brain, I slept till reveille disturbs.'

On arrival at Folkstone, the 14th Royal Warwicks boarded the SS *Invicta*, whilst the 16th boarded the *Princess Victoria*. During the crossing they were escorted by Royal Navy destroyers. Boulogne was reached around 10 am. After landing the troops it is probable the ships were used for men returning on leave or hospital cases, because, by 4.15 pm, the SS *Invicta* was back in Boulogne with the 15th Royal Warwicks on board. After disembarkation they marched two miles to join the other two City Battalions on the bleak windswept hills overlooking Boulogne. The 14th were in St.

Martin's Camp, whilst the 15th & 16th were in Ostrohove Camp. These tented camps were built by the BEF for the use of newly arrived troops in transit to the front. Sergeant Arthur Cooper of the 14th Royal Warwicks (No.65, A Coy, Selly Park Road, who prior to the war was employed at the General Electric Company, Witton), kept a diary of his war service. The following entry are his first observations on reaching France:

'Away we went, singing through the streets of Boulogne, but we didn't sing for long. We came to a splendid hill for testing motor bikes. We got up it after a lot of swearing and saw lines of tents. As we thought we were going into huts this was not so good. The Captain came and told us that we were only there for 24 hours. That bucked us up a bit. When we were on the march, dozens of boys came for cigs and anything else that we could give away. It seems that they start smoking at about eight years old here. The people seem to be a very poor lot.'

There are many first-hand accounts by British Soldiers which indicate their reactions after landing in France for the first time. As they marched from the docks, many were greeted by cheering French people who gave them flowers, sweets, etc. However Lieutenant Alan Furse (14th Royal Warwicks) remembered an entirely different attitude:

'On our first march on French soil the pavé roadway was very difficult at first, especially for those with well nailed boots. We marched away from the docks through the streets and the first thing that astound-

ed us was the apathy of the French inhabitants. They had evidently got so used to the sight of our troops that they rarely looked twice at us. This was very disconcerting to us, just landed in France all filled with the idea that the war would soon be over, now that we had arrived and incidentally feeling that a better battalion had never crossed over. (In this last supposition I think we were not far wrong, for I never came across any City Battalion in France which was composed of a greater proportion of fit, thinking men than ours). We marched from the docks up a very narrow street straight up the hill at the back of the town. It was a very steep incline and progress was quite slow. After about a mile and a half of this we fell out for ten minutes. There were small cottages on the side of the street and the men were soon on good terms with the inhabitants, accepting water and apples which were offered freely. Our big drummer, Latham (D coy, No.937), created much fun by nursing a small baby whilst the mother looked on apprehensively. After about another mile of this steep hill we arrived at the camp at the top.'

Being only transit camps, conditions were very primitive. Twelve men were assigned to each tent, and given one blanket each. As night drew on the temperature dropped to well below freezing. The men tried to make themselves as comfortable as they could, with no bedding they lay on the cold hard floor. Some men huddled together so they could share two blankets, others were so cold, they could not sleep, they walked around the camp with the blanket wrapped around themselves. The freezing temperature seemed to be the least worry to some of the men. Being 'Brummies' their first priority was alcohol, as Sergeant Arthur Cooper (14th Royal Warwicks) later recalled:

'We soon found the canteen and collected some beer. Oh! what beer! worse and worse gets the beer of the poor 1st B'ham! it was just coloured water! dear! dear! Ernie did carry on some. We soon carried on to the YMCA, penny a cup of tea, then away to our twelve in a tent and slept the sleep of the weary.'

Reveille next morning, 22 November, sounded at 06.30 am. French interpreters were attached to the 15th & 16th Royal Warwicks on this day. The 15th had the service of Captain Louise Nozal, whilst the 16th had the very impressive sounding Rene Lecointe, *Brigadier Fourrier du 19 Escadron au train classe 1898, Matricule No. 1166.*

The 15th & 16th spent the rest of the day in readiness to move later in the evening. The 14th were also taking things easy until after dinner, when Major Charles Playfair the 2/ic of the battalion thought it a good idea that the men should go

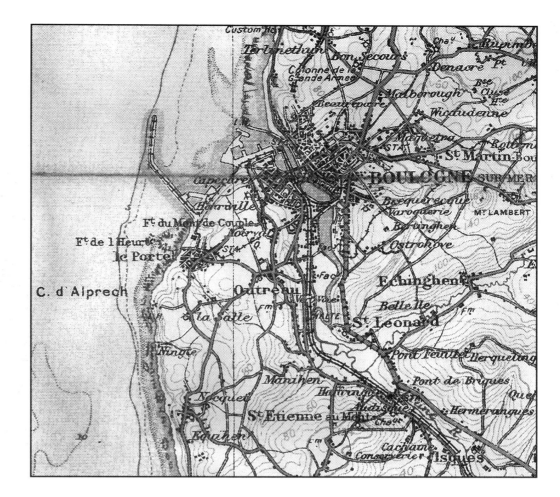

on a route march with full packs. They left the camp at 2.30 pm and arrived back three hours later, after covering six miles on slippery pavé roads and of course returning via the steep hill from Boulogne. After a couple of hours rest the 14th with the other two battalions marched to the Boulogne Gare Central Railway Station. The 14th left at 8.30 pm, the 15th around 10 pm and the 16th at 00.30 am on 23 November.

The three Birmingham Battalions along with the rest of the 32nd Division were now heading for the same destination, Conde Railway Station near the village of Longpré, a few miles south-west of Abbeville. The Division was to have a few days acclimatisation in the area to the north-west of Abbeville. It was here that the various Transports from each battalion, which had left England a couple of days earlier, rejoined having made their way from Le Havre via Pont Remy. Living in the age of mobile telephones, radios and computers etc, it is hard to imagine how, with only the basic communication system that was available at the time, one division let alone several made their way from the British Isles to France and reached the right area. Apart from the infantry there were the artillery and ammunition columns, divisional engineers and field ambulances. Then there were the ancillary units such as Signal, Cyclist and Veterinary Companies. In fact it was a great feat of logistics.

After reaching Longpré there then commenced a gruelling 12 mile (19 Km) march to each battalion's billeting village. This became a nightmare march for many of the men, especially those of the 14th Royal Warwicks, who had done a route march the previous afternoon. To make matters worse the

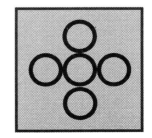

roads were covered in a sheet of ice, giving no grip to heavy nailed army boots. Lieutenant Alan Furse in command of number three platoon of A Coy, 14th Royal Warwicks, remembered it well:

'About 2 am we suddenly stopped and had to hurriedly turn out finding ourselves at the station of Longpré. We soon found that we had twelve and a half miles to march to our billeting area, to a small village of Vauchelles about two miles from Abbeville. Here we have an example of our Staff work. Our train had passed through Abbeville on the way to Longpré and although there was every convenience for detraining at Abbeville we were taken further on and so given a long march. We soon started off with the dawn mist breaking over the frozen roads, very slippery. Everyone was carrying a greatcoat and an extra pair of boots in addition to the heap of unnecessary things we had brought out and this weight soon began to tell on us. On that march over 300 hundred men fell out in all."

The men of the 14th Royal Warwicks were exhausted due to the lack of sleep on the three previous nights. The first night travelling from Codford to Folkestone, the second night freezing in the transit camp at Boulogne and the third travelling down from Boulogne to Longpré. The route march on the previous day did not help either. After a few months in France, this march would be considered an evening stroll. During the morning of 23 November, as each battalion reached their destination, the men were allotted to their billets. The 14th were at Vauchelles-les-Quesnoy, the 15th at Bellancourt and the 16th at St. Riquier. In most cases the men were billeted in barns, but C Coy of the 15th Royal Warwicks, along with its officers, were billeted in an empty château at Monflieures, about a mile

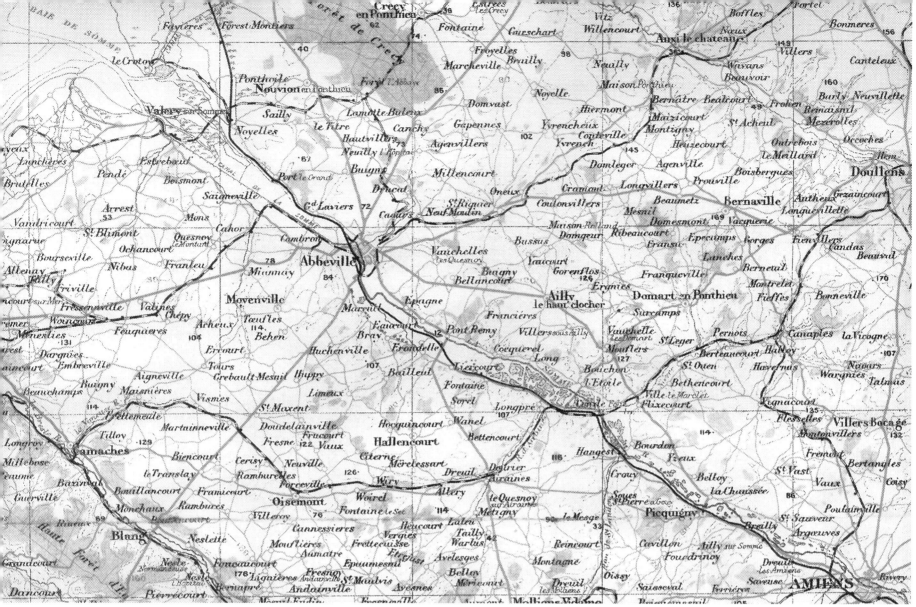

away. The other ranks were in the out-buildings whilst the officers stayed in the sumptuously furnished château itself. As each platoon was told off to their billets the first priority was to catch up on some sleep. The rest of the day would be left for resting.

The poor Company officers of the 14th Royal Warwicks only had their heads down for an hour or so when they were woken up with orders to report to the Battalion HQ as soon as possible. Here they were given a concise telling off from the CO, Lieutenant-Colonel Murray, concerning the number of men who had fallen out during the march from Longpré. Feeling very chastened they went back to bed.

The battalions remained in these billets four days. Each day there were inspections for kit and iron rations, general training and route marches. The novelty of the new surroundings soon wore off and the men quickly settled down and made contact with the locals in the cafés and estaminets trying to learn everything they could of the country. I must make mention here of the farms that the men were billeted in. Unlike ours, French farm buildings were laid out in the shape of a square with the living quarters on one side and the other three sides being stables and barns. Perhaps one thing the men

could not get quite used to was the piling up in each courtyard of all the farm refuse into very large dung-heaps on which chickens would spend most of their time.

Whilst at Vauchelles the CO of the 14th Royal Warwicks was still disturbed with the way 300 or so men dropped out of the march from Longpré. This feeling caused the following comments in the diary

Above: From an official map supplied by the War Office. The 32nd Division acclimatisation area to the east of Abbeville.

Below: An example of a typical French farmyard, with the dung heap in the middle.

of Sergeant Arthur Cooper:

'A route march at 8.30 am today as far as Ailly. CO frequently comes down the line and says a few words on marching discipline. When we get back the CO parades all NCOs and talks very seriously about things. Any NCO who does not bring men up for breach of discipline will be stripped of his stripes. If this don't work more serious measures will be taken. Tells us that we have not been trained properly. Any man who is brought up on serious crimes, or frequent breaches of discipline, will be SHOT! (Takes a very serious view of the Army, does our CO) After dinner the CO takes the battalion and wears the men out over a ploughed field.'

During this four day period Lieutenant Alan Furse became Mess President for A Coy, 14th Royal Warwicks, Officers' Mess. Writing home to his parents we get an insight as to how the officers of the 14th dined compared to the other ranks:

'I am responsible for the food and the cooking and I will tell you what I am giving them today. Breakfast: tea, three rashers of bacon, bread & butter and jam. Dinner: pork chop, cabbage, potatoes, a cake bought from a neighbouring town and two litres of Bordeaux. (The latter is some stuff and only one franc per litre). Tea: bread & butter, tea and jam. Supper: chops

Below: Men of the 15th Royal Warwicks resting during the march, as they made their way in stages to the Bray Front. *Birmingham Library Services*

(not pork), and chips, bread & cheese, coffee & liquors. (Benedictine is 6d per half pint).'

The company cookers for the other ranks of the

14th were in the middle of the main street running through Vauchelles. Men from each platoon would fill a large dixie to be shared out and eaten back in their billets. Sergeant Arthur Cooper of the same battalion wrote the following on the same day as Lieutenant Furse; we see how the men fared.

'No bread today, but some bacon for breakfast. Dinner, stewed bully beef, (very salty). Such tea! used to be better when we could buy tuppence worth of Brandy, but they have stopped us buying spirits. Somebody said that the men did not leave enough for the officers. May be so.'

On 27 November 1915, the 32nd Division made its next move, this time to Vignacourt, about twenty miles away. The march was to be done in two stages. The Birmingham battalions set off around 8 am and reached their first stage around noon after about ten miles of marching. The 14th billeted at Bouchon, 15th at L'Etoile and 16th at Mouflers. The weather for these couple of days was very cold with as much as eight degrees of frost; even the contents of the men's waterbottles had frozen. Vignacourt, a long straggling town of around 20,000 inhabitants, was reached next day about 1 pm. Much to the disgust of the officers and the men, they were kept standing in the town square for three hours until the 'powers that be' had finished their lunch and billeting instructions were issued.

Although thirty odd miles behind the lines, Vignacourt could boast that in the early days of the war it was one of the furthest towns reached by the Germans in what was known as 'the race to the sea'. (In reality this was not a race, but a series of flanking movements, each army trying to overtake the other and hoping to get behind, until eventually the Belgian coast was reached.) Lieutenant Alan Furse (14th Royal Warwicks) recalled that according to the French women who owned the premises being used as a billet for A Coy Officers, eight Uhlans (German cavalry troops) were ambushed and killed by French gendarmes outside her front door.

During the two day stay at Vignacourt all men of the Division were given lectures on the use of new gas helmets by the Chemical adviser of the Third Army. The gas helmet in question was known as the PH helmet. It was made of grey flannel and saturated with a chemical concoction. This completely covered the head and was long enough to be inserted into the collar of the tunic. On the 29th, to instil confidence in the use of these gas helmets, every officer and other rank passed through a gas filled room wearing one. On the morning of 1 December 1915, the 14th and 15th Royal Warwicks left Vignacourt, with the 16th remaining for another day. This was also a journey made in two stages, the 14th made for Pont Noyelles and billeted for the night whilst the 15th made for Coisy. A thaw had now set in and it had started to rain. Now, as the battalions were reaching the back areas of the line, they came into first contact with mud. The roads

were covered in liquid mud, and it was often at least two inches thick!

The next day they reached their destinations, the 14th were now at Sailly Laurette, whilst the 15th moved to La Houssoye and the 16th had marched to Pont Noyelles to take over the billets that the 14th had vacated.

The 32nd Division would soon take over part of the front line, but before doing so all the infantry battalions belonging to the division would have to undergo a period of trench instruction from more seasoned troops. 95 Brigade of the 32nd Division, which comprised our three Birmingham Battalions plus the 12th Gloucesters were to be temporarily attached to 13 and 15 Brigades of the 5th Division. Unknown to the New Army troops, this temporary attachment would soon be made permanent.

The 5th Division

At the outbreak of war the 5th Division was quartered in various parts of Ireland, such as Dublin, The Curragh, Kildare, Belfast and, Londonderry. The Division was soon mobilised and as part of the British Expeditionary Force, landed at Le Havre on 16 August 1914. Seven days later the Division was involved in the opening action at Mons, soon to be followed by Le Cateau, the retreat to the Marne and the Battle of the Aisne. During October 1914 the Division was involved in the first battles in Flanders and saw extremely heavy fighting at La Basseé. At the start of November 1914 a German offensive tried to reach the Channel Ports and with out any respite the Division moved up into the area around Messines and Ypres. In common with other divisions, the 5th became separated for a few short hectic weeks. Brigades, battalions and artillery Batteries were split up and sent where they were needed most to plug gaps in the line. For a time the 5th Division was a name only, but by the end of the month it had reformed. With winter approaching, both sides settled down into trench warfare and battalions were brought back up to strength with reinforcing drafts.

All was relatively quiet until the following spring. April 1915 saw the battle for the German held Hill 60. In reality this was not a hill but was a large mound of excavated earth from a railway cutting placed on top of a ridge. Still, it gave excellent observation for the whole area which explains why it was the scene of three weeks of the most savage fighting. The hill was taken and lost on several occasions and it was the site of the most severe hand-to-hand fighting. German counter-attacks were beaten off not only with rifles and bayonets but also with picks and shovels. It was during these actions that the division was bombarded with gas for the first time. After all this fighting, no ground was taken.

The 5th Division stayed in the Ypres sector until July when relieved by the 46th Division. They then went into rest in the area between Poperinghe and Hazebrouck. By the beginning of August 1915 the Division had moved south to the Somme and was stationed in the district between Bray and Querrieu, south of Albert. This move was in preparation for relieving the French who were holding the line from the Somme River to La Boisselle. Along with the 51st (Highland) and 18th (Eastern) Divisions, the 5th formed part of the newly formed X Corps.

5th Division at the Bray Front

The three Infantry Brigades of the 5th Division took over the following sectors of the Line: The 14th were on the Somme River at Frise, just to the north of Maricourt; the 13th from Maricourt to a ridge overlooking Mametz; and the 15th were stationed to the left of the 13th, on a line running through the Bois Francais to the Tambour between Fricourt and La Boisselle. The extreme right hand position of the British line finished at the Moulin de Fargney approximately a mile south-east of Maricourt. From there the ground turned to marshland in which no permanent defences could be made. Trenches were then resumed at the village of

Below: Divisional sign of the 5th Division. A yellow diagonal on a blue background.

Frise, which was the start of the French line.

The width of No Man's Land on the Divisional front varied from 50 to 150 yards, but at the Bois Français the distance became as little as five yards. The Division had inherited an excellent trench network from the French, nothing like the low breastworks that they were used to previously in Flanders. Dug in chalk and clay these trenches were up to ten feet deep and consisted of firing, support and reserve trenches with many communication trenches in between. Rest villages, four miles behind the lines, were connected to the front line by long communication trenches known as 'Boyaux'. Deep dug-outs with wooden bunks covered in chicken wire were other facilities that until now our men had never dreamt of.

The Bray front prior to the 5th Division taking over was fairly quiet. The French and Germans had a live and let live policy and it was very quiet indeed. It was so peaceful that fishing took place for a time in the millpool at the Moulin de Fargney, which was in our front line position. Shellfire was few and far between. Until the 5th Division artillery was settled in various emplacements behind the lines, French batteries covered the Division for a while. They had an elaborate scheme for retaliatory fire which was retained with a few minor modifications during the divisional stay on this part of the front. The Germans were allowed two shells per sector per day, anything more brought down a burst of rapid fire on the German trenches, until they had ceased. If the Germans shelled a village behind our lines, for example Carnoy, then in return Mametz was heavily shelled. Montauben was shelled for Maricourt and Curlu for Vaux. Now the British were here, the Bray front soon began to liven up. It was High Command policy to take the initiative and not let the German front line troops rest. This was done by taking command of No Man's Land with nightly patrols with the aim of finding out information about the opposing troops. General Kavanagh, GOC 5th Division, in a further aid to harass the German troops opposite, obtained three elephant rifles, one for each part of the Brigade front. They did excellent destruction to German loop hole plates but on most occasions they were more of a danger to the user rather than the intended target. At this time in the war the British one-and-half-inch trench-mortar was first introduced, which proved successful. This fired a 30lb (13.6 kg) football shaped shell attached to a rod and was accurate up to around 700 yards (640 metres). Before the new trench mortar was established, more medieval forms of warfare were in operation. Huge catapults were erected in the trenches for hurling jam-tin bombs. Later the West Bomb-thrower came into use, spring operated, the range could be adjusted and a good rate of rapid fire could be had. For a time then, shortly before the arrival of the Birmingham Pals, this part of the Somme became more active than hitherto.

Birmingham Battalions at the Bray Front

Here, was where the Birmingham Pals were to gain their first experience of trench warfare. A quiet sector, good deep trenches, in fact a 'cushy' start to their war. As 1915 drew to an end, Mother Nature would frustrate both sides. After the severe frosts, rain had started and, with the thaw, trench walls had started to collapse and slide in. For their introduction to war, for the time being, the enemy

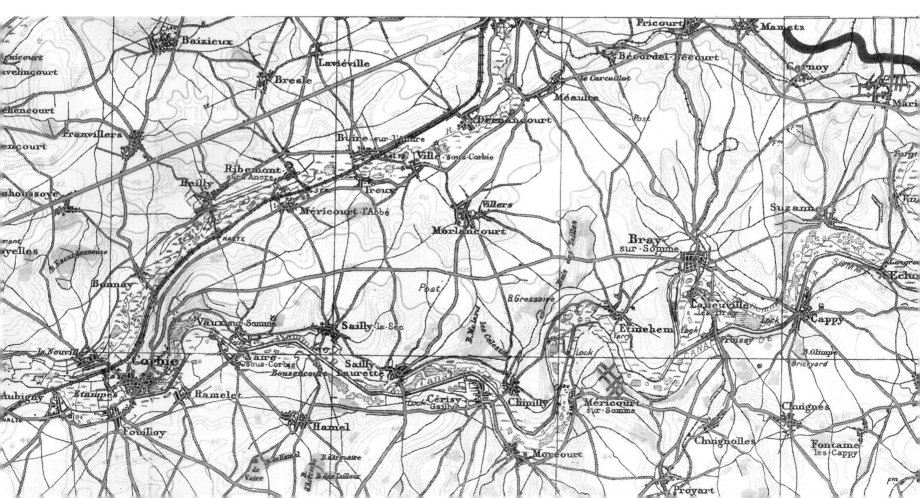

was not going to be the Germans but MUD!

To recap, by Friday 3 December 1915, the 14th Royal Warwicks were at Sailly Laurette. The following day they were joined by the 15th Royal Warwicks. The 16th Royal Warwicks were to stay at Pont Noyelles until 6 December, from where they would then go to Vaux sur Somme until December 11th in preparation for their turn in trench instruction. It was now, prior to moving into the trenches, that each battalion formed a Headquarters Company. This was done by transferring specialists such as signallers, clerks and machine-gunners. Sailly Laurette was about ten miles behind the front line, but the distant rumble of artillery fire could now be heard for the first time. Sergeant Arthur Cooper (14th Royal Warwicks) made the following observations in his diary before moving up to the trenches:

'Another week gone! Going foot flagging again. CO says eight and a half miles. Found out he was a bad judge of distance as it was about twelve. Passed some reserve trenches and can hear the guns booming every now and again. Quite a few fellows faint on the wayside again. Most of the way the mud was over our shoe tops. At last we get to our to-day's destination. Strike a fairly decent barn and a plentiful supply of water, which is a rare thing in France. A strange thing happened to-day. We saw a French woman who had recently washed!

'A.S.C. canteen here, so we do fairly well.'

The 14th Royal Warwicks were the first of the Birmingham Pals to experience the trenches. On the afternoon of 3 December, A and B Coys under the command of Captain J S Robinson paraded in front of the CO, Lieutenant-Colonel Murray, to receive a 'pep' talk before setting off to march another five miles closer to the front line. The two companies made for the village of Etinehem and billeted for the night. Etinehem was also where the 5th Division HQ was situated for the duration of the stay on the Bray front. Whilst at Etinehem, Lieutenant Alan Furse (14th Royal Warwicks) wrote home to his parents, at School Road, Moseley:

Friday December 3rd, 1915. 8pm

'We have done our short march up towards the trenches and so many strange things have happened that I feel I must try and sit down and write you a diary of this day.

'I arose at my billet in the last small village (Pont Noyelles) at 7am. I had been sleeping on a stone floor with only my valise and had not had a very good night, so was quite ready to get up. We break-fasted in the kitchen off sardines and a small piece of bacon and after getting some of the mud off our clothes, proceeded to go round to our men's billets to inspect their rifles.

'Billet is rather a wrong expression for the places where they sleep, but it conveys any outbuilding with a roof and some straw to lie on. That filled up the morning

and after dining off a suspicion of bully beef and whisky, we fell in at the market place. Here the Colonel addressed us and gave us a few tips before going into the trenches. As you understand only two companies were going forward, with Captain Robinson in command.

'We then started off on our march and after five miles we landed in the very small village (Etinehem) we are in now. I have never seen such mud in my life as we ploughed through on the road here. It is absolutely no exaggeration to say that for nearly two thirds of the way there was two inches of liquid mud and such mud as I have never seen before. I might mention that whilst on the way the guns could be heard quite distinctly and whilst on the top of a rise we saw two shells burst on a hill about two-and-a-half miles distant. On arriving here we got the men into barns and then proceeded to look for some place for ourselves.

'We finally found the place I am now writing from. It is a room with a stone floor about the size of our front room with one bed, one table and six chairs in it. Captain Robinson is sleeping in the bed and "Betty" (nickname of 2nd Lieutenant J W Lythgoe) and I on the floor. The other two have at present gone out to look for some provisions and I am sitting on my valise on the floor arrayed in my pyjama trousers and vest (my pyjama coat is now lost) writing this letter to you on a copy of the Tatler dated November 4th. I have also got a "Gold Flake" in my face and I was able to buy twenty tonight. I nearly went mad when I saw them.

'The most hindmost trench is about 50 yds outside this village although I understand the firing line is 4 miles away but when I look out of the window I can plainly see the searchlights. I have just had reported a 'Zep' has passed over here although I did not see it myself. A house about 50 yds from this was wrecked two days ago by a shell but of course they would not do any by night because of the difficulty of getting the range so I am alright until daybreak. You can buy "BASS" here and there are twelve pint bottles staring me in the face on the table. Here's good luck to you and by Jove it does taste good.

'Tomorrow we go to another place two miles up, for a bit of instruction, I expect, and then on Sunday night go for our first dose in the trenches. I always thought when I was in England that I should feel too excited to do anything as soon as I heard the guns and knew I was going in the trenches but although I have heard and seen so little of it yet I do not think any more of it than if I were listening to the Trams on the Moseley Road. It really sounds bravado to say it and I always thought it was when I heard of it but I can now assure you that it is so. What your feelings are when you get right into it, of course, I do not know."

The following day, Saturday 4 December, the Officers and Sergeants of A and B Coys, 14th Royal Warwicks, moved up to Bray sur Somme. By this stage in the war the village had been shelled heavily and was pretty much knocked about. Of course this was very interesting to the men of the 14th, it was their first sight of destruction. They marched straight through Bray and onto the road leading to Carnoy. On reaching Bronfay Farm they halted until dark before going any further. They were now in easy reach of German field guns. As soon as it was dark they set off. The trench system in front of Carnoy bulged into the German lines, forming a salient. The road they were walking on was covered in mud and pitted with shell holes causing the men to stumble. Star shells were going off on three sides. Lieutenant Alan Furse in a letter home stated that 'he had fallen twice and was as black as a sweep' when they arrived at their destination. The whole effect must have been a terrifying first experience to the novices of the 14th.

Nearing the Peronne road they heard their first bullets and, just as they were crossing a brow of a hill near to the reserve trenches, a spurt of German machine-gun fire welcomed the Birmingham Pals to the war. Captain Robinson, on reaching the support line, reported to the CO of the 2nd KOSBs (Kings Own Scottish Borderers). Here the small group of officers and sergeants were separated into two groups, one remained in the reserve trenches running through Carnoy whilst the other went up to the firing line. Much to their horror, the party going up to the front line watched their guide climb out of the communication trench and begin to walk across open country. After about a mile they came to another communication trench, approximately 500 yards (457 metres) from the main front line. They dropped down into the trench and then they understood, despite the danger that lurked from stray bullets, shrapnel and shell splinters, the reason why they had walked as far as they could in the open. They were now standing thigh deep in liquid mud!

When they eventually made it to the front line, the mud was even deeper. In some parts it was nearly waist high with instances of men sinking up to their armpits. This was nothing like the firm, deep and dry trenches of Salisbury Plain, where the men had recently trained. 'We had not imagined that such conditions could exist', was the view of Private J E B Fairclough. On reaching the front line, they came under instruction from men of the 2nd KOYLIs (Kings Own Yorkshire Light Infantry). Referring again to Private J E B Fairclough (writing in the battalion history), are his recollections of this period of time:

'The regular battalions to which we were attached for instruction looked after the new soldiers very well and we owed them what little comfort we did obtain. The old hands realised our greenness, but they treated us as guests and by their unselfishness, advice and help ungrudgingly given, taught us excellent lessons in the comradeship of the Western Front.'

Apart from his diary, I have very little information about Sergeant Arthur Cooper (14th Royal Warwicks). He may be on several group photographs, but at the time of writing, he has not been identified. Judging by his down to earth sense of humour and his liking for beer, he must have been a Brummie. He was in the first party to go into the trenches and his comments were written soon afterwards. His first impressions of trench instruction differed vastly from those of Private Fairclough

'Well we got there and each NCO got posted with the occupiers, KOYLIs, 5th Division, and some of the lads too they were ! Got as much information as I could out of my chap, which was not a great deal.

'If we don't make better soldiers than these chaps, I will eat my hat.'

The night passed fairly quietly with no casualties for our amateurs. But there was a very lucky escape from death for two subalterns of A Coy during the early hours of Sunday morning, 5 December. They were Second-Lieutenants 'Laddie' Higgins and Ernest Fanthom Hingeley. Both men were attempting to have a couple of hours sleep in a dugout. However, due to the very wet conditions, the soft earth began to cave in on them. It was only the fact that Higgins was still awake that saved them. Both these Officers had enlisted into the ranks of the 14th Royal Warwicks; Higgins from Linden Road, Bournville was commissioned in May 1915, whilst Hingeley from South Grove, Erdington, was commissioned in March 1915.

The second party that remained in the reserve trenches with the KOSBs also had a quiet night, but they too had a narrow escape on Sunday morning. It was their first experience of a German 'Whizzbang' (light shell) so called because they were of such high velocity they could not be heard coming. It landed in a kitchen dug-out, wounding two cooks and destroying the breakfast. It was explained later that too much smoke had caused the attention. Nearby to where this shell landed, was Lieutenant Alan Furse; his reactions were expressed in a letter to his parents:

'As this was our first shell it naturally upset us a bit and it took an hour or two to get over it. We were next told to go and draw gum boots and directed to a small building in the village (Carnoy) through which these trenches ran. By some mistake

Betty (Second-Lieutenant Jeffrey Wentworth Lythgoe, from St Paul's Vicarage, Tipton) and I went to the wrong one and our first sight on entering was that of a poor fellow who had been killed the night before. We then found we had gone into the mortuary.'

During the morning it was the turn of the second party to make their way up to the line and be reunited with the first. They were issued with gum boots from men who had just come down from the line. On the inside the boots were wet and muddy, making an uncomfortable start to the party's first encounter of front line trenches. To make going easier they took the same short cut as the first party and climbed out of the reserve trench and walked across meadow land. Later in the day, it was the turn of the rank and file of A and B Coys, 14th Royal Warwicks, to move up and be reunited with their officers and NCOs. They marched from the village of Etinehem under the command of Captain William Hereward Ehrhardt. As the men neared the front line guides led them through a maze of communication trenches, half-filled with liquid mud. I suppose the mud was daunting enough, when seeing the trenches for the first time. But due to the wet weather, the trenches nearer the front line were slowly eroding away, causing numerous bits of decaying French soldiers to protrude out of the walls. Once re-united with their officers and NCOs, A and B Coys were to spend the next three nights in the front line. Private J E B Fairclough remembered his first night quite clearly:

'At length we reached what looked like an open drain full of mud. This, we were informed, was the front line. Sentries were posted and we began the night's vigil in surroundings completely strange, and with no idea of what might appear out of the darkness. The situation was very different from what we had imagined. We seemed to have reached the depth of misery. It was a cold, dark night, and there we were squatting on a wet fire step with no shelter of any description. Later on we treated such a case as all in the day's work.'

Sergeant Arthur Cooper, being in the advance party, was there to greet his men on their arrival. Unable to keep up his diary whilst in these dreadful condition, the following is his account after coming out of the line on 8 December. For then it was the turn of C and D Coys to receive their first turn of trench instruction:

'I almost cried when I thought of them coming through the mud, but they arrived, good lads, very merry and bright. I got my sentries posted and the rest settled down in the mud as comfy as possible under the circumstances.

'We were very glad when daylight came and a bit later on, a drop of rum to warm us up. (I wish I had that teetotal MP who *asked in the House of Commons why troops at the front had Rum served out. I would soon show him why!) All our T.T.'s swallowed it quickly! Three whole spoonfuls every day!*

'Well the days of the 5th & 6th passed off, we popping at the Huns and they at us. On the night of the 6th some bombers of the next battalion went and played hell with a section of an advanced German trench (on the evening of 6th/7th December a raid took place by each battalion on the Divisional front). *Our guns all along the line of course supporting them and I think that most of the men shook a bit and thought of home. Our officer Mr Lythgoe, came along and had a few words in each direction, which steadied the fellows a good deal and soon got used to the row. I believe that all soldiers on their first bombardment are a bit nervy. However, as I said, we soon got used to that and the next day one could have seen Ernie and myself shaving quietly to the tune of the guns (in very muddy water). Water was scarce and food fairly*

so, which was a cause of a good deal of the men's suffering. Could not get them anything hot, although I managed to cook a drop of Oxo on a fire which Joe got together for a few minutes.

The night of the 8th came, when we were to get out and I am not ashamed to say that we were all glad to go. Perished for four days in mud, with nothing hot to eat and practically no sleep. Six pm (8 December) *and the word came down to get packs on and be ready to start. Our packs were a solid block of mud and our rifles a solid rod of mud. However we had to wait for six hours before we started and I will never forget that journey through the trenches. The sight of our other companies who relieved us were enough to make one cry. I pitied them but bucked them fellows up as much as possible who came to my section. We got finally out of the trenches at four am and had to go about eight miles. We had a rest on the way for about an hour and then later on got some very welcome hot cocoa and cake at a village. After that we all got warm once again, our packs seemed a lot lighter and we finally arrived at our destination* (Chipilly) *at twelve noon, fairly happy.*

'Most of the fellows lay down in the barn and went straight to sleep for sixteen hours without waking and without food, so you can guess what they felt like. I stripped and had a good wash, got some nice hot stew and followed their example.'

In another letter to his parents, Lieutenant Alan Furse gave his account of what life had been like for the previous few days:

'Several officers have told me that they think the conditions this winter are as bad if not worse than they were last and I find that the only way to get through four days under these conditions is to be continually thinking what you will do when you get back to rest camp. Anyone who has not been in the trenches cannot understand the conditions. Whilst on your tour of duty round the front line you are floundering in a trench, knee deep in mud and both sides are slimy with mud so that you have nothing clean to steady yourself by and when you get back to your dugout to rest, you have the same slimy walls and at least a foot of mud on the floor.

You soon learn not to drop things as of course they are useless afterwards and great trouble it is to find somewhere to put a thing down.'

One young lad of the 14th Royal Warwicks, still only sixteen years old, was Private Alfred Cowell (No.1225, A Coy). Dispirited by his first taste of trench warfare, it caused the following comment in a letter home to his mother:

> 'I got in on the Dec 5th. I am fairly well in health nothing to call ill just fed up. We are in the trenches and I shall be very glad when we are out of them again as this mud is up to your neck no swank. When I get to England again I bet you a quid I stop and I'll chance being shot as it is awful.'

In another letter to his mother, Private Cowell wrote that there were three other under-age members of the battalion whose mothers had claimed back and were soon to be discharged. He explained to his mother that this was done by their mother's writing to the War Office and enclosing their Birth Certificates. They were due to return to England on 26 December. Private Cowell asked if his mother could do the same for him. She did, and he was discharged as under age on 31 January 1916.

Four months later he re-enlisted, this time in the Lancashire Fusiliers and five months after that transferred to the Royal Garrison Artillery. After the war finished he re-enlisted and spent the next two years in Jamaica.

Birmingham Pals First Casualties

Prior to leaving the trenches on 8 December, the 14th Royal Warwicks had its first two casualties. Private Arthur Hackett (No.1202, B Coy), had the sad honour of being the first man of the three Birmingham Battalions to be killed in action. He was shot by a sniper. Private Hackett, aged 31, lived at Springfield Road, Kings Heath. His family home was not far from Springfield College, Moseley, the former training establishment of the 16th Royal Warwicks. His army service number shows that he was not an original volunteer to the battalion of September 1914. Perhaps living so close to where the 16th Royal Warwicks were training inspired him to enlist into E Coy of the 14th Royal Warwicks, which he did on 20 March 1915. He was killed 266 days later. Private Hackett is now buried in Carnoy Military Cemetery. The other casualty was CSM James Mole Kitchen, who received a stomach wound after being hit by a bullet from a German sniper. He died of his wounds on 16 December, (No.1088, B Coy, from Minstead Road, Gravelly Hill). CSM Kitchen, aged 24, was an old boy of King Edward's Aston and is buried in Carnoy Military Cemetery.

HQ, C and D Coys stayed in the same trenches until 11 December, then the whole battalion came together again. A, B and C Coys were allocated canvas tents and dugouts in Billon Wood, whilst HQ and D Coys were billeted nearby in the ruined outbuildings of Bronfay Farm. For the next few days the 14th Royal Warwicks now became the battalion in reserve and each day men were supplied to carry rations and supply working parties for trench repairs. Thanks to Sergeant Arthur Cooper, we can now get a fair idea of what life was like while out of the line:

Friday, December 10th 1915 (Etinehem)

> 'We all woke up feeling better after our rest, just what a sight all our clothes were! Greatcoats, tunics, trousers, puttees, boots, all a wet heap of mud! We had to set to work cleaning them. First rifles and then scrape, scrape at our clothes with our jack-knives. (In the history of the 14th Royal Warwicks, the author relates that one of the ways used to get the mud off their rifles was to tie a few together and dip them into pools of water.) We did that up to dark and came to the conclusion that we would sooner have the trenches, bad as they were. After tea Jo and I struck and went and found some weak French beer.'

Saturday, December 11th

> 'Cleaning once again, along with rifle inspections up to 1 pm. At 2pm we are off on the march, feeling light-hearted and happy, and merrily singing along the muddy way. But, don't think we looked like the First Birmingham Battalion! We did not. More like an orderly crowd of madmen who had seen bad times!
>
> 'We were told that we were going into dugouts just behind the first line (Billon Wood). When we arrived, I was appointed a decent dugout with three beds in it. They are made of poles with wire stretched across, and some straw in. We settled down and had a good night's sleep, after once again cleaning our rifles.'

Sunday, December 12th

> 'I did not know that it was Sunday, until I commenced to write this. Great event of the day. Post comes in! Had to continue the cleaning of clothes, also a CO's rifle inspection. Our other two Companies came out of the trenches and join us here. They had a chap killed and one or two wounded. Chief casualties through the weather and condition of trenches. They had a very rough time, like ourselves. The Huns were rattling most of the night, but they did not keep us awake long.'

Monday, December 13th

> 'Up at 4am. No time for breakfast, and off to the front line on a working party, pumping the water out and attempting to clean out the mud from some of the deep parts. Got very hungry as time wore on. Had some fun with the Dukes (2nd Duke of Wellington's, West Riding Regiment, 13 Infantry Brigade). They don't care a damn for the Germans. They were firing bombs and blowing up a German trench. Great

fun! I think that most of the Germans got out during the day, very little doing, started strong at night though. One of the Dukes was just off to Old Blighty on holiday. Lucky devil!

'They are good lads. Gave us their tea, and one gave us a cake. We were starving by this time. Had nothing since the day before and it was 3 pm then. I think that these regular soldiers would halve their shirts with a chap who hadn't got one. (As you can see, Sergeant Cooper, has changed his opinion of regular soldiers). Finally started back at 4.30 pm, whacked to the world! Had to get one of the chaps out of a mud hole. He was in it up to the neck. Poor fellow he was a sight, and was very hurt when I cussed him for dropping into it. These holes are made by shells and then get filled with mud. Of course all the roads and paths round here are full of them.

'Had some good stew when we got back and a cup of hot cocoa. Got a bit of fire going and was quite happy. Bit of luck! Tomorrow going to have a bath in the village below. Hope the rumour proves true. We do indeed want one. Had a bit of a sing-song and off to bed. We see a great many air machines here, chiefly British, but a big German was up today, a big double decker. Our fellows fly over their lines dodging the shells. Don't seem to mind them much either!'

Tuesday, December 14th

'Up at 6 am. A suggestion of breakfast, and then fell in for the treat of the three weeks that we have been in France! Down to the village of Bray sur Somme we went.

'Well! The baths were not anything like Kent Street (In Birmingham). We had to stand in tubs, small ones, and warm water dropped through four little holes in the pipe, but it was good enough and we rubbed and drubbed until we were clean. I was surprised how clean we were. Of course our heads and feet were bad, but otherwise we were all right. Somebody had borrowed my boots when I got out, but I didn't do so badly. This bath really belonged to the Royal Engineers and they were getting clean clothes, socks etc. Of course we, being the First B'ham, did not get anything. I was an RE, to the tune of a clean pair of socks and pants (at the cost of 3d!).

'We got half an hour off to buy stuff to take to the trenches with us tomorrow. We need some too, but perhaps we shall not be quite so short of food this time.

'As the Huns had been shelling the road, we had to march back in small parties. We

got back safe and sound though. Had some good stew for dinner.

After tea, we had a very nice bit of fire, and a merry party round. The post arrives. Parcels! No luck! One for Jo though. Sent the parcels round. Had a good time. Feel quite full. Cake with one. Good stuff with Stanley Rudder (No.1120, A Coy). Fine little chap is Stan! Xmas Pudding with one, Butler 592, almonds and raisins, and more cake, another half of pork-pie with Jo and cocoa. Quite a night of nights. Off to bed where I am writing this. Goodnight! I am sleepy. All the boys are at it already.'

For comparison, the following is a letter written on the same day as Sergeant Cooper's previous diary entry. It is written by Lieutenant Alan Furse to his fourteen year old brother Claude, back home in Moseley:

'Since writing home last we have come back about half a mile behind the firing line in a big wood (Billon) where we are resting until tomorrow night, when we go in again until Sunday morning and then what we are going to do, I do not know.

'Have been back to a village about two miles from here today and had my first bath since I arrived in this country. There were three baths fixed up in a barn and a big steam engine keeping up a continuous supply of hot water. It was absolutely great.

'After sending the men back to bivouac under a Sergeant, three of us went round this little village to see if there was anywhere we could get some decent food. After two or three failures, I at last explained in frightful French to an old lady that the three of us wanted dinner and going back an hour later we had an egg omelette, steak and chips, wine and coffee and I have never enjoyed a meal like it before. Whilst we were in the big square opposite Headquarters, a bugle call went for everyone to stand out of the streets and you all have to put your backs up against a wall whilst a Taube (German Aeroplane) went overhead. He did not drop any bombs today, although he is in the habit of doing so. It is a grand sight to see the anti-aircraft guns firing at an aeroplane, little puffs like bunches of cotton wool suddenly appearing all round the plane, until he gets out of range. I have not seen one hit yet, although they get very close.

'When in the trenches last, a nose cap from one of these shells fell within twelve feet of me and buried itself two foot in the soft mud. One of the men dug it up, but of course I could not keep it, as it had to be handed in to Headquarters.

'Whilst we were walking back to the

wood today, a couple of shells fell about 100 yards away and kicked up a deuce of a row, they were however only small ones. They are called Whizzbangs because they are of such high velocity and you get no warning of their arrival, just the whiz through the air and then the explosion. The ordinary shells sound just like a boat going through water as it goes over your head and in the ordinary way you get about two seconds advice of its arrival. The trenches we are going to occupy tomorrow night are only 75 yards from Fritz. So we may have a bit of fun there. We have been sending small fatigue parties every day to clear up the mud a bit. I believe now the conditions are a lot better. We had a very sharp frost last night and it was lovely here this morning, but it has now thawed again and as you can imagine, the mud is again awful. I don't know how long this will take to get to you as of course posts will begin to get a bit congested this time of the year, but if you do not get another before Xmas, here's wishing you all a very happy Xmas and a prosperous New Year.

'I am always thinking of you all and hope to be back with you soon.

'Your Loving brother, Alan.'

15th Royal Warwicks at Maricourt

Whilst the 14th Royal Warwicks were in the line the 15th & 16th had been occupied with general training and equipment inspections. It was 13 December when B & D Coys of the 15th Royal Warwicks left Sailly Laurette and marched via Bray to the village of Suzanne. Here, they moved into a tented camp in the grounds of a château. This was to be the battalion rest area during its stay on the Bray front. Meanwhile the 16th Royal Warwicks were dispersed between Chipilly and Etinehem

Above: 15th Royal Warwick's tented camp in the grounds of the château situated in the village of Suzanne.
Birmingham Library Services

Left: The château ruins in Suzanne
Birmingham Library Services

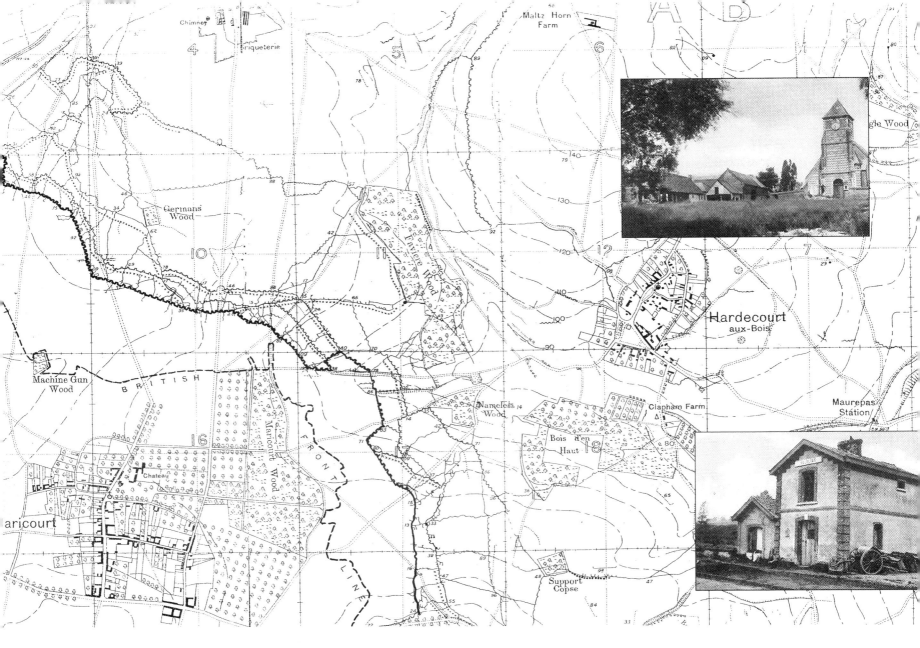

Above: British Trench Map showing the front line near Maricourt, where the 15th Royal Warwicks first experienced the trenches. **Inset above:** The German held village of Hardecourt as it was at the time the 15th Royal Warwicks entered the trench system opposite. **Inset below:** Maurepas Railway Station.

ready for their period of instruction. The method of preparing the men for the trenches was similar to the 14th Royal Warwicks, with Officers and NCOs going into the line first. The 15th Royal Warwicks were attached to the 1st Manchesters and 1st Devon's in front of Maricourt. The 16th Royal Warwicks were to be attached to the 1st Cheshires and the 1st Bedfords in front of Carnoy. In the history of the 2nd Birmingham Battalion, Captain Charles Bill wrote the following:

'On the following morning (14 December) the Officers and NCOs of both companies (B & D) *went into the line at Maricourt for 24 hours instruction and the Battalion suffered its first casualties, two NCOs being killed.* (Both from D Coy, 14 Platoon. They were No.870, Cpl Daniel Joseph Greasly, aged 25 from Alum Rock. The other was No.831 Cpl Percy Taylor Broomfield, aged 31 from Marston Green. Both men were originally buried in a small cemetery in Maricourt. During sometime in the 1920s all those buried there were exhumed and re-buried in Cérisy Gailly Military Cemetery, near the village of Chipilly.) *In the evening 100 men from each company had their introduction to the job of finding a working party, that scourge of the infantry supposed to be at rest. The next morning B & D went up by platoons, each platoon being attached to a company for twenty-four hours. During this tour we had our first officer casualty Second-Lieutenant Ernest Geoffrey Crisp, the Battalion Bombing Officer, going out with a bombing patrol of the 1st Devons. During the raid he was hit by a bullet and while making his way back to our lines was hit again by shell fire and died of his wounds. We felt this loss very keenly, for Crisp was a charming man and a keen officer and it was a great shock to lose a friend so early.* (Before the war Second Lieutenant Crisp, aged 24, lived in Evesham and worked in the Daventry Branch of Lloyds Bank.)

'B & D Coys completed their platoon period of training and then without coming out took over sections of the line as complete companies for another forty eight hours, afterwards returning to Suzanne.'

21 December was the last day of trench instruction for A & C Coys of the 15th Royal Warwicks. Before leaving the trenches to rejoin the rest of the battalion at Suzanne, a shell exploded in a dugout killing yet another NCO, the third from the battalion in seven days. He was 28 year old Sergeant Albert Horton (No.225, A Coy, from Falconer Road near the General Hospital), who was the Company Physical Training NCO. Before the war Sergeant Horton was well known in the gymnastic circles around Birmingham. He also took an active role at the Bristol Road Wesleyan Church and Sunday School. He was also buried in the Cérisy Gailly Military Cemetery.

In fact A & C Coys did not get much relaxation after their first experience of these atrocious conditions. For next day, 22 December, the whole battalion marched back to Maricourt. It was now the turn for the battalion to take over a section of the front line. The 15th Royal Warwicks relieved the 1st East Surreys in the A4 trench sector. Here the front line trenches ran parallel approximately 100 yards (91 metres) in front of Maricourt Wood. The first tour of duty in the front line was undertaken by A, B & D Coys, whilst C Coy was placed in reserve, in Maricourt. This was to be the home of the 15th Royal Warwicks for the next month; due to the appalling conditions the front line troops were relieved every 48 hours. Captain Charles Bill, the CO of C Coy, wrote the following:

'The only progress by day was to dig one's elbows into the sides of the trench

Above: This photograph of No Man's Land was taken from the 15th Royal Warwick's front line trench at a forward sap known as the 'Listening Post'. In the distance, to the left, what appears to be a white smudge is in fact the excavated chalk of the German front line. *Birmingham Library Services*

Left: December 1915, Maricourt front line trench. On the right is Second Lieutenant H Anderson (from Park Road, Warley Woods) of C Coy, 15th Royal Warwicks.

113

and tug and heave until one leg slowly and suckingly emerged, lower it into the mud as far in front as one could stride and then proceed to extricate the rear leg by the same manoeuvre.'

Thigh length gum boots were issued for the men to wear in the front line, but at times these proved unsuccessful, as in the case of Private H Ironmonger (No.502, C Coy of St Albans Road, Moseley). On one occasion he became stuck fast and when he was eventually hauled out he was minus his gum boots and trousers. For a period of time the poor man had to make do with his legs shoved through holes in a couple of sand-bags.

Trench reliefs and the bringing up of rations were mostly carried out in the hours of darkness. The company in reserve had the daily duty to supply men to take hot food and drink to the front line. Dixies containing the food were slung between a pole and carried on the shoulders of two men. One can imagine, in these conditions the enormous task that ration carriers had to overcome. If and when these men actually made it to the front line, most of the contents had by then spilled out and what was left was stone cold. Private William Bridgeman of the 15th Royal Warwicks wrote of his experiences, and in 1930 his story was serialised in the *Birmingham Evening Despatch*, under the title 'Sheet & Blanket Soldiers'. For many years, until his retirement, William Bridgeman was an Art Teacher at King Edward's School, Aston.

The following is his account of life in the mud of Maricourt:

'Gradually, almost unconsciously we become used to prevailing conditions. Quiet it certainly is, but for the disturbing 'whizz bangs' which seem to skim the trench at all times and with terrifying swiftness. The continuous downpour of the last few weeks is followed by intense cold. 'Trench Feet' and the waist deep thick liquid mud constitute our greatest menaces. If one happens to step from the centre of the

Above: Second Lieutenant H Anderson, taken at the 'Listening Post'. *Birmingham Library Services*

Right: German Minenwerfer (trench mortar).

trench without first plumbing its depth with the long 'bean' stick which we all carry, drowning will probably be the unheroic fate of anyone less than 7ft tall. These awful sump holes are a source of dread and much profanity, especially after dark. The liquid mud tops even our thigh length gum boots.

'During the period in the line many of us suffer intense pain due to 'trench feet.' The feet become sodden within the rubber casing and swelling makes the removal of the boots impossible without cutting. Frostbite is accounting for quite a number of casualties. It is an extremely painful malady which I hope to stave off by a daily massage with a nauseous 'dubbing' unction just issued.

'Fighting is occupying our thoughts less and less. Our one desire is to be as comfortable as possible.'

Riding down from Codford
On an Eastern train,
15th Royal Warwicks
Leaving Salisbury Plain
Far away behind them,
Off to France they go
Eager for the trenches
Eager for the foe.

From Boulogne to Longpré,
Continental train,
15th Royal Warwicks

On the move again.
Carriages in darkness
Save for candle-light
"Nap' and 'Farmer's Glory"
Far into the night

Soon arrived at Longpré,
Packs put on again,
15th Royal Warwicks
Got out of the train;
Marched about twelve kilos,
Place called Bellancourt.
15th Royal Warwicks
Tired and very sore.

Stayed there three or four days...
Wish we were there still,
Many Royal Warwicks
Went to Abbeville.
Visited the cafés,
Nearly bathed in wine,
Wrote home fervent letters:
'Think this life is fine'.

Marching ever trenchwards,
Ankle deep in mud,
15th Royal Warwicks
Rampant after blood.
Thoughts of Bosches' legions...
Kaiser Billy's hordes...
Dreams of picks and shovels,
Pistols, guns and swords.

First we went to L'Etoile

I WONDER WHEN THE BLINKIN' TIDE GOES OUT TED.

Then to Vignacourt,
Five days there, then Coisy,
Then to La Houssoye,
What with endless marching
Life seemed in a maze,
Till we came to Sailly...
There we stayed ten days.

When ten days were over
Trouble then began,
One December morning
Moved up to Suzanne;
Stayed there under canvas,
Only two days more.
Final destination
Muddy Maricourt.

Wading up the trenches,
Cleanly days are past,
15th Royal Warwicks
"In the soup" at last.
Chance of week-end passes
France to Kingdom Come
15th Royal Warwicks
WANT TO GO TO BRUM!

Pte R B L Moore 'Ricardo' (No.1010, 15th Royal Warwicks)

16th Royal Warwicks

The 16th Royal Warwicks began their trench training on December 15th. They were attached to 15 Infantry Brigade, who were occupying the C1 and C2 sub-sector in front of Carnoy. At first only the CO, Lieutenant-Colonel De Trafford, along with two officers and eight NCOs of A Coy were attached to the 1st Cheshires, with those from B Coy attached to the 1st Bedfords. The remaining men of the two Companies moved up the next day. The first casualty to the 16th Royal Warwicks occurred on 18 December when Private W N Carr (No.1299, A Coy, from Lightswood Hill, Warley) was wounded and evacuated. This was also the same day that C &

D Coys moved up to the front line, meanwhile A & B Coys moved back to Etinehem.

On 21 December, the battalion suffered its first man killed in action when Private Arthur Facer (No.826, D Coy, from Aston Street, Gosta Green) was killed by sniper fire. A close friend of Private Facer was Private James Randle (No.991, D Coy). In a letter to his girlfiend, Miss Ethel Hill of Clissold Street, Hockley, he had this to say about D Coy's first tour in the trenches and his own lucky escape:

'Raining biggest part of the time. Mud and water up to my thighs so you can tell what a state I was in when I come out. The worst part about it is the food, we get now and again one loaf of bread between 11 men. My dear I don't want you to get upset when you see the casualty list. One of my biggest pals got bowled over first night, he was only joking with me in the daytime about making his will out. It is right what they say about keeping your head down, the first night in the trenches I fired about 50 rounds and next morning when I threw a tin over the parapet the Germans fired at it, also at a few bits of paper. At dinner time when I was about to start on my dinner, a few of the boys started to come by so I stood on the platform upright head above the trench for about five minutes. The Germans must have been asleep because they never fired. When I found out what I was doing, I fell at the bottom of the trench. That will never happen again as long as I am out here.

'I have said all for present so I will close now wishing all of you a happy new year.
So God be with you till we meet again, Jim.
Sadly Jim never saw Ethel again, he was killed on the Somme later in the year, before he had a chance of leave.

Christmas 1915

With the second Christmas of the war drawing near, all three Birmingham Battalions had now received their baptism of fire. Trench reliefs and periods of duty with their new Brigade comrades soon became a matter of routine and before long the men had settled down to their new conditions. The slow trickle of casualties that had now begun, were more often than not due to lack of trench experience, as a moment of forgetfulness with a head just showing above the parapet would mean another notch on a German sniper's rifle. The 14th Royal Warwicks were next in the trenches on 14 December. Their last tour of trench duty before Christmas, during the relief of the 1st Royal West Kents Sergeant Benjamin Bertram Barlow (No.854, D Coy, from Highfield Road, Washwood Heath) received a fatal bullet wound from yet another German sniper. Sergeant Barlow died in Hospital at Rouen and was buried in St Sever Cemetery. Before

Below: Made of tin-plate, this is the lid of the container that held the plum pudding that each Birmingham Pal received during the Christmas of 1915.
Dorothy Holder

A CHRISTMAS GREETING
FROM THE
LORD MAYOR,
LADY MAYORESS
AND
CITIZENS OF
BIRMINGHAM.
·1915·

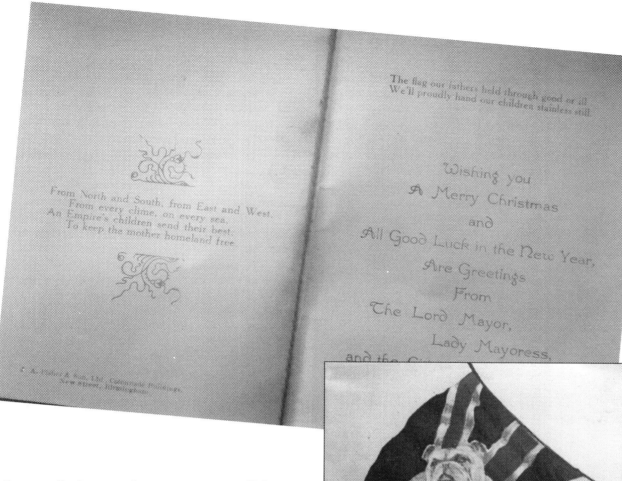

Left: The Christmas Card each Birmingham Pal received from the Lord and Lady Mayoress and the citizens of Birmingham.

the war Barlow, aged twenty, was a well known YMCA footballer and a member of the Nechells Park Wesleyan Church.

The Germans did not have it all their own way, each battalion formed their own sniping sections; as was remembered by Captain Charles Bill in the History of the 15th Royal Warwicks:

'The only real activity in the line was amongst our snipers, good shots, specially trained, and formed into a sniping section who were practically free lances acting under the orders of a sniping sergeant. They made themselves posts, cunningly hidden in the edge of the wood, used rifles fitted with elaborate telescopic sights and to their pals in the companies they later recounted tales of wonderful bags. I think they would have made good anglers.'

The 14th Royal Warwicks were relieved by the 1st Royal West Kents on 18 December. They marched via Bray sur Somme to the village of Froissy, situated on the bank of the Somme canal. They cleared the trenches around 7 pm and found they had another six miles to go. Even though they were extremely tired, hungry and covered in mud they marched well, especially when they were told they were to be billeted in huts this time. Visions of Sutton Park came to mind, but alas no such luck, half a company per hut. Off came their packs and equipment, the clean up would wait until the next day. The first priority was sleep. The 14th Royal Warwicks were to remain at Froissy until 27 December. During this period of atrocious trench conditions, the GOC 5th Division, Major-General Kavanagh, offered a prize for the best suggestion

for keeping the mud and water at bay. In the end, the only solution was for the men who were at 'rest' to return daily to shovel the mud over the parapet. Even then, during very wet conditions, the liquid mud remained at the same level. As you can guess, the majority of men from the 14th Royal Warwicks, did not receive much rest.

With Christmas approaching, the Birmingham Pals were not forgotten by the citizens of their City. All men of the three battalions each received, a Christmas pudding, Christmas card and a bottle of 'Bass' beer provided by the Lord Mayor and Lady Mayoress on behalf of Birmingham. The 15th Royal Warwicks came out of the line on Christmas Eve and spent Christmas Day at Suzanne. The battalion was due back in the trenches on Boxing Day, therefore a lot of work involving the cleaning of equipment etc, was put in on Christmas morning, before the men were allowed to relax and enjoy themselves. Sadly, the 16th Royal Warwicks were to be in the trenches for their first Christmas.

Once again we can thank Lieutenant Alan Furse and Sergeant Arthur Cooper of the 14th Royal Warwicks for writing accounts of their second tour of duty in the trenches, and life out of the line, leading up to the second Christmas of the war:

Wednesday, 15 December, 1915 (Sergeant Cooper's Diary):

'Up we got, early off to the trenches once again today. Some of them start at 5.30 am. Our Platoon Sergeant is one. Hard luck. Leaves me in charge.

'Two or three inspections during the day, away we go at 3.45 pm paddling through the mud. I am told that the trenches are a bit better. Overland, not through the communication trench mud. A bit of luck and nobody hit. And still another bit of luck, a very decent dugout, and a bit of fire soon on. The poor lads are not allowed in the dugouts though. What sleep they can get, they have on the muddy parapet, the hour they are off duty. This is where the NCOs do touch. Still we look after them as much as possible. A drop of tea etc.

'Raining like the very damn outside! I am on 12 to 2 am.'

Thursday and Friday, 16 and 17 December (Sergeant Cooper)

'A nasty day too. Still we are fairly merry and bright, but rather muddy. Up to our leg tops. We are in dugouts just in the rear. Our lads have a good name amongst the regulars here. They stuck it well during their first trial under the hardest conditions. We have four of the West Kents in here now. Bombers, good lads, but there is very few of them left. They have been in some of the big scraps.

'Didn't sleep well. 17 in a muddy little dugout. Just room to sit down and very cold. Sooner be in the first trench. No hot tea and water short.

'5 pm and back to the front line and our comfy little dugout. The Huns are very merry and bright sniping away. Had a fellow come over the front. Lucky fellow to get in. He was stuck in the barbed wire. Missed his way. Three of our lads had him covered while I questioned him, and the Huns peppered away. He was scared when we got him down. Had a good feed tonight. Not on army rations either. A nice drop of Rum 10 pm, Jo don't like it and Harry don't (I do) and do well. Goodnight! Bit of Kip!'

Saturday, December 18th (Sgt Cooper)

'I am again a bit mixed up about the dates, but I believe I left off Friday. It is impossible sometimes to write daily.'

'I was on duty from 12 until 2 am but the night was fairly fine, and the time soon went visiting the sentries. The fellows were standing it much better than they had done the previous visit, but they were still fairly used up. The mud absolutely wears one out. Having a decent dugout and a fire enables me to get the boys something hot during the night, which bucked them up a lot. As I think I said in my last notes, the men are not allowed in the dugouts during the night at all, and during the day there is no time for sleep, which means that they get practically no sleep for three days and nights. It is a hard task and one which you would think it impossible to get used to, but they will do it well after a few visits.

'The trenches which we occupied this time were slightly better than the others as regards mud, but we were nearer to the German lines (about 100 yards in one place between us) and it was not very safe to pop one's head up.

'Well! we were to be relieved about 6 pm, so that was one thing to look forward to, but where we were going to we did not know. Our great trouble was water. One bottle between each three men and no tea or drinkables came up. The food was a bit better though and will no doubt improve as we go on and take over our regular trench. Had a welcome letter from Gladys and the 'Post' (Birmingham Weekly Post) from Dad. I expect that the 'Post' will have the photos of our three killed in next week, so look out and send me one. A Coy have had no casualties yet, and I hope we shall continue to have good luck.

'Well to get on with the tale.

'We had just finished packing our packs and cleaning our rifles, when the word comes along that the relief is coming. Early too, 5 pm, and in the K's troop (West Kents), all merry and bright, swearing like good troopers do. As soon as they are posted, off we start our homeward way. Get clear of the trenches around 7 pm. Very slow work. We learn we have about six miles to go. Hard work when one is covered with mud from head to toe and perhaps a wet greatcoat and already too heavy pack.

'The Captain comes down and tells us that we are going into huts. That cheers us and we go singing merrily along with old Jo and myself doing our best to keep things going. Very different from the return after our first visit. All the boys kept together and marched well, although they were so tired and hungry.

Much cheered when the captain of another Company, which we pass on the road, shouts out "Well marched, A Company". Those are the sort of things that make the men put their last bit of back into it and stick it.

We arrive at the huts. No! Not Sutton huts, but somewhere to lay one's head. There is a raised boarding and which is where we lie on to sleep, and then a narrow passage for walking. I am told that they are German huts, but I don't know for sure.

'We get some tea, then off to bed. Half a Company per hut (75 to 100 men), and not room to turn over, so, don't do so badly. Jo keeps me awake with the usual snoring, but having just room enough to give him frequent jabs in the stomach with my elbow I soon get to sleep, and the next thing I know it is 7 am next morning.'

Sunday, December 19th (Sgt Cooper)

'I know that it's Sunday, because of Church Parade. Once again the day of cleaning commences, and we are all hard at the scrape, scrape, scrape against our tunics, trousers, equipment etc, not to mention rifles, which require a good day's work to get them right again. Turn out for inspection and pass fairly well owing to the energy displayed with our useful friend the jack-knife. Church parade at 3 pm. Would you believe it, and my toes have not been warm for days. First one we have had since we landed. Forgot almost that there was such a thing as a Sunday in the week. We sing hymns and get colder.

'After the service which took place in a field just behind where our guns were banging away, our CO says a few words about what men on active service get shot for. By the way the sermon was about peace. It seems that quite a few ought to be shot already ! After tea Jo and I go off to Bray, about two miles away, and find some Worthington. Quite like home ! Get a useful parcel from Dad, enclosing one of his usual long letters. Still Jo and I enjoy the HP (sauce) and boiled ham for tea. Quite like Xmas. Everybody handing things round. Xmas puddings etc. Everybody happy!'

Extract of letter written to his parents, by Lieutenant Alan Furse, Sunday December 19th:

'We have just found out how to get whisky and have got a dozen bottles in so that we will be all right in the future, but if you can possibly manage brandy, it will be very useful. I do not take it as a drink but always have a flask full on me in case the men are taken bad and I haven't seen any decent brandy here yet.

'We arrived here (Froissy) at 10.30 pm, last night, after three days in the trenches and are now in huts for a day or two by the side of the canal. It was simply awful this time. The rain and frost was causing the trenches to fall in and there was nowhere less than knee deep of very cold mud.

'I should like one pair of socks as soon as possible and a further supply at regular intervals of two to three weeks. Also two refills for my pocket lamp which I dug out of 2ft of mud after having dropped it. I got the other refills from Halfords (TEC Red Seal 3 volt No.PL7).'

Monday, December 20th. (Sgt Cooper's Diary)

'Parade 9.30 am, CO inspects the rifles, clothing etc. He gives us a tip that the anti-frostbite grease issued for the feet in the trenches, is good for cleaning equipment. It is!

'The K's (West Kents) told me in the trenches that the grease is all right for the feet if applied in the proper way. We are ordered to rub it on the feet once a day at least. **They say it is good for the feet if you light a fire with it and then warm them!**

'Of course, I can't say, but I should think that they are right, being 'old Soldiers' they should know best.

'Just thought of settling down to write a few of the letters I owe when I am warned for guard. As the captain said that he was trying to get us into the baths tomorrow, I thought it hard luck. Found out since that it is cushy, as I believe the boys are going off at 4 am to the trenches on fatigue, chucking mud over the parapet. We have one guard over a prisoner here. No, not German, and one over some coal (we have a lovely fire!)'.

Tuesday, December 21st (Sgt Cooper)

'One or two things struck me as strange here. For one thing I expected all the villages that are within reach of the German guns, to be blown to bits, but they are not. In fact the village about three miles behind the trenches we occupied hardly shows any signs of shells. Also we see many Frenchmen's graves dotted about apparently where they fell, with their little wooden cross up. Looks very sad. Another thing, each road leading to a village has a crucifix up at the entrance. None of these has been damaged in any way. On guard at 5.30 pm. A nice rest, but not enough of it. Had a quiet drink of bad French beer (nothing changes, does it! TC) with Jo, and got to bed early.

Tuesday, December 21st, a letter written by

Lieutenant Alan Furse:

'My Dearest Mater,

Very many thanks, for your long letter tonight. Besides the parcel I had from you with puddings, I have since had two others, a real good box of 50 cigars and a packet of Kunzle chocolate (A now defunct, but once well known, Birmingham chocolate cake bakery). Nearly all of us have an Xmas parcel coming and two have already arrived. Tonight we had a lovely boned turkey and a yuletide pudding with rum sauce and I am now smoking one of Charlie's excellent cigars and feeling thoroughly satisfied with life.

'What you hear about brandy and port are not correct, but we are now able to obtain whisky alright. No wine seller is allowed to sell brandy to any soldier and officers cannot get it either. Whisky we get from the Expeditionary Force Canteen.

'We are absolutely in the lap of luxury now. We discovered last night a small inn on the other side of the canal to where the huts are and now sleep in a bed and have a nice little room for the mess. We are really in quite a safe portion of the line, as fighting goes, out here, and provided you take reasonable care the odds are on your being unscathed after twelve months of this.

'It is just possible tonight that we may not have to go into the trenches for Xmas Eve, but it is not settled yet, at any rate I'll bet we are cheerful wherever we are.

'There is to be no handshaking with Germans this year as there was last and strict orders have been issued about it. I have spoken to several men and one officer who shook hands and exchanged souvenirs with Fritz last Xmas.

'One of the Fritzs came over into our trenches the other day and gave himself up, saying he was fed up with the war. He was only a kid about nineteen but seemed very clean and well fed from what I hear. It is not a common occurrence round this part of the line but happens about once a month.'

Wednesday, December 22nd (Sgt Cooper)

'Went digging up to the communication trench. Very hard work chucking mud over an 8ft parapet.'

The same day, Lieutenant Alan Furse:

'We are still resting here by the side of the canal in about 3 inches of mud and have just heard we are to be here until Monday next, so that we shall be able to spend a comfortable Xmas day in billets and huts, instead of the trenches.

'We are fixing up for all the officers to have a great night at a Café on Xmas night. It is sure to be some evening.

'I and my platoon have been up for hot baths today, a great event. The men have a stable set apart with tubs all over the floor and hot water pipes along the roof. There is a spray of hot water dropping into these tubs in which they stand and wash. The water is beautifully hot and there is nothing like it to buck you up. Our baths are palatial tin ones also in barns with clean water and two towels for each customer. Afterwards a pint bottle of real ENGLISH BEER. The French beer always makes me think that a Frenchman tasted some English beer about twenty years ago and yesterday tried to make some like it, only to put about three times too much water in and used a very dirty barrel.'

Thursday and Friday, December 23rd & 24th (Sgt Cooper)

'Digging parties. Rifle inspections etc. Get a couple of busy days.

'Poor old Butty very ill (Probably Private Leigh Butler, No.592, A Coy). As you no doubt can see, I am behind with this diary. I have been so busy, being in charge of the platoon. Mr Lythgoe not on parade, and the Sergeant is Orderly Sgt. Leaves me in charge, and keeps me very busy. Have to chase two recruits up to Company Punishment for not obeying orders.'

Saturday, Christmas Day, December 25th 1915 (Sgt Cooper)

'Had quite a good day under the circumstances. Rifle inspection and a parcel from home. Chicken, a little gamey, but very enjoyable all the same.

'Went to one of the quaintest services that I have ever been to. It was held in a café, about forty of us there. At 11.30 am, Jo and I went to another service, which we shall remember for a long time. This was a communion Service held in another café. About ten of us attended. In the next room we could hear all the fellows ordering beer, and kicking up a row, and also the banker of the 'Crown & Anchor' shouting 'who will have a bit more on so & so and so & so.' This is a gamble that goes on a lot out here.

'This service struck me as the most solemn I have ever been to.

'Did not get any mid-day dinner, being Xmas day, but had it at 5.30 pm. Boiled mutton, and very nice to, what there was of it. As there was only two joints, each as big as dad carves for 231, they did not go to much for each of 50 to 60 men.'

The 'Whizz-Bangs'

With the City Battalions still temporarily attached to the 5th Division, Christmas would be the first time that the men would have seen the Divisional concert party, the 'Whizz-Bangs'. Over the Christmas period the concert party staged a Pantomime at the Brigade HQ at Bray sur Somme. It was in this 'Panto' that the well known Birmingham light entertainer, Corporal Will Kings (No.783) of the 14th Royal Warwicks, made his debut (during the early 1950's, Will Kings became one of the original cast of *The Archer's* radio serial). When the divisional reorganisation occurred in January, many members of the concert party left, to be replaced by men from the three Birmingham Pals battalions. As previously stated, the 15th Royal Warwicks had only two days out of the line over Christmas. Private Wilfred Bridgeman of the battalion's Lewis Gun section, wrote the following concerning his first Christmas in France:

'The greater part of the day out of the line is spent in an effort to remove the mud which has almost obliterated any traces of khaki from our uniforms. Spit and polish parades, fatigue drills, equipment inspection all contribute to the feeling that 'thank God we shall soon be back in the line again.'

'Our first Christmas is a memorable affair. Parcels have arrived, they are many. Everything is shared, each producing from many wrappings offerings which from some have doubtless meant much sacrifice. Still the pride and heroes of our City, we receive countless gifts of woollens of all sorts, socks, mittens, helmets, belts. We are overwhelmed with them and often intrigued at the usefulness of some of the articles. But the spirit is there, and we are grateful anyhow. They do not embarrass as does one gift, a body shield of chain mail. The poor devil who unwraps it, is chaffed unmercifully before he flings it through the window.

'As gunners (Lewis) our leisure commences early, as soon as the guns are cleaned, oiled and put ready for action again. We have our own 'fatigues' which take the place of guard duty. We foregather in our favourite estaminet and drink, talk and later when the Artillery chaps join us, I am usually pressed into service on the piano. There with the help of much thin beer and wine I accompany a raucous voice that pays little heed to my time and tune. The latter is usually given to me by humming and 'you know chum, "The old rustic bridge by the Mill," goes like this. I'll help you carry on.

'I carry on, a merry evening ... The rocking glasses line up along the top of the piano. Some I drink, quite a quantity is spilled into the works. I am glad it is thin stuff and as one of the crowd puts it, "It'll bost yer, afore yer boozed!"'

By 4.30 pm, 26 December, the 15th Royal Warwicks had returned to Maricourt and relieved

Left: The 5th Division Concert Party, the 'Whizz Bangs', circa 1916, who by then comprised of four members of the 14th Royal Warwicks, of whom two can be definitely identified. In the back row, Left to right: Buckley, Fleckner and Pte Edward Turley (No.1171, B Coy, 14th Royal Warwicks). Front row: Cpl Will Kings (No.783, C Coy, 14th Royal Warwicks), Smith, Skinner, Davies and Buchanan. In his *The History of the 15th Royal Warwicks* written by Captain Bill, he mentions that Corporal G Barker (No.1068, of Gravelly Lane, Erdington) of C Coy was a pianist with the concert party.

the 1st Devons in the front line. On 28 December the battalion took over the Maricourt reserve line. For the next two days 321 men were attached to 184th Royal Engineers Tunnelling Company at Carnoy. Here, 107 men per eight hour shift, were employed for mining operations.

Christmas Day Misery for the 3rd Birmingham Battalion

The 16th Royal Warwicks had a miserable first Christmas in France. The battalion was in the front line at Carnoy from the 23rd until the 27th December. As mentioned earlier by Lieutenant Alan Furse in a letter home, the unofficial Christmas truce that occurred in 1914 was not to be repeated and trench life continued as normal. On Christmas Day, men from B Coy, 16th Royal Warwicks, were employed for digging new support trenches behind Carnoy. The area came under heavy shelling from German 5.9 Howitzers, which resulted in nine casualties, mostly from number eight platoon. Four were killed outright and two more died of wounds the same day. They were:

No.518, Private Robert Roy Burlison from Small Heath, born in Edinburgh.

No.1169, Private William Edward Castle, from Coventry Road, Small Heath. Before the war Private Castle was employed as a Warehouseman and prior to that was a pupil at the Ada Street Council School.

No.296, Private Harold Coley from Claremont Street, Old Hill.

No.1176, Private Sydney Herbert Johnson from Wilton Road, Sparkhill.

CASTLE, WILLIAM EDWARD, Drummer, No. 1169, B Coy., 16th (Service) Battn. (3rd Birmingham) The Royal Warwickshire Regt., s. of Job Castle, of 241, Coventry Road, Small Heath, Birmingham, Carter for the Birmingham Corporation, by his wife, Rebecca, dau. of the late A. Clutterbuck; b. Small Heath, Birmingham, co. Warwick, 8 May, 1895; educ. Ada Street Council Schools, Birmingham; was a Warehouseman; served five years with the Boy Scouts; enlisted 13 Jan. 1915; served with the Expeditionary Force in France and Flanders from 21 Nov. 1915, and was killed in action near Bray 25 Dec. following, by the bursting of a bomb while digging trenches. Buried at Bray. Captain (now Major) Graham Deakin wrote: " He was killed while digging in a support trench on Christmas Day by a shell. We buried him in a little cemetery a mile behind the line. He was a nice lad, always cheerful and obliging, and we are sorry to lose him, for he always did his duty well," and Corporal S. Clark: " Having been in my charge for 12 months, I had the opportunity to notice the splendid way in which he always carried out his duties which were allotted to him, and he will be deeply mourned by his comrades in the Band and all those with whom he came in contact." *Unm.*

William Edward Castle.

No.470, Private Harold Edmund Taylor from Gladstone Road, Sparkbrook.

No.466, Private Arthur Enoch Tudor from George Arthur Road, Saltley.

Amongst the casualties was RSM Peter Swain Morgan (No.856, from Kidderminster) who died from his wounds on New Years Eve. RSM Morgan was fifty years old and a former NCO in the Coldstream Guards. He had worked in the lighting department of the Saltley Railway Works prior to the outbreak of war. On 27 December the battalion was relieved and returned to Bray sur Somme. After a good rest and 'clean up', the men could open their parcels from home and enjoy their Christmas dinner.

During these cold, wet, muddy conditions, the men for warmth wore their large bulky greatcoats, The goatskin jerkin, a common sight in old photographs were not in great numbers yet. One can imagine the difficulty of wading through thigh deep mud wearing an army issue greatcoat. This brings me to an interesting little story that Ted Francis (No.1114, A Coy) told me, concerning an attempt to make life a bit more easy wading through the trenches. Ted recalled that he and his comrades sliced about 2ft from the bottom of their greatcoats with their jack-knives. Later, when out of the line, they were threatened to be put on charges, but so many men had adopted this new fashion that nothing came of it.

Divisional Reorganisation

With the start of the New Year, 95 Brigade of the 32nd Division, (Our three B'ham Battalions plus the 12th Gloucesters) was officially transferred to the 5th Division, replacing 14 Brigade. The Gloucesters remained in 95 Brigade and were joined by the 1st Devon's, 1st East Surreys and the 1st Duke of Cornwall's Light Infantry. The 14th and 15th Royal Warwicks exchanged places with the 2nd Duke's (West Riding Regt.) and the 2nd KOYLIs in 13 Brigade. Meanwhile the 16th Royal, Warwicks exchanged with the 1st Dorset's in the 15th Brigade, the Regular battalions now moving into the 32nd Division. This reorganisation was not popular amongst the old battalions at first, as Private J E B Fairclough (No.396, B Coy) recalled in the history of the 14th Royal Warwicks:

'The 5th division had a wonderful fighting reputation. As one of the original divisions of the BEF, it had seen service at Mons, and was concerned in the immortal stand at Le Cateau. Since then it had been engaged continuously in heavy fighting round Ypres, and the present sector at Bray was its first taste of comparatively quiet trench warfare. We are very new to the war game, but we were fortunate to join this famous division and share in its further successes. The Divisional tradition

counted for much and proved an incentive for us to make ourselves the equals of the more war-experienced regular battalions and maintain the high reputation of the division.

January 1916

It was New Year's Eve 1915, when the 14th Royal Warwicks had completed their third tour of the trenches. The battalion was relieved by the 1st Royal West Kents and made its way back to the reserve lines in Billon Wood and Bronfay Farm. An hour before midnight the Germans opened up with machine-guns and blasted the trenches with high explosive and shrapnel. Our own artillery opened up in return. For a while this part of the Bray front in the early hours of New Year's Day 1916 was an absolute inferno. This resulted with one man being killed (Private Thomas Hall, No.1169, D Coy, from Sutton Coldfield) and two others wounded. On reaching the safety of Billon Wood, Sergeant Arthur Cooper and Lieutenant Alan Furse soon put pen to paper:

Saturday 1 January, 1916 (Sgt Cooper)

'We came back last night from the dugouts and we are now under canvas. A dickens of a journey it was too. Overland, mud up to our eyebrows. First one and then another stumbles over wire and down a shell-hole and goes sprawling in the mud. Bullets sing by, but no-one is hit. A Coy has a clean sheet up to the present, touch wood! I am glad that girls are not allowed to come into the army. The swearing that goes on is something terrible!

'We are in a nice little camp now, fairly close up, but they cannot touch us here.

'Started the New Year well, went and had a bath and a change. Very enjoyable too! Also had a parcel from Gladys.

'The boys had a bit of bad luck. Started out on a fatigue and did not get back until 1 am. Carried big iron bomb-proof covers for dugouts* (made of corrugated iron and because of their shape, commonly known as Elephant backs) *up to the front. They are making some good ones here now.

'They are shelling all round this place like Hell now. Old Jo has just gone across with a bathing parade. I hope that he is OK. We are quite all right down here though. A nice place for a rest. Our guns have started to answer them back now, getting quite interesting! It is very difficult to tell whether it is our guns firing, or their shells bursting, unless you can see them. The reports are very similar. I have not seen a gun of ours since I have been here. It is wonderful how they hide them.

'I was just about to have a nice quiet* hour when THIS business started to rattle the place.'

Extract from a letter written the same day by Lieutenant Alan Furse:

'We had rather an interesting time the last four days in the trenches. Our Coy was in reserve about 400 yards behind the firing line and we were responsible for getting food and water up to the three companies in the firing line. Also, keeping all the communication trenches clear.

'I had a bit of excitement one day. I took a party of twenty up with scoops and shovels to shift mud out of a trench just behind the firing line. Fritz evidently spotted the mud being slung over the side of the trench and decided that it was contrary to Rules and Regulations, and started shelling us. He dropped six shrapnel rounds on us in about two minutes, but by keeping well down in the bottom, we were none of us hurt. Two men had bits of shell hit them but it only produced a bruise and did not penetrate the clothing.

'When they had finished shelling we initiated the better part of valour and 'opped it.*

Sergeant Cooper resumes his diary the next day, 2nd January, Sunday:

*'Had a nice quiet day. The rest of the boys had their bath and your humble had a sleep. Quite a few got parcels and we had a good time at night handing same round. I had one from Gladys and enjoyed the Pork-Pie etc.

'Jo arrived safely from his trip to the farm. Been shelling quite a lot today again. Had a nice quiet night and got to bed early. Had a bit of fun in the night. The boarded floor of the tent had a slope towards the entrance. During the night, twelve of us woke up and found ourselves in a hopeless muddle, one pile of blankets, equipment and our poor selves. Quite a struggle to extricate ourselves and get righted. Couldn't understand what had happened and everyone blamed the others for rolling on top of them!'*

January 3rd, Monday (Sergeant Cooper)

*'Digging party to front trenches 4 am. Not so good. Fairly fagged. Wrote a letter or two and stuffed ourselves on the good things the parcels had brought us.

'Sent Jo out to find the rum at about 8 pm. He unfortunately shouted for it, and found that it had not arrived from HQ. As he had made such a noise about it, the Sergeant Major* (CSM Robert Malin, No.1030) *sent poor old Jo and four men to fetch it from HQ. No joke for Jo. Through barbed wire entanglements and mud up to their knees for about a mile. Came back* *and used some awful swear words about me sending him to find it. Of course we all enjoyed the joke and the rum. Gave him some hot milk and rum, which smoothed his temper a lot. It will be a long time before he goes out again and complains about our rum ration being late!'*

The 14th Royal Warwicks spent four days in reserve at Billon Wood. As usual, men were supplied daily for trench clearing fatigues. By January 4th the battalion was back in the front line. This was to be the last tour of front line trenches on the Bray Front for the 14th Royal Warwicks. Over the next three nights the men had their first experience of No Man's Land when wiring parties went out to within 100 yards of the German front line. In a letter home to his parents, Lieutenant Alan Furse described his experiences:

'At 6 pm, six men of A Coy crept out over the parapet and started cutting away the barbed wire over the place where the new trench was to be and put down sandbags to mark where the trench was to be dug. When this was finished a party came out with shovels and we started digging and by means of reliefs we dug until 5 am the next morning and during that time we dug a trench 110 yds long and 3ft deep with a parapet in front thus joining up the trenches at each end which before had been cut off from one another. During the next three nights we again dug for eleven hours and when we came away you could walk all along the new trench without ducking your head at all. All this was done with Fritz just over 100 yds away and we never had a casualty although they were firing with rifle and machine guns all night as of course they could hear us but could not locate us. The nearest thing I had was a bullet which struck the ground between my extended fingers whilst I was getting out of the trench.'

Leaving the Bray Front

Proud of their performance, of the three previous nights digging, A Coy of the 14th Royal Warwicks could still boast a 'clean sheet', not one casualty so far. As mid-January approached, the 5th Division was now due out of the line for rest, to be replaced by the 30th (New Army) Division, whose infantry brigades comprised mostly Pals battalions raised in Manchester and Liverpool. The 14th Royal Warwicks were relieved by the 19th Manchesters (4th Manchester Pals). The Man-chester men took over trenches that were now, due to the hard work put in by the men of the 5th Division, in very good condition. It was now possible to walk the front line with mud only ankle deep. By 20 January the front occupied by the 5th Division now came under

orders of General Fry, GOC 30th Division.

The 14th Royal Warwicks were the first of the Birmingham Pals to leave the trenches. The battalion reached Vaux sur Somme on 9 January, and after a day of rest and cleaning up, the men started a period of general training. On 19 January they were inspected by the 5th Division GOC, Major General Kavanagh. Much work had been put in by the battalion in preparation for this inspection, but their turn out was viewed with much disapproval by the General as not being up to 5th Division standard. Of this, Private J E B Fairclough, made the following comment:

'Consequently a smartening up regime was instituted, weekly parades were held for the Colonel's inspection, until the battalion presented a really smart appearance. After this severe lesson, about which one must be candid and admit was needed, there was never further need to grumble at the turnout, and the battalion could compare favourably with any unit of the division.'

1st Birmingham Battalion in Isolation

Meanwhile German Measles had broken out amongst the men of the 14th Royal Warwicks and it soon spread. Therefore the battalion was kept in isolation at Vaux sur Somme for the next two months and was attached to various divisions. Contact cases were kept in isolation in the château of the village, whilst the rest of the battalion carried out training along the Bray-Corbie road. Working parties were organised for road repairs around the village, and large sump holes were dug to drain away the vast quantities of mud. Private J E B Fairclough recounted that whilst at Vaux Sur Somme, an order had appeared encouraging British troops to fraternise with the local French troops whose positions were nearby. The story continues:

'One day there appeared before the company on road work a French General and his staff. A well known character of the company, a typical Brummie, bearing in mind the latest order, approached the General, saluted smartly and, what he thought was good French, greeted the great man thus: "BON SOD, MANURE". To the credit of the French General the salute was gravely returned and then he rode away.'

Increase in German Artillery

As the month of January, 1916 progressed, German artillery fire slowly increased along the Bray front. This slow build up led to a successful operation on 28 January on French trenches, south

Above: French troops
marching through the
village of Vaux sur
Somme. Due to the
German Measles
epidemic, the 14th Royal
Warwicks were kept in
isolation here for two
months.

of the River Somme. The the result was that the village of Frise was surrounded and the French garrison captured. Apart from the increase in German shell-fire, German patrols became more active in No Man's Land. Until the Liverpool and Manchester Pals of the 30th Division were familiar with the trenches they were taking over, they too had to undergo a few days trench instruction with Fifth Division troops (similar to the Birmingham Battalions in December 1915). The 16th Manchester's (1st City Battalion) took over the front line trenches at Maricourt from the 15th Royal Warwicks for a two day spell on 6 January. It was during the change-over period, two days later, when the Birmingham men were returning, that a German bombing patrol was successfully repulsed, with no casualties reported. Two days later, 10 January, the 16th Manchesters took over the front line; this time the 15th Royal Warwicks marched back to Suzanne. A further march of eight miles, the following day, saw the battalion at Morlancourt. The 15th Royal Warwicks had now left the Bray Front. By 15 January the battalion had made its way to Sailly Laurette. Here the battalion was billeted in barns and commenced a period of general training.

Below: German Field
Gun position.

209

More Misery for the 3rd Birmingham Pals

On 30 December, 1915, after a short three day rest, the 16th Royal Warwicks returned to the 'C2' sector of trenches in front of Carnoy. It was New Year's Day, 1 January, 1916, when the battalion suffered its next fatality; Sergeant Frank William Grove (No.331, B Coy) from Shustoke, near Coleshill. But it was towards the middle of the month, when the German artillery were 'softening up' the front line for their forthcoming attack on the French, that the 16th Royal Warwicks casualties began to increase even further. But I am afraid the compiler of the battalion War Diary did not clarify matters for posterity. All he gave was just a brief statement, either in the trenches or out, and the number of casualties received on that day.

With the increase of German shell-fire, it was decided that 15 Infantry Brigade (of which the 16th Royal Warwicks were now part) should stay behind and support the 30th Division, in case of an attack on our lines; which never materialised. The days leading up to the German attack on the French on 28 January, coincided with a severe bombardment on our lines, especially on the river crossings between Bray and Frise. So, while the 14th and 15th Royal Warwicks were now out of the line, the 16th moved back into the front line on 21 January.

On 25 January, the War Diary records that the battalion had re-occupied and cleared the front line trenches numbered 72, 73 and 74. It was here that Captain George Frederick Victor Heaven, of B Coy, became the first officer of the battalion killed. Captain Heaven, aged twenty-four, came from Grove Avenue, Moseley, and was a former member of the Birmingham University Officer Training Corps. By the time the 16th Royal Warwicks were finally relieved by the 2nd Queens (91 Brigade, 7th Division) on 1 February, the month of January had seen nine men killed and thirteen wounded. All those killed are now buried in the Citadel New Military Cemetery, Fricourt. 15 Brigade reached the rest of the 5th Division , who were now in the vicinity of Corbie, on 3 February. Four days later the Division had marched to an area north of Amiens, and here it stayed until the move north to Arras less the 14th Royal Warwicks who were in isolation at Vaux sur Somme. Apart, that is, from the twenty-nine Birmingham Pals, from the three battalions, who were killed on the Bray Front.

Chapter Six

The Arras Front

The next destination for the 5th Division was Arras. Orders were issued for the move to begin on Friday 25 February, 1916. This resulted in the Division being transferred into XI Corps, under the command of Lieutenant-General Sir J L Keir.

Meanwhile, the 14th Royal Warwicks still remained at Vaux sur Somme in isolation. The 15th Royal Warwicks left Sailly Laurette for Talmas on 30 January. Here the battalion spent a few days general training until 8 February. Then after a couple of days at Coisy the battalion arrived at Fourdrinoy on 13 February. It was here that the battalion was introduced to the new hand grenade known as the Mills Bomb. This new hand grenade was of Birmingham invention and manufacture. The battalion dug trenches and practised the art of throwing these new bombs. The 16th Royal Warwicks meanwhile, stayed at Molliens Vidame until 24 February and from there marched via Caullion and Picquigny to Belloy sur Somme and then billeted for one night. The next day the battalion made its first move northwards to Candas.

The divisional move coincided with a severe cold spell; snow and ice made the roads very slippery. Marching through a north easterly blizzard did not help matters either. The 15th Royal Warwicks left Fourdrinoy on the 24th and marched nine miles to St Vaast en Chaussée. Another march the following day saw the battalion reach Doullens. Here the men found out there was no hot food for them. The transport sections of the battalions which included the company field kitchens were delayed twenty-four hours in the arctic conditions. The horses could not get a foothold and progress was very slow indeed. To make matters worse, the French were using the same roads marching south to Verdun. Throughout the division this move to Arras was often referred to as 'The Retreat from Moscow,' after the war Private William Bridgeman of the 15th Royal Warwicks remembered this episode in the *Sheet and Blanket Soldiers*:

'We move under leaden skies in a cold easterly wind. Snow blows across the countryside horizontally. Halting in this is more trying than moving. A cold numbness settles upon the limbs, giving us the feeling that prolonged inactivity will be fatal. We must keep moving. This is the longest and most trying trek we have experienced. We arrive late and very weary at a town of considerable size (Doullens) *and are billeted in the maltings of a brewery. This is fitted up quite comfortably with wire netting bunks. Rations are not issued, it is late, the limbers are fast in a snow drift some distance back, we are told. We hold a consultation, decide it is too late to forage and sleep until ten next morning.'*

The 15th Royal Warwicks stayed at Doullens for three days. Here the other ranks were occupied on snow clearing fatigues. The battalion left the town on 29 February and marched to Coullemont. Their next destination was Dainville where they arrived on 2 March. After leaving Candas, the 16th Royal Warwicks, moved into Doullens for a couple of days and then on March 1st arrived at Coullemont in preparation for their move into Arras. The Division was now ready to exchange places with the French 34th Division.

Arras

Arras, is the principal City of the Artois region of northern France. In former times Arras was once under Spanish occupation. The evidence of this was shown around the city's two main squares, The Grande and Petite Places; they were surrounded by

Below: British troops in the Grande Place at Arras.

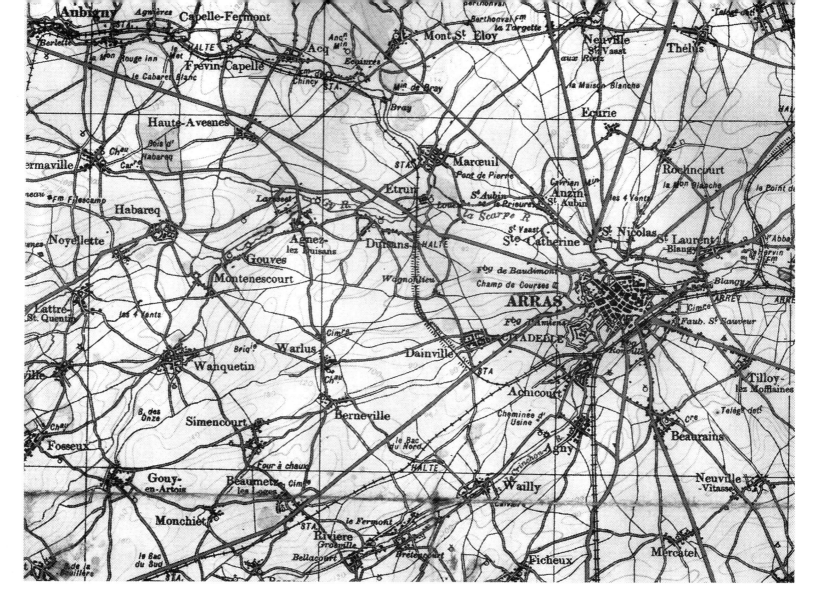

Above: A section from a 1915 official War Office map showing the outlying villages around the eastern outskirts of Arras.

Right: The City of Arras

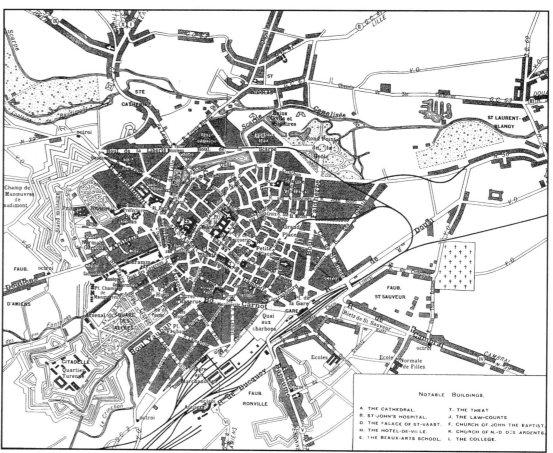

NOTABLE BUILDINGS.

A. THE CATHEDRAL.
B. ST JOHN'S HOSPITAL.
D. THE PALACE OF ST-VAAST.
H. THE HOTEL-DE-VILLE.
E. THE BEAUX-ARTS SCHOOL.
T. THE THEAT
J. THE LAW-COURTS
F. CHURCH OF JOHN THE BAPTIST.
K. CHURCH OF N.-D DES ARDENTS.
L. THE COLLEGE.

many fine specimens of Spanish architecture. Prior to the war, Arras had around 26,000 inhabitants. When forward patrols of German cavalry entered Arras during September 1914, many citizens fled. Within two weeks the French Army had retaken most of the city except for the eastern suburb of Blangy. When trench warfare began in earnest during the winter of 1914-15, the Germans were able to cling to a trench system in the eastern part of the city. Here, amongst the rubble and the ruins, the opposing forces were only buildings apart. Similar to Ypres, Arras occupied a slight salient into the German lines which was overlooked from the north by Vimy Ridge, and from the south by high ground at Beaurains. By March 1916, when the British XI Corps was due to take over the line, Arras had by now received a fair amount of bombardment, but it was never to take on the appearance of complete devastation as Ypres. The prominent larger buildings of Arras, the Cathedral and the Hotel de Ville (Town Hall), had now been reduced to ruins; they made excellent ranging marks for German artillery. The railway station received a daily ration of shells and was a fairly unhealthy place to be. Important

road junctions were also shelled frequently, in the hopie of catching troops, moving into and out of the city. Arras was sited on deep underground quarries and there was ample accommodation in the deep cellars that most buildings possessed. Due to this, a few hundred inhabitants had remained in the city, some of whom would soon be making a profitable if not hazardous living by selling food, lace and souvenirs to the British troops about to occupy the city.

5th Division at Arras

By 4 March 1916, the 5th Division had completed the relief of the French. The divisional front was from the River Scarpe on the outskirts of Blangy northwards to the lower slopes of Vimy Ridge. The Divisional front was divided into four sectors J1, J2, K1 and K2.(see map). On the extreme right (J1) the line was among the houses of St Laurent Blangy to the river bank. This consisted of barricades, trenches and fortified houses, with access to some of these positions being via tunnels and through cellars. Part of the support positions in the J1 sec-

Above: View of Arras, looking north-east. Taken from a British Observation Balloon sited near the Citadel of Arras that housed the Headquarters of many units. The reserve, support and front line trenches (out of picture to the right) could be reached in safety by an underground network of tunnels.
IWM Q60774

129

tor was the remains of a candle factory. The ironical fact about this part of the line was that candles were in abundance but were not needed as most of the dug-outs had lights connected to an electricity supply fed from the German lines.

From the river the trench lines ran northwards, roughly parallel, with No Man's Land varying in width from 100 to 150 yards. Where the lines crossed the Arras-Bailleul Road, No Man's Land narrowed to about 50 yards. From here the trenches continued northwards until curving west in an arc around the village of Roclincourt. The trenches were now on the lower slopes of Vimy Ridge. When the trenches crossed the Lens Road, they then turned northwards up to Neuville St Vaast and the slaughter ground of thousands of French troops. Their loss was the result of many unsuccessful attempts to take Vimy Ridge. These four sectors covered a total divisional front of approximately three-and-a-half miles. The Divisional artillery took up position amongst the gardens and the ruins of Arras, which provided them with good cover. The trenches dug by the French were in good order and the ground similar to that of the Somme, clay and chalk.

Communication trenches to the Divisional front radiated from the suburb of St Nicholas. Those leading to J1 and J2 sectors were named after months of the year; for example 'January Avenue' which led to positions near the River Scarpe. Those communication trenches that led to K1 and K2 were named after days of the week; for example 'Wednesday Avenue' followed the route of the St Nicholas-Roclincourt Road. The general routine for

the 5th Division for the next few months would be, whilst three companies of a battalion were occupying front line trenches, the fourth company would take up position in the reserve trenches known as the Redoubt line. Also on this part of the front just behind the front line were a series of strong-points known as 'Works', starting with 'A Works' near the right of the front and finishing with 'J Work' on the left. These positions were usually occupied by the Lewis Gun teams.

As previously mentioned, when the 5th Division was on the Bray front, the one-and-half-inch mortar was introduced. On 19 March 1916, whilst on the Arras front, the Division received the new Stokes three inch mortar. This new mortar, with a maximum range of 1,250 yards, had an automatic ignition, firing as soon as the bomb reached the bottom of the tube. Several could be making there way to the German lines within seconds. It soon became a most valuable weapon for the infantry in the trenches. The introduction of the Stokes Mortar coincided around the same time when Trench-Mortar Batteries were organised on a permanent basis. Heavy and Medium Trench-Mortars now formed part of the Divisional Artillery. The Light Trench-Mortars (Stokes three inch) were for infantry use and therefore a Battery was formed for each Brigade in the Division. The three Batteries came under the orders of the Divisional Trench-Mortar Officer (Captain Hewson), and the 13th, 15th and 95th Light Trench-Mortar Batteries came into being. Further assistance was given to the Division by a Battery of old French 220 mm *Mortiers*, which were sited near the Citadel of Arras. They were muzzle-loading mortars of very old pattern and were fired from the vent. Apparently the French artillery soldiers looked as old as the guns they were firing. Gunpowder was weighed out onto scales, as different ranges required different amounts of charge. After ramming the charge home the shell was loaded into the top of the mortar. The sight of this battery must have caused much amusement to the British Tommy; but their shooting was very accurate. Once the range had been set, a rapid rate of fire was obtained. The 5th Division held this part of the line until relieved by the 14th (Light) Division on 21 June 1916. When the Divisional History was published after the war, the stay at Arras produced the following summary:

> *'The situation was generally quiet, and with the exception of one or two short periods, remained so during our four months stay in the area, which were perhaps the happiest months of the whole war; the quietness of the front, and the comforts of Arras, and a fine summer, all helped to this end. Although close to the front, the town was rarely shelled by Heavy Artillery, but there was a small daily ration of field-gun fire.'*

Unfortunately the one or two short periods that

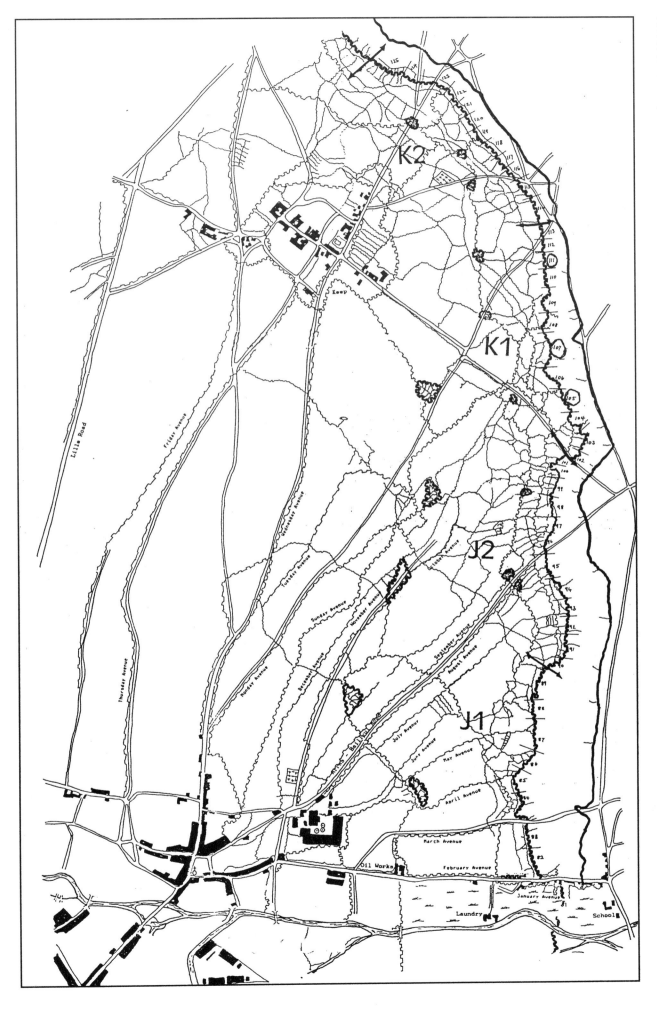

Left: Map of the 5th Division front line from March to June 1916. The front was split into four sections: J1, J2, K1 and K2. The three craters marked near K2 front line were known as Clarence, Cuthbert and Claude; the aftermath of a German trench raid on 4 June 1916 (see page 154). Communication trenches to the front lined radiated from the suburb of St Nicholas.

were not quiet, sadly, concerned the Birmingham battalions. the 15th Royal Warwicks especially. To give a day by day account of the Birmingham Pals on the Arras front would make dull reading. Therefore I will take each battalion in turn. First I will detail their movements and then elaborate on the important happenings concerning them.

14th Royal Warwicks (1st Birmingham)

* 10 March, left Vaux sur Somme to rejoin the 5th Division. Marched to Villers Bocage and billet for the night.
* 11 March, Doullens for one night.
* 12 – 13 March, Grand Rullercourt.
* 14 March, Agnez les Duisans. The battalion rejoined 13 Brigade. 15 - 20 March, K1 support line, Thelus, Observatory and Bosky Redoubts.
* 21 – 27 March, K1 front line trenches.
* 28 March – 3 April, Habarcq, rest and general training.
* 4 – 11 April, J2 support lines. (H.Q. and B company as mobile companies in August Avenue. Three platoons of C Company in Nicholas redoubt, the other in Bosky. D Company in reserve at the candle factory. A Company as Brigade reserve in Arras.)
* 12 – 19 April, J2 front line trenches. (B Company in trenches 90-92, C in 93-95, D in 96-98 and A in 99-100.)
* 20 – 27 April, Habarcq, rest and general training.
* 28 April – 4 May, K2 support lines. (A and D Companies in Roclincourt. B and C in Arras.)
* 5 – 10 May, K2 front line. (B in 114-122, C in 117-122, A in 123-125 and D in Roclincourt.)
* 11 – 16 May, K2 support line.
* 17 – 22 May, K1 front line.
* 23 – 28 May, Duisans, rest and cleaning up.
* 29 May – 4 June, K2 front line. (D in 114-122, A in 117-122, B in 123-125 and C in Roclincourt.)
* 5 – 10 June, K2 support line.
* 11 – 17 June, K2 front line. (A in 114-122, D in 117–122, C in 123-125 and B as mobile reserve in Roclincourt. 18th - 20th June, Duisans, rest.
* 21 – 24 June, Lattre in billets.
* 26 – 27 June, front line trenches near Wailly.
* 28th June, planned attack called off, battalion back to Agnez les Duisans. (H.Q. and B Companies) the others at Gouvres.

Before I carry on with the events of the Arras front it may be of interest to find out what happened during the battalion's isolation period. Prior to the outbreak of measles that swept through the battalion, Lieutenant Alan Furse was selected to go to Le Havre for three weeks. He was to learn horse-riding and the care of horses. The purpose was so that he could act as the battalion Transport Officer if duty called. Before leaving for Le Havre he had a few painful days having a 'crash course' under the guidance of the battalion transport Sergeant. His batman, No. 1106, Private S G Suffield, (in letters home referred to as his servant) accompanied him, but having shared a tent with a soldier who had a

Below: Lieutenant Alan Furse of the 14th Royal Warwicks at Le Havre during his horse riding course.

fever, he had to be isolated, which caused the following remarks in a letter home concerning his replacement:

'The man I got to carry on for me was a KOSB and I never want another Scotch servant as long as I live. He was never there when I wanted him and he smoked considerably more of my cigarettes than I did myself'

Part of his training consisted of learning to drive a brewer's dray through Le Havre down to the beach, load up with pebbles and return to the camp. Within three days he and other members of the same course, had bent a tram, torn a wheel off a light trap, knocked over a barrow of oranges and finally upturned the mess cart from another camp smashing eggs and breaking bottles of wine! On returning to the battalion at Vaux sur Somme he then undertook a Lewis Gun course. Whilst the rest of the division was marching up to Arras amid the arctic blizzards, splendid practice was had by shooting snowmen at 200 yards.

How did Sergeant Arthur Cooper fare during this period of isolation? Apart from trench digging and road mending fatigues, there were plenty of route marches and the company drill practice was reminiscent of Sutton Park. Before the snow set in, a few inter-platoon football games were played with Sergeant Cooper scoring a few times. He also played for the battalion football team in a couple of matches. Sergeant Cooper seemed to be a bit of an all rounder. The day before the battalion moved north to Arras, the men were given practice on the ranges. A good standard to achieve was fifteen rounds per minute. Sergeant Cooper hit the bull fifteen times in fifty six seconds and was congratulated by the Commanding Officer, Lieutenant Colonel Murray.

On 15 March, 1916, the 14th Royal Warwicks came back into divisional life, when they took over the support lines of K1 sector. The battalion was extremely lucky to get there in one piece. It was nearing dark as the battalion reached the outskirts of Arras. The men fell out and had a short rest. Unknown to all, where they rested was known as 'Dead Man's Corner', at frequent intervals the Germans would shell this area quite fiercely. Ignorant of this, after half-an-hour, they got up and continued with their journey. A lucky escape indeed and they soon learned to give this spot a wide berth in the future. Perhaps being out of the line for so long made the men a bit 'rusty', as in this first tour in support, they had two men killed and four wounded. The first man of the battalion to be killed on the Arras front was No.144, Private Sidney Smith, A Company. He was 26 years old and came from Bournville Lane. Killed on 17 March, he is buried in Cabaret Rouge British Cemetery, Souchez. During this period of support the battalion received two drafts of men from the 17th (Reserve) Battalion, thirty five men in total. According to the war diary they were 'very good stamp, physically and intellectually.' To give an example of the knowledge the Germans had of British movements, when the battalion took over the front line on 21 March, a shout rang out from a German listening post of 'good old Brum'. In his memoirs, Lieutenant Alan Furse recounted his first impressions of Arras:

'On the night of the 15/16th we marched from Agnez along the Arras Road to Arras and from there into reserve trenches. The road is the highest point for miles around and as we marched up we had a fine view of the lines round here, picked out by the Very Lights going up. I took my platoon into Observatory Redoubt and very comfortable we found it. There was a nice big dug-out for the men and I shared one with the Brigade Machine Gun Officer, a very nice chap. We were in the front of a salient about 300 yards behind the front line and in daytime had a fine view of the German lines. We were shelled very little whilst in here and were able to get a lot of work done in the way of improving the redoubt. On the 20th Fritz shelled Company H.Q. rather badly but although we were only 30 yards away we were left alone. On the 21st I had a nice job of clearing out some old French dug-outs and don't think I ever remember such smells. As fast as we got to the earth we had to sprinkle Jeyes to be able to keep on. They are unsanitary hounds and seem to be able to exist in anything. On the night of the 20/21st we moved up into the front line trenches (K1), or so they were called. They really consisted of four advanced posts over the mines and although the trenches were in fairly good condition it was a nasty eerie job going from one to another during the dark hours. One dug-out was part of the entrance to one of the mines and was devilish draughty, but as it rained practically throughout our six days up here we were "jolly glad of it". We were about forty yards off Fritz in most places and carried on lively games with him all day with rifle grenades with occasional interruptions from his Minenwerfer. This was a very large trench mortar, throwing a fifty pound shell like a torpedo which exploded with a terrific noise but did not do a great deal of damage. On the 25th I had my first casualty, Arthur Lilly being wounded by a rifle grenade, but not very badly. After bandaging him up in four or five places we got him safely away to hospital, little thinking in just over a year he would come back to the identical trench as an officer and be killed by a sniper's bullet. On the night of the 26/27th we were relieved and marched back to Habarcq for six days rest and as no one had had their shirt off for thirteen days it was not before it was needed !'*

Private Arthur John Lilly (No.343), whom Lieutenant Furse mentions was formerly a Gents Outfitter from 'The Mount', Reddicap Hill, Sutton Coldfield. He ended up in an Edinburgh Military Hospital. On recovery he was commissioned into the 2/6th Royal Warwicks. Here Lieutenant Furse gets his facts wrong because the 2/6th Battalion was at Tertry, clearing roads and filling in a huge crater at the crossroads when Lilly was hit by a sniper. Second-Lieutenant Lilly is buried in Saulcour Churchyard extension.

When the battalion arrived at Habarcq, Sergeant Cooper made the following entry in his diary on 28 March:

'Well, at eleven o'clock last night we were very anxiously awaiting the Norfolk Regiment, who were to take our places behind the sand bags and mud. They arrived, and we very quickly and quietly exchanged places at the posts and filed off towards the communication trench, which we went down for a bit and then pushed each other up over the top. It was a fairly dark night, but the Germans were sending up a great many lights, which make all around them as light as day. Their guns and machine guns banged away at times, but nothing seemed to drop our way. It's a weird experience, a long file of men, each man has to carefully watch the man in front. If he disappears he's down splashing away in a shell hole and you have to avoid it. If you should fall in on top of him, look out for trouble, because he is just about in the temper to get hold of your head and keep it under the water until you are drowned. After the snow and rain for six days the top was very sloppy, and I had one or two very risky skids getting over trenches and on the brink of Johnson holes. (A certain type of German shell on exploding gave off clouds of black smoke and was known as a 'Jack Johnson', he being the World Boxing Champion at the time.) Some of these holes are big enough, and have enough water in them, to get a decent swim. At last we arrived at Arras. Here everyone was anxiously enquiring how far we had to go. They were all very weary, as they had not had a sleep for six days, at least not a proper one. They can if they like go to sleep one hour out of every three between 8 p.m. and 4 a.m., also the previous six days in support they got very broken nights, so really they had not had a night's rest for twelve days. Well, to start with, through the town we had to move by platoon, as they sometimes shelled it. Number 1 platoon got lost, took the wrong

Above: Private Daniel Howell (No.113, A Coy, 1 Platoon, 14th Royal Warwicks) was killed by a German sniper whilst on sentry duty, in the K1 front line trenches, on 25 March 1916. Twenty-one year old Private Howell came from Glanyaefon Terrace, Johnstown, Carmarthen. Prior to the war he had worked for sixteen months on the staff of the Export Department at the General Electric Company, Witton, Birmingham. Private Howell is buried in the Cabaret-Rouge British Cemetery at Souchez.

Above: After their first spell in the Arras trenches the 14th Royal Warwicks rested at Habarcq from 28 March to 3 April. Whilst there, the Divisional Concert Party the 'Whizz-Bangs' put on a show. In the photograph taken in April 1916, the Old Mother Riley character belongs to the 55th Divisional Concert Party, but is a good indication of how these men looked, dressed for action. *IWM Q511*

a mug of water, cleaned my teeth in it first, shaved next, and then washed neck and face with the shaving brush, and had to pinch my thirst a bit to do that, so one appreciates a wash with plenty of water after being in the trenches for a time!'

The few days spent at Habarcq were put to good use in hand grenade throwing practice. On the lighter side our friend Sergeant Cooper, tried his hand at a game of Rugby for the first time, when A Coy played HQ Coy, he admits to a few mistakes, but was very pleased with his performance, as A Coy only lost 4 points to nil. During this stay at Habarcq the CO arranged a battalion six-a-side football competition. It took place on the Saturday and Sunday 1/2 April. In all twenty teams from the battalion entered; the winners to receive sixty francs. Yes, you know what's coming... Sergeant Cooper organised a team from No. 1 platoon, and at the start of the competition were given the odds of 12 to 1 to win. After putting six goals past No. 9 platoon, in the semi-final, with Sergeant Cooper scoring five, they were firm favourites. They did win, they beat HQ Company four nil, in front of a crowd of around two thousand. Sergeant Cooper as Captain of the victorious side not only collected the sixty francs from the CO, Captain Robinson gave thirty francs, and the platoon CO, Second-Lieutenant Lythgoe gave another sixty. Between them, the 150 francs worked out at roughly about £1 each; not a bad sum in those days.

The winning team was:

No.43 N A Matthews as Goalkeeper
No.1132 C B Keatly as Back,
No.79 F G Smith as Halfback
No.193 W E Hall as Forward
No.1277 T G Devey
No.65 A K Cooper

It may be of interest to know that Smith, Hall and Cooper were all employees of the GEC at Witton.

The Divisional Concert Party, the 'Whizz-Bangs', put on a show whilst the battalion were at Habarcq. The concert party by now had four members of the 14th Royal Warwicks. Towards the end of this spell at Habarcq the CO, Lieutenant-Colonel Murray, was pleased to report that nearly all the ranks of the battalion could now reach fifteen rounds per minute, rapid firing.

By 4 April the battalion was back in reserve trenches of J2 sector. In this spell in reserve the majority of the ranks were put on mining fatigues. This meant carrying sandbags full of spoil, to be disposed of and disguised from German observation aircraft as being chalk it was easily identified The following are Sergeant Cooper's views:

'The sappers we are carrying for are New Zealand men. Never seen such workers. Our fellows say they have a pick in each hand, hold the sandbags in their teeth and fetch the rock down into the bag with both the upward and downward stroke (they are real hefty lads). One thing is cer-

way out and found the rest of A Company after about an hour's marching across ploughed fields and such like. We found them and also the field kitchen, which provided a mug of hot tea for each of us. That was a God-send indeed. After that we marched, and marched, keeping as merry and bright as possible by singing and generally kicking up a row. During the ten minutes fall out which we got every hour about 90% would drop off to sleep on the roadside. Eventually between 5 and 6 a.m. we arrived at our rest camp, (Habarcq) and were settled in wooden huts to sleep the sleep that only a Tommy experiences. The boys marched well. So far as I know no one in the company fell out, which was a good performance, when one considers the twelve days they had had, followed by a seven hour route march. We were complimented by the Captain for the way the company had stuck to it. What a sleep we all had. The cooks woke us up and brought us our breakfast, and then I knew no more until dinner time, after which I got up and did a bit of cleaning. Never enjoyed a wash more in my life. Used two full buckets of clean water straight from the well. I had washed in the trenches in a quarter of

tain, that we have to fetch about ten times as many bags full as we used to for our Royal Engineers.'

The next tour of front line duty commenced on 12 April. The battalion relieved the Royal West Kents in the front line of J2. This part of the front line was known as 'Knife-Rest Corner'. During the fourth day of this tour the battalion was informed that they were sitting practically on top of a German mine. Because of this, a new section of trench had to be dug about fifty yards behind the existing one; which would be used as a new front line trench if the mine blew. This uncertain situation caused the following comment in Lieutenant Alan Furse's diary:

'Of course it made things a bit strained as we never knew when some careless beggar would set it going. We had to start digging trenches like fury every day and night and I also had a lot of barbed wire to put out in front. I never seemed to fancy my chance standing up about 40 yards from the Hun driving 2 inch stakes into the ground with a large wooded mawl. It was muffled, of course, with a pad of sand-bags but every stroke sounded as though it could be heard in Berlin. There were also a lot of French men in No Man's Land who had

been dead a long time and this did not tend to make the job any sweeter.'

On the night of 17 April, a party of men from B Coy were out wiring. In the light of a German flare Private Thomas Sanders (No.272, from Hagley Road) was hit by a sniper. The bullet entered his thigh and passed out through his stomach. Captain William Ehrhardt on seeing the unfortunate plight of Sanders, went to his assistance with a view to bring him back in. Probably the same German sniper fired again this time hitting Captain Ehrhardt. The bullet hit him in roughly the same body area as Sanders. However, the bullet did not pass through Ehrhardt, it split in two. One piece lodged near his spine, the other piece, plus bone fragments, going into his stomach. Very soon Lieutenant Emile Jacot was on the scene and with the assistance of Sergeant Jimmy Weatherhead (No.1086, from Hanley, Staffs). Both men displayed great courage and energy in bringing the wounded men back. Sanders, Ehrhardt and Jacot were old boys of King Edward's School in New St, Birmingham. The Headmaster, Mr Heath, received the news in a letter written by Lieutenant Jacot a few days later:

'I need hardly say they both took it as one would have expected of them. Ehrhardt's only concern was that Sanders should be moved first, while Sanders kept entreating us not to worry about him till we had got the Captain in.'

Both men were taken to the 14th Field Ambulance in Habarcq. Captain Ehrhardt underwent surgery almost immediately to remove the fragments from his stomach. At this time in the war it was estimated only one man in a hundred survived from the type of wounds that Ehrhardt received. For a few days he hovered between life and death, eventually he managed to pull through. (Captain Ehrhardt was discharged when well enough, though he still had part of a bullet in his back) Not so for poor Private Sanders, Gangrene had set in and he died on 20 April and was buried in Habarcq Communal Cemetery Extension. The battalion was back at Habarcq on the 20th April. During this period all the NCOs and other ranks were given what was known in army slang as 'the merry knock'. Each man was inoculated for Paratyphoid, not in the arm but in the chest. The men were then given a couple of days off to recuperate. Whilst out of the line, the acting Quartermaster, RQMS B Anderton (No.1062, of Strensham Road, Moseley), went back to England for a course whilst awaiting a commission. His duties were temporarily taken over by Lieutenant Alan Furse who now had to leave A Coy for a while.

The next tour of the line saw the battalion in the K2, Roclincourt sector for the first time. On 11 May, balloons were seen to drift over No Man's Land from the German lines.

Above: Captain Emile Jacot

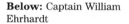

Below: Captain William Ehrhardt

Left: For a few days, Captain Ehrhardt, hovered between life and death. But as soon as he was able he wrote to his parents giving details of his wounds and a diagram of where the bullet entered his body.
Clive Hereward

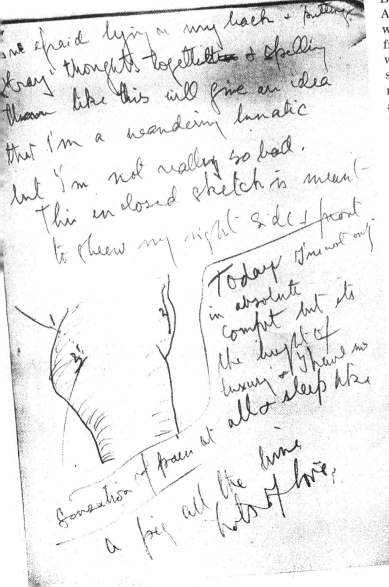

Above: Private John Leslie Dain, No.882, D Coy, 15 Platoon, 14th Royal Warwicks, from Bridgenorth, Shropshire. Died of wounds 4 July 1916, aged twenty-three. A former employee of the Ironbridge branch of Lloyds Bank, he is buried in Ste Marie Cemetery, Le Harve.

They were about six foot in diameter and red in colour. After one was shot down it was found that copies of German newspapers, printed in English, were attached. The story in the papers concerned the Irish Rebellion in Dublin. Perhaps German intelligence thought that Irish troops were opposite and hoped to cause a feeling of unrest. This tour consisted of two periods in reserve trenches and two in the firing line, a total of twenty six days. This resulted in three men killed and a half dozen wounded for the period. After this tour, instead of Habarcq, the battalion rested in Duisans.

On 29 May the 14th Royal Warwicks began their last tour of duty on the Arras front. This was another return to the K2 sector. They started off this time in the front line. After a quiet and uneventful six days, with no casualties, the battalion was due to be relieved by the 1st Royal West Kents on the evening of 4 June. The full description of the day's events will be revealed in the section concerning the 15th Royal Warwicks, who at the time were in K1 front line trenches. Twice in that afternoon the German artillery blasted the trenches of the 15th Royal Warwicks. In the evening three mines exploded and, in the ensuing confusion, an estimated five hundred Germans attempted to enter our front line positions. During the next period in the reserve line, many men were supplied for working parties. This was to straighten out the front line around the mine craters. The three craters were afterwards

known as Clarence, Cuthbert and Claude, after a song that was popular amongst the division, sung by the 'Whizz-Bangs'. Also on 4 June Lieutenant Alan Furse was off on leave back home to School Road, Moseley. By sheer coincidence his elder brother, Second-Lieutenant William Furse of the 21st Northumberland Fusiliers, was also home on leave. William was an original member of the 1st Birmingham Battalion, No.399, B Coy. He was commissioned on 23 September 1915. This would be the last time the brothers would meet. Within three weeks of their leave, William was destined to be one of the twenty thousand or so men who were killed on the first day of the Somme.

The 14th Royal Warwicks left the Roclincourt sector on 17 June for Duisans. Meanwhile, south of Arras, the 55th Division were making preparations to attack the German lines south of Wailly. This was due to happen two days after the Somme offensive had begun. This for a time was the proposed next destination for the 5th Division. Therefore the Division began a period of intensive training for the proposed attack. The plan was eventually called off; but not before the 14th Royal Warwicks had relieved the Territorials of the 7th Kings Liverpool Regiment on 26 June. Patrols were sent into No Man's Land to report on the German wire and trenches. A big daylight raid was carried out by a battalion of the Kings Liverpool Regiment on the afternoon of the 28th. So little was the retaliation,

Right: A group of NCOs and men from B Coy of the 14th Royal Warwicks. Taken when the battalion was out of the line at Lattre near Arras, 24 June, 1916. *Back row left to right:* L/Cpl Jewitt; Pte Stirling (No.494, from Alcester Road, Moseley); Pte E N Parker (No.300, from Harbourne Road); Pte Rowe; L/Cpl J Deakin (No.325, from Spring Road, Edgbaston and wounded on 23 July 1916). *Front row:* Pte Gabriel (No.1155, from Oxford Road, Acocks Green, killed in action 30 July 1916); Sgt Jenks (No.632, from York Road, Handsworth, wounded 23 July 1916); Pte Brown. *Miss Rose Deakin*

that the men of the 14th Royal Warwicks were able to stand up and get a good view of the Liverpool men on the raid.

After the attack was called off the battalion marched back to the vicinity of Arras. Here it split up for billeting purposes, half at Gouvres, the rest at Agnez les Duisans.

The 14th Royal Warwicks had come to the end of its association with Arras for 1916. Within a year the 1st Birmingham Battalion would return for another tour of duty to this part of the front, but as we find out, was to a large extent only the name that came back.

15th Royal Warwicks (2nd Birmingham Battalion)

* March 3 - 5, J1 support. A Coy in Arras, Rue De La Mont-De-La-Piet.
* March 6 - 9, J1 front line trenches.
* March 10 –14, Hauteville for rest and clean up.
* March 15 – 21, K2 support trenches. D Coy in Arras.
* March 22 – 25, K2 front line.
* March 26 – April 3rd, Agnez les Duisans. Rest and clean up.
* April 4 – April 11, J1 support. (C & D in the redoubt line. A & B as reserve, billeted underneath the vaults of the museum in Arras.)
* April 12 – 20, J1 front line. (D Coy in reserve at the Oilworks)
* April 21 – 27, Agnez les Duisans. Rest and clean up.
* April 28 – May 3, K1 support. (A as mobile company near Bosky Redoubt. B in Thelus and Observatory Redoubts. C in Arras. D in St Nicholas.)
* May 4 – 11, K1 front line. (C in reserve in Thelus and Observatory Redoubts.)
* May 12 – 16, Duisans, rest and clean up.
* May 17 – 23, K1 front line.
* May 24 – 28, K1 support.
* May 29 – June 4, K1 front line. (D in reserve, Thelus and Observatory Redoubts.)
* June 5 – 11, Duisans, Rest, clean up and roll call.
* June 12 – 16, K1 front line. (B in reserve, trench 40.)
* June 17 – 20, K1 support line.
* June 21, Battalion relieved by the 8th Rifles of 41 (Light Infantry) Brigade, 14th Division. The battalion then proceeded to Agnez les Duisans. For the next few days all available men were required to help dig new artillery emplacements.

Weather conditions were still very cold with much snow on the ground when the 15th Royal Warwicks took over the support trenches of J2 on 3 March. After a quiet three days of acclimatisation in the new sector the battalion then moved into the front line on 6 March, relieving the 1st Royal West Kents. The trenches here were more 'lively' than those on the Bray front. The Germans were quite active with rifle grenades and trench mortars and daily casualties soon began to mount up. It was also during this

first tour of the front line that the CO, Lieutenant - Colonel Harding, made an unusual discovery whilst exploring their new positions:

'I was looking over our new line with Captain Tatlow, one of my Company Commanders and a most capable and gallant officer, when we discovered a small tunnel freshly made, leading from our front line to the Hun trenches which were at a point about 60 yards away. That night we decided to explore and find out where the tunnel led. With a lit candle in one hand and grasping my revolver in the other, I proceeded with cautious mien, closely followed by Tatlow. The aperture was dark and damp and in a crawling position we were just able to get along at a snail's pace. We did not know the direction in which we were going, for we had no compass. Once started we hated to return without finding the reason of this underground aperture, and candidly, proceeding was equally distasteful. The candle, burning none too brightly, did not improve our dubious contemplation, and it was with an assumed nonchalance I shot the encouraging remark over my left shoulder to Tatlow that we should soon come to the end, what end, however seemed rather remote. He replied with the lugubrious information that he thought he heard German voices. I think he was right, for we had not got much farther before the aperture took an upward turn and I saw a glimmer of light and distinctly heard talking. Yes, undoubtedly we had come to the German line and also unquestionably a German sentry was standing or sitting in close proximity to ourselves. Two courses now stared us in the face – either proceed and be captured or shot, or ignominiously

Above: Captain Archibald Tatlow, OC of B Coy, 15th Royal Warwicks.
(see text left)

Below: Standing in a communication trench in the Arras support lines is: left, Second Lieutenant C L Jeffery and right Captain G M Turner; both of C Coy, 15th Royal Warwicks.
Birmingham Library Services

Right: 15th Royal Warwicks in the J1 sector, front line trench, March 1916. *Birmingham Library Services*

Far right: Captain G M Turner, second in command B Coy, with trench periscope. *Birmingham Library Services*

Below: Captain Charles Bill (with pipe), OC of A Coy with Second Lieutenant H Anderson. *Birmingham Library Services*

return. Unanimously and without hesitation we chose the latter and did so as noiselessly and quickly as possible. But even this was easier said than done, for it was inadvisable to come right out in the open and the tunnel was so small that it was

impossible to turn about whilst inside. The only alternative was to crawl backwards with our face to the enemy. This we did, but we had not proceeded far before our presence became known to the Germans, for we could distinctly hear voices at the mouth of the hole. No shots, however, were fired at us, and eventually we got back to our line smothered in dirt but rather pleased with ourselves. We immediately posted a sentry at the mouth of the tunnel on our side, and I expect our friends the enemy at the other end of the tunnel had adopted a similar precaution and were ready and hoping for a return visit which did not materialise.'

The War Diary for the battalion gives little information for this first tour of the trenches at Arras. Two men were killed and four men were wounded during this period, with only a cursory mention in the diary on the relevant dates. Fortunately the little 'Boots' pocket diary of Private Archie Brown

(No.586, C Coy, from Station Road, Harborne) has survived the ravages of time. Even though his entries were brief, he paints a better picture than the War Diary. He mentions that he is fed up. It is snowing and very cold. The men are only on half rations. Shrapnel landing amongst them from our own guns, firing at German aeroplanes, was a common occurrence. Making his way to the trenches one night with a ration party, carrying a dixie, he was fired at by a sniper. The bullet went through the dixie. He witnessed one man wounded by a rifle grenade, which resulted in both his feet being blown off. He also mentions the gruesome sight of the rotted remains of French soldiers hanging in the barbed wire. Concerning these gruesome sights, Private H V Drinkwater's (No.161) diary mentions that shellfire hitting the front line exposed many dead French soldiers that had been buried in the parapet.

The first period of rest for the battalion was spent at Hauteville, a small village a few miles east of Arras. Apart from heavy snow the only other item of interest during this period was when a bomb dropped from a German aeroplane and blew out the wall from the Officers' mess. Luckily no one was injured.

On 15 March began the battalion's second tour of the Arras front. This time it was the K2 sector near Roclincourt. The snow of the previous few weeks had now cleared. With a spell of warm weather during this period the battalion experienced dry trenches for the first time since arriving in France. When the front line trenches were taken over on 22 March, it was found that No Man's Land was roughly fifty yards wide, and in some parts as little as thirty yards. During the early hours of 25 March, the battalion sent out it's first patrol into No Man's Land. The patrol, from D Coy, was headed by Second-Lieutenant G S F Dale (from Lozells Road, Handsworth). Accompanying him were two sergeants and five other ranks and a good supply of

Above left: Captain Charles Bill *Birmingham Library Services*

Above: Near A Coy HQ, J1 front line trench sector, April 1916. Second Lieutenant H Anderson on the left. *Birmingham Library Services*

139

inspected by Sir Douglas Haig on 30 March. On the day, the battalion lined the roads of the village as guard of honour for the Commander in Chief. He must have had pressing matters; he and his entourage drove through the village at 3 pm, without stopping to inspect the battalion. The battalion returned to the trenches on 4 April. This time in J1 support line lasted for seven days and then they moved into the front line for a further nine. During the period in support, some of the men were attached to the 59th Coy, Royal Engineers for mining duties. On 2 April, Captain F H Timings, the former CO of D Coy who was left behind at Codford Camp, rejoined the battalion. However, because D Coy was now commanded by the twenty year old Captain Roland Gough, Captain Timings was attached to C Coy instead. On the night of April 16th, Captain Timings went out with a wiring party and was soon under German observation. Of this episode, Captain Bill (C Coy) wrote the following:

'We had at the time a limited supply of recently issued steel helmets, which we used for patrols and wiring parties. When this party was fired on they proceeded to crawl on all fours back to our front line with the bullets pinging off the wire around them. While doing so, Timings, realising that the largest part of his anatomy was offering an extremely vulnerable target to the enemy, tried to put up a protective screen by holding his tin hat behind him. Progress under these conditions, however, was slow and arduous, so he compromised by putting his tin hat back on his head and crawling into our lines backwards. They all got back safely and the next night went out again and completed their work without interference.

Not long after this incident Captain Timings was sent home with Trench Fever and did not return to

Above: March 1916, the Commander in Chief of the BEF, Sir Douglas Haig who was due to inspect the 15th Royal Warwicks. *IWM Q485*

hand grenades. The patrol came upon a German working party, which they attacked. Twenty-two Mills bombs were thrown in all. How many casualties were inflicted is not known, but after two-and-a-half hours the patrol returned safely.

Agnez les Duisans, was the rest village for the battalion's next period out of the line. The first few days were spent cleaning uniforms and polishing buttons. The men were informed they were to be

Right: Roclincourt, April 1916. Entrance to the cellar dugout that was home to C Coy HQ when the 15th Royal Warwicks were in the K2 sector support trenches. Second Lieutenant H Anderson is on the extreme left of the group, whilst standing second from the right is Captain F H Liddell the battalion's Adjutant. The original cellar to the ruined house became the living quarters whilst a further room had been dug below the cellar for sleeping quarters. It was as safe a spot as one could hope for, provided, that a German shell did not land on the cellar steps. *Birmingham Library Services*

the battalion again. The battalion came out of the line in the early hours of 21 April (Good Friday). Three men had been killed and six wounded during the previous few days. The battalion returned to Agnez les Duisans for the Easter period. The CO, Lieutenant-Colonel Harding, along with all the other commanding officers of the British Third Army, took part in a conference at Auxi-le-Château. Meanwhile back at Agnez the rest of the battalion cleaned up, had various inspections and parades. Whilst here all ranks were given lectures on 'care of arms' and 'defence schemes'. For these few days out of the line the weather was glorious; hot and sunny. Men who had been to lectures were off duty from 17.30. The early evenings would see them lounging by some riverbank, dozing and soaking up the last couple of hours of sunlight. The war far behind in their thoughts, with no worry of a trench mortar or a rifle grenade dropping on them here. But, the CO returned from his conference which signalled a return to the trenches. Thus the last day before going back to the line was spent on parades, inspections and a route march. A gas helmet practice rounded the day off. 28 April saw the battalion back in the support lines; this time in K1.

When in support one tends to think that the men are sitting in their dugouts, hanging around, waiting to stem a possible German breakthrough if the front line trenches are breached. Apart from those who were on sentry duty, officers servants, sanitary men, machine gunners and signallers, most men of a battalion's fighting strength (around 600) were used for hard manual labour. As darkness fell, all along the front line thousands of troops of both sides would be slowly making their way up communication trenches carrying stores, ammunition, rations, barbed wire, tools and wood for the shoring up of trench walls etc. As an example, take the 15th Royal Warwicks during this next period in the reserve trenches. A fair number of men would be working eight hour shifts attached to the engineers on tunnelling duties. Others would be keeping the trenches in a state of proper repair. Then as darkness fell the fetching and carrying commenced, while others repaired or rewired the defences in No Man's Land. Every night whilst both sides busied themselves in the darkness, the artillery of both sides would be blasting away. As daylight approached, the work would stop, a chance for a few hours' rest before the routine began all over again. A fine example of what the other ranks were expected to try and convey up to the trenches concerned Private H V Drinkwater:

'I was detailed with other fellows to carry iron girders from St Nicholas to the firing line. Arrived at St Nicholas at 8 p.m., we found the girders weighed 3 hundredweight each (152 kg). Four men to a girder, we started to carry them. A dark night pouring with rain, we slipped over in the trenches and kept falling into sump holes, nearly bent double with the weight.

So we got out of the trench onto the top and immediately slipped into a shell hole, down came the girder. We were now fairly saturated. We got back into the trenches again but had the greatest difficulty getting the things around the traverse. At midnight we had got about half way and the language was foul. The prospects of another four hours of this was too much. We dumped the things in the trench, there was a state of rebellion in the air as we made our way back to the billets. Arrived back in a filthy condition, had to take all my tops off to hang them up to dry. I expect we shall hear something about this in the morning.

'We were awakened this morning and told by the sergeant we were under open arrest for not finishing our job last night, personally I did not mind a button, I rolled over and went back to sleep again. Later in the morning we had a parade in front of the Captain. he did not say much except that we had to finish the job tonight. So at 4 p.m. we paraded and carried on where we left off last night. With the help of a little daylight and no rain, things went a little better. But two miles of traverses to carry such things is too much. We got to the firing line about 10 p.m. barely able to lift an arm and scarcely able to crawl back to our billet. We arrived back at 11.30 p.m., we lit up a fire and cooked anything we could find.

The battalion moved into the front line, K1 on 4 May. It had been decided that the battalion would make a raid on the German trenches during the next period of front line duty. Written after the war the former CO, Lieutenant-Colonel Harding, had this to say about one of the youngest captains in the British Army:

'The officer who was in charge of this raid was Captain Gough. It was his express wish to have command and, knowing his undeniable capability and resources, I gladly acquiesced. Gough was very young and, at the time of the raid, was not, I think, 20 years of age. He was a 'cheery bloke,' adored by his company and beloved by his brother officers, including myself.'

In preparation for the raid, on the night of 5 May, D Coy sent out two patrols into No Man's Land. The object was to inspect the German front line and the condition of the barbed wire. A sample of wire was taken and brought back for inspection. The next few days shellfire was heavier than usual. On 7 May, the battalion received its heaviest bombardment since its arrival in France. A, B, and D Coys were in the front line, whilst C was in reserve at Observatory and Thelus Redoubts. The bombardment commenced at 09.30 am and increased with

Above: Captain Percival Edwards, OC of A Coy, 15th Royal Warwicks. Wounded on 19 May 1916.

Below: Major Richard Jones, Second in Command, 15th Royal Warwicks and former Principal of the Birmingham University Training College. Killed in action 21 May 1916.

Above: Private Claud White, No.749, 15th Royal Warwicks. Note the braided chin strap, and just above and behind the cap badge is sewn a piece of ribbon: Royal Blue with two narrow yellow stripes. It is some kind of Divisional/Brigade/Battalion identification patch. Or, it may be an unofficial embellishment – the wearer appears to be an 'old sweat'.

Right: May 1916. Three men of C Coy, 15th Royal Warwicks, in K1 front line trench, 109 section (see map, page 131). On the left is Private Claud White (No.749, 12 Platoon). *'Nocker' White*

intensity between 2.30 – 3.30 pm. It finally ceased around 6.30 pm. Apart from sentries, most of the men were safe in the deep dugouts; a thankful legacy from the former French occupiers of the divisional front. It was reckoned around 2000 shells passed over onto the battalion front. Fortunately only one man was killed (No.579, Private Charles Bristow of Albert Road, Aston) and around twenty wounded. The most damage occurred in the vicinity of Sunday Avenue and Observatory Redoubt. During the next two days and nights the Germans continued to bombard the area with shell and shrapnel to deter working parties repairing the damage received.

It is possible that this bombardment was a practice for the forthcoming German raid that was due on 4 June. The bombardment received was almost identical. Perhaps the Germans would now study air photographs and wait for intelligence reports on the results of the bombardment. Secrecy was at a minimum at Arras, especially with the remaining civilian population so close to the front line. This was an ideal place for a German spy network to operate. The easiest way for information to pass through our lines to the Germans was via the River Scarpe which flowed through Arras in a westerly direction. In his diary, Private Drinkwater explained that it took a few weeks to realise this was happening, but eventually a net was strung across the river. Hollowed out lengths of stick or small tree branches were found with messages inserted.

The battalion returned to Agnez les Duisans on 12 May. Captain Gough took D Coy to another, more secluded village, further from the front. Here with the aid of air photographs, the company dug dummy trenches and rehearsed for the forthcoming raid. Captain Gough, along with his Company Sergeant Major (No.1031, CSM Clayton), made nightly visits into No Man's Land and explored as close as possible to the German lines. This enabled

him to obtain the correct distance and lie of the land that he and his men would soon traverse.

The battalion returned to the same front line trenches of K1 on 17 May. After three months of hard work a British mine was to be blown up on 19 May. This mine, designated K14, was dug to countermine a German one heading for our lines which had been discovered. The idea was, by blowing up our mine it would destroy the German tunnelling and in the confusion our side would capture and consolidate the crater. One wonders if the River Scarpe spy network must have still been in operation during this period. K14 was due to be blown at 08.00, and A Coy of the 15th Royal Warwicks were to occupy the crater. The German mine blew first at 04.30. Knowing the British troops opposite would attempt to take the crater the Germans had concentrated machine guns and trench mortars on the spot. This then was the scenario that A Coy found themselves in. A member of A Coy at the time was Private Drinkwater who wrote the following in his diary:

'Captain Edwards, our company Captain, crept out over the parapet to investigate the damage and was met by a fusillade of bullets from the German line. He stopped one through the shoulder and one in the head, the latter would have been fatal had he not been wearing his steel helmet, another instance of their usefulness. Lieutenant C W Davis (of Pershore Road, Edgbaston) *took over as company commander. When Captain Edwards was hit an engineer who happened to be watching, sprang onto the parapet and crawling on his stomach reached Captain Edwards and dragged him in. The engineer was awarded the Distinguished Conduct Medal.'*

Despite the German attempts, A Coy occupied the crater with only a few casualties and started to consolidate. The next evening, the second in command of the battalion, Major R A Jones, made his way to the crater to supervise the defence work. Just after midnight (21 May) a rifle grenade exploded killing Major Jones, Lance Corporal W J Hundy and wounding three others. One of the men at the crater was Private Drinkwater:

'I helped carry the N.C.O. to the dressing station and, on uncovering him, found him to be one of my pals, a very descent fellow, we had been together since the first days of joining. I could not recognise his features, they where blown away. Could only tell by his identity disc. He was one of two brothers, the other a stretcher bearer, unaware of his identity, dug him out and carried him back.'

Known to some as that 'blue-eyed bleeder,' to most, more affectionately, 'the Major', the death of Major Jones was a sad loss, not only to the battalion, but also to Birmingham University. Before the

war he was Principal of the University Training College and Commanding Officer of the university Officer Training Corps. The stretcher bearer who did not realise he was digging out his dead brother was Private Hubert Hundy (No.220, from Park Road, Hockley). His brother, Lance Corporal William Hundy, had the distinction of being the first man attested into the 2nd Birmingham Battalion; his service number being 1. Before the war William Hundy was employed at Bryant and Sons in Winson Green.

The crater was transformed into a good strong position out in No Man's Land. To reach it a sap was dug from the original front line. Sentries were posted in there each night. The crater was only yards from a German listening post. Great care and concentration had to be taken to make sure German patrols did not creep around the lip of the crater and attack the sentries from behind.

Trench Raid

The planned trench raid by D Coy was to take place on the evening of 22 May. Thus for the next tour of the trenches D Coy were placed in support trench 40. Captain Gough had chosen two officers and sixty other ranks for the raid. The raiding party was split into two groups 'right' and 'left'. The German front line was to be entered at two points. Some men were designated 'blockers'; their job was to prevent Germans moving up the trenches, from either side or up along communication trenches. Other men were designated 'bombers'; once in the German front line, they would hurl hand grenades over the traverse of the trench. Bayonet men would then rush round the traverse to finish off any German with hostile intentions or hopefully, by now, so demoralised they would surrender and be taken prisoner. Other men designated as 'support' were to stay in No Man's Land to give covering fire to the men on leaving the trenches and assisting any wounded.

RAIDING PARTY: D COY, 15TH ROYAL WARWICKS
Command: Captain Roland Gough

LEFT PARTY
No.1a
1446 Sergeant George Scrivens
939 Private Herbert Brown
     Station Road, Harborne
762 Private Albert Eyre
     Anderson Road, Erdington
921 Private Herbert France
     Carlton Terrace,Waterworks Rd, Ladywood
1207 Private B E Field

No.1b
933 Sergeant Charles Cottrell
     Great Colmore Street, B'ham
1200 Private Walter Gossage Anderton Street,
     Ladywood
817 Private James Ryley
     Prince Albert Street, Bordesley
851 Private Horace Timmins Coleshill
982 Private John Sadler
     Shaftsbury House, Rounds Green, Oldbury

No.2a (Blocking Party)
     Lieutenant R A Wilton in command

914 L/Cpl Frederick Parkes Berners Street, Lozells
920 Private Christopher Hollis
     Grantham Road, Smethwick
966 Private Frederick Foster
     Woodbridge Road, Moseley
911 Private Harry Denchfield
     Mansel Road, Small Heath

No.2b
836 Sergeant Albert Maspero
     Leatherhead, Surrey
808 Private L J Snape
     Albert Road, Handsworth
     Private Hawker
825 Private A H Smith

Left: Wash and brush up trench style. Unidentified officers of the 15th Royal Warwicks.

Private Jackson
1562 Private B Smith

No.2c
972   Cpl S Davis
        South Road, Handsworth
964   L/Cpl S A Griffiths
        Bloomsbury Street, Vauxhall
777   Private R F Knight
        Stirling Road, Edgbaston
970   Private Harry Tetstall
        Blackthorne Road, Smethwick
901   Private L G Coleman
        Balsall Heath Road
876   Private George Robbins
        Sutton Sreeet, Aston
1258 Private Charles Shergold
        Ernest Place, Vicarage Rd, Aston

SUPPORTS FOR LEFT PARTY
445   Cpl A E Purchase
        Resevoir Road, Ladywood
1356 Private W Ogborn
1296 Private W J Greaves
798   Private G H Richardson
        Shenstone Road, Cape Hill
803   Private H A Hathaway
        Somerset Road, Harborne
1000 Private Harry Griffiths
        Belgrave Road, Balsall Heath
882   Private Sidney Pearson
        Ladywood Road
1641 Private E T Southall

SIGNALLERS
848   Private   Francis Cowles

Great Arthur Street, Smethwick
807 Private F Rowley
        Elkington Street, Aston

RIGHT PARTY
No.1
794   Sergeant S B Smith
1202 Private William Norgrove
        Stockwell Grove, Handsworth
867   Private A E Fazey
        Wentworth Road, Harborne
        Private Hitchman

No.2
1765   Private A F Green
         Private   Dance
         Private   Hewson
         Private   Mills

No.3
Corporal Greaves
1389 Private Ronald Baugust
         Harborne
913 Private Albert Hitchings
        Wollaston near Stourbridge
858 Private L A Jones
        Linwood Road, Handsworth
862 Private J T Humphreys

SUPPORTS
873 Cpl L J Lawson
799   L/Cpl W Peake
        Galton Road, Bearwood
1709 Private Ferdinand Cheetham Lozells
852 Private H S Turner
        Quinton
1667 Private Green
1613 Private Archibald Hewitt
        Walsingham Street, Walsall
         Private Newbury
1288 Private E Appleton
942 Private F S Thomas
        Hinstock Road, Handsworth
977 Private George Hewitt
        Greenfield Road, Harborne

On the afternoon, of 22 May, there had been an intense trench-mortar bombardment upon the German wire facing the 15th Royal Warwick's front line. The object was to cut gaps in it for the raiding party to enter. Afterwards the Royal Flying Corps reported that the wire was well cut. The raid was timed to start at 10 pm, Captain Gough brought the party up to the front line as darkness fell. Here they had some food and a rest before the raid started. As a feint our artillery blasted another part of the German line. A telephone had been placed in No Man's Land and once the raid had started, Captain Gough could keep the CO, Lieutenant-Colonel Harding, well informed; he in turn had a direct line to Brigade Headquarters.

At ten minutes before zero hour the men desig-

Above: Leaflet published by the War Office giving guidelines concerning the collection of intelligence.

nated to enter the German lines crawled out into No Man's Land and lay down in front of our wire. At 10 pm our artillery opened up with a concentrated bombardment on the German front line. On this signal, the raiding parties began to crawl forward. Their place was then taken over by the support parties. After five minutes the artillery barrage moved forward onto the German support line to form a protective curtain of shellfire. This was the signal for the 'right' and 'left' parties to get up and move forward at a steady double.

The Right Party

It was now that the raid went disastrously wrong. The gaps in the wire, that had been reported by the RFC, had now been filled by hastily built wooden frames covered in barbed wire. These had been hurled from the German front line. Thus, these obstacles had to be cleared before the raiders could continue. Under the glare of their star shells the Germans opened up with machine gun and rifle fire from their front line. Sergeant S B Smith (No.794) of the 'right' party, undaunted by the enemy fire, proceeded to cut the wire. He did not last long and collapsed with bullet wounds to his head and left hand. Fortunately, Sergeant Smith had noticed that the enemy trench was full of German soldiers.

Though seriously wounded he still had enough strength to shout and order the rest of the 'right' party to retire. By giving this order Sergeant Smith probably saved the 'right' party from being wiped out. As the party slowly made it's way back across No Man's Land, Private J T Humphries (No.862), from the cover of a shell hole, managed to lob eight hand grenades into the German front line trench. Apart from Sergeant Smith, who managed to crawl back to our lines, four other men of the party were wounded making their return. They were: Privates A E Fazey, J S Barr, H S Turner and A F Green. All the 'right' party got back except Private Mills, who was missing.

The Left Party

This party was less fortunate; Second Lieutenant R A Wilton was leading when the hail of fire commenced from the German front line. By then the leading members of the party were approximately twelve yards from the German wire. Second-Lieutenant Wilton was hit in the chest, but continued to stagger forward. Before collapsing he saw a gap in the German wire and shouted 'go on boys!'. There was a path through the wire at this section; or was it a deliberate ploy of the Germans to funnel the men to one area and make them sitting ducks?

If so, the plan worked. Following on the heels of Second-Lieutenant Wilton was Sergeant Cottrell and Private A Smith. They were the next to be hit. Privates John Sadler and Herbert Brown managed to get through the wire unscathed and reached the German parapet; a distance of approximately twenty yards. On seeing this, Sergeant George Scrivens shouted 'go on number one'. He then must have been shot; he was not seen again. The two men who reached the parapet were both shot, Private Brown was last seen tumbling into the German trench. Someone now shouted the order to retire. It's possible they were the last orders given by Sergeant Albert Maspero after seeing the impossibility of the situation. But before he started to retire he, too, was shot. Private Frederick Foster saw the sergeant collapse into the barbed wire.

In trying to get to the Sergeant, Private Foster became another casualty. Five surviving men of this leading group sought the safety of the nearest shell crater. These were Privates Denchfield, France, Gossage, Ryley and Timmins. On entering the crater they found the seriously wounded Second-Lieutenant Wilton and Sergeant Cottrell. Just as this group reached the safety of the crater, Denchfield was killed and France was wounded. Whilst in this crater, Private Ryley decided to try and drag Second Lieutenant Wilton back to our lines. Two other wounded men trying to get back were Privates Hollis and Smith.

Private Ryley found that trying to drag Second-Lieutenant Wilton over the shell-pocked No Man's Land was an impossible situation. Therefore he decided to leave the subaltern in the safety of a shell-hole and come back with help. The remainder of the left party had now returned to the battalion's front line trench.

During all this activity we must remember that the sky was aglow with German star shells and this section of No Man's Land must have been as bright as daylight. Not only that, German artillery had begun a heavy retaliatory bombardment whilst the relentless rattle of German machine-gun and rifle fire swept No Man's Land. As men from both parties began scrambling back to our lines, Second-Lieutenant A G French asked if Second-Lieutenant Wilton was back. When no one answered he said 'come on Corporal Purchase, lets go and get him'. Off they went, towards the German line. On the way Corporal Purchase came across the wounded Private Foster, who then led the Corporal to where Sergeant Maspero was hanging limply in the German barbed wire. He was found to be dead. Unfortunately, Private Foster somehow got himself badly snagged up in the wire. Corporal Purchase now had to let Second Lieutenant French go his own way while he helped poor Foster. Unknown to Second Lieutenant French, Wilton was now in a shell hole some forty yards back from the German line, where Private Ryley had left him. Thinking that Second-Lieutenant Wilton was still somewhere in the vicinity of the German wire, Second-

Lieutenant French continued to look for him.

Poor Corporal Purchase, in trying to free Private Foster from the barbed wire had himself got tangled. From his position at the barbed wire he saw Second-Lieutenant French strive to get within twelve yards of the German front line. He then saw him crumple and fall into a wire entanglement. This was soon followed by a blast from a German hand grenade very close to where Second-Lieutenant French was hanging. Unable to release Private Foster, Private Purchase managed to break free and decided to return for help. In the crater, near the German wire, that had once sheltered seven men from the left party there were three men still alive. One of them, Private Timmins, decided to go for help. In the confusion he went the wrong way and headed towards the German lines (see his account later). The other two men were Privates Gossage and France. Private France had received a bad wound to the shoulder and was now crying for water. Leaving Private Timmins wandering around No Man's land, Private Gossage then made his way back to fetch help. Soon after Private France managed to struggle the remaining distance over No Man's Land and reached our lines.

Captain Gough was still in No Man's Land with the field telephone. On seeing the men return, he asked for our artillery barrage to stop. When he returned, he was given a brief account of what had happened. He then asked Lieutenant Anderson of C Coy to collect the men together and have a roll call. Gough, concerned that his two officers were still missing, decided to try and find them himself. Private Ryley, who had dragged Second-Lieutenant Wilton to a shell hole, was to act as guide. Two other men in the party were Private Jacobs and Corporal Purchase who carried a stretcher. By good luck, Second-Lieutenant Wilton was found and carried back to our lines.

By this time Lieutenant Anderson had completed the roll call. Gough was given the details of which men were still out in No Man's Land. Volunteers

from C Company went out and searched for the missing men. Without being asked, Captain Hewson (Trench Mortar Officer) and Lieutenant Tremlett, (Forward Observation Officer, 52nd Battery, Royal Field Artillery) both went out to help search for the missing. Captain Gough decided to try again with the assistance of Corporal Purchase and Private W J Greaves. Again, Private Ryley acted as guide. The party extended five paces apart and slowly made their way to the German lines. Unfortunately Ryley had lost his direction and after an unsuccessful search returned. Back in our lines again, Captain Gough had another roll call taken. He decided it was possible for one more search before dawn. Privates Hewson and Dance went in search of Private Mills. He also detailed Privates Ryley and Gossage to search the area of the shell hole, where men had sheltered after the attack had failed. This time they took a rope. Anyone found, dead or wounded, would have to be dragged back rather than carried. Captain Gough, Corporal Purchase and Privates Ogborn and Jacobs made their way as close to the German front line as possible. With the sky still illuminated by star shells they searched in vain for Second Lieutenant French. Meanwhile Private Gossage not feeling too good, returned back to our lines.

Private Foster, who was tangled in the barbed wire, had managed to free himself. He was eventually found by Private Ryley. Foster was barely alive, it would soon be daylight. If he was not brought in now, Foster would have to stay out all day and probably bleed to death. Ryley probably realised he had not got much time, so he decided to tie a rope around Foster's feet and slowly began to drag him back across No Man's Land. Under the hail of German lead Private Ryley crawled with Private Foster in tow. Slowly creeping on all fours from cover to cover. Then every now and again he stopped to pull the unconscious body of Foster to him; before continuing his slow journey towards our lines. Private Ryley managed to get Foster back, but sadly he was found to be dead. Captain Gough and his party returned just before daybreak. A final roll call was to be taken, before the men were allowed to get their heads down. The final act of this night's tragedy was about to happen. There occurred an accidental explosion of a hand grenade amongst some of the surviving members of the raiding party, killing Private G Hewitt. Seven others were wounded, Lance-Corporal S A Griffiths, Privates F Cheetham, L G Coleman, J T Humphries, C Shergold, H Tetstall and F S Thomas. Private Coleman had also received a slight wound during the raid. In his memoirs, written after the war, the CO, Lieutenant-Colonel Harding, had this to say of the raid:

'Three times that night Gough went 'over the top' to bring in wounded comrades. Mercifully he was untouched, but when I saw him after the attack he was humiliated by the want of success and heartbroken by the decimation of his small but gallant company.

'Sad and dejected, on the following day, Gough and I attended the funeral of Major Jones. Unquestionably of late the Battalion had struck a bad patch, but unperturbed by our numerous casualties during the past few days, they had enhanced their reputation as a fighting unit.

'Subsequently, I recommended Gough for the Military Cross and one or two of his company for the Distinguished Conduct Medal, but inasmuch as the raid was a failure, my recommendations were turned down. To me, this decision seemed arbitrary and unfair, for the failure lay in the fact that the artillery preparation was insufficient to cut the wire although at the same time it was sufficient to notify the enemy of our attack.

'Too late we recognised the fact that in all our offensive movements the artillery bombardment which of necessity preceded the attack to destroy the wire entanglements, warned the enemy and the assault was, therefore, no surprise to them, and it being no surprise, they made the necessary arrangements for repulse.'

The men recommended for gallantry awards were:
Captain Gough: DSO
Second-Lieutenant R A Wilton: MC and Mention in Despatches
Second-Lieutenant A G French:
No.794 Sergeant S B Smith: MM
No.445 Corporal A E Purchase: DCM
No.817 Private J Ryley: DCM

Not all those recommended were turned down, Second-Lieutenant R A Wilton was awarded the Military Cross.

The next day the following communication was received from Divisional Headquarters:

The Divisional Commander wishes to thank the 15th Battalion, The Royal Warwickshire Regiment, for their very gallant effort to enter the enemy's trenches last night.

Their non-success seems to have been entirely due to the fact that the enemy was not surprised, and they did not cease their efforts until half the attacking party had been killed or wounded. The fact that the enemy was ready may perhaps have been due to our wire cutting with trench mortars during the afternoon. On the other hand the affair may have been given away by injudicious talking throughout the Division.

The G.O.C. directs all Commanding Officers to impress on all ranks the necessity fore absolute secrecy with regard to impending operations. They are never to be mentioned or talked about except as a

Above: Rifle inspection – an important feature of life at the front, where mud persisted.

matter of duty. Offenders against this order will be most severely dealt with.
(Signed)
R.A.CURRIE,
Lieutenant-Colonel,
General Staff, 5th Division.

On the evening of 23 May, two of the missing men crawled back to our lines. These were Privates Mills and Timmins. They had stumbled upon each other in No Man's Land and took shelter in a deep shell hole that was partly filled with barbed wire. They had spent all day approximately twelve yards from the German front line. The following is the report Private Timmins made on returning:

'*On the night of May 22nd, we started our raid at 10 o'clock. On reaching the German barbed wire the Germans opened rapid fire on us: also their artillery opened and bombarded us heavily. The German trenches were found to be very heavily manned and the order was passed to retire. Having several casualties we thought it advisable to attend to them immediately. We got them into a shell hole. Private Ryley then assisted Mr Wilton back to our trenches. I attempted to get back for some water (for Private France) also a stretcher, as the casualties were so badly wounded that we could not get them back without a stretcher without causing much loss of blood. I went in the wrong direction and got within five yards of the German parapet: they discovered me and shot, but fortunately missed. They also threw a bomb which hit me on the cheek and failed to explode. I lay in a shell hole for some time, then made my way, (as I thought) to our trenches, but again I found I had reached the German lines. It was getting light by now so I thought it wise to get into a shell hole. When looking for a shell hole I was challenged by Private Mills. I joined him in the shell hole. We then dug our hole larger with jack-knives and lay there from 2 am until 10 o'clock the same night. During the day we found that our line was directly in front of us, and that we were about 25 or 30 yards from the Germans. At 10 o'clock we made our way slowly towards our lines and crept in through the obstacle trench. When challenged by the KOSBs we explained our circumstances and were allowed to come over the top. Much to our delight we found ourselves in 109 trench. I would like to mention that the KOSBs Officer and NCO's were very good and considerate to us.*
I am, sir,
Respectfully yours,
(signed)
851 Private Timmins, 'D' Coy.
P.S. Sir, I have omitted to state that Sergeant Cotterill (sic) was in the same shell hole that I was in at 10 o'clock May 22nd, and he had half his head blown away.'

Private Horace Timmins was born in Handsworth, his family probably moved to Coleshill, but on enlisting into the battalion he gave his address as C/O Mrs Gibbs, Bickenhill Lane, Marston Green. He was killed by shell fire on 29 August 1916, when the Division was serving on the Somme front. He is commemorated on the Thiepval Memorial to the Missing and also on the War Memorial in Coleshill. After the war his family moved to Stourbridge.

The body of Second-Lieutenant Alan George French (from North Farm, Loughton, Essex) was never found. He is named on the Arras Memorial, along with Sergeant Cottrell, Privates Brown, Sadler and Denchfield. Private Frederick Foster, who was hauled across No Man's Land by Private Ryley, is buried in Faubourg D'Amiens Cemetery, Arras (also the site of the Arras Memorial). In the same cemetery lies the former employee of the Dunlop Rubber Works, Aston, Private George Hewitt, who was killed in the accidental hand grenade explosion.

Three more men involved in the raid died of their wounds over the next few days. Private Herbert France who had crawled back over No Man's Land was taken to the Operation Centre at Habarcque. He died on 24 May and is now buried in Communal Cemetery there. Private Charles Shergold, wounded in the hand grenade incident, succumbed at a Casualty Clearing Station and is buried at Aubigny Cemetery. Sergeant George Scrivens, who was last seen near the German wire, was found by a patrol out in No Man's Land. This occurred when the battalion were back in K1 front line commencing 29 May. Sergeant Scrivens was found on the night of 31 May/1 June. He had lain for eight days badly wounded, eating grass and daisies to keep alive. He was taken to the Casualty Clearing Station at Aubigny. At first he rallied but sadly he died on 11 June, he also, is buried in the cemetery there.

The first few days back in the trenches were fairly quiet, with just a few men being wounded. On the last day of May, the War Diary entry tells us that the strength of the battalion is now 943, nearly a hundred under strength, and that the C Company front is more lightly held than the others due to the casualties of late. June is heralded in by an increase of trench mortars and more than the usual artillery bombardment. This resulted in two killed and four men wounded in the first two days. On 3 June, the CO, Lieutenant-Colonel Harding returned to England for a short leave. He visited Birmingham where he was the guest of the Lord Mayor and his wife, Mr and Mrs Neville Chamberlain. Whilst in the City he paid a visit to the mother of Captain Gough:

'Mrs Gough had heard her son had been killed, and I was glad to be in a position to assure her that when I left him only a day or two previously he was quite fit, and also I had the pleasure of recording her son's distinguished conduct in the trenches. After leaving Mrs Gough, I went to the Town Hall, where many kind ladies were diligently making and forwarding to France all sorts of useful articles for their City Battalions. I assured them how much their work was appreciated by 'the Boys,' and thanked them on behalf of the Battalion.

'Later I paid one or two visits to the parents of those in my Battalion who were recently killed. This is a sad and painful duty, yet it was a pleasure to find how much my visits to these sorrowful parents were appreciated.'

During this period, Captain Bengough, attached from the Cheshire Regiment, took over command of the battalion. It was under his command that the next significant occurrence in the battalion's history took place. The following is an extract from the history of the 5th Division, published after the war:

'During June, matters became more lively on the front; on the 4th the Germans, having bombarded our position all day, in the evening exploded five mines simultaneously near the Arras-Bailleul road. In the confusion ensuing on this explosion they carried out a raid, and succeeded in penetrating into our line, but were quickly driven off, not, however, without our sustaining some loss; three of these mines

Below: The parents of Private Herbert Brown (No.939, from Station Road, Harborne) who was posted as missing after the trench raid on 23 May, had this published. Copies were probably distributed among relatives, friends and Herbert's former work colleagues.

15th ROYAL WARWICKSHIRE REGT.,
B.E.F.
May 26th, 1916.

Dear Mr. Brown,

It is with deep regret that I have to inform you that your son, Pte. H. A. Brown, 15/939, is "missing."

He was the first man of a party which went out 22/5/16, to raid the German trenches, and when the party came back he was "missing."

He was a very gallant soldier, and by myself and by his comrades will be very deeply missed.

Please accept my very sincere sympathy in your loss.

Yours sincerely,
REG. J. GOUGH,
Captain.
O/C D Coy.,
15th Royal Warwickshire Regt.

———

B.E.F.
May 27th, 1916.

Dear Mrs. Brown,

It is with the greatest regret that I learn that your son, Pte. H. A. Brown, is reported "missing."

He with many others took part in a raid on the German trenches, and nothing more has been heard of him. The party showed great bravery on that night, and everyone of them is considered by all of us as heroes.

Please accept the deepest sympathy of all his platoon comrades and also myself, as his platoon officer.

Yours sincerely,
L. JACKSON,
2nd Lieut.

———

FRANCE,
May 26th, 1916.

Dear Mrs. Brown,

No doubt you've already heard from your son Arch. about the sad end of his brother Herbert.

As his platoon sergeant I should like to offer my heartfelt condolences to you. I, too, miss him very much, as he was one of my best. Really, though I don't think we should give up hope, because although he went over to the German lines as a soldier, no one can say he was wounded. His conduct on that night was fine.

It is poor comfort I know to read the cold word "missing," but we must trust in God to know what is best, although it's so hard at times like this.

Please forgive me if I've put my feelings too bluntly, but I can assure you that a letter of this description becomes no easier with repetition.

Believe me to be,
Yours most sincerely,
C. RONALD WHITE,
Sergeant.

formed huge craters just in front of our original front line, which were afterwards known as 'Cuthbert,' 'Clarence,' and 'Claude,' the names being taken from a song in vogue with the 'Whizz Bangs' at the time.'

German Trench Raid

Sunday 4 June, 1916, was the last day of the present spell of front line duty for the 15th Royal Warwicks. The 2nd KOSBs were due to relieve the battalion during the evening. The weather was glorious and the front line was very quiet, perhaps too quiet. There was none of the usual artillery fire or trench mortars that had been prevalent over the past few days. Most thoughts would be on being relieved and spending the next few days resting and cleaning up. At 4 pm sharp, the Germans started a concentrated bombardment of the battalion's front line (trenches 102 to 110) and that of the 1st Norfolks who were on the right. The bombardment was more intense on the centre stretch of the battalion's front line position (trenches 102 to 107) being held by B Coy. On the left hand fringe of this barrage was C Coy commanded by Captain A C Bill:

'Where the centre Company was, the shelling was terrific and the whole area was obliterated in the smoke of bursting shells and mortar bombs. Our support line and communication trenches were also heavily shelled, and within a few minutes all telephone communication was cut, companies being isolated from the battalion headquarters and the latter from brigade. For three hours we stood in our places and waited while this went on, until 7 p.m. the bombardment suddenly ceased.'

Private H V Drinkwater of A Coy (trenches 102 to 105) was on sentry duty when the bombardment began, and he wrote the following account in his diary on 6 June:

'During the early afternoon got our equipment together and the trench in a state of readiness to hand over immediately the relief arrived, without delay. Precisely at 4 p.m. the Germans opened fire with their artillery on the front line, support and communication trenches. On the right the Norfolks were getting it, on the left I could see B Company trenches going up in the air. I was on sentry at the time and stuck it a few minutes. A shell landed in front and another behind, blowing in the parados and smothering me with dirt. This appeared to be no ordinary bombardment, so I made for a shelter, hopeless if a shell hit it, but useful to stop shrapnel. I found some of the other fellows gathered there, casualties were occurring rapidly and the rain of shells kept coming. Fellows hit were calling for stretcher bearers, at

Below: German 21cm Mortar and crew. Used effectively for dropping shells into entrenched positions.

4.30 pm it was evident we were in for something, the shell fire was furious.

'The trenches, both in the firing line and the supports, were going up in all directions. The passage became blocked and telephone wires broken. We tried to get into communication with Company Headquarters, but could get no reply. It is a thrilling sensation to be in a bombardment because when one knows that the shells are being concentrated on a comparatively small area of ground, dozens at a time, he would be a very bold man who says he doesn't get the wind up. Jones (Private G A Jones, No.211, from Jockey Road, Sutton Coldfield) came into the shelter, badly hit in places. I undressed him and bandaged him up whilst Jinks (Private Philip Jinks, No.1369 of Earls Court Road, Harborne) stood at the exit of the shelter, ready in case the Germans came over. Philip Page, like a brick, kept on going along the trench in spite of the shells, and dragging into cover anyone he could find wounded. Having barely bandaged Jones when Eastwood (Private E G Eastwood, No.156 from Wylde Green, Sutton Coldfield) came rushing in along the sap from the crater (K14 from the 19th May), and gave us to understand that the shelter had been blown in, and the sentry group buried, he was standing in the doorway when the shell landed on the top burying the fellows and blowing him out, he then collapsed. Jinks and I gathered what picks and shovels were lying about, and crawling along on our hands and knees, made along the sap to the crater. We had crawled about fifteen yards when a shell landed on top of the trench, partly burying us, and it was some moments before we could pull ourselves together. I felt the force of the explosion force my head into my body, apparently it was a few seconds before I was able to see. By this time it was impossible to go on, no trench remained in front just a mound of earth thrown up by succeeding shell bursts. To go back was futile, so we crawled to the nearest shelter, by this time the shell fire was augmented by rifle grenades and trench mortars. The ground vibrated with explosions and the air was thick with acrid sulphurous fumes. The shelter consisted of a corrugated iron placed over the top of the trench. We were unable to go backwards or forwards, we appeared fairly in the midst of it. We made the best of it by dragging down bags of earth, against which we crouched in the bottom of the trench, hoping for the best. Occasionally I could feel the supports of the shelter wobble as a shell close by fell and

Above: German Minenwerfer position

exploded, and all the time awful fumes came drifting backwards, fairly choking us. I couldn't recognise Jinks, his face was covered in dirt, so we hung on. We could do nothing else, six o'clock came, shells were still pouring over and I did not for a moment think we should get out of it alive. At seven o'clock it ceased as suddenly as it started.

'We made our way back to the front line

Below: A section of K1 front line after a three hour German artillery bombardment. June 1916. *Birmingham Library Services*

151

dazed, we apparently had forgotten why we had left it, we could not recognise it. It was a series of holes, no real trenches remained. Some fellows were lying about dead, some wounded, some alive, one of whom enquired about the fellows in the shelter. Then I remembered why I had left the line, gathering up what picks we could find, a sergeant and myself crawled back over the top and into the crater. It was a wretched site, young Cooper (Private David Cooper, No.194 of Meadow Hill Road, Kings Norton) *wedged in a doorway, dead, the remainder buried under the shelter. We dug for two hours, uncovered first Patch,*

Below: Another view of the of the results of a three hour bombardment on a section of K1 front line trench. June 1916. *Birmingham Library Services*

then Baker, both dead (Privates Frederick Patch, No.150 from Marchmont Road, Bordesley Green and Oswald Baker, No.15/1584 from Melton Road, Kings Heath). *Sergeant Ashby had some signs of life in him, so, leaving those we could not help, we carried Ashby* (Sergeant F W Ashby, No.110 from Highfield Road, Saltley) *down to the front line, or what remained of it. I handed him over to stretcher bearers and cleaned our rifles for anything that might happen. We were reduced to a handful of men. Page came along. I was very glad to see him alive, also Bates* (Private William Bates, No.296 from Murdock Road, Handsworth) *another Lance Corporal, and we sorted ourselves out, taking what cover remained.'*

By now the trenches in this area, from the front line down to and including the support line had ceased to exist. Parties were put to work straight away to unblock the communication trenches. Telephone lines from each company were cut, information was passed on by runners and in the confusion, incorrect information was being fed into Battalion HQ. Captain Bengough, the acting CO, was informed that apart from the damage all his companies were all right. The real fact was that C Coy on the left had suffered few casualties and minor damage. A Coy on the right had suffered severely and their trenches were partially wrecked. B Company in the centre had been blown to pieces – all its officers casualties and the trenches completely smashed. Captain Bill, OC C Coy, made his way into the shambles of what was B Coy front line to try and make contact:

'I found one of their subalterns with about two sections of men, and he told me that he thought the rest of the Company were all right. It afterwards transpired that he did not know the worst, as he and his handful of men were practically all that were left of the Company. Their line had been completely obliterated, and deep forty-foot dugouts, where most of the officers and men were seeking shelter, had been blown in by eleven inch armour piercing shells and the occupants had been killed and buried.'

The OC of B Coy, Captain Archibald Tatlow (Molineaux Street, Derby) and his second in command Lieutenant John Larkins (from Penns Lane, Sutton Coldfield) were amongst those killed whilst sheltering in these deep dugouts. (The shells that caused this havoc were probably from German Naval Guns.) Meanwhile the OC of A Coy, Captain C W Davis, had managed to make his way back to Battalion HQ. He reported that he had re-organised his Company and they had formed a succession of posts in shell holes along his front, and that they were being strengthened as far as circumstance permitted. Captain Bengough ordered D Coy, who were in reserve, to move up into the support lines to assist in clearing the trenches; with a view to holding the support line where it was still defensible. He also sent up Lieutenant G S F Dale, D Coy (from Lozells Road, Handsworth), the Battalion Bombing Officer, to take over command of what was left of B Coy. Because the concentrated shelling in the area of B Coy was so destructive, Lieutenant Dale did not make it to the front; he lost his direction. Therefore the survivors of B Coy were not able to be re-organised.

When a similar bombardment occurred on 7 May, (previously mentioned) the German artillery sent over sporadic barrages to deter work on repairing the trenches. This was not the German plan of action this time. All remained quiet until 9 pm. Then suddenly the shelling started again, with the same severity as before. Fifteen minutes later the Germans blew three large mines, one in each section of the battalion front. Two of the mines missed their mark and exploded in front of our lines, under what remained of the barbed wire. The third exploded under C Coy's front line in trench 105. Captain Bill of C Coy recalled:

'When I went down the line to find out what had happened I found a huge crater, which could have contained a small house, completely blocking further progress. The mine had gone up directly under the trench. I therefore sent Sergeant Wright (Sergeant R A Wright, No.662 of Haslucks Green Road, Shirley) *to work his way round it and bring me a report as to how the men in the trench beyond were faring. On the way back in the dark he stumbled against a steel helmet and found it was on the head of a man who was buried up to his neck.* (Private W H Trueman, No.596 from Balsall Heath Road) *I gave Wright some men and they managed to extricate Truman and one other man* (Private Frederick Jolly, No.1492 from Neatishead, Norwich), *who were the only survivors of a sentry group which had gone up with the mine.'*

After the mines exploded the German artillery now began to shell the rear communication lines with a mixed barrage of shrapnel and gas shells. A westerly wind was blowing at the time and the gas had little effect. The barrage did catch the 2nd KOSBs near to 'Dead Man's Corner', on the Arras-St Pol Road. Here they suffered thirty men killed as they were making their way to relieve the 15th Royal Warwicks. The intense shelling that was on B Coy front moved back onto the support lines to act as a screen. This was now the signal for the Germans opposite to leave their trenches and assault the entire length of K1 front line position. Private H V Drinkwater in C Coy trenches, continued his account of the second stage of this eventful day:

'They opened up again all along the front with artillery of all calibres, our guns replying with equal ferocity. It was pitch dark and shells were leaving backwards and forwards, shrapnel exploding overhead lit up the trench and by reflections I saw other fellows doing as I was doing, kneeling down against anything that affords protection. This had been going on for some ten minutes when I was conscious of a sudden whirl in the air, and knew the barrage had been lifted from our line onto the support, at the same moment it was shouted along that the Germans were coming over. It will always be a matter of joy to remember how the fellows all thoroughly well shaken, jumped out from their different place of cover and got to business with their rifles. This was our first experience of a bombardment practically to ourselves and well it was stood, in spite of the fact that there was no cover. Each man stuck to his post and blazed away into the darkness. Raper and Middleton (Privates Claud Raper, No.141 from Clapton, London and James Middleton, No.89 from High Park Road, Smethwick) *went down, killed by a rifle grenade, then Jinks hit by another.* (Private P G Jinks, No.1369) *We took him into a shelter, but he was going fast, his leg had been practically blown off. Stayed with him to the end and saw him go west.'*

After the war, Drinkwater wrote further on the death of his comrade, Private Jinks who is now buried in Faubourg D'Amiens Cemetery, Arras:

'We were lying close to each other when the shell or rifle grenade landed close to his legs, and we carried him into a shelter which was nothing more than a sheet of corrugated iron laid over the top of the trench, and on top of which some sandbags had been placed, no protection against anything but shrapnel. Outside the air was livid as shrapnel was bursting very much like flashes of lightning, come and gone in an instant, but coming with great rapidity with its attendant explosion and scattering of bullets. It was amongst this inferno and with the knowledge somewhere not far away the Germans were in our trench and might be along any moment, that I had to render what aid was possible. Probably a hopeless cause under best conditions, here was hopeless, and I could do little else than kneel by his side.'

Within twenty seconds of the three mines exploding, the divisional artillery was in action, and no doubt this must have caused havoc amongst the Germans crossing No Man's Land. By now every man was at his post firing their rifles as fast as they could into the darkness of No Man's Land; around 5,000 rounds would be used by the battalion this night. It was estimated that up to 600 Germans attempted to cross over into our trenches. Those attacking A and C Company's trenches were

Above: Lieutenant John Larkins from Penns Lane, Sutton Coldfield.

Below: Captain Archibald Tatlow from Derby. Both these officers were killed on 4 June 1916 and are buried in Faubourg D'Amiens Cemetery, Arras.

Below: Eighteen year old Private Percy Alfred Antrobus (No.15/1643) who came from Maxstoke near Coleshill, Warwickshire. Killed on 4 June 1916
Geoff Taylor

ROLL OF HONOUR

LANCE-CORPORAL L. F. AND PRIVATE E. J. BROMWICH

Sincere sympathy is being extended to Mr. and Mrs. Wm. Bromwich, of High Street, Sutton Coldfield, in the severe affliction they have sustained in the loss of two of their sons on active service. Both through their family and their employees they have been well represented at the front, and the reflection that they have evidenced such a fine patriotic spirit throughout, should in some measure help to temper the blow that has now fallen on them Of their four sons the three younger were members of the "Only" Battalions. One of them, Corporal Harold Bromwich, after being in hospital for some weeks past is, it is understood, returning home on leave this week. Of the other two, Lance-Corporal Leslie Frank Bromwich has been officially reported as killed in action on June 4, and Private Edgar John (Eddie) Bromwich as missing. While in the case of the latter there is still an absence of official confirmation, intelligence from private sources seems to preclude the least hope that he has escaped the fate of his brother; indeed, letters of sympathy received from some of his old comrades are quite circumstantial in referring to the sad affair. No official statement is available as to how the fatalities occurred, but unofficially it is understood that a mine explosion was primarily responsible.

PRIVATE E. J. BROMWICH.
(Photos by Speight, Sutton Coldfield.)

Private Edgar Bromwich was the elder of the two lads, and the second of the four sons. He was 25 years of age, and immediately prior to enlisting he was assisting his father in his business at Sutton. Formerly, he was for three years in the Sutton office of the Birmingham Gas Department, and three years at the head office in Birmingham. He was an old Grammar School boy, and took a keen interest both in football and swimming

LANCE-CORPORAL L. F. BROMWICH.

Lance-Corporal Leslie Bromwich was the youngest of Mr. W. Bromwich's sons, and was only 19 years of age. From the Sutton Grammar School he passed on to Hanley Castle School, near Worcester, and did remarkably well. He was no less successful in sport than in scholastic work. Twelve months before the war broke out he was articled to Messrs. Squiers and Co., chartered accountants, Colmore Row, and he gave promise of a brilliant career. It is significant of the good opinion both lads enjoyed among their comrades, that one of the latter should now write "We all feel their loss very keenly, but this consoling thought I would offer you—and to my mind it is a great consolation—they both died nobly doing their duty."

repulsed by the intense rifle and machine gun fire. This was greatly assisted by the 14th Royal Warwicks on the left, and the 1st Norfolks on the right. The attackers entered what had been the B Coy front line at trenches 105 and 106. The actual figure of how many Germans entered is not known. They made their way as far as the support lines. They attempted to bomb their way along into A and B Companies' trenches, but were repulsed. From the support lines the raiders then turned left and got behind trench 104. 'The Germans came in on the left, of those that got into our trenches, only a few got out again, they were either bayoneted or bombed', wrote Private Drinkwater of the frightful and gruesome situation the men now found themselves in as friend and foe met face to face.

How long the raiders were in our trenches is not known for sure, but the German artillery barrage slackened off at around 9.40 pm. When they were eventually driven off, they had left behind large numbers of bombs and other equipment, This was probably going to be used for smoking out dugouts and for blowing in mine shafts. Of course there was nothing left to destroy. The earlier barrage in the afternoon had seen to that. The area was in such a state of disarray and confusion, that next morning as day broke, odd Germans were found in the honeycomb of support trenches that were in the sector at the time.

By 11.30 pm on the evening of 4 June, all was quiet. The battalion was at 'stand to' until 1.30 am, 5 June. By 4.30 am the 15th Royal Warwicks had been relieved by the 2nd KOSBs with no further casualties. Private Drinkwater, further added in his diary:

'As we left the trenches in the early hours, we left it a mess of shambles. Most of us possessed pocket torches, and whilst some stood on sentry, others went along the remnants of the trenches looking for wounded. Many we found were dead, they made a frightful sight for the most part. The KOSBs carried on as soon as they arrived and got away what wounded remained.'

The next morning the OC of 13 Infantry Brigade, Brigadier-General L O W Jones, personally inspected the trenches. He later reported 'that he had difficulty in discovering where they ought to have been'. There was also the question of how many prisoners the Germans had managed to take back with them; in the same report the Brigadier was of the opinion that 'most of the unaccounted, would most likely be buried and very few taken prisoner'. Three men of a Lewis Gun team were missing, but the gun was saved. The only piece of equipment missing was a Stokes Mortar, the crew all casualties, taken from the rear of trench 104. The KOSBs with the assistance of men of the Divisional Cyclist Company and others from 95 Brigade, had cleared the front and support lines by daybreak. As much wire as possible was replaced.

In sections of the trenches that were completely devastated, the only shelter the men had were shellholes. The 15th Royal Warwicks on being relieved made their way down to Arras. There they had to stay in the vaults underneath the pre-war Army Barracks. It was the policy that no troops were allowed to use the streets of Arras during daylight hours. Private H V Drinkwater continued in his diary:

'All our rations had gone to Duisans, where we should have arrived the night before. Under these circumstances there is always someone to come and rescue, and in this case it was the Australian and New Zealand miners; within an hour of our arrival, they had dixies of hot tea for us and gave us their spare rations. We stayed there all day and came on here (Duisans) at dark, ending a disastrous period for the battalion.

'We are not a cheery crowd tonight, already most of the fellows have wrapped themselves in their blankets and are fast asleep, with this finished, I will follow suit.'

The next morning, 6 June, the roll was called. B Coy could only muster one officer and thirty-six men. There were still forty-four men unaccounted for.

'The roll call was somewhat pathetic, standing in the open, and as a name was called and unanswered, we had to say if we saw the fellow killed or knew if he had gone down the line wounded', Drinkwater recalled. Later the same day, he continued, 'this evening Kilby (Private F D Kilby, No.72 from Oakwood Road, Sparkhill) asked me to join the Lewis gun section, I shall do so. Of the battalion originals they are most intact. The idea of when the battalion was formed, that friends served together, has long well passed in the last 18 days'.

The total casualty figures for the 15th Royal Warwicks on Sunday June 4th 1916, were:

Officers killed	3
Other ranks Killed	63
Other ranks d.o.w	4
Officers wounded	2
Other ranks wounded	25
Other ranks shell shock	8
Other ranks P.o.w	9
Total	114

Of those men killed or died of wounds, fifty three were from the original volunteers of September 1914. Eight of these still lie to this day, in a collapsed dugout forty foot underneath the ground; these men are named on the Arras Memorial. The others were found and they now lie buried in Faubourg D'Amiens Cemetery at Arras. We have to thank Private Drinkwater for the Prisoner of War figures; writing in his diary after the war, he mentions meeting former acting CSM P C Kennard, who was captured during the raid. (Incidentally, Kennard, like Drinkwater, was from Stratford upon Avon), which caused this following comment:

'He had just returned from Germany, referring to the raid and his capture, he told me he was eventually taken before some German Colonel. When learning that he came from Stratford upon Avon, he said how much he liked the town. He was staying there on holiday a short time before the war broke out. Which may or may not be true, he (Kennard) *was well treated according to the usage of war'*.

Acting CSM Kennard's name appeared in the *Birmingham Daily Post* casualty list, as a PoW, on 19 September 1916, more than four months after he was captured. On the same day, a total of eleven Royal Warwickshire Regiment soldiers' names were released. In theory they could have all been captured on the same day. Two of them have service numbers, completely different from that of the City Battalions and I have therefore ignored them. Five of the remainder were B Coy men, and the other four had numbers corresponding to men who were drafted into the 15th from the 17th (Reserve) Battalion, they were:

By consulting the

Acting CSM Kennard, No.418,
Private W C Allen, No.315
Private P J Davis, No.1465
Private H S Perigo, No.1460
Private H S Pratt, No.442
Private Bolus, No.1703,
Private Boulton, No.1821
Private Jones, No.1589
Private Simms, No,1330

CWGC Register of Faubourg D'Amiens Cemetery,

the average age of those original men who were killed were in the mid twenties, but there were the exceptions, such as Private Ernest Bennitt (No.326 from Harborne), aged forty-three. Then, at the other end of the age scale were the likes of Private Arthur Franklin (No.1497, from Durham Road, Sparkhill), aged eighteen. Even younger were Privates Stanley Holt (No.1187 from Edgbaston) and John Ludlow (No.902 from Langley), who were seventeen. By far the youngest was Private Willoughby Greaves (No.1252 from Tintern Road, Aston) aged sixteen. Young Willoughby, who left his job at the Wolsley Sheep Shearing Company at Witton, had originally enlisted into E Coy of the 14th Royal Warwicks on 27 May 1915, when he must have only been fifteen years old. His father was serving with another regiment on the Western Front at the time. Two brothers were amongst those killed. Both Lance Corporals, they were Edgar and Leslie Bromwich of High Street, Sutton Coldfield. The family Catering business still survives to this day.

On the morning of 8 June, the men of the 15th Royal Warwicks attended a memorial service to their fallen comrades; it was held in an old barn which also doubled up as the divisional cinema hall.

After the service a parade was held in order to hold an enquiry of why several men (those who had been in the thick of the bombardment, and probably in hand-to-hand fighting with the Germans) returned from the front line with a different rifle from the one they were issued with. This would come to light after a kit inspection. Men who did not have their issued rifles had to report to their Company Commanders and explain the reason why. One of those questioned was Private Drinkwater:

Below: A section of K1 front line trench system, photographed after the German trench raid. The mound in the rear middle is the lip of the mine crater that was blown under the trenches held by B Coy, 15th Royal Warwicks on 4 June. *Birmingham Library Services*

Above: A section, this time of, K2 front line trench system. The mound, rear right, is the lip of the mine crater that blew adjacent to trench 111. An excellent picture that depicts a British front line trench. The ledge running along the bottom row of sandbags was the fire-step. The top of the sandbags looking out towards No Man's Land was the parapet. Beyond the sandbags can be seen the barbed wire pickets, supporting the barbed wire. The mound of earth to the right was known as the parados. Then in the middle of the picture, an entrance to a dugout can be seen.
Birmingham Library Services

Right: An unidentified officer of the 15th Royal Warwicks, peeking into No Man's Land, June 1916. The end of the trench has been blocked off and beyond is the mine crater which was blown under B Coy's front line on 4 June.
Birmingham Library Services

'The explanation was that ours either got so hot or dirty whilst firing that we exchanged it for the nearest cool one lying about. He understood all this but he had to hold the enquiry. It gave one the impression that someone didn't understand the war; it was about time such customs were scrapped.'

In the afternoon of 8 June, the battalion was paraded before the GOC of the 5th Division, Major-General R B Stephens; he spoke a few encouraging words and complimented the men on their recent action. Over the next couple of days or so the men were allowed to take it easy. Parades, cleaning of equipment and kit inspections still took place This was so the men did not dwell too much on the loss of so many friends.

On 10 June, the acting CO, Captain Bengough was taken ill and sent to hospital; he was replaced by Major Anderson of the 2nd KOSBs. The following day the battalion prepared to move back to the same front line trenches of K1 and relieve the 2nd KOSBs. The battalion moved back into the front line on the evening of June 11th; B coy, due to the recent casualties, were this time in reserve in trench 40. Two platoons from B Coy, 14th Royal Warwicks (who were in K2 front line trenches), took over a section of the 15th's front line to further assist in making the trenches fully manned. The 2nd KOSBs had worked hard over the previous seven nights. A new front line trench had been dug in front of Clarence, Cuthbert and Claude craters. This was to be the last five days of front line duty

for the battalion, the 5th Division were soon to be relieved. Each night during this tour the battalion sent out wiring parties. A Coy had a wiring party out on the night of 13 June, and were heavily shelled by a German trench mortar battery. Returning safely back to their lines, the party resumed the work the following night.

During the first two days of this tour, a further two men had been killed and three others wounded. The War Diary for these few days reports the situation as very quiet, with just the occasional artillery burst or a Whizz Bang coming over. On June 15th, a Whizz Bang smashed through the parapet and exploded in part of the trench held by A Coy, wounding the Company CO, Captain C W Davis, and three other ranks. Four men were killed outright, Second-Lieutenant William Farley, Corporal Chester Homer (No.87 from Hampstead Road, Handsworth) and Privates Harry Hopkins (No.204 from Harborne) and Vincent Reeve (No.173 from Alcester Road, Moseley). Nearby, when this incident happened, was Private Drinkwater, 'I was in a dugout at the time I heard the explosion; I went up into the trench and saw these fellows lying about, a sickly site when one knows them so well'. The death of the thirty-eight year old, Second-Lieutenant William Farley was another sad blow to the original surviving men of B Coy. Farley had been their CSM throughout their training period until he received his commission on 22 November 1915. Previously, he had served in the ranks of the South Staffordshire Regiment for eighteen years, finishing with the rank of Sergeant. Prior to the war Second-Lieutenant Farley had been a member of the Birmingham Parks Police unit. Buried in

Above: From left to right: Second Lieutenant's C L Jeffery and F C Ball (who appears to be wearing a French steel helmet) and Captain C A Bill in K2 front line, June 1916. Beyond them is the rear lip of one of the mines blown on 4 June.
Birmingham Library Services

Left: Sergeants of D Coy, 15th Royal Warwicks taken towards the end of the battalion's tour of the Arras front. Back row, left to right: G A Perkins, P S Brown, C R White, Unknown.
Middle: T H Philips, E S Braddock (CSM), A Knight.
Front: Sgt W J Greaves, T E Wood
Arthur Knight/ Peggy Carter nee Braddock

157

Above: Most of the 15th Royal Warwick's who were killed at Arras are buried in the Faubourg D'Amiens Cemetery. This photograph is probably the Cemetery in June 1916, showing the graves of some of the men killed on 4 June. The Cemetery was made by the various Field Ambulances who set up nearby. In June 1964, four old comrades of the 15th Royal Warwicks (Tom Buckler, Sidney Dark, Walter Harper and Roland Pritchard) made a pilgrimage back to the Western Front. Their visit was featured in a series of articles published in the *Birmingham Post* in July 1964. In one article, one of them stated that the 15th Royal Warwicks started the Cemetery, and it was the battalion's Padre (Captain C Williams) who consecrated the first plot.

Faubourg D'Amiens Cemetery, he left a wife and four children.

The battalion moved into K1 support trenches on the evening of 16 June, being replaced by the 2nd KOSBs. For the next few days men were supplied for mining duties. By 21 June the 15th Royal Warwicks were at Agnez les Duisans and for the next six days, working parties were found for digging gun emplacements. On 29 June D Coy moved to Crossville were the men were used for carrying ammunition in preparation for the proposed Wailly attack in which the 5th Division was due to assist the 55th Division. After the attack was cancelled the battalion said goodbye to the Arras front on 2 July. On leaving the Arras sector the battalion was two Officers and 187 other ranks below strength. A total of 104 men of the 15th Battalion had been killed or died of wounds during the three months at Arras; Captain Bill of C Coy was to recall:

> *We had come out of the line after our month at Maricourt knowing very little more of active service conditions than when we went in, but in our three months in the Arras Sector we had our baptism in the horrible side of modern war and saw something of its stark ghastliness and hideous cruelty.*

When at Arras we relieved
The French, we were deceived

In the temperature of that delightful spot.
We thought it pretty 'cool,'
But we found Fritz was no fool
For he gave us the best of what he'd got.
He sent over by the score
'Sausages,' and, furthermore,
Other things that were not good to look upon;
And the nicest time by far
Was when we said 'Au Revoir'
To that shell-bespattered crater-strewn K1.

'Ricardo' alias Private R B L Moore,
No.1010, 15th Royal Warwicks

16TH ROYAL WARWICKS (3RD BIRMINGHAM PALS) 15TH INFANTRY BRIGADE

* March 9 – 14, J2 support trenches. (A and D Companies at St Nicholas. B, C and one platoon of A at Arras)
* March 15 – 21, J2 front line.
* March 22nd - 26th, Habarcq in billets, rest and clean up. March 27 – 30, K1 support trenches. (A in St Nicholas, B in Arras plus one platoon of C, C in Observatory and Thelus Redoubts, D in trench 40 and Chalk Farm)
* March 31 – April 3, Front line K1. (A in trenches 102-105, C in 106-109, D in 110-113 and B in support)
* April 4 – 7, K1 support trenches. (A in Observatory and Thelus Redoubts, B in Trench 40 and Chalk Farm. C at St Nicholas and D in Arras)
* April 8 – 11, K1 front line trenches. (A in support, B in 102-105, C in 106-109, D in 110-113)
* April 12 – 19, Habarcq in billets, rest and clean up. The evening of the 19th spent in Arras, readiness to take over trenches. April 20th - 23rd, J1 support trenches. (B and D in support, A, C and HQ in Arras)
* April 24 – 27, J1 front line trenches. (A in 81-83, C in 84-86, D in 87-89. B and HQ in the Oilworks)
* April 28 – May 1, J1 support trenches. (A in Forester Redoubt, C in trench 19, B, D and HQ in Arras)
* May 2 – 5, J1 front line. (B in 81-83, C in 84-86, D in 87-89, one platoon of A with D, one in 'A' works and two platoons in the Oilworks. Two Lewis Gun teams from the battalion in the detached post to the right of trench 81)
* May 6 – 10, Agnez les Duisans, rest and clean up. May 11 – 16, J1 front line. (C in 81-83, B in 84-86, A in 87-89. D in support, Oilworks)
* May 17 – 22, J1 support trenches. (A and HQ in Arras, B in St Nicholas, C in Oilworks and Forester Redoubt, D in Forester, Nicholas and Boskey Redoubts)
* May 23 – 29, J1 front line. (D in 81-83, B in 84-86, A in 87-89. C in support, Oilworks)
* May 30 – June 3, Agnez les Duisans. (D plus twenty men from A and B to Arras)
* June 4 – 5, J1 support trenches.
* June 6 – 13, J1 front line trenches. (C in 81-83, B

in 84-89, A in 90-94, D in reserve. Part of J2 sector was now being covered)
* June 14 – 20, J1 support trenches.
June 21st, Relieved by 10th Durham Light Infantry, 43 Brigade, 14th Division. The battalion then moved to Manin: where, over the following days, most men of the battalion were occupied in the digging and burying of cables along the Dainville-Wailly Road.

The 16th Battalion experience of trench life, on the Arras front, was no different from that of the other two Birmingham Battalions, or in fact from the rest of the division. When not occupying front line trenches, the majority of the men were used most of the time for mining fatigues; a human chain, hundreds of men passing sandbags of spoil, down the line, to be disposed of, out of sight from enemy observation.

Prior to moving into the Arras trenches, the battalion was billeted at Hauteville; and on 7 March a draft of 99 men under the command of Lieutenant J Hamilton arrived from the 17th (Reserve) Battalion back in England. Lieutenant Hamilton, on the formation of the battalion, had enlisted into the ranks (No.876), and was commissioned 2 January, 1915. The few days before going into the trenches, letters would be sent home, requesting food items to supplement their rations and to make life a bit more tolerable. Bandsman Charles Jeffs (No.918) writing

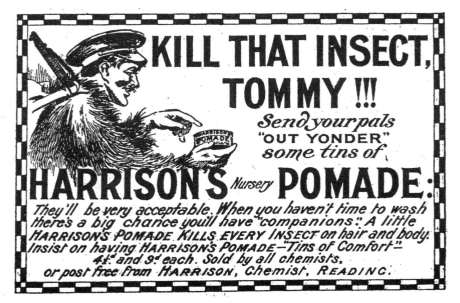

back home to Sutton Coldfield ask his parents to send him, 'a fruit cake, also some Pears soap, and will you get me a fourpence halfpenny tin of Harrisons pommade' and then he underlined the next portion, 'no other vermin killer will do.' The battalion moved into J2 front line on March 15th; writing on the same day, Private J Randle (D Company, No.991), in a letter home stated:

'We are in for twelve days, so I expect to have a rough time. Our Batt (sic) had a draught sent out to them, and the lot that came only look youngsters, I feel sorry for them myself, especially

Left: Three men of the 16th Royal Warwicks photographed on the rubble adjacent to the Hotel de Ville (Town Hall) in Arras; a favourite haunt of French photographers. Seated in the middle is Private Frank Brazier, No.770, D Coy, 13 Platoon, from Yardley Wood Road, Moseley. Note the fashion of attaching their cap-badge to the cover of their steel helmet.

Left above: Private Charles Jeffs, No.918, D Coy, 14 Platoon
Irene Ducker

Left, below: Flea infestation was rife amongst men in the trenches. Running a candle flame along the seams of uniforms and underclothing; thus killing the eggs was a favourite pastime for off duty troops. Others tried 'Harrisons Pomade', sent from home, like Private Charles Jeffs. This may be an 'Old Soldiers' story, but I have heard that fleas loved this ointment and thrived upon it!

Above: Hotel de Ville, Arras, prior to the war.

Below: The same building, circa 1916

Below: Private Frank Arthur Newey, No.957, D Coy, 15 Platoon, 16th Royal Warwicks. From Talbot Road, Bearwood. Awarded the Military Medal aged seventeen.

one. He was on rations carrying with me to the firing line, when a shot hit a pal, and he fainted. I only wish I could stop one like it, you know a Blithy (sic) one that would keep me in England for about three months. What makes the people think the war is going to be over soon, if they were out here, they might change their opinion. My friends and myself are out to get a D.C.M., the one it will be is a District Court Martial, so keep a smart look out in the papers.'

On the same day as writing the above letter, the battalion suffered its first casualties on the Arras front. Two men were wounded and Private F W Pegrum (No.961, D Company, 15 Platoon) was killed; the effects of German rifle grenades. Within two more days, another seven men had been wounded by the same devices. On the evening of 21 March, the battalion was relieved by the 1st D.C.L.I. of 95 Brigade. Before being relieved the battalion suffered one more casualty, when Private J W Knight (No.178) was wounded by what was known as an Aerial Torpedo. Private Knight, from Wednesbury, on recovery, was drafted back into the 2nd Royal Warwicks, and was killed during the Battle of Bullecourt, 4 May, 1917.

The battalion spent the next four days out of the line at Habarcq; on the eve of returning to the line Bandsman C H Jeffs, writing home, seemed full of optimism, 'The war is looking very bright for us, and they all seem to think the end of the summer will see the last of it.' On 27 March, the battalion returned, this time, to K1 support trenches; having relieved the 2nd KOSBs. On 30 March, four men from C Company were wounded by shellfire whilst in Observatory Redoubt. The next day the battalion took over from the 1st Norfolks in the front line. In this tour of the front line, lasting four days, took place the death, by sniper fire, of Private Leonard Byewater (No.16/1590). Born in Stroud, Gloucestershire, he and his twin brother, Arthur, were living in Aston when they both enlisted into the depot company of the battalion.

First Decorations for the City Battalions

The next front line spell commenced on 8 April, again in K1. Two days later on the 10th, German Trench-Mortars accounted for six casualties from D Company; three men were killed, they were: Privates L Hicks (No.893), R H Patterson (No.1166) and R G Salmon (No.1011). On the same day two acts of bravery occurred, which resulted in Privates F A Newey (No.957) and J E Kelly (No.1300), both being awarded the Military Medal. There is no mention in the war diary for any heroic action on this day, (in fact the compiler of the battalion war diary on the Arras front, was a man of few words) but on the battalion's next tour of front line duty, commencing 24 April, this time in J1 sector, was the following statement: 'The C in C awards the Military Medal to 957 Newey, 1300 Kelly.'

D Company were in trenches 110-113 at the time, and the feat of bravery came about as Newey and Kelly both went into No Man's Land in broad daylight, under heavy and concentrated machine-gun and rifle fire, to assist a wounded comrade; rendered first aid, and after several hours, brought him back to our lines.

Private Frank Arthur Newey from Bearwood, was only seventeen years old at the time the incident occurred; he was only just turned sixteen when he enlisted into the battalion on its formation. He was presented with his medal by the G O C 5th Division, Major-General R B Stevens DSO, when the battalion was out of the line, at Agnez les Duisans, on 31 May. He said, 'there were many gallant acts done in the front line trenches, which unfortunately, were never brought to light, and the decorations reflected not only on the men but also the whole battalion.' He also expressed 'his appreciation of the excellent way the battalion had acted in the past and his confidence in the readiness with which they would respond to any future call'. Private Kelly was not mentioned by the General, nor is he mentioned in the article about Private Newey, published in the *Birmingham Daily Mail* on 5 June. We know Kelly was wounded, because he received his medal from Lieutenant-Colonel Diver, the CO of No.1 Convalescent Camp, back at Sutton Park. In a picture published he is seen with his arm in a sling. Writing home to his girlfriend Ethel, on 1 May, Private Jim Randle, gives us a better observation of why a man should not be out in No Man's Land in broad daylight:

'The first honours for the City B's came to our battalion. Two Military Medals, higher than DCMs, [which they were not in fact] both of them in my platoon. One is a great friend of mine. I think you have seen him on the station (Snow Hill) when I had a weekend. Do you remember a crowd of boys round a girl one Sunday night on the station? Come to see one of the boys off, he got in my carriage, only a youth about 17. Artful bounder not quite so innocent as myself, what a reception they will get when they reach Brum. There was one out on the top looking for souvenirs, when he got hit, of course these two went and dressed his wound under fire, when one of them got shot through the arm (Private Kelly), he stayed with him for three hours and bullets were whizzing over him all the time, what a sensation for him, one bullet blew a button off his tunic and ripped his jersey. I have given up looking for souvenirs myself, it is not worth risking your head for bits of iron. Two or three of us go over every night, when it is dark, to see if there is any

Germans out working, of course we are safer out on top, than in the trench at night.'

On 25 April, the D Company Lewis Gun position which was sited in trench 87, received a direct hit from a German 77mm shell; luckily no one was killed, but two men were wounded. One of these was the Adjutant, Lieutenant Marcel J Martin; he had enlisted into the battalion (No.944) on its formation, and was commissioned in January 1915. Two days later, on the 27th, there was a joint divisional artillery and trench mortar battery operation on a suspect German Minenwerfer position opposite the trenches that the 16th Royal Warwicks were holding. Whilst the bombardment was in progress all the men, except sentries, withdrew from the front line trenches 81-83, back to the support lines. This was done as a precaution, in case of a German counter-barrage; which of course happened. The Germans retaliated strongly with high explosive, shrapnel and trench-mortars. The battalion's front line trenches were soon pretty badly knocked about, especially in the area around trench 82 and February Avenue. Twenty three year old, Private Reginald Hands (No.41), from Sommerville Road, Small Heath, was killed by a direct hit; four other men were wounded, whilst another was evacuated with shell shock. On the evening of the same day, the battalion was relieved by the 1st Norfolks, and then it took over J1 reserve lines, and the men for the following five days would be used for mining fatigues. The battalion returned again to the same front line trenches on 2 May, the next day there was another joint operation bombardment upon a German position known as 'Six Arbres'; this

time 15 Brigade trench-mortar battery was assisted by French heavy artillery. The war diary states that 'the shooting was good and much damage occurred', the Germans retaliated once again, but little damage was done.

The battalion was relieved on the evening of 5 May, and the next five days was spent at Agnez les Duisans. On the 9th a successful battalion sports meeting was held; the weather was bad, in a letter home Private Jim Randle commented, 'there was plenty of good English beer knocking about'. One can imagine, a good time was had by all. J1 was again the section of trenches the battalion returned to on 11 May, this time for a nineteen day tour, twice in the front line and once in support. On the 18th an interpreter, by the name of Maurice de Lubersac, was attached to the battalion. On the 20th, the war diary reports that Private A Gibbs (No.1213) was returned to base on account of his age being only eighteen; yet only the previous month Private Newey had won the Military Medal whilst seventeen. Newey, as previously stated, returned back to Birmingham, and was there for his eighteenth birthday, but he had returned to the battalion with no questions asked. Two months later Private Newey was wounded in the fighting around Longueval on the Somme. The battalion was back in the front line again on 23 May, the next day shellfire accounted for another six men wounded whilst Private Tranter (No.1019) was wounded by sniper fire. During the early hours of the 26th, the detached post near to the river Scarpe, south of January Avenue, dispersed a German patrol out in No Man's Land. Afterwards a patrol from D Company discovered a German hat, which denoted

Above: A group NCOs from the 16th Royal Warwicks, photographed amid the rubble of the Hotel de Ville, Arras, May/June1916. Unfortunately, I cannot put names to faces. The book *The Birmingham City Battalions Book of Honour*, contains a photograph of every platoon of all three battalions, with a list of names. However, it does not tell you where the men are seated. Most of the Sergeants pictured above are featured in the book and belong to D Coy, but their names cannot be pinpointed.
Gwyneth Pearman/Chris Coogan

Above: Sergeant Thomas Cooks, No.1107, D Coy, 13 Platoon, 16th Royal Warwicks. After an artillery bombardment, during May 1916, he was hospitalised with concussion of the spine. After the war, Sergeant Cooks lived at Billesley Lane, Kings Heath.
Ray Westlake Archives

Below: Private Frederick Jones, No.16/1616, from Aston. He was wounded whilst the battalion was in the J1 trench sector in June 1916. He eventually died from his wounds on 3 February 1918 and is buried in Witton Cemetery, Birmingham.

Above: Private Edward Hughes, No. 905, D Coy, 14 Platoon, 16th Royal Warwicks. Wounded in June 1916 at Arras. On recovery he was posted to the 10th Royal Warwicks, and whilst serving with them was killed in action on 10 April 1918. He is now commemorated on the Tyne Cot Memorial. Private Hughes, who came from Small Heath, worked in the DC Test Room of Chamberlain & Hookham, New Bartholomew Street, Birmingham.

the previous owner had belonged to the Bavarian Infantry. (Opposite the British 5th Division at the time was the 1st Bavarian Division.) The battalion was relieved on 29 May by the 1st Bedfords; the majority of the battalion went back to Agnez les Duisans, but D Company, plus twenty men from A and B, made their way to Arras. This was probably for the award ceremony of the Military Medal, given to Private Newey, that occurred on 31 May, by the G O C 5th Division.

The five days spent at Agnez were so quiet, that they did not rate a mention in the daily war diary; except for Thursday 1 June, there is a mention that the battalion horse show took place at 3 pm. The battalion was now approaching its last tour of duty on the Arras front, for 1916. On the evening of 4 June, whilst the 15th Royal Warwicks were being heavily shelled, the battalion was due to relieve the 1st Cheshires in the support lines of J1 sector. The battalion was moving up the St Pol-Arras Road when the mines exploded in front of the 15th Battalion's trenches; the road came under heavy shellfire, fortunately no one was injured and the relief continued unhindered. Two days only were spent in the support lines, and on 6 June the battalion took over the front line of J1. The same day, the CO of the battalion, Lieutenant-Colonel A C De Trafford, left to take over command of the 15th (Reserve) Battalion, of the East Yorkshire Regiment, which was stationed at Seaton Delaval, near Whitley Bay, on the North East coast.

Back in the trenches, the weather was glorious, and the mud was now gone, it gave the men a different outlook on life. The 16th Royal Warwicks had so far lost the least men of the three Birmingham Battalions since arriving in France; they had not gone through the nightmare which the 15th Battalion had suffered. So after six months of cold and muddy conditions, working as navvies instead of soldiering, the change in weather, was a chance for them to get out of the trenches, do some fighting and get the war over with. This I think is apparent in the letter written to his girlfriend Ethel, by Private Jim Randle of D company; it was posted on 6 June:

Just a line to let you know I am amongst the land of the living. I have been very busy doing one thing and another, that I have had no time to write, but as long as you get an F.C. (Field Service Post Card) you'll know I am still merry and bright. There are one or two of us who keep smiling and no German will knock the smile off, if we can help it, and we are bursting for a good scrap, just to see what it's like.

'There's things happening out here we are not allowed to mention, because the people around Birmingham might get the wind up, (perhaps Jim is referring to the 15th Battalion losing so many men) *and feel sorry for us. It's been a fine war this last day or two, all of us are having a glorious time, as I always said, there were better days in store for us.'*

On 8 June, the Germans bombarded the front line positions very heavily using Trench-Mortars, but it soon stopped when the divisional artillery took retaliatory action. No casualties occurred during this bombardment, but Private B Edwards (No.1226, D Company) was accidentally shot by Sergeant L Bryan (No.771, D Company), whilst he was unloading his rifle. Around 9 pm on the same day a German aeroplane flew low over the front line positions, machine-gun and rifle fire blazed away at it, but it continued safely back to the German lines. On the evening of 10 June a seven man patrol from A Company went out into No Man's Land under the command of Lieutenant John de Reimer Phillip. They were out for nearly two hours, and got to within 30 yards of the German wire, before all returned safely to our lines. On the evening of the 13 June the battalion was relieved by 1st Bedfords, and moved into the reserve lines of J1. The next evening at 11 pm the BEF adopted 'British Summer Time' and the clocks were put forward one hour. On the 16 June, the last man to be killed, whilst the battalion was on this tour of the Arras front occurred. Private Arthur Bywater (No.16/1575) was shot by a sniper, he was the twin brother of Leonard, who was killed two months earlier in the same fashion.

The 10th (Service) Battalion, Durham Light Infantry, who were in 43 Brigade of the 14th (Light) Division, moved into the line on 20 June. HQ and D Company of the 16th Royal Warwicks were the first to be relieved; moving to billets for the night in the villages of St Quentin and Lattre. B Company remained in the Redoubt line of J1, whilst A and C Companies were still labouring away on mining fatigues. The next day, all companies of the battalion regrouped around the village of Manin.

The total casualties of the 16th Royal Warwicks whilst on the Arras front amounted to: nine killed in action, two died of wounds, one died of sickness, and forty-one wounded, a total of fifty-three men. The 16th, during the early days of training, had fewer of the original volunteers commissioned, and in the first seven months on the Western Front, had so far sustained the least casualties. Therefore, as the 5th Division prepared to leave the Arras front, of the three Birmingham Battalions, the 16th was still predominantly made up of original volunteers from October 1914. On 27 June the battalion marched to Wanquentin, and around 700 men daily, spent the last three days of the month burying cables along the Dainville-Wailly Road; whilst further south, the biggest bloodbath in the history of the British Army was about to start...THE SOMME.

Chapter Seven

The Somme: July to October 1916

Background to the Somme offensive

During December 1915, a military conference took place between the British and French High Commands. The main topic on the agenda was the whereabouts for the next major Allied offensive on the Western Front. Both sides were in full agreement that a joint large scale attack should take place. But where? Haig favoured the Ypres front. The preferred area for the French, and the one decided on, was that astride the River Somme; where the two Armies met. However in February 1916, the German Army took the initiative and launched a major offensive on the French lines surrounding Verdun. Since the beginning of the war France had lost considerable territory to the Germans and was determined to hold Verdun at all costs despite the terrible loss of life which would occur. Consequently, the proposed plans for the joint British and French offensive on the Somme had to be modified. The prediction by the French High Command was that their army could hold Verdun until June 1916, at the latest. The only answer was a smaller offensive, still on the Somme, but with the British forces bearing the main thrust of the attack.

By 1916 The British Expeditionary Force in France and Belgium was of a completely different calibre from that which had landed in August 1914. By mid-1916 the British Army was composed mostly of volunteers. who, prior to the outbreak of war, were untrained in the use of arms. Apart from the Regular and Territorial Divisions, there were now twenty-five 'New Army' Divisions serving on the Western Front. Therefore, with this lack of experience in mind, the British High Command decided that a prolonged and concentrated artillery bombardment (lasting days) would devastate the German lines. Thus, the inexperienced British troops would only have to walk across No Man's Land meeting minimal resistance whilst 'mopping up'. The plan involved a combined assault by the British Fourth and French Sixth Armies from the village of Chilly, south of the River Somme northwards to the village of Serre; a straight line distance of around 22 miles. (The actual front line distance was a lot more, if you take

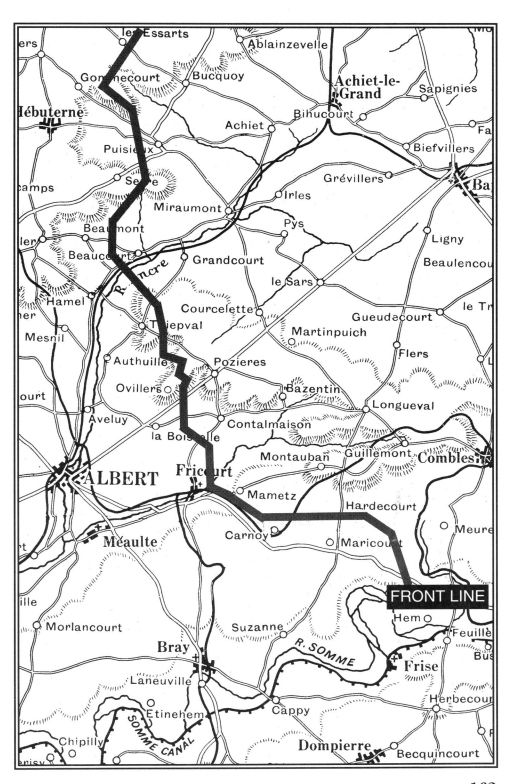

into account the meandering trench system). There was also to be a diversionary attack involving two Divisions of the British Third Army. This was to take place approximately a mile North of Serre, at Gommecourt. If all went well and a breakthrough occurred, three British Cavalry Divisions would be ready to exploit the open ground towards Bapaume and push the Germans back towards Arras. Whilst to the south, if all went to plan, the French would be giving flanking cover to the British.

The British front to be assaulted, by General Rawlinson's Fourth Army, was from Serre down to Maricourt; around eighteen miles in trench length. Twelve British divisions would be used for the attack; four of these were Regular Army, whilst the other eight were New Army divisions. The Third Army diversionary attack on Gommecourt was to be made by two Territorial divisions. Lord Kitchener never found out how his volunteer new army would fare; heading a military mission to Russia, he died on June 5th 1916, whilst a passenger on HMS *Hampshire*. The cruiser was near to the Orkney Islands, when it struck a mine and sank with nearly all hands.

As previously stated, the British plan was kept quite simple. One-and-a-half million shells of various calibres would saturate the German lines over a five day bombardment. Then, a few minutes before zero hour, a series of mines would be blown under the German lines. It was estimated that all the infantry had to do was walk across No Man's Land at a steady pace, mop up and consolidate the captured trenches. Meanwhile, the artillery would then turn their attention to the German second line, and then the German third line. The infantry following up each time until the envisaged breakthrough occurred. Then it would be the turn of the Cavalry to exploit the open ground beyond.

The plan was simple, but did not take into account the deepness of the German dugouts. The bombardment suffered by the German troops was horrendous and terrifying, but they survived. For those men chosen for sentry duty, up above in the trenches, it meant almost certain death. After such a heavy bombardment it was thought that the German barbed wire would be completely destroyed, but, in most parts it was still intact.

At 07.30, 1 July 1916, the Battle of the Somme began. It was a beautiful summer morning. For a few seconds all went quiet; the artillery had ceased briefly whilst adjusting sights before continuing the barrage on the German second lines. Along the British Front all that could be heard was the sound of whistles; the signal to climb out of the trenches and make for the German lines opposite. But thanks to their deep dugouts the Germans were waiting. After being subjected to the most horrific bombardment in the war, so far, they were out to seek amends. Hundreds of machine guns, along the German front, were hauled up from the safety of the dugouts and brought into position as zero hour approached. Poised and ready to wreak death

amongst the estimated 100,000 British Troops soon to move forward. As our men left their trenches the German machine guns were soon brought into action. To make matters worse, No Man's Land was by now pitted with hundreds of shell holes; making the crossing slower and themselves easier targets. Those who got across, then encountered the un-cut German barbed wire. Here, they met withering rifle fire from men who had spent the last few days in hell; no mercy was shown to those 'Tommies' entangled in the barbed wire. On this day, the largest loss of life sustained in the history of the British Army, took place. Probably within thirty minutes or so of zero hour, the best part of the 20,000 men had been killed, and around 36,000 wounded.

There was a slight success on 1 July, the German positions at Mametz and Montauban were taken. In fact these were the German lines overlooking the trenches occupied by the Birmingham Pals, when they were introduced to trench warfare the previous December. It was here that the Birmingham Battalions were destined to return in the near future.

Birmingham's Territorials on Saturday 1 July

A mention here, must be made concerning the fate of two other 'Birmingham Battalions', on the morning of 1 July; the 1/8th and 1/6th Territorial battalions of the Royal Warwickshire Regiment. Being Territorials, these battalions were composed mostly of Birmingham men. The 1/6th along with the 1/5th, shared the same drill hall in Thorp Street, Birmingham, whilst the 1/8th were based at the drill hall in Nelson Road, Aston: a stone's throw from the Villa ground. The 1/7th were based in Coventry but many of the recruits came from all parts of Warwickshire. These four territorial battalions formed 143 Infantry Brigade of the 48th (South Midland) Division.

For the opening day of the Somme offensive, the 48th Division was part of VIII Corps of the British Fourth Army. The Division was manning the line between Gommecourt and Serre. On this part of the Somme front there was no attack on 1 July. The 1/6th and 1/8th Royal Warwicks were temporarily attached to 11 Brigade of the 4th Division; which was to attack over the area of ground known as the Redan Ridge. This area lay between the hamlets of Serre and Beaumont Hamel. The formidable German strongpoint known as the Quadrilateral lay before the 1/6 and 1/8th Warwicks (The Quadrilateral or as the Germans called it the *HeidenKopf*, was in the land now occupied by the largest cemetery on the Somme, Serre Road No.2) To the right of the 4th Division, was the 29th Division, whose objective was Beaumont Hamel (now the site of the Newfoundland Memorial Park). On the left of the 4th Division was the 31st, whose

attack on Serre has been painstakingly researched and documented in earlier 'Pals' histories of this series. The 1/8th Warwicks were in the first waves to go over. Off they set, three paces apart, rifles at the port with bayonets fixed. A few minutes later it was the turn of the 1/6th Royal Warwicks. On the sixth anniversary of the opening day of the battle, the following account was written in the *Birmingham Daily Mail*:

'The 1/8th Battalion leapt forward from the front line. Seven minutes later and the four companies of the 1/6th Battalion were following them over No Man's Land. Already the ranks were decimated by shells and machine guns. The 1/8th took what was left of the German front and support lines; together the two battalions reached the third line and the near edge of the Quadrilateral. On the left the 31st Division were hung up below Serre. Munich Trench on the right was unattainable to the rest of the 4th Division.

'The Battalions made good their objectives, the Quadrilateral and the cutting beyond. By 11 am 2nd Lt J G Cooper was the only officer of the 1/6th Battalion untouched, and a dwindling handful of men of the 1/6th and 1/8th was left amongst the heaps of dead and dying to man the Quadrilateral against counter-attacks from both flanks and the crossfire of the German machine guns. It was useless to remain, impossible to go forward.

'In the evening the 'Battalions' were ordered to withdraw to their old lines. Four companies by sunset (1/6th) were reduced to the strength of two weak platoons. The Brigadier of the 11th Infantry Brigade, General Prowse, whilst lying mortally wounded, spoke the epitaph of the 1/6th and 1/8th Battalions: "I did not before think much of Territorials, but by God, they can fight."'

The 1/8th Royal Warwicks suffered in total 588 casualties, one of those killed was the CO of the battalion Lieutenant-Colonel E A Innes; whilst the 1/6th suffered 457 in total. In the attack, 170 men of the 1/8th and 110 men of the 1/6th were never found; they are now named on the Thiepval Memorial.

Before resuming the history of the Birmingham Pals, it may be of interest to know that six of the original volunteers to the 14th Royal Warwicks, who were commissioned during their early days of training, were killed on July 1st, they were:

588 Ferdinand Eglington, Captain, 1/5th South Staffs from Newton Row, Sparkhill.

236 Frank Fawcett, Second-Lieutenant, 1/5th South Staffs from Clarence Road, Moseley.

234 Francis Freeman, Second-Lieutenant, 19th Lancs Fusiliers (3rd Salford Pals) from Gillot Road, Edgbaston.

399 William Furse, Second-Lieutenant, 21st Northumberland Fusiliers from School Road, Moseley.

175 Horace Jones, Second-Lieutenant, 1/6th North Staffs.

764 William Sanby, Second-Lieutenant, 20th Northumberland Fusiliers from Hazelwell Hall, Kings Heath.

One other former volunteer to the 1st Birmingham Battalion died of wounds on 1 July; but he was not serving on the Somme front at the time. He was Second-Lieutenant Alfred Neuman (formerly No.812, from Doris Road, Small Heath)

Above: Beaumont Hamel, Royal Warwicks Resting: Saturday 1 July 1916. Beaumont Hamel was in German Hands until November 1916. On 1 July the northern end of the village was part of the objective of the British 4th Division, which included the 1st Royal Warwicks in 10 Brigade. The 1/6th and 1/8th Royal Warwicks were also attached to the 4th Division for the attack upon the Quadrilateral Redoubt, further north of the village. The soldier lying on his back fourth from the right appears to have a horizontal battlefield identification patch sewn onto the canvas cover of his steel helmet. Thus with the help of Mike Chappell's book, *British Battle Insignia 1914-18* published in the Osprey, Men-at-Arms Series, I believe the patch to be green. Therefore, this is a section of men from the 1st Royal Warwicks. The man third from left has a Royal Warwicks cap-badge on his helmet. The soldier 4th from left is wearing shorts, this helped ease the irritation caused by fleas in the crease of the trouser behind the knee. Second from right is wearing a blue and white signaller's brassard. His signalling implement is on the ground underneath a rifle.
IWM Q733

of the 12th South Wales Borderers, 40th Division. The incident happened during a practice session throwing hand grenades. One was accidentally dropped, Second-Lieutenant Neuman quickly picked it up, but the grenade exploded before he had a chance to throw it away. Prior to the war, Alfred worked for the Birmingham Education Department and was a former pupil of King Edward's School, Camp Hill. Alfred is buried in Marles Les Mines Communal Cemetery.

The first day of July also happened to be the twenty-fourth birthday of Lieutenant Alan Furse of the 14th Royal Warwicks. His brother William was killed on that day; the following is his account of this day, written after the war:

> 'I gave a little dinner at the mess we had, in honour of my birthday and we really had a topping evening. The occupants of the farm came in and drank my health, although a little bewildered by the tremendous gun firing which could be heard. This was, of course, the commencement of the great Somme show, (over forty miles away!) and little did I know, as I celebrated my birthday, well into the morning of the 2 July, that my best pal had gone to his long rest, and there was lost the whitest man I ever knew.'

It was 7 July, the 14th Royal Warwicks were still billeted at Magnicourt when Lieutenant Alan Furse received the telegram from home, telling him of his brother's death. On 1 July, Second-Lieutenant William Furse, had been attached to the Trench Mortar Battery of 102 (Tyneside Scottish) Brigade, 34th Division. The objective of this Brigade was the village of La Boisselle; here the opposing trenches were so close together, that No Man's Land was a mass of overlapping shell holes, known as the 'Glory Hole'. After the initial attack, Second-Lieutenant William Furse, with the rest of his Trench Mortar Battery, were making their way across No Man's Land, their object being to set up the battery in the captured German trenches. Apparently William stopped to light his pipe, and was then hit by a stray bullet and mortally wounded. He was taken back to the British lines, but soon died. Alan Furse found out from William's former comrades that he had been buried near to where he fell. Over the following couple of weeks, Alan tried to establish the exact spot with a view to visiting the grave if he had the chance.

5th Division returns to the Somme

For the first two weeks of July the 5th Division remained part of GHQ reserve, and all battalions of the division underwent a period of general training, with many tactical exercises being carried out. On July 2nd, the 14th Royal Warwicks were by now billeted around the village of Magnicourt, and it was here the battalion was inspected by the divisional GOC, Major-General R B Stephens. Afterwards he told them of the success and breakthrough near the Battalion's old sector in front of Carnoy. There was no mention concerning the 5th Division moving south at present. The 14th Royal Warwicks were still preparing for the proposed attack at Wailly, which had now been re-scheduled. Apart from telling the battalion the present situation on the Somme Front, the General also gave the men a pep talk of the proposed attack on Wailly. Sergeant Arthur Cooper of the 14th Royal Warwicks wrote the following concerning the General's visit in his diary entry on 2 July:

> 'He told us that our battalion, with another one, were chosen to do the good work for our Brigade. He is very nice and is sure that we shall jolly well kick the jolly Boche out of the jolly trenches into jolly kingdom come. He's jolly well right too and he is a jolly fellow.'

Preparations for what was known as the 'Wailly Stunt' continued until 13 July. In this period the Division was under orders to be ready to move at three hours notice. On this date the 16th Warwicks were issued orders to march to the village of Berneville, which was near to the Wailly positions. This order was suddenly cancelled and the battalion was to be prepared to move at a minute's notice. Orders had come through. The 5th Division was to move to the Somme as quickly as possible. Throughout the division all surplus kit and excess baggage was reduced to a minimum, and by the early evening of 13 July, the 5th Division started to march south, towards the never ending rumble of the guns of the Somme.

The weather was hot and the roads dusty, but the division meandered southwards in a series of night marches, which made the going more pleasant. Nevertheless, the going was still severe. During this march south, 13 Infantry Brigade on its own (which included the 14th and 15th Warwicks), with all its transport, occupied three miles of road. Lorries motored up and down the roads, picking up those who fell out. Forty-five miles were covered in forty-five consecutive hours. By 16 July, the 5th Division had deployed around the area of Lahoussoye-Bresle-Ribemont-Heilly, a few miles south west of Albert. Rumours had been circulating throughout the division that a break through by Cavalry had occurred near Bazentin. 'Visions of chasing a defeated foe over open country arose, only to be shattered later by the news of the actual situation,' wrote Brigadier General Hussey in *The 5th Division in the Great War*.

To explain how these rumours began also gives a better background picture to how and where the 5th Division and the Birmingham Pals would be involved in the Somme battles of 1916. Since 1 July, the front line from Ovillers up to Serre had remained the same. It was the gains from 1 July, from La Boiselle to Maricourt that were by now

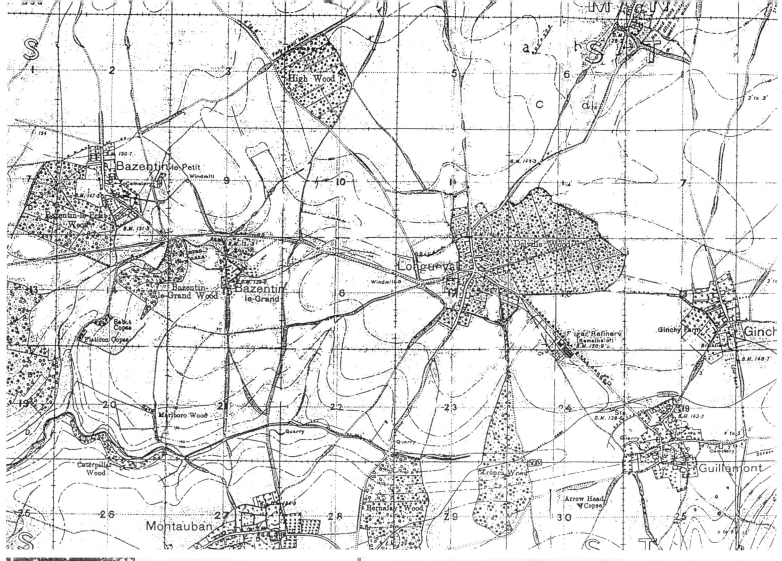

being

Above: The area of the Somme, the 5th Division and the Birmingham Pals would soon be heading for.

Left: German PoWs repairing a road, whilst a long column of British troops march by. On leaving the Arras Front, 13 Brigade, which included the 14th and 15th Royal Warwicks, occupied three miles of road, during the march to the Somme battlefront. *IWM Q3909*

exploited and German positions were slowly being pushed back. At dawn on 14 July, 22,000 men of the XIII and XV Corps of the British Fourth Army launched an attack upon a 6000 yard frontage of the main German second line trench system, from Bazentin le Petit to Trones Wood. Similar to the tactics of 1 July, three cavalry divisions, would be ready to break through and secure three objectives:

2nd Indian Cavalry Division, High Wood; 1st Cavalry Division, Leuze Wood: 3rd Cavalry Division, Martinpuich.

Lessons had been learnt since the tragic losses incurred on 1 July. On this attack there was to be no prolonged artillery barrage, just a five minute concentrated bombardment from all available guns, beginning five minutes before zero hour. During the hours of darkness the six attacking Brigades,

167

Right: Walking wounded, Dernancourt July 1916. Two miles south-west of Albert, the village of Dernancourt became the location of many Divisional Field Ambulance Units. The main railway line nearby, was used to evacuate wounded to the coastal hospitals at Etaples or back to England. When the 5th Division returned to the Somme in July 1916, the 13th Field Ambulance ran the XV Corps MDS for lying wounded in Dernancourt. The 14th Field Ambulance ran the MDS for walking wounded near the village of Becordel and the 15th Field Ambulance the ADS on the Mametz – Montauban Road.

Below: A map showing how the Battle of Bazentin Ridge progressed prior to the 5th Division moving into the line on 19 July.

consisting of 22,000 men plus supporting troops, had assembled in secrecy in No Man's Land, approximately 500 yards from the German trenches. No alarm by the Germans had been raised, and hardly any casualties occurred on the British side. At 03.00 am, further north across the River Ancre, the 4th and 48th Divisions discharged smoke as a diversionary tactic. As zero hour approached, some battalions began crawling closer to the German trenches. The attack went to plan, and the Germans offered minimal resistance and by 10 am the British had taken a salient of 6000 yards of what was known as the Bazentin Ridge. The objectives on the right, Longueval and Delville Wood, were the only stumbling block of the day. The Germans were very strongly fortified here, resulting in only a small area of Longueval being taken.

The Germans had now retreated to a partially constructed trench system known as the Switch Line. This line passed through the north-eastern corner of High Wood. From the newly captured Bazentin Ridge, the British troops now occupying the former German trenches had an excellent view of High Wood; and for the time being it looked deserted. During the morning of 14 July, senior

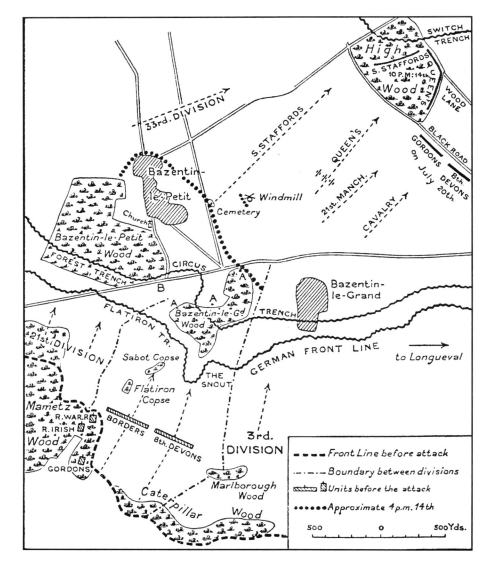

British staff officers walked up the slopes towards High Wood, with no German troops seen or any shots fired at them. The Wood had hardly been shelled, so its appearance would be almost as it looks now. In fact, an artillery Forward Observation Officer belonging to the 7th Division, Second-Lieutenant Probert, took a few 'pot-shots' at some large water tanks high up in the trees that were used for observation purposes. 'They gave a very pleasant resonance when I fired my revolver into them to see if there was anyone at home', he would later recall.

Fresh British troops were on hand ready to exploit the situation. Sadly, this never happened, the infantry were ordered to remain on the ridge whilst the cavalry would be called up to take High Wood. Two regiments of the 2nd Indian Cavalry Division were ordered up to High Wood, early on the morning of 14 July. They were the British 7th (Princess Royal's) Dragoon Guards and the Indian 20th Deccan Horse. But this took time, patrols from the cavalry had to reconnoitre the best route towards High Wood, taking into account that most of the way the ground was littered with shell craters and strewn with old trenches. The cavalry would not get to the captured ridge until late afternoon; thus giving the Germans enough time to sort themselves out and prepare for any more attacks. As the cavalry moved up through the support lines one squadron each of the 7th Dragoon Guards and the 20th Deccan Horse were seen to be still carrying lances; a stirring sight indeed. On seeing this, one can understand why rumours were soon rife about a breakthrough. A joint infantry/cavalry operation was decided on. Two infantry battalions (1st South Staffs and the 2nd Queen's of 91 Brigade, 7th Division) were ordered to advance on High Wood, whilst the Cavalry would advance to the right of the wood. Both cavalry and infantry set

Left: Battle of Bazentin Ridge: Friday 14 July 1916 Wounded soldiers of an unknown Regiment (though the battlefield recognition patches on their shoulders are a good clue to their identity) being transported on the light railway that ran from Trones Wood, via Bernafay Wood back to Casualty Clearing Stations near the village of Carnoy.
IWM Q166

off from the vicinity of Crucifix Corner, to the right of Bazentin le Petit. The two infantry battalions entered the wood around 8 pm. Very soon a position was consolidated diagonally across the middle of the wood. The 7th Dragoon Guards and the 20th Deccan horse, some armed with lances, most with sabres drawn, charged across the ripening cornfields up a long slope towards the German Switch Line. This was the high ground between High Wood and Longueval (an excellent view of this area, can be gained by standing on the road running by Caterpillar Valley Cemetery). On reaching the high ground the cavalry came under shellfire from the village of Flers, situated about one-and-a-half miles further on. They also encountered heavy crossfire from German rifle and machine guns situated in the Switch Line and from a sunken road running from eastern corner of High Wood known as Wood Lane. The 7th Dragoon Guards charged some German infantry that were hidden in little pockets amongst the standing corn, killing fifteen with the lance and capturing thirty-two. It was now twilight, and with the height of the corn the Germans became hard to detect. The 20th

Below: 20th Deccan Horse moving up to High Wood: Friday 14 July 1916
Some of these Troopers and their horses would be killed during the charge on the evening of 14 July. Their bodies still there when the 14th Royal Warwicks took over a section of Black Road on 20 July. The stench was so bad from the bloated horses that parties of men crawled out into No Man's Land, wearing gas masks, to bury them.
IWM Q825

Deccan Horse had also taken a few prisoners. In doing so they had encountered machine gun fire from Delville Wood. A total of 102 officers and other ranks had become casualties amongst the cavalry. As darkness fell they dismounted and occupied a line along the Longueval-Martinpuich Road.

The scene has now been set. Over the following few weeks this small sector of the Somme Front from High Wood, via Wood Lane, Longueval to Delville Wood, was going to cost the lives of thousands before any further breakthrough could occur. It was in this portion of the line that the Birmingham Pals would next see action.

Six months earlier this area of the line was considered 'cushy'. Now the 5th Division was amid the bustle and commotion of the back area of the Somme. There were units of all arms, in bivouacs, tents transport lines, whilst ammunition and stores of all kinds, had accumulated at a convenient distance behind the front lines. Miles of new railway line had been laid, both standard and narrow gauge, to handle all these stores. The villages of Fricourt, Mametz and Montauban, which had previously overlooked the lines held by the division, were by now heaps of rubble. On returning to this back area with the 14th Royal Warwicks, Sergeant Arthur Cooper wrote the following on his first impressions:

'By the look of things there is something doing. Plenty of prisoners come through and troops with souvenirs such as German helmets, pipes etc. We are getting along well on this front. Our guns are as thick as flies and there is a continuous bombardment.'

On 18 July the 5th Division, along with the 7th, came under the command of XV Corps of the British 4th Army. Orders were issued that, at 03.30 am, 20 July, the 3rd, 5th, 7th and 33rd Divisions were to make an assault. The 3rd Division was to take Longueval and finally clear Delville Wood; the 33rd Division was to take High Wood, whilst the 5th and 7th Divisions were to take the high ground between the two woods. The ultimate objective for the Fourth Army was the German Switch Line. The first objective for the 5th and 7th Divisions was to secure approximately 800 yards (730m) of the Martinpuich-Longueval Road, by now known as Black Road. This was the road that the 7th Dragoon Guards and the 20th Deccan Horse retired to and partly entrenched before withdrawing on the morning of 15 July. Orders were issued for 13 Brigade (14th and 15th Royal Warwicks) to move on to Black Road to strengthen the position and hold it, whilst 20 Brigade (7th Division) were ordered to head for the second objective. This was 300 yards (275m) across the cornfield towards the Switch Line. The target was a farm track, running parallel with Black Road, known as Wood Lane. The 5th Division's 95 Brigade were to relieve troops from 76 Brigade (3rd Division) along the Longueval end of Black Road; whilst 15 Brigade (16th Royal Warwicks) were to concentrate in a state of readiness along the Mametz-Montauban road.

Final preparations were made with the dumping of packs and greatcoats. For the first time since arriving in France the men adopted battle order, 'this incident alone being sufficiently wind-raising as to what lay before us' as Captain A C Bill (15th Royal Warwicks) later recalled. On the evening of 18 July men of 13 Brigade spent their time around the village of Meaulte. The new acting Transport Officer of the 14th Royal Warwicks, Lieutenant Alan Furse, remembered this evening at Meaulte

Right: Church Bell, Montauban July 1916. On 19 July, the 14th Royal Warwicks rested along the roadside running south of the village. It was near here that Sergeant Cooper, dozed on a mass grave of twenty-five British soldiers. In regards to the main figure in the photograph, it can be seen how an important item of kit puttees had become. They were essential for storing eating utensils.
IWM Q4281

quite vividly after the war:

'We spent only one night here, but this was our first real insight into what a push means. Day and night the road was one long line of ambulances and walking wounded and occasionally a battalion which had been relieved would march through with a total strength of about 150 instead of 600 or 700. Although we realised what losses these men had, it never seemed to occur to us that we might be the same, but then of course we had not been blooded then.'

The following day, 19 July, 13 Brigade marched up to the line. Going through rubble that was once Fricourt, they passed the 5th Division's new HQ; a position known on trench maps as 'Rose Cottage' but in reality a Nissen hut and a few tarpaulins stretched over poles amid a shell torn field. On reaching the ruins of Montauban, the men rested along the side of a road that ran to the south of the village. The brigade then waited, so they could arrive at their allotted positions during darkness; of which Sergeant Arthur Cooper of the 14th Royal Warwicks recalled:

'We marched through the German old first and second line of trenches towards the present front line. Ye Gods! What a maze of trenches they had. We stayed for a time on the side of the road for dinner and to wait for dusk before getting nearer. I

dropped off to sleep on top of a filled in shell hole, and found when I woke up a little board stuck up explaining that it was the grave of twenty-five Tommies. The smell about this part of the country was simply awful. Hundreds of men had just been buried and this place was littered with equipment and everything else which soldiers usually carry. At about 6 pm we march on again. We got a fairly thick shelling on the way too. A Coy was lucky and got through whole but the other companies lost quite a few. Of course the Huns knew the nooks and corners some. It was an awful march up to the trenches. The stink from the dead horses and the dead Tommies who lay about was chronic.'

Another member of the battalion who remembered this day was Private J E B Fairclough. He described his feelings thus:

'All around us the artillery was continuously in action and the noise was deafening. Little did we realise what lay before us, and because we were new to this type of warfare, ignorance shielded us from too much anxiety.'

For the proposed attack on 20 July, the 15th Royal Warwicks were in reserve. Therefore when the brigade resumed its march from Meaulte towards the front line, the 15th Royal Warwicks parted company and sought shelter in abandoned German

Above: Bazentin Ridge near Bernafay Wood: Wednesday 19 July 1916. On the day this photograph was taken the 14th and 15th Royal Warwicks were in the same sector. The 14th had moved into former German trenches on the Bazentin Ridge to the north of Bernafay Wood, whilst the 15th were in the village of Montauban on the western edge of the wood. The German PoWs are hauling a freshwater cart up towards the fighting zone. The unidentified stretcher bearers are taking a wounded British soldier away from the front. *IWM Q804*

trenches that were near to the road running from Caterpillar Wood to Bernafay Wood. It was there that Private H V Drinkwater had a chance to catch up with his diary:

'We eventually arrived here at 5 p.m., in the German trenches facing those trenches we occupied when we came out last November. The cavalry, we can all see for some distance, is like one mass of ploughed ground. German equipment, helmets, broken rifles scattered all round, it looks as though they had a taste of what we had on 4th June. It is very extra-ordinary to occupy trenches at which we gazed for so long, wondering what it was like 'this side', now we found out.'

With the 15th Royal Warwicks in reserve, the rest of 13 Brigade continued towards the front via Caterpillar Valley, which was soon to be the home of the Divisional artillery. Caterpillar Valley runs eastwards from roughly between Mametz and Mametz Wood towards the northern end of Bernafay Wood. The valley was packed from end to end with artillery pieces of all calibres, which kept a continuous barrage upon the German lines. In return the German artillery swept the valley at several intervals, day and night.

On reaching their destination, 13 Brigade moved into former German trenches, captured on 14 July, situated near the road from Longueval to Bazentin le Grand. Caterpillar Valley was to the rear, whilst in front of the ridge the ground sloped down and then rose again up towards the opposite ridge, now the site of the German Switch. The 2nd KOSBs took over the front two lines, the 14th Royal Warwicks the third, whilst the 1st RWKs, dug themselves in further back as support.

The Battle Commences

Zero hour was 03.30, 20th July. Under an artillery barrage the 8th Devons and the 2nd Gordon Highlanders (7th Division) began their attack on Wood lane. They set off from the eastern vicinity of Bazentin le Petit i.e. the sunken lane that runs from Crucifix Corner to the Windmill; a good three quarters of a mile from Black Road. Once they reached a certain position, the barrage moved forward onto the German trenches at Wood Lane. Black Lane was reached with little difficulty. Following closely behind the attacking troops were three companies of the 2nd KOSBs, from 13 Brigade. The men from the 5th Division remained on Black Road to strengthen the position whilst the Devons and Gordon Highlanders continued towards Wood Lane. Unfortunately, these two battalions met a well-defended German trench running down the lane. Crossfire from machine guns situated in High Wood and Longueval, and German marksmen hidden amongst the corn resulted in both battalions being cut to pieces. For an hour or more, surviving men of these battalions tried to dig themselves in about 25 yards (22m) from Wood Lane but eventually they gave up and had to crawl back to Black Road where the 2nd KOSBs were positioned. Plans were considered for a second attempt to take Wood Lane. But, because the 33rd Division had failed to clear High Wood, it would have been futile to make a further attack. The Devons and the Gordon Highlanders had suffered, between them, nearly 400 casualties. The positions remained the same on Black Road during the daylight hours of 20 July.

The 14th Royal Warwicks had by now moved into the second line along the Bazentin Ridge, behind the reserve company of the 2nd KOSBs. On the evening of July 20th, the 14th Royal Warwicks were ordered to relieve the KOSB's on Black Road. During the same day, Lieutenant Alan Furse was in charge of taking the rations up to the battalion;,prior to its moving off later in the evening. This caused the following account in his diary:

'On the 20th we moved up via Fricourt to Mametz and here I delivered two days rations by the wayside, and this was the last time I saw the battalion as I used to know it. As they moved off on their final stage to the trenches I stood by the side of the road saying goodbye, and Betty (Second-Lieutenant J W Lythgoe, A Coy) called me to him and gave me five Francs to get some Players cigarettes for him when he came out.'

The area that 13 Brigade now found themselves in, was a salient. The support lines on the Bazentin Ridge and the new front line along Black Road, could be clearly seen by German artillery observers around Leuze Wood and the village of Ginchy to the east. The result was that German artillery was very accurate with its shelling of Black Road. In fact the salient around Longueval was liable to receive shelling from all directions except the south-west. Another unpleasant feature in the vicinity of Black Road was the numerous dead horses, resulting from the cavalry action on the evening of 14 July. Due to the hot weather, the smell of these bloated horses was horrendous. Before the 14th Royal Warwicks moved up onto Black Road, small groups of KOSBs, wearing gas-masks had crawled out into No Man's Land to try and locate some of the offensive smelling carcasses. When found, pits were then dug next to each horse and it was then dragged in and covered over. As darkness approached A and B Coys of the 14th Royal Warwicks along with two Coys from the 1st RWKs proceeded to relieve the Devons, Gordon Highlanders and the KOSBs that were spread along Black Road. The RWKs took over the left side of the line, the 14th Royal Warwicks the right. On the morning of 21 July, after the relief was completed, Sergeant Arthur Cooper of the 14th Royal Warwicks continued his diary:

'At night we went forward again and dug ourselves in about two or three hundred yards from the enemy. During the night we got it rather badly. They shelled us while we were digging and lost quite a lot of men. Perhaps I was fortunate in leaving No.1, (Sergeant Cooper was transferred from No.1 Platoon to No.3, the day before.) as they had the worse dose. Old Joe and the Platoon Sergeant and a dozen of them were hit. Only three were killed though. I should most certainly have been with them had I still been with the Platoon. Ernie's is only a scratch and I expect he will come straight back. Although the boys were dropping fairly thickly and the dead men and cavalry horses laying about upset the atmosphere some, our fellows worked like niggers. It was a real Bairnsfather scene here.

'Well we dug and scraped holes for ourselves under the bank of this road and got a bit of shelling from their shrapnel. We lost about thirty whilst we were doing it, which made us a fairly weak company as we were nothing like full strength before we started. We were to go over the top at night and find out how strong Fritz was in front and unfortunately our idea of how his trenches lay was rather vague. When I got word that Butler of my old section was hit I got out of my hole to go and see him. They were a bit further down the road. Ye Gods! it was thick. One had to keep one's mouth shut to save breathing lead. Any way my journey was of no avail, he had gone to his long rest when I got there. I had tears in my eyes that were not caused by gas shells when I came back to my hole. He was a nice lad. Only eighteen years old now and I had been more or less a father to him for almost two years. (Private Leigh Stanley Latham Butler, No.592, came from Wellington Road, Handsworth; though probably buried near to where he died, his remains were never identified and he is now named on the Thiepval Memorial.) *It was funny that day digging ourselves holes. The boys who were hit, but not seriously, would walk down the road wishing the other lads 'Goodbye' and collecting messages for Blighty before they went, and old Fritz's snipers were up in the trees round about peppering away. I should think he's lost all his good shots. They were about two to three hundred yards away and couldn't hit a haystack in an entry. So far as I heard, their bag was one stretcher*

Below: A well known Somme photograph of an eighteen pounder field gun and crew in action pose for the Official Photographer. A frequent find on visiting the battlefields, especially after the ground has been ploughed, are the nose-cones of the various different calibres of shells used. The nose-cone always survived the explosion.
IWM Q4066

Right: During a heavy artillery bombardment, the majority of casualties were caused by the white hot jagged shell splinters, of all sizes, ripping through the air, slashing, slicing, severing and splitting anything they came in contact with – more often than not human flesh. You only have to walk over today's former battlefields to see the many jagged shell shards of various sizes that have come to the surface and litter the ploughed fields (especially evident after heavy rain). The example, right, is a buckle off a section of British First World War webbing. The shell splinter is only the size of a garden pea, yet the force was enough to imbed it in this 1.5 mm section of brass buckle.

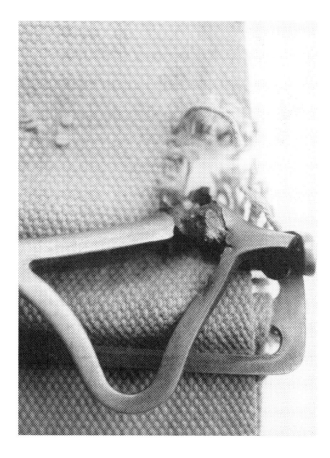

Below right: German Observation Balloon. The position that 13 Brigade occupied along Black Road, could be viewed from several areas of the German Lines, thus allowing very accurate fire from German artillery.

Below: Captain Emile Jacot, 14th Royal Warwicks, wounded by shell splinters on 20 July.

bearer. The fellows who fetched the breakfast, dinners and teas had to walk across the open fields for about a thousand yards and the old snipers going 'pit-a-pat' all the time. The fellows weren't afraid though. Their only trouble was that by accident the dixey might get a hole through it and all the tea or stew run out before they got to us. We got our sniper's looking for their's, but they had covered themselves in too well. We had no luck.

'Old Ernie, the blighter, hopped it with my shaving Kit. At least the one we were both to use. You see we were travelling light for business, had handed our packs and greatcoats in, so only had our haversacks to carry things in, including grub. So Ernie and I were sharing towels and a few other things which we had of necessity and now he's gone and I can't shave to-day!'

Whilst the general staff decided the strategy for the next attack, the 14th Royal Warwicks and the 1st Royal West Kents stayed on Black Road for the next two days. All this time both battalions came under very heavy and concentrated German artillery fire. Amongst the men of the 14th Royal Warwicks that was wounded by flying shell splinters was Second-Lieutenant E W Jacot (B Coy). Hit in several places, the most serious being in the chest, Jacot still rendered very valuable aid in the dressing and caring for the wounded of his platoon, before allowing himself to be taken to a dressing station. On the evening of 20/21 July, Second-Lieutenant J T Turner along with Sergeant Jimmy Weatherhead

(No.1086, B Coy) carried out excellent reconnaissance work and gained valuable information out in No Man's Land between Black Road and the German line along Wood Lane. 'Yank' Turner, a former Sergeant in C Coy before being commissioned, was awarded the Military Cross for this patrol. He transferred to the RFC in September 1916; Sergeant Weatherhead was killed in the forthcoming attack.

The 15th Royal Warwicks were still in support on the upper slopes of Caterpillar Valley, about 1500 yards north of Montauban. They were also on the receiving end of some heavy German artillery fire, the battalion's experience for these two days was later recalled by Captain A C Bill:

'Overlooked by the German positions at Ginchy to the east, it was made the target of much artillery fire. There was hardly any cover for the detachments, only holes dug in the ground covered with corrugated iron and earth, which afforded little protection against the 'Caterpillar Valley Barrage' which swept relentlessly down the valley at intervals during the day and night.

'A cross-roads from Montauban to Bazentin cut the valley at the eastern end, and our position was roughly on the north section of this cross-road where it was slightly sunken. My own men (C Coy) were in trenches about a hundred yards in front of it, the officers and our servants hacking out holes for themselves in the side of the road. Sleep that night was impossible. Shelling was continuous, but far worse was the bark of a 60-pounder battery firing directly over our heads from a position directly behind us. The ear-splitting crack

was terrific and we were so close we felt the blast every time it fired. The next day, the 21st, the battalion came in for a little shelling, losing Second-Lieutenant W R Pratt (A Coy, from York Road, Edgbaston) and nine other ranks all wounded. In the morning we sat tight and watched the slaughter going on in Caterpillar Valley just below us. Guns, ammunition wagons, ration wagons, infantry marching up, wounded walking or being carried down – the road held a continual stream of traffic, with the German guns searching for it. At the cross-roads a quarry was being used as a dressing station. I saw one large shell drop right into it and a dozen or so men came running out, but from the number of casualties continually being passed in and out that one shell must have done a lot of damage.'

Even though Caterpillar Valley was subject to this intense artillery fire, the horses for all the artillery pieces were still kept in it. On the afternoon of 22 July, the Germans opened up with a sudden concentrated bombardment and in order to prevent huge loss, the horses were cut lose, 'and stampeded terrified down the valley towards Fricourt in a cloud of dust and shell smoke', as the 5th Division History recalled. It took a few hours to collect them, and luckily only a few were lost.

The 16th Royal Warwicks along with the rest of 15 Brigade were still in reserve, for the time being. The 16th were in a state of readiness and entrenched to the west of Montauban in an old German trench known as 'Montauban Alley'. Each man carried extra ammunition and those not carrying a pick or shovel had extra hand grenades in their packs. The reason for this was that the brigade would be ready at a few minutes' notice to move into the front line, to check any possible German counter-attack that might occur on the divisional front.

Attack on Wood Lane

On the morning of 21 July, a conference, attended by all the Corps Commanders of the British Fourth Army, was held to plan the next assault upon the German lines. It was decided to resume the offensive on the Switch Line on the evening of 22/23 July. Unfortunately synchronisation along the Fourth Army Corps front was not to be achieved in the final plan of attack.

To tie up with an assault on the village of Pozieres by the Australians, the attack on the left flank of Black Road was to start at 12.30 am and 01.30 am, 23 July. To the right of Black Road, to tie up with the French, the assault was to begin at 03.40 am, 23 July. Smack in the middle, along Black Road, was 13 Brigade of the 5th Division. Here there was a problem. Between Black Road and the Switch Line was an obstacle; the German occupied Wood Lane. Therefore. a preliminary attack was required to take and hold Wood Lane before any attempt on the Switch Line could be attempted. This preliminary operation was to begin at 22.00 on the evening of 22 July. The 14th Royal Warwicks and the 1st Royal West Kents were to take Wood Lane. Once taken and consolidated, at 01.30, 23 July, the 2nd KOSBs would then 'leap frog' Wood Lane to attack the Switch Line. Wood

Above: 8 inch Howitzers, the Somme: July 1916. In the book *The 15th Battalion Royal Warwickshire Regiment (2nd Birmingham Battalion) in the Great War,* written by Captain Charles Bill (C Coy), the following passage could certainly be describing the scene above:
'In the morning we sat tight and watched the slaughter going on in Caterpillar Valley just below us. Guns, ammunition wagons, ration wagons, infantry marching up, wounded walking or being carried down - the road held a continual stream of traffic, with German guns searching for it.'
IWM Q3981

Lane was, and still is, a farm track running in a south-easterly direction from the eastern corner of High Wood towards Longueval.

The section of Wood Lane that would be the objective of the 14th Royal Warwicks lay on slightly lower ground than Black Road, approximately 320 yards away. From where the 14th Royal Warwicks were entrenched No Man's Land sloped very slightly upwards for approximately 250 yards, then crested down to the German positions. There were only a few yards difference in height, but it meant that from the 14th Royal Warwick's trenches, all that could be seen was corn and thin air. But, from the German point of view opposite, any person standing at full height coming over the slight crest would stand out like a sore thumb. There was still enough corn standing to crawl through and not be seen, even though in parts it had been flattened by shellfire, cavalry horses and the infantry attack on 20th July. The corn also gave excellent cover for German snipers, as Private Walter Nash (14th Royal Warwicks, No.1495) found out:

'An Indian Lancer and his horse lay dead in the corner of these oats. I had no boot laces – only pieces of string. So I said to a mate that I was going to see what this Indian had got in his haversack in the way of spare laces. I stooped to get at his haversack when – bing! An oat stalk had toppled over no more than six inches from my head. Make no mistake; those Hun snipers were very patient and crafty.'
The Hell They Called High Wood by Terry Norman.

Nowadays, if you stand at the 'T' junction half way along Black Road, which was roughly the position of A Coy, 14th Royal Warwicks, 1100 yards in the distance can be seen the New Zealand Memorial, and the site of the German Switch Line. Wood Lane can only be seen as it leaves High Wood, it then sinks out of sight.

Following up their successful reconnaissance on the evening of 20/21 July, Second-Lieutenant J T Turner and Sergeant Jimmy Weatherhead 'carried out a very plucky and successful reconnaissance of the enemy's line, in broad daylight, in order to supplement the information gained overnight.' This occurred on the morning of 22 July. The rest of the day was spent in preparation for the evening attack. The objective for the 14th Royal Warwicks was approximately 500 yards of German trench; from where the German line entered Wood Lane to the machine-gun strongpoint at the road junction.

The 1st Royal West Kents were to continue the attack from the 14th Royal Warwicks' immediate left up to High Wood. There were rumours of another German strongpoint somewhere in the eastern corner of High Wood, which gave Lieutenant-Colonel Dunlop the CO of the Royal West Kents much consternation. His concern was totally justified. Nowadays, if you stand by the eastern corner of High Wood, with the water-filled mine crater behind you; you can see the whole of No Man's Land that the West Kents and 14th Royal Warwicks were to attack over. A machine gun here would wreak havoc among men attacking from the British Front Line.

However, the 51st Division on the left of the 5th Division gave assurance that High Wood would be secured before the flank of 13 Brigade be exposed (this was to be achieved by one platoon from the 1/4th Gordon Highlanders of 154 Brigade). Still not satisfied, Lieutenant-Colonel Dunlop, made arrangements for one platoon of C Coy (Royal West Kents) under Lieutenant Peachey to make their way along the side of the wood and co-operate with the Gordons in the location and elimination of the strongpoint. The artillery bombardment concentrating upon the German Switch Line began at 4.30 pm. Then, at 8 pm, the range was adjusted to concentrate upon Wood Lane. A and B Coys of the 14th Royal Warwicks, who were already entrenched along Black Road, were to make the attack.

13th Infantry Brigade Front Line Position 22/23 July 1916

SWITCH LINE

HIGH WOOD

Strongpoint

WOOD LANE

No Man's Land

Objective of 14th Royal Warwicks on the evening of 22/23 July

BLACK ROAD

1st RWK's

Approximate battalion boundary line

B Coy

14th Warwicks

A Coy

100 yds

Strongpoint

front line included 100 yards east of "T" junction, and 100 yards, south of junction

PONT STREET

LONGUEVAL

Meanwhile C and D Coys moved up to close support, ready to take over the vacated trenches when the attack was under way. Apart from A and B Coys, a special bombing party was also formed from within the battalion. This party, along with one section of the 59th Field Company, Royal Engineers and one machine-gun section from 13 Brigade Machine Gun Company were required to make their way along the road running east from Black Road, to storm a German strongpoint positioned at the end of Wood Lane. If successful, the Royal Engineers were to re-build it facing the Switch Line; the machine-gunners manning the position; whilst the bombing party were to continue down the German communication trench, that led to the village of Longueval, create a block and hold it.

In addition to the normal 120 rounds of ammunition that each man of the battalion carried, they were also issued with an extra bandolier to be slung over their shoulders. Every man also carried two hand grenades in his pockets. Once the German line was taken, these grenades were to be handed in to form dumps along the line in case of any counter-attack. The men in A and B Coys of the 14th Royal Warwicks were also required to carry across with them all the spades that the battalion had in its possession. On taking the German line the order was that a thin skirmish line no more than 150 yards in front was to give cover against any counter-attack whilst the rest of the men consolidated the newly won trench to face the Switch Line. The Operation Orders for the attack, issued to all at 5 pm, made this quite clear:

'All ranks must bear in mind that a counter attack is sure to come. It may even come as they are entering the enemy's trenches. In either case they must be prepared to meet it swiftly and with full force. Hesitation is fatal: if such counter attack comes whilst they are entering the trenches, a quick bayonet charge is certain to have the required effect. If it comes when the men are in position, rapid fire will meet the case.'

By 9.00 pm the 15th Royal Warwicks, who were in reserve for the attack, had moved up into the old German trenches that run along the Longueval-Bazentin le Grand Road. Private H V Drinkwater later described the scene:

'Eventually arriving at 9 pm at a shallow trench about half a mile from the firing line. The artillery were in full swing firing over into the German lines an awful barrage of shells. The sky was livid with shell explosions and on our right a wood appeared to be on fire.' (Delville Wood)

Over the Top

Along the length of Black Road, the men of the 14th Royal Warwicks and the 1st Royal West Kents prepared themselves for the task ahead. Perhaps at the back of their minds lay the knowledge of what had happened two nights previously, when the Devons and Gordon Highlanders had been cut to pieces. The very same obstacle now lay before 13 Brigade. However, there was the reassurance that as zero hour approached the artillery barrage had intensified in the region of Wood Lane; no troops could have stood up to such concentrated fire. It was going to be a walk over; it was only a preliminary operation anyway. Unfortunately, even though the barrage looked destructive, it was missing Wood Lane.

Above: Corporal Henry Herrick, No.635, D Coy, 14th Royal Warwicks, from Washwood Heath Road, Saltley. Killed, aged twenty-five, during the attack on Wood Lane. Thiepval Memorial.

Below: Heilly Station Casualty Clearing Station. Quite a few Birmingham Pals who were wounded on the evening of 22/23 July ended up at No.36 CCS at Heilly Station (situated about three miles north-east of Corbie). Some did not make it any further and are buried in Heilly Station Cemetery. The walking wounded in the photograph are a mixture of Grenadier Guards and Royal Fusiliers.
IWM Q1256

The first five minutes went exactly to plan. At 9.50 pm, A and B Coys of the 14th Royal Warwicks, along with those from the 1st Royal West Kents, made their way into No Man's Land. For the time being, due to the lie of the land and the darkness, they remained unobserved by the Germans in Wood Lane. Just before the slight crest towards the German lines, A and B Coys of the 14th Royal Warwicks spread out to form two long waves. For the next five minutes the men lay down, took cover and waited for the whistle that would signal the assault to take Wood Lane.

At 10 pm, the whistles sounded, the men stood up and began their determined rush to the German line. It was now that events turned disastrous for the men of 13 Infantry Brigade. In the book *The 5th Division In The Great War*, the attack merited the following brief description:

'They were met with a heavy counter-barrage and streams of lead from the numerous machine guns, and, after suffering severe casualties, they were forced to retire to their jumping off line'.

Translated, 'severe casualties', meant that the 14th Royal Warwicks suffered a total of 485 casualties during the attack; of these, 194 were killed. The 1st Royal West Kents also suffered severely with a total of 421 casualties. There were a further 140 casualties from D coy of the 15th Royal Warwicks who moved up and supported the 14th Royal Warwicks. The end result was over a thousand men either killed or wounded. For a preliminary attack only!

The principal cause for the disaster that befell 13 Brigade was the failure of the artillery barrage to destroy the German positions along Wood Lane. The cause of this can be found in the following account from the History of the 1st Royal West Kents, published after the war:

'It has been said previously that the enemy was not much damaged by our artillery fire. The latter, in fact, was almost ineffective, the batteries having only been notified of the coming attack at 8 pm, when it was already getting dark. It was then too late to register properly on the enemy trenches, which were out of sight. Hence the artillery support, though heavy, was very inadequate, and this through no fault of the gunners, who were necessarily groping in the dark.'

Once the attack was underway, the men of 13 Brigade made perfect silhouetted targets under the light from German star shells. The two machine-gun posts situated at either end of Wood Lane criss-crossed No Man's Land like a scythe. The Germans entrenched along Wood Lane stood shoulder to shoulder causing further carnage with rifle fire and grenades. Meanwhile a retaliatory German counter-barrage blasted No Man's Land with a vengeance. In this mayhem the 14th Royal Warwicks found themselves in a very unhealthy predicament. Despite these conditions, 'everyone went forward with great determination and spirit. It is most distressing under the circumstances that they should have been up against what was undoubtedly an impossible proposition', as the CO, Lieutenant-Colonel Murray later wrote in the Battalion War diary.

Thirty-five minutes after zero hour, Lieutenant-Colonel Murray had still not received an official report of how the attack was going. Wounded and stragglers were dribbling back to the jumping off line; all with the same story that both A and B companies had been shot to pieces. At 10.35 pm it was decided to send two platoons of D Coy to

support A Coy. Soon after, the remaining two platoons from D Coy went over to support B Coy. It was 11.20 pm when a runner got back with an official report, stating that A and B Coys had failed to reach their objective and unless reinforcements were sent up, they would have to retire. Lieutenant-Colonel Murray then ordered C Coy to advance and support those already in No Man's Land. Receiving no further information, but sensing the situation was becoming critical, Lieutenant-Colonel Murray at 11.50 pm requested the help of two companies from the 15th Royal Warwicks. In the battalion War Diary written the next day, Lieutenant-Colonel Murray states that he sent two men who knew the ground well to guide the two companies of the 15th up to Black Road, and 'from subsequent events it transpired that these two companies lost their way and were not used in the attack at all. I am enquiring into the matter from the two guides I furnished.' The account by the CO was probably written not long after the attack, and with such a huge casualty list and the confusion of what had happened, he was not yet fully aware of all the facts. Exactly what did happen to these two companies? The 15th Royal Warwicks were entrenched along the Longueval-Bazentin le Grand Road. Captain A C Bill, (OC, C Coy) continues where Lieutenant-Colonel Murray left off:

'The trench was already full of troops and the congestion and the confusion made it extremely difficult to keep in touch with one's men or to pass messages to one's officers. The night was pitch dark save for the incessant flashes of guns and bursting shells and the glare from the star shells in front; and the din of battle all round us was deafening. Soon after the attack had been launched orders came along that Gough with 'D' and I with 'C' were to move up and support the attack. Then came the job of extricating our men from the general mix up. Gough's company was lower down the trench, near where it was crossed by a track which led up to High Wood, and he took his men up along this track. To move my men down through the crowded trench to the same place I felt to be almost impossible, so I led them over the parapet from where we stood. We moved in single file and it was a slow and arduous business, for every man was carrying an extra bandolier of ammunition slung around him and a canvas bucket full of Mills bombs, in addition to his normal fighting kit. The Lewis gun teams carried, in addition to their guns and normal supply of ammunition, as many extra loaded drums as they could possibly manage. I had overlooked the possibility of there being other trench lines between us and our objective, and we got about half-way when we came across a trench held by the 2nd KOSB's, who were lying in close support. This delayed us badly, as it took some time in the darkness for the file of men to negotiate this deep trench, laden as they were, but eventually we all got across and the remainder of the going was much more easy. We struck Gough's track further up and tailed in behind some Highland Division troops (51st) moving up to High Wood. It is fatal to move quickly in file formation in the dark because of the difficulty of the rear troops keeping in touch, but we had the luck to get up through some unpleasant shelling without losing many men. A short distance behind the road which was our immediate objective (Black Road) I called a halt and went forward with one man to find out how the position stood. The trench from which the attack had been launched was very narrow and shallow and was obstructed in many places by dead and wounded men. I could learn nothing here as to how the attack had gone, but further along towards High Wood I found a company of the 14th Royal Warwicks under Captain Bryson (C Coy). Two of their companies had gone over and simply disappeared, apparently decimated, and they themselves made another effort to reach the enemy line while I was there, but were held up by heavy fire and forced to return. I told Bryson I would fetch my men up, though what to do with them when I got them there I didn't know. It was obvious from what had happened that the trench which had been attacked was untouched by our gun-fire and to order the company to attack would mean their utter decimation, as had happened to the 14th Royal Warwicks and the West Kents. Yet we were sent to support the attack!'

Captain Bill was now in a dilemma, ordering C Coy into the attack he realised was useless, what would be best? Occupy Black Road and stay put, and then face the wrath of higher command; but at least his men would be spared, or attack. Because of the delay in getting to Black Road, Captain Bill did not know that Captain Gough with D Coy had gone into the attack just after midnight, and were now suffering the same fate as the 14th Royal Warwicks, with Captain Gough being severely wounded in the process.

Arthur Knight of Sutton Coldfield, was only two months old when his father, Sergeant Arthur Knight (No.782, D Coy, from 'The Builder's Arms', Nelson Street, Ladywood) was killed during the attack. In 1966 he met up with some of the survivors of D Coy to find out more of the father he never knew. He interviewed the former CSM of D Coy, Ernest Samuel Braddock (No.930, of Oliver Road,

Above: Sergeant Thomas Wood, No.751, D Coy, 15th Royal Warwicks, from Rugeley. Killed during the attack on Wood Lane, 23 July 1916, aged thirty-five. Thiepval Memorial.

Below: Private William Stubbs, No.996, 14th Royal Warwicks, from Poplar Avenue, Edgbaston. Killed 23 July 1916 aged twenty. A former employee of Lloyds Bank, Acocks Green. Thiepval Memorial.

Above: Private Reginald Milnes Blakemore, No.342, 15th Royal Warwicks. Died of wounds, 1 August 1916, after the attack upon Wood Lane. Reginald was the son of the former Landlord of the Red Lion Public House in Knowle, Warwickshire. He is buried at Heilly Station Cemetery and also commemorated on the Knowle War Memorial.

Above: Acting Company Sergeant Major Thomas Philips, No.38, D Coy, 16 Platoon, 15th Royal Warwicks. Killed in action during the attack upon Wood Lane. Sergeant Philips who came from Regent Road, Handsworth is buried in Caterpillar Valley Cemetery.

Below: Sergeant Arthur Knight, No.782, D Coy, 13 Platoon, 15th Royal Warwicks, from the Builder's Arms Nelson Street, Ladywood. A former Jeweller who worked at Regent Place. Killed during the attack on Wood Lane, 23 July. Buried in Caterpillar Valley Cemetery.

Below: Private William Curtis, No.64, A Coy, 1 Platoon, 14th Royal Warwicks. Killed during the attack upon Wood Lane. William, aged twenty-nine, was the Head of the Osram Light Department at the General Electric Company, Witton. He was also Captain of Erdington Football Club and played cricket in the Birmingham Suburban League. He left a wife, Florence, Holly Road, Handsworth. His parents lived at Minstead Road, Erdington. Thiepval Memorial.

Ladywood) then living in Harborne; and just retired from the post of Town Clerk to Halesowen:

> *'We were in a trench alongside a sunken road* (Black Road) *and the Germans were in a position along a ridge connecting High Wood and Delville Wood* (Wood Lane). *The attack was made up rising ground, at night, against machine-gun fire from the Germans. My difficulty was to keep the men in extended order as they instinctively bunched together for self-assurance in the dark. The night was so black that it was not possible to see what was happening. You would see a man fall here and there, but who it was or what had happened to him, you didn't know. I found myself in a shell-hole with D Coy CO, Captain Gough, and another man. Captain Gough was badly wounded in the right thigh and we did what we could to help him. A man from the KOSBs dropped into the hole and as he bent over Captain Gough, he suddenly fell on top of him. He had been shot through the head. We could not get a stretcher for Captain Gough, so we got a ground-sheet under him and carried him back to HQ.*

> *'When it was all over and we had retreated to our lines, I took a roll-call. There were thirty odd men and no officers. We asked what had happened to so and so and perhaps someone would say they had seen him hit. Someone said they had seen Sergeant Knight badly wounded and he never came back.*

> *'Arthur was a very great friend of mine. He was a man that you liked very much. He had a dry sense of humour. When Captain Gough asked who I would have for Platoon Sergeant, I said, "why Knight of course, who else?" He was very good with his men. He was always quiet with them. He did not shout or lose his temper, but they knew who was in control.'*

Unlike many of his comrades, Sergeant Arthur Knight's body was recovered and buried in a battlefield grave or a small cemetery in the vicinity. In 1921 his body was exhumed and re-interred in Caterpillar Valley Cemetery.

Returning to the events of C Coy and whether Captain Bill should lead his men into an impossible situation. The decision was soon out of his hands. Before he had chance to move back to his company a whizz-bang landed too close for comfort, which resulted in injuries on the inside of his arms and legs. He later counted sixty-one small wounds, fortunately none contained metal. Before Captain Bill was taken to the dressing station, he sent a runner back to where C Coy were still waiting, to inform Captain H Anderson (from Park road, Warley Woods) of what was happening and guide Anderson and the rest of C Coy up to Black Road.

The message never reached Anderson, and whilst waiting for Captain Bill to return, he had C Coy move into an old German trench, just behind the road. It was not until dawn that Captain Anderson, moved C Coy into the front line trench. One of those who now moved into the front line was Private H V Drinkwater:

> *'Arriving at what was once an old German trench and appeared to be our firing line, we joined the rest of the Brigade, Kents, KOSBs, 14th Royal Warwicks, all mixed up together, what was left of them. We filled our rifle magazine and fixed bayonets, no one seemed to know what we had to do, as we peered over the top waiting for something to happen. We were unable to see what was going on, we appeared to be looking at a cornfield, the wild growth obscuring what little one could see in the darkness.'*

Continuing now with the 14th Royal Warwicks. No definite news reached Lieutenant-Colonel Murray until 02.25, 23 July, when Captain Bryson informed him of the situation by field telephone. The CO had realised by now that all the companies that had advanced to make the attack had been completely cut up and had become totally disorganised.

On the left flank of the 14th Royal Warwicks, twenty men from a platoon of B Coy, 1st Royal West Kents, under Lieutenant Scott, had managed to occupy and consolidate approximately 40 yards of the German line. These men clung on for four hours and even though the 2nd KOSBs (who were to attack the Switch Line 01:30 am) were ordered up to support the West Kents, only a few managed to get to the captured part of the German trench. As dawn was breaking, the trench was given up and the surviving men of the West Kents and KOSBs were ordered back to their jumping off line. The Royal West Kents could only muster 250 men in the front line afterwards.

It was now futile to consider any further attacks upon Wood Lane. The best possible plan was to reorganise and consolidate the original front line and close support lines, with those men who had managed to make their way back from No Man's Land and prepare for any possible counter-attack. Many of the wounded still lay out in the cornfield, having managed to crawl into shell craters. They would now have to lie there all day until darkness before they could attempt to make their way back in, or before men could go out and look for them.

Before the attack was under way, one NCO of the 14th Royal Warwicks, Sergeant W B Davies (No.333, from Broughton Road, Handsworth), took stock of his bearings, in relation to the one tree that was standing alone in the featureless landscape in front of Black Road. During the attack Sergeant Davies was wounded early on, he dropped into a shell hole, and looking back to the jumping off line saw the silhouette of the same tree in the distance. Scrambling along on hands and knees, Sergeant

Davies, made his way towards the tree and on his way managed to locate various other wounded men. He finally reached the tree with twenty men in tow. Private H T Hughes (No.166, A Coy) was an employee at the General Electric Company, Witton before the war. Though wounded he had an amazing piece of luck, as recalled in the book *The Hell They Called High Wood* by Terry Norman:

'He had gone through the stream of fire from High Wood's eastern corner when he became aware of a searing sensation in both his hands. He dropped his rifle before realising that his hands were useless, having been drilled through almost simultaneously by bullets. He looked around in the colourfully splashed light of soaring and falling star-shells to see that he was near the German wire and on his own. Incapable of further action, Hughes simply turned round and walked dazedly through the cross-fire again to the battalion trench. Not another bullet hit him.'

Even though the 14th Royal Warwicks were cut to pieces, we can assume some men actually got into the Wood Lane trench, similar to those men of the Royal West Kents. Unfortunately no man who may have reached Wood Lane survived to tell the tale. One man, Private William Benfield (No.510, from High Barnet, Herts and a former employee of the GEC), was reported last seen hand-to-hand fighting in the German trenches; he is now remembered on the Thiepval Memorial.

Another confirmed sighting was that of Lance Corporal Arthur Dowler (No.876 from Church Lane, Handsworth and an 'old boy' of Handsworth Grammar School). He was seen to reach the German parapet before being killed with a bullet through the head. Private Richard Taylor (No.1247, A Coy, from Vicarage Road, West Bromwich) is buried at Lebucquiere Communal cemetery Extension, which was behind the German lines in 1916. Presumably, he made it as far as the German trenches before being killed. Private Walter Nash (No.1495) managed to get within 10 yards of the Germans and was able to throw a couple of hand grenades before he himself was on the receiving end of a German grenade which knocked him out cold for several hours. When he eventually came to, he was found and taken prisoner. Before he was escorted to the back area the wound on his face was examined. Part of a compressed milk tin was found to be embedded in his face and was removed with a pair of pliers. Private Nash spent the rest of the war working in a coal mine in the Ruhr district of Germany.

Another who was killed was Private Harold Mills, (No.1147, A Coy) who was due to be articled to a firm of Birmingham Solicitors prior to the outbreak of war. At first he was medically rejected, but managed to enlist into the battalion's reserve company in January 1915. A comrade who survived the attack wrote the following to Mill's parents at Ravenhurst Rd, Harborne:

'The company was in dead ground for about 150 yards and sustained few casualties, but on advancing into the open it was met by a terrible fire on its flanks from machine guns in High and Delville Woods; it got into the enemy's barrage fire, and was met by most of their contrivances, including gas shells and liquid fire shells. The men were knocked over like nine-pins, and our attack was utterly smashed; all the officers who took part were killed or wounded.'

Private Mills' parents were also told that he was buried where he fell, which probably meant he was put in a shell hole with his upturned rifle as a marker. Unfortunately, this area of No Man's Land was to see plenty of death and destruction over the ensuing weeks. Private Mills' grave, like so many others, would never be found, obliterated by further gunfire.

Sergeant Cooper's Nightmare at Wood Lane

Our old friend Sergeant Arthur Cooper of the 14th Royal Warwicks, was also wounded in the attack. He lay out in No Man's Land for a good number of hours. The following is the complete extract of the final part of his diary written whilst aboard a hospital ship bound for England, three weeks after the attack took place:

'I am on board the hospital boat Panama now, waiting to sail for Blighty, I came on board last night but we did not sail because some Hun Subs are outside. They sank five boats yesterday and I believe this port is closed till they catch them. We are kicking up our heels here waiting and impatient to get home, so I thought that it would help to keep my blood cool and keep my temperature down and therefore save unnecessary medicine, to continue to write a few notes. I don't know that I can remember a great lot about what's happened lately, the last fortnight or so, but I will do my best.....

'I think the date was 22 July. At ten o'clock pm we got over the top and filed away into the gloom. I had my section in file behind me, which was the way we were to go forward until we were fairly close. This offers a small target for artillery fire, but of course as soon as the rifle fire gets hot we have to extend into line. I think that they must have had scouts well out in front of their line, as fairly early their guns opened out like Hell and so did the rifle and machine-gun fire. They must have had hundreds of the latter. We extended and

Above: Private Thomas Riley, No.976, 14th Royal Warwicks, from Lancaster. A former employee of the Birmingham Reference Library killed 23 July 1916. Thiepval Memorial.

Below: Private Frederick James Patrick, No.3, 14th Royal Warwicks, from Reservoir Avenue, Edgbaston. Received a slight head wound on 22 July. After the second attack on 30 July he was promoted to Sergeant. An employee of the Birmingham Reference Library. After the war he returned to his job and eventually became the Head Librarian of Birmingham.

Below: Private Percy Garner, No.7, 14th Royal Warwicks. A former employee of the Birmingham Reference Library, died of wounds 23 July 1916. Thiepval Memorial.

went forward at the double. The boys were dropping fairly thickly then and the line was very thin. I got to within about twenty yards of their trench where I could see the line of machine guns and rifles spitting fire, when I felt a sudden twinge through my right arm, which knocked my rifle out of my hand. I stooped to pick it up and at the same time I got a bash on the head with shrapnel and saw some real stars floating about. Then I knew no more for I can't say what period, but I came round some time later not feeling very well. Fritz was peppering away, so I knew that the boys had not moved him on this journey and that made me sad. Anyway I soon found out that the spot where I lay was not a very healthy one. I stood a good chance of stopping one from both ways, so I decided to move as soon as I possibly could, also taking into consideration Fritz's bits of lead which I was praying would cease before light set in. They did not, the swines kept on, so I decided to take my chance and crawl if I could. I tried two or three times before I got away and then only got a few yards before I dropped exhausted. Eventually and by small degrees I got about twenty yards and dropped into a bit of a shell hole. I dropped on the top of some other fellow. I don't know who he was, but he yelled out and some time after disappeared. He tried to get me to go on, but I absolutely could not and kept dropping off unconscious. Some time during the night I heard a voice asking me who I was. It was Tommy Thompson out of No. 3 platoon. He was hit in the thigh (Private Victor Herbert Thompson, No.311, of Beaufort Road, Edgbaston).

'By the way, we have just started for Blighty 9 am, August 12th

'Tommy and I could not give one another much help, I had lost a lot of blood through my head and arm by this time.

'The bally boat has stopped. I wonder what the matter is?, I wish this boat would go on. We have been stuck here in the open sea for half an hour. Must be a Sub, I think.

'Well Tommy began to worry me to get a move on with him, but we BOTH wanted help and neither one of us could help the other. I asked him to try and get in himself and I would come as soon as I could, but he couldn't shift. I thought that there was a good chance of us finishing our young careers there, as we were not likely to improve stopping out with our wounds not dressed. Oh! I forgot to say that I had a field dressing put very roughly on my head. I don't know if it was in the right place. I don't think it was. The fellow whom

I dropped on when I first got into the shell hole put it on for me. Of course he couldn't see in the dark and I was not very sure where it was at the time.

'There was blood all over my head. Well I dropped off again and when I came to, morning had broken. That meant staying there until dark at any rate because we were in view of Fritz and he would have soon finished us off if we had crept out. I thought to myself, what a cheerful and bright day we were going to have. I had dropped my equipment in the first place. I couldn't carry it and I hadn't even got a drop of water. The happy day wore on. Each side was shelling heavily and we were in the middle. Well not quite as we were only about forty yards from Fritz and I think that most of the shells which were shaking us were our own. Not very cheering lying down there thinking every minute that one of your own shells was going to wipe you out. Later in the day Tommy got hit again with shrapnel and so did I. This time in the left arm, not at all seriously though, mine was very slight, but I am afraid that my friend's was worse. So we went on through the day and when night fell we were both worse than we had been the previous night, but I made up my mind that we had got to get in and tried to kid Tommy to get a move on, but I couldn't shift him. In the end I started off on my own, crawling a very few yards at a time and how I eventually got there I have no idea. I remember the sentry challenging me and I could just say who I was. I then tried to get a couple of the fellows to come with me for Tommy, but they would not let me go, so I explained where he was and they said they would fetch him, I don't know if they ever found him. (Unfortunately not, Private Victor Herbert Thompson was never found. He is named on the Thiepval Memorial.)

'Two fellows, I think they were wounded, helped me down to the trench dressing station and I only remember being carried in the stretcher, a motor ambulance, more dressing stations, in one where they gave me some beef-tea, which I gulped down red hot. I hadn't had anything, not even a drink, for about thirty hours. Then another motor ride to the rear and then the hospital, I woke up when the orderly was getting my clothes off. I had my wounds dressed and was washed all over and put into clean sheets. Ye Gods! What rest! Like dropping into heaven, but Oh my head! Someone was surely hitting it with a stick! It did give me Jib! I also found that I could not open one eye and I could only see very little out of the other and only stand having it open for a very short time. I was rather afraid that my right eye was done in through the wound in my head.

'I had about four or five days absolute agony and then underwent an operation to my head. I was sort of semi-conscious all the time during the operation. They seemed to be cracking all the bones in my head. It was just about the worst hour I have ever spent in my life. After that I gradually improved and on about the twelfth day my head was not singing and got my first night's sleep that I had in hospital. Previously my head at night got worse and worse until morning, when I was absolutely worn out. I didn't tell you I found a pal in Hospital. Private Newman, the son of the Tobacco people (No.319, W H Newman of Margaret Grove, Edgbaston), he was out of No.2 platoon. We got our beds put side by side and now we were getting better it was a great comfort to have a pal. On about the 6th I opened my right eye and by doing so just missed another operation which the doctor intended making that day. I was very lucky.

'My sight was improving fast now and I could read a bit, which made things a lot better for me. I began to take interest in my food, which is always a good sign and also had two servings of pudding. The sisters here are absolute Angels and the doctor is a very nice man and also a very clever one. He told me on the 9th that he was sending me home, and on the 11th, I got carried on board and here I am still, 4 pm, 12th, stuck still just outside the Harbour.

'We stayed outside the harbour until about 6 pm, and then off we went. I went to sleep and woke up at Southampton. I had my ticket marked No.3 District, which is Birmingham and the Midlands, but although there was a Midland Railway train in for Birmingham and the North, to my great disappointment I was not put on it. Instead I got landed on a London and South Western Railway train and eventually arrived at Waterloo Station. I felt a bit fed up about it, but it was good to be in Blighty. The country looked lovely on the train journey. France in parts looks beautiful, but it don't beat dear England. Well I was deposited in J 1 ward, King George Hospital, Waterloo Road, London SE and here I am on August 16th rapidly getting better.'

On recovery Sergeant Arthur Cooper was not passed fit for active service, he finished the war in England on training duties. Apart from finding out that Sergeant Cooper came from 231, Selly Park Road, nothing else about him has come to light. I

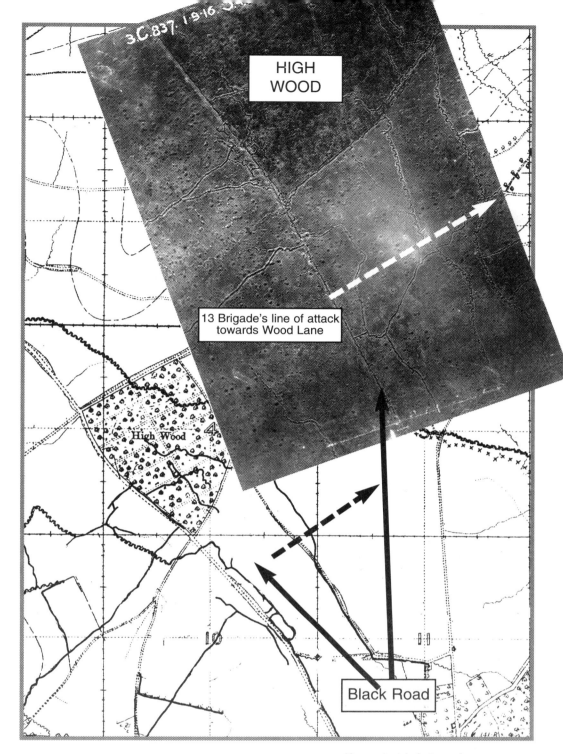

Above: Aerial photograph of southern corner of High Wood taken on 1 September 1916.

hope he had a long and happy life after the war.

Tragic Results of the Attack on Wood Lane

Before resuming with the history of the Birmingham Pals, it may be of interest to know that there were thirty-seven sets of brothers serving within the ranks of 14th Royal Warwicks (this also included three sets of three brothers) and there were a further eight sets from the 15th Royal Warwicks, that could have taken part in the attack on Wood Lane. They may not have all been involved in the attack because it was the policy for about 150 men or so to remain with the transport and HQ Coy to act as a nucleus to rebuild the battalion in case of high casualties; which with the 14th Royal Warwicks sadly happened.

Above: Platoon Sergeant Charles Clements, No.102, B Coy, 6 Platoon, 14th Royal Warwicks. Killed during the attack on Wood Lane 23 July. A former Regular who served with the Royal West Kents in the South African War. He was employed at the General Electric Company, Witton as the Company Engineer before enlisting into the 1st Birmingham Battalion. He left a wife and three children at Francis Road, Stechford. Thiepval Memorial.

Below: The sector of the Somme Front that the 5th Division was now serving on, had advanced nearly four miles from the German trenches that confronted Montauban on 1 July 1916. This resulted in a four mile zone of devastation with bodies, equipment and weapons of both sides strewn across the old battlefield. The rifles found by the salvaging party in the photograph, have all got bayonets fixed, thus denoting their former owners had probably become casualties whilst 'going over the top'. *IWM Q3994*

Another result of the attack was that the command infrastructure of the 14th was badly depleted with such a huge loss of Officers and NCO's. Ten Officers were killed or died of wounds whilst the NCO's suffered the loss of one CSM, eleven Sergeants, five Corporals and twenty-four Lance Corporals. Several more NCO's were amongst the wounded. Of all the brothers in the 14th Royal Warwicks, only one pair were killed during the attack, these were Privates Alfred and Arthur (No.149) Farnell (both from A Coy, 3 platoon), whose parents lived in Leonard Road, Handsworth. Alfred (No.150) worked for the Birmingham Tramways Department at the Council House and left a wife at Railway Terrace, Nechells. Their bodies were never identified and they are both commemorated on the Thiepval Memorial.

There were another two brothers from the 14th who were killed within a few hours of each other. Born at Churchill near Kidderminster and both Lance Corporals. They were Collins Jones (No.1134), killed by shellfire prior to the attack (His remains were found after the war and some trace of his identity still remained, because he is now buried in the post-war created Delville Wood Cemetery.) The other brother, Charles Jones (No.1135) was killed during the attack; he was never found and is named on the Thiepval Memorial. They were not original volunteers from September, 1914. They both enlisted into E coy on 1 January 1915. Of the 194 officers and men of the 14th Royal Warwicks who were killed in the attack on Wood Lane, 116 of these men were never found, or their remains were never identified. They are all commemorated on the Thiepval Memorial. The majority of men who were found and identified are now buried in Caterpillar Valley Cemetery.

The remains of Lance Corporal Alfred Jones (No.174, A Coy, from Landsdowne Street, Winson Green) from the 14th Royal Warwicks who was 'missing' and named on the Thiepval Memorial, were later found and identified in the mid 1930's. His father was notified by the Imperial War Graves Commission that the remains of Alfred had been buried in the largest cemetery on the Somme battlefield, Serre Road No. 2. (This cemetery was originally for those men killed on 1 July, 1916 and the later battles of November the same year. After the war the cemetery was enlarged twice, in 1922 and 1934, this was to make room for more and more British and Commonwealth soldiers whose remains were being found in all parts of the former battlefields).

Birmingham Pals: Aftermath

Along Black Road, the rest of 23 July continued with the occupation and consolidation of the trench and in patrol work to recover the dead and wounded. The 13th, 14th and 15th Field Ambulances, the medical units of the 5th Division, recorded that after the attack on Wood Lane, over 600 lying cases and about 2,000 walking wounded passed through their Advanced Dressing Stations. As news of the disastrous outcome of the attack began to filter through to the support lines of the 14th Royal Warwicks, Lieutenant Alan Furse, waited for news of his comrades. He wrote the following account about the morning of 23 July:

'At daybreak we were out on the road trying to get news of our battalion. We found the men who had been wounded, but were able to walk, crawling along the road towards the dressing station close to our lines and they all told the same tale of miserable failure. We helped them into motor charabancs, which were waiting to take them back to hospital, and gathered what scanty news we could of those we

knew well, but each only knew what had gone on just around him and definite news was very scanty. It was a nasty sight to see all our fellows so cut about and I remember well how badly Carroll was hit (Sergeant R Carroll, No.528, from Dolman Road, Aston). *A little later poor Jolliffe was brought in on a stretcher wounded in the stomach and he only lived an hour or so'* (Private Leslie Jolliffe, No.176, from Grove Avenue, Moseley; not far from Lieutenant Furze's own home in School Road).

Whilst waiting for news, Lieutenant Furze probably carried with him the packet of Players Cigarettes that were intended for his friend and fellow officer 'Betty', but he, unknown to Furse, had been killed. Captain Jeffrey Lythgoe, aged 25 was the son of the Vicar of St Paul's Church, Tipton. He was a former Dudley Grammar School and old boy of King Edwards, New Street. Prior to the war he had worked for the Alliance Assurance Company and had served for five years in the ranks of the Territorials. After enlisting into the battalion, Lythgoe had been a Sergeant in D Coy before being commissioned.

The 15th Royal Warwicks suffered a total of 141 casualties during the attack, thirty-four men being killed. One of those was the twenty-eight year old Private Percy Jeeves (No.611), the promising batsman and medium paced bowler of Warwickshire County Cricket Club. Not a Brummie, his family home was in Craven Street, Ravensthorpe, West Yorkshire. As a professional Percy Jeeves played forty-nine matches for Warwickshire between 1912-14; he has no known grave. Lieutenant-Colonel Colin Harding, the CO of the 15th Royal Warwicks, recalled the following in his memoirs after the war:

'Later, when proceeding to the scene of the action, I met amongst the many wounded a stretcher bearing my dear old friend, Gough, (Captain Roland Ivor Gough, CO D Coy; aged only twenty) still smoking his inevitable cigarette, bespattered with mud, pale as death but cheerful. He had been shot through the thigh and had a compound fracture. As we shake hands, Gough gives me a few heart rending details of the loss of life and the attack, needlessly apologises for its failure and passed on. We never met again.'

As evening approached, on 23 July, 13 Brigade was relieved by the 95th. The 16th Royal Warwicks were placed in reserve and took over positions on the slopes around the quarry along the eastern end of Caterpillar Valley. On Black Road, the 14th Royal Warwicks were relieved by the 1st Bedfords. After the relief, 13 Brigade made their way towards a former German fortified trench system known as Pommiers Redoubt which was situated on the south side of the road between Montauban and Mametz. The brigade entered the redoubt around 2 am, 24

July. When the remnants of the 14th Royal Warwicks wearily made their way back, Lieutenant Alan Furse was waiting. He later recalled the following:

'All that day (23rd) Timmie and I waited on that little road and saw our wounded coming in and later on received a message that our battalion would be relieved about midnight. We were allotted a piece of bare open field as camping ground and so as quickly as possible we got up a tent of sorts for the officers and got a supply of waterproof sheets for the men. We then waited on the Mametz-Montauban Road in the pitch dark for signs of the battalion. Shortly after one o'clock they came with A Coy leading, which now consisted of Lieutenant HIGGINS AND ONE PRIVATE. The other companies were not quite so bad but the battalion could only muster just over one hundred all told. Those who were left were in a very exhausted condition then I went to take my final orders from the CO, I found him sitting on the side of an old shell hole with his eyes full of tears and he told me of his awful feelings at the wonderful men he had lost.'

Fortunately, quite a few men disobeyed orders, and kept diaries. One in particular that survived belonged to Private W B Whitmore of the 14th Royal Warwicks (No.133, A Coy, from Rutland Road, Bearwood). Being a member of the

Above: Another sad duty as the battle zone moved forward was the job of removing the pay books from the dead for identification. The Germans entrenched along Wood Lane would hold out for a few more weeks. Thus, No Man's Land, adjacent to Wood Lane, where the bodies of many Birmingham Pals now lay, would be pounded by artillery from both sides. This is why so many are now commemorated on the Thiepval Memorial. *IWM Q23562*

Battalion's Quarter-Master Stores section, he mentions the attack but does not elaborate. However, he did write down for posterity the names and numbers of five A Coy men who survived the attack unscathed and two others who, like Sergeant Arthur Cooper, had spent forty-eight hours in No Man's Land seeking safety in a shell-hole.

Survivors:
Lt H L Higgins (Linden Road, Bournville)
1359   Cpl G T Smith
1637   Private W E Harrison (Ashted, B'ham)
1678   Private Cooper
15/614 Private. Dutton (Minstead Road, Gravelly Hill)
Returned from shell-hole:
593 Private A Bullivant
114 Private D W Harris (Gladys Road, Bearwood)

Finally before finishing with this tragic episode in the history of *The Missing City Battalions*, It is only fitting for Private J E B Fairclough (No.396, B Coy) to have the final word. The following are his comments recorded in the *First Birmingham Battalion in the Great War*:

> *'The first parade on Pommiers redoubt was a very sad one: a battalion had practically disappeared, leaving a mere handful to carry on its fine traditions. It is comforting to remember that the companies went to the charge in magnificent style, never faltering or hesitating, in face of a murderous fire, and Birmingham has reason to be proud of her sons and of the courage they displayed in the face of hopeless odds. Our first attack did not succeed, but in that magnificent effort and failure the City 'Pets' proved their worth in iron manner.'*

Pommiers Redoubt

After the sombre roll call of the 14th Royal Warwicks at Pommiers Redoubt, work was soon begun on the reorganisation of the depleted companies. A draft of one officer and sixty other ranks arrived during the day. These were the first recruits resulting from the Derby scheme. This scheme was introduced by Lord Derby prior to conscription, whereby men could volunteer for service, but were not called for until needed. The War Diary of the 14th Royal Warwicks states that these Derby men had very little experience, having only had eighteen weeks' training before being sent to France. However, they were 'physically very fine and with good intellect.' Later in the day the CO, Lieutenant-Colonel Murray, addressed the survivors of the battalion to thank them for their gallant conduct on the evening of 22 July. On 25 July, the GOC 5th Division, Major-General Stephens, addressed the battalion and 'thanked them for their very gallant conduct' and pointed out that although the attack failed 'no blame whatever attaches to them.' Also in reserve at Pommiers Redoubt, were

the 15th Royal Warwicks, but not having suffered the severe casualties as those of the 14th, the majority of men were put to work digging communication trenches under heavy and continuous shellfire, luckily with no casualties.

An officer of the battalion, who was wounded in the attack, died of his wounds on 24 July, he was Second-Lieutenant Christopher St John Tyrer, from Lyndon Road, Sutton Coldfield. He was one of four brothers who enlisted into the battalion. They were the sons of the Reverend Frank Tyrer, who was the Vicar of Moxley, near Darlaston (Second-Lieutenant Tyrer is buried in Heilly Station Cemetery, Mericourt-L'Abbé).

Whilst both sides were continually bombarding each other day and night there was little front line activity on the divisional sector for the time being. To get men, ammunition, stores and rations up to the fighting zone at High Wood, Longueval and Delville Wood, the sheltered Caterpillar Valley became choked with units of all the services. Consequently, the German shellfire was most severe there and the surrounding area. On 24 July the 16th Royal Warwicks were still in reserve in Montauban Alley. Between 06.00 to 06.30 am, concentrated German shellfire resulted in the battalion receiving its first casualties on returning to the Somme. Four men were killed by direct shellfire, another eleven were wounded, whilst four others suffered shell shock. The men killed were: Privates Albert Ackrill (No.1366) from Ladywood, Charles Birch (No.788) from Nechells, Ernest Hastings (No.16/1711) from Leamington Road, Sparkbrook and Harold Green (No.1205) from Cox Street West, Balsall Heath. Nothing remained of them to bury, they are all named on the Thiepval Memorial.

Sad News for Lieutenant Alan Furse

During the 14th Royal Warwicks period of rest and reorganisation at Pommiers Redoubt, Lieutenant Alan Furse received news concerning the whereabouts of the battlefield grave of his brother, Second-Lieutenant William Furse who had died of wounds on 1 July. William was an original 'Birmingham Pal' who was commissioned in September 1915 to the 21st Northumberland Fusiliers (102 [Tyneside Scottish] Brigade, 34th Division). The following is Alan's account of the events, written after the war:

> *'I got the Sergeant Carpenter a man named Chare (Sergeant Frederick Chare, No.530, from Coventry Road, Small Heath) to make me a cross out of a piece of old oak and then rode across to the Bapaume Road to find the spot. I left my groom and the horses on the road and struck out across country and eventually found the trench which was fairly well described by map reference. I erected the cross right on the*

E 3.

grave and after arranging a cross of white stones on the top of it, took two or three photographs.'

After the war, William's remains were transferred to the Bapaume Post Military Cemetery that is situated near the former Tara Redoubt overlooking La Boisselle.

The 15th Royal Warwicks continued supplying men for fatigues, digging new trenches and carrying and fetching etc. Heavy shelling was still in process as the War Diary records. Nonetheless,

2' Lieut T.A. FURSE
14th Royal Waricks.

2' Lieut W.H. FURSE Di'N'1
is buried in QUEMART
STREET Map. Ref X 19 6 6·8
Sheet 57 D. S.E 1/20,000

_____ Capt
Staff Capt
102 (Tyneside Sc. Mil.) Bde

14 8. 16.

the CO, Lieutenant-Colonel Colin Harding, thought it was still safe enough for a spot of horse riding. This resulted in a tragic incident, which is recounted in his memoirs:

'We had gone back about four or five miles from the front for a short rest, and although we were in the trenches, we were supposed to be out of the reach of ordinary shelling. Such being the case, I sent for my horse, which was stabled a few miles again further back and it was brought up to me by Doyle, my groom. My charger was a very brainy mare devoted to Doyle and Doyle to the horse. In this instance, he rode up his own horse and led mine, and I had hardly mounted when the enemy started sending over a casual shell or two. As my men were resting outside their trenches, as soon as the shelling commenced I rode round ordering them to take cover. Whilst so doing, a shell pitched between the horse Doyle was riding and my own; Doyle and another man was killed, also Doyle's horse. The impact threw me out of my saddle and I was dazed; clinging to my horse's neck we rushed helter-skelter till we were suddenly brought to an abrupt stoppage by a trench. Friends came to my assistance. I was shaken but not wounded. My horse was hit but not seriously, but the poor dear was sadly frightened as was its rider. God moves in a mysterious way, and why Doyle and myself did not cross to the Unknown together I shall never quite understand.'

The CO's groom was Lance Corporal Frederick Doyle (No.539) of Esme Road, Sparkhill. Two other men were killed by the shell, not one, as the CO recalled; they were: Corporal Joseph Jervis (No.823) who left a widow at Dolobran Road, Sparkbrook and Private Walter Middleton (No.539) of Bath Row. All three are now buried in Danzig Alley British Cemetery which is sited on a former German trench system to the west of Pommiers Redoubt.

On the evening of 25/26 July a stray German shell landed in the Divisional Ammunition dump which was situated near the village of Mametz. A few men suffered shock but fortunately no one was killed. However, Lieutenant Traill, according to the Divisional history, who was in charge of the dump, was blown nearly 100 yards into the cemetery! In all approximately 100,000 rounds of ammunition of all types was lost.

16th Royal Warwicks (3rd Birmingham Battalion) at Longueval

During the evening of 26 July the 5th Division's 15 Brigade relieved 95 Brigade on the southern outskirts of Longueval. The following day, 27 July at 07.10 am, would see the resumption of the British Fourth Army's offensive upon Longueval and Delville Wood. This task would be a joint venture between the 5th Division's 15 Brigade and the 2nd Division's 99 Brigade. If successful, the Fourth Army would be in a better position to launch a further attack upon the German Switch Line; which was due to commence on 30 July. 15 Brigade were to attack the northern portion of Longueval and the western edge of Delville Wood, whilst 99 Brigade had the job of clearing the rest of Delville Wood.

Below and right: The village of Longueval under German occupation, before the Somme offensive of July 1916.

188

As both brigades got into position and prepared for the assault the German artillery kept up a heavy barrage on the southern approaches to Longueval. In return, the British artillery had guns of all calibres firing on the northern approaches of the pulverised remains of what were once Longueval and Delville Wood. Consequently, the attack was to take place within a curtain of incessant shellfire; once inside all communication with the outside world would cease. News back to Brigade HQs of the progress of this forthcoming attack would depend on any survivors getting through this ring of destruction.

For 15 Infantry Brigade the 1st Norfolks would lead the attack, closely followed by the 1st Bedfords. The 1st Cheshires were to form a defensive flank whilst attacking a German strongpoint on the left (this was probably the machine-gun strongpoint situated at the end of Wood Lane that decimated the 14th Royal Warwicks on 22 July). The 16th Royal Warwicks were to be in close support near Sloane Street in the south-eastern outskirts of the village, to be called on when needed. An excellent account of what conditions were like at Longueval at this period of time are described in the memoirs of R B Talbot Kelly (*A Subaltern's Odyssey*, published in 1980 by William Kimber) who at the time was a Forward Observation Officer for 52 Brigade Royal Field Artillery, of the 9th (Scottish) Division. He went up to Longueval on Sunday, 16 July. One can only imagine, the ghastly surroundings that he found himself in and which had worsened eleven days later when the 16th Royal Warwicks had moved into the ruined village:

'Through stifling heat, and an endless curtain of shells, my signallers and I entered the smashed trenches before the village. Here we walked for over half a mile on half-buried German dead. Every

Left: Longueval Church before it entered the battle zone.

Below: An example of a fortified German held village with trenches running between the fortified buildings. Longueval may have looked liked this before it was pulverised into becoming a brick coloured stain on the landscape

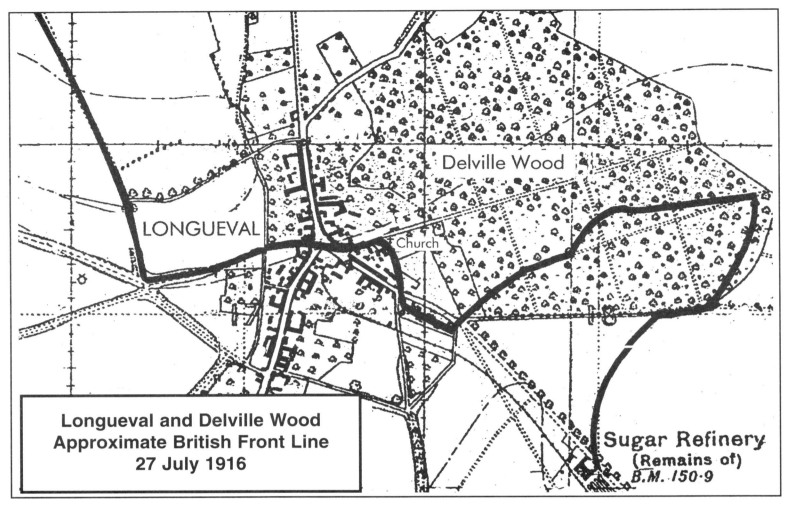

**Longueval and Delville Wood
Approximate British Front Line
27 July 1916**

step was on the ground that yielded to the foot, as the dead body below the layer of yellow clay gave to our weight. Sometimes a boot, removing a lump of earth, disclosed the nose or hand of the corpse below us. The village itself we entered up a sunken road between shattered orchards. The shambles on this road was beyond description, and the stink of death almost overpowering. Here the dead were just blasted, swollen and putrid bits of men, now a rotting head, now a pair of fleshless legs hung on a tree-stump. In one place I almost tripped upon the barrel of a man's torso, no legs nor arms nor skin had it, and the bowels ran out from the tunnel of the ribs to form a fly-blown horror on the road. And the village itself was no better; street upon street of incredible destruction and death. Outside one cottage lay three dead Germans with faces smashed in so that they were insets in a saucer of skull. And in a great shell-hole, filled with blood and water, sat a dead Highlander and a dead German, gazing, with sightless yellow eye-balls, into each other's faces.'

At 06.10 am, 27 July, 369 British artillery pieces were brought to bear upon Longueval and Delville Wood. For the first time a 'creeping barrage' was to be used. It was not as sophisticated as those that

were developed later in the war but from zero hour, 07.10, the barrage was to leap forward at three intervals of 90 minutes. The infantry were then to rush forward and consolidate each time until the village and wood were cleared. However, under the ruins of Longueval there was a honeycomb of tunnels connecting many fortified cellars which gave the German defenders ample protection. As the attack got under away, the Divisional History now takes over:

'Parties of Germans came up from the cellars and dug-outs, and took up positions among the ruined buildings. The Norfolks pressing forward, were checked, and the barrage went on in accordance with the time-table, leaving the Germans in the village free of shellfire. The fight now developed into a struggle between the opposing infantry amid the ruins of the village within a ring of artillery fire.'

Within an hour of the attack beginning, the Norfolks were held up by machine-gun fire. By 08.15 the 16th Royal Warwicks were ordered up in support. At 09.00 A and B Coys had moved into trenches near the village cross-roads. Here the battalion came under the temporary command of the CO of the 1st Norfolks, Lieutenant-Colonel Stone. At 12 noon Captain H Richardson of the 16th Royal Warwicks (OC, A coy, from South Littleton near Evesham) reported that two of his

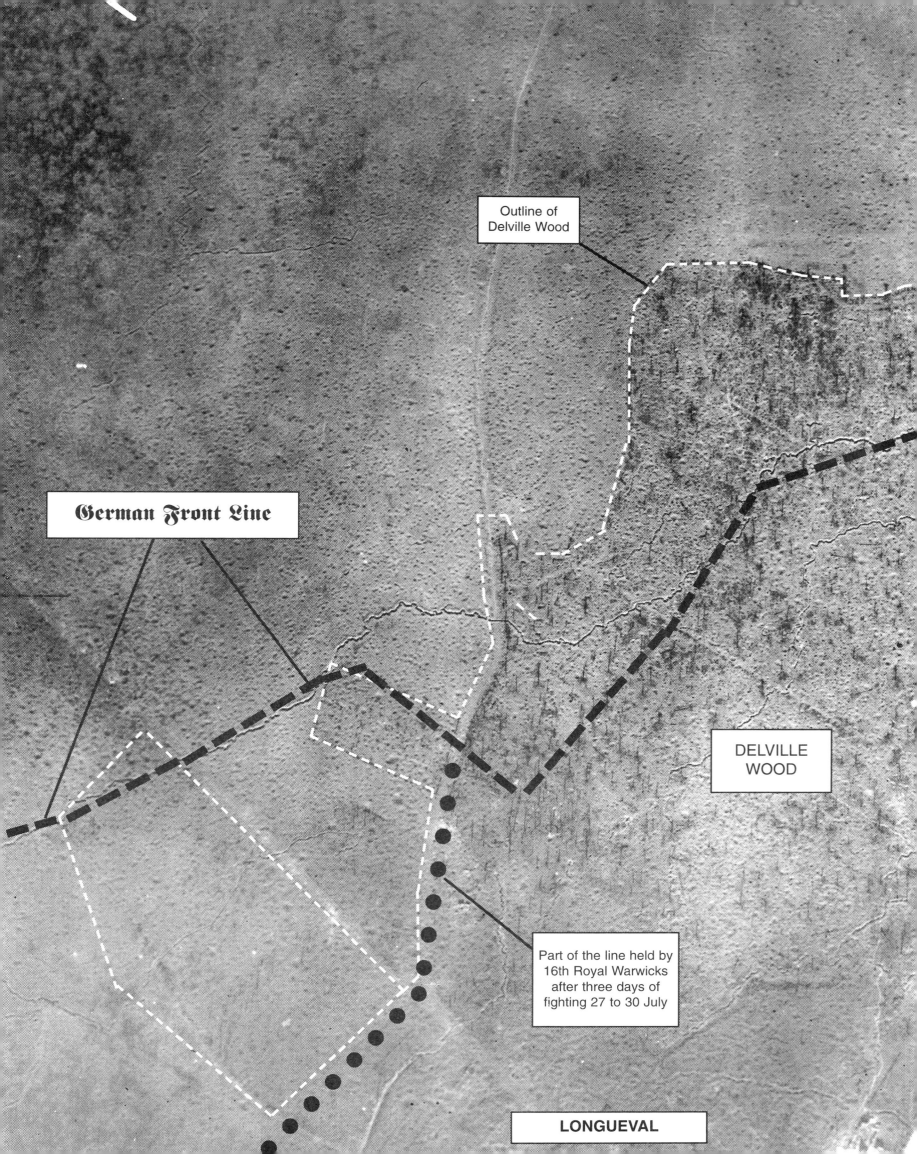

Outline of
Delville Wood

German Front Line

DELVILLE
WOOD

Part of the line held by
16th Royal Warwicks
after three days of
fighting 27 to 30 July

LONGUEVAL

platoons had got detached from the rest owing to the fact that the officer in command had become a casualty. Later in the afternoon B coy had reported that two of its platoons had become detached because of further officer casualties. It is now that the battalion War Diary mentions the gallant conduct of CSM W Baker:

'CSM Baker was left in charge of these two platoons and acting on his own initiative (having received no definite orders from his Coy Commanders) he led the two platoons under his command straight up into the firing line and joined up with the Norfolk and Bedfordshire Regiments.'

No.1188, CSM Baker was not an original volunteer to the 3rd Birmingham Battalion, but a pre-war regular from the 2nd Royal Warwicks. He had been wounded the previous year at the battle of Loos and on recovery drafted into the battalion.

Gradually, as the day wore on, 15 Infantry Brigade slowly gained more and more of the village. From ruin to ruin they went bombing cellars, rushing houses and hunting down machine-gun nests until most of Longueval had been cleared. At 17.30 orders were issued for B Coy, 16th Royal Warwicks, to form a defensive flank on a line running roughly from the ruins of Longueval Church to the northern end of Trones Wood.

Before continuing, the reader may be interested to know of a Birmingham man who was involved in 99 Brigade's attack on Delville Wood. During the fierce fighting Sergeant Albert Gill of the 1st Kings Royal Rifle Corps was killed whilst displaying great prowess as a platoon leader and was later posthumously awarded the Victoria Cross. Sergeant Gill, a Regular soldier for seventeen years, left a widow at 2, back of Cope Street, Spring Hill, Birmingham. As the day wore on, Lieutenant-Colonel Dudgeon, the CO of the 16th Royal

Warwicks, and the rest of the HQ Coy moved up to the forward HQ of the 1st Norfolks in the ruins of Longueval. Then, at 19.10, D Coy were ordered up into the battle whilst the remnants of A Coy moved into the support lines to the south of the village. He also ordered two platoons of C Coy along with a Lewis Gun section to move and establish three strongpoints in the sunken road known as 'Piccadilly', near where the HQ was now operating. Five attempts were made in trying to send the message through. The shellfire was so heavy that each runner was killed in trying to get through. This leads to the sad story concerning the last few lines of probably the last letter written by Private James Edward Randle (D Coy, No.991) to his girlfriend Ethel Hill of Clissold Street, Hockley. the letter was written before the 16th Royal Warwicks had moved to the Somme front. Private Randle was also the company barber when out of the line:

'I suppose Fred as told you about the luck my friend 'Windows' (Pte Walter Moss, N0.921) *and myself as had. We only get together now when we get out of the trenches, owing to one being a bomber and the other being a company runner and barber. I THINK I HAVE FINISHED GOING INTO THE FIRING LINE NOW I AM A COMPANY RUNNER, NOT SO DANGEROUS....'*

Private James Randle, whilst acting as a runner, was killed at Longueval on 27 July. According to his friend 'Windows', when writing his condolences to Ethel a couple of months later, 'Jim met his death quite instantaneously, and I doubt much he ever felt any pain whatever.' Private James Randle is another name on the Thiepval Memorial. Perhaps Jim met his death along with his Platoon CO, Second-Lieutenant Rowland, which is covered in a later paragraph. At 22.30, Lieutenant Alfred Henry Sayer (the son of a former Birmingham Lord

Below: The rubble that was once the village of Longueval. This photograph taken in September, of troops carrying duckboards up to the new front line, gives an idea of the terrain the 16th Royal Warwicks had to deal with.
IWM Q4265

Mayor) attempted to make his way from the Norfolks HQ back to the outskirts of Longueval to find out if any messages had come through from Company Commanders. Again, to show how intense the shellfire was, the distance he had to cover was approximately 600 yards. This took Lieutenant Sayer near enough an hour-and-a-half to complete. Finally, he managed to get a message to the CO of C Coy that two platoons and a Lewis Gun team were needed in Longueval. Under the guidance of Lieutenant Sayer the body of men moved off at 00:15 (28 July), but, with all the landmarks having been completely obliterated they managed to lose their direction. Lieutenant Sayer managed to re-locate the Norfolks HQ, and finally reported to the CO at 03:30, eight hours after the first orders were issued.

However, Lieutenant Sayer's epic journey was a complete waste of time. On reaching the Battalion HQ he found out that 15 Infantry Brigade were now in the process of being relieved by 95 Brigade. The 16th Royal Warwicks were .ordered back to Pommiers Redoubt; all except two platoons of D Coy. They were to be attached to 95 Brigade until the evening of 28 July.

The shellfire was continuous all through the 28th and the village was shrouded in a cloud of dust and smoke. Despite the shellfire, 95 Brigade consolidated the line along Duke Street unopposed. The following day, 29 July, the 12th Gloucesters occupied a line a further 500 yards north of Duke Street. (At the cross-roads near to Caterpillar Valley Cemetery, there now stands a memorial cross in commemoration of the 12th Gloucesters action on July 29.) For the two days of close support that the 16th Royal Warwicks were in Longueval, the battalion suffered 267 casualties, of this number, a total of fifty-seven men were killed; forty-five of those killed were never recovered. It is another indication of the hellish conditions that prevailed in and around Longueval and Delville Wood. One survivor of the battalion's experience at Longueval was, at the time, nineteen year old Second-Lieutenant Thomas Eric Pearman, Platoon CO of D Coy (Second-Lieutenant Pearman came from Ryton-on-Dunsmore, Warwickshire, and was an old boy of King Henry VIII school, Coventry. He enlisted into the ranks of the battalion, aged seventeen, No.674, and was commissioned in March 1915). Sixty years later he wrote a brief memoir relating to the 27/28 July 1916:

'We now came into the evening barrage laid down purposely to stop the supports reaching the line. As we were going forward one could see in front the splintered trunks of what once had been Delville Wood. The Norfolks ahead must have been in the wood. I think I envied them, at least it seemed to me that anywhere in the world would have been more comfortable and less terrifying. We were told to enter along the edge of the wood with its blasted trunks and burning shrivelled branches. Here the barrage reached a crescendo; field guns and howitzers had obviously linked all their fuses to the edge of the wood and rained their high explosives like a hail storm. It didn't seem possible to escape. The ground was so churned up, however, that cover from machine-gun fire was easy and a certain amount of cover from shrapnel, but nothing gave protection from the high explosive which rained without cease and which if it didn't get a direct hit, just buried. We hadn't even the comfort of moving – either backward or forward, and the orders were to stay put until required. Would we ever be required?... Would any of us be there to be required, to answer a call?

'To relive the mental torture I thought of God and heaven. Here was hell. At school and in church we prayed 'The Lord's Prayer' and I partly remembered it. Nursery prayer did not seem very appropriate here. Perhaps if I prayed God would do something. 'Our Father' seemed a long way away and the prayer, even when gabbled, did not stupefy or over reach the awful horror and fear. So the prayer as a whole petered into 'Our Father', 'Our Father' in endless repetition. It must have worked, because I slept or fainted, at any rate lost consciousness, and eventually opened, my eyes to a warm silent world with the sun blazing down. There were more of my platoon near me. Perhaps they were buried in the shell pocked soil, but by moving slowly down the edge of the wood some survivors materialised out of holes and we just lay there, gulped some of our water and food and waited. Then came a Company runner with orders to close out Company Headquarters. There was Jimmy Holme the O.C. with the remainder of another platoon lying in a slit trench along what had been a hard road. Jimmy had been in the French Foreign Legion and still had the lice marks on his back. He had been a student in Paris before the war and very much a man of the world. Jimmy kept me sane for the next four or five hours by reading extracts from the Gourmet's Guide to Europe *and telling me of the mouth watering dishes which could be had at some of the famous hotels and restaurants. I did not realise at the time that this was one of his great acts of courage. But I did later, and now sixty years later, still do so.* (Captain James Edward Holme was later killed when the 5th Division was serving in the Ypres Salient, 9 October 1917 and he is

Above: Private Jim Randle, No.991, D Coy, 16th Royal Warwicks. Killed at Longueval on 27 July 1916. Jim who was born at Bradley, near Wolverhampton, is now commemorated on the Thiepval Memorial. (See page 98).

Below: The last Field Postcard sent by Private Jim Randle, posted on 4 July 1916, to his girlfriend Ethel Hill of Clissold Street, Hockley. Her last letter to Jim, written after his death, was returned with the following remark across the envelope 'Killed in action, return to sender'.

NOTHING is to be written on this side except the date and signature of the sender. Sentences not required may be erased. If anything else is added the post card will be destroyed.

I am quite well.

I have been admitted into hospital sick and am going on well. wounded and hope to be discharged soon.

I am being sent down to the base.

I have received your letter dated _____ telegram _____ parcel _____

Letter follows at first opportunity.

I have received no letter from you lately. for a long time.

Signature only. J. E. Randle

Date 4/7/16

[Postage must be prepaid on any letter or post card addressed to the sender of this card.]

(93509) Wt. W3497-293 2,250m. 4.16 J. J. K. & Co., Ltd.

commemorated on the Tyne Cot Memorial).

'The evening barrage had started up again but fitfully, perhaps only a near shell burst every five or six minutes. We had a few casualties but stretcher bearers could brave it up and down the road and it was fairly good going for the walking wounded. The Norfolks had taken their objectives and we were all to be shortly pulled out. They didn't want us here.

'I remember taking what was left of my platoon back to the edge of the Wood where there were far fewer standing trees where I had spent the early morning. There we linked up with another subaltern named Rowlands (Second-Lieutenant Rowland Evan Basil Rowlands, the name is correct, D Coy, 9 platoon) who had survived untouched... He told me he was quite certain he was going to be killed and I tried to cheer him up. Shortly afterwards I felt an urge to check up on my platoon further on. When I came back to meet Rowlands he was not there, nor the men who had been there with him. A giant shell had taken the lot, or buried them. I can remember scratching in the earth, calling Rowlands and then losing consciousness. I came to with Jimmy Holme pushing the neck of his whisky flask between my lips. Sadly for him I drank the lot. He could not, or would not, believe me when I said I was looking for Rowlands but thought I was crazy. And Rowlands could never tell any of us where he was.'

14th Royal Warwicks, the Second Attempt on Wood Lane

On 28 July back at Pommiers Redoubt 13 Infantry Brigade made preparations for the evening move back to the front line at Longueval. During the day, the 14th Royal Warwicks had received another draft of 152 other ranks. The majority of the men, though physically sound, had received little training. A small percentage of the men were veterans from 1st and 2nd Warwicks who had been out to France before, and had recovered from wounds. The 14th Royal Warwicks along with the 2nd KOSBs were ordered to take over the line along the lower segment of Black Road to the junction of Pont Street and Duke Street and eastwards to the junction with Piccadilly.

The 15th Royal Warwicks were again to be in reserve, and they were to occupy old German trenches to the west of Montauban, near to Caterpillar Wood. Prior to this move the battalion, whilst at Pommiers Redoubt had been supplying around 450 men daily on fatigues for 95 Brigade, carrying rations and water etc.

On 29 July, the 16th Royal Warwicks, now back

at Pommiers Redoubt, supplied two working parties. The first was an officer and twenty-five men carrying sandbags up to the front line. The other party of 125 men under the command of Second-Lieutenant J D Dell, carried wounded from Longueval back to the casualty clearing station. This work was carried out successfully under very heavy shellfire. For this the battalion was congratulated by the Brigadier-Generals commanding 15 and 95 Brigades. (Br.Gen M N Turner and Br.Gen Lord E C Gordon-Lennox.) This resulted in the following letter, received by the CO of the 16th Royal Warwicks, Lieutenant-Colonel R M Dudgeon:

'The Brigadier General Commanding desires to express his entire satisfaction in the way the working party of 120 men detailed to carry sick and wounded from Longueval last night carried out their work. The Brigadier General Commanding 95 I.B. also expresses his entire satisfaction in the thorough way in which this duty was performed.

'The Brigadier General Commanding wishes to express his admiration to those who carried out this duty.'

(Signed) W. Tyrell Brooks, Captain, 15 Infantry Brigade

As previously mentioned, the next phase of the attack for the British Fourth Army was about to begin. The objective of XV Corps, which consisted of the 5th and 51st Divisions, was to clear the orchards north of Longueval and take as much of Wood Lane as possible. Zero hour for the attack was 6.10 pm, 30 July.

This time it was the turn of C and D Coys of the 14th Royal Warwicks to make the attack, whilst A and B Coys were to remain in close support. The 2nd KOSBs were to be on the right of the 14th, whilst 153 Brigade of the 51st Division were on the left. This time the attack was to be launched in daylight. Writing in the 16th Royal Warwicks War Diary, the CO, Lieutenant-Colonel Murray, was of the opinion that companies assembling for the attack would be in full view of a probable German observation post situated on the high ground north of Longueval. By 02.00 on 30 July, C and D Coys of the 14th Royal Warwicks completed the take-over of the firing line along Black Road without sustaining any casualties. This time the battalion was to the right of its position a week earlier. Patrols were then sent out into No Man's Land to reconnoitre in view of the proposed attack. Running eastwards from the trenches now occupied by the 14th Royal Warwicks was a partly dug trench started by the 95 Brigade, the aim of which was to connect a series of strongpoints that were forward of the British line. Orders were given for the men of C and D Coys to 'dig themselves in as rapidly as possible, and improving by all means in their power this line of trench,' as the War Diary put it. This meant prior to the attack the jumping off point was now approximately 150 yards nearer

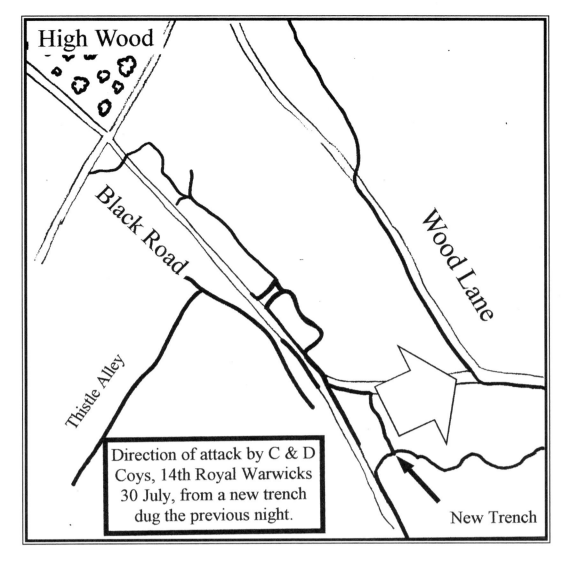

High Wood

Black Road

Thistle Alley

Wood Lane

Direction of attack by C & D Coys, 14th Royal Warwicks 30 July, from a new trench dug the previous night.

New Trench

Above: Map showing the second attack upon Wood Lane.

to the German line.

A preliminary bombardment began at 3.45 pm, with the main bombardment starting an hour later; increasing intensity towards zero hour. From the German point of view, an attack was now imminent. The German artillery response was equal to ours, and again Longueval was surrounded by a wall of fire, thus causing communication problems to the various Brigade Headquarters once the attack was under way. At 5.50 pm, C and D Coys left their trenches and under cover of the corn advanced until reaching striking distance of the German lines. Out of sight of the Germans the two companies formed two waves and crouched down in the corn and waited for Zero Hour. On their left flank were the 1/5th Gordon Highlanders (153 Brigade 51st Division) and on their right the 2nd KOSBs. Each man carried an extra bandolier of ammunition plus two hand grenades. At 6.05 pm the attack got underway.

From Lieutenant-Colonel Murray's point of observation the battalion was soon lost to sight in the corn. A few minutes later the sound of machine gun and rifle fire could be heard. First reports as to how the attack was faring came in around 6.30 pm; it looked pretty grim. The battalion had come under very heavy frontal and flank fire and both companies had been badly cut up. Two patrols were then sent out to get in touch with the attacking troops in order to get definite news. It was not the

news that Lieutenant-Colonel Murray wanted to hear, odd groups of men were widely dispersed seeking cover in shell holes approximately forty to fifty yards from the German trenches.

On hearing the news B Coy of the 15th Royal Warwicks were ordered up to reinforce the original jumping off line being held by A and B Coys of the 14th. Second-Lieutenant 'Laddie' Higgins, was by now the 14th's Intelligence Officer (Higgins was the only officer of A Coy, to come out of the previous attack on 22 July, unscathed) and at 6.45 pm was sent forward to try and reorganise the front two companies out in No Man's Land. His aim was to try and get the men, by digging, to connect the shell holes and form a new line. Unfortunately due to the few men that were left, he reported back that he did not think that they could do much good. On the left flank the Highlanders who were attacking Wood Lane had also been cut to pieces and had gone to ground and were digging in around 200 yards in front of their jumping off line. To the right, the 2nd KOSBs had come under very heavy shell-fire in the north western edge of Delville Wood, but a machine-gun section had managed to clear the wood and dug in. Here in isolation these few men beat off enemy counter-attacks and endured shell fire from our own guns for several days. Finally having received no support and running out of food and water, they retired back to our lines, then being held by the 17th Division. The 1st Royal West Kents

(with only a fighting strength of 175 other ranks) who were in support of the KOSBs, were so further weakened by shellfire that the 1st Bedfords (15 Brigade, 5th Division) were also sent up in support, whilst the 16th Royal Warwicks moved into old German trenches to the west of Longueval. (These being on the reverse slope of the ridge, along the Longueval-Bazentin le Grand Road.)

The attack had ground to a halt, the only thing to do now was to reorganise the original line. At 01.00 am, 31 July, the remaining men of C and D Coys, 14th Royal Warwicks, were ordered back to the original front line. Relieved by the 15th Royal Warwicks at 03:00 am, the 14th made their way back to Pommiers Redoubt to count the costs of another heavy toll upon its ranks. With the 16th Royal Warwicks being in close support, for a short time, all three battalions of the Birmingham Pals were occupying the same sector of trenches.

Reasons for Failure

In the War Diary of the 14th Royal Warwicks, the CO, Lieutenant-Colonel Murray, wrote the following observations concerning the attack:

> 'I think it very probable that the Germans have a post of observation on the slope facing DELVILLE WOOD about point S 11 b 0/5 from which they can observe our lines and see Coys assembling for the attack.'

> 'They undoubtedly have machine guns on the slope immediately behind their front line trench. This slope commands our line of advance.'

> 'I am of the opinion that the Artillery preparation was too short

> 'The German trenches are reported to have been badly smashed up at one point, vis: S 11 c 8/8, but the remainder of the line had escaped Artillery fire.'

> 'Throughout the bombardment the heavies were dropping very short, and at times shells landed behind and into our own front line trench. A very large percentage of these shells were, luckily for us, blind.'

> 'I reported this matter to the Brigade on three or four occasions, but even up to the very end the heavies were undoubtedly off their targets and probably did little damage to the German trenches.'

> 'I am of opinion that under cover of the corn fields, a successful infantry attack could be launched at the German trenches without Artillery preparation, which of course informs the enemy of our intention, and gives him time to prepare manning his trenches.'

Major-General Stephens, 5th Division CO reported back to XV Corps HQ that his brigades, who by now were well under strength, were exhausted for any further attack on this front and he urged that a fresh division be given the task. His wishes were granted and it was arranged that the 17th (Northern) Division (New Army) was to replace the 5th on the night of 1 August.

The 15th Royal Warwicks occupied the front line opposite the strong point at the end of Wood Lane and were attached temporarily to 15 Brigade when it relieved the 13th on the evening of 31 July. Despite heavy and continuous shellfire which made digging very difficult the day was spent consolidating the trenches between strongpoints; resulting in thirty-five casualties and of these thirteen were either killed or to die of wounds. Enemy shellfire also concentrated along the support trenches, to the west of Longueval, that were still occupied by the 16th Royal Warwicks. Still counting the cost of the casualties suffered on 27 July, the 16th received another twenty more whilst in support. The two Birmingham Battalions remained in these positions until around midnight of 1 August; the 15th were relieved by the 9th Northumberland Fusiliers and the 16th by the 12th Manchesters.

> 'Our first period of participation in the Battle of the Somme was over, and a hard-earned battle honour had been added to the record of the old 5th Division; Longueval will always be remembered by those who were there as the place where there was a more intense and continuous shellfire than any other in the whole course of the War.' 5th Division in the Great War

From 19 July until 1 August, the fourteen days the 5th Division were in the line, the combined total of men who died in the service of the three Birmingham Battalions was 422; with approximately 750 further men wounded, the majority of all these being the original volunteers. The worst hit by far was the 14th Royal Warwicks, its total casualty figure for the last fourteen days had been twenty-two officers and 632 other ranks. The following is how Private J E B Fairclough (B Coy, No.396) remembered the next few days, taken from his book, *The First Birmingham Battalion in the Great War:*

> 'A day was spent at Pommier (sic) Redoubt, and the 5th Division, now only a skeleton and very exhausted, was relieved by the 17th Division. The battalion marched back to tents about 2 miles north-east of Dernacourt, and during this period of rest, bathing parades in the Ancre at Buire were very much appreciated as the weather was blazing hot. It was possible to take stock of the position and realise how very few of the old battalion had survived the two ghastly attacks. The First Birmingham Battalion had practically ceased to exist, for very few of the original officers and men were left. When the

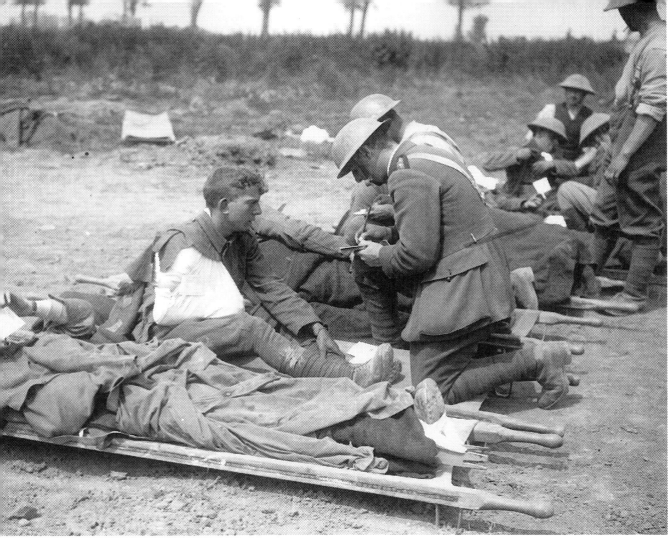

division was relieved, 16 officers and 289 other ranks constituted the full strength of the battalion. Comrades of many months had disappeared, the fate of many was unknown, and many were gone beyond recall. It was a sad time: numerous old associations, formed in happier training days and strengthened by common hardship during the winter of 1915 were broken, and although there was no parade of sentiment, the losses were keenly felt.'

5th Division at Rest

On 2/3 August the Division entrained at Edgehill Station near Buire, and moved back approximately forty miles behind the front line to an area of French countryside, south east of Abbeville. Here, after a few days rest and clean up, hundreds of new drafts were received bringing the division back to near full fighting strength and training for future offensives began. The 14th Royal Warwicks bivouacked by the village of Etrejust, the 15th at Villars-Campsart and the 16th at Le Quesnoy.

500 men were drafted into the 14th Royal Warwicks in the first two weeks of August, many had only two to three months training. There was also a mixture of men who had formerly served with the 1st, 2nd, 11th, 15th and 16th battalions of the Royal Warwickshire Regiment, all had war

service and had now recovered from slight wounds. A draft of thity-five men came from the 1st and 2nd Worcesters, causing the following comment in the 14th's War Diary: 'a fine body of men, all with war service, but they are not happy at being transferred from their own battalions.' By far the greatest number of new drafts, 195, were Territorials from the Huntingdonshire Cyclist Battalion. The War Diary continues:

'with but a few exceptions well set up and physically sound. Have done practically no infantry training throughout their average service of nineteen months. Have fired only thirty to forty rounds on a range and thrown but one live bomb. Have been employed throughout their service on night patrol work along the east coast.'

Many other Hunts Cyclists were drafted into the 1/5th, 1/7th and 1/8th Territorial Battalions of the Warwickshire Regiment at this time also.

With the arrival of so many new men into the division, preparations were started to get battalions up to the required standard, and practise hard learned lessons gained from the previous three weeks on the Somme. The following list is an example of the training put in by the men of the 16th Royal Warwicks during this so called period of rest, from 6 to 23 August; and no doubt very similar to that of the rest of the division:

Physical training; bayonet fighting; platoon

Below: An anonymous Hunts Cyclist. Nearly two hundred Hunts Cyclists were drafted into the 14th Royal Warwicks during August 1916.

Steve Farrant

Above: A behind the lines scene of soldiers from various regiments getting water.
IWM Q4028

Below: Troops resting in Bivouac. Looking at their leather equipment and their cap badges, this appears to be a New Army battalion of the Royal Fusiliers.
IWM Q1155

and company close and extended order drill; musketry instruction; Lewis gun instruction; bombing classes; signalling; sniping and scouting.

Company training, consisting of :

(1) Methods of advancing under fire and the use of ground
(2) Training in the conduct of infantry patrols
(3) Fire and formation in battle
(4) Intercommunication and passing of orders
(5) The assault, pushing forward of patrols after assault
(6) Attack and defence of a wood
(7) Attack and defence of a village

On 11 August, the 14th Royal Warwicks received orders that all the original surviving members of the battalion were to be granted a forty-eight hour

pass for anywhere in France except Amiens or Paris. (The reader may now think, how very kind of the 'powers that be' to be considerate to these men of the 14th Royal Warwicks. But, before they were allowed to leave camp, they all had to be inoculated for Para-Typhoid, the side effects making some of the men very poorly.) Le Treport on the coast proved the most popular choice for the men. Perhaps another reason was because there were also four military hospitals in Le Treport, and many friends who had been wounded in the attacks on 22 July and 30 were probably recovering here. Private J E B Fairclough (B Coy, No.396) recalled this very valuable forty-eight hours respite from the horrors of war:

'Parties left the camp on Friday morning (11 August) *for Airaines, where the hotel in the town had a rush lunch hour providing pork-chop and chip meals for the excursionists. No journey to the seaside was ever more eagerly anticipated than this. The amenities of hotel life at Mers were in marked contrast to life in Dead Horse Valley. Sea bathing; meals served on tables with white cloths; turning into a clean bed at night; all came as echoes of former days. We had a real taste of civilised life, and succeeded for a short time in forgetting the army and the Somme. The scene on Monday morning* (14 August) *at Le Treport railway station was reminiscent of Sunday evenings at Sutton. Some delay occurred in admitting the troops to the platform, and the troops therefore took the matters into their own hands and stormed the gates to get in the train, much to the consternation of the French railway staff. Walking back from Airaines to the camp at Etrejust one party met a group of four walking in the opposite direction. Enquiries were made, and the*

party returning to the battalion was informed 'We are going to England to become chaplains, you are going back to Delville Wood on Thursday!'

Return to the Somme

On Thursday 24 August, the 5th Division made its way back to the Somme front, though Delville Wood was not to be the destination this time. The Division reached the area around Dernancourt on 25 August. The 14th and 15th Royal Warwicks going into bivouac in 'Happy Valley' near Bray sur Somme, whilst the 16th stayed in a camp known as the Sandpits which was situated near the village of Meaulte. Still part of the British Fourth Army, the 5th Division now came under the umbrella of XIV Corps commanded by Lieutenant-General, the Earl of Cavan.

The following day, 26 August, the 5th Division relieved the 35th (Bantam) Division that was entrenched on the slopes of what was known as the Maltz Horn Ridge. The divisional front, about a mile in length, lay between Angle Wood on the right (the boundary between the British and French Army) and Arrow Head Copse on the left, the junction with the British 20th Division. The front line was taken over by 95 and 13 Brigades, with 15 Brigade (16th Royal Warwicks) being in reserve. The 1st Royal West Kents and the 15th Royal Warwicks took over a front line that had only been taken two nights previously. I must add here that the front line taken over by the division was not a continuous one. There was a fairly well established trench system from around Maltz Horn Farm running up to Delville Wood, but the area in which the 15th Royal Warwicks now found themselves

was not yet properly established. They found themselves on a 600 metre front, with slight slope of 50 metres, finishing in the vicinity of Angle Wood. A, B and C Coys of the 15th Royal Warwicks relieved the 20th Lancashire Fusiliers, whilst 'D' Coy stayed in reserve in Hardecourt. In support were the 2nd KOSBs and 14th Royal Warwicks. The 14th were in a former German front line trench known as Silesia Trench, north of Maricourt, which was taken by Pals battalions from Liverpool and Manchester on 1 July 1916. These were the trenches that overlooked the Birmingham Pals, when they first arrived in France, the previous December.

Whilst in reserve the men of the 14th had a chance to investigate. 'We found several dugouts still full of Huns, but on account of the smell we refrained from souvenir hunting,' Lieutenant Alan Furse recalled. The 15th Royal Warwicks now had the distinction of being on the extreme right of the British Western Front trench system. 'Relief difficult owing to bad lines of communication', was the entry for the evening of 26 August in the War Diary. Lieutenant-Colonel Colin Harding, the CO, elaborated further in his memoirs:

'To get there we had to pass Maricourt, but, alas, it could not now be recognised as the Maricourt where, more than a year ago I rested with the King Edward's Horse. (Harding was 2nd in command of this battalion prior to him becoming CO of the 15th Royal Warwicks.) *I remember that journey, alas, too well. We had to pass through a sort of tunnel where the place was simply littered with dead. To pass through we had at times to crawl over them. At other times my foot splashed*

Below: Fricourt Road near Albert: September 1916. This road must have one time come under German observation, hence the camouflage screen draped on the trees to the left. The troops resting along the roadside appear to be from the Hampshire Regiment. Possibly the 15th Hampshires of 122 Brigade, 41st Division. Whilst the troops marching are from the New Zealand Division. Both of these Divisions were involved in the offensive on 15 September.
IWM Q 4346

the open, to our objective where I meet an enraged British Battalion Commander from whom I have orders to take over and who has been expecting us for hours. I enquire for the trenches and the position of our flanks, but he does not know and seems to care less. Finally he disappears and leaves me to find out where my responsibility begins and ends.

'There are no dugouts, no shelter for my men or myself. The Battalion forms some sort of line and finally hitches on to the French troops on one flank, the other flank seems in the air'.

It was 02.30 am, on 27 August, when the 15th Royal Warwicks had completed their relief. Opposite and overlooking them was 'one of the strongest redoubts ever made by the engineering skill of the Germans', to quote the divisional history, better known as Falfemont Farm. Just over a mile behind the farm lay the small town of Combles, which was to be the eventual target for the next British-French mid-September offensive. Surrounded by hills, Combles, had not received much shelling up till now, and the Germans had turned the town into a veritable fortress. Apart from a very good trench system in and around the town, tunnels criss-crossed underground connecting fortified cellars. Combles would be a very tough nut to crack. It was decided that the best plan of attack was for the British and French to go either side of the town and get in via the back door. On the British part, the high ground in the vicinity of Leuze Wood, would first have to be taken. Which now brings us back to the 5th Division; before the British could be in a position to attack Combles, the next action for the ever dwindling Birmingham Pals was to be the attack on Falfemont Farm.

The farm was situated on the front end of a spur, with the ground dropping away approximately fifty metres (165 ft) on three sides and behind it, about half a mile, was Leuze Wood, or to the British Tommy, Lousy Wood. 29 August was the date planned for the joint venture of the British Fourth and French Sixth Armies, but this was cancelled and moved to 3 September. The British part of the attack was to be on a front more or less four miles in length, from High Wood down to Angle Wood. It may be of interest to note that the failed preliminary operation, involving the 14th and 15th Royal Warwicks attack upon Wood Lane, on 22 July, was still one of the objectives for the attack, after six weeks of bitter fighting the Germans were still firmly entrenched there.

Getting back to the 15th Royal Warwicks, as darkness fell on the evening of 27 August, the battalion was ordered to commence digging a new front line trench, 200 yards nearer to Falfemont Farm. In spite of the heavy German shellfire, by dawn on the morning of 28 August, the 15th had completed a new trench on a 400 yard front, averaging four foot deep. The men returned to their

Above: Guides near Trones Wood, September 1916. When a divisional relief took place they would take the fresh incoming battalions, who had not served in the sector before, up to the front line. The two soldiers are from an unidentified battalion, the private on the right, is wearing the leather 1914 pattern equipment that was issued mostly to the New Armies. He, also, has a signallers cloth patch, two crossed flags, sewn on his left arm. The mud indicates that this photograph was taken at the beginning of September 1916, when heavy rain showers were experienced across the Somme battlefield. In fact, a comment in the War Diary of the 14th Royal Warwicks, on 10 September, describes the trenches and surroundings 'a sea of stinking mud'.

through a quagmire of putrefied remains. It was dark. To strike a match would have been fatal. I remember Captain Davenport, who was ably leading his Company, struggling through this uncovered cemetery with many of his men was knocked out by a shell. I remember the resulting chaos which followed for I was just behind my faithful Liddell. (Captain F H Liddell, the Adjutant. Enlisted into the battalion as a Private, No.499, from High Street, Solihull and ended the war with the rank of Major with the Military Cross and Bar and was Brigade D.A.A.G. for the 17th Division.) Another officer takes Davenport's place and I tell them to carry on. For the moment I do not know what happens to Davenport and the other wounded. Forward, forward, is the word of command, and under the fire of a hellish bombardment, we struggle on, in and out of shell holes, but now, thank goodness, in former positions for the hours of daylight, whilst the German artillery spent the rest of the day attempting to undo their endeavours. Despite heavy rainfall and the difficulty of getting hot rations up the line, the men, to quote the War Diary, were in 'good spirits'. In his memoirs, the CO of the 15th Royal Warwicks, Lieutenant-Colonel Colin Harding, drew some of his information from the diary of his Batman Private Sidney Silver (No.1213), and the following are Private Silver's thoughts for August 28th:

'Shelled to Hell. Some of the wounded look ghastly. Had some warm shaves here to-day. Poor old Stokey knocked out to-night among many others. Fed up a bit. Hottest shop we have had together. Things warming up.'

But the Shellfire had taken its toll, Lieutenant A W Davenport, Second-Lieutenant R W Travis and one other rank were wounded and sadly fourteen others were killed. One man in particular was the left hand bowler, who had made several appearances for Warwickshire County Cricket Club, Sergeant Harold Bates (No.617, C Coy). Harold, prior to the war, had also worked on the ground staff at Lords. his brother, Len Bates (No.644, C Coy), survived the war and played 440 games for Warwickshire between 1913-35. They were the sons of John Bates, the groundsman of the Edgbaston Cricket Ground, and both attended Tindal Street School in Balsall Heath. Samuel is now commemorated on the Thiepval Memorial.

As darkness approached on the evening of 28 August, the 15th Royal Warwicks made preparations for another night of hard slog. Strengthening the new trench was the priority, with the further addition of strongpoints being consolidated and communication trenches made back to the old front line also dug. The left flank of this new 400 yard trench was in the air and several attempts to get in touch with the 1st Royal West Kents failed. As this new front line was becoming established, the battalion now sent out patrols to study the wire in front of Falfemont Farm. Of course, all this did not go on without the Germans knowing, and severe shelling continued to make life uncomfortable; causing another thirty-four casualties. During the daylight hours of 29 August, the battalion now occupied the new front line trench. The reader here may get a picture in mind of a neatly sand-bagged, zigzag trench system with fire step, parados and parapet etc. The 15th Royal Warwicks now occupied a front 400 yards long, which in reality were shell craters inter-connected via a ditch. Persistent rainfall caused this new trench to collapse in many places, whilst in the afternoon the German bombardment was most severe, with 'C' Coy receiving the greatest attention. Again, the CO's Batman, Private Sidney Silver, wrote in his diary:

'Been shelled all night, and to-day with heavy thunder storm with shelling worse

than ever. French officer who came along says this is worse than 'Verdun'. Fritz dropped fifteen 5.9s in succession in front of our hole. He had no luck. Concussion, rotten rain and shelling makes our hole fall in.'

On the evening of 29 August, the 15th Royal Warwicks were relieved by the 2nd KOSBs. In the face of heavy rain, atrocious conditions under foot, a pitch black night and shellfire, all made the relief extremely difficult. The 15th were out of the front line by 03.30 am, 30 August. The battalion made its way back to Casement Trench, losing another thirty-four casualties on the way. 'Men very tired and somewhat worn after the strain of shellfire for three days', to quote the War Diary. On reaching Casement Trench, the men slept soundly until the following morning. One hundred and thirty-two casualties was the outcome for the three previous days in front of Falfemont Farm, thirty-three men of these being killed. One of those was Private Eric Tyrer (No.1126, A Coy), the second son to be killed of the Reverend Frank Tyrer, the Vicar of Moxley, near Darlaston. Another son, Raymond (No.212), had been severely wounded. The fourth son to join the battalion, Frank, (No.213) had been commissioned a few months earlier. So distressed by the loss of two of his sons, the Reverend Frank

Above: Advanced Dressing Station situated along the Montauban /Guillemont Road. On returning to the Somme, the Field Ambulances for the 5th Division were sited at the following locations: The 14th Field Ambulance at Dive Copse and Bronfay Farm, the 15th Field Ambulance at Corbie and the 13th Field Ambulance, for lying wounded, at Dernancourt.
IWM Q4247

Below: Private Sidney Silver, No.1213, 15th Royal Warwicks. CO's Batman.

Above: Captain Reg Gough DSO, 15th Royal Warwicks, died of wounds received on 23 July 1916 leading D Coy in the attack upon Wood Lane.

Below: Regimental Sergeant Major George Frederick Downes, No.1048, 14th Royal Warwicks. Wounded during the fighting of late September 1916. In the history of the battalion, Private J E B Fairclough, gave us this insight of 'Dicky' as he was affectionately known throughout the rank and file:

'In those early days, at Sutton, because we were new to army discipline, he had appeared very strict and a veritable martinet, and we certainly did not then appreciate that what he did was for our good. No one was more grieved than he, when he knew that the battalion which he had cared for so assiduously had been cut to pieces by machine-gun fire at Wood Lane. For behind that seemingly fierce manner of his was a generous and affectionate nature.'

Regimental Sergeant Major Downes who had been awarded the DCM and been 'mentioned in despatches' left the battalion in June 1917 to take a commission.

Dave Vaux

Tyrer, decided to retire on health grounds in April 1917. On the same evening the 15th Royal Warwicks were being relieved, the 14th Royal Warwicks relieved the 1st Royal West Kents. 'B' Coy under the command of Captain Neal were ordered to dig a forward assembly trench, to be used as a 'kicking off' trench for the impending attack. The 14th remained in the line for another two nights, then on the evening of 31 August, 13 Infantry Brigade was relieved by 15 Brigade. It was now the turn of the 16th Royal Warwicks to move into the front line, and by 03.15 am, 1 September, the men were occupying the new front line dug by their comrades of the 15th Royal Warwicks. Before the story continues, it was on the last day of August that the CO of the 15th, Lieutenant-Colonel Colin Harding, was sent down the line feeling unwell. After undergoing an examination in one of the many British Hospitals in Rouen, he was found to be suffering from Appendicitis. He was evacuated back to England for an operation, and was later discharged on medical grounds. When well enough, he rejoined the British Foreign Service and became the Provincial Commissioner to the Gold Coast Colony in West Africa. In the New Year's Honours List of 1917, he was awarded the DSO. In his memoirs he recounts further contact with Captain Roland Gough, wounded on 23 July:

'Whilst at the Base Hospital, I hear that Ray Gough is also there. Learning of my arrival he sends me a short pencilled note saying (of course) that he is getting on all right and expressing profound regret that I am so ill. Previously I had recommended Gough for the DSO, and by the same kind surgeon who had brought me Gough's note, I sent back a message that my recommendation had been endorsed and that the well deserved DSO had been bestowed on Gough. I remember the MO saying that my message would do his patient more good than all the medicine he could give him. Also I remember his saying that I was not well enough to see Gough and that he, Gough, was in a desperate condition and causing his fond mother who was with him very great anxiety. On my return to England, I was sent to Netly Hospital for a few days; from there, with little regret, I was shipped to the Stoodley Hospital at Torquay, where under the care of experienced and kind nursing friends, the operation was performed. It proved more serious than contemplated – complications occurred and further service at the front was improbable, if not impossible.

'Whilst at Stoodley Hospital, I heard that Ray Gough had to undergo a further operation. I telegraphed wishing him a speedy recovery. My wish never materialised, for the return post brought me a heartbroken letter from his mother, who

was with him to the last, informing me of his death. 'Death's but a path which must be trod, if men would ever pass to God.' Ray Gough had passed that way and God's right hand would welcome this gallant boy to the realms of above.'

Acting Captain Roland Ivor Gough, only twenty years old, died from his wounds on 14 October 1916. His award of the DSO was for conspicuous gallantry in action leading 'D' Coy on the evening of 22 July. The following is the *London Gazette* notice of his award, dated 22 September 1916:

'He led his men with great dash under heavy machine-gun and rifle fire, and though his company suffered severely, he reached the enemy's trenches, where he was dangerously wounded. Nevertheless he continued to direct his men until exhausted.'

Roland Gough was the son of Arthur, a Birmingham butcher, who had two shops, one in Broad Street the other along the Hagley Road. He is now buried in St Sever Cemetery, Rouen.

Attack on Falfemont Farm

To recap, the British Fourth and French Sixth Armies were to attack eastwards at twelve noon on Sunday September 3rd, 1916. The objective for the 5th Division was to secure the spur that overlooked the town of Combles, i.e. Leuze Wood. The German machine guns in Falfemont Farm had such an excellent field of fire, that carnage would be wrought upon attacking infantry who came into their range. It was decided that before the main assault a preliminary attack by 2nd KOSBs of 13 Infantry Brigade was to be launched upon Falfemont Farm at 9 am. Two days before the attack, 1 September, the 16th Royal Warwicks were occupying the newly dug assembly trenches opposite Falfemont Farm.

During the morning the CO of the 16th, Lieutenant-Colonel Dudgeon, attended a meeting at 15 Brigade HQ. The outcome was, that in order to assist the main attack, two strongpoints in the enemy's line were to be reconnoitred and if possible taken and consolidated. On the same evening at 8.25 pm, two patrols of eighteen men each, the first commanded by Second-Lieutenant J Hughes, the other by Sergeant E F Sparkes (No.212, A Coy, from Hope Street, West Bromwich) made their way into No Man's Land.

To take and consolidate a strongly fortified position such as Falfemont Farm was a tall order and in hindsight an impossible task for thirty-six men. The two patrols returned by 10.15 pm, with Second-Lieutenant Hughes wounded and two men missing, having been pinned down for most of the time by machine-gun fire and hand grenades. It was reported that the German wire was strong and intact and that there were in fact four machine-gun strongpoints in its defences.

At 8 am, the following day, 2 September, the British artillery bombardment began on the 4th Army front. On the 5th Division sector, the German artillery retaliated by heavily shelling the area around Angle Wood. The 16th Royal Warwicks, endured a day of almost continuous bombardment, suffering nearly thirty casualties, until being relieved in the evening by the 2nd KOSBs. By 3 am on 3 September, the 16th were back in Casement Trench; but only temporarily, for the battalion was under orders to be prepared to move back to the front line at a moment's notice.

Along with the 2nd KOSBs, the 14th Royal Warwicks had also moved into the front line in readiness for the attack. The 15th Royal Warwicks had also moved up in close support, to take over the trenches soon to be vacated by the 2nd KOSBs. Apart from fighting kit and extra ammunition, each man carried a sandbag containing two days iron rations. There were also distributed picks, shovels, wire-cutters, rockets and flares. Operation orders were issued, the evening of 2 September and the early hours of the 3rd were spent by Company Commanders and senior NCOs explaining what was required of each company. Watches were synchronised at 06:10 am. Word was also passed around that at present German morale was badly shaken and if a German counter-attack took place, 'steadiness and coolness is all that is necessary.'

The object for 13 Brigade was the German line from Wedge Wood to a position known as point 48.

From the assembly trenches Falfemont Farm was out of view. Therefore a detachment of six signallers from the 14th Royal Warwicks moved up into a detached forward post to make sure a good line of communication existed back to Battalion HQ. Sadly the post came under view of German artillery observers, resulting in heavy shelling. One shell made a direct hit on the post killing four of the six signallers; already it was an ill omen for the impending attack. As stated earlier, the 2nd KOSBs were to make a preliminary attack upon the north-western corner of the Farm to point 48, in order to prevent the French troops of the 127th Regiment being caught in enfilade fire. The following is the entry in the 14th Royal Warwick's War Diary concerning this preliminary attack:

'The 2nd KOSBs advanced to the attack very gallantly and in splendid order. They were lost to sight over the ridge and from that moment until about 5 pm the situation at the Farm remaining obscure as no message came back from the 2nd KOSBs.'

To some observers, it was thought that 'no news was good news' and the KOSBs were in the defences of the Farm, but in reality the majority of the men who left our line in perfect order were either dead or wounded on the slopes leading up to German barbed wire. Without warning to the Divisional or Brigade HQ's, the battery of French artillery who were to blast away at the Germans in Falfemont Farm covering the KOSBs as they made their way up the slope, were called upon to deal

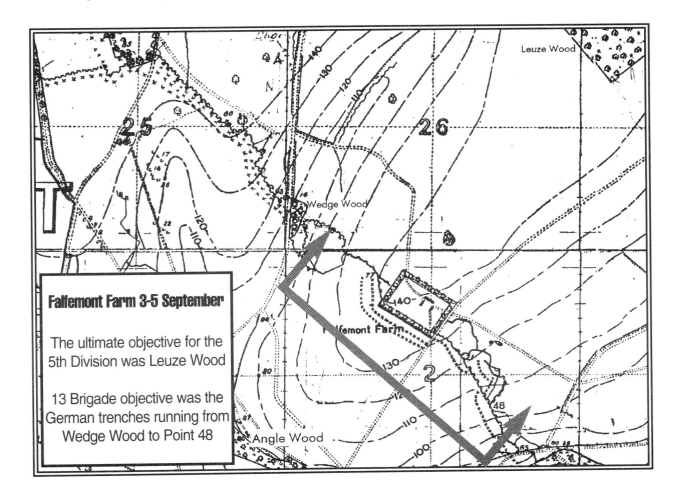

Falfemont Farm 3-5 September

The ultimate objective for the 5th Division was Leuze Wood

13 Brigade objective was the German trenches running from Wedge Wood to Point 48

Below: Company Sergeant Major Ernest Samuel Braddock, No.930, 15th Royal Warwicks
Mrs Peggy Carter

Below: Lance Corporal Charles Illingworth, No.74, A Coy, 4 Platoon, 15th Royal Warwicks, from Cartland Road, Stirchley. Killed during the attack on Falfemont Farm, 3 September. Charles was a former employee of Lloyds Bank, Bristol Road. Thiepval Memorial.

with a German counter-attack further south. The tragic result was that the leading waves of 2nd KOSBs were cut down from machine-gun and rifle fire, suffering nearly 300 hundred casualties.

The main Fourth Army attack commenced at 12 noon. On the left portion of 5th Division front, it was the turn of 95 Brigade, led by the 12th Gloucesters and 1st Duke of Cornwall's Light Infantry, attacking the German line south of Guillemont to Wedge Wood. In conjunction with 95 Brigade, two platoons of C Coy, 14th Royal Warwicks, attacked the German line in the valley to the right of Wedge Wood; this position was an old German artillery emplacement known as the Gun-pits, but now a formidable strongpoint.

The Gloucesters and the DCLI successfully took the German front line, which nearly resulted in a tragic accident for one Birmingham soldier. Prior to the attack starting, one of the battalion runners for the 14th Royal Warwicks (these men were used for carrying messages between the Battalion HQ to the front line etc), Private Hedley Vickers (No.289, B Coy) was returning from the front line. Mistaking his direction, he made for the German line instead. With him, was the runners' mascot, a small dog. On nearing the enemy's lines, shots rang out, killing the dog but only wounding Private Vickers. He was taken prisoner and temporarily kept in a dug-out. When men of the 1st DCLI took the German line and searched the dug-outs, they found Vickers, and thinking he was a spy, wished to kill him there and then. He managed to convince them who he was and safely made it back to our lines. A picture now springs to mind, I can imagine these men from the Cornwall Regiment shouting down the dug-out 'who goes there?' and a voice replies in a Brummie dialect 'Oorite, ow yo gooing'... Meanwhile the attack by C Coy of the 14th Royal Warwicks had ground to a halt, for the time being, amongst the shell craters in No Man's Land, pinned down by machine-gun fire from the Gun-pits and flanking fire from Falfemont Farm. According to Private J E B Fairclough (No.396) in the history of the 14th Royal Warwicks, 'so fierce had been the bombardments in this region that the ground was churned up and broken until it was the consistency of sea-sand piled into hillocks and sunk into pits.'

At 12.30 pm the CO of the 14th, Lieutenant-Colonel Murray, ordered the remaining two platoons of C Coy plus the remnants of the two platoons who were in No Man's Land to resume the attack on the Gun-pits. Despite artillery, machine-gun and infantry fire, the men of C Coy gradually made their way forward, crater to crater, along the valley. Nearing 1 pm, it was now the turn of A and B Coys, of the 14th and 15th Royal Warwicks, to renew the attack upon Falfemont Farm. Keeping as close as possible behind a creeping barrage, the 14th were to attack the left hand side of the farm and down the slope towards Wedge Wood, whilst the 15th had the same objective as the 2nd KOSBs, the Farm to point 48. The plan, was that the 2nd

KOSBs should now have taken this position (but as we know they were mostly dead or wounded), resulting in the 15th Royal Warwicks passing through and consolidating the high ground near to Leuze Wood. This would also have given the 14th Royal Warwicks cover on its right flank. At the same time, D Coy of the 14th, were ordered up to assist in taking the Gun-pits. Sadly D Coy, officers became casualties at the outset and the men became split up and disorganised and failed to carry out its orders. About this, the CO was not too happy, as we will see later in the chapter.

Both battalions left the assembly trenches on time and in good order and deserved a better fate than what was in store for them. Before even meeting any withering machine-gun fire, the attack went disastrously wrong, the creeping barrage, supplied by our own artillery, started to land BEHIND the attacking troops. As casualties started to mount up D Coy of the 15th Royal Warwicks were also ordered up into the attack. In 1966, fifty years after the event, a survivor of the 15th Royal Warwicks, CSM Ernest Braddock (No.930, D Coy) related the following:

'There were two companies who were to attack ahead of us. When the time came, the first company went forward and just lay down. The second company did the same. Then it was our turn. When the whistle blew nobody would move. Being CSM, I was at the rear, so I ran forward calling on the men to move. I had no sooner got to the front when I was hit by a bullet inside the left thigh. That was the end for me.'

On recovery CSM Braddock, who came from Oliver Road, Ladywood, took a commission in the Tank Corps. Before the war he had been a member of the Birmingham University Officer Training Corps.

It will not be a surprise to find out that the attack ground to a halt on the slopes leading up to Falfemont Farm. As news slowly filtered through of the situation back at Brigade and Divisional HQ's. It was decided to bring up from reserve the 15th Infantry Brigade. For by now the front line jumping off trenches were manned by wounded and a few stragglers. At 6.30 pm B Coy of the 16th Royal Warwicks, under the command of Captain F Dingley, and one company of the 1st Cheshires attacked the German line from the right hand corner of the farm down to Oakhanger Wood. This, too, was met with intense German machine-gun fire and petered out amidst the shell craters of No Man's Land. There were also reports that a large force of German reserves had made their way across open ground from Leuze Wood to strengthen the defences of the farm. During the early evening it was decided therefore not to renew the attack for the time being.

The following is the report of the attack of A and B Coys from the War Diary of the 14th Royal Warwicks:

'As it transpired the 2nd KOSBs had failed in their attack on the farm. The 14th Royal Warwicks had therefore to advance with their right open to the concentrated fire from machine-gun and rifle fire of Falfemont Farm. Under these conditions the impossible was being asked. Both Coys advanced very gallantly and in splendid spirit, but, at once coming under very heavy machine-gun fire and losing heavily they began to wither away. A Coy on the right bore the full brunt and soon dwindled away to a few remnants, which however continued to advance in the most undaunted manner. B Coy on the left, suffered almost as severely but struggling on managed to occupy and hold the front trench of the position, just south of Wedge Wood. In conclusion I would say that the behaviour of the battalion was, throughout, magnificent, and it was by no fault of theirs that the attack failed.'

There was some good news to be had, the 95 Brigade on the left portion of the Divisional front had taken its third objective, the Ginchy to Wedge Wood Road. After many repeated attempts C Coy of the 14th Royal Warwicks had taken the Gun-pits and the front loop of the German trenches in the valley leading up to Wedge Wood. This had happened by the gallant and individual efforts from two C Coy officers, Captain. Arthur Addenbrooke and Second-Lieutenant H Barrow. With a display of great bravery, Captain Addenbrooke, wounded in both feet, along with seven men, five of these also wounded, fought their way into the isolated Gun-pit

and captured seventeen prisoners and two machine-guns.

Undoubtedly the man who must receive the greatest accolade is Lance Corporal H W Perry (No.465, C Coy of Hall Road, Handsworth). Seeing that a German machine gun was holding up the advance and that immediate action was imperative, he attacked the gun-pit single-handed, resulting in the death of seven of the enemy and captured the gun. With both officers being wounded he took charge of the consolidation of the position and held on until being relieved at 9 pm. For this action Lance Corporal Perry was awarded the Distinguished Conduct Medal. He was soon promoted to Sergeant and later took a commission in the battalion. Before the war Lance Corporal Perry was the Captain of Aston Old Edwardians Association Club, secretary of the Perry Barr Cricket Club and he worked for Messrs. W Canning and Co. of Birmingham.

Captain Addenbrooke was Mentioned in Despatches for the action. To many a British Tommy, an ideal situation whilst serving in the front line was to get a 'Blighty' i.e. a wound, not too serious, but enough to get you back home to England and get a respite from the trenches. On first observation this is what Captain Addenbrooke achieved. He ended up in a London Military Hospital, but complications set in, and four weeks later, on 5th October, he died of his wounds. Captain Arthur Addenbrooke, a former master of Epsom College, is now buried in St John the Baptist Churchyard, Kidderminster.

Two other men, both from the 15th Royal Warwicks, had *London Gazette* citations published

Above: Lance Corporal H W Perry DCM

Below: Battle of Guillemont: 3 -6 September 1916. This photograph was originally featured in the weekly magazine *I Was There*, published in the 1930's. It was identified by former Private L F Ayres as a group of stretcher bearers from the 5th Division's 14th Field Ambulance unit. As can be seen, webbing and personal equipment are strewn everywhere. Probably, many casualties from the attack on Falfemont Farm passed through this Advanced Dressing Station. By consulting the Operation Orders found in the War Diary of the 14th Royal Warwicks, this could be the advance medical post set up in Casement Trench where it crosses the Maricourt to Bernafay Wood Road
IWM Q4221

the same day as Lance Corporal Perry's. I can only assume these were awarded for the same action on 3 September, because the 15th's War Diary does not give the men any mention. Both were awarded the DCM. The first was to Private H R Huskisson (No.205, C Coy) who came from Lodge Rd, Winson Green. 'He went forward alone with a machine gun under very heavy fire, displaying great courage and initiative.' The second was awarded to CSM J H Nash (No.215, A Coy) from George Road, Gravelly Hill. 'He gallantly led forward a handful of men under intense fire. Later, he rendered most valuable services in reorganising the line and evacuating the wounded.'

As darkness approached on the evening of 3 September, survivors of 13 Brigade started to make their way back from No Man's Land to the jumping off trenches that were now occupied by 15 Brigade. In the early hours of 4 September, the survivors of the 14th Royal Warwicks were in Dublin Trench and those of the 15th in Casement Trench. It was now time to count the cost of the day's operation. The 14th Royal Warwicks suffered 86 killed and 216 wounded, whilst the 15th Royal Warwicks had 66 killed and 165 wounded. As before very few of these men were ever found to be buried in a known grave. Those that were are now

buried in Delville Wood and Guillemont Road Cemeteries. The majority of those killed are now named on the Thiepval Memorial. Each man killed, represents a tragic story for grieving relatives, but some stories that have emerged seem more tragic than others. Take the case of Private Henry Wilfred Brassington (No.255) who came from Station Road, Wylde Green. He was a former Bishop Vesey pupil and an old boy of Ratcliffe College, Leicester. Two years before the war broke out he met with a cycle accident and a series of operations to his foot were needed. He was barely out of the Doctors' hands when war broke out and his foot was still proving troublesome. Disregarding this problem he enlisted into the 3rd Birmingham Battalion (16th Royal Warwicks). He stood his initial training well, but after the move up to Wensleydale his foot began to give him trouble. He then transferred into the 17th (Reserve) Battalion, whilst awaiting a discharge. Feeling he needed to do something worthwhile for his country, he volunteered to work on a hospital ship, but this fell through. Still awaiting his discharge he was put in a draft and sent out to join the 15th Royal Warwicks in June 1916. Private Brassington, aged nineteen, was killed on 3 September and is now buried in Delville Wood Cemetery.

Below: In the vicinity of Guillemont: September 1916. Another sad duty that had to be performed after an attack. Prior to going into the line, a battalion would adopt Fighting Order, which required the men to leave their heavy packs in a specified dumping area. Afterwards, those packs belonging to casualties had to be sorted so that letters and personal effects could be sent back home.
IWM Q4245

Another sad story is that of Mr and Mrs Jones of Radnor Road, Handsworth. Still grieving for one son, Lance Corporal Noel Jones (No.831) who was killed on 22 July, with the 14th Royal Warwicks, after the attack upon Falfemont Farm, they were informed of the death of their second son, of the same battalion, Sergeant Hubert Jones (No.342). Both had served in 12 Platoon of C Coy; and now they are reunited in name only on the Thiepval Memorial.

There were another two brothers serving in 12 Platoon, these were Private D Whitcombe (No.260) and Cpl B Whitcombe (No.785) from Farm Road, Sparkbrook. Both had been wounded in the second assault on Wood Lane on 30 July. They had another two brothers, one an officer in the RAMC, whilst the other was a Chaplain to the forces. They were the sons of Edmund, who was the Medical Superintendent of the Birmingham City Asylum at Winson Green. All four brothers were old boys of King Edward's High School in New Street. Private Beresford Whitcombe, was formerly a Gas Engineer and at 27 the youngest of the four. He had made a speedy recovery and was soon passed fit to rejoin the battalion, which he did on 2 September, just in time for the attack on the Gun-pits. He is another man with no known grave. Private James Harvard Evans (No.503, A Coy) of the 15th Royal Warwicks was mortally wounded during the attack, but at some stage he did an act of bravery in the field, which a survivor would recall. What it was for, I have failed to discover, But Private Evans of Douglas Road, Acocks Green was awarded the Military Medal. He did not get to find out though, because he died in a hospital at Le Treport on 11 September and is now buried in Mont Huon Military Cemetery.

Falfemont Farm: Second Attempt

On the evening of 3 September, it was now the turn of the 1st Norfolk and 1st Cheshire Regiments to hold the front line opposite Falfemont Farm. The 16th Royal Warwicks went into close support by Angle Wood. As daylight approached on the morning of 4 September, the preliminary British artillery bombardment resumed. The 5th Division front was covered by the artillery of the 35th and 56th Divisions, whose gun emplacements were situated in Chimpanzee Valley and around the southern end of Bernafay Wood. The assault on Falfemont Farm was to be renewed at 3 pm. Because of the success that 95 Brigade and C Coy of the 14th Royal Warwicks had achieved the previous day, the division was now in a better position to launch an attack.

The 1st Bedfords started off from Wedge Wood and were to make their way up to the Farm by bombing their way from traverse to traverse along the German trenches. These were the trenches that the 1st Cheshires were to attack from the front. The

1st Norfolks attacked the Farm down to point 48. As soon as the Norfolks left the jumping off trench, A and D Coys of the 16th Royal Warwicks replaced them. As might be expected the Norfolks were mowed down by machine-gun fire. A few men actually broke through and got in the Farm's defences on its south west corner, but were soon repulsed.

At 3.40 pm two patrols of the 16th Royal Warwicks went forward to observe the situation. The first was led by Corporal G Wells (No.100, A Coy, from Hampton Road, Handsworth) and the second by Lance Corporal A R Walter (No.242, A Coy, from Grove Street, Redditch). Both patrols returned with the news that the Norfolks were pinned down by very heavy machine-gun fire. For the moment it was impossible to reach the farm from a frontal attack. Whilst the German defenders were occupied with defending from the front, the Bedfords had slowly bombed their way up through the German trenches to meet up with a company of Cheshires who had worked their way around the left hand side of the spur. By 4 pm the northern and western corners of the farm had been taken. This had resulted in the taking of 130 German prisoners and several machine-guns.

A and D Coys of the 16th Royal Warwicks were ordered up to support the Norfolks in a further attempt to take the Farm. B and C Coys of the 16th then moved up into the front line. The gallant men of the Norfolks had slowly inched their way closer to the Farm from shell-hole to shell-hole and as soon as the 16th Royal Warwicks were close enough to support them, another unsuccessful attempt was made to storm the defences. Meanwhile patrols from the Bedfords and the Cheshires had made their way to the crest of the spur, in front of Leuze Wood. Later in the evening the 1st Devons of 95 Brigade had moved up and consolidated a line within the wood. No further German reinforce-ments would now be able to make their way to the Farm. With the cover of darkness both the Norfolks and the 16th Royal Warwicks began to dig in along the south eastern approaches to the farm. Then at 10.15 pm the CO of the 16th, Lieutenant-Colonel Dudgeon, made his way up the slopes, with orders that A and D Coys were to dig trenches (saps) forward towards the farm. By 3 am on the morning of September 5th one company of 1st Norfolks had gained a footing in the defences. Just over an hour later, Lieutenant-Colonel Dudgeon along with Lieutenant-Colonel Stone (CO, 1st Norfolks) made another inspection and reported back that the trenches sapped towards the Farm had been well carried out. The saps were approximately 220 yards long by three feet deep. The following is how the taking of the Farm was explained in the Divisional History:

'A fierce hand-to-hand fight was now raging around the Farm buildings and enclosure, and gradually the garrison was reduced, and the numerous machine guns

Above: Sergeant Henry Checketts, No.873, D Coy, 15 Platoon, 14th Royal Warwicks, from Oldfield Road, Balsall Heath. Henry, an old boy of King Edward's Camp Hill, and a former employee of the Birmingham Reference Library was killed on 3 September 1916. Thiepval Memorial.

Below: Private Harry Carr, No.15/1379, 16th Royal Warwicks, from Witton. Aged twenty-five, Harry, was a former employee of the General Electric Company, Witton. He was killed performing his duties as a stretcher bearer on 3 September. Thiepval Memorial.

destroyed or captured.'

Once the Farm had been taken, patrols pushed along the trenches down the slope to point 48, each traverse being taken methodically; first hand-grenades would be thrown over the traverse, on explosion, men rushed around to mop up. Any German left standing either surrendered or died by the bayonet. By 7.30 am the whole objective was taken. An hour later B and C Coys of the 16th Royal Warwicks were ordered up to establish strongpoints along a line running from the southern corner of Leuze Wood down the slope towards the light railway line at the start of Savernake Wood. C Coy was to get in touch with 95 Brigade on the left and B Coy with the French on the right. This operation was successfully carried out by the battalion; and by 3 pm, the 16th Royal Warwicks were relieved by the 7th Royal Irish Fusiliers of the 16th (Irish) Division. The same night the rest of the 5th Division was withdrawn and replaced by the Territorials of the 56th (London) Division. Just after midnight, now 6 September, the 16th Royal Warwicks, were in bivouac near Billon Farm, south of Carnoy. For the next few days the 5th Division would converge in the area known as the Citadel, which was sited along the Fricourt-Bray sur Somme Road.

There was now a period of rest and re-organisation. In the book *Soldiers Died in the Great War*, for the Royal Warwickshire Regiment, those men of the 16th Royal Warwicks who were killed during the period of the 3, 4 and 5 September, have been put down as 3 September. The War Diary gives casualty figures covering a six day period from 31 August to 5 September. These figures, for all ranks, comes to 195 wounded and 61 killed.

Two of the youngest members of the 16th Royal Warwicks were killed during this period, both aged eighteen. The first was Private Charles Howe (No.599) whose family home was Plymouth. The other was Private Lawrence Dance (No.18, A Coy) from Birchfield Road, Perry Barr. Lawrence, prior to the war, showed great promise as a pianist and organist. Yet another sad tale concerns Private Albert Grimes (No.834, D Coy), from Victoria Road, Erdington. He had been wounded and bandaged up at an Advanced Dressing Station of another battalion. Being able to walk he was then sent to a Casualty Clearing Station. He was never seen again.

'Magnificent Performance'

Prior to moving back to Billon Farm, the CO of the 16th Royal Warwicks wrote the following extract in the War Diary, concerning three of his senior officers:

'During the operations 31 August to 5th Sept round Falfemont Farm, Captains Parry, Dingley and Phillip did exceptionally good work and proved themselves to be gallant and able leaders. They were quick in grasping the situation and after losing all their officers and a large proportion of their NCO's they still maintained control of their Coys and carried out the operations allotted to them.'

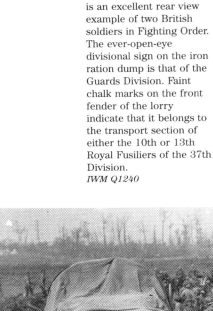

Below: Behind the lines, September 1916. Standing behind the column of German PoWs is an excellent rear view example of two British soldiers in Fighting Order. The ever-open-eye divisional sign on the iron ration dump is that of the Guards Division. Faint chalk marks on the front fender of the lorry indicate that it belongs to the transport section of either the 10th or 13th Royal Fusiliers of the 37th Division.
IWM Q1240

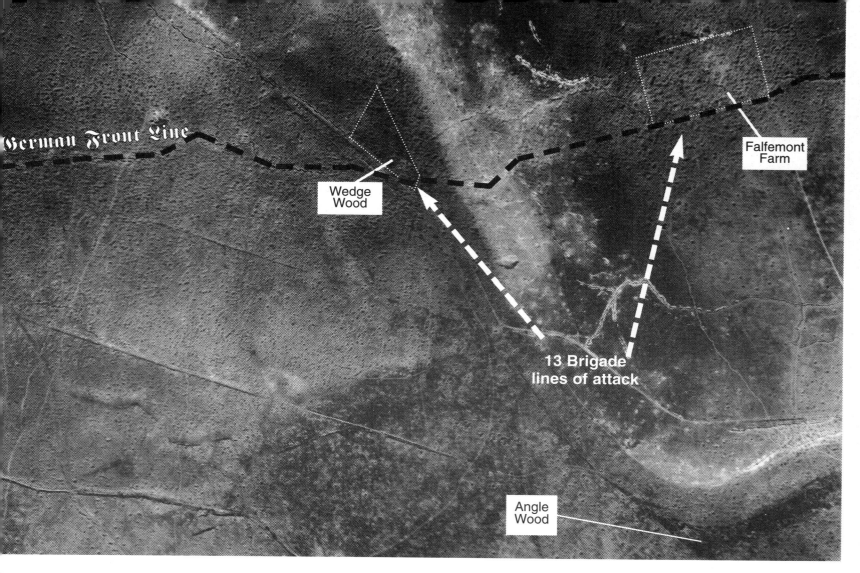

German Front Line

Wedge Wood

Falfemont Farm

13 Brigade lines of attack

Angle Wood

Whilst the division was out of the line for the next few days, many messages of praise were received, not only from the GOCs of the XIV Corps and the Fourth Army, but one from the man at the top Sir Douglas Haig, which contained the following passage:

'I wish to thank all ranks of the 5th Division for the very highly successful part they bore in the recent operations. The 5th Division has been of the utmost assistance to the complete success of the operations, and all ranks very gallantly carried out their allotted tasks.'

The GOC of the 5th Division, Major-General R B Stephens, took it in turn to address each Brigade of the Division. The following are parts of his address to 13 Infantry Brigade, concerning their failure to take Falfemont Farm on September 3rd:

'I know you fellows think that you failed, but you must understand that you were asked to do the impossible.

'The 2nd KOSBs and 14th Royal Warwicks advanced gloriously and with the utmost gallantry. Their advance was witnessed by officers of the General Staff. I am very sorry that the Brigade failed to carry through their objective, through no fault of yours, but owing altogether to some error on the part of the artillery preparation, you had to advance with practically no artillery support.'

'The advance was pushed on with the utmost determination and perseverance. You have had bad luck in the last three shows, the two previous ones being in the High Wood and Wood Lane areas, but I know that whatever 13 Brigade are asked to do in the future, they can be relied upon to carry through, as they have done in the past.

'I can trust 13 Brigade to do anything on earth.'

On addressing 15 Brigade Major-General Stephens made the following comments:

'I cannot too warmly express my admiration of the fine soldierly qualities again displayed by all ranks during the recent operations.

'The taking of Falfemont Farm, a most important and strongly defended post, was a magnificent performance and is one of the greatest successes accomplished during the war.

'This was made possible by the good handling of their battalions by Commanding Officers and the devoted conduct of all ranks.

'Heavy working parties were required when the Brigade was not in the line and these did excellent work.'

Above: Aerial view of Falfemont Farm, 13 September 1916. Taken eight days after 15 Brigade had occupied the strongpoint following fierce hand-to-hand fighting. Falfemont farm is the rectangular feature towards the top right hand corner. Angle Wood can be seen in the bottom right hand corner. The white chalk line between shows the British forward trenches dug prior to the attack. *IWM Q58646*

209

Above: Private Lewis James Dealey, No.361, B Coy, 6 Platoon, 15th Royal Warwicks. He received a foot wound in the attack on Falfemont Farm 3 September 1916. On recovery he was posted to the 11th Royal Warwicks. During the fighting in the vicinity of Monchy-le-Preux on 23 April 1917 he was severely wounded. He died of his wounds 29 April and is buried in Aubigny Communal Cemetery. Lewis lived at the Smethwick end of City Road, and was a former employee of the Oldbury branch of Lloyds Bank.

The few days spent out of the line were used for resting and cleaning up. New drafts to replace casualties were absorbed into platoons. There were kit inspections and daily sessions of drill and physical training.

The Divisional concert party the 'Whizz-Bangs' made an appearance whilst the division was out of the line, and to celebrate the success of the previous few days, they had contrived a parody of a popular song of George Robey's, called 'Another little drink won't do us any harm.' The following is the chorus:

'There was a famous Div. went to take a
    certain farm,
They put the wind up Fritz and caused him
    great alarm,
But the Corps Commander said,
When he heard what they had done,
Well! another little stunt won't do 'em any
    harm.'

Amongst all the praise and back slapping going on, Lieutenant-Colonel Murray, the CO of the 14th Royal Warwicks, was still fuming about D Coy, and their failure in the attack upon the Gun-pits. His thoughts though, were kept private and nothing officially entered into the War Diary. The last time Lieutenant Alan Furse was mentioned he was still temporarily in charge of the Battalion's Quarter-Master's stores, which he had been doing for the previous few months. According to letters home he was settled in this role. With the death of his brother Bill on July 1st, his parents back home in School Road, Moseley, no doubt thought that with Alan working behind the lines he had more chance of surviving than being in the front line. The following is taken from Lieutenant Furse's memoirs, written after the war:

'The Battalion came back to the lines on 6 September and I again started the job of refitting everyone. I was getting very sick of this as the men seemed to lose their equipment on purpose and I suggested to the CO a method by which deductions could be made from pay for other than actual losses in action. I think this made me somewhat unpopular, but I was not to remain as QM for much longer. We now heard that Falfemont Farm had been taken on the 5th and the line was directly in front of Leuze Wood.

'On 8 September, the CO sent for me and told me that owing to the losses of senior officers, he wanted me to take over D Coy from Lieutenant B Turner and I was to leave the NCOs to look after the QM department. I accordingly moved my belongings from the transport lines into battalion tents and started the duties for which I was totally unprepared. I had been away from all company duties for over five months and consequently had not seen all the latest instructions issued for trench warfare.

'On the afternoon of 8 September, the CO, told me to parade D Coy as he wished to speak to them. He then came and told them that at the last attack on Falfemont Farm, they had not done their duty and if he did not accuse them of cowardice he implied it very strongly. It can easily be realised that to a man just taking over a company of about 150 strong, this was terribly discouraging for a start, and as my subs (Second-Lieutenants) were all young and inexperienced, I could not look forward with any pleasure to the next show. Stan came over about tea-time and gave me a few tips on my new job.'

Stan, by the way, was Captain Rupert Stanton Baugh DSO, Grenadier Guards. The Guards Division were in the vicinity of Guillemont. Captain Baugh, from Wake Green Road, Moseley, was an original volunteer in the battalion. Given No.365 and he was commissioned in February 1915 to become Second-Lieutenant in B Coy, 6 Platoon, before transferring to the Guards.

Lieutenant Alan Furse did not have to wait long before the 'next show'. The mid-September offensive was about to start, to be known as the Battle of Flers-Courcelette and was to be the first offensive that tanks were to be used. Whilst the division was still out of the line, Private J E B Fairclough (No.396) of the 14th Royal Warwicks, recalled in the Battalion history the first time tanks were seen:

'During our stay at the Citadel, rumours reached us that peculiar new engines were to be seen in the vicinity, and investigation revealed to us our first view of the Tanks, which were preparing to go into action. They certainly looked monstrosities, and it seemed uncanny to see these huge machines with such names as 'Creme de Menthe' and 'Cherry Brandy', waddling around, climbing over trenches and negotiating huge shell-holes with ease. Doubt has been cast on the wisdom of putting these tanks into action before we had large numbers of them, but it can be safely said that they gave confidence and put new spirit into the attacking troops. At this period, it appeared that every attack was bound to fail owing to overwhelming enemy machine-gun fire, but when it was seen that the machine-gun posts were flattened out and subdued, thus making the infantry advance much easier, the spirits of the attacking troops rose to a remarkable degree.'

Lieutenant Alan Furse had also seen some tanks on 6 September, they were on the high ground behind Mametz. He and fellow officers made their way over to investigate, and recalls that they 'were lucky enough to get there just as the Prince of Wales was getting out of one.' The Prince of Wales was attached to the Staff of the XIV Corps for the recent operations and was a regular sight on a bicycle visiting Divisional and Brigade HQs.

It was decided to rest some battalions who were to take part in the forthcoming offensive. Therefore on the evening of September 10th a composite Brigade was formed to take over parts of the line temporarily. Under the command of Brigadier General L O W Jones it comprised 13 Brigade (14th and 15th Royal Warwicks), the 1st Devons and 1st East Surreys of 95 Brigade, the Divisional Pioneers, 6th Argyll and Sutherland Highlanders and 15 Brigade Machine Gun Company. Meanwhile the rest of the 5th Division moved to Morlancourt. The 15th Royal Warwicks were placed in reserve and they spent the next few days in Chimpanzee Trench. The 14th Royal Warwicks, 1st R W Kents and the 2nd KOSBs occupied the newly taken ground by Leuze Wood, which overlooked Combles and faced the Germans in Combles Trench and Loop Trench. The Composite Brigade had relieved 169 Brigade of the 56th (London) Division, who had suffered numerous casualties trying to take the aforementioned positions.

For two days the 14th Royal Warwicks dug in and consolidated their position under very heavy shellfire. On 11 September the battalion was extremely lucky to have suffered only four men killed and ten wounded, yet on the extreme left of D Coy, the Royal West Kents suffered so severely that they had to be withdrawn and replaced by the 1st London Regiment. The next day the 14th Royal Warwicks suffered another three killed and twelve wounded. During the evening the battalion was relieved by the Devons of 95 Brigade, and the men made their way back to the former German trenches at Falfemont Farm. They occupied the trenches attacked by the 2nd KOSBs. The war Diary recorded that:

'All ranks very glad to have seen the last of Leuze Wood, a wood no longer but a churned up network of shell craters, with bare and battered tree trunks, partly standing but more often broken and twisted masses littering the ground. Enemy and our own dead everywhere and athough our men worked hard at burying, a lot still remained to be done when they left.'

Lieutenant Alan Furse, now commanding D Coy of the 14th, left a very vivid account of Leuze Wood, which makes very interesting reading:

'We spent the night of the 9/10 in open trenches in the pouring rain and all around us within 50 yards in all directions were batteries of the new 'four-fives', a mobile light Howitzer with a particular sharp bark on firing. (The 14th had spent the night in Germans Wood, near to Casement Trench.) On the morning of the 10th the CO told us that we were to go into Leuze Wood. According to Brigade instructions the Huns were only five yards from the trenches which we were to take over and we all carried bombs in our pockets in expectation of a lively night. The humorous part also was that we were shown detailed plans of the trenches we were to take over, but when we arrived we found nothing but a shallow ditch and a few scattered shell holes. About 10.30 pm we moved off in pitch dark and marched in single file about three miles to the wood. (The 14th Royal Warwicks relieved the 1/16th London Regt. [Queens Westminster Rifles] of 169 Brigade.) We expected to have a hearty reception of bombs but to our surprise found things quite quiet on the edge of the wood. I got the Company lying down in extended order and went forward with my CSM and runner to try and locate the position. I could not find any continuous trenches and could not find anyone to take over from. I had been told to take over from a London Regiment and after about half an hour, I found a machine gun with two men and three wounded lying by it. They told me that the London Regiment had been gone some hour or more and it must be that they thought they were being relieved by someone on their left or right, but even then I cannot understand their leaving any wounded behind them. The fact remains that at least 200 yards of our front line was unoccupied (but for a machine gun) for over an hour.

'We decided upon a line and having linked up with the Coys on the right and left started digging in. We dug until daylight and then had enough to get under cover. As very little rifle fire was directed at us and we could not exactly locate the Hun front line, being on a downward slope, we went on digging in daylight, but soon stopped as they turned a battery of 5.9's on us. They continued this attention all through the day but although they blew the trench in, in several places, we had no casualties during the day. Every few hours I had to send a report to Battalion HQ behind the wood and had one runner shot through the hand. At night they started on us with Whizz-bangs and we had about a dozen casualties, but we were gradually getting deeper and safer.

'On 11 September we saw a wonderful advance by the French on our right when they took Maurepas and reached the Bapaume-Peronne Road. As we were only a little over a mile away I could see the French troops quite plainly through the glasses and saw the results of their

came from Hagley Road and was an old boy of King Edward's, New Sreeet. He died, aged 29, at home a few weeks after the end of the war, 3 December 1918. He is now buried in Brandwood End Cemetery, Kings Heath.

The Battles of Flers-Courcelette and Morval

This battle known as Flers-Courcelette will go down in history as the first in which tanks were used in warfare. It was launched on the morning of Friday 15 September and met with partial success, but ground to a halt in front of the three villages, that were in the fourth line of the days objective. These were Gueudecourt, Lesboeufs and Morval. Thirty-two of the available forty-nine tanks made it to their allotted jumping off line. Of these, only twelve played an effective part in the attack. Our story concerns the ground gained opposite Morval, for it is here that the 5th Division next came into the line and were to play another decisive part.

After leaving Leuze Wood, 13 Brigade made its way back to Mericourt. On 15 September, the same day as the offensive began, Lieutenant-Colonel Murray, the CO of the 14th Royal Warwicks, took over temporary command of 13 Infantry Brigade and Major Charles Playfair, the Proof-Master of the Birmingham Gun Barrel Proof House in Banbury Street, was given temporary command of the battalion. The strength of the battalion on this day was given as twenty officers and 537 other ranks, with the following comment in the War Diary:

'The spirit of the battalion is as good as ever but considerable difficulty is being found in getting suitable officers to train and lead them. Only young and very inexperienced youngsters are now being posted.'

On 16 September, the 5th Division was ordered up to the vicinity of Waterlot Farm, to the north-west of Guillemont. According to the War Diary of the 14th Royal Warwicks this had now become 'a sea of stinking mud'. All landmarks had disappeared, the area was a barren wasteland of old trenches, pock-marked with thousands of shell holes; the villages of Guillemont and Ginchy could only be recognised by the brick stains left in the mud. Private H V Drinkwater (No.161), 15th Royal Warwicks, writing in his diary gives us an excellent view of what conditions were like during the divisional move back up to the front line. It may be of interest to the reader that the quotes used by Private Drinkwater in this section of the taking of Morval were also featured in *I Was There, The Human Story of The Great War* 1914-18, published in the late 1930's:

'At 9 o'clock we moved out of the village (Mericourt), the 14th Royal Warwicks, ourselves (15th), the West Kents and K.O.S.B. A vile morning, rain still coming

barrage. *They advanced quite slowly with slung rifles and heard afterwards from our officers who were attached to them for liaison purposes that the men advanced smoking and singing and perfectly confident behind the screen of bursting shells.*

'12 September was a terribly hot day and poor old Wilson (of the New Hudson Cycle Company) *got a terrible dose of shell-shock. He was in charge of C Coy on my right. A whizz-bang burst just outside the trench near him and he went completely mad, trying to scratch a hole in the ground and barking like a dog. We tried to calm him down but finally had to send him back over the top in daylight in charge of two men.*

'On the night 13/14 September we were relieved and went back about a mile to Falfemont Farm, where we had beautiful old German dugouts finished off inside with concrete and well finished wood. I had my first attack of Scurvy here and had no food for the next twenty-four hours, being continually sick. In the afternoon of the 14th the CO came round and complimented the Coy on its improved behaviour in Leuze Wood and I was delighted to be able to tell the men.'

Lieutenant Arthur Edward Wilson to whom Lieutenant Furse refers, was an original volunteer to the battalion (No.283), but within a few weeks of training was commissioned and became the Officer Commanding 13 Platoon, D Coy. Lieutenant Wilson

down in torrents, with every prospect of a soaker.

'We had no idea of our destination or what position we were going to take up. We passed through Morlancourt and rested for dinner outside what was once the village of Montauban at 4 pm. Of the village hardly a brick remained, there was not a wall two feet high. The whole place in the early days of the Somme offensive had been moved skywards and lay in all directions a mass of bricks and shell-holes. Rain was still coming down and had been doing so all day. Without exception we were soaked to the skin, for we had been marching all day through it, with only a few minutes interval every hour for rest. In spite of the hard travelling we were bitterly cold from a keen wind blowing.

'Travelling was bad, the roads were inches deep in mud, congested with traffic of every description, ambulances coming down from the line and ammunition columns and transport going up.

'With our Lewis gun carts we were unable to keep pace with the Batt. We had ropes onto the carts, but the mud beat us in the end and we got stuck, and the Batt. went on, leaving us to follow.'

The next attack by the British Fourth Army was planned for 25 September, and was a continuation of the attack from 15 September. The objective for the XIV Corps were the villages of Lesboeufs and Morval. The latter was the objective of the 5th Division. Before the offensive could be resumed, the ground gained on the 4th Army front had now to be consolidated. Communication trenches now had to be dug back to the former British front line. Patrols were sent forward to explore and find out where new front line and assembly trenches could be dug. For the time being, the spade was more important than the rifle.

Below: Advanced Dressing Station, September 1916. A Canadian official photograph, probably taken in the region of Martinpuich /Courcelette. It shows the hectic action that took place at any ADS on the Somme battlefront during an offensive. Here, wounded are given an initial check up, a basic dressing, to stem any flow of blood, and a shot of morphine to dull the pain. They were then sent on to the casualty Clearing Stations further down the line. Those severely wounded, who seemed hopeless cases were usually given morphine to ease their suffering and left to die quietly.
IWM C0754

The 5th Division sector was on a frontage of roughly 2000 yards (1800 Metres) from the northern edge of Bouleaux Wood to the eastern slope of the Ginchy-Telegraph Hill. 95 Brigade took over the right sector and 15 Brigade the left. By 02:30 am, on the morning of 19 September, A and D Coys of the 16th Royal Warwicks had relieved the 1st West Yorkshires of the 6th Division and were under orders to patrol ground to the east of Morval. Four strong-points were ordered to be dug at given map references and immediately on completion to be manned by four Lewis Gun teams. These in turn would give cover whilst the men finished digging a trench connecting up these four strong-points. The new trench was completed by 05.00 am, and two patrols had gone out about 300 yards in front to reconnoitre the German line opposite. Even though the patrols came under German rifle fire, it was thought that the line was lightly held.

During the daylight hours the German artillery intermittently shelled these newly dug trenches. during which Captain F Dingley and eight other ranks were wounded. Then as darkness approached, further trenches were dug. This time a trench was dug to meet up with the former German trench to the right of a strong-point known as the Triangle. At some point along this trench, as it made it's way down to front Morval, it was still occupied by the Germans. 'Excellent work' and 'very gratifying' were the laudatory messages received from both Brigade and Divisional HQs for the work carried out by the 16th Royal Warwicks in very wet and windy weather.

The following night volunteers were called for, from the ranks of the 16th Royal Warwicks, to form a bombing platoon under the command of Captain Bubb. At 05.45 am on 20 September, this platoon was to make their way down the German trench, closely followed by men of 60 Brigade (20th [Light] Division), who were to make good any ground gained by the bombing platoon. If all went to plan, C Coy of the 16th Royal Warwicks would then relieve 60 Brigade when the situation was clear. It was also arranged for a spotter plane from the RFC to fly over early in the morning when flares could then be lit, showing the new forward position, thus enabling our own artillery to increase their range.

At 08.45 am, it was reported that the bombing attack had failed, for what reason, the War Diary does not state. But during the following daylight hours the German artillery was very active and information was passed to all companies that according to a German PoW, a counter-attack was imminent. It never materialised and on the same evening the 16th Royal Warwicks were relieved by the 1st Norfolks. By 03.00 am, 21 September, the 16th Royal Warwicks were back in the former German front line, south-east of Guillemont.

With zero hour approaching for the next attack, 25 September, 15 and 95 Brigades were brought out of the line for a few days rest, and the Divisional front was now taken over by 13 Brigade. The 15th Royal Warwicks stayed in reserve but the 14th took over the left hand sector on the evening of 22 September and, according to the War Diary, spent a quiet two days with nothing to report, until moving back to the support lines, south east of Guillemont on the night of 24 September. Lieutenant Alan Furse of the 14th, who was now OC of D Coy, divulged a very interesting account of these few days leading up to 24 September. He begins by describing the scene in the aftermath of the Guards Division who had fought at Ginchy on September 15th:

'On 20 September, I walked to the other side of Ginchy with an artillery officer and saw the casualties which the Guards had had in taking the village. I have read in the histories of the war of the wonderful precision with which they advanced on the day, but the lines of them dead had to be seen to be believed! In several places as many as thirty of them lay in a perfect straight line where they had been swept down by a machine gun in their advance over the open. I came back through Guillemont and there saw literally heaps of Guards and Huns lying all mixed up where they had been killed by shellfire in the close quarter fighting for the village.

'On the night of 21 September, we went forward from Waterlot Farm through Guillemont along the light railway (or rather where it used to be) up to the top of the crest before Morval, into some very decent trenches. For the next two days the weather was wonderful but as we were entrenched almost on the skyline of the hill we had to keep very close in. On the 22nd we watched a wonderful aeroplane fight over our lines, the result of which was that the British plane was shot down. The pilot landed upside down in full daylight between the two lines of trenches, but managed to make his way into our lines suffering from only slight concussion. He had some grub with me in my dugout and explained as the plane was only slightly damaged he would have to salvage it, and before leaving for his aerodrome that night to report, he asked me to be good enough and throw a bomb or two on the plane that night so that he could report it badly damaged and would not have to come back and salvage it.

'That evening the CO came round and explained that although we were really due for a decent rest, we had got to join in the attack on Morval, either in the front line or support. Our job for the first two nights was to dig a straight communication trench down the hill in front of us, and it did not seem a very nice job to *tackle. At night the CO sent up a guide to show us where to dig, and I started off on a very dark night at the head of fifty men in single file. The so called guide led us to within about ten to fifteen yards of the Hun front line and only found out his mistake when we ran into the barbed wire guarding the Hun line. With as little noise as possible we turned the head of the line straight back and were lucky enough to get out of it without being spotted. In a place like this, it is impossible to pass word down the line to 'about turn' as some silly ass is sure to shout and then you are 'for it'. But afterwards when we were able to laugh about it, it seemed very funny to have been playing the old game of follow my leader under such circumstances. We did a very good dig that night and again on the following one and only had one casualty from a stray bullet. On the night of the 24 September we moved back about a mile to some old German trenches east of Guillemont, which were to be our starting place at zero hour for the attack on Morval.'*

Battle of Morval 25 – 28 September

A more apt name for this attack, would have been, the Battle of Morval-Courcelette, for those two villages occupied the ends of roughly a nine mile arc along which ten British Divisions were to assault. The goal of the 5th Division was Morval, with 15 and 95 Brigades carrying out the attack whilst 13 Brigade had the supporting role and were to occupy the jumping off trenches when the attack was under way.

A steady bombardment began on the German lines at 07.00 am 24 September until 6.30 pm, the same day. It then recommenced the following morning, the day of the attack, at 06.30 am. To suit our French allies attacking in the vicinity of Combles and who did not favour dawn attacks, zero hour was set for 12.35 pm. With all the activity in No Man's Land, digging assembly trenches etc, the Germans must have known that an attack was imminent, but once dawn had passed, which was the usual British time for 'going over the top', perhaps they thought they had another days grace. Well they did not, and with no intensive bombardment prior to the attack to alert the German defenders, the attack was launched.

Then the bombardment began in earnest. Behind a succession of creeping and stationary barrages, sixty-four battalions of British and Dominion troops, wave after wave, slowly made their way, in a series of leaps and bounds, to their objectives.

The Norfolks were first 'over the top' for the 15 Brigade, they were to take a section of the main

German front line trench in front of Morval. Closely following the creeping barrage, they had taken the Brigade's first objective by 12.50 pm. Whilst the Norfolks were on their way, the remaining battalions in the Brigade moved forward one trench. Next to go were the 1st Bedfords, followed by the 1st Cheshires and lastly it was the turn of the 16th Royal Warwicks accompanied by men of the Divisional Pioneer battalion, 1/6th Argyll & Sutherland Highlanders, and the 2nd Home Counties Royal Engineers. The battalion leap-frogged the three previous battalions and, about 6 pm, had reported to be digging a line in open country around 450 yards (410 metres) east of the village. At the same time, reports were relayed back to the Battalion HQ to say that our own shellfire was landing on the newly won ground and causing casualties amongst the battalion. German troops were still clinging on in isolated groups amongst shell craters and old practice trenches near to where the 16th Royal Warwicks were digging in, and snipers were having a field day. Private Thomas Alfred Jones of the 1st Cheshires was so aggravated by this that he crawled out and shot three German snipers, whilst another 102 German soldiers surrendered to him. He marched them back to our lines; for this exploit, Private Jones was awarded the Victoria Cross. As darkness approached patrols from the 16th Royal Warwicks went forward to try and take these trenches, but met with no success. Reinforced by men from the Norfolks and Cheshires, the Warwicks held the line for another twenty-four hours. The following evening a strong German patrol approached the line and was driven off by rifle and machine-gun fire. At midnight the 16th Royal Warwicks were relieved by the 1st Leicesters of the 6th Division and at 04.30 on the morning of 27 September had reached Oxford Copse, on the western outskirts of Maricourt. The following account of the taking of Morval comes from the Divisional History:

Above: An aerial view of Morval taken on 30 September 1916. The 5th Division attacked from left to right.
IWM Q58378

'On the left 15 Brigade carried the
village of Morval with a rush; a half-
hearted opposition put up by the Germans
still in place was quickly overpowered,
and, after mopping up the dugouts and
cellars in the village, the troops moved out
into the open country east of the village.
Among the prisoners captured in the
village was the German Town-Major, who
remained faithful to his post, probably
thinking that discretion, in the shape of a
strong dugout, was the better part of
valour.

'By nightfall the final objective running
southward from the Moulin de Morval had
been consolidated. The whole attack had
bee carried through exactly to plan and
time-table, a truly remarkable feat.'

What of 13 Infantry Brigade, during the capture of
Morval? As the waves were going forward for the
main attack, 13 Brigade made its way in a series of
reciprocal moves until reaching the jumping off
line. 'All ranks acted splendidly and carried out the
orders as if on parade', was the remark in the 14th
Royal Warwicks' War Diary. But, it is also a good
excuse for me to quote from the last few
paragraphs of the memoirs of Lieutenant Alan
Furse (14th Royal Warwicks, D Coy):

'On the night of 24 September, we moved
back about a mile to some old German
trenches east of Guillemont, which were to
be our starting point at zero hour on the
attack on Morval. At zero hour, on the 25th,
we started off as a Company in line in
extended order to do the mile to the
trenches we had last occupied on the top of

the hill. Every gun within miles was firing
without ceasing and even by putting your
mouth to anyone's ear and shouting you
could not make yourself heard. Under
these conditions it was very difficult to
control a hundred and fifty men spread
out in line, with about two yards between
each, but I was so excited that I tried to do
it by shouting, as a result, by the time we
had done the first mile, I was absolutely
hoarse and could hardly make myself
heard even in a dug-out. Whilst covering
this mile we had to pass through several
barrages but we reached our first trenches
without a single casualty. On reaching
these trenches on the crest we got down
into them and were able to see the
wonderful results of our barrage on the
village of Morval about three-quarters of a
mile away, over the valley on top of the
next hill.

'By this time our front line had taken the
first two Hun lines and were getting into
the village itself and with the glasses I was
able to see the Huns getting up in bunches
from their trenches in front of the village
and retreating through it. At this point
some Brigade machine gunners put up two
guns in our trench and we were able to see
the results of their fire on these bunches of
Huns. After about twenty minutes in these
trenches we got orders to advance to the
next line in the valley in front, and in
going through the barrage we lost a good
few men on the slope. It was during this
part of the advance that a German shell hit

216

the ground within a foot or so of me, without exploding fortunately, but the pressure of wind from it was enough to knock me over.

'We spent about twelve hours in the valley and had a hell of a time. When the Huns are on the retreat like this and are continually taking up new positions, they can only get accurate ranges by map reference and as this valley we were in was clearly marked and they themselves had dug the trench in which we were occupying, they gave us something to go on with. Almost continually during these twelve hours they plastered us with salvos of medium heavies and we were very lucky indeed to have only another ten or twelve casualties in the company during that time.

As soon as night fell the CO came round himself and explained that we were to go on up the hill towards Morval and dig in on a new line, so as to form a support trench for the men in the village itself and also so as to get into some position which would save us from the heavy shelling we were getting. He came up with me and showed the line we were to dig on and we started on the job at once. Here we had an example of the wonderful Staff work which was being done. The CO was able to tell me the exact spot where I would find picks and shovels dumped, although the ground had only been taken a few hours before. We set to with a will because we knew that if we showed so much as an eyelid in the morning, we should be blown out of it. With my two Subs and our servants, I dug a very reasonable dug-out that night and before morning carried over sufficient

railway sleepers to form a splinter proof roof. By morning the whole of us were underground although the trenches were very rough and as we were behind the village I thought it was safe to go on digging for a while after daybreak. Very soon , however, the Hun put up a 'Sausage Balloon' and as dirt was flying out of our lines we were spotted and greeted with salvos of whizz-bangs, so we settled down in the bottom and waited for dark again.

'We got shelled at intervals all through the day and had about six more casualties, and at about 4 o'clock the CO came over the top to see how we were getting on. He complimented us on our digging and on hearing that our officers' grub had been blown up sent some more biscuits and jam from his own mess.

'For the two days that we were in these trenches we had all our water in petrol cans and it had a lot of oil with it. It was here we actually strained our drinking water through a sock, and I am sure that it was drinking this mixture of oil and water that finally finished off my teeth.

'On the night of 27 September we were to be relieved and as we had been in the front area for rather a long time, we were very glad of it.'

Soon after coming out of the line, Lieutenant Alan Furse was hospitalised suffering from Pyorrhoea (gum disease) and Scurvy (vitamin deficiency) and within a few months was discharged as medically unfit for further service. Later in life he became the senior partner in the Birmingham firm of Cox & Furse, Chartered Accountants. During the Second World War he became the commander of the Birmingham City Police Constabulary Reserve; for which he was awarded the MBE.

Below: The Battle of Morval 25 September 1916. Here we can see German PoWs carrying the wounded of the 5th Division back to the Casualty Clearing Stations. A hatless German, walking towards the camera on the left, can be seen carrying a wounded British soldier's rifle. Their pose gives the impression that they are moving quite quickly. With the smoke of shellfire in the background you can understand why.
IWM Q1311

Farewell to the Somme

With the attack on Morval being an overwhelming success and casualties comparatively light compared to earlier attacks (the 14th, 15th and 16th Royal Warwicks had 50 killed in action between the 24-26 September) it was still a weary and worn out division that made its way to the Citadel Camp near Fricourt on September 27th. But the news soon circulated that the division was being withdrawn and to make an immediate move northwards to Givenchy. 'One remembers vividly the relief experienced when it was known that our share in the battle had concluded and that we had finished with the Somme,' recalled Private J E B Fairclough, in the history of the 14th Royal Warwicks battalion.

As a farewell gift to the division, that night a German night bomber scored a direct hit amongst the bivouacs and killed some men of the 1st Bedfords, a harsh stroke of luck for men who had survived the horrors of the Somme battles.

The total casualty figures for the 5th Division from 19 July until the end of September amounted to 559 Officers and 11,186 other ranks. General Rawlinson, GOC Fourth Army, to which the division had belonged for its tour of duty on the Somme, sent the following tribute:

'The conspicuous part that has been taken by the 5th Division in the battle of the Somme reflects the highest credit on the Division as a whole and I desire to express to every officer, NCO and man my congratulations and warmest thanks.

'The heavy fighting in Delville Wood, Longueval, the attack and capture of Falfemont Farm line and Leuze Wood and finally the storming of Morval are feats of arms seldom equalled in the annals of the British Army. They constitute a record of unvarying success which it has been the lot of few Divisions to attain and the gallantry, valour and endurance of all ranks has been wholly admirable. It is a matter of great regret to me that the Division is leaving the Fourth Army but after three strenuous periods in the battle front they have more than earned a rest.

'In wishing all ranks good fortune for the future, I trust I may one day have this fine Division again under my command.'

That was the 'Top Brass' summary of the Division's experience on the Somme front. In a letter home to his mother, Private Frederick John Hughes (No.15/1434) of the 16th Royal Warwicks, gives his brief version of what the Somme was like at the sharp end:

Below: Battle of Morval 25 September 1916. Once take by the 5th Division the ruins of Morval were consolidated in case of German counter attacks. Here we can see some unidentified 5th Division troops. Men from the 'sharp end of war', judging by their weapons and equipment.
IWM Q4419

Nov 4th

'Dear Mother,

I am sending you some souvenirs in the shape of a German soldier's Pay Book. I took it off him at Morval, he would not require it any more, my last engagement was there. There are some views of Arras. That is the first place I was at when I first came out here. The engagements I have been in are as under

Longueval, Delville Wood, better known as Devil's Wood, Falfemont Farm and Morval.

I am now at La Bassie and near Festerburt and Neue Chappelle. In those engagements we lost some men. At Falfemont Farm after going over the top we came out under 200 strong. Shells dropped like hail stones. This is being posted for me in England. Edgar Wray was killed in the Falfemont Farm scrap. (L/Cpl Edgar Wray, No.487, B Coy from St Pauls Road, Balsall Heath) *We only had one officer and sergeant left and 50 men, the French troops were on our right they fought like Hell. The Royal Irish relieved us there about 3 in the afternoon. We were dead beat as we had hung on night and day.*

'The shelling at Longueval was the worst that has ever been in all the war. As we were shelled from 3 points, the boys dropped left and right but on we went. A barrage of fire is terrible, it is one line of shells and that is the sort of thing we face in these pushes. It is easy where I am now. I go out on patrol at night looking for Fritzy's patrols. That is in No Man's Land.

'Well I could say a lot about the War but I would rather not. I often think we are past the days of civilisation when we can look at arms and legs without a shudder...'

The letter was not posted in England because it was never finished. Private Frederick Hughes, was killed five days later by German trench-mortar fire. The unfinished letter was found amongst his personal effects sent on to his parents. Edgar Wray who was mentioned was not only his best pal, but the brother of Frederick's fiancée, Miss Ethel Wray. Like many women who lost their loved ones during the war, she never married.

Even though the casuality list was considerably lower, for the attack on Morval, compared to earlier actions in which the Birmingham Battalions took part, the overall figure for those who were killed or died of wounds is quite considerable. The following figures are the total of all ranks who DIED (not the wounded) whilst serving in the three battalions from 20 July until September 28. It also includes a few who died of their wounds during the first few days of October:

14th Royal Warwicks (1st B'ham) **403**

15th Royal Warwicks (2nd B'ham) **204**
16th Royal Warwicks (3rd B'ham) **178**
Total **785**

515 of these men, were never found, or their remains could not be identified. They are now commemorated along with another 77,000 missing in action, British and Dominion troops, on the Thiepval Memorial.

Of those 785 who died, 471 were original volunteers who sailed to France the previous November. If we include the wounded in the total, as you might guess, it was a very different three Birmingham Battalions leaving the Somme than when they first arrived. There was still a core of original men still serving within the battalions. Quite a few, due to the casualties, would now be NCOs. Many of the original volunteers who were wounded, when fit, would return to fight another day. A few of the wounded made it back to their original battalions. Many more were drafted to other battalions within the Royal Warwickshire Regiment. Sadly many of these former Birmingham Pals, fresh from Officer Cadet Battalions, can be found amongst the casualty lists after the German Spring offensive of March 1918.

Before finishing with the Somme, I think the last word should be left to 'Ricardo' alias Private Richard Louis-Bertram Moore (No.1010, B Coy) the amateur poet of the 15th Royal Warwicks. Private Moore was wounded in the action at Falfemont Farm on 3 September. He wrote the following whilst recovering from his wounds. It was published in the *Birmingham Daily Post* in December 1916 and is a fitting tribute to the Birmingham Pals:

'CHOCOLATE SOLDIERS ALL.'
There were three battalions raised in 'Brum'
About two years ago,
They dres't us in blue
And put us on view
And petted us don't-yer-know.
They put us in billets at Sutton,
Paid 19 and 3d. a head,
Lived on the best,
Thought it a jest,
And the populace were not the least impressed, For the wiseacres smiled and said:
'They're only for people to look at,
'That's what they've been raised for;
'They're only chocolate soldiers,
'They'll never go to war.'

Then we were shifted to Wensleydale,
And, after six weeks up there,
They moved us again,
Down to the Plain,
And khaki we had to wear.
We'd finished with billets for ever
And laid the blue on one side,
We went thro' the mill
At bayonet drill

Above: Private John Deakin, No.325, B Coy, 7 Platoon, 14th Royal Warwicks, from Spring Road, Edgbaston. Wounded during the attack on Wood Lane, 23 July 1916. Like many of his comrades he decided to take a commission on recovery. He is pictured whilst a Cadet at the No.11 Officer Cadet Battalion.
Miss Rose Deakin

Above: Private Frederick John Hughes (see text left) killed in action 9 November 1916.
Les Philips

Above: Platoon Sergeant John Eldridge, No.885, D Coy, 15 Platoon, 14th Royal Warwicks, who was wounded during the attack upon Wood Lane 23 July 1916. Many of the original volunteers who were wounded decided on recovery to take a commission. Sergeant Eldridge, who came from Alfred Road, Sparkhill, was commissioned to the 2nd Kings Royal Rifle Corps and was killed in action on 18 September 1918. He is buried in Berthaucouer Communal Cemetery, Pontru, France.

Below: Silver Wound Badge given to men who were discharged after being wounded on active service.

Right: As the 5th Division left the Somme Front, winter was fast approaching. Conditions would soon be deplorable, with the battlefield turning into a quagmire. The two soldiers in the photograph are wearing leather jerkins. The soldier on the left has a sandbag tied around his rifle to stop mud getting into the mechanism. They are both wearing the 1914 pattern leather equipment, which indicates they are probably from a Kitchener's New Army battalion.
IWM Q4498

And divisional schemes which were harder still,
And still the knowalls cried:
'They're only the City Battalions
'So spick and span and spruce:
'Birmingham's chocolate soldiers,
'For ornament, not use.'

Then we were shifted from Salisbury Plain,
And, after that, in due course
By train and ship
We took a trip

To the jolly old B.E. Force.
An' ever since then we've been scrappin'
Or restin' (that means fatigues).
And the boys shaped well
'Mid the shot and shell
And we've been in places that rivalled hell
And marched for many leagues:
But we often say to each other now
(it's a joke we can't forget):

'They said we were 'Chocolate Soldiers,'
'But we haven't melted yet.

Chapter Eight

La Bassée Front; October 1916 to March 1917

On 29 September 1916, the 5th Division left the Somme Front. From the Citadel Camp (near the present day site of the Citadel New Military Cemetery, near Fricourt) the division made its way back to a main railway junction situated near to the village of Dernancourt. Here the various battalions went to their designated pick-up points: the 14th Warwicks entrained at 'Edgehill Station', the 15th, 'Grovetown' and the 16th, 'Happy Valley'. There followed a short two day rest in the region of Abbeville, before the division continued the move to another section of the Western Front.

This time the powers that be were kind to the 5th Division; instead of returning to the Somme, and the horrendous conditions that would be encountered with the onset of autumn and winter, the division moved further north, past Arras, to the vicinity of Béthune. This was to be the division's winter quarters for the next six months. The section of the line that the division took over was known as the La Bassée Front, and by 5 October, the 5th Division had replaced the 31st. The 7,500 yard front (6.8 Km) in question was divided into three sectors: Cuinchy, Givenchy and Ferme du Bois. Béthune, which had so far received very little German artillery attention, became the site of Divisional HQ and various other training centres; for example, Infantry schools, Sniping schools, Lewis-gun Schools and Trench-mortar schools. This was a very quiet front and it was an ideal opportunity to bring the division back to full strength and commence training in comparative safety. The 14th and 15th Royal Warwicks during their stay on this front were mostly in and out of the line fronting the villages of Festubert and Givenchy, whilst the 16th Royal Warwicks operated further north.

Apart from German artillery, the only hostile actions received were daily doses of trench-mortars or the constant threat of German snipers. It was soon established that a German Bavarian Division, who like the 5th Division had taken heavy casualties on the Somme, were on the opposite side of No Man's Land; all they wanted was a peaceful time. But they did not get it. It was High Command policy to harass the German lines continually, to wear them down, to keep their sentries on edge, wondering when it was their turn to be raided. No Man's Land was patrolled nightly and at least two raids on the divisional front were carried out each week during the six months on this front. Similarly to the previous year, the Christmas of 1916 saw an increased bombardment from the British artillery. Starting on 24 December and lasting four days a slow continual bombardment with periodic bursts of rapid fire made sure no fraternisation took place. Of the three Birmingham Battalions, it was the 16th

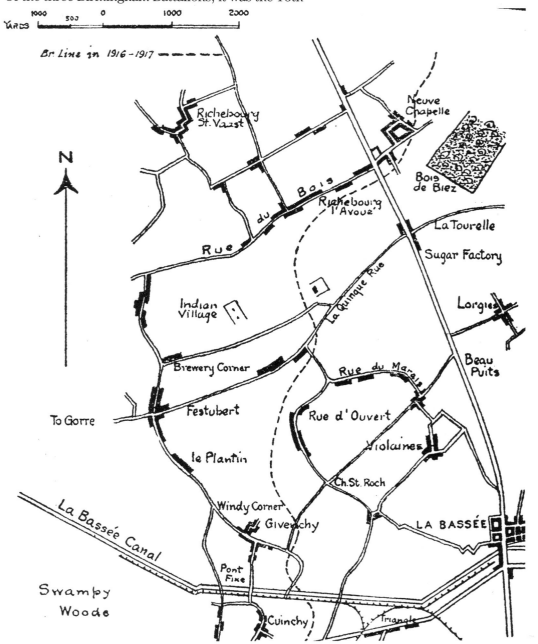

Royal Warwicks who made the first raid on this front. On 9 October Lieutenant G H Hadley and two other ranks entered the German trenches and remained in them for over an hour without discovering any signs of the enemy! After one patrol of the 15th Royal Warwicks an unusual German early warning system was reported when geese were discovered penned up near to the front line barbed wire. Another example of how quiet the war was on this section, was when during the early occupation of this sector, young boys and girls would come up to the support lines selling *Daily Mails* and chocolates. This habit, however, was soon stopped. During the first few weeks of the new year severe frosts, down to minus 22 degrees, were experienced; the worst in France for thirty years. As you can guess the casualties for this tour of the front were low indeed; between them, the 14th, 15th and 16th Royal Warwicks had only around fifty men killed, and of these only ten were original volunteers to the battalions. One of these was the unfortunate Private Stanley Hulbert (No.1292) of the 14th Royal Warwicks who was reported in the War Diary, on January 13th, 1917, to have been hit by friendly fire from a Lewis-gun Private Hulbert, aged twenty, had been previously wounded on two other occasions. He was formerly an employee of the London Insurance Company and lived in Finch Road, Aston. He is buried in Béthune Town Cemetery. Towards the middle of March the 66th (East Lancs) Division (Territorials) arrived from England, and after a short instructional period replaced the 5th Division on the La Bassée Front. The 5th Division made its way to the Bruay district (around 5 miles south west of Béthune) in preparation for forthcoming actions collectively called the Battle of Arras.

Vimy Ridge and the Battle of Arras; April to September 1917

It was now spring, and with the better weather and dry conditions it was time for the Allies to put into operation plans that had been meticulously formulated for the 1917 offensives. However, the Germans had an ace up their sleeve, so to speak, and took the initiative. For many months the German Army had been constructing a new defence system, many miles behind their present front line, which shortened the length of their trench system considerably. It was known as the Hindenburg Line, running south from Arras to the French sector to the north-west of Soissons. In parts, the Hindenburg Line was approximately fifty miles further back from the previous front line. Whilst on the Somme front, where there had been around 1,000,000 casualties, on all sides, in six months and in some places what only amounted to yards gained the Germans had moved back around fifteen miles! Consequently, the British plans for the forthcoming offensive were re-arranged for a large scale assault upon roughly a fifteen mile section of the Arras Front, to begin on Easter Monday, 9 April 1917. The Canadian Corps under Lieutenant-General Sir Julian Byng, which consisted of the 1st, 2nd, 3rd and 4th Canadian Divisions, were given the task to take the northern portion of the attack; the seemingly impregnable Vimy Ridge.

On leaving the La Bassée Front, the 5th Division now came under the command of the Canadian Corps. 13 Infantry Brigade (1st Royal West Kents, 2nd KOSB's, 14th and 15th Royal Warwicks) were attached to the Canadian 2nd Division for the assault on Vimy Ridge. Why 13 Brigade you may ask? Well, this may have been something to do with the assistance given to Canadians, by 1st Royal West Kents and the 2nd KOSBs of 13 Brigade, during a gas attack in the vicinity of St Julian (about 3miles north east of Ypres) on 24 April, 1915. In the history of the 1st Birmingham Battalion, Private J E B Fairclough later recalled:

'The operation in which we were to take part had for its objective the capture of Vimy Ridge. The success which attended

this venture was both immediate and lasting. The spectacular capture of this renowned stronghold had a sound moral effect, and Vimy Ridge remained in our hands all through the war and was a very tower of strength in the dark days of 1918. It formed a hinge on which all our operations turned in those days when the fate of the Empire hung in the balance. Running south easterly from Givenchy-en-Gohelle, the ridge gradually falls away, losing itself in the country north of Arras. The western slope, except in front of Souchez, is fairly gradual, but over the summit the ground falls abruptly to the east, and from the top of the ridge an expansive panorama of the plain stretches away as far as the eye can see.

13 Brigade and the 5th Division artillery, with all its guns assembled in the village of Neuville St Vaast, were attached for the attack to the 2nd Canadian Division. The remainder of the 5th Division remained in reserve, ready to move forward if wanted. In the capture of Vimy Ridge, there was only one British Brigade concerned – 13 – and thus the two

Birmingham Battalions helped to maintain the prestige of the Motherland in that historic attack.'

The 13th Brigade's involvement in the capture of Vimy Ridge came during the second phase of the attack, once the original German front line had been taken and consolidated. It was the Royal West Kents and the KOSBs who took the fighting role on the day. Their objective was Goulot Wood, which was sited on the steep front slope of the ridge. Once taken, C and D Coys of the 15th Royal Warwicks, who were in close support, helped reinforce the newly gained position in case of any German counter-attack. Meanwhile, A and B Coys of the 14th Royal Warwicks were used to carry ammunition, stores and trench mortars up to the consolidating troops whilst C and D Coys made two strongpoints along the Arras – Lens Road. Casualties for 13 Brigade were very light, seven officers and 230 other ranks; which reflects the professionally executed attack formulated and put into force by the Canadian Corps. Of these casualties, the 15th Royal Warwicks lost three men killed and fifty wounded, whilst the 14th had only five men wounded.

On 14 April, the 16th Royal Warwicks, came into the action, when 15 and 95 Brigades along with the

Above left: Goatskin jerkins became an essential item of kit whilst in the trenches during the winter of 1916-17. Middle, Private Charles Jeffs, No.918, D Coy from Station Road, Fernhill Heath, Worcs. Right, Private Harry Hopkins, No.362, B Coy, from Medlicott Road, Sparkbrook. Both served in the 16th Royal Warwicks. *Irene Ducker*

Above right: An example of the weather conditions on the opening day of the Battle of Arras. British troops at Arras, 9 April 1917.

Above: Corporal George Dyer, No.874, D Coy, 15 Platoon, 14th Royal Warwicks, from Warren Road, Washwood Heath. Wounded, 9 April 1917. An employee of the Birmingham Reference Library. *Steve Farrant*

Left: British troops marching through Arras, 13 April 1917 *IWM Q3094*

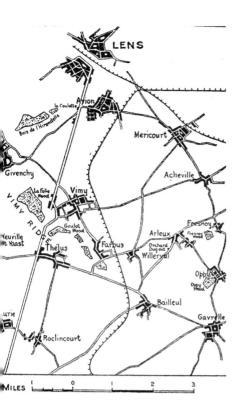

Above: Private Harold Wright, No.592, C Coy, 11 Platoon, 15th Royal Warwicks, from Westfield Road, Kings Heath. Died of Wounds 24 April 1917. Harold was a former employee of Kings Heath branch of Lloyds Bank.

Right: Arras front, 8 April 1917. Fixing scaling ladders, in the jumping off trenches prior to the offensive. On right hand side of the trench can be seen 'toffee apple' bombs that were fired from a Stokes 3ins Light Mortar. *IWM Q 6204*

3rd Canadian Battalion began pushing the Germans back towards Lens. They were held up by strong German resistance on the outskirts of the village of La Coulotte, approximately 3km south of Lens. Here a hastily dug trench line was established and held for three days; until they were relieved. During an ensuing attack, by the same two brigades, on April 23rd, the 16th Royal Warwicks were in support at La Chaudiere. By 1 May, The 5th Division had left the Canadian Corps, and came under the control of the British XIII Corps commanded by Lieutenant-General Congreve VC. The other divisions in the Corps were the 2nd, 31st and 63rd (Royal Naval), and for the next four months operated in the vicinity of Arleux, Oppy and Fresnoy. Whilst in this area, the 5th Division HQ was located in Roclincourt, where the Birmingham Battalions saw service twelve months previously. The stay on this part of the front started badly for the division. The village of Fresnoy was lost to a determined German attack on 8 May, and over the following days all the battalions of the 5th Division were involved in trying to regain the lost village. Artillery fire from both sides was intense, the fighting was savage; hand-to-hand, bayonet charges and bombing attacks. Various parts of the village changed hands many times with isolated pockets holding out and keeping the Germans at bay for hours on end.

During this period the casualty figures for the three Birmingham Battalions were quite high. The 14th Royal Warwicks lost 115 men due to shellfire between 5 and 8 May, whilst only holding the line; of these forty were killed. During the bombardment, one shell killed three officers: Captain Turner and Lieutenants Barrow and Vince. Bernard Turner (Francis Road, Edgbaston) and William Vince (Lyttleton Road, Edgbaston) were both original volunteers to the 1st Birmingham Battalion. The 15th Royal Warwicks were involved in an assault on Fresnoy beginning at 02:00 on 9 May. Before the men even got to the German positions many casualties were caused by shellfire catching them whilst crossing No Man's Land. Despite these early losses men of the 15th Royal

Warwicks reached their objectives in and around Fresnoy, but because they were now weak in numbers and both flanks in the air, the remaining men had to pull out and return to the jumping off line. During this failed attack the battalion lost 206 men; sixty of these were killed. Once back in the jumping off trench, the 15th Royal Warwicks were relieved by the 16th, who then suffered four days of concentrated artillery bombardment, in which twenty five men lost there lives.

Oppy Wood Attack: 16th Royal Warwicks

The most exceptional episode during the divisional stay on this front was the attack by all four battalions of 15 Brigade on 28 June (1st Norfolks, 1st Cheshires, 1st Bedfords and 16th Royal Warwicks) on Oppy Wood. This was combined with an attack on trenches south of the wood by battalions of the 31st Division. The 16th Royal Warwicks' final objective was a section of German third line trench, south of Oppy Wood, known as Wood Trench. The Divisional history now takes over:

'This wood (Oppy), which was only an acre or so in extent, had long stared us in the face, and was the home of many enemy OP's (observation posts), machine guns, and trench-mortars – a very desirable spot to annex to our territory. The 15th Brigade carried out the operation with all four battalions, disposed as follows: 16th Royal Warwicks on the right, Cheshires right centre, Norfolks left centre, and the Bedfords on the left, all of whom had a week's previous training behind the line. The preliminary task of the artillery was to completely destroy all wire, but not blot out the trenches, so our men, after the capture, should find some shelter. This was done to the entire satisfaction of the infantry. The weather during the day was sultry, culminating in a thunderstorm and a heavy downpour of rain in the evening:

Three views from the opening day of the Battle of Arras, 9 April 1917.

Left: Captured German MG 1908 machine gun and crew.
IWM Q5123

Below: German POW's carrying British wounded.
IWM Q5124

Bottom: German POW's carrying stores.
IWM Q5180

the daily artillery fire went on as usual with no notable increase, though the enemy may have suspected something, as he put down a heavy bombardment for a few minutes on the assembly trenches, causing a few casualties; but the 15th Brigade were undismayed by it.

Suddenly, at 7:10 pm, the thunder of the Heavy Artillery Counter-Batteries and the intense barrage of the Field Artillery broke forth with a crash: at the same time the Howitzers put up a thick smoke screen on the North, to cover the left flank from observation. Our troops advanced rapidly, keeping close under the barrage, in which they had the greatest confidence, charged the trenches, and carried the front line at 7.15, before the enemy had time to man his machine guns. The attack was a complete success; the enemy trenches were strongly held, but only on the left, where the objective was deeper than on the rest of the front, was there any opposition. The German reply was feeble and disjointed; it was six or eight minutes before a definite barrage was formed, and, by that time, the position had been won, and a large batch of prisoners had been sent back. By 9 pm all battalions were busy digging and consolidating the line, and Royal Engineers and Pioneers had been sent across to help them. The captures amounted to two officers and 141 other ranks, besides a number of machine guns and trench-mortars; and the 31st Division, who had been equally successful, took about the same number. Our casualties in killed and wounded were ten officers and 342 other ranks.'

In this successful operation, the 16th Royal Warwicks, took a total of forty-two prisoners, and

Right: Oppy Wood, objective of the 15 Brigade, 28 June 1917. *IWM Q28787*

Above: Acting Corporal Thomas Bicknell, No.504, C Coy, 9 Platoon, 16th Royal Warwicks. Reported 'missing' during the fighting around Arleux village 8 to 15 May 1917. Three months later he was reported as being a PoW. *Dave Bicknell*

Above: Company Sergeant Major E Callow, No.868, D Coy, 15 Platoon, 15th Royal Warwicks, from Chantry Road, Handsworth. Wounded May 1917.

Above: Private Charles Morgan, No.1339, D Coy, 13 Platoon, 14th Royal Warwicks, from Lennox Street, Lozells. This photograph was taken whilst out of the line, June 1917. *Mrs Bentley*

Right: Lewis Gun team, June 1917. The men can be seen wearing the 1917 pattern small box respirator. An excellent rear view can be seen of the 1914 pattern leather infantry equipment. Underneath the water bottle can be seen the leather bag that contained the entrenching tool. The handle is attached to the bayonet scabbard. *IWM Q6777*

226

several light machine guns and a trench-mortar. During the attack, the battalion only suffered four other ranks killed, and three officers and 32 men wounded. For this action Second Lieutenants N E Jervis and J Hughes and Company Sergeant Major W Baker were awarded the Military Cross, and seven other ranks the Military Medal. The Battalion War Diary describes the acts of gallantry for the Military Cross winners, but not the others:

2nd Lieutenant N E Jervis

'Although wounded in the head by a machine gun he remained in charge of his Coy and directed them throughout the attack'.

Second-Lieutenant J Hughes (as Lieutenant, killed at Passchendaele 9-10-17)

'Bombed a dugout killing the occupants and captured a machine gun'.

> CSM W Baker

'Bombed a machine gun which was getting into action, thereby saving many casualties'.

On 9 July, when the battalion was out of the line, Divisional Routine Orders stated that the main German trench captured by the 16th Royal Warwicks on 28 June would now be known as Birmingham Trench and a the communication trench nearby to be known as Brum Street.

Military Medal winners, 28 June 1917:

22	Sgt P O Edge (Highbridge Road, Sutton Coldfield)
1156	Sgt A Hughes
12704	L/Sgt A E Handel

30086 Cpl W Guest
10189 L/Cpl F Barratt
362   Private H Hopkins (Medlicott Road,
         Sparkbrook)
11517 Private H Hill

Parchment Certificate, June 28th 1917:

29   L/Cpl A Gissing (St Agnes Road, Moseley)
1728   L/Cpl W H Walpole
30184 L/Cpl H Bowd
1640   Private W Huckvale

Trench Raid: 15th Royal Warwicks

Another episode worth mentioning during this period was a successful trench raid undertaken by twenty-six men from B Coy of the 15th Royal Warwicks in the early hours of 16 July, upon part of a German front line trench, north of Oppy Wood. The raid was commanded by 2nd Lieutenant A C Coldicott, an A Coy officer temporarily attached to B, whilst the senior NCO was Sergeant John Gates (No.1354). In the history of the battalion, Captain C A Bill wrote the following concerning the incident:

'On the second night Coldicott took ten men out to reconnoitre and on the third and fourth nights he took the full party of twenty-six out to accustom them to the way across. Demolition of the enemy wire was carried out by Trench-mortars and Artillery during each day. In the early morning of the 16th July the raiding party left our lines and took up a position about 150 yards (137m) from the German wire. Zero hour had been fixed for 02:30 am, when oil projectors and the artillery opened on the enemy wire, lifting at Zero plus one minute on to his trench. At Zero plus three the Artillery formed a box barrage, shrouding off the area to be raided and the party entered the front trench. A prisoner of the 13th Bavarian Infantry Regiment had been captured in a shell hole a few yards in front of the trench and brought in and another German near him was killed. The trench had been badly knocked about by our gun-fire and was found to consist mainly of shell holes connected by imperfect sections of trench about thigh deep. This somewhat upset the pre-arranged plan of working down the trench, and fighting resulted in attacking the enemy at sight with revolver, bomb, and bayonet. A party of three or four Germans were bombed in one place without hope of escape and several more were known to have been bayoneted. The raiding party remained in the enemy line for about twenty minutes and penetrated to his second line before withdrawing

Above: June 1917, men from the Dorset Regiment, cleaning salvaged rifles. *IWM Q6095*

under cover of a stopping party.

'By this time an intense enemy protective barrage was being put down on our own front line and Coldicott decided to dispose his party in No Man's Land until thing quietened down. He himself came in to report the situation and then rejoined his men. At 03.20 the gun-fire slackened and the whole party came in with the exception of one man badly wounded, who was brought in shortly afterwards in broad daylight by Private French (No.15057 of Long Itchington, Warwicks). The raid was highly successful, eight or ten of the enemy being known to be killed and one prisoner taken. Our casualties were one man slightly wounded, one slightly injured by a fall, and the one seriously wounded already mentioned who afterwards died of his wounds'.

After the raid the following letter was sent by Major-General R B Stephens, GOC of the 5th

Below: The remains of a German 5.9 Field Gun in the vicinity of Gavrelle, 27 June 1917. *IWM Q5529*

Division:

> *'The Corps Commander has directed me to congratulate Lieutenant-Colonel Miller of the 15th RWR on their most successful raid on the night of 15th/16th. The careful preparations, the reconnaissance and the dash with which the raid was carried out reflect the greatest credit on all concerned'.*

The leader of the raiding party, Second-Lieutenant Arden Cotterell Coldicott, a twenty year old former pupil of King Edward's School, Birmingham, was awarded the Military Cross. Unfortunately, he was reported 'missing' after a similar raid a year later when the battalion was on the Nieppe Front. Records show that he died of wounds as a Prisoner of War, and he is buried in Cologne Southern Cemetery, Germany. Sergeant John Gates (from Woodland Road, Handsworth) the senior NCO was awarded the Military Medal, along with Private John French; who by the way was another man who would not see out the war. Private French was killed later in the year at Passchendaele. With regards to Captain Bill's account of the raid, he mentioned 'oil projectors' used against the German trenches. These were the British answer to the German flame-thrower. Organised by units of the Royal Engineers known as 'Special Companies'. cylinders of oil, as many as 200 to 300 at a time were electrically fired from a device similar to a Trench-Mortar, and once contact was made with the ground, were ignited.

An interesting entry in the 14th Royal Warwick's War Diary on 13 August 1917, was that Sergeant Edward Wallace Williams (No.281, A Coy, from Sandon Road, Edgbaston) who had been killed in the attack on 'Wood Lane' on 23 July 1916, had been awarded the Military Medal. No other information, just that. One wonders what information came to light concerning Sergeant William's act of gallantry, and where that information is now. Perhaps someone someday could enlighten me. Sergeant Williams MM is buried in Caterpillar Valley Cemetery.

On 7 September, 1917, the 5th Division was relieved and the brigades moved to a quiet back area for rest and training. It is worth mentioning, that whilst out of the line the GOC of the 5th Division (Major-General R B Stephens) instituted a Divisional Platoon Competition. Nearly 200 platoons entered, and the eventual winners were No.5 Platoon, B Coy, 16th Royal Warwicks, commanded by Lieutenant Wilfred Evelyn Littleboy; who was presented with a silver cup. In less than four weeks Lieutenant Littleboy, who had enlisted in 1914 straight from the sixth-form at Rugby School, would be dead. He was killed on 9 October 1917 during an attack upon Polderhoek Château, Lieutenant Littleboy's family home was at Saltburn-by-the-Sea, Yorks and he is buried in Hooge Crater Cemetery, Belgium.

Third Battle of Ypres: September to November 1917

To many who have read up on the First World War, areas where heavy fighting took place around the Ypres Salient are quite well known and trip off the end of the tongue, for example the Menin Road, Sanctuary Wood, Hellfire Corner, Clapham Junction, Zillebeke, Zonnebeke, Passchendaele, Hill 60, Gheluvelt and Polderhoek Château; Polderhoek who? Yes, Polderhoek Château. It was an impregnable fortified ruin, about half a mile north

Above: Panoramic view of the ruins of the Cloth Hall, Ypres, September 1917.
IWM Q2829

of the Menin Road at Gheluvelt, that withheld all attacks that the British Army could throw against it. Polderhoek remained in German hands until finally evacuated in the retreat of August 1918. Even though the 5th Division was involved in the Third Battle of Ypres for a short duration, it was six weeks of pure misery in the worst fighting conditions imaginable, and the objective ... Polderhoek Château.

There had been no major breakthrough during 1917. The Germans had withdrawn to the Hindenburg Line earlier in the year. In April Vimy Ridge was taken and the Battle of Arras fought. In June, south of Ypres, the Germans had been blown off Messines Ridge. Therefore, up till now, from the Allies' point of view, 1917 had been comparatively successful as regards ground gained. The next big offensive, whilst weather conditions were still favourable, was the Battle of Third Ypres; the objective, the high ground near the village of Passchendaele. Eventually the ridge was taken, but instead of weeks it took four months, and in doing so 90,000 Allied soldiers alone, were reported as 'missing in action.'

The battle commenced on 31 July, 1917, with the main objective for the British and Dominion troops, Passchendaele Ridge. Unfortunately, when the battle commenced so did the rain, it came down in torrents. To set the scene and envisage the terrible conditions that ensued, it is best to quote from somebody who experienced them. Private J E B Fairclough, still with the 14th Royal Warwicks, gave the following account:

'Since the beginning of the offensive in August, the weather had been vile, turning the flat land into a veritable sea of mud. The postponement of the original date for the opening of the offensive, owing to French unpreparedness, had robbed us of several days' fine weather, and when the offensive did start on the altered day it heralded in also the wettest autumn that had been known in Flanders for nearly forty years (it is on record as being the worst weather in Belgium for 75 years). Constant shelling had broken down the barriers which held the water courses in position with the consequence that the ground became flooded and shell holes formed series of small lakes. Incessant rains converted the already waterlogged ground into a quagmire so that duckboard tracks were the only means of moving about in the forward areas. Any straying from these marked paths meant serious trouble and for the heavily-laden infantry, journeys up to the front line were grim adventures, but even these were not to be compared with the return journeys when the men were soaked with mud and exhausted by attacks and front line work. These duckboard

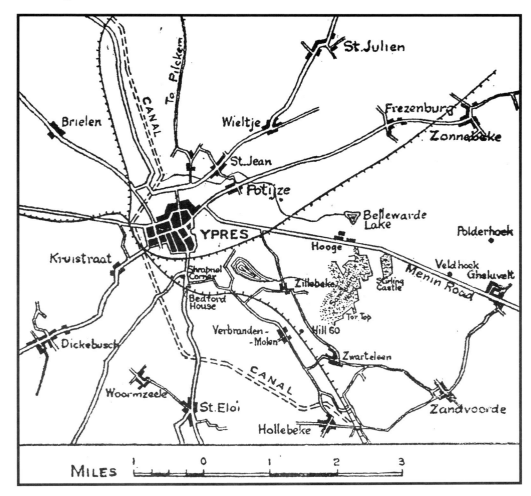

Above: Polderhoek Château under German occupation, prior to it's devastation. The huge cellar, that a large building like this would have, would be reinforced with a thick concrete lining and roof. After British artillery reduced the building to one huge pile of rubble, all that was left was an impregnable concrete box bristling with machine guns.
IWM Q55578 (19)

tracks were well marked and proved excellent targets for enemy artillery. Many wounded never reached the casualty clearing stations but perished in the mud, some after many hours of agony, gradually sinking lower and lower until they were finally completely immersed. However, the mud sometimes proved to be a blessing in disguise, for shells would often embed themselves so deeply in the mud before exploding that one would receive only a plastering of mud: uncomfortable, but distinctly better than flying steel.

'Continuous trenches in the forward areas were impossible, either to dig or maintain: companies would take over lines of shell holes and then hang on in these with no shelter of any description, at the mercy of the continual rain and ceaseless shelling. In fact these lines of waterlogged shell holes were at once a danger and a defence. They were the only possible method of holding the ground but were dangerous to their occupants inasmuch as they often contained sufficient water to drown a man.

'It is impossible to convey an adequate impression of the physical conditions prevailing in the Ypres salient in the memorable autumn and winter of 1917. To move at all demanded the greatest physical pluck and endurance, but when the extra handicaps of darkness and incessant heavy shelling were added to the appalling state of the ground, then the achievements of the regiments who carried through the operations in that stricken area assume the proportions of an epic struggle, and stand out as heroic achievements, even in those days of great events.

'The Germans did not rely on the generally accepted form of trench system for defence, owing to the nature of the ground and the heavy casualties they had

suffered. They had decided on defence in depth, and constructed lines of small concrete forts known as 'Pill-boxes'. These had walls and roofs about three feet thick and were proof against direct hits from the smaller-sized shells, although some of the larger ones survived direct hits from eight inch howitzers. These pill-boxes were manned by machine gunners who fired through narrow loopholes: thus they were themselves practically immune from rifle and machine-gun fire which did not penetrate the slits.'

Ted Francis (No.1114, 16th Royal Warwicks) was a grand old gentleman, and was the only Birmingham Battalion veteran that I ever made contact with. Sadly, Ted died in March 1996. Ted's worst memories of the war came from Ypres. He remembered how the dead were dragged along by their feet, and heaped in huge piles, like animals. But his worst recollection was the order concerning any man who may have slipped into a shell hole. Even if it was your best pal, you had to leave him; because in trying to rescue him, others could end in the same predicament. Even after eighty years Ted could still recall their cries for help as they slowly sank to their death. Captain Arthur Bill of the 15th Royal Warwicks described how a party of A Coy came upon one unfortunate soldier who had slipped off the duckboard track and was now thigh deep in what seemed bottomless mud. They tried to help with rifles under his armpits but there was no foothold. They had to leave him; duty called. Two days later when returning from the line, the same soldier was still there, but this time only his head was showing and he had gone raving mad.

After a month's training the 5th Division, on 24 September, transferred to X Corps of the British Second Army and two days later the division concentrated in the vicinity to the west of Bailleul. Here 13 Infantry Brigade temporary left the division and moved nearer to Ypres to become reserve for a 59th Division attack (177 and 178 Brigades) towards Gravenstafel, commencing on 26 September. Fortunately the attack was successful and the their services were not required thus, on 29 September 13 Brigade had rejoined the division. On the same date it is mentioned in the War Diary that the 14th Royal Warwicks received a draft of 196 men, all from the cavalry, i.e. Dragoon Guards, Hussars and Lancers.

After a couple more days training the 5th Division relieved the 23rd Division during the evening of 1 October. The Divisional front began at a position near the Menin Road about 1000 yards (914m) west of Gheluvelt and then northwards to roughly an area known as Carlisle Farm, near to Polygon Wood. Due to the extreme conditions and boggy ground, most of the action, concerning the 5th Division, for the next few weeks would concentrate between the two streams, the Ruetelbeek to the north and the Scherriabeek to the

south. Opposite the divisional front, and midway between the two streams were the remains of Polderhoek Wood and the ruins of Polderhoek Château. Before continuing the reader must erase from their mind the thought of trenches; as Private Fairclough explained there were none, the front line was now a series of connected shell holes. When mention is made of a wood, think of shattered and splintered tree stumps for streams, think of an impassable morass where heavy shelling had broken barriers resulting in the flooding of low lying land. And for Château, well, by now it was a mound of rubble, but below ground level the large cellar had been turned into a reinforced concrete bunker with many concealed entrances and tunnels to various strongpoints. Viewed from our lines it stood out like an island amid a sea of mud; a veritable fortress. Dotted here and there in what was once the château grounds were concrete pill-boxes, perhaps from ground level they may have appeared to be positioned higgledy-piggledy, but each one was sited with deadly precision. They each provided covering fire to others and the whole of No Man's Land could be raked with lethal machine-gun fire. The support line for the division was in the area by the Menin Road known as Stirling Castle and various Brigade Headquarters were situated in the tunnels of Tor Top near Sanctuary Wood. When it was time to be relieved, the men made their way back via Bedford House to either Scottish or Ridge Wood camps which were situated near Dickebusch Lake. Burgomaster Farm, on the western side of the lake, became Divisional HQ. When returning to the front line, Bedford House was where the troops had their last hot meal and drink for several days. From then on the only way of moving was by the duckboard tracks. In places there were up tracks and down tracks but in parts there was just one. If one battalion moving up the line happened to meet another moving down, one of them had to get off and stand in the mud whilst the other passed. Perhaps, this worked well in daylight, but imagine

the difficulty on a pitch black night; no wonder many men completely vanished. One fatal slip into a water filled crater whilst laden down with spare ammunition, bombs and rifle would no doubt mean certain death by drowning. Apart from these tracks, the whole landscape was a vast wilderness, 'Everything that ever grew had completely disappeared, all traces of buildings had vanished and as far as the eye could see was nothing but a waste of utter and demoralising desolation,' was how Captain Bill of the 15th Royal Warwicks recalled the Ypres Front.

A major attack starting on 4 October had been planned in the region and the 5th Division objective was a line past Polderhoek Château. The 1st Royal West Kents and the 2nd KOSBs were to carry out the attack whilst the 14th Royal Warwicks were in close support and the 15th Royal Warwicks in reserve. An ominous warning of what lay ahead, perhaps, occurred on 1 October when a reconnoitring party from the 14th Royal Warwicks consisting of five men under the command of 2nd Lieutenant A V Holley went up to find as much as possible about the front line. They never made it, the whole party became casualties caused by shellfire, with one man being killed. Even more casualties befell the battalion during its move up from Bedford House to the support lines that straddled the Menin Road roughly between Tower Hamlets and Northampton Farm.

Under a creeping barrage the attack began at 06.00 Thursday 4 October. All went well at first. In the first hour many outlying pill-boxes had been cleared by the KOSBs and numerous prisoners taken, but as the attacking troops got nearer to Polderhoek château they were checked by withering machine-gun fire from the Château and the numerous pill-boxes close by. To the right of the KOSBs the 1st Royal West Kents, had not only the château defences to deal with but also heavy machine-gun fire from the direction of Gheluvelt. Amongst all this destruction, there was also another form of killing machine that the attacking

troops had to contend with; low-flying German aircraft were strafing the battlefield with bomb and bullet. However, the Division's 95 Brigade fared slightly better. Their proposed route of attack was along the low land by the Reutlebeek stream; an impassable bog. Therefore the 1st Devons and 1st DCLI pushed on along higher ground towards the village of Reutel and managed to get behind the château and reach their objective, a position known as Juniper Hill. The Germans were very reluctant to give up Polderhoek Château and, as darkness fell, there commenced a total of eight determined counter-attacks in mass formation, and even though our artillery caused them heavy losses the 13 and 95 Brigades fell back to the outer perimeter of what once had been the château grounds. With regards to the Birmingham Battalions, three companies of the 14th Royal Warwicks were called upon to reinforce the newly gained ground whilst the 15th Royal Warwicks did extremely important work in keeping the attacking troops supplied with ammunition and stores. In doing so, the Military Cross was awarded to Captain Walter Goodwin (from Bristol Road, B'ham, who originally enlisted into the ranks of the 1st Birmingham Battalion and was commissioned in May 1915) the OC of B Coy, an indication of how significant the work was. The following day, 5 October, was spent trying to construct some type of defensive position in the newly gained sodden ground. Then during the evening 15 Brigade relieved 13 Brigade, with the 16th Royal Warwicks taking over the support role from the 14th and 15th Battalions, who now made their way back to Ridge Wood. In the War Diary of the 14th Royal Warwicks, the CO, Lieutenant-Colonel Murray, had this to say:

'I must bear testimony to the splendid courage, spirit and endurance shown by all ranks throughout a very arduous and trying time. Owing to the intense blackness of the night, and very violent nature of the enemy's shellfire and the almost impassable going over the shell pitted obstacled and trackless area, leadership and march discipline were put to a severe test. On no single occasion did Coys fail to assemble on their positions to time.'

There was one little incident worth mentioning that happened prior to the attack when C Coy of the 14th Royal Warwicks were taking up their support positions. One half of the company was in the charge of CSM 'Brummie' Heath (No.410 CSM E Heath), and the other of Sergeant Jimmy Davenport (No.544, from Park Road, Moseley). After Sergeant Davenport had got his men into position, he then made his way to see how his pal, CSM Heath, was getting on. 'Oh! we've buried him,' was the answer to his enquiry. On further investigation, Sergeant Davenport established that CSM Heath had looked dead, but their were no signs of wounds or blood, just a dent in his tin helmet. Fortunately, Sergeant Davenport had doubts and suspected that CSM Heath might only be unconscious. His suspicion was correct, after digging up the body it was found that CSM Heath was only concussed. For gallant conduct during the 4 October the following decorations were awarded to members of the 14th Royal Warwicks:

Military Cross
> Second-Lieutenant C H Platt
> Second-Lieutenant R G Warren

Military Medal (Bar)
> 73 Corporal W E Tongue MM (Stamford Road, Handsworth)

Military Medal
> 544   Sergeant James Davenport
> 28407 Private W Lunn
> 32428 Sergeant E S Burke
> 1447   F E Ralphs
> 16003 L/Sgt J Howe

Below: Heavily laden Australian troops making their way towards the front line via a duckboard track that snakes precariously around the edges of shell holes, 12 October 1917. What look like mere puddles in the photograph, are probably deep enough for a weary heavily burdened soldier to drown if he should slip into one. Picture yourself in the same scene, but this time at night in pitch darkness, and imagine a German artillery barrage gets too close for comfort. Your natural instinct would be to dive for cover...
IWM E (AUS) 985

18295 F J Shirley
29880 L/Sgt W Robertson
30274 A Smith
20896 Private A A Cooper
1324 W Webb
16439 R H Holloway
1142 T Williams

16th Royal Warwicks Attack on Polderhoek Château

Orders were received for a resumption of the offensive, with the same objective as that on 4 October. This time it was the turn of 15 Brigade and at 05.20 am 9 October, two companies of 1st Norfolks and three from the 16th Royal Warwicks ventured forth under a creeping barrage in another attempt to take Polderhoek Château. It was during the Somme battles of 1916, that we last heard from Private Harold Victor Drinkwater (No.161, 15th Royal Warwicks). By October 1917, he was now Second Lieutenant Drinkwater, having been commissioned into the 16th Royal Warwicks. Twenty years or so after the war, part of his diary, concerning the attack on 9 October, was published in the magazine *I Was There! The Human Story Of The Great War Of 1914-1918.*

'Towards early morning, on 8 October, about 3 a.m., I went over to D Company headquarters and found my own Company Officer and two or three more discussing things in general. They appeared to me to be sitting in a trench that was open to the direction from which the shells had been coming. After giving them my views on their position I moved away to what seemed to me a safer position some twelve yards away. I had barely got there when a shell lobbed into the middle of them. I hurried back on hearing their shouts, and found them in an awful mess. My own Company Captain and D Company Captain were both hit, also Stanley Henson (Second-Lieutenant). Stretcher-bearers came along and we quickly bandaged them up and got them out of the way. There were three men besides, one badly hit. We were only able to find parts of the other two, they seemed to have stopped the full force of the shell (These two men were probably Captain James Holme and Lieutenant George Sanders; they are both named on the Tyne Cot Memorial). *Morning came, orders followed later that we had to relieve the firing line that night. As a battalion we had lost heavily whilst in this position and we were glad of the prospect of getting away from it. The shellfire had by now become intense at intervals. We left the trenches when it was dark. Walters* (Second-Lieutenant W L Walters) *acting as*

Captain in the place of Captain Burns (Captain F B Byrne, wounded October 6th). *The ground was in a fairly bad state, shell-holes were full of water, the ground deep in mud and the men heavily laden with picks, shovels and sandbags. We moved slowly and cautiously, winding round shell-holes and trying to find firm parts of the ground to walk on. I led the way for my platoon, Sergeant Badger bringing up the rear* (No.1242, from Leopold Street, Highgate, B'ham): *although we had only some 500 yards to travel, it took us some two hours to do it.*

'My platoon was sent slightly to the left in support of D Company, who were occupying the front line; we arrived in a perfect salvo of shells. I got my men into a trench which was to be their billet for the time being. They had scarcely settled down when a shell dropped amongst them, killing four.

'It was a dangerous position. I therefore moved them up closer to D Company and then got into my headquarters, which was a cellar belonging to a lodge, which in turn belonged to a château (Polderhoek Château). This must have been a magnificent place in peace time. Situated on a rise, surrounded by woodlands and with an extensive view across valleys and hills. The view was now all that remained. The château had disappeared and the adjacent country utter desolation. We held the lodge, the Germans held the château. No actual buildings, except walls of the lodge or château existed. They had long since been blown down by artillery. It was the cellars in both instances that were occupied.

'The cellar I found was occupied by D Company and brigade machine gunners

Above: In the vicinity of Pervyse, Belgium, 30 July 1917. Two English nurses who set up a field hospital behind the Belgian trenches, north of Ypres. Left is Baroness de T'Serclaes MM, and on her right Miss Mary Chisolme. It may be of interest to note that the ambulance was paid for by the citizens of Sutton Coldfield. *IWM Q2660*

as their H.Q. (15 Brigade Machine Gun Company), *but the most welcome sight of all was to see a candle burning. I had not had a light for nights past, and its glow was very cheery. The recent occupancy was evident by the amount of German equipment strewn about. The sides of the walls were reinforced by blocks of concrete. We had reached another stage and wondered what was going to happen next. We were only fit to be literally carried out of the line at the first opportunity and given a night's sleep and some food (rations which had been sent up from the rear in double quantities seldom reached us; the carriers were either killed or unable to get through the barrage). Small parties got through occasionally, and it was on these that we relied for sustenance. I had scarcely been in the cellar a few minutes when such a party arrived, bringing a supply of rations and rum.*

'*Under these conditions we fondly looked for relief, but instead I had a message at 10 p.m. by runner from Walters, asking me to go to his headquarters. Stuffing my pockets with grub and a bottle of whiskey from D Company rations in case he was without food or rum, I returned with the runner, taking Sergeant Badger. Rain was pouring down; our condition was pitiable. Personally, my boots were full of mud and had been so for some days, and I was fairly*

wet through either by rain or perspiration. We were, without exception, all the same. We followed the runner over what seemed to be about a mile of ground. Although it was a very short distance, he had to stop every few yards to take his bearings. We found Walters at last. With him was Hutchinson (Second-Lieutenant C L C Hutchinson). They were standing up to their knees in mud and water. They had no covering. Their shack, a ground-sheet stretched across the top of the trench, had fallen in. They were both shaking as if they had a bad attack of the ague and could scarcely speak from cold. I handed them down into the trench the whiskey and food. Their expression of thanks was rather pathetic. With this tonic they recovered somewhat, and Walters told me he had operation orders for an attack on the château at dawn. It was impossible to do anything there. Rain was still coming down hard. So they both climbed out of the trench, and back we all went to the cellar and studied the scheme for the attack, or that part which applied to us.*

'*The scheme appeared sound on paper; but our condition made success improbable. We wished that those Staff Officers concerned somewhere, high up in rank, who had ordered the attack had undergone the same conditions as ourselves during the past week. There would not then have been this absurd affair. We heard afterwards that when the*

Below: Autumn 1917, the barren wilderness of a typical front line position during the Battle of Passchendaele. Trenches in the forward areas were impossible, either to dig or uphold. When in the front line, troops occupied shell holes with no cover of any description, sub-jected to endless rain and continual shelling. To the rear a Hotchkiss machine gun crew can be seen. In the forefront, a battlefield grave, with a hastily made cross, made from the debris lying around.
WM E (AUS) 807

Brigadier first received the orders, he tried to get it stopped, knowing very well the result must be disastrous in our weak condition. Walters and Hutchingson (sic), having got a good idea of the scheme, returned to their platoons, whilst Sergeant Badger and myself got our platoon NCOs a few at a time down in the cellar and explained the general idea. Although as conscious as I was of the improbability of success, they made no word of comment, but took their orders and went up the steps and out into the night to their sections. It was well done.

'The whole battalion were attacking the château and two pill-boxes, supported by the Norfolks on our left. Rain was coming down steadily as I moved forward with my platoon some fifty yards to the jumping line; so were German shells, and another of my men went west. I met Lieutenant W O Field (finished the war as Captain with an MC and Bar), *the Battalion Intelligence Officer*. He told me he had been unable to mark out our position; he had been unable to get any tape. So I took my general direction from a stump of a tree that he had pointed out.

'As each successive Very light went up in the district I got a few more of my men in position and quickly had them in line. Other officers were doing the same, so I went along to find out who were on my right and left. There was the usual confusion. It was fine overhead now, but pitch dark. The men seemed tired and done up, and in places were laying down in thick mud. The officers had no clear idea of what units were on their right and left of their objective, and like myself, were trying to find out and get some idea before the attack. I was unable to find Walters anywhere. He appeared to be lost. No one had apparently seen him after he had left me at the cellar. I was afraid he had got knocked out on the way back. I met one or two officers. They were all having casualties from falling shells and the men were naturally getting nervous.

'We were going over in two waves: A, B and C Companies, supported by the Norfolks on our left. Our particular objectives were the two pill-boxes, A Company and the Norfolks dealing with the château; my platoon were in the first wave.

'Punctually at 5.30 a.m., just as day was breaking, the barrage opened on the château and pill-boxes. We advanced and in less than two minutes we were among the Germans, who were laying out in shell-holes around them. Keeping well in line, we received and inflicted casualties, but our men were going strong, taking a prisoner here and there, and according to plan my platoon were keeping their eye on and making straight for the pill-boxes, the Germans running before as we advanced.

Above: Smoke from exploding shells can be seen from this shell hole situated near the Gravenstafel Road, 27 September 1917.
IWM Q2418

Below: Second Lieutenant Harold Victor Drinkwater, 16th Royal Warwicks. An original volunteer to the ranks of the 2nd Birmingham Battalion, No.161, A Coy, 2 Platoon, from John Street, Stratford upon Avon. His account of the 16th Royal Warwick's attack upon Polderhoek Château begins on page 237

Above: A fatigue party of Irish Guardsmen resting whilst carrying duckboards to the Langemarck sector, 10 October 1917.
IWM Q6053

I was left-hand man of my platoon, so that I could keep them from straying with the party who were attacking the château. Glancing along the line as we closed up to the pill-boxes, I saw my bombers crawling on their hands and knees close up, trying to find an opening to drop in bombs.

'My platoon machine-gunner, who was advancing with me, and slightly to the rear, carrying a Lewis gun, fell hit in the head. Hearing him fall down I looked round quickly and quickly back again, and saw a German stretched out in a shell-hole. I let fly with my revolver. He was not more than ten yards away, I missed, and he got up and bolted towards the pill-boxes, while I dropped into the shell-hole he had just left. Bullets were flying about in all directions, so I stayed a moment, glanced to the right, saw our men were still crawling up to the pill-boxes, whilst on the left our other men, A Company and the Norfolks appeared to be getting around the château. It all took only a moment and I was up again and going forward. We seemed to be making good headway, when for some unexplained reason my platoon and the remainder of the battalion on my right began to retire. Glancing to the right I found that there was not a soul between myself and the pill-boxes, and looking quickly backward I saw the battalion

retiring and were some fifty yards to my rear. I dropped into a shell-hole and glanced to the left. Our men were still attacking the château. I waited, thinking that perhaps they had retired for some good reason and would come back again. Although the attack on the château and the pill-boxes was one scheme as a whole, that upon the château was made from a slightly different angle, so that there was a gap of a few hundred yards between myself and their right hand man.

'I was within twenty yards of the pill-boxes, and knowing them to be occupied by Germans, I dodged from shell-hole to shell-hole, and lay down beside a fallen tree trunk out of their line of fire. I had a good view of the château being attacked (I was within a hundred yards of it). The Germans were putting up a good fight. One German from the top of the ruins was slinging bombs amongst our men. I could see him, but apparently they could not. But still our men kept crawling closer, taking cover in shell-holes and behind fallen trees. I waited some ten minutes for our men on the right to return. They did not do so and seeing Germans emerge from the pill-boxes, less than thirty yards away, I watched my opportunity and, like a frightened rabbit, bolted over the rise in the ground, and obscured from their view, made my way to the rear to try and find my platoon. On the way back I picked up C. with a bullet through the leg (this was probably Second Lieutenant Frederick George Crisp). we stopped in a shell-hole and I put a bandage round the wound. It was of no consequence, and scarcely bleeding. Together we bound up one or two fellows we saw lying about, a fairly nerve-racking ordeal, we knew the fellows so well, and then made our way back to where we thought our men had retired and our front line trench. We had nearly reached there when we must have come under observation from the pill-boxes. At any rate, a machine gun was turned on us and C. joined the great majority with a bullet in the brain (we were walking arm in arm). [Second Lieutenant Crisp has no known grave and is commemorated on the Tyne Cot Memorial] I dropped down, and finding him beyond aid, I crawled on my stomach, tumbled into the trench almost on to the top of Walters (Second Lieutenant W Walters), who was lying in the mud on the top of a couple of dead Germans with a piece of shell through his chest. The attacks, both on the château and on the pill-boxes, were failures. Gopsill (platoon commander) was the only one to reach the château, and he was taken prisoner. In both cases we got to within a dozen yards, but could not push the attack home.(Second Lieutenant J E Gopsill from Golden Hillock Road, Small Heath, had registered his name with the *Birmingham Daily Post* as a volunteer for the Birmingham Battalion on its inception. For reasons not known he was not accepted. He then probably enlisted into the 10th Royal Warwicks, my theory is based on the fact that a Lance Sergeant J Gopsill, No.4870, was wounded with the 10th Royal Warwicks in January 1916. This, after a period of recuperation and then a period of training with an Officer Cadet Battalion, ties up with Second Lieutenant Gopsill's commission in June 1917. He was repatriated in December 1918.) *I found the remnants of the battalion in charge of a lieutenant, as Senior Officer, and two Second Lieutenants, and the men half-way up to their knees in mud. I waded along the trench and found Sergeant Badger. He had got the remains of the platoon together. From him I gathered that when the men had got to the pill-boxes they heard the word given to 'retire.' They should have known that it did not come from us, as the command is never given in the British Army. The Germans may have shouted it, or what is more probable our men were too exhausted to carry on.*

'*Leaving them in charge of Badger, I went back along the trench. Sewell had put himself in charge* (Lieutenant W Sewell). *Hutchinson and Wilkes* (Second-Lieutenant H H Wilks) *were the only other two officers who had got back, and Hutchinson was fairly well hit but carrying on for the time being. We organised ourselves in case of counter-attack. Slightly wounded men* waded up and down the trench, collecting and cleaning ammunition and handing it out to those who were short. Hutchinson, Wilks and myself divided the line roughly into three parts and each took command of a part. We had a good field of fire and there was no great emergency, so I went back and saw Walters. He looked a 'gonner' and said he felt as much (Second-Lieutenant W L Walters survived the war).

'*Time was now about 8 a.m. Shortly afterwards Germans appeared on the opposite slope of the valley. We opened fire as they came down. They came no farther but occupied some old trenches. Towards dinner-time, assuring ourselves that the Germans did not intend to attempt to reach our front line, we took things more easily. The men were very exhausted but they set too to try and clear the trench of mud. It was a hopeless task. We were in it up to our knees; but it served to keep us occupied. With night came rations, a good supply of rum was got through. We all warmed up under its influence.*

'*Later on Field, the intelligence officer, and Percy de Vene were sent up to reinforce us* (this was probably Lieutenant A S Devine). *We hoped they had come as guides to take us back, but apart from the fact that they had orders to join us, they knew nothing about what was likely to happen.*

'(The Powers that be had ordered another attack on Polderhoek Château which was to be 'assaulted at all costs' during the early hours of 10 October, this time by one battalion; the 14th Royal Warwicks. But, because of the short notice given to organise, the ignorance of the ground and tracks by all ranks, the pitch blackness of the night and the

Below: The remains of a German pillbox in the vicinity of St Julian, 12 October 1917. *IWM Q6060*

Above: Debris around the entrance of a captured German pillbox. During the Battle of Passchendaele, captured pillboxes and blockhouses usually became Battalion /Company HQ's or Advanced Dressing Stations for the wounded. The walls and roofs were about a metre thick and could survive direct hits from large calibre shells, However, because the entrance now faced the German lines, there was always the chance of a shell landing in the opening and killing all those inside.

extremely deep mud, only A Coy under the command of Captain Herbert Clements managed to reach the assembly position at around 03.30 am.)

'We waited, hoping for relief. Hutchinson, who was hit in the morning, went down with the ration party. We waited all night. Towards dawn a runner came through from Battalion HQ to say we were being relieved that night. The men 'bucked up' considerably at the news, and we all tried to settle down for the day and await night and relief. The day passed miserably dull and cold, raining at intervals. At dusk the men got ready to move away and we anxiously watched for relief. Midnight came and no relief. At 3 a.m. we saw a number of men appear from the back and thought at last relief had arrived; but from the officer in charge we gathered that they had not come to relieve us but to reinforce us, and we were not being relieved that night. They were a company of 14th Royal Warwicks, with orders to reinforce us and attack again next morning. Quite memorable was the meeting and subsequent discussion between Sewell and the Captain of the 14th. Sewell pointed out with all eloquence the impossibility of our men attacking, what was left of them could barely stand (the 16th's War Diary makes the comment concerning the men's lack of hot food for nearly five days during which they were soaked to the skin and had very little rest or sleep). *Whilst agreeing, the 14th Captain had orders to carry out the attack. They sat in the pill-box covered in mud, clothes, hands and face. By the light of a candle it was apparent how much each felt his responsibility. At daybreak the Captain went along the trench to see the position, and was sniped through the head. If this was intentional it was bravely done. Only a few moments before I had warned him of the dangers of the trench. By some means the second attack was cancelled* (Captain Herbert Clements, aged twenty-nine and a native of Clapham, London, died of his wound soon after; he is named on the Tyne Cot Memorial.) *The men were almost ready to shoot themselves, or anyone else who came near them, as they took their packs off to stick it for another night. However, the reinforcement from the 14th Royal Warwicks took off some of the strain, allowing our men to relax.*

'Before daybreak another ration party got through, bringing rum, cigarettes and food. They had had an awful time getting through. They said it was impossible to dodge the German barrage and they had had considerable casualties. My food for the two preceding days had been a piece of bread on the first and a piece of bread and cheese on the second, both taken from the dead. The rum, cigarettes and food were issued to the men. The cigarettes were particularly welcome. Some of them had not had a smoke for days. The ration party was followed by a runner from B.H.Q., saying that relief was coming that night for certain. With that news we settled down for the day. The men had for the most part scooped holes in the side of the trench, and in these they sat, their legs hanging in the mud.

'De Vene (Lieutenant A S Devine) took Hutchinson's place, and with Wilks we took alternate hours throughout the day on duty in the trench, spending the remainder of the time in the pill-box. To get to the pill-box entrance was difficult, a shallow and dry trench led to it, the trench was not more than two feet deep and led off from our front line. Three of our men were sniped and lay dead in the doorway before we able to discover that we were being fired at from the pill-boxes (in the château grounds); we crawled backwards and forwards on hands and knees.

'The day dragged on. The Germans on their part were quiet, we had no desire to disturb them. Half the men's rifles would *not fire, they were choked up with dirt. No Lewis guns were in action, they also were choked. We had one brigade machine-gun left and that was minus the tripod. The gunners fired the gun by holding it on the parapet. We waited for night to come.*

'*Sergeant Badger got ready what remained of my platoon, so that when the relief did arrive we could get quickly away. Towards 8 p.m. I was on duty, feeling too dead to wade up and down the trench. I sat in a cubby hole and dozed, like the men not on duty, hanging my feet in the mud. I was awakened by a sentry coming along and reporting that the Germans were using signal lamps in the valley; so we all prepared for an attack. No attack developed, and we were still waiting when the relief arrived (7th Bn Rifle Brigade, 14th Division). They reported that the Menin road was being very heavily shelled, and as far as they could gather so was the surrounding district.*

'*I was the only officer left of my company, and getting the men together as best I could, I told them of the conditions and warned them that if anyone fell out on the way no help could be given; that we had to go for all we were worth, to stop and help one man might mean half a dozen being hit. We set out, Percy de Vine leading the way and taking with him a company, or the remnants of a company, which had not an officer left.*

'*We had not gone far when shells came buzzing over. De Vene, not sure of the way, was leading us over shell-holes and mud, the men slipping in all directions. Travelling over such would have been difficult for fit men; to us it was a form of torture as we wound round the craters. Representing half a battalion, we must have presented a pitiable spectacle, a few dozen men and a couple of officers. It was a blessing, perhaps, that the night was dark, the language was foul, and our appearance equal to the language.*'

Counting the costs

On being relieved by the 14th Division during the evening of 11 October, the 5th Division made for the neighbourhood of La Clytte – Westoutre (about eight miles south-east of Ypres) for a period of rest and a chance to clean up. Of the three Birmingham Battalions, the 16th Royal Warwicks had suffered the most with just over 300 men becoming casualties between 5 – 11 October. Ninety-four of these were killed and another ten died of their wounds. This first tour had also claimed the lives of fifty and 103 wounded from the

15th Royal Warwicks and thirty-five men and 140 wounded from the 14th Royal Warwicks. With the conditions so appalling, it is easy to understand why the majority of these men who were killed had no known grave; they are now remembered on the Tyne Cot Memorial. Twenty-five of these men were original volunteers to the battalions in 1914. The following men from the 16th Royal Warwicks received the Military Medal for gallantry and devotion to duty during this period:

1229	Private (A/Sgt) C Garland
32894	Private M K Dady
658	Cpl C W Owen
10590 or 10150	H Garratt
1705	L/Cpl R Holt
32784	D Henderson
51	L/Cpl William Jarvis
1269	A E Lea
267	Private Charles Bunce
32966	G H Wilding

Of those named above, Private Charles Bunce (No.267) was a stretcher bearer and his award was for meritorious work whilst attending the wounded in No Man's Land. His ribbon was presented to him by General Plumer when the battalion was serving in Italy. At the end of the war, Private Bunce re-enlisted into the Royal Warwicks and by 1932 had attained the rank of CSM.

Polderhoek Château: Third Attempt

If the next attack upon Polderhoek Château was to be successful it was apparent that a carefull well-organised effort would be required. Therefore no further attacks were planned whilst the 14th Division held the line. As you can guess, the infantry of the 5th Division did not get much rest whilst out of the line. The battalions were once more 'topped up' with new drafts, and again many of those who were drafted to the Birmingham Battalions were ex-cavalry and by now there were also a fair sprinkling of former Army Service Corps men. A specially constructed training course marked out by tapes and coloured flags had been constructed for the infantry of the 5th Division to practise over. The final practice session on 20 October had been watched over by the Corps Commander Lieutenant-General Sir T L N Morland DSO. 26 October had been chosen for a determined push towards the German held positions at Gheluvelt, Polderhoek and Passchendaele. The official name given to this forthcoming offensive was the Second Battle of Passchendaele. Consequently, when the 5th Division relieved the 14th Division on Tuesday, 23 October, the front line was as they had left it. Apart from one thing, for now there was even more mud. As the author of the divisional history put it, conditions were now 'indescribable.' It had rained virtually every day since 3 October. Concentrating on Polderhoek, this time the attack would be carried out by three battalions of 13 Brigade; the 14th and 15th Royal Warwicks and the 1st Royal West Kents. The 2nd KOSBs were in support. As before, the vicinity around 'Bedford House' would be the forward dump for the transport departments of various battalions, and the place where the men had their last hot meal before going up the line. In the War Diary of the 14th Royal Warwicks there is a comment relating to the Transport section, where the author does not pull his punches: '2 ranks wounded & 1 missing – probably blown to bits.' This unfortunate young man was nineteen year old Private John Williams (No.19288 from Horseley Heath, Tipton). Private J E B Fairclough of the 14th Royal Warwicks recalls the return journey up to the front line in the battalion history:

'Since our last tour there had been no improvement in the general conditions; it had rained incessantly for the whole of October and the ground steadily got worse. The route to the trenches was extremely bad and caused much fatigue, mud in places being over the knee. All round were visible signs of heavy losses of mules and horses, and the duckboard tracks were receiving constant attention from enemy artillery. On one occasion a shell was seen to drop on the track in front of a horse and limber. The horse was wounded and plunged off the track with the consequence that horse, limber, and driver were quickly swallowed up in the mud and lost.'

In agreement with Private Fairclough, the battalion War Diary for this period also describes the awful state of the ground with one simple statement, which says it all, 'heartbreaking'. To make matters worse, low flying German aeroplanes made a habit of strafing troops making their way along the meandering duckboard tracks. By 23.00 on the evening of 24 October, 13 Brigade had relieved 42 Brigade of the 14th Division. The following day was spent by Company Commanders and senior NCOs in reconnaissance of the German front line defences and the ideal locations for assembly areas where the battalions could form up prior to the attack starting; which would be taped out when darkness fell. Around 04.00 on 26 October the attacking troops made their way to the taped lines and assembled in their order of waves. This was approximately 100 to 150 yards west of Polderhoek Wood. The 14th Royal Warwicks' objective was the château and ground approximately 300 yards to the east and south of it. The left flank was to be taken care of by the 15th Royal Warwicks, whilst the 1st Royal West Kents had the impossible task of wading through the quagmire along the valley of the Scherriabeek to cover the right flank. Apart from the 5th Divisional Artillery, two additional divisions artillery were attached, and to show we meant

Above: Polderhoek Château, and grounds, as it appeared before the war. Copies of this photograph were issued to officers prior to the first attack on 4 October 1917. It bore little resemblence to what they found. *Taylor Library*

Right: Polderhoek Château, the grim reality – a water-logged, dreary wasteland with a low ruin, fortified to resist attacks. *Taylor Library*

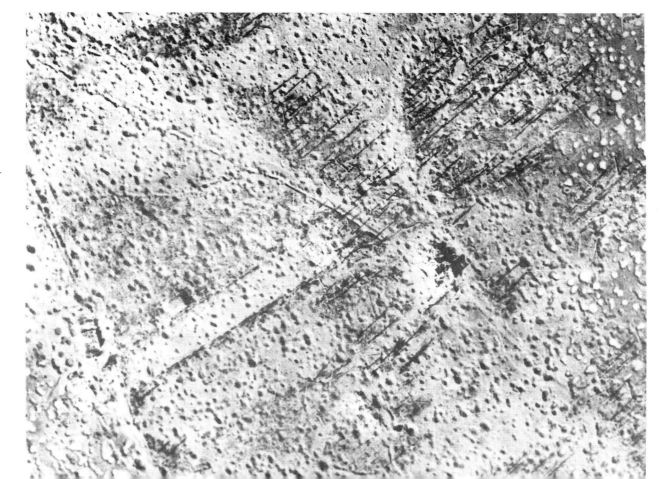

business machine guns were placed every ten yards to give covering fire over the heads of our attacking troops.

At 05.40 on Friday 26 October, the Second Battle of Passchendaele began. 'At 5.40 a.m. – Zero Hour – I watched the troops going over the top. They were apparently in good order and disappeared into the wood.' So wrote Lieutenant Col Murray, the CO of the 14th Royal Warwicks. Nothing was heard of how the attack was developing until the first wounded started to trickle back some forty minutes later. One of the first back to 14th Warwicks' HQ was CSM Carl Plenderleith, with wounds to his chin and hand (No.753, a former pupil of King Edward's Aston who came from Highfield Road, Saltley). He reported that most of the platoons were well on to and past the château, and that many Germans were fleeing under our fire, and that around thirty prisoners were waiting to be sent down. He also reported that machine-gun fire from the right was very severe. This was the first indication that the 7th Division attack upon Gheluvelt was not going well.

After the attack had got under way, A and D Coys of the 14th Royal Warwicks met a very stubborn resistance from the German troops amongst the ruins of the château and the surrounding pill-boxes. The Royal West Kents struggled bravely onwards but found themselves in an impossible situation with the combination of an impassable morass to cross and heavy machine-gun fire to contend with from the right in the direction of Gheluvelt. This also meant that the right hand company of the 14th's, B Coy, were 'up in the air' and many casualties had occurred from the same machine guns that had caught the Royal West Kents.

To the left, the attack by the 15th Royal Warwicks began well, until C Coy reached the clearing to the north of the château. Here they met withering machine-gun fire from the château, causing considerable casualties. Adrenalin was running high. Disregarding the machine-gun fire C Coy pushed on, the Germans before them were 'bolting like rabbits' as Captain Bill (CO C Coy) recalled, and that 'the Lewis gunners were firing from the hip,' in pursuit. During this period all C

Coy Officers became casualties, including Captain Bill (a bullet fracturing his thigh bone), except for Second-Lieutenant A H Thorp. He led the remnants of the company towards the final objective. Unfortunately, he slipped into a shell-hole and got stuck, and was later rescued and made prisoner by the Germans.

During the assault, D Coy of the 15th Royal Warwicks, commanded by Captain D A Rutter, had slightly veered off course and they had pushed up towards the 14th Royal Warwicks who were held up in front of the château. With the aid of a Lewis gun team and a bombing party from B Coy, (15th Royal Warwicks), under the command of Captain Walter Goodwin, the château was rushed, and after some very heavy hand-to-hand fighting, was cleared of Germans. The 14th Royal Warwicks, meanwhile, had taken a pill-box on the immediate right of the château and then pushed on a further sixty yards and started to consolidate the ground gained. Polderhoek Château was now in our hands, though machine-gun fire from several German pill-boxes in the vicinity still made a section of the ruins untenable. Around a hundred German prisoners were taken from the château defences, including a battalion commander. To the left of the château, A and C Coys of the 15th Royal Warwicks were now around 300 yards past the château, and at their objectives, but on their own. Once the Germans had realised the château had been taken, a tremendous artillery barrage saturated the area and immediate plans for a counter-attack were put into action. Reinforcements were needed, but communication lines back to the jumping off line and the battalion HQs were difficult to maintain in these gruesome conditions. By mid-morning the Germans were seen massing for determined counter-attack from the front and a threatened encircling manoeuvre to the right flank. This was now a critical time for the remnants of the 14th and 15th Royal Warwicks. By now all the Lewis guns and the majority of the rifles were unable to fire; they were choked with mud, even the cartridges in the men's pouches were covered with slime. In some parts of the battlefield men were sinking waist deep in the going. In these circumstances, with a German counter-attack imminent and no idea if reinforcements were on the way, Captain Rutter (D Coy, 15th Royal Warwicks) who had command of the château ruins had no alternative, and made the decision to fall back. In doing so, the remnants of all the other companies involved in the attack did the same and they made their way back to their original start positions. This resulted in the Germans immediately re-occupying Polderhoek Château. By 11.30 it was all over, 13 Brigade were in the same position they had started from. So too were the men of the 7th Division, their attack upon Gheluvelt had also failed. During the evening, the 14th and 15th Royal Warwicks were relieved by the 1st Bedfords.

Casualty figures were high. Between 24 and 27

Above: Second Lieutenant Keith Saxby Curtis, 14th Royal Warwicks, killed during the attack upon Polderhoek Château 26 October 1917. Commemorated on the Tyne Cot Memorial. Keith, from Ivy Road, Handsworth, was a former pupil of Handsworth Grammar and King Edward's High School, New Street. He enlisted into the 1st Birmingham Battalion (No.624) and became a Corporal in C Coy, 10 Platoon. He was wounded in the second attack on Wood Lane, 30 July 1916, and on recovery took a commission into the regiment. The white band around his service hat was worn during his Officer Cadet training.

Above left: During the Battle of Passchendaele it was common for German aircraft to strafe British front line positions. Here is an example of a British Vickers machine gun firing at low flying aircraft. *IWM Q5172*

Above: Private H Coles, No.1475, 14th Royal Warwicks, from Saltley. Awarded the Military Medal for gallantry and devotion to duty during the attack upon Polderhoek Château, 26 October 1917.

October the 14th Royal Warwicks sustained 78 men killed in action, eight died of wounds and 162 wounded. During the same period the 15th Royal Warwicks had 79 killed, seven die of wounds and 114 wounded. As you might guess, the majority of those killed have no known grave. Many were posted as missing in action. Like many others, they are commemorated on the Tyne Cot Memorial.

The combined total of dead for the two battalions came to 172. About one hundred of these men were drafted in from other regiments, i.e. various cavalry regiments and the Army Service Corps. By looking ahead at future actions and sifting through the casualty lists, it is clearly seen that many of the men who would replace these casualties of October 1917 would now come from the Royal Engineers, Army Ordnance Corps, various infantry regiments and even a sprinkling from the Army Veterinary Corps. From the action of 26 October, of all those killed only ten men were original volunteers from September 1914. There were a few men killed who were original volunteers, for example men who were commissioned to other battalions and men who had been previously wounded, but had been drafted back to another battalion within the Regiment. Fifteen Royal Warwickshire battalions were engaged at one time or another during Third Ypres. For Gallant conduct on 26 October, Private F Shirley (No.18295) of the 14th Royal Warwicks was awarded a Bar to his recently awarded Military Medal, whilst the Military Medal was awarded to Privates H Coles (No.1475) and J W Haynes (No.30209). It seems however, the officer looking after the 15th Royal Warwicks' War Diary at this period of time was a man of few words. He made no mention of any gallantry awards for the battalion.

Captain Arthur Bill of the 15th Royal Warwicks, as you may remember, received a nasty wound; a bullet had fractured his thigh bone. Fortunately for the captain a batman was around to supervise his withdrawal from the battlefield. Prior to the battle it took the battalion over seven hours to get from Bedford House to the jumping off positions. How long did it take if you were seriously wounded? The following is Captain Bill's hair-raising account written after the war:

'My company stretcher-bearers , having tied my legs together in rough splints, got men on a stretcher, and one of our batmen who stayed with me took my revolver and brought along half-a-dozen prisoners, of the many we had taken, to carry me out of the fight. He had to go back a bit to find these fellows and it required considerable determination on his part, coupled with the persuasive power of the little gun, to get them to come back into the unhealthy, reeking wood. They got me up shoulder high, my faithful batman bringing up the rear, and we started of at about 06.30 for a thoroughly thrilling day, my own condition being such that I could only lie patiently and hope for the best, expecting every moment to be upset by my swaying, slithering bearers and landed in the mud. We missed our way for a start, and instead of passing through our support lines near Battalion Headquarters we fetched up by a pill-box alongside the Menin Road in the neighbouring sector. Here we had to pass through an intense barrage which the German guns were putting down. Two of the German bearers were killed by shell splinters while they had me on their shoulders. I was sorry for them but even more sorry for myself as I fell with a crash upon my broken thigh. Here my remaining bearers were made up into a batch with other prisoners and sent on down the line under escort and under almost as heavy a fire from their own guns as they had previously experienced from ours.*

'The pill-box was being used as a First-Aid Post and was already crowded with wounded, with numbers of other stretcher cases lying around outside. Rumours came along that the enemy was heavily counter-attacking in front and every available man in khaki grabbed a rifle and 'stood to,' even the Red-Cross men stripping off their armlets ready to fight if the Germans came through. For an hour or more this hell went on and I made up my mind that it would be quite impossible to get through alive. Those of you who do not know war cannot conceive the torment of mind and body which hundreds and thousands of men suffered while lying maimed and helpless on the battlefield incapable of that action which so often alone preserved men's sanity. Pray God you never may know it.

'The threatened attack, however, did not materialise and attention was again concentrated on the job of getting the wounded away. A whole battalion was engaged in this area as stretcher bearers. I remember they were all very young - boys of eighteen to twenty they seemed, and I marvelled at the wonderful courage and devotion to duty they showed. Their job was to carry from the First-Aid posts down to the Field Ambulances and magnificently they did their splendid work, through hellish barrages and suffering casualties all the time. We made up a convoy and started down the Menin Road. That sounds a simple matter until you realise that not one vestige of the original surface of this main highway could be seen. Every inch had been shell-shot as well as the ground on both sides, until the whole was nothing but a broad strip of interlocked shell craters, half-full of mud and water. And to

this confusion must be added the fallen trees which had originally made it an avenue as is the usual in the French and Belgian main roads. To indicate the most navigable route through this devastation a broad white tape had been laid down wandering hither and thither, over and round - and along this our bearers slowly wended their way. Added to this there was continual shellfire, and as I watched the shells bursting perhaps 50, perhaps 100 yards ahead of us, I wondered whether we should get safely past that spot before a particular gun fired again or whether we should be just in time to stop one.

'After a mile or so of this we left the road and took a duck-board track on the left which wandered down the valley through Dumbarton Lakes, behind what was left of Inverness Copse. And here again we were in trouble, for flying low, backwards and forwards, on a figure of eight course was a German aeroplane, machine-gunning the stretcher parties as they came down. We were on a down track only – there was no up traffic at all, so that even the excuse that the stretchers might have looked like machine guns could not be made, and to their everlasting discredit the German airmen must be convicted of deliberately firing on wounded troops being evacuated from battle. Two of the lads carrying the stretcher in front of me were struck down and my bearers stepped over their dead bodies lying on the duck boarded track.

'At 6 o'clock that night – nearly twelve hours from the time we started down – I reached the Clearing Station and was operated on.'

After a long spell in hospital in England, Captain Bill returned to light duties with the 3rd Reserve Battalion of the Royal Warwicks, who were stationed at Dover, in June 1918. During the Army of Occupation in Cologne, he was given command of a Leicesters' battalion. In November 1919, Major Charles Arthur Bill was demobilised.

Above: A mule laden down with barbed wire and screw-in pickets. These Tommies seem to be carrying everything bar the kitchen sink! However, a mule only went so far, then it was the turn of the poor soldier when another form of transport was used...Shanks's pony! *IWM Q5172*

Right: Anzac Ridge, 26 October 1917. To get rations, ammunition, stores etc. up to the battle zone, wooden sleepers were laid to make firm roads across the barren shell pocked wasteland. The were known as corduroy tracks. They became ideal targets for the German airforce and these roads were continually strafed or searched out by artillery fire. Either side of these tracks was always littered with bloated horses and mules and shattered General Service wagons and ammunition limbers.
IWM E (AUS) 1241

Above: Second Lieutenant Leonard Tansell, 14th Royal Warwicks.
Pat Tansell

Farewell to Flanders

The attack on 26 October was the last concerning the involvement of the 5th Division's three Warwickshire battalions. On November 6th the 5th Division made one final attempt to take Polderhoek Château. This time the 95th Brigade were chosen for the task. The attack was to be made by the 1st Devons and the 1st Duke of Cornwall's Light Infantry. Again they met a stiff German resistance and the attack broke up into isolated groups having their own private battles with various pill-boxes. This time the attackers could only get to within seventy yards of the château, and by mid-afternoon the attacking troops were back at their jumping off line; except for a party of DCLI troops who captured a largish pill-box in the château grounds and defied all attempts by the Germans to dislodge them.

Further north, Canadian troops had taken the ruins of the village of Passchendaele. Just a mile from the village, nowadays, is Tyne Cot Cemetery and the Memorial to the Missing. This is the largest Commonwealth War Graves Cemetery with 11,900 graves and the memorial panels contain the names of nearly 35,000 with no known grave. Between them, the 14th, 15th and 16th Royal Warwicks had 400 men killed or died of wounds whilst the 5th Division was on the Ypres Front.

On the evening of 15/16 November troops of the New Zealand Division relieved the 5th Division; it was time to say goodbye to the Ypres Front. 'Cookhouse' rumours were rife, Italy was favourite, but for the time being the 5th Division moved to the district of Nielles Les Blequin, about 16 miles (25k) west of Boulogne. As usual, now the division was out of the line, the battalions were brought back to strength, deficiencies in kit made up, and a period of training commenced. On 17 November, the 14th Royal Warwicks received a draft of eight junior subalterns. One of these was Second-Lieutenant Leonard Tansell from Stoke Prior near Bromsgrove. His background makes interesting reading.

Leonard Tansell was born in 1885, one of ten children; his father, Joseph, was a farm labourer. On leaving school, which in those days was probably around the age of twelve or thirteen, young Leonard followed his father and become a farm hand at Cooksey Green Farm, near Bromsgrove. Deciding that farming was not the life for him, at the age of seventeen, Leonard signed up for eight years with the 2nd Battalion Worcestershire Regiment. Most of his service was with the Signal Section, but he did spend seventeen months with the Regimental Police. Six years of his service were spent in India. In 1908, whilst in India, Leonard Tansell became the Forces Heavyweight Boxing Champion of India. The following year he lost his title to Bombardier Billy Wells; a famous name in the annals of British Boxing. On leaving the Army in May 1910, he transferred into the Reserves. Leonard once more tried his hand at farm labouring. But not for long, within a year he had joined the Birmingham City Police Force and was posted to 'E' Division.

With the sudden rush to the colours at the start of the First World War, as we have seen at the start of this book, Regimental Depots were jammed full of new recruits with not enough experienced instructors to go round. Volunteers from the Birmingham Police Force, and others around the country, with military experience were called for. Police Constable Tansell soon found himself at Budbrooke Barracks putting new recruits through their paces. On 27 November 1915, Leonard Tansell resigned from the Police and enlisted into the 1/6th Royal Warwicks (143 Brigade, 48th South Midland Division T.F.) and was posted to France to become Company Sergeant Major of C Coy (No.4862). He was Commissioned on 30 May 1917, and presumably after a period of training with an Officer Cadet School, Second-Lieutenant Leonard Tansell was posted to the 14th Royal Warwicks.

It transpired that rumours concerning a divisional move to Italy were true; Second-Lieutenant Tansell was in luck. The Birmingham Battalions were going on holiday.

Chapter Nine

Italian Front: December 1917 to April 1918

For two years the Italian – Austrian Front had been high up the mountains along the entire length of the eastern Alps with both sides aspiring to break through to the plains. On 24 October 1917, along a twenty-five mile front (40km) that flanked the River Isonzo, a joint Austro-German offensive began. Within nineteen days the Italian Army had been pushed back around eighty miles (130km). Consequently the Allies sent promptly twelve Allied divisions (five British and seven French) from the Western Front to assist the badly demoralised Italian Army. Fortunately, whilst this colossal feat of logistics was beginning, the Austro-German Army started to outrun their lines of supply, trying to keep in contact with the retreating Italians. Therefore, on reaching the River Piave, the Italian forces now had a breathing space.

All bridges along the river were destroyed and the Italian Army dug in and consolidated on the western bank.

The five British Divisions sent to Italy were: the 5th, 7th, 23rd, 41st and 48th (South Midland). Sixteen battalions of the Royal Warwickshire Regiment saw active service during the First World War and it might interest the reader to know that eight of these battalions saw service in the Italian Expeditionary Force. They were: the 2nd, 1/5th, 1/6th, 1/7th, 1/8th Territorials and the 14th, 15th and 16th Service Battalions. It may also be of interest to note that six of these battalions originated in Birmingham.

Between 27 to 29 November most of the 5th Division (including the 14th and 16th Royal Warwicks) had managed to entrain for Italy. Then, due to the German counter-attack at Cambrai, all rolling stock was required to ferry reinforcements to the front. (20 November 1917 saw the start of the British offensive at Cambrai in which 476 Tanks were first used en masse. After the initial success of pushing the Germans back some six miles and taking around 10,000 prisoners, the Germans counter-attacked on 30 November and nearly all ground gained, was lost.) Due to this delay, a composite brigade was formed of the remaining battalions of the 5th Division, which included the 15th Royal Warwicks, and remained in the area of St Pol until December 10th. Again, we look towards Pte J E B Fairclough for his account concerning the 14th Royal Warwicks' long trek to Italy:

'The journey occupied six days, and to men whose outlook had so recently been confined to the Ypres Salient, a journey through the heart of France came as a visit to another world. Although the trains crawled along, with no heed to scheduled stops, the leisurely pace suited our mood. There were numerous unauthorised halts, and the troops took advantage of these to get hot water from the engine driver to make tea; or to obtain food from the natives; or to roam about the permanent way in the casual fashion peculiar to the British Tommy. Some of these halts were of several hours duration, but invariably the engine driver started off again without giving any warning. Even then, for the most part, one could catch up the train, so leisurely was our progress. If tea was being made, one had time to gather up the utensils, sprint along and

The 5th Division's move to Italy, November 1917

Below: IWM Q1995 The frequent form of transport for British troops in the Great War was cattle trucks. The journey to Italy took six days, with the trains crawling along in a leisurely fashion making many unscheduled stops that lasted hours.

board the train before it had gathered speed.'

What Private Fairclough did not mention was the mode of travel used at the time; dirty, smelly trucks that could accommodate either eight horses or forty men. Unfortunately, these forty men carried weapons, equipment, ammunition, rations and tools. This was due to the fact that they might have had to detrain rapidly and enter a battle zone immediately on reaching Italy.

The long and interesting journey took the trains past Paris southwards to the Mediterranean seaport of Marseilles and then, amid glorious sunshine and scenery, along the French Riviera. The journey continued along the Italian Riviera until reaching Genoa; then the trains turned eastwards. Bit by bit, the 5th Division dribbled in and concentrated in numerous billeting villages north of the Po River about twenty miles south-west of Padua. Whilst the division slowly came together the troops had plenty of time to acclimatise to their new surroundings. The 14th Royal Warwicks were billeted in the village of Noventa Vicentina. Here, posters and placards, written in Italian and English, adorned the walls with sentiments such as 'England For Ever,' Private Fairclough continues:

'We had a new language difficulty to combat but, with the usual resource of the British Army, this was soon overcome. It was not long before we acquired a smattering of the language, and by pantomime and a few phrases from Italian in a Month, we were able to make ourselves understood. In the early days QMS Denham of D Coy (No.322, Alfred Denham of Dudley Park Road, Acocks Green), went on a shopping expedition, accompanied by one of the cooks, to purchase some pork. Neither of them understood a word of the language, but Denham pointed to the joints hanging in the shop, and the cook proceeded to cut up what was required, while the shopkeeper looked on. Denham wrapped up the meat, and then by signs asked how much there was to pay. More signs indicated the amount required and when this was paid up, the shopkeeper smiled and our men departed, with everyone satisfied. Surely, true economy of words!'

In another incident Private Fairclough told of how one night, in a local inn, two King Edward's old boys had met some Italian theological students who were working for the Red Cross. A convivial evening ensued, with Latin being the common language to them all. One of the original volunteers to the 14th Royal Warwicks was the battalion tailor, No.1077, Sergeant P Moretti, who came from Birmingham's Italian community. Before long he became the battalion's interpreter. Mind you, there was one incident in which those concerned had wished Sergeant Moretti had kept his mouth shut. It happened after some 14th Royal Warwicks had just finished an enjoyable meal at a café. Of course having no gist of the language, nobody really knew what they had ordered or had eaten and a debate broke out about the bones and what animal they belonged. Enter Sergeant Moretti; after a quick chat with the proprietors he informed the diners that they had belonged to a dog!

The Commander in Chief of the British Forces in Italy was General Sir Herbert Plumer, and the 5th and 48th Divisions composed X1 Corps commanded by Lieutenant-General Sir Richard Haking. Together with the French X11 Corps and one Italian Corps, the British X1 Corps were put into the line that occupied the foothills of the Dolomites, in the region of Mount Grappa and the town of Asiago. For the time being the 5th Division was placed in Corps Reserve, to be used either to reinforce or counter-attack when required.

As soon as the Composite Brigade had rejoined the 5th Division a move northwards was made and by December 17th the various battalions had reached their billeting villages that they would occupy for the next five weeks. The 14th Royal Warwicks billeted at St Giorgio di Brenta, the 15th at S. Anna Morosina, and the 16th at Campo S. Martino. 'And it can safely be said that this period was one of the most pleasant periods spent by the battalion on active service,' recalled Private Fairclough on the 14th Royal Warwicks stay at St

Above: December 1917, British troops marching from a railway station after arriving in Italy. *IWM Q26531*

Giorgio. From these villages small parties of officers and men took it in turn, every three days, to survey the forward area and take instruction in the art of mountain warfare. Thus began many interesting expeditions of various units of British infantry, with the aid of alpenstocks and spiked fitments attached to boots, slowly winding their way up goat tracks to around 6,000 ft up into the snow line. Here Italian engineers had blasted trenches out of the rock and made machine-gun emplacements on ridges opposite similar defences on the Austrian side. The various transport units had the worst experiences; they had the strenuous task of training horses and mules to carry rations and equipment up the slippery mountain paths, and many a weary soldier grabbed a passing mule by the tail for a pull up the mountain! There was one consolation though; once the top of these perilous mountain tracks were reached there was often found a drinking establishment selling 'vino rosso' at very low prices.

Christmas of 1917 arrived, and probably the best Christmas of the war in the view of the 5th Division troops. The majority of men had both Christmas Day and Boxing Day at leisure and according to the Divisional History 'it was kept in good old-fashioned style'. Each company had its own special Christmas dinner provided from the Divisional Canteen funds. Roast beef and pork, poultry, Christmas puddings, wines and beer. Rooms were decorated and officers made their rounds exchanging compliments akin to pre-war barrack life. Afterwards it was back to billets and cafés for more festive eating and drinking with impromptu concerts finishing the night off. On New Year's Eve 1917, the HQ Coy of the 14th Royal Warwicks (which still probably included many original volunteers to the battalion) held a supper and smoking concert. At midnight Colonel Murray standing on a table, led the singing of 'Auld Lang Syne' and soon afterwards he was carried out shoulder high back to his mess.

This period whilst in Divisional Reserve also saw, when weather permitted, many inter-battalion football and rugby matches. There were also boxing tournaments and cross-country runs. On 24 December came the first issue of the newsletter *The Warwick News* edited by Lance Corporal Harper and printed out on the duplicator in the 14th Royal Warwicks' orderly room. In one issue he reports on a very early 'International' football match when C Coy of the 14th Royal Warwicks played an Italian side from the 14th Regg. Fanteria Dimarcia; C coy won.

Talking football, in the New Year's Honours List (Military), the Distinguished Conduct Medal was awarded to No.896 RSM J W Windmill of the 16th Royal Warwicks for the part he played in the battalion's tour of Passchendaele. His citation read:

'For conspicuous gallantry and devotion to duty. He invariably displayed great courage and ability in operations when

conditions were exceptionally bad, and set a splendid example of courage and determination.'

Before enlisting into the 3rd Birmingham Battalion, RSM Windmill had been a schoolteacher in Brierly Hill, having trained at St Peter's Teacher Training College in Saltley, Birmingham. He had also been a regular player for Aston Villa Football Club and had been a member of the victorious English Cup winning side of 1905.

River Piave

In the middle of January 1918 orders came for the division to take over part of the front line. So, after five weeks of strenuous toil up and down the mountains in preparation, the 5th Division was sent to the flat plain bordering the River Piave instead! On 27 January 1918, the British 5th Division relieved the Italian 48th and 58th Divisions on a front of around 4.5 miles (7.3 km) extending from

The Italian Front was the most pleasant part of the Birmingham City Battalion's overseas active service. When out of the line, there were no afternoon parades and sport of all kinds was encouraged.

Top: A football match between the Worcesters and the RAMC.
IWM Q26357

Middle: Drums and bugles of an unknown British Battalion. After the horrors of trench warfare it was time to spruce up and look like soldiers again.
IWM Q26645

Bottom: Officers Steeplechase meeting.

the village of Nervesa southwards to the village of Palazzon.

When the river was in full flood, which happened about two or three times a year, the watercourse at Nervesa was 400 yards (365m) wide, whilst at Palazzon it spread to around 2,000 yards (1800m) wide. Most of the time the river flowed with a very strong current through several rivulets leaving many islands of shingle and sand; thus when the river was low it was possible by 'island hopping' to cross No Man's Land to Austrian positions on the far bank. Now that the Austro-German offensive had quietened down, the Italians on the Piave front had a live and let live policy; consequently, the Italian divisions on the neighbouring front to the British 5th Division were not too happy concerning the offensive attitude it undertook right from the start as they would be bound to be on the receiving end of some type of retaliatory counter-barrage. According to Arthur Russell who was serving with the 13th Brigade Machine Gun Company at the time: 'They seemed quite happy to sit in their trenches doing nothing but drink their ration of wine.' On further investigation, once the relief was under way, Arthur also discovered that the dugouts used by Italian officers had white cloth covered tables laid out with glasses, cutlery and crockery and were waited upon by white-jacketed mess orderlies. The whole appearance reminded him of a Gentlemen's Club in London rather than a front line dugout.

Another aspect of the relief that the Italians were not happy about was that a sector held by one Italian division was now taken over by one British brigade. This put the Italians who were being relieved into a state of panic, especially when a post held by twenty or so Italians was taken over by four Tommies. This resulted in Company Commanders of the British battalions signing some type of disclaimer 'a most elaborate four-page document in Italian of which they probably understood not a word,' according to Captain C A Bill in 15th Royal Warwick's history. On the divisional front, the destroyed bridge known as Ponte Priula was roughly the Brigade boundary; and the sector from Nervesa to the bridge was held by the 14th and 15th Royal Warwicks during the first tour of the front line. No sooner had the division taken over the front, than patrols were sent out nightly to search the islands for the enemy on a similar errand. Prisoners taken in the first couple of weeks were surprised to find they had been taken by British troops; this was due to the fact our sentry groups wore Italian helmets at the start to keep the relief a secret.

Once the Divisional artillery had settled in, and with the aid of aerial photographs, Austrian artillery positions were on the receiving end of some heavy barrages. Due to this, the divisional front and back area was virtually free from Austrian artillery bombardments. Also, with No Man's Land being so wide, the front line troops were little troubled with sniping or machine-gun fire. The only irritation the division had to put up with were the nightly visits from the Austro-German airforce. Night after night they flew over and trenches, roads and villages were bombed; causing more structural damage rather than heavy casualties. But, once their stock of bombs had gone, they would then fly low following the roads with machine guns blazing away and sporadically a column of marching men were caught out in the open with no cover, resulting in many casualties. Fortunately, Birmingham's three City Battalions never had this experience; and whilst in Italy the 14th, 15th and 16th Royal Warwicks between them had only six men killed in action. On 2 February, 1918, the 16th Royal Warwicks relieved the Royal West Kents in the Nervesa sector and an interesting item in the War Diary on February 8th describes a patrol led by Second Lieutenant Ward who 'wore camouflage dresses of white sheets with holes for head and

Text visible on photograph: Ponte Priula 2490 / 400ft 10 2-18-14 / OSTERIA DI PONTE / E PRIULA / TO STAZIONE SUSEGANA

arms.' Then on February 15th a party of 16th Royal Warwicks under Captain C C Lacon, consisting of Lieutenant C Partington, Second Lieutenant Rogers, Second Lieutenant Filer and fifty other ranks successfully carried a ferry-rope across the Piave and anchored it on the opposite bank. Apart from the nightly patrols across the river during the divisional stay on the Piave Front another extremely important development in the men's training took place in daylight hours. Targets were hung out on the barbed wire that was laid out across the river bed and many hours plus thousands of rounds of ammunition were spent in rifle practice. Very soon the proficiency in marksmanship and rapidity in firing had improved throughout the three infantry brigades. Unknown at the time, this was to have far-reaching effect when the 5th Division returned to France in the near future.

Sham Attack

As a morale raising exercise for the Italian Army a small offensive was planned to take place at the beginning of March. The idea was for the Italian Third Army to retake ground between the old and new Piave Rivers near Venice. To coincide with this attack, and to keep Austrian reserves at bay, the British 5th Division were ordered to make a

crossing of the Piave in the vicinity of the Ponte Priula and establish a bridge-head for forty-eight hours. The 16th Royal Warwicks were to be the

Below: The 5th Divisional Front extended from Nervesa to Palazzon.

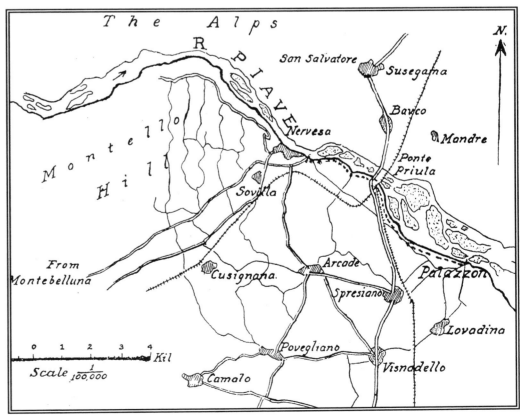

Above: Whilst the 14th Royal Warwicks were in Italy, Private Frederick Arthur Woodcock, No.286, B Coy, 5 Platoon died of sickness back in Birmingham. Frederick, aged 34, was an old boy of King Edward's Camp Hill and a former employee of the Aston Road branch of Lloyds Bank. He is buried in Brandwood End Cemetery, Kings Heath.

vanguard of the 15 Brigade's crossing near the bridge whilst the 14th and 15th Royal Warwicks were part of the 13 Brigade's feint attack further down the river.

To assist 15 Brigade's crossing of the river, sixteen Venetian gondolas and their gondoliers had been commandeered and were put under the control of Lieutenant Stone RN and five sailors from HMS *The Earl of Peterborough*, which was stationed at Venice. Along with the 250,000 rounds of ammunition brought up for the infantry, the division was also to have the support of a huge number of heavy and light artillery batteries and various types of trench-mortars of all calibres. No doubt the feint that the 5th Division was to participate in would be a good public relations exercise between the British and Italian Chiefs of Staff; and perhaps the British were keen to show the Italians how a war should be fought. I would imagine that the Italian liaison officers attached to the division would have been suitably impressed by the thoroughness of planning put in by Brigadier-General Oldman, the GOC of 15 Infantry Brigade. For an example, in the War Diary of the 16th Royal Warwicks, there are fourteen pages of Operation Orders concerning the crossing and what to do when the battalion got there.

By 1 March, 1918, the 5th Division was in a state of readiness for the main Italian attack to begin. Unfortunately Mother Nature stepped in and within a couple of days starting with a fine drizzle the weather grew worse until storm-like conditions prevailed. By the early hours of 3 March the River Piave had risen over twelve inches (30 cm) and twelve hours later the river had risen a further 36 inches (90 cm). By 4 March the islands had completely disappeared under a deafening roaring white-water torrent containing all types of debris brought down from the mountains.

Considering that the success of the operation depended upon forty men of the 16th Royal Warwicks wading across and securing the bridge-head, the attack was postponed until 9 March to allow the river to subside; it did not. This led the Italians to ask for a modified plan. Then, they asked for just a bombardment instead. Finally the whole operation was cancelled and all the stores, ammunition, equipment, gondolas etc had to be returned from where they came. Soon afterwards, between 15 to 21 March, the 5th Division was relieved by the Italian 48th Division.

While the 16th Royal Warwicks never had a chance to play their part in the crossing of the Piave, there was one enjoyable episode that transpired from the proposed joint Army-Navy venture. On 16 March the CO of the 16th Royal Warwicks, Lieutenant-Colonel Graham Deakin, along with the Battalion Football team and the Divisional Concert Party, The Whizz Bangs, were invited to Venice as guests of the officers and crew of HMS *Earl of Peterborough*. The party were met at Mestre and conveyed by launches to the ship.

After lunch a football match was played in Venice, the 16th Royal Warwicks beating the Bluejackets three goals to two. Finally the day was rounded off with a concert given by the Whizz Bangs.

On leaving the Piave Front, the 5th Division congregated in the region of Vicenza with the intention that, after another period of instruction on mountain warfare, the Division would spend the spring in the valleys and hills of the lower Alps; in the region of the Asiago Plateau. It was a very pleasing outlook indeed. Of course, the Army had to go and spoil things.

France: 21 March 1918: The German Spring Offensive

There follows a brief outline of events that took place in the early months of 1918, culminating in the German Spring offensive. An excellent account is to be found in Martin Middlebrook's *The Kaiser's Last Battle*.

Briefly, on 21 March 1918, along a sixty mile front that encompassed the old Somme battlefields of 1916, the German Army launched a major offensive known as 'Operation Michael'.

After the collapse of Russia (the new Bolshevik regime signed an armistice with Germany in December 1917), the German Army was now numerically superior to that of the Allies. But, once troops from the USA were shipped over in significant numbers, this advantage would soon be lost (the USA declared war on Germany on 6 April 1917). Therefore, with over seventy Divisions at their disposal in this area alone the German plan was to force a wedge between the British and French forces. The French would of course be intent on saving Paris, leaving the main German thrust to concentrate on destroying the British Army and pushing the remnants back to the Channel ports. At this period of time the British front line, in the area of the German attack, was thinly manned but supported by a series of detached strongpoints of barbed-wire redoubts bristling with machine guns and mortars.

For the Spring Offensive the Germans adopted new tactics. After the opening artillery barrage had smashed the front line, German troops would then funnel between these redoubts and assault the reserve lines with the intention of breaking through to open country beyond. The isolated redoubts would then be placed under siege by 'mopping-up' troops and slowly destroyed.

Fortunately for the German forces, thick fog on the morning of the attack was an added bonus. Quite a few British battalions manning the redoubt line fought to the last man. Others carried on until their ammunition supply ran out and then surrendered. Very soon the British Fifth Army was in a fast and furious retreat. In many cases battalions were sacrificed in staging rearguard actions so other units could get to safer ground.

Within a few days the Germans had forced a forty mile deep salient into the British line, but the assault had taken place over ground that had been ravaged by three years of war. Thus the Germans soon outran their line of supplies. The offensive lost momentum and ground to a halt.

Due to the events happening in France it was decided to recall two British divisions from the Italian Front: the 41st and the 7th. The 41st Division returned first, but as advanced parties from the 7th Division were on the move the Italian High Command were alarmed by the thought of the British abandoning them. Matters were soon resolved, but a delay had occurred in getting these badly needed troops returned to France. Thus, to get the 7th Division assembled at a railhead would take more time. However the 5th Division were already out of the line, so orders were promptly changed and the 5th Division was recalled instead. This decision the Divisional history recounts:

> '*The fighting spirit of the 5th Division arose and asserted itself, and all and every one prayed that they might be sent back to rejoin the ranks of our hard-pressed comrades in France.*'

But I think that Private Fairclough writing in the 14th Warwicks' history probably summed up the attitude of the majority of men, 'Our worst fears were realised, however, and on 1st April – an auspicious day – the 5th Division commenced entraining for France.' A total of sixty trains conveyed the Division back to France, and by 7 April 1918, the infantry brigades of the 5th Division had assembled in the area between Doullens and Frevent.

Divisional Reorganisation

On 10 January, 1918, whilst the 5th Division was in Italy, there began a major divisional reorganisation concerning the British Army. The roots of this change stemmed from the British Prime Minister's (Lloyd George) concern of the huge casualty lists with seemingly nothing to show for them. Therefore, via the War Cabinet and the Army Council, Lloyd George was hoping to deter Haig from making any offensive plans. This was

Above: Stosstruppen (Stormtroops). German "shock" troops put to good use in the 1918 March offensive.
IWM Q42263

Below: Battle of the Lys, 13 April 1918. British Troops just returned from the front line.
IWM Q367

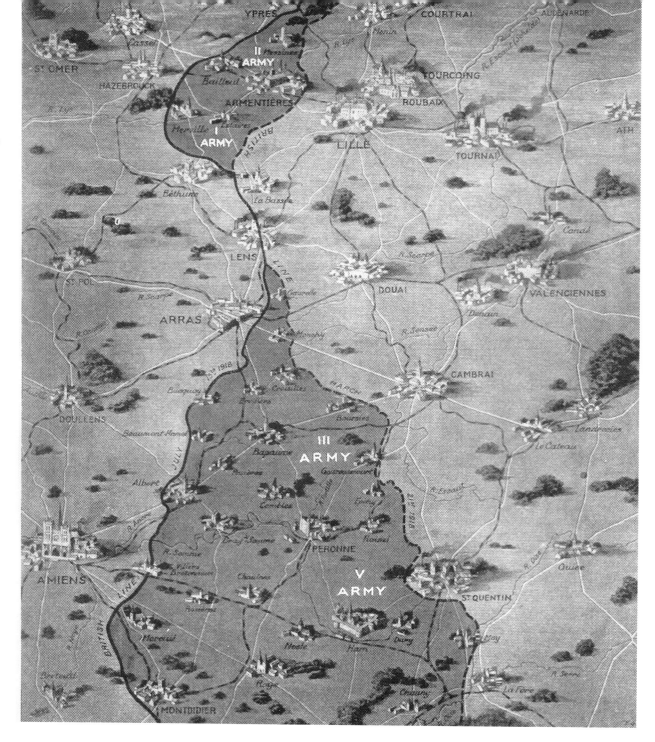

Right: German gains of 1918. The March offensive is the large shaded section, whilst the top shaded part is the April offensive, and subsequently where the 5th Division returned to the Western Front.
I was There Volume IV, edited by Sir John Hammerton.

done by holding back reinforcements in the UK for the BEF in France and Belgium. This meant many divisions were well under strength after the huge casualties from the Battles of Passchendaele and Cambrai.

One way round this was to reduce the size of the Infantry Brigade from four battalions to three. In all, 141 battalions were surplus. Some were juggled around and put into different brigades and other divisions. But the majority of the disruption was caused amongst the New Army and Second-Line Territorial battalions. Many of these were disbanded and the men used to top-up under-strength battalions in the same division.

For some reason or other, whilst in Italy, the 5th Division perhaps did not receive these orders or the powers that be chose not to heed them. If they had, then out of the three Birmingham battalions and the 12th Gloucesters, three of them would have

gone or, at least, been sent elsewhere. Fortunately, due to the dramatic events happening in France on the Division's return, thoughts of any reorganisation were put on hold until the closing weeks of the war, which will be dealt with later.

Nieppe Forest: April to August 1918

On arriving back from Italy, the 5th Division were ordered to relieve a Canadian division in the front line near Beaumetz, south-west of Arras. On 9 April the Division commenced its move towards the battle-zone. This day also coincided with the launch of the second part of the German Spring Offensive; Operation Georgette. The main thrust of the German attack was concentrated to the south of Armentières and was markedly fierce on a sector of the front held by the 2nd Portuguese Division. This division had been occupying an extended but comparatively quiet sector for a long time and were about to be relieved. Prior to the attack the German artillery had softened up the whole attacking front with an estimated 40,000 gas shells. The 2nd Portuguese Division soon collapsed and German troops began making deep inroads behind the British front line. This period of Great War history and actions that ensued including this German push were collectively known in Great War terminology as The Battle of the Lys.

Orders were issued for the 5th Division to cancel the relief of the Canadians and return to the area it had just left (Doullens and Frevent) and be ready to move at a moment's notice. On 11 April the Division entrained north towards Aire, a few miles south-west of Hazebrouck. Here the 5th Division came under the command of the British First Army and was placed in reserve for twenty-four hours. In this region the situation was critical. A gap had now opened in the British line in the region of Merville, and Hazebrouck was threatened. So precarious was the situation, that on this day, Field-Marshal Haig issued his famous Special Order Of The Day:

'There is no other course open to us but to fight it out ! Every position must be held to the last man; there must be no retirement. With our backs to the wall, and believing in the justice of our course, each one of us must fight on to the end. The safety of our homes and the freedom of mankind depend alike upon the conduct of each one of us at this critical moment.'

On the morning of 12 April, at Thiennes, the GOC 5th Division, Major-General R B Stephens met the senior officers of XI Corps, to whom the 5th Division now belonged, to discuss the current situation. It appeared that apart from stragglers there were no troops defending the front adjacent to Merville. The 5th Division was ordered forward to form a 2,000 yard front on the eastern edge of Nieppe Forest, opposite Merville. Then, once this position was established, they were to launch a counter-attack and retake Merville. However the exact German position was unclear. Merville was definitely in German hands and scattered patrols

were reported to be making their way towards the forest; some might even have begun to infiltrate the Forêt de Nieppe which was about 6 miles wide and 2 to 4 miles in depth.

Orders were issued for 13 Brigade to move through the forest, southwards via Tannay, and for 95 Brigade to move on a north-easterly bearing through the forest via Pre-a-Vin and La Motte. Packs and extra equipment were dumped, and by mid-day on 12 April the men of the 5th Division, in open order, began to break through the undergrowth of the western edge of Nieppe Forest. Leading 13 Brigade through the forest were the 14th and 15th Royal Warwicks. Above the sound of snapping branches and virgin scrub being trampled underneath British ammunition boots, and an occasional alarmed animal darting through the

Above: Field Marshall Douglas Haig – 'Every position must be held to the last man'. Order of the Day, 11 April 1918
IWM Q3255

Left: March/April 1918. Remains of British 6 inch 26 cwt Howitzer.
IWM Q44439

plodded by, pushing their possessions in carts and trucks. Fear, desperation and courage alternately showed in these usually stolid faces.'

Meanwhile, Corps HQ decided on a change of plan and issued a change of orders. Now, a line was to be established from Robecq in the south, through the forest to La Motte Château. Providentially, before these new orders had reached the forward battalions, they had cleared the eastern edge of the forest and begun to dig in approximately 100 to 200 metres outside. Major-General Stephens (GOC 5th Division) then urged the advantage that this line would have over one that ran through the forest. Sanction from Corps HQ was given. The foresight of this development was amply demonstrated in the hectic days that were to follow. By now, German artillery was in range and shrapnel was finding its mark amongst the men as they cleared the forest.

First touch with forward German patrols was made by C Coy of the 15th Royal Warwicks at around 5:15 p.m. The battalion had emerged from the forest near the hamlet of Le Corbie and some Germans were found to be holding some brickfields and adjacent houses. With the help of two platoons of B Coy an attack was carried out. Within an hour the enemy had been displaced. After an unsuccessful counter-attack, the Germans moved back to a strongly defended line on the south side of the Canal de la Lys. Though successful, the 15th Royal Warwicks had been welcomed back to the Western Front with a vengeance. Nearly one hundred casualties had been sustained, ten of whom were killed.

During the advance, one of the battalion's original volunteers, CSM J Glover (No.242, from Sutton Coldfield) was wounded for the third time since arriving at Boulogne in November 1915. Miraculously a bullet had passed completely through his neck without touching a vital spot. Calmly and without fuss he tied a field dressing around his neck as one would a scarf, and with a wonderful sense of devotion to duty carried on his job. Another original battalion man wounded in this incident was Lieutenant C L Jeffery (from Murdock Road, Handsworth) who had been commissioned from the ranks in May 1915 at Sutton Park. Lieutenant Jeffery had been hospitalised in June 1916 suffering from Trench Fever and had only returned to the battalion prior to the move to Italy. Talking of Italy, remember that I mentioned the newly commissioned former Birmingham Police Constable, Second Lieutenant Leonard Tansell; he and the CO, Lieutenant-Colonel Murray, were both hit by shrapnel and had to go back down the line. The command of the 14th Royal Warwicks was taken over by Captain R C Watts MC. By late evening on 12 April, a line had been established ,albeit only a series of shallow pits dug with entrenching tools, on the eastern side of Nieppe Forest and contact had been secured with the

brush, could be heard the sound of an isolated German howitzer, reckoned to be many miles to the south. The Germans had advanced at a much faster rate than their artillery and likewise the 5th Division's artillery still had a fair bit of catching up to do for their guns to cover the advancing troops. This episode is clearly remembered in the 14th Royal Warwicks' history:

'The weather was fine now, and as we crashed through the undergrowth, we contrasted the bustle and movement with the stagnation which had prevailed on the Piave. Occasionally, through a clearing, we would catch a glimpse of the open country away to the east and, although it was impossible to see any great distance, yet the ominous black columns of smoke which rose up from behind the trees, told a tale of burning villages and dumps.

'A few stragglers of other divisions were met, and pathetic sights were witnessed when streams of refugees, taking with them what household goods they had managed to gather, passed through the battalion lines. This was the first time that most of us had seen a civil population fleeing before an oncoming enemy. Women, children and a few old men

Guards Division on the left and the 61st Division on the right.

As dawn broke on the morning of 13 April, the men of the 14th and 15th Royal Warwicks faced the direction of Merville and were ready for any emergency. Apart from their hastily dug pits there was no other sign of war.....as yet. They gazed upon farmland unscarred by war; an occasional cow could be seen grazing in the distance. If the Germans had made a determined attack now, probably, the divisional line would have broken. Luckily, it is reputed that the delay was caused by the Germans liberating all the wine from the cellars in Merville. As yet no reserves had come up in support, the artillery was still not in a position to give covering fire, ammunition was low and the Divisional Transport was still on the march; resulting in the lack of barbed wire and tools to consolidate their defensive screen. Early in the morning men in grey uniforms were seen approaching the 14th Royal Warwicks' position. They were fired on, however they were found out to be stragglers from the Portuguese Division.

A quick diversion from the story here. Ted Francis was a lovely old gentleman who sadly passed away in March 1996, Ted was a veteran of the 16th Royal Warwicks. Whilst the 14th and 15th Royal Warwicks were in the front line at Nieppe Forest, the 16th were in reserve. Ted told me that one day he and a few others from the battalion were chosen for special guard duty. He told me it was at a château and it involved Portuguese troops. La Motte Château on the western side of the Nieppe Forest became XI Corps HQ and it was also a collecting area for rounding up the Portuguese troops who had broken during the initial German attack. Therefore Ted's story must concern this period of time. Even though the Château was in a war zone, the staff did not like the idea of anyone walking across, or lounging upon, the château lawns. But, to the many dishevelled and unkempt Portuguese soldiers it was an ideal place for an afternoon siesta. Consequently it was Ted's duty to guard the perimeter of the lawn and in Ted's own words the only way to keep the Portuguese off the grass was a, 'boot up the backside!'

Returning now to the morning of 13 April. German artillery had by now caught up with their infantry. A very heavy bombardment on the divisional front began at 10 a.m., which was soon followed by determined attacks upon various parts of the front throughout the whole day. The division now began to reap the rewards of the many hours and thousands of rounds fired in the daily target practice whilst on the Piave Front in Italy. From their minimal defensive position, with only rifles and machine guns, 13 and 95 Brigades beat off attack after attack throughout the afternoon and evening of 13 April. Fortunately, an old Army ammunition dump near Aire had been discovered and supplies were gradually sent forward. The story is continued in the 14th Royal Warwick's history:

> ' The supply of ammunition often proved a source of great anxiety, for at times the front line was reduced to five rounds per man; all spare ammunition was kept for the Lewis and machine guns. officers' servants, grooms and all extra men were used to carry up ammunition, which was dropped at the edge of the wood and from there it was fetched by the front line companies.'

TWO AND A QUARTER MILLION ROUNDS were sent up to replace the expenditure in the front line on 13 April.

The 14th Royal Warwicks' position was in the vicinity of Les Lauriers., and part of their line ran through Le Vertbois Farm. Here the Germans penetrated and the battalion was forced to withdraw. More attacks followed, but the Germans could not gain any further advantage. On the evening of 13 April, Major St J S Quarry (Royal Berks Regt.) took over command of the battalion, with orders to retake Le Vertbois Farm. Major Quarry gallantly led B Coy and successfully re-captured the farm, but in doing so was killed (Major Quarry is now buried in Merville Communal Cemetery Extension). Again, Captain R C Watts MC took over command of the battalion. However, after consideration, the staff took the decision that the farm formed a too exposed salient; so it was later evacuated.

The following day, 14 April, was just as hectic. Concerning this day, the divisional history recounts:

> 'All these attacks were preceded and accompanied by bombardments, and it was extremely difficult to move up any reinforcements through the belt of fire. The task of breaking them up devolved upon the infantry and machine guns in the front line, who had been there from the beginning, and who stolidly stood their ground with the utmost gallantry and steadiness.'

In the evening, the 14th and 15th Royal Warwicks were relieved. During the two day period holding the line the 14th had sustained 169 casualties of whom fifty-eight were killed or died of wounds. The 15th had about eighty casualties; of these twenty-five were killed. As per usual, once out of the line there was no time to rest. Both battalions were soon digging support trenches in the forest.

By now the 5th Divisional artillery was in place, and even though the German attacks continued throughout 15 April, concentrations of enemy troops forming up ready to attack were smashed by our artillery and dispersed. By 16 April it was evident that the German Push was dying down. They began to dig and wire their front line. According to the Divisional history 'their dead lay thick in the fields in front'. The history then continues:

Above: Company Quarter Master Sergeant F P Cornforth, C Coy, 14th Royal Warwicks, from St Oswald's Road, Small Heath. For his part in getting vital stores, equipment and ammunition to the front line on 13 April 1918, he was Mentioned in Despatches.
Dave Vaux

Above: Sergeant Richard Alban Wright, No.662, 14th Royal Warwicks. Killed in action, 13 April 1918, aged 22. He was an original volunteer to the 2nd Battalion (15th) C-Coy, 12 Platoon. He lived at Haslucks Green Road, Shirley and before the war was an employee of the highgate branch of Lloyds Banck. He is Buried in Merville Communal Cemetery Extension.

'In these three days the 5th Division had saved the situation on this part of the Western Front, and had stopped the German thrust on the important town of Hazebrouck. The infantry, fresh from their four months in Italy, had gone into the attack with a marvellous dash and spirit, and their steadfastness in withstanding the furious and continuous onslaughts of the enemy was magnificent.'

'Well done 5th Division! The Corps Commander congratulates all ranks on their steadiness and gallantry.'
General Haking (GOC XI Corps)

'I wish to express my appreciation of the great bravery and endurance with which all ranks have fought and held out during the past five days against overwhelming numbers. It has been necessary to call for great exertions, and more still must be asked for, but I am confident that in this critical period, when the existence of the British Empire is at stake, all ranks of the First Army will do their best.'
General Horne (GOC First Army)

Even though the German thrust had been halted on the divisional front, the German attack was renewed to the north (Bailleul and Kemmel) and to the south (Givenchy). The plan was to drench the western side of the forest with mustard gas and attack the 5th Division via the flanks. Fortunately, because of General Stephen's (GOC 5th Division) decision to consolidate the forward line east of the forest, many gas casualties were avoided.

The line in front of Nieppe Forest became the divisional home for the next three months. From the shallow rifle pits dug on 12 April a comprehensive trench system developed and spread back through the forest. Pill-boxes were constructed by Royal Engineers and cellars of houses were reinforced with concrete. Troops from the 7th Canadian Railways Corps laid a narrow gauge railway through the forest which was excellent for transporting reliefs, ammunition and stores. Many more tracks were added by the Divisional Royal Engineers, radiating through various parts of the forest. The greatest enemy to the troops, whilst occupying the support lines, was mustard gas shells. Gas patrols organised by the R.A.M.C. continually scoured the forest looking for gas filled shell-holes. Once found they were sprinkled with chloride of lime and filled in. A common sight in the forest was to see a procession of gas-blinded men being led to a dressing station. On 29 April, Brevet Lieutenant-Colonel R H C Nunn DSO, took over command of the 14th Royal Warwicks, but it was short lived; within five days he was hospitalised after being badly gassed. Again, Captain R C Watts MC assumed command. Mustard gas was a new development by the Germans in 1917, and the Divisional history had this to say:

'This mustard-gas was a distinctly new departure. With very little odour, and no immediate signs of any discomfort or danger, it was very persistent, penetrating the dug-outs and remaining on the ground for several days, and causing casualties. It produced temporary blindness and affected the throat and lungs, and even burnt the skin through the clothes. The surest panacea was to evacuate the shelled area at once, and not approach it again until the shell-holes had been sprinkled with chloride of lime and filled with earth, as the sun's rays brought out the noxious fumes, even when there appeared no trace of the gas about.'

The normal routine of holding trenches resumed on the divisional front. Every night patrols went out into No Man's Land to harass the German front line. Small raiding parties were also commonplace as it became apparent the morale of the German troops was deteriorating.

Raid by 16th Royal Warwicks

By the beginning of June 1918, 15 Brigade were holding the front in the Arrewage sector. Around midnight on the evening of 3 June, a party of men from the 16th Royal Warwicks raided a section of the German positions that ran along the Arrewage – Les Puresbeques Road. The raid was led by Second Lieutenant Harold Victor Drinkwater and comprised six sections of C Coy: thirty-nine men in total. Orders for the raiding party were simple: 'To kill and capture as many of the enemy as possible, and secure an identification.' Apart from two Mills grenades, a rifle with bayonet attached and twenty-five rounds of ammunition, no other equipment was carried; nor any identification.

After fifty minutes the raiding party returned with two prisoners from the 103rd Saxon Regiment. Second Lieutenant Drinkwater was wounded in the first two minutes of the raid, but

Below: Nieppe Forest, 8 July 1918.
IWM Q6846

256

carried on throughout it; which earned him a Military Cross. Nine other ranks were also wounded, apparently none of them were the result of German retaliatory fire. They were due to shrapnel from our own artillery barrage landing short. Some shells even landed in our own lines; one destroyed A Coy's Lewis Gun post, wounding four men. Matters were put right with the following telegram from the Brigade GOC acknowledging the error:

'Congratulating all ranks on their excellent raid and very much regretting their unnecessary casualties.'

'Operation Borderland'

Though the morale of the German troops opposite the divisional front was low, it had not spread through to the German artillery. With us having the upper hand in the nightly raids across No Man's Land, the 5th Division still occupied a pretty unhealthy spot with its back close up to the wall of Nieppe Forest. Apart from the daily dosing of poisonous gas, a form of trench fever given the name P.U.O. spread through the support lines in the forest in epidemic proportions. The fever took the form of a very bad case of flu and left the sufferer completely devoid of energy. The epidemic did not die down until around 20 June; by then fifteen officers and 340 other ranks alone from the 14th Royal Warwicks had been hospitalised.

As previously mentioned, hardly a night went by without a raid or patrol on the 5th Division front. Most nights German prisoners were captured or German deserters made their way to our lines. Subsequently, towards the end of June 1918, the time was thought ripe for a British offensive. Therefore, it was decided to launch an attack upon a three mile section of the German front line opposite Nieppe Forest and push it back a mile; thus allowing the 5th Division breathing space. A similar plan was to be launched on the 31st Division front who were on the left of the 5th Division.

The attack, known as 'Operation Borderland', planned for Friday, 28 June 1918, was a complete success, as the Divisional History relates:

'At 6 a.m. the artillery, who had been reinforced with two Brigades, and the Trench Mortars, opened an intense bombardment lasting four minutes; the barrage then lifted, and the infantry advanced under it, passages through our own wire having been cut overnight. The men displayed the greatest eagerness to come to grips with the enemy, and, though at first there was some opposition from machine guns, these were quickly disposed of either with bombs or bayonet, and the objectives were all gained up to time.

'Immediately the attacking troops had reached their final goal, strong patrols were pushed forward with Lewis Guns, and brought most effective fire on the demoralised enemy, while the Royal Engineers, under cover of darkness, destroyed the bridges over the Plate Becque. A great number of the enemy were killed in this attack; in front of Itchen and Bonar Farms alone were 200 dead, and in one place 37 Germans were found heaped together, all of whom had been bayoneted.'

'Operation Borderland' 15th Royal Warwicks

A week before the attack was launched the 15th Royal Warwicks were out of the line at Tannay. For three days the battalion practised for the attack over a specially laid course. The battalion took over a section of the front line on the evening of 26 June. As soon as the relief was complete, a patrol of twelve men under the command of Second Lieutenant J W Streater went out to examine the enemy wire. On their return he reported that the wire would not form much obstacle.

At zero hour 6 a.m., A Coy on the right, D Coy on the left and B Coy in support rose from the assembly trenches and moved through our wire and closed up under the divisional artillery barrage. hammering the German trenches. As soon as the barrage lifted A and D Companies quickly entered the trenches in front of them. Little opposition was offered and, 'the defenders were bayoneted or otherwise dealt with and a few prisoners sent back to Battalion HQ,' to quote the War Diary. The attack went according to plan, every time our barrage lifted each objective was reached and cleared, although the battalion did receive some harassing fire from German machine-gun fire on their right flank, south of the River Bourre.

By 08:15 a.m., the 15th Royal Warwicks had reached their final objective and with the help of C Coy who were in reserve, tools and ammunition were brought up to the assaulting companies and a new front line trench was established. To give a good field of fire, crops in front of this new line were cut down with bayonets. A patrol under the command of Lieutenant C S Preston accounted for another ten Germans retreating to the far side of the Plate Becque River. By nightfall all the divisional assaulting battalions had dug in and linked up. Wire entanglements had been erected and patrols were roving around the new front. The casualties for the battalion amounted to 111. Two officers were killed and one died of wounds, whilst the other ranks had twenty-six killed and another six died of their wounds over the following few days.

The officer who died of his wounds was twenty-one year old Captain Arden Coldicott MC, who came from Henley-in-Arden, Warwickshire. He is not mentioned in the War Diary as wounded and missing but is referred to by Captain C A Bill in the battalion history. Presumably Captain Coldicott was wounded and was picked up by a party of retreating Germans. He died of his wounds on 14 August, 1918, and is buried in Cologne Southern Cemetery in Germany. This also gives me a chance to correct the records concerning the other two officers that were killed. The first was Second Lieutenant Reginald Morris who is listed in casualty lists and the Tannay British Cemetery Register (where he is buried) as being a member of the 8th Royal Warwicks; he was in fact attached to the 15th Battalion. The same goes for the second officer killed on 28 June, Second Lieutenant George Rose, who is buried in Thiennes British Cemetery. He was attached from the 7th Royal Warwicks.

The success on June 28th was the first operation undertaken since the retreat during March, and congratulations poured in from the Top Brass, emanating from Sir Douglas Haig down to Brigade level.

Once the new divisional front was established, the same old routine of trench warfare resumed, though now it was much quieter than before and July was an uneventful month. At the beginning of August a blueprint for another attack, this time called 'Operation Partridge,' was put into preparation. But, on 7 August, the 5th Division was relieved by the 61st Division. One week was spent in the vicinity of Aire. Then on 14 August, the 5th Division moved to the eastern side of St Pol near Frevent and was placed in GHQ Reserve.

Below: Abandoned German 7.7cm field gun and dead gunner. An unofficial snapshot taken during the German retreat.

Final Operations: August to November 1918 – The Advance to Victory

At dawn, Thursday, 8 August, 1918, on a fourteen mile front roughly ten miles (16 km) east of Amiens, a joint Allied offensive was launched (British Fourth Army and the French First Army).

Beforehand the build-up to the operation had been shrouded in secrecy; even the Allied front line troops did not know an attack was planned until a few days before it was due. Reinforcements were brought up to the line at night. The main thrust was in the vicinity of Villers Bretonneux and involved the Canadian and Australian Corps. Further north, across the River Somme, the British III Corps covered the flank.

Another different ploy used in this attack involved the artillery, or lack of it. There was no softening up barrage beforehand to forewarn the six under-strength German divisions, on whose front the attack lay, that an offensive was about to be launched. This time, the bombardment coincided with Zero Hour (04:20), then, led by 456 British Tanks, the Australians and Canadians crossed No Man's Land and swept over the German front line. Apart from the extreme flanks, an advance of eight miles was achieved. Momentum was lost as the Fourth Army troops reached the old Somme battlefield of 1916. Here they encountered a desolate wasteland of old trenches, deep shell craters and rusting barbed wire entanglements. In four days, the British Fourth Army had taken 21,000 prisoners.

The next phase of the offensive was planned for 21 August. This time it was the turn of the British Third Army, commanded by General Sir Julian Byng, whose task was to strike in a south-easterly direction between Albert and Arras. From this period of time until the end of hostilities, the 5th Division now belonged to the Third Army's IV Corps commanded by Lieutenant-General Sir G Harper. IV Corps consisted of the 5th, 37th, 63rd (Royal Naval) and New Zealand Divisions (the 63rd was replaced later with the 42nd Division).

To explain fully the complex series of overlapping movements with divisions passing through one another, brigades leap-frogging other brigades pushing back the Germans, first to the strongly defended Hindenburg Line and then to the borders of Germany, would no doubt fill another book. From 21 August until 11 November, the 5th Division took part in the following operations:

SECOND BATTLES OF THE SOMME

21-23 August	Battle of Albert 1918
21 August	Capture of Achiet le Petit
23-24 August	Capture of Irles and Loupart Wood
26 August	Capture of Beugnatre
30 August	Advance West of Beugny
31 Aug- 3 Sept	Second Battle of Bapaume

Right: Battle of Albert, 21 August 1918. The fog that shrouded the battlefield cleared around 9 am. This then allowed an official photographer to record scenes following in the wake of the 5th Division's two mile advance. Here, 5th Division troops are seen moving up to assembly positions.
IWM Q11213

Second Battles of the Somme 1918

At 04:55 a.m. (Zero Hour), Wednesday 21 August, the British Third Army attacked on a front of nine miles, from Moyenneville to Beaucourt. During the night a mist had thickened until the whole of the front was densely shrouded. Working on compass bearings only, the attacking troops made their way successfully through the thick fog, and the German line was broken in the first rush. In the area that concerns us the 37th Division had advanced 2000 yards and reached its objective, the high ground east of Bucquoy. Once reached, it was the turn of the 5th Division's 15 and 95 Brigades (13 Brigade in reserve) with the help of twelve Mark IV Tanks to pass through and take the next objective, a line just short of Achiet-le-Petit. It is

now time for the 16th Royal Warwicks to enter the battle.

At zero hour the 16th Royal Warwicks had moved forward in the rear of the 1st Bedfords and according to the War Diary, the heavy mist had thickened with the smoke of our artillery barrage and, 'it was impossible to see more than a few yards.' During this push forward, the enemy put down practically no barrage and no casualties were incurred. A halt was made near Bucquoy, then at 06:15 the battalion moved forward to their objective, taking several prisoners and machine guns on the way. Despite the thick fog and dense smoke, Achiet-le-Petit was reached with no problem. There were two objectives left for the division. The first was a steep and strongly defended railway embankment to the east of the village. The second was known as an 'exploiting objective' a position to aim for if all went well during the attack. In the case of the 16th Royal Warwicks it did, and they made for a crest of a hill on the far side of the railway embankment.

At the forefront of 16th Royal Warwicks attack, was its CO, Lieutenant-Colonel Graham Deakin,

Above: Battle of Albert, 21 August 1918. 5th Division troops advancing in file in the vicinity of Achiet-le-Petit.
IWM Q11504

Below: Battle of Albert, 21 August 1918. An overrun German position. Scrutinising the original photograph with a magnifying glass, these two soldiers appear to be from the New Zealand Division.
IWM Q11227

and during the crossing of the railway embankment, the battalion encountered a battery of German Artillery that was firing in the direction of the advancing 95 Brigade. Accompanied by a few men, Lieutenant-Colonel Deakin himself shot down the gunners.

The mist that shrouded the battlefield suddenly lifted around 9 a.m. and it was discovered that the right of the battalion's flank was at least 1500 yards further forward than the rest. By 12 noon, after a few German counter-attacks, a divisional line was consolidated, but in doing so the 16th Royal Warwicks had to withdraw and take up a position on the northern side of the railway to conform with the line held by the rest of the division. It may be of interest to note that if you count the march to the assembly position prior to the attack, the 16th Royal Warwicks covered fifteen miles in sixteen hours. The Division as a whole had advanced two miles and had captured over 500 prisoners. During the operation the casualties for the 16th Royal Warwicks had been remarkably light: five officers wounded and one missing (the missing officer was Lieutenant H S Sanders from Caterham, Surrey, who had been drafted into the battalion on 16 August from the 2/6th Royal Warwicks. His body was later identified and is now buried in Adanac Military Cemetery, France). From the other ranks there were sixty casualties, of which eleven were killed/died of wounds (One of the officers wounded was Captain A H Sayer MC who with his brother were original volunteers to the 1st Birmingham Battalion. They were the sons of a former Lord Mayor of the city, Alderman Henry James Sayer). During the advance the 16th Royal Warwicks took around 350 prisoners, three 77 mm Field Guns, four 5.9 Guns, twenty machine guns, two trench mortars and large amounts of rifles and equipment. The CO, Lieutenant-Colonel Deakin, made the following conclusion in the War Diary:

> 'It is impossible to describe the difficulties of this attack owing to the heavy mist, which caused units to lose direction entirely. Added to that the whole country was totally unknown to everyone. At the same time the mist undoubtedly saved us many casualties. The troops showed the utmost dash and keenness and many gallant acts were performed during the day.'

The night of 21 August and the following day were spent in consolidating the positions gained. Orders were received for the offensive to be resumed on

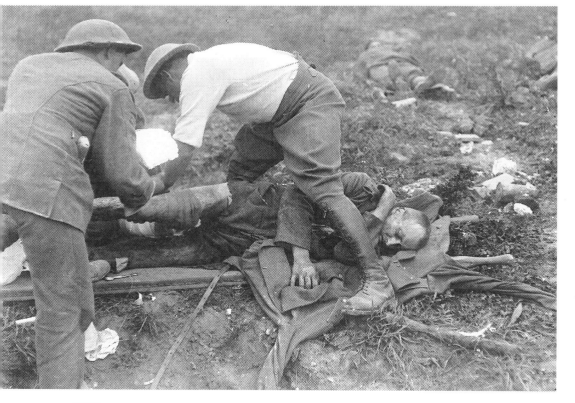

23 August. Objectives this time were the village of Irles and a ridge south of the railway embankment. Of course this time there was no fog and the Germans had also had time to strengthen their line. Again, the 16th Royal Warwicks were in the forefront and had to cope with three lines of barbed wire defended by a large number of machine-guns. Zero hour was 11 a.m.; the 16th Royal Warwicks advanced under a creeping barrage with D, C and A Coys, whilst B were in reserve. The battalion were soon met by very heavy and accurate machine-gun fire from all sides. It was here that the second son of the former Birmingham Lord Mayor, Alderman Sayer, Captain Leslie Sayer MC, commanding A Coy was killed 'leading his men in a magnificently gallant manner'. Twenty-five year old Captain Leslie Sayer lived at 'Beech Croft', Belle Walk, Moseley. He is now buried in Shrine Cemetery, Bucquoy. In spite of the withering gunfire the battalion pushed on and gained their objective by 11:45 a.m. During the consolidation of the ground gained, the battalion continued to come under continual fire, resulting in nearly all the officers and NCOs becoming casualties. After the attack the War Diary made the following comment:

'It is impossible to realise the difficulty of the whole of the attack on the 23rd without seeing the ground. The determination with which the railway embankment on the right was tackled can be judged from the fact that over twenty-three machine guns were captured on a fifty yard front (about this, the Divisional history states that each had a great heap of empty cartridge cases by its side), and in another portion of the railway one platoon of the East Surreys worked round a small trench and captured 100 prisoners and twelve machine guns. Over 150 machine guns in all were captured by the right brigade.

'The whole attack was a very gallant piece of work, the advance of the 16th Royal Warwicks without a check to their final objective with a formidable trench system, running both at right angles to and across their line, was especially brilliant.'

The day's work was not over yet. The attack upon the village of Irles had been held up just short of the village. Therefore the decision was taken to order 13 Brigade into action and take Irles and exploit the ground already taken during the morning. The 1st Royal West Kents were given the task of taking Irles, the 14th Royal Warwicks' objective was to advance towards Loupart Wood, whilst the 15th Royal Warwicks were to take the high ground above the village of Grevillers. The attack went well and the brigade's objectives were reached. Had not darkness beaten them, the 14th Royal Warwicks could have taken all of Loupart Wood as well. The day had been completely successful.

At 4 a.m. on 24 August the New Zealand Division passed through the 5th Division front to continue the push. Meanwhile, the 5th Division was now used as close support; to be ready at a moment's notice. Over the following few days, as the advance continued, the various battalions of the 5th Division had little rest. Each battalion was to be made ready at a moment's notice. Used in a close support role the division followed on the heels of the 37th and New Zealand Division, adding extra fire-power to an attack if it was held up or to be on hand if a German counter-attack materialised. Over the three day period 21-23 August, between them the 14th, 15th and 16th Royal Warwicks had a combined total of over seventy men killed. To give an idea how often the division was used over the ensuing days, a further 110 were killed until the 5th Division was relieved on 4 September.

On 2 September, the 16th Royal Warwicks were ordered up to support the 1st Cheshires who had been held up in an attack upon the village of Beugny. Unfortunately, German observers had accurately pin-pointed the battalion's position and it was soon heavily bombed by German aircraft. Around ten bombs fell amongst D Coy causing eighty casualties; of these 14 were killed. Next morning at dawn, the 16th Royal Warwicks advanced on the village of Beugny without any interference from the enemy. Once there, orders were given for the battalion to carry on and pursue the retreating enemy. Le Bucquiere was reached by 11 a.m. The advance continued until the 16th Royal Warwicks came under close range of German 5.9 guns. They took cover in some old German trenches, and in the evening the battalion was relieved. In the battalion War Diary, the CO, Lieutenant-Colonel Deakin had this to say about this episode:

' The fighting on the 2 and 3 September especially was remarkable for the exceptional endurance displayed by the men, who after continuous fighting and no real settled rest for fourteen days, had to advance five miles across country, carrying Lewis guns, panniers, picks and shovels.'

A problem that an advancing Army encounters whilst pursuing a retreating enemy across battle scarred ground is the outrunning of their line of supply. During this period the weather was intensely hot. In their retreat the Germans destroyed many wells and those that survived were inadequate to supply the needs of a thirsty battalion. Lorries laden with water tanks followed the advancing battalions and Royal Engineers boring new wells managed to keep the men supplied. The main problem was keeping the advancing troops stocked up with the copious amounts of ammunition being used. By now, large numbers of Lewis Guns were fairly distributed amongst a battalion, and they could fire a 47 round pannier in six seconds).

Two new tactics were devised and they worked

the cost had been high; 210 officers and 4065 other ranks. In this period nearly two hundred men of the three City battalions had been killed, and as one might imagine only a handful were from the original volunteers of September 1914. They were:

Private Arthur Bosley, No.528, 16th Royal Warwicks. He lived at Stretton Grove of Chesterton Road, Sparkbrook. Killed on 24 August he is buried in Adanac Military Cemetery.

Corporal Charles Clarkson, No.292, 16th Royal Warwicks. He lived at Stratford Street, Sparkhill. He died of wounds on 24 August and is buried in Bagneux British Cemetery.

Private David Millar, No.948. An original volunteer with the 3rd Birmingham Battalion, he was killed on 24 August serving with the 14th Royal Warwicks. Born in Small Heath, he is now commemorated on the Vis-en-Artois Memorial.

Above: Battle of Albert, 21 August 1918. German POW's and wounded under escort of soldier from the 5th Division. The Tommy has a German MG 08 machine gun on his shoulder.
IWM Q11214

Below: Gas casualties arriving at an Advanced Dressing Station in Croiselles. Though a sad picture it gives an excellent view of British troops in fighting order.
IWM Q7293

extremely well. The first was to utilise the Mark 1 Gun Carrier Tank. This variation of tank carried either a 60 pounder gun or a 6 inch howitzer. Their success was limited, but it was found they were an ideal vehicle for transporting large quantities of supplies and ammunition to the fighting zone. The second new method of keeping the front line supplied with ammunition was via the RAF, in particular 59th Squadron, which looked after the 5th Division. This is also an indication of the improved signal methods of 1918. Within thirty minutes of asking, an aircraft would drop supplies of ammunition by parachute at the requested drop point.

During this first phase of the advance the 5th Division had advanced nearly fourteen miles, but,

Private Thomas Norton, No.932, 16th Royal Warwicks. A Birmingham man, from whereabouts I have not found out. Killed on 23 August, he is buried in Adanac Cemetery.

Sergeant Arthur Thompson, No.997, 15th Royal Warwicks. He lived at Green Lanes, Wylde Green. Killed on 30 August, he is buried in Vaulx Hill Cemetery.

Lance/Sergeant Major Wakelin (Major was his Christian name), No.748, 16th Royal Warwicks. A Winson Green man, he was killed on 24 August and is buried in Adanac Cemetery.

SP. TR. 27/55
17.3.18-12

Battles of the Hindenburg Line

Between the 4 and 13 September the 5th Division rested in the various villages around the northern outskirts of Bapaume. The 14th Royal Warwicks bivouacked near the village of Sapignies, the 16th Royal Warwicks near the village of Biefvillers and the 15th Royal Warwicks camped in a quarry roughly halfway between these two villages.

During this rest period the battle zone had now moved forward a few more miles; thus when the 5th Division relieved the New Zealand Division the front line ran from high ground east of Gouzeaucourt Wood to the south-west of the village of Trescault. Opposite ran a daunting obstacle: a well defended and strongly fortified section of the outer defences of the Hindenburg Line known as African Trench. Beyond that lay the main Hindenburg trench system, backed up by even more barbed wire and trenches of the Hindenburg Support Line.

A comparatively quiet period ensued over the following few days. During darkness patrols went out and tested the strength of the German defences. On the morning of 18 September, the 15th Royal Warwicks gave covering fire with rifles and Lewis guns to the 2nd KOSBs failed attempt to take a section of African Trench.

At 05.20 a.m. (Zero hour) on 27 September, the British Third Army resumed the offensive. African Trench was the objective for 13 Brigade. If all went well, 15 Brigade were then to pass through and take the village of Beaucamp and then 95 Brigade to leap-frog and push towards the north-east of the village of Villers Plouich. Over the next three days the brigades of the 5th Division paid the price of trying to break through this formidable obstacle that lay before them. By 9.30 a.m. on the 27th the 1st Royal West Kents had got a foothold in African Trench and they were soon followed by the 14th and 15th Royal Warwicks. Unfortunately the 14th Royal Warwicks were bombed out of a greater portion by determined German counter-attacks which caused the 15th Royal Warwicks to retire

Above: A section of the Hindenburg Line. The Front line is on the left of the picture with three bands of barbed wire (the dark lines) in front for protection. The support line is protected by two bands of wire. On the right of the picture is the reserve line. Communication trenches can be seen connecting all three trench lines.
Aero Films C16783.
Brendan Quinlen

Above: September 1918, the war is not going well for them yet this German 1st Guards Regiment is looking quite cheerful.
IWM Q55403

back to the jumping off line.

The 16th Royal Warwicks attacked in close support to the 1st Bedfords and according to the War Diary, 'despite the hostile barrage, advanced in perfect order.' By 8 p.m. the new Divisional front lay along the Gouzeaucourt – Villers Plouich railway. Early the following morning, 28 September, 95 Brigade made good progress which had a knock-on effect and caused the German resistance to weaken opposite 15 Brigade front. Thus, by 9:30 a.m. the Royal West Kents took African Trench with little resistance. Later on, at 11 a.m., the 14th and 15th Royal Warwicks occupied Lincoln Reserve and Smut Trench.

The next obstacle on the divisional front was a section of the Hindenburg Line. Opposite the division was an immense amount of wire and many strongly-fortified trenches. The task of taking this position was given to 15 Brigade; thus, at 4 a.m. on 29 September, the offensive resumed. The 16th

Royal Warwicks followed up closely on the heels of the 12th Gloucesters. Fortunately, by now the German infantry had no thought of fighting to the last man. They still wrought destruction with their deadly machine guns and artillery, but as soon as a position seemed likely to be overrun, they withdrew. By 7 a.m. troops from the 16th Royal Warwicks had taken the village of Gonnelieu. During the early hours of 30 September, the 5th Division was relieved. The Hindenburg Line had been breached; the second phase of the final advance had been completed.

Heavy Casualties

During this last episode of fighting the 14th Royal Warwicks had three company commanders killed: Captain Hughes, A Coy, Lieutenant Jones, C Coy and Captain Izon, D Coy. Captain Charles Walter Hughes was thirty-eight years old and an original volunteer to the battalion. From Woodbridge Road, Moseley, he enlisted in the ranks, No.382, and was commissioned into the battalion in February 1915. He was hit in the head by a German sniper and died of his wounds on 1 October. Captain Hughes is now buried in Grevillers British Cemetery. There were approximately 190 casualties from the other ranks; of these around fifty were killed.

The casualties of the 15th Royal Warwicks were around 120 wounded and forty-four killed. Prior to an attack a battalion always left a number of dumped personnel as a nucleus to rebuild the battalion in case of heavy casualties. For the first time in two years, the CO, Lieutenant-Colonel G S Millar, and the Adjutant, Major G A Wilmot, were left behind. The honour to take the battalion into action went to Major Percival Charles Edwards

Below: A British Lewis Gun team, August 1918.
IWM Q11256

DCM,
the
second in command. He was last mentioned when, as Captain and C Coy commander, he was badly wounded whilst the battalion was serving on the Arras front in May 1916. Sadly he was killed near the battalion HQ near a position ironically called Dead Man's Corner. Thirty-nine year old Major Edwards was an original officer volunteer in the 2nd Birmingham Battalion. His parents lived in Wellington, New Zealand but he and his wife lived in Knowle prior to the war. He is now buried in Lebucquiere Communal Cemetery and is also commemorated on the Knowle War Memorial in the Parish Church.

The 16th Royal Warwicks also suffered a large number of casualties. In fact by 11 a.m. on 28 September the War Diary tells us that the battalion fighting strength was by now only eight officers and 240 other ranks. Casualties for 27-28 September amounted to approximately 325, of these around fifty were killed. During the attack B Coy, commanded by Captain W Sewell, had advanced further than any other company. Consequently, the Germans managed to encircle them and they were cut off from the rest of the battalion for a number of hours. Captain Sewell skilfully managed to withdraw his company and rejoin the rest of the battalion. In doing so he was seriously wounded for the third time in three years and earned himself the Military Cross. After the war, Capt Sewell MC, became a member of the 3rd Birmingham Battalion Dinner Club. In the 1927-28 list of members he gave his address as Harrison Street, New Orange, New Jersey, USA.

Major Francis Parry had served with the 3rd Birmingham Battalion since its formation. Sadly he was killed whilst leading C Coy on 27 September. Major Parry was thirty-six years old and his parents

lived in Newbold Terrace, Leamington Spa. He is now buried in Gouzeaucourt New British Cemetery.

During the attack upon the Hindenburg Line, the 5th Division had the assistance of one section of A Coy, 11th Tank Battalion; which were by now using Mark V tanks; this version of the Mark V tank was specially built for crossing 14 ft wide German trenches. They were made 6 ft longer. This brings me now to relate a story told to me by the late Mr Ted Francis (No.1114, 16th Royal Warwicks).

PRIVATE TED FRANCIS (3rd Birmingham Battalion)
Early in my research, I had letters published in the local Birmingham Press asking for information from relatives concerning men who had served in the Birmingham Battalions. One afternoon the telephone rang and a voice asked me if I still wanted information. As this gentleman spoke to me, I took it for granted he was going to explain, like many others who contacted me, that his father

Above: British Mark 1 Gun Carrier put to use carrying stores and ammunition in the trail of an advancing division during final few months of the war. This photograph was taken on 25 August 1918 in the vicinity of Irles. A number five can be seen on the right hand armoured cab. Therefore, this could be the carrier attached to the 5th Division. It was estimated that one carrier with its crew of four could carry a load which would otherwise require nearly three hundred men. *IWM Q61069*

Above: Private Ted Francis, No.1114, A Coy, 1 Platoon, 16th Royal Warwicks.

Left: German troops with flame-thrower versus a British Tank. *IWM Q55426*

had served in one of the battalions. As always I had my computer print-out nearby that I had been compiling of all the original volunteers. 'Do you know much about the 3rd Birmingham Battalion?' he asked, 'Why, was your father in it?' I replied. 'No, I was.' Talk about being gobsmacked. After picking myself up off the floor, I asked the gentleman his name. 'Ted Francis,' he replied, and then hurriedly flicking through my print-out, I spotted him. 'Was your number 1114?,' 'Yes,' 'Were you in A company, 1 Platoon?,' 'Yes,' 'Did you live at the Glassmaker's Arms, Granville Street?,' 'Yes,' 'Were you wounded three times?,' 'Was I?, you seem to know more about me than I do myself!' Almost before Ted had put the phone down I was knocking at his door. Even though he was ninety-six years old, and had his daughter living close by, he was fiercely independent and lived on his own in a house with a long back garden which needed a pair of binoculars to see the end (which by the way was beautifully maintained). He had not long come out of hospital, he had fallen off a ladder whilst trying to repair guttering on an outhouse roof! Another remarkable fact was that he had only given up driving at the age of ninety-four. After a few visits we had got to know each other well.

One afternoon he gave me a small piece of folded paper to look at, thin, tatty and much ravished by time. Ted and his brother Harry had made a pact, they both swore they would not take promotion. Ted was no coward, but after experiencing his first bout of trench warfare at Bray in December 1915, he realised that to be an NCO, was an unhealthy career move for a front line fighting soldier. Life expectancy was very short. These were the guys who got out of a trench first, to call the others on. Of course they were the first to get hit. Even though he always declined promotion, Ted always volunteered for the nightly patrols in No Man's Land. By doing this he got out

of the mundane life of carrying rations and stores up to the trenches.

As I unfolded this piece of paper, Ted told me it was the nearest thing he had to a medal and he was very proud of it:

'A' COMPANY, 11TH TANK BATTALION
30th September 1918

I wish to convey my thanks to you for the excellent work you did whilst attached to my Company. The Tank Commander of the Tank to which you were attached, and also the Section Commander, speak extremely highly of your work in putting up a smoke barrage for the Tanks on September 27th 1918.

Signed, Major R A Freeman
O.C. A Coy 11th Tank Battalion
1114 Private Francis, E.
16th Royal Warwicks.

To continue our story, on 27 September four A Coy tanks were to operate on 15 Brigade front. Volunteers were called for; three men per tank were required to walk behind the lumbering vehicle and fire off smoke grenades from their rifles over the tops of the tanks. After firing his stock of grenades, Ted was allowed to climb inside the tank for safety. Ted reckoned that most of the other volunteers became casualties. To repeat, these Mark V tanks were longer to cope with the width of the German trenches. Obviously, the Germans dug their trenches even wider! This is what happened to the tank in which Ted was now a passenger. It ditched into one of these extra wide trenches. Finding they could do nothing else the Tank CO decided that he and the crew should make a hasty exit and make their way back to the jumping off line. Before leaving the tank, Ted unhitched one of the tank's machine-guns and carried it back. Afterwards, the officer told him he could not recommend him for a

Below: German troops ready and waiting. It is said that after August 1918, the German Army was worn down with attrition, demoralised and surrendered quite readily after only showing token resistance. However, the families of nearly 450 14th, 15th and 16th Royal Warwicks men who were killed from 21 August to 11 November 1918, would tend to disagree.
IWM Q45483

medal, but give him the letter to pass on to his own battalion CO. Not one to make a fuss, he did not bother. If he had, I think, maybe, he would have been awarded a Military Medal.

Divisional Reorganisation

On 1 October the 5th Division came out of the line and moved to the vicinity of Ytres. The British Army's divisional reorganisation of three battalions to a brigade rather than four had come into effect in February 1918. Up till now the 5th Division had turned a blind eye and continued to function with four battalions to a brigade. The division was now under pressure from the High Command to come into line with the rest. With the end of the war seeming to be days away rather than months, perhaps matters would have been resolved then. Unfortunately, at the beginning of September Brigadier General L O W Jones, the GOC of 13 Brigade, died of pneumonia. He had been in command of the Brigade since the end of 1915, and had been respected by all the men under his command. His successor was Brigadier General A T Beckwith. With a new command came a change of plans and consequently the reorganisation was ordered to take effect by 1 October.

But which battalions should be disbanded and moved? Sadly, the 15th Royal Warwicks drew the short straw, so to speak. Probably, the decision of which Birmingham Battalion to disband was made easier for the Divisional Top Brass after an incident that occurred on 29 September. After the 15th Royal Warwicks had secured parts of Lincoln Reserve and Smut trenches they came under heavy German artillery fire. In this bombardment gas shells landed very near to the Battalion HQ causing thirty casualties; amongst these were the CO, Lieutenant-Colonel G S Millar, the Adjutant, Major G A Wilmot, and the Regimental Sergeant Major W H Lemmon (No.857, from Sedgeley, near Dudley. An original volunteer into the ranks of the 3rd Birmingham Battalion). Thus with no top management left, so to speak, it became an easy enough choice for one of the battalions to be disbanded. On 30 September, the last entry in the 15th Royal Warwicks' War Diary was written by Captain A E Stehn and was a simple statement, 'Battalion withdrew to Ytres'.

The other battalion in the division to be disbanded was the 12th Gloucesters of 95 Brigade. Two other moves were made. The 1/6th Argyll and Sutherland Highlanders, who had been the Divisional Pioneer Battalion, were transferred to the 51st Highland Division; their role was now to be undertaken by the 14th Royal Warwicks. Apart from road mending and filling bomb craters, the 1st Birmingham Battalion took no other part in the fighting during the last six weeks of the war.

This then left the 16th Royal Warwicks. They transferred from 15 to 13 Brigade. The division did not lose the disbanded personnel, they topped up other battalions in the 5th Division. Many of the 15th Royal Warwicks, especially any original men still surviving, transferred into the 14th and 16th Royal Warwicks. In fact the 14th and 16th's War Diaries mention they both had 200 former 15th Royal Warwicks joined their battalions. Thus, on 4 October, the 16th Royal Warwicks left the 15 Brigade area around Neuville and marched to Ytres area to join 13 Brigade. The battalion was played out of camp by the Drums and Bugles of the 1st Cheshires and marched past Brigadier-General Dudgeon (GOC 15 Brigade), who himself had commanded the battalion for a period of time.

The Advance Continues

On 8 October the British Third and Fourth Armies resumed the offensive. The problem now was that each village in the line of the advance was inhabited by French civilians. It soon became the practice for our artillery to shell heavily the outskirts of the villages, usually where the Germans placed their machine guns, and then as the artillery fire moved forwards use shrapnel over the inhabited parts. As the fighting zone reached each village the French civilians took refuge in their cellars. After four years of occupation, a few broken windows and minor damage was the least of their worries. The first large town that the Division liberated was Caudry, which for a period became the home of the Divisional HQ. For the first time in four years French flags were unfurled and dangled from nearly every house, whilst the townsfolk sang their national anthem as the 5th Division troops marched in.

Between 12 to 19 October the 14th Royal Warwicks were employed in the vicinity of Caudry repairing roads and filling in large craters blown by the Germans on retiring. By now the 16th Royal Warwicks were entrenched on the eastern side of the River Selle, and on 13th October suffered thirty-five casualties from 'heavy enemy harassing fire,' to quote the War Diary.

On 20 October the 5th Division resumed the advance. The task allotted to the 14th Royal Warwicks was to repair the roads behind the advancing battalions. On this day the battalion had twenty-two casualties resulting from German artillery fire. One man was killed, Private Charles Buckle (No.38600, from Wandsworth, London), the last man of the 14th Royal Warwicks to be killed in action. The objective given to the 16th Royal Warwicks and the 2nd KOSBs was the main road and railway on the eastern side of the river. Zero hour was 2 a.m. and an hour later their objective was taken and very soon troops from 95 Brigade had passed through to carry the advance westwards. During the attack the 16th Royal Warwicks had 43 casualties of which twelve were killed; none of whom were original volunteers to the battalion. The following message came from Major-General J Ponsonby (GOC 5th Division):

'Please convey to the 16th Royal Warwicks, 2nd KOSBs and 1st Royal West

Kents, my high appreciation of the skilfully conceived and gallantly conducted attack on 20 October, when heavy losses were inflicted on the enemy at small cost to themselves. The natural strength of the position had been increased by trenches and wire obstacles, and the enemy had every intention of holding it at all costs, as is evident by statements of prisoners and the number of enemy's dead found on the battlefield. Yet the position was captured at a loss trifling in comparison with that inflicted on the enemy.'

'The Brigadier wishes to express to all ranks of the Brigade his admiration for their work and spirit during the last few days in the line and operations of today. He attributes the success of the attack on the railway line to the vigilance and some excellent patrol work by the Royal West Kents giving valuable information, and to the splendid dash of the 2nd KOSB's and the 16th Royal Warwicks, combined with method and precision in carrying out the orders given to them concerning mopping up and the closeness with which they followed up the barrage, giving the enemy no time to recover himself.'

This high note is an opportune time to close the War History of the Birmingham Pals. Hostilities continued until 11 a.m., 11 November. But after the attack on 20 October the 16th Royal Warwicks took no more part in any more fighting. Their war was now over. After a few days out of the line, 13 Brigade were placed in Divisional Reserve and by the time they resumed their place in the line it was virtually all over. On 11 November the 16th Royal Warwicks were on the march from Pont sur Sambre to Rue Haute. When hostilities ceased at 11 a.m. The 14th Royal Warwicks were repairing roads in the vicinity of Pont sur Sambre.

To finish, I think the following quote concerning the last three months of the war history of 14th, 15th and 16th Royal Warwicks is a fitting tribute. It was made by Third Army Commander, General Sir Julian Byng:

TO ALL RANKS OF THE THIRD ARMY

'The operations of the last three months have forced the enemy to sue for an armistice as a prelude to peace. Your share in the consummation of this achievement is one that fills me with pride and admiration.

'Since 21 August you have won eighteen decisive battles, you have driven the enemy back over sixty miles, and you have captured 67,000 prisoners and 800 guns. That is your record, gained by your ceaseless enterprise, your indomitable energy, and your loyal support to your leaders. Eleven Divisions of the Third Army (Guards, 2nd, 3rd and 62nd, 5th, 37th, 42nd and New Zealand, 17th, 21st, and 38th) have been continuously in action since the beginning of the advance, and borne the brunt of the operations.

'May your pride in your achievements be as great as mine is in the recollection of having commanded the Army in which you have served.'

Below: King George V at Le Quesnoy, 2/3 December 1918 – three weeks after the war had ended. The 16th Royal Warwicks were in the village at the time of the King's visit. In the background on the right can be seen the King's two sons. Edward, the Prince of Wales and Albert (right) who later become King George VI.
IWM Q9755

Chapter Ten

Conclusion

After the Armistice the 5th Division remained in the vicinity of Le Quesnoy until mid-December. This was a strange period to get adjusted to; especially those who had endured so long in the fighting zone. They were still on active service but demobilisation was now on everyone's mind. Also the quietness, with no sound of artillery or machine-gun fire in the distance, took a time to get used to. In the 14th Royal Warwick's history, J E B Fairclough explained that after 11 a.m. on 11 November there was no excitement, just a dull, numb feeling that now, after three years overseas, we should definitely get back to 'Blighty.' The following is his account of what the first few hours of peace felt like:

> 'To raise the head without thought of precaution against what might be in front or on either flank, into free, still air was the first pleasure of the great release. To lie down that night in a big barn beside unscreened braziers, with one's smiling companions who talked until sleep overtook them, and, when the last happy babbler had dropped off, to hear the long forgotten sound of a horse's feet trotting evenly on a hard road under a full moon crowned all that had gone before. Each man had but one thought in those miraculous first hours: : "I – even I, myself, here – have come through the war." To scorn the shelter of sunken roads, hedges, walls or lines of trees, and to extend in unmartial crowds across the whole width of a Pavé, were exercises in freedom that he arrived at later.'

Demobilisation was going to be a long, slow process. Therefore, to keep the men fit and amused sporting activities of all kinds were encouraged on a daily basis. Thus began various knockout competitions, mostly of football and Rugby. According to the War Diary, on 3 December, the 16th Royal Warwicks marched to Le Quesnoy to see the King. Whether he saw them is not recorded. On 13 December the 5th Division began a march into Belgium, stopping every night and finding billets in various villages on the way. The Divisional area was to be midway between Namur and Wavre. On 22 December the 16th Royal Warwicks had reached their billeting village of Leuze. The

battalion had marched 90 miles (144 km) in nine days. The 14th Royal Warwicks at first were billeted at Meux, but the billets were found to be unsuitable, so after a few days the battalion moved to Eghezee. On 22 December, the first batch of men to be demobilised from the 14th Royal Warwicks, left for England. They were eight coal miners. Demobilising men who were needed for important jobs, even though they may have been in the services a short time, caused much disquiet throughout the British Army during the winter of 1918-19, especially from men who like the original Birmingham Pals, had signed up for three years or the course of the war. These men thought that they should be first to go. However, it was not to be, though one wonders how many men, slipped the Orderly Room Corporal a few bob, to change their pre-war occupation to miner? It just seems strange that over a five day period in late December 1918, there were nearly fifty 14th Royal Warwicks

Above: End of war photograph of surviving original officers to the 16th Royal Warwicks. Back row left, Lieutenant Thomas Pearman. Third from left, Captain W S Stebbing MC. Front row, left, Captain John de Reimer Phillips. Right, the CO, Lieutenant-Colonel Graham Deakin DSO.

demobilised because they were coal miners. Then suddenly it stops. Perhaps this little dodge to get out of the army was discovered?

Christmas 1918

I know the war had finished and the men were fed up, because they wanted to go home. But you would have thought the 14th Royal Warwicks would have had a bit of a party. The battalion War Diary states that 'The officers held their 4th Xmas dinner in the field.' It seems that the 16th Royal Warwicks had a more cheerful time. On Christmas Day there was a football match, Officers versus Sergeants (I take it that the Sergeants won, as the officer who wrote the War Diary did not mention any score!). Then during the evening the battalion concert party, 'The Brum Boys' gave a concert in the local hall, whilst the Leuze village band joined in also. But, due to lack of provisions, Christmas Dinners were postponed until the New Year.

January to April 1919

This is now the period that the majority of men were demobilised. Parties of men left daily for the UK. Not everybody was to be demobilised, by the way. Some officers and other ranks (the number is not mentioned in the War Diary) of the 16th Royal Warwicks were drafted to the 2/7th Royal Warwicks (I do not know if this was compulsory or

voluntary), who were to remain in France until November 1919. The same goes for the 14th Royal Warwicks, two officers and ninety-nine other ranks were posted to the 2/6th Royal Warwicks who were employed guarding German PoW's at Dieppe until September 1919.

There is one more important date in the history of the 14th and 16th Royal Warwicks. On a freezing cold day in the village of Leuze, with two inches of snow on the ground, both battalions received their colours (the King's Silk Union Flag), on 4 February 1919. The Colours were presented by IV Corps Commander, Lieutenant-General Sir G M Harper KCB DSO. Lieutenant-Colonel Murray DSO, the CO of the 14th Royal Warwicks, commanded the parade. The Corps Commander was received with a General Salute, and after a short service and a consecration of the Colours by a senior Army Chaplain, the battalions marched past in column and close column. The following day, in celebration of the presentation, companies of both battalions partook in a 'splendid and plentiful meal, including pork, beer etc., and was highly appreciated by everyone.'

By the end of February 1919 both battalions had been reduced to 15 Officers and 140 other ranks. At some time in March 1919, the CO of the 16th Royal Warwicks, Lieutenant-Colonel Graham Deakin DSO, returned back to Birmingham with the battalion concert party, 'The Brum Boys.' They were soon first on the bill at the Grand Theatre of Varieties in Corporation Street. By April 1919, there was only the war Diary of the 14th Royal Warwicks being kept. From the last couple of pages we find out that on 14th April, the last remnants of the battalion arrived at an embarkation camp at Antwerp. Three days later, 17 April 1919, the 14th and 16th Royal Warwicks embark for the UK. On reaching their demobilisation camp at Oswestry, Shropshire, both battalions were disbanded. The following list is the cadre of the 14th Royal Warwicks that reached Oswestry (original volunteers have their address):

Commanding	Major W Wilberforce DSO, MC
Adjutant	Captain A H Handford
Quarter Master	Lieutenant W Dadd MC
	2nd Lieutenant G F Baxter

200943		acting RSM G H Houghton DCM
6412		acting CSM A J Smith
265202	Sgt	F G Ball
5067	..	P Whelan
14/1395	..	E J Clarke (E Coy recruit 1915)
34118	..	J M Ferguson
14/441	..	J H Lusty (The Cottage, Sandon Road, Edgbaston)
14/707	Cpl	W S Sharman MM (College Rd, Wake Green, Moseley.)
10653	..	H Joseph
6578	..	W E Biddlecombe
15/683	..	E C Gandley (Sherborne Street, Ladywood)

14/1238	L/Cpl	E W Owen (E Coy recruit, 1915)
5373	..	H Vodden
15/171	..	G H Bailey MM (New Spring St, Brookfields)
15/721	..	G Millar (address unknown)
23465	Pte	Morris
48222	..	W Taylor
15/202	..	A Wilkinson (Colbourne Road, Tipton)
15/30	..	H Commander (Morville Street, Ladywood)
15/689	..	A H Rogers (Nursery Road, Harborne)
38407	..	W Lunn
30295	..	E Baldock
32605	..	J H Anderson MM
16/1880	..	A Ashwin
14/1410	..	A O Palmer (Newport Road, Moseley)
29005	..	A Browning
27690	..	W Coldicott
23226	..	R Hennessy
28444	..	F Lewis
24354	..	E E Murdock
15/45	..	H W Pumphrey (Lee Bank Road)
1304	..	J Phillips
13/704	..	H F Smith (address unknown)
35002	..	A P Waldron
22699	..	W Woodhall
50470	..	O E Ward
14/1504	..	W E Weaving
22655	..	S Yeomans
15183	..	H P James
43697	..	A H Toney
15/425	Sig.	A J White (address unknown)

Epilogue

Even though the story of the 'Birmingham Pals' is finished, I have not. I will still strive to collate as much information as I can about these men and their war service. No doubt once this book has been published quite a few more facts, photos, ephemera and reminiscences will emerge. I am sure Pen & Sword Books (address at front of book) would pass any such information on to me.

Before finishing, I think the reader would find it interesting, to find what happened to some of the men who have been mentioned in the book.

First I would like to tell you about Private **Ted Francis** of the 16th Royal Warwicks, who was last mentioned during the action of 27 September 1918. Shortly after his episode with the tanks, Ted was sheltering in a dugout during a German artillery barrage. The roof of the dugout was strengthened with railway sleepers. One shell landed too close for comfort, the roof collapsed and one of the sleepers crashed down and fractured Ted's ankle. By the time the war had finished, Ted

was in hospital in Scotland. Like many, Ted returned to Birmingham to find his pre-war job, that was promised to be kept open for him, filled. He found work in a pub near Evesham. After marrying he returned to Birmingham to set up home and start a family. He found work at Birmingham Wholesale Market and became employed by Fyffes; for whom he worked well into his seventies. Even though Ted's ankle mended, over the years the bone where the break occurred grew and grew until he had a lump the size of a tennis ball on his ankle. As Ted approached the last few years of his life, he entered hospital many times. But whatever his ailment, it was always his ankle that became the talking point. One Doctor even offered to cut it off with a saw! Ted declined the offer as the lump gave him no discomfort or affected the way he walked. Ted's brother Harry (No.23) who was wounded in early 1916, became a corporate accountant with offices in Suffolk Street.

Captain **William Hereward Ehrhardt**, 14th Royal Warwicks, who received bullet fragments in his spine and stomach (page 147) ended up in a military hospital at Brighton. He was eventually discharged from the Army with an extraordinary souvenir; a German bullet still lodged in his spine. At the time it was a very difficult operation to perform to try and remove. So, in constant pain

Above: Once demobilisation took place, those original Birmingham Pals who had proudly marched through the city's streets on Saturday 13 March 1915 (see page 79) slipped quietly back into normal life
IWM Q30501

and with the aid of a walking stick he resumed his career in law. Instead of working in Patents he specialised in the matter of Reparations when the war had finished and Versailles Treaty was signed. He was called to the Bar and considered 'one of the most brilliant barristers of his generation'; Sadly his wife Doris, whom he married in 1920, died soon after giving birth to a daughter, Daphne, in 1922. This was the same year that William decided to enter politics, and was accepted as a Conservative candidate for the next General Election. Since being wounded in April 1916, William had undergone eleven unsuccessful operations to remove the bullet in his spine. But he decided to risk everything on one final operation. This time the bullet was removed; unfortunately infection set in and he died on 23 June 1923. It is said that but for that German sniper's bullet, King Edward's High School, Birmingham, might have had their first Old Edwardian Prime Minister.

In the same incident that Captain Ehrhardt was wounded, his old schoolfriend and brother officer, Captain **Emile Jacot** assisted him back to our lines. Later, whilst the battalion was serving on the Somme, Captain Jacot was wounded in the lungs (page 188). By the time he was passed fit for active service the war was in its final days. He was first posted back to the 16th Royal Warwicks, before transferring back to the 14th in December 1919. The war had interrupted his studies at Queen's College Oxford, were he was reading English Literature. Captain Jacot returned to Queen's College and earned a distinction in the Shortened Course of the Honour School of English Literature (a course designed for ex-service personnel). His lungs had mended well enough for him to row in the Queen's Eight and he also had trials for the University Rugby team. Whilst at Oxford he had a book of satirical verse published entitled 'Rolls'.

On leaving Oxford, Emile Jacot entered the Slade School of Art in London, and was a pupil of Havard Thomas. He also married a fellow artist by the name of Maeve Wolf. Whilst there he published another book, this time a children's book, *Nursery Verseries*. He had his young niece in mind when he wrote the poems and drew the sketches. In 1925, Emile Jacot, was awarded the prestigious Rome Scholarship in Sculpture. His new place of study was the British School in Rome. Perhaps the new climate in Italy affected Emile Jacot's lungs. Having relatives in Switzerland he decided that a spell of mountain air would be good for him. Unfortunately it had the opposite effect, and he died in Switzerland in March 1928, aged twenty-nine. His ashes were sent home and placed in the family plot in Curdworth Cemetery, Warwickshire. The Chairman of the school, W Goscombe John, had this to say of former Captain Emile Jacot:

'The British School at Rome has lost one of its most brilliant students and sculptors an artist of exceptional promise and power.'

Although this has nothing to do with the

Above: Emile Jacot

Below: Lieutenant Charles Carrington MC

Birmingham Pals, I thought the reader would like to know about Emile Jacot's younger brother, Conrade Jacot. He had joined the Royal Flying Corps at Castle Bromwich Aerodrome. He had no problem in getting his 'wings', but he was too young to serve in France. Because of this he became bored with the daily routine at Castle Bromwich, consequently he was apt to take unnecessary risks whilst flying. It is said that he used to fly low over the family home, in Perry Barr, and drop a parcel of his dirty washing in the grounds for the maid to pick up! Unfortunately he took one risk too many. Flying too low whilst coming to land at Castle Bromwich, his plane hit telephone wires and crash landed. Conrade Jacot was killed; he was still a few days short of his seventeenth birthday. He is also buried in Curdworth Cemetery.

Private **Charles Carrington** (No.247) was last mentioned when I quoted from several of his letters during the formation and early training days of the 1st Birmingham Battalion. He was commissioned on 19 February, 1915, into the 9th York and Lancs. Because he was too young for overseas service he remained in England when the battalion went to France. With the influence of his uncle, Captain Philip Carter, who was serving in the 1/5th Royal Warwicks (Territorials) he transferred to the same battalion. Lieutenant Carrington was awarded the MC in 1917 for service in the Battle of Passchendaele. After the war he had a long and distinguished academic career and became an expert on the history of the British Empire and the Commonwealth. He also published a number of books. The most well known, to those with an interest in the First World War, was entitled *A Subaltern's War*, written under the pseudonym of Charles Edmunds and published in 1929. Two others on the same subject were *The War Record of the 1/5th Battalion The Royal Warwickshire Regiment* published by Cornish Brothers of Birmingham in 1922, and *Soldier From the Wars Returning* published in 1965.

Nothing more is known about Private J E B Fairclough who was the author of the *First Birmingham Battalion in the Great War*. He left the battalion in October 1917. He is not named in the casualty lists, therefore I presume he was commissioned. A small book was published after the war 'For private circulation only,' entitled, *13th 14th & 15th Field Ambulances, Diary of their Movements in France, Italy and Belgium 1914 –1919*. These were the Field Ambulance units serving the 5th Division. In a list of names of officers who served in the 13th Field Ambulance, there is a Captain J B Fairclough. Could it be the same? Answers please on a postcard...

Little is also known about 'Ricardo' the 2nd Birmingham Battalion Poet; or to give him his proper name and title Private **Richard Louis-Bertram Moore**. After the war he published a book of poetry called *The Warblings of a Windy*

Warrior, nothing else is known about him. The same goes for Second Lieutenant Howard Drinkwater, whose diary was quoted from during the Somme and Passchendaele periods. He was wounded in June 1918 and on recovery was posted to Egypt. Shortly after the war, whilst still in Egypt, he happened to be in the vicinity when a local went berserk with a pistol and a stray bullet ricocheted off the pavement and hit Drinkwater in the foot.

Captain **Charles Arthur Bill**, the author, of the History of *The 15th Battalion Royal Warwickshire Regiment (2nd Birmingham Battalion) in the Great War*, (published by Cornish Brothers, Birmingham, 1932) was born in 1887, at Oaken, near Wolverhampton. His Who's Who entry in the 1953 *Birmingham Post Year Book* states that he was educated at Wolverley School, Worcestershire. But it does not mention that he was also an Old Boy of Birmingham's Central Secondary School in Suffolk Street. By the time Captain Bill recovered from his wounds received in the attack upon Polderhoek Château, page 258, the war was over. He was then given command of a young soldiers' battalion in the Army of Occupation. By the time he was demobilised he held the rank of Major. He was recalled to the colours in 1939 and finished the Second World War as a Lieutenant-Colonel. He became a certified Glider Pilot and became Chairman of the Midland Gliding Club. In The 1950's he was living in Harborne.

Thomas Eric Pearman was last mentioned on page 207 when, as a young Second-Lieutenant with the 16th Royal Warwicks he described the horrors of Longueval. He served with the battalion until the end of the war. On 24 November, 1918, Lieutenant Pearman transferred to 15 Brigade HQ. Before being demobilised he served for a period of time in Russia. He then served with the Nigerian regiment until 1923. At the outbreak of the Second World War he rejoined the Army from the Reserve. He went with the BEF to France as Major in command of 11 Works Labour Company (Pioneer Company). In May/June 1940 the Pioneer Companies combined to form a scratch force called the 'Beauman Division'. Lieutenant-Colonel Pearman commanded 'P' Battalion. The Division tried to hold the Seine after the Dunkirk evacuation. In the *War History of the Royal Pioneer Corps* an incident is mentioned of Thomas Pearman swimming across the Seine to recover boats that could be used to rescue troops on the north bank facing the advancing Germans. The Beauman Division was eventually driven up the Cherbourg Peninsular by Rommel's Armoured Division. On 17 June 1940, the division was evacuated from Cherbourg. Back in the UK he was appointed the Commandant of the Pioneer School of Instruction. By the end of the war he had achieved the rank of full Colonel, had been awarded the OBE, CBE and twice mentioned in despatches and held the position of Deputy Director of Labour. Colonel Thomas Eric Pearman

died on 9 December 1979.

The Teacher from Kings Norton Council School and former pupil of King Edward's Camp Hill, Private Arthur Guy Osborn, was last mentioned on page 65. He continued with his training with the 1st Birmingham Battalion until July 1915 when he had by then attained the rank of Sergeant. He was then commissioned to the 12th (Service) Battalion, South Wales Borderers (119 Brigade 40th Division). Captain Arthur Osborn was killed in action on 6 May 1917 and is now buried in Fins British Cemetery, Sorel le Grand, France.

Although I would like to, I cannot mention every volunteer to the Birmingham Pals. Therefore, I would like to bring to the reader's attention a few others worthy of recognition. On page 56 I have mentioned Private **Charles Leatherland**, who later became Lord Leatherland. Another original Birmingham Pal who received the same honour was Sergeant **William Frederick Jackson** (No.669, C Coy, 14th Royal Warwicks). He was wounded in June 1916. In 1933 he entered politics and won Brecon and Radnorshire for Labour. In later life he was knighted and later given the title Lord Jackson of Glenstone.

On enlisting into B Coy of the 2nd Birmingham Battalion, the two Apps brothers were living in Aston Street (near Birmingham Fire Station). Private A E Apps, No.320, remained with the battalion and was awarded the Military Medal in 1918. The other brother, **Ernest William Apps** served in the ranks throughout the Somme battles and took a commission into the 2nd Wiltshire Regiment in 1917. He has a *Who's Who* entry as long as your arm, therefore suffice it to say that he was the Managing Director of Thomas Woolf Ltd (a well known Birmingham furniture firm) and Lord Mayor of Birmingham 1956 to 1957. Another well known figure at the time in Birmingham was former Captain **Alfred Henry Sayer** Military Cross & Bar, he became Chairman of the City Magistrates; a post also held by Lieutenant-Colonel Graham Deakin DSO, the CO of the 16th Royal Warwicks.

Sergeant **Will Kings** (No.783, 1st Birmingham Battalion) became a regular with the 5th Division Concert Party, the Whizz-Bangs. After the war he became a member of the 'Fol-de-Rols' Concert Party whose summer shows were very popular at various seaside resorts in the years between the wars. During the Second World War he did valuable work touring home and abroad with ENSA. Afterwards he devoted much of his time to radio broadcasting in the Midlands region. He was one of the original cast of 'The Archers' radio serial, playing the character Ben White. Will Kings died in November 1955, aged sixty-seven. Another well known Midlands radio broadcaster in the 1950s was **Thomas Kemp** (No.429, 1st Birmingham Battalion). Prior to the war and for a few years afterwards he was a schoolmaster. He then became Technical Librarian to Birmingham City Libraries.

Above: Captain Thomas Pearman

Above: Sergeant Charles Leatherland

Bottom: Private Thomas Kemp

Above: Private William Spearman

Above: 16th Royal Warwick's Lamp of Remembrance.

His main interests lay with the theatre and writing. In 1935 he became Drama Critic for the *Birmingham Daily Post* and broadcast on the same theme for local radio. In 1943 he published a book entitled *The History of the Birmingham Repertory Theatre*. This brings me to the sad story of a friend and former comrade of Thomas Kemp, Private **William Spearman** (No.761, 1st Birmingham Battalion). William was a signaller with the battalion and served throughout the war. Whilst in Belgium and waiting for his turn to be demobilised, he sent the following note home:

'You may expect me home in a little more than a week now, am leaving here Tuesday. Will save all the news until I see you. Cheerio, until then Will.'

On 3 March 1919, within two weeks of being back home in Birmingham, he died of pneumonia or Spanish Flu as it was then known. Private Spearman was given a military funeral and is now buried in Brandwood End Cemetery, Kings Heath.

Finally, this brings me to Lieutenant **Alan Furse**. He was last mentioned towards the end of the Somme chapter. During January 1919 he was instrumental in forming an old comrades association of former Birmingham Pals. From these early meetings there soon emerged three old comrade associations, one for each battalion. There is also evidence that some of these associations formed smaller groups such as the 'C' Company 1914-15 Club of the 2nd Birmingham Battalion. Dinners were held annually around the anniversary of the Armistice. After the Second World War, during the 3rd Birmingham Battalion's annual reunion, it became a ritual to light the 'Lamp of Remembrance' during the two minutes silence. It was made by a Birmingham Silversmith, Mr William Hickman, a former member of the battalion (No.1157, D Coy, who as Lance Corporal suffered shell-shock during the battalions experience at Longueval, 27 July 1916).

In all 2,400 Officers and men were killed in action, died of wounds or sickness whilst serving in the three Birmingham Battalions of the Royal Warwickshire Regiment. The Birmingham City Battalions' Memorial stands to this day in the Birmingham Parish Church of St Martin's, in the Bull Ring. It was unveiled on Sunday 12 November 1933.

This book is dedicated to the memory of these men:

'THEIR NAME LIVETH FOR EVERMORE'

Birmingham Battalions' Gallantry Awards

The following list of honours, decorations and awards is compiled from the "London Gazette," the battalion War Diaries, and the 14th and 15th histories published after the war. The majority of gazettes only gave the regiment and not the battalion. Thus, this list may not be complete; but it is as complete as I can achieve with the information at hand prior to this book being published.

Abbreviations:

DSO	Distinguished Service Order
DCM	Distinguished Conduct Medal
MBE	Member of the Order of the British Empire
MC	Military Cross
MM	Military Medal
MSM	Meritorious Service Medal
MID	Mention in Despatches
PC	Parchment Certificate
BCdeG	Croix de Guerre (Belgium)
FCdeG	Croix de Guerre (France)
ICdeG	Croce di Guerra (Italy)
SMMV	Silver Medal for Military Valour (Italy)

Name	Rank	No.	Award	Gazette	Bn
aron H	L/Cpl	844	MM	11/11/16	14th
dams S G	Pte	50201	MM	14/05/19	16th
ddenbrooke A	Captain		MID	04/01/17	14th
lexander J P	Pte	33788	MM	21/10/18	15th
llsop W W J	Pte	35215	MM	24/01/19	16th
nderson F H	Pte	32508	MM	17/06/19	16th
nderson J H	Pte	32605	MM	14/05/19	14th
pps A E	Pte	320	MM	28/01/18	15th
rkell W	A/Cpl	277	MM	14/01/18	15th
shford T H	Pte	40590	MM	11/02/19	15th
agshaw J F	L/Cpl	1196	DCM	17/04/19	15th
ailey G H	Pte	171	MM	20/08/19	14th
ailey R H	Captain		MID	30/05/18	14th
aker W	CSM	1188	DCM	13/02/17	16th
aker W	CSM	1188	MC	17/09/17	16th
anks G	Pte	34486	MM	11/02/19	15th
arrett F	L/Cpl	10189	MM	21/08/17	16th
arrow H	Captain		MID	08/07/19	14th
arwell W	L/Cpl	30208	MM	24/01/19	16th
eale A	Pte	1199	MM	12/03/17	15th
eaver F	Sgt	506	DCM	03/09/19	16th
eere W H	Pte	50582	MM	14/05/19	14th
erry H L	Sgt	1427	MID	08/07/19	14th
ill C A	Captain		MID	18/12/17	16th
lood J	Cpl	724	MM	18/07/19	16th
lower W J	CSM	9653	MID	30/05/18	14th
lundell H J	Pte	10580	MM	11/02/19	15th
ond S L	Pte	35234	MM	14/05/19	15th
ooker R H	Pte	33876	MM	24/01/19	16th
owd H	Pte	84	PC	26/06/17	16th
radley A E	CQMS	529	MM	20/08/19	16th
rewer C P	Cpl	676	MID	30/05/18	15th
ristow P	Sgt	29890	MM	14/05/19	14th
romwich J	Pte	2	MM	14/05/19	16th
rown A S B	Pte	34468	MM	14/05/19	14th
rown C J	Sgt	355	MSM	18/01/19	14th
rown C J	Sgt	355	MID	18/12/17	14th
ubb W	Pte	27694	MM	24/01/19	16th
unce C E	Pte	267	MM	28/01/18	16th
urgess G J	2nd Lieut		MC	26/07/18	15th
urke E S	Sgt	32428	MM	28/01/18	14th
urnell S J	Pte	35247	MM	14/05/19	16th
utler W	Pte	34741	DCM	11/03/20	16th
aley A J	Cpl	20684	MM	24/01/19	16th
allant W A	Pte	24886	MM	11/02/19	15th
allow E J	Sgt	868	MM	23/08/16	15th
arroll R	Sgt	528	MM	11/11/16	14th
aswell J R	Cpl	55	MM	13/09/18	14th
attell A F	Cpl	1121	MSM	03/06/18	16th
lark F H	Cpl	287	MM	24/12/18	16th
larke F	Cpl	287	MM	24/01/19	16th
oldicott A C	2nd Lieut		MC	09/01/18	15th
oldicott W H	Pte	201361	MM	11/02/19	15th
ole R B	2nd Lieut		MID	30/05/18	15th
oles H	Pte	1475	MM	04/02/18	14th
ollins W	RQMS	625	MID	22/05/17	15th
onnolly W P	2nd Lieut		MC	04/10/19	16th
ook W J	Cpl	6	MID	04/01/17	16th
ooke A L	Pte	537	MID	04/01/17	14th
ooper A A	Pte	20896	MM	28/01/18	14th
ope B J T	Cpl	1642	MM	11/02/19	14th
ope H	Sgt	1120	MSM	03/06/19	16th
ope H	Pte	1120	MID	18/12/17	16th
ornforth F P	Sgt	540	MID	30/05/18	15th
ouch O P	L/Sgt	34	MMbar	06/01/17	15th
ouch O P	L/Sgt	34	MM	21/09/16	15th
raven J A	Cpl	1657	MID	30/05/18	16th
ulliford A L	Lieut & QM		MID	27/12/18	16th
Culliford A L	Lieut & QM		MID	30/05/18	16th
Cutts H E	CSM	797	MID	18/12/17	16th
Cutts H E	CSM	797	DCM	03/06/18	16th
Dadd W	Lt & QM		MC	03/06/19	14th
Dady M K	Pte	32894	MM	28/01/18	16th
Dance H J	Sgt	1598	MM	14/05/19	14th
Darby M	Pte	1939	MM	30/01/20	14th
Dark F	CQMS	1033	MSM	03/06/19	14th
Davenport J H	Sgt	544	MM	21/01/18	14th
Davies B V	Sgt	30366	MID	18/12/17	14th
Davis H	Sgt	1049	MM	09/12/16	14th
Davis H R	Pte	1069	MM	21/09/16	15th
Deacon C H	Pte	25724	MM	11/02/19	15th
Deakin G	Lieut Col		MID	27/12/18	16th
Deakin G	Major		MID	18/12/17	16th
Deakin G	Major		MID	04/01/17	16th
Deakin G	Lieut Col		F LdH	15/12/19	16th
Deakin G	Lieut Col		DSO	02/12/18	16th
Denham A C	CQMS	322	MSM	03/06/18	14th
Dimmock A A	Cpl	300259	MMbar	23/07/19	16th
Dimmock A A	Cpl	300259	MM	14/05/19	16th
Dow F W	CQMS	1105	MSM	18/01/19	14th
Dow F W	Sgt	1105	MID	04/01/17	14th
Downes G F	RSM	1048	MID	04/01/17	14th
Downes G F	RSM	1048	DCM	09/07/17	14th
Dyson W	Pte	1314	MID	30/05/18	15th
Eaton T	Pte	23290	MM	11/02/19	15th
Edge P O	Sgt	22	MM	21/08/17	16th
Edwards P DCM	Major		MID	27/12/18	15th
Evans J	Reverend		MC	03/06/19	14th
Evans J H	Pte	503	MM	19/02/17	15th
Farrimond W	2nd Lieut		MID	30/05/18	15th
Farrimond W	2nd Lieut		MC	15/10/18	15th
Fee G	Pte	33730	MID	08/07/19	14th
Field W O	Captain		MCbar	02/12/18	16th
Field W O	Lieut		MC	03/06/18	16th
Fifield G	Pte	35861	MM	14/05/19	14th
Filer C J	2nd Lieut		MC	02/12/18	16th
Fisher W E	Sgt	148	MM	11/05/17	16th
Ford H	2nd Lt		MC	02/12/18	14th
Foster W T	A/Sgt	18441	MM	24/01/19	16th
Francis G M	Pte	1835	MID	27/12/18	16th
Franklin C	Pte	50226	MM	14/05/19	16th
Fraser D	Pte	34088	MID	08/07/19	14th
French R P	Sgt	38262	MM	14/05/19	14th
Friend D R	Cpl	567	MM	09/12/16	16th
Fuller A J	Pte	326	MID	30/05/18	16th
Fuller A J	Pte	326	FCdeG	10/10/18	16th
Gannaway J L	Cpl	541	MID	18/12/17	15th
Garland C	Sgt	1229	MM	28/01/18	16th
Garratt H	Pte	10590	MM	28/01/18	14th
Gascoigne G	Sgt	2002	MID	04/01/17	14th
Gates J	Sgt	1354	MM	17/09/17	15th
Gibson A H	Captain		MID	27/12/18	14th
Gissing A	L/Cpl	29	PC	28/06/17	16th
Glaze B C	Pte	13	MSM	03/06/19	14th
Glover J	Cpl	242	MM	21/09/16	15th
Good H	Cpl	1105	MSM	03/06/19	15th
Goodwin W B	Lieut		MC	06/04/18	15th
Gordon A E	L/Cpl	395	DCM	03/06/19	15th
Gough R I	Captain		MID	04/01/17	15th
Gough R I	Captain		DSO	22/09/16	15th
Griffiths W H	2nd Lieut		MC	02/12/18	16th
Guest W	Cpl	30086	MM	21/08/17	16th
Gumnell A O	Pte	235262	MM	14/05/19	16th
Haddon A L	Sgt	383	PC	28/09/18	14th
Haderer P T S	Sgt	511	MM	13/03/19	15th
Hales A A	Sgt	160	MID	08/07/19	16th
Handel A E	L/Sgt	12704	MM	21/08/17	16th
Hands N	2nd Lieut		MC	01/01/18	15th
Hanson T R	L/Cpl	380	MM	11/11/16	14th
Harding C	Lieut Col		MID	04/01/17	15th
Harding C	Lieut Col		DSO	01/01/17	15th
Hardy T	Pte	27558	MM	11/02/19	15th
Harman J	Pte	32458	DCM	15/11/18	14th
Hartley J	L/Sgt	901	MM	16/11/16	16th
Harvey H	CQMS	36	MSM	03/06/18	16th
Harwood A W	Lieut		MID	30/05/18	16th
Harwood M W	Lieut		MID	08/07/19	16th
Harwood S G	Cpl	33915	MM	17/06/19	16th
Hayes F W	CSM	918	DCM	03/06/18	14th
Haynes J W	Pte	30209	MM	04/02/18	14th
Hazleton C L	Pte	1251	MM	24/01/19	16th
Henderson D	Pte	32784	MM	28/01/18	16th
Henry C DCM	Sgt	1660	BCdeG	15/04/18	16th
Herbert C L	2nd Lieut		MID	30/05/18	15th
Hewlings A	Sgt	1746	MM	07/10/18	16th
Higgins H L	2nd Lieut		MC	25/11/16	14th
Hill H	Pte	11517	MM	21/08/17	16th
Hocking W	Pte	25388	MM	24/01/19	14th
Hollick P H	2nd Lieut		MID	22/05/17	15th
Holloway R H	Pte	16439	MM	28/01/18	14th
Holt R	L/Cpl	1705	MM	28/01/18	16th
Hopkins H	Pte	362	MM	21/08/17	14th
Hopton F V L	Cpl	226	MID	08/07/19	15th
Houghton G DCM	CSM	200943	MID	08/07/19	14th
Howard R E	Pte	1221	MM	20/08/19	16th
Howe J	Sgt	16003	MM	28/01/18	14th
Huckvale W	Pte	1640	PC	28/06/17	16th
Hudson A H	Pte	9253	DCM	17/04/18	14th
Hughes A	Sgt	1156	MM	21/08/17	16th
Hughes A V	Pte	339	MM	14/05/19	16th
Hull E E	Pte	23421	MM	14/05/19	14th
Huskisson R	Pte	205	DCM	13/02/17	15th
Inman F	Pte	242243	MM	11/02/19	15th
Irwin H J	Pte	910	MM	11/11/16	14th
Jackson J H W	Captain		MID	05/07/19	14th
Jackson T E	Pte	24869	MM	11/02/19	15th
Jacobs W C	L/Cpl	975	DCM	17/04/18	15th
James A H L	Cpl	47	MID	08/07/19	16th
Jarvis W E	L/Cpl	51	MM	28/01/18	16th
Jervis N E	2nd Lieut		MC	17/09/17	16th
Johnson C	Pte	617	MM	11/02/19	15th
Johnson W H	Pte	23459	MM	14/05/19	14th
Jones F G	Pte	169	MM	21/09/16	14th
Jones G A	Pte	211	MM	17/06/19	16th
Jones J	Pte	33909	MM	17/06/19	16th
Jones M	Sgt	15842	DCM	02/12/19	15th
Jones T J	Sgt	519	SMMV	07/01/19	15th
Jones T J	Sgt	519	MM	29/08/18	15th
Jukes G	Pte	19588	PC	28/09/18	14th
Kaye H H	Cpl	920	MM	09/12/16	16th
Kaye H H	2nd Lieut		MC	02/12/18	14th
Kelly J E	Pte	1300	MM	03/06/16	16th
Kendall M H V	Lieut		MC	03/06/19	14th
Knight H F	Sgt	932	MID	27/12/18	16th
Lane A O	CSM	398	MID	30/05/18	16th
Langford T	Pte	32628	MM	11/02/19	14th
Langford T	Cpl	32628	DCM	10/01/20	14th
Latham A E	Cpl	48347	MM	14/05/19	15th
Lawton G	Pte	34448	MM	11/02/19	14th
Layton D L	Sgt	67	MM	17/09/17	15th
Lea A E	Pte	1269	MM	28/01/18	16th
Leach J	Sgt	4424	MM	24/01/19	14th
Leatherland C	A/CSM	1073	MSM	03/06/19	16th
Leatherland C	Pte	1073	MID	27/12/18	14th
Lee H	Sgt	804	MSM	03/06/18	14th
Lemmon W	A/RSM	857	MID	22/05/17	16th

Lemmon W	RSM	857	BCdeG	15/04/18	16th
Liddell F H	Lieut		MC	01/01/18	15th
Locker A C	L/Cpl	940	MM	11/11/16	14th
Lorimer E L D	Cpl	1467	MSM	03/06/19	14th
Lowe C E	L/Cpl	937	PC	07/10/17	16th
Lucas A	Sgt	1452	MID	30/05/18	14th
Lucas A	A/CSM	1452	BCdeG	15/04/18	14th
Lunn W	Pte	28407	MM	28/01/18	14th
Lyons H H	Cpl	29886	MID	30/05/18	14th
Machin E	CSM	9243	MM	16/08/17	15th
Madgwick W	Pte	25033	MM	11/02/19	16th
Manning C V F	2nd Lieut		MC	01/02/19	14th
Manning S	Pte	29914	MM	14/05/19	14th
Marks L Y	Pte	34141	MM	11/02/19	15th
Martin H R	Cpl	35313	MM	24/01/19	14th
Mason E	Sgt	427	MM	28/01/18	15th
Matthews W J	Pte	24892	DCM	02/12/19	16th
McFarland E J	Pte	32820	MM	14/05/19	15th
McHale P	Sgt	17622	PC	28/09/18	14th
McHale P	Sgt	17622	MSM	03/06/18	14th
McHale P	Sgt	17622	MID	18/12/17	14th
Mckenzie T	CSM	1975	MC	01/01/17	16th
McKenzie W J	Sgt	32807	MM	14/05/19	15th
Mercer W J	Pte	549	MM	11/11/16	15th
Miller G S	Lieut Col		MID	04/01/17	15th
Miller G S	Lieut Col		MID	30/05/18	15th
Miller G S	Lieut Col		MID	27/12/18	15th
Miller G S	Lieut Col		DSObar	15/10/18	15th
Miller G S	Lieut Col		DSO	03/06/18	15th
Millidge P	L/Cpl	28443	PC	28/09/18	14th
Moakler R J	Sgt	254	MM	09/12/16	15th
Mooney N	L/Cpl	32474	MM	07/10/18	14th
Moore T	Pte	202905	MM	24/01/19	16th
Morris H	Pte	945	MM	24/01/19	16th
Murphy N	Pte	34210	MM	07/10/18	16th
Murray L	Lieut Col		MID	15/06/16	14th
Murray L	Lieut Col		DSO	01/01/17	14th
Nash J H	CSM	215	DCM	13/02/17	15th
Neal D	Captain		MID	04/01/17	14th
Neighbour S J	CQMS	455	MSM	18/01/19	14th
Neighbour S J	CQMS	455	MID	30/05/18	14th
Nesbitt R	Cpl	34228	MM	24/01/19	16th
Newey F A	Pte	957	MM	03/06/16	16th
Newey H	A/Sgt	305886	DCM	15/11/18	16th
Nicholls G H	L/Cpl	1605	MM	28/01/18	15th
Nicholls G W	Pte	33726	MM	24/01/19	14th
Nicholson L E	Pte	30176	MM	14/05/19	14th
Nind F T	Cpl	1655	MM	17/06/19	16th
Nock L A	Sgt	414	MID	18/12/17	16th
Nolan P DCM MM	2nd Lieut		MC	02/12/18	16th
Norton E	Sgt	956	MSM	18/01/19	16th
Nown F G	Pte	16385	MM	11/02/19	15th
Oliver E H	Pte	33868	MM	11/02/19	16th
O'Malley J M	Pte	47	MM	09/07/17	15th
O'Sullivan O	Captain		MC	03/06/19	15th
Owen C W	Cpl	658	MM	28/01/18	16th
Page A F	2nd Lieut		MC	01/01/18	15th
Page C H C	Pte	675	MID	27/12/18	16th
Parker J G H	Pte	202619	MM	11/02/19	15th
Parrish S	Cpl	16430	MM	14/05/19	15th
Parrott A S H	Pte	34303	MM	11/02/19	15th
Parry F A	Captain		MC	14/11/16	16th
Parry W H	QMS	1062	MSM	18/01/19	14th
Parsons A	Pte	32910	MM	11/02/19	16th
Patrick F J	Sgt	3	MID	30/05/18	14th
Pavitt W G	Pte	458	MSM	18/01/19	14th
Peart G C	Cpl	301	MM	11/11/16	14th
Perry H W	A/L/Cpl	465	DCM	13/02/17	14th
Peyton R R	Pte	432	MID	30/05/18	15th
Phillpot G E	2nd Lieut		MC	01/02/19	14th
Pilditch F L	L/Cpl	75	MM	09/12/16	16th
Pilgrim A C	Pte	18314	MM	24/01/19	14th
Platt C H	2nd Lieut		MC	06/04/18	16th
Playfair C	Major		MID	04/01/17	14th
Plenderleith C B	CSM	753	DCM	17/04/18	14th
Pool W J	Cpl	129	MSM	03/06/19	14th
Powell T H	Pte	25392	MM	24/01/19	14th
Powell W T	A/Sgt	30094	MM	24/01/19	16th
Pykett G F	Lieut		MID	30/05/18	16th
Pykett G F	Lieut		MC	01/01/19	16th
Ralphs F E	Pte	1447	MM	28/01/18	14th
Randle J	Pte	992	MM	13/11/18	16th
Read C	Sgt	998	MID	08/07/19	16th
Rees H D	Captain		MC	03/06/18	14th
Reeves H M	Pte	1246	MM	24/01/19	16th
Rhodes R V	Pte	48246	MM	11/02/19	16th
Richards J H	L/Cpl	204	MM	21/09/16	16th
Richardson G	Sgt	30329	DCM	11/03/20	14th
Richardson W E	2nd Lieut		MC	01/02/19	14th
Richmond F W	Captain		MID	04/01/17	14th
Riley J A	Pte	1005	MM	13/11/18	15th
Rivers J E	Pte	1247	MM	18/07/17	16th
Roberts J A	L/Cpl	1139	MM	09/12/16	14th
Robertson W	Sgt	29880	MM	28/01/18	14th
Robotham W E	Pte	5545	MM	14/05/19	15th
Rolles N	2nd Lieut		MC	01/02/19	14th
Ross C	Cpl	32483	MM	24/01/19	16th
Rowland W E	Sgt	443	MID	04/01/17	16th
Rudge C	Cpl	1352	MM	24/01/19	14th
Sadler E J	CSM	1032	MID	04/01/17	15th
Salmon D	Sgt	1121	MM	11/11/16	14th
Saul G	Cpl	713	MM	11/02/19	16th
Saunders J E A	Pte	1446	MM	14/12/16	14th
Sayer A H	Captain		MCbar	03/06/19	16th
Sayer A H	Captain		MC	01/01/18	16th
Sayer L	Captain		MCbar	02/12/18	16th
Sayer L	Lieut		MC	01/01/17	16th
Schofield W F	Pte	1070	MID	30/05/18	15th
Seaman S H	Pte	22373	MM	14/05/19	15th
Sewell W	Lieut		MID	30/05/18	16th
Sewell W	Lieut		MC	02/12/18	16th
Sharman W S	Pte	707	MM	07/10/18	14th
Sharp W G	Pte	28050	MM	14/05/19	14th
Sharp W G	Pte	28050	FCdeG	10/10/18	14th
Shepherd A	Pte	15305	MM	24/01/19	14th
Shirley F T	Pte	18295	MMbar	04/02/18	14th
Shirley F T	Pte	18295	MM	28/01/18	14th
Siddons F C	Lieut		MC	03/06/18	16th
Silver S H	Sgt	1213	MSM	18/01/19	15th
Silver S H	Sgt	1213	MID	30/05/18	15th
Smith A G	Cpl	710	DCM	17/04/18	14th
Smith A T	Sgt	491	MID	22/05/17	15th
Smith A	Pte	266635	MM	14/01/18	14th
Smith A T	Sgt	491	BCdeG	15/04/18	15th
Smith G J	Pte	709	MM	07/10/18	14th
Smith G O	Pte	30276	MM	07/10/18	14th
Smith G T	L/Cpl	1359	MID	22/05/17	14th
Smith S B	Sgt	794	MM	10/08/16	15th
Snead T E	A/CQMS	9618	ICdeG	17/05/19	16th
Solomon W J C	Pte	1341	MSM	03/06/18	16th
Sorge A V	Pte	732	MM	09/12/16	14th
Sparkes C	Pte	389	MM	24/01/19	14th
Sparkes E F	Sgt	212	MM	16/11/16	16th
Spencer G T L	Lieut		MBE	03/06/19	14th
Starbuck T	Pte	1009	MM	21/09/16	16th
Stebbings W S	Lieut		MID	18/12/17	16th
Stebbings W S	Lieut		MC	01/01/19	16th
Stehn A E	Captain		MID	08/07/19	15th
Stephens F J	Pte	48202	MMbar	14/05/19	14th
Stephens F J	Pte	48202	MM	11/02/19	14th
Stokes N J	Pte	139	DCM	11/03/20	14th
Stone W H	Lieut		MC	15/10/18	15th
Tandy E E	Cpl	8626	MSM	03/06/19	14th
Taylor W A	CSM	9663	DCM	15/11/18	16th
Thompson T	A/L/Cpl	1278	MMbar	29/03/19	16th
Thompson T	A/L./Cpl	1278	MM	24/01/19	16th
Tongue W E	Cpl	73	MMbar	23/02/18	14th
Tongue W E	Pte	73	MM	09/12/16	14th
Towner C R MM	Cpl	32499	MMbar	14/05/19	14th
Tranter F E	2nd Lieut		MID	04/01/17	16th
Tranter H	L/Cpl	1019	MM	18/07/17	16th
Travis R W	Lieut		MID	27/12/18	15th
Tuffley D W	Sgt	1181	MID	18/12/17	14th
Tuffley D W	Sgt	1181	DCM	03/09/18	14th
Turner A	L/Cpl	24897	MM	24/01/19	16th
Turner A E	Sgt	724	MM	11/11/16	14th
Turner J T	2nd Lieut		MC	01/01/17	14th
Usher F C	Sgt	32494	MM	14/05/19	14th
Varnon T H	Pte	17910	MM	24/01/19	14th
Walpole W H	Pte	1728	PC	28/06/17	16th
Ward E L	2nd Lieut		MID	04/01/17	15th
Ward E L	2nd Lieut		MC	17/09/17	15th
Ward G F	2nd Lieut		MID	30/05/18	16th
Warren R G	2nd Lieut		MC	06/04/18	14th
Watson B	Pte	733	DCM	14/11/16	16th
Watson O E	L/Cpl	926	MM	18/07/17	16th
Watts R C	Captain		MID	22/05/17	14th
Watts R C	Captain		MC	01/01/18	14th
Webb W	Pte	1324	MM	28/01/18	16th
Wedlock H W	Sgt	260319	DCM	15/11/18	16th
Whyman J	Pte	9711	MM	11/02/19	15th
Wilberforce W	Captain		DSO	01/02/19	14th
Wilcox E A	Sgt	515	MID	27/12/18	15th
Wilcox E A	Sgt	515	DCM	11/03/20	16th
Wilding G H	Pte	32966	MM	28/01/18	16th
Wilks H R	2nd Lieut		MC	06/04/18	16th
Williams E W	Sgt	281	MM	28/07/17	14th
Williams H	Pte	136	MM	24/01/19	14th
Williams J	Pte	48337	PC	28/09/18	14th
Williams J	Lieut		MID	08/07/19	16th
Williams T	Pte	1142	MMbar	24/01/19	14th
Williams T	Pte	1142	MM	28/01/18	14th
Wilmot G A	Captain		MID	18/12/17	15th
Wilmott G A	Captain		MC	01/01/19	15th
Wilton R A	2nd Lieut		MC	27/07/16	15th
Windmill J W	CSM	896	MID	22/05/17	16th
Windmill J W	RSM	896	MC	01/01/19	16th
Windmill J W	RSM	896	DCM	17/04/18	16th
Windsor C	Sgt	267788	MM	24/01/19	16th
Woodward W	Sgt	12910	MM	11/02/19	16th
Woolsey J S	Pte	32497	MM	24/01/19	14th
Wright H	L/Cpl	25127	DCM	15/11/18	14th
Young E J	Pte	36001	MM	24/01/19	16th
Young S B	Pte	21909	MM	11/02/19	16th

DISTINGUISHED CONDUCT MEDAL

Lance Corporal J F Bagshaw,1196, 15th Royal Warwicks
When in charge of a Lewis gun section, he handled his gun and section at all times with the greatest initiative and resource. On one occasion when left with no officers and very few men, he penetrated the enemy's lines and brought his gun to action. After the war Lance Corporal Bagshaw lived at Druid's View, Aldridge.

Company Sergeant Major W Baker,1188, 16th Royal Warwicks
On 27 July 1916, at Longueval, he assumed command of and led his company with great courage and determination, and performed consistent good work throughout.

Sergeant F Beaver, 506, 16th Royal Warwicks
During the fighting from 21 August to 2 September 1918, he rendered most valuable services by manning advanced observation posts under heavy fire, and reporting the progress of operations most accurately. On 2 September 1918, he maintained an observation post in an exposed position under considerable shell fire for over five hours until wounded doing valuable services at a somewhat critical time. Sergeant Beaver came from Charles Road, Small Heath and had been wounded at Longueval in July 1916.

Private W Butler, 34741, 16th Royal Warwicks
For marked gallantry and devotion to duty as a stretcher bearer from 25 February to 11 November 1918; especially during the heavy fighting around Achiet le Petit between 21 to 23 August 1918. He did excellent work, making numerous journeys with wounded under heavy fire and saved many lives.

Company Sergeant Major H E Cutts, 797, 16th Royal Warwicks
During a long period of severe fighting, he rendered most valuable services by his courage, determination and cheerfulness under heavy fire and most trying conditions. His utter disregard for his own safety greatly inspired the men of his company. After the war, Company Sergeant Major Cutts, who had been wounded three times, lived at Norfolk Road, Erdington.

Regimental Sergeant Major G F Downes, 1048, 14th Royal Warwicks
Prior to leaving the battalion in June 1917 to take a commission, Regimental Sergeant Major Downes, had consistently performed good work throughout. He had set at all times a fine example to his men when under heavy fire. He was wounded during the action at Falfemont Farm, 3 September 1916.

Lance Corporal A E Gordon, 395, 15th Royal Warwicks
In charge of a section of stretcher bearers, he consistently showed gallantry and devotion to duty. During operations on 28 April, 28 June 1918 and during August 1918 he displayed great zeal under most trying circumstances, and great skill dressing and bearing the wounded. He set a fine example to those with him. Lance Corporal Gordon who came from Darwin Street, Highgate, had been wounded during September 1916 whilst serving on the Somme.

Private J Harman, 32458, 14th Royal Warwicks
During an attack he took command of a Lewis gun team, and used the gun with excellent effect against enemy machine guns until it was put out of action. He then led his men in a bombing attack upon a German machine gun post that was holding up the advance, killing all the team. He set a splendid example of determination and resource.

Company Sergeant Major F W Hayes, 918, 14th Royal Warwicks
At all times, during two years active service, he displayed great courage, energy, ability and performed his duties regardless of personal danger. Under trying conditions and heavy and accurate shell fire, he controlled and encouraged all ranks. Regimental Sergeant Major Hayes (his rank at the end of the war) lived at Evelyn Road, Acocks Green. On enlisting into the battalion in September 1914 he gave his address as the Central Fire Station.

Private A H Hudson, 9253, 14th Royal Warwicks
He carried out his duties as a company runner with fearlessness, energy and ability on all occasions. Private Hudson came from Coventry.

Private R Huskisson, 205, 15th Royal Warwicks
Displaying conspicuous gallantry, courage and initiative, he went forward alone with a machine gun under very heavy fire (During the Somme battles of September 1916). During June 1917, Private Huskisson, who came from Lodge Road, Winson Green, was wounded.

Lance Corporal W C Jacobs, 975, 15th Royal Warwicks
As a member of the signal section, he continually went out and repaired telephone lines broken by very intense shell fire. It was greatly, owing to his splendid work, that communications were maintained at critical moments.

Sergeant M Jones, 15842, 15th Royal Warwicks
During the second attack on Gouzeaucourt, 27 September 1918, Sergeant Jones organised a bombing party and led them up a communication trench inflicting heavy casualties to the enemy. When the stock of grenades were used, he returned to organise a second party and again penetrated the German defences. This time he acted as first bayonet man. A German bombing party was met and were soon repulsed. It was chiefly owing to his fine courage and initiative that his company were able to consolidate their newly captured position.

Corporal T Langford MM, 32628, 14th Royal Warwicks
During the attack upon Gouzeaucourt, 27 September 1918, Corporal Langford showed conspicuous gallantry and leadership of a platoon. After suffering heavy casualties he gained the objective, but was forced back by a bombing attack. He collected men from other units, and consolidated his position. Subsequently, he led a bombing attack with six men, and regained part of the trench he had lost.

Private W I Matthews, 24892, 16th Royal Warwicks
During the operations that breached the Hindenburg Line, 27 September 1918, Private Matthews first fought as an infantryman for ten hours. Then, as darkness fell, he spent the following twelve hours bringing in the wounded, going in some cases through the enemy outpost line. Again, on 29 September, he did fine work under very heavy fire, dressing and carrying wounded in the open for several hours. His grit and devotion to duty were admirable. It is interesting to note that Private Matthews, from Alfred Street, Handsworth, volunteered in August 1914, but was soon discharged as medically unfit. However, he re-enlisted in 1917, and was eventually demobilised in November 1919.

Company Sergeant Major J H Nash, 215, 15th Royal Warwicks
Unfortunately, throughout the service life of the 15th Royal Warwicks, the various officers who maintained the War Diary kept matters close to their chests. Therefore I can only assume that CSM Nash's award was for an act of gallantry, during the attack upon Falfemont Farm, in September 1916. He led forward a handful of men under intense fire. Later, he rendered most valuable services in reorganising the line and evacuating the wounded. Company Sergeant Major Nash lived at George Road, Gravelly Hill.

Acting Sergeant H Newey, 305886, 14th Royal Warwicks
During the battalion's advance towards Loupart Wood, 23 August 1918, acting Sergeant Henry Newey, earned his award for gallantry and resource. During the night after the attack, his company were heavily fired on by an enemy machine gun from a flank. He led his section behind the position, bayoneted the team and captured the gun; showing splendid initiative and courage. In doing so Sergeant Newey was seriously wounded and died in hospital on 24 August. Sergeant Newey was twenty-six years old and left a widow, Lilian, at Laburnum Avenue, Brunswick Road, Sparkbrook. He is now buried in Bagneux British Cemetery, near Doullens.

Acting Lance Corporal H W Perry, 465, 14th Royal Warwicks
The incident that resulted in the award is described on page 209. Lance Corporal Perry was later commissioned into the battalion and ended the war as Second Lieutenant.

Company Sergeant Major C B Plenderleith, 753, 14th Royal Warwicks
Acting as a platoon commander, CSM Plenderleith, on several occasions in active operations, invariably displayed great courage, energy and ability. Before the war, CSM Carl Plenderleith, lived at Highfield Road, Saltley. Afterward he lived at Clowes Cottage, Earlswood. He played full-back for the Aston Old Edwardians Rugby Club for two seasons before emigrating. His brother, W Plenderleith (No.773), who also served in the 14th Royal Warwicks was wounded at Arras in April 1916.

Sergeant G Richardson, 30329, 14th Royal Warwicks
From 21 August to 18 September 1918, Sergeant Richardson, showed consistent gallantry in five successive actions. When his seniors became casualties he took on responsible positions during the fighting, inspiring those under him with confidence. Sergeant Richardson, a Peterborough man, was wounded leading his platoon near the village of Gouzeaucourt.

Corporal A G Smith, 710, 14th Royal Warwicks
As a member of the battalion's Headquarters signal section, Corporal Smith and his linesmen, were out mending lines continuously for sixteen hours under intense shell fire. It was due to his energy and total disregard of danger that communications were maintained. After the war, Sergeant Alfred George Smith served in the 51st (Graduated Battalion) during the Army of Occupation. Sergeant Smith came from George Street, Lozells, and was an official in the City Engineers and Surveyors office at Birmingham Council House.

Private N J Stokes, 139, 14th Royal Warwicks
As a battalion signaller, he displayed untiring energy near Havrincourt Wood, where the shelling was particularly severe, as the valley end of the wood was under direct observation. He showed consistent gallantry in the very arduous work of keeping up communications from June 1917 to November 1918. An Oldbury man, before the war, Private Stokes was living at Brighton Road, Balsall Heath.

Company Sergeant Major W A Taylor, 9663, 16th Royal Warwicks
When all officers of the company had become casualties, CSM Taylor, took command and led the company forward to their final objective (27 September). Single-handed he attacked and silenced a machine gun killing three of the team. He set a splendid example of determination and courage to his men, and his leadership was brilliant. During August 1916, CSM Taylor had been wounded whilst serving with another battalion of the regiment and was drafted to the 16th on recovery. Originally from Rugby, he lived at Trafalgar Road, Moseley, after the war.

Sergeant D W Tuffley, 1181, 14th Royal Warwicks
Whilst in charge of the battalion transport, he succeeded in conveying to the front line a very large quantity of ammunition which was badly needed at the time (Nieppe Forest, 13 April 1918). It was necessary for his limbers to proceed along a road which was continuously shelled by the enemy. Thereby, It was largely due to his perseverance and courage that the ammunition got through. Unfortunately, forty year old Sergeant Tuffley died on 21 December, 1918, most probably due to the "Spanish Flu" epidemic that was prevalent at the time. Before the war, Sergeant Tuffley was a well known Master Haulier and Reserve Police Constable in Sutton Coldfield. He is buried in Sutton Coldfield Cemetery. His widow, Ada, lived at Coles Lane, Sutton Coldfield.

Private B Watson, 733, 16th Royal Warwicks
Whilst the battalion was in action at Longueval during July 1916, Private Watson, won his award for conspicuous bravery as a stretcher bearer. All through the day and night he attended the wounded in the open and helped carry them to an aid post, utterly regardless of heavy shell fire.

Sergeant H W Wedlock, 260319, 16th Royal Warwicks
Whilst in command of a platoon during an attack, Sergeant Wedlock displayed great gallantry and exceptional powers of leadership. Later, he withdrew his men under heavy fire with perfect coolness and in excellent order. Subsequently, he rendered good service in taking charge of reinforcements, utilising them to the best advantage. His reports to HQ were excellent.

Sergeant E A Wilcox, 515, 16th Royal Warwicks
From 25 February 1918 until the end of hostilities, Sergeant Wilcox rendered valuable services by his courage and good leadership. On one occasion he took command of his company, and led them forward to their objective in face of heavy machine gun and shell fire. Ernest Arthur Wilcox was an original volunteer to the 2nd Birmingham Battalion (15th Royal Warwicks), enlisting into C Coy, 10 Platoon. His address prior to the war was Victoria Road, Aston. After the war he became a member of the "C Coy Club 1914-15, 2nd Birmingham Battalion." In 1922 he was living at Fentham Road, Birchfield.

Regimental Sergeant Major J W Windmill, 896, 16th Royal Warwicks
When the battalion encountered the horrendous conditions of the Ypres salient in October 1918, RSM
Windmill invariably displayed great courage and ability. He set a splendid example in operations when conditions were exceptionally bad, and set a splendid example of courage and determination. After the war, RSM Windmill was an original member to the 3rd Birmingham Battalion Dinner Club. He was then living at Grove Park, Wall Heath, Kingswinford.

Lance Corporal H Wright, 25127, 14th Royal Warwicks
After an attack, an enemy machine gun was interfering with work of consolidation. Lance Corporal Wright showed conspicuous gallantry when he went forward and attacked the position with hand grenades. At the second attempt he killed four of the enemy and captured seven others, including the gun. He showed splendid determination and initiative.

Birmingham Battalions' Roll of Honour

The following roll is made up of all the officers and ranks who were killed in action, died of wounds or sickness whilst serving in the 14th, 15th and 16th Royal Warwicks. Further information on each casualty can be found by consulting *Soldiers Died in the Great War 1914-19*, Part 11, *The Royal Warwickshire Regiment*, published by J B Hayward & Son in association with the Imperial War Museum's Department of Printed Books. Thus, the following information is usually found therein: place of birth, where enlisted, place of residence on enlisting, killed in action, died of wounds or died (sickness or accidental death) and also the soldier's former battalion if he was transferred.

Extra information may also be found in the cemetery registers supplied by Commonwealth War Graves Commission. A complete set of CWGC registers and *Soldiers Died* are kept at the Birmingham Reference Library. Otherwise for a small fee the cemetery register information can be supplied by the CWGC, 2 Marlow Road, Maidenhead, SL6 7DX, Tel: 01628 34221. Other information can sometimes be found in the 'Rolls of Honour' published in the local press during the war years.

For example the first man on the roll is Corporal A Abbott, No.15621 of 15th Royal Warwicks. By consulting the above books we find out that Alfred Abbott died of wounds received in action. He was born in Kidlington (Oxfordshire) and enlisted at Coleshill (Warwicks) and at the time was living in Minworth (B'ham). The register for the Bethune Town Cemetery, supplies the following: he was married to Olive, who by the time the register was compiled (mid 1920's) had remarried and her surname was now Hitchman living at The Green, Minworth.

Sometimes the register entry gives a bit more information, but many entries give only the soldiers burial plot.

Three soldiers in the list, Corporal W E Jarvis (MM), No.51 and Privates T H Richards, No.972, and E G Silk, No.80 are buried in Canadian Cemetery No.2 and Haplincourt Communal! This is being investigated by the CWGC as the book is going into print.

The largest amount of casualties occurred during the Somme battles of 1916, when the original Birmingham Pals were decimated. From July to October nigh on 800 men of the three battalions were killed or died of wounds. A year later, the two months spent at Passchendaele (October/November 1917) took a heavy toll upon the three battalions, with 400 being killed. The last eight months of the war was equally fierce with over 600 being killed.

Of the 2,334 officers and men, in the following roll, that died serving in the three City Battalions, 1,121 of them, nearly half, have no known grave. Their remains have never been identified.

Please note that cemeteries and memorials unless otherwise stated are situated in France.

Abbreviations used:

Br - British

Com - Communal

Cem - Cemetery

Ext - Extension

Mil - Military

Abbott A	Cpl	15621	15th	23/12/16	Bethune Town Cem
Abbott F C	L/Cpl	28388	14th	13/04/18	Ploegsteert Mem Belgium
Abbott P Z	Pte	25406	14th	15/09/18	Grevillers Br
Ablin T W	Pte	38354	15th	25/07/18	Tannay British Cem
Ackland L H	Pte	32610	14th	08/02/19	Newdigate Churchyard UK
Ackrill A J	Pte	1366	16th	24/07/16	Thiepval Memorial
Adam R	Pte	30128	15th	03/09/16	Thiepval Memorial
Adams A	Pte	32509	14th	26/10/17	Tyne Cot Memorial Belgium
Adams A G	Sgt	843	14th	23/07/16	Thiepval Memorial
Adams E J	L/Cpl	19146	14th	04/10/17	Tyne Cot Cem Belgium
Adams H S	Pte	29888	14th	13/04/18	Ploegsteert Mem Belgium
Adams J B	Pte	1206	14th	23/07/16	Caterpillar Valley
Adams W E	Pte	20567	15th	03/07/17	Duisans Br
Adcock D	Pte	52202	16th	27/09/18	Vis-en-Artois Memorial
Addenbrooke A	Captain		14th	05/10/16	Kidderminster Ch'yard UK
Adderley W E	Pte	24895	16th	10/10/18	St Sever Cem Ext, Rouen
Airey A	Pte	32689	15th	14/04/18	Ploegsteert MemBelgium
Alcock A S	L/Cpl	754	16th	06/10/17	Tyne Cot Memorial Belgium
Aldgate W	Pte	242145	16th	30/05/18	Tannay British Cem
Aldred F W	Pte	28389	14th	25/05/18	Tannay British Cem
Aldridge A J	Pte	497	16th	27/07/16	Thiepval Memorial
Aldridge W G	Pte	28041	14th	27/09/18	Vis-en-Artois Memorial
Alexander F H	Pte	1133	14th	23/07/16	Thiepval Memorial
Alexander H J	Pte	32659	15th	08/10/17	Tyne Cot Memorial Belgium
Alexander J P	Pte	33788	15th	29/06/18	Aire Com
Allchin W C	2nd Lt		14th	26/10/17	Tyne Cot Memorial Belgium
Allcock L	Pte	27474	14th	07/05/17	Orchard Dump Cem
Allen A	Pte	847	16th	03/09/16	Thiepval Memorial
Allen A W	Pte	1168	14th	23/07/16	Caterpillar Valley
Allen C B	Pte	30	14th	23/07/16	Caterpillar Valley
Allen H H	Pte	1002	15th	30/04/16	Faubourg D'Amiens
Allen I H	Pte	32885	16th	09/10/17	Tyne Cot Memorial Belgium
Allen J T	Pte	30129	15th	24/09/16	Guards Cem
Allen N	Captain		14th	14/04/18	Merville Com Cem Ext
Allen R	Pte	16633	14th	15/06/17	Duisans Br
Allen T A	Pte	36516	14th	27/09/18	Vis-en-Artois Memorial
Allen T A	Pte	40928	16th	23/08/18	Vis-en-Artois Memorial
Allen T G	Pte	36556	16th	30/09/18	Grevillers Br
Allen W	Pte	11075	14th	04/10/17	Tyne Cot Memorial Belgium
Allison J M	Sgt	1161	15th	27/09/18	Lebucquiere Com
Allso P A	L/Cpl	252	16th	27/07/16	Thiepval Memorial
Allum W	Pte	30201	14th	03/09/16	Thiepval Memorial
Alton J	Pte	22397	15th	08/05/17	Arras Memorial
Anderton S	Pte	565	14th	23/07/16	Caterpillar Valley
Andrew G H	Pte	25234	14th	14/04/18	Ploegsteert Memorial Belgium
Andrews G P	Pte	32742	15th	04/10/17	Tyne Cot Memorial Belgium
Andrews J	Pte	34503	14th	29/05/18	Thiennes British Cem
Andrews W H	Pte	22651	15th	28/07/17	Roclincourt Mil Cem
Ansell F B	L/Cpl	251	16th	27/07/16	Thiepval Memorial
Anstey J D	Pte	28	14th	23/07/16	Caterpillar Valley
Anstey T R	Pte	317	15th	03/09/16	Thiepval Memorial
Anthony A J	Pte	35217	14th	19/09/18	Metz-en-Couture Com Br Ext
Anthony F A	Pte	203415	15th	26/10/17	Hooge Crater Belgium
Antrobus A P	Pte	15/1643	15th	04/06/16	Faubourg D'Amiens
Appleton A	Pte	22047	15th	26/10/17	Tyne Cot Memorial Belgium
Appleton W T	Pte	35815	14th	08/07/18	Tannay British Cem
Archer J A R	Pte	245162	16th	11/11/18	St Sever Cem Ext, Rouen
Arculus H	L.Cpl	1056	16th	26/09/16	A.I.F. Burial Ground
Arkell H S	L/Cpl	759	16th	06/10/17	Godewaersvelde Br
Asbury E	Pte	19771	14th	14/04/18	Ploegsteert Memorial Belgium
Asbury W J	Pte	503	14th	23/07/16	Thiepval Memorial
Ashby J E	Pte	11882	15th	08/02/17	Bethune Town Cem
Ashford A G	Pte	28391	14th	23/03/17	Bethune Town Cem
Ashmall A J	Pte	38350	16th	23/08/18	Vis-en-Artois Memorial
Ashmead T F	Pte	1253	14th	30/07/16	Thiepval Memorial
Ashton J E	Pte	19139	14th	04/10/17	Tyne Cot Cem Belgium
Ashwell W J	Pte	30219	14th	26/10/17	Tyne Cot Memorial Belgium
Askew W C	Pte	32435	14th	02/05/18	Morbecque British Cem
Aspery W T	Pte	27929	16th	23/08/18	Vis-en-Artois Memorial
Aspey A	Pte	34195	14th	14/04/18	Caberet Rouge
Aspinall F T	2nd Lt		16th	01/08/16	Dantzig Alley Br
Astell G H	Pte	203710	15th	26/08/18	Vis-en-Artois Memorial
Astley S L	Pte	21592	16th	05/11/17	Tyne Cot Memorial Belgium
Aston P W	CSM	1260	15th	29/08/16	Thiepval Memorial
Atkins P F	Pte	279	15th	04/06/16	Faubourg D'Amiens
Atkins W	Pte	300061	16th	20/06/18	Thiennes British Cem
Attwood F C	Pte	16/1785	15th	04/04/16	Arras Memorial
Attwood L	Pte	34697	16th	11/11/17	Tyne Cot Memorial Belgium
Audley W	Cpl	7232	15th	28/06/18	Ploegsteert Memorial Belgium
Austen F	Pte	27299	15th	27/09/18	Gouzeaucourt New Br
Ayres J	Pte	32868	16th	23/08/18	Adanac Mil
Ayto J W	Pte	52239	16th	01/09/18	Favreuil Br
Bacon J	Pte	1732	16th	26/06/18	Aire Com
Baddeley F	Pte	23555	15th	10/05/17	Aubigny Com Cem
Badham W H	Pte	1455	14th	23/07/16	Caterpillar Valley
Baggott G J	Cpl	118	16th	26/09/16	Thiepval Memorial
Baggott J	Pte	1300	16th	03/09/16	Thiepval Memorial
Bagley M	Pte	50241	16th	24/08/18	Adanac Mil
Bagnall J	Pte	200836	16th	28/10/17	Tyne Cot Memorial Belgium
Bagshaw C E	Pte	26348	15th	16/09/18	Grevillers Br
Bailey B T	Pte	48205	14th	27/09/18	Gouzeaucourt New Br
Bailey H	Pte	16/1959	15th	23/07/16	Thiepval Memorial
Bailey H W	Pte	16915	14th	03/09/16	Thiepval Memorial
Bailey J G	Pte	43447	16th	02/09/18	Favreuil Br
Bailey S G	Pte	772	16th	04/09/16	Abbeville Com
Baker A J	Pte	1342	15th	03/09/16	Thiepval Memorial
Baker E H	Pte	35223	16th	27/09/18	Vis-en-Artois Memorial
Baker F J	Sgt	235140	16th	23/08/18	Queens Cemetery
Baker J S	Pte	522	16th	27/07/16	Thiepval Memorial
Baker O E	Pte	1584	15th	04/06/16	Faubourg D'Amiens
Baker R	Pte	9326	14th	29/03/18	Padua Main Cem Italy
Baker W	L/Cpl	558	14th	04/10/17	Tyne Cot Memorial Belgium
Baker W W	L/Cpl	785	16th	03/09/16	Delville Wood
Bakewell A	Pte	16/1650	16th	27/07/16	Thiepval Memorial
Bakewell W	Pte	244153	16th	23/08/18	Adanac Mil
Baldwin W	Pte	9426	15th	28/07/16	Thiepval Memorial
Ballard G	Pte	1071	14th	05/10/17	Tyne Cot Memorial Belgium
Ballard T J	Pte	241729	15th	28/05/18	Tannay British Cem
Balleny W G	Pte	334	15th	23/07/16	Thiepval Memorial
Barker A	Sgt	3854	16th	09/08/17	Roclincourt Mil Cem
Barker J	Pte	16833	14th	12/09/16	Thiepval Memorial
Barker W	Pte	17753	14th	08/07/17	Orchard Dump Cem
Barker W	L/Cpl	17604	16th	09/10/17	Hooge Crater Belgium
Barlow B B	Sgt	854	14th	23/12/15	St Sever Cem, Rouen
Barlow M R	Pte	1382	14th	04/06/16	Faubourg D'Amiens
Barlow P C	Pte	30217	14th	03/09/16	Thiepval Memorial
Barnacle C W	Pte	14/1701	14th	23/07/16	Thiepval Memorial
Barnett L P	L/Cpl	3214	15th	03/09/16	Thiepval Memorial
Barnfield H	Pte	505	16th	01/02/16	Citadel New Mil
Barnsley W	Pte	50219	16th	02/11/18	Brierley Hill Churchyard UK
Barratt F J	Pte	855	14th	23/07/16	Caterpillar Valley
Barrett A	Pte	358	14th	23/07/16	Caterpillar Valley
Barrett B T	2nd Lt		15th	12/04/18	Ploegsteert Memorial Belgium
Barrett E	Cpl	30125	15th	26/09/16	Guards Cem
Barrett F	Sgt	333	15th	03/09/16	Delville Wood
Barrett P	L/Cpl	22505	16th	28/10/17	Hooge Crater Belgium
Barrett W J	Pte	1421	14th	23/05/16	Faubourg D'Amiens
Barrett W T	Pte	1708	16th	30/05/18	Tannay British Cem
Barrett W V	2nd Lt		16th	28/09/18	Grevillers Br
Barrow C H B	Pte	1149	14th	03/09/16	Guillemont Rd
Barrow E S K	2nd Lt		14th	08/05/17	Orchard Dump Cem
Bartholomew W	Pte	38895	14th	08/07/18	Tannay British Cem
Bartlett F	Pte	16/1813	16th	27/07/16	Thiepval Memorial
Bartlett H	Pte	16/1968	15th	06/10/16	Grove Town
Barwell W	L/Cpl	30208	16th	01/09/18	Favreuil Br
Bassett W	Pte	15/1581	15th	04/06/16	Faubourg D'Amiens
Bassnett C H	Pte	494	16th	27/07/16	Thiepval Memorial
Bast E A	Pte	50576	14th	27/08/18	Vis-en-Artois Memorial
Bastable H J	Pte	1201	16th	01/01/17	Gorre Br & Indian
Bate W T	Cpl	1006	15th	20/05/17	Etaples Mil
Bates G	Pte	332	15th	04/06/16	Arras Memorial
Bates S H	Sgt	617	15th	28/08/16	Thiepval Memorial
Bates T H	Pte	15813	14th	03/09/16	Thiepval Memorial
Bates W	Pte	17376	14th	30/07/16	Thiepval Memorial
Baugh C E	L/Cpl	511	16th	27/07/16	Thiepval Memorial
Baugust R H	Pte	1389	15th	03/09/16	Thiepval Memorial
Baxter A E	Pte	36100	14th	26/08/18	Vis-en-Artois Memorial
Baxter C	Pte	235117	15th	26/10/17	Tyne Cot Memorial Belgium
Baxter C A	2nd Lt		15th	08/10/17	Hooge Crater Belgium
Baxter E H	Pte	203393	15th	26/10/17	Hooge Crater Belgium
Bayliss T	Pte	1387	16th	14/05/17	Arras Memorial
Bayliss W H	Pte	17837	14th	03/09/16	Thiepval Memorial
Beach G B B	Pte	34290	15th	27/07/18	Thiennes British Cem
Beale A	Pte	1199	15th	09/07/18	Aire Com
Beale J H	Pte	22354	14th	26/10/17	Tyne Cot Memorial Belgium
Beale W E	Pte	22704	15th	05/10/17	Tyne Cot Memorial Belgium
Beames C T	Pte	1644	15th	12/06/16	Faubourg D'Amiens
Beard P L	Lieut		15th	09/09/16	Abbeville Com
Beardmore J H	Pte	34127	15th	29/10/17	Lijssenthoek Mil Belgium
Bearman R	Cpl	32798	15th	27/05/18	Tannay British Cem
Beasley C F	Pte	23762	14th	26/10/17	Hooge Crater Belgium
Beaumont C E	Pte	988	15th	09/05/17	Arras Memorial
Beddard A J	Pte	104	14th	13/04/18	Tannay British Cem
Beddoes C E	L/Cpl	50453	14th	17/10/18	St Sever Cem Ext, Rouen
Bedford C E	Pte	16822	14th	30/07/16	Thiepval Memorial
Bedford G	Pte	18720	16th	19/09/16	Thiepval Memorial
Bednall B C	Pte	1254	15th	30/08/16	Thiepval Memorial
Beer F	Pte	1306	14th	04/10/17	Tyne Cot Cem Belgium
Belcher E J R	L/Cpl	28549	16th	18/04/18	Ploegsteert Memorial Belgium
Belcher J	Pte	43425	14th	07/09/18	Ration Farm Mil Cem
Bell C F	Cpl	527	16th	17/10/16	Le Touret Mil
Bell R	Pte	32692	15th	04/10/17	Hooge Crater Belgium
Bellamy F W	Pte	14/1646	14th	23/07/16	Serre Road Cem No.2
Bellamy W M C	Pte	1603	14th	23/07/16	Knightsbridge Cem
Bember A	Pte	32663	15th	04/10/17	Hooge Crater Belgium
Benbow G E	Pte	48427	16th	23/08/18	Adanac Mil
Bench F G	Pte	22675	14th	10/03/17	Brown's Rd Mil, Festubert
Benfield B W	Pte	510	14th	23/07/16	Thiepval Memorial
Bennett C H	Cpl	274	16th	07/10/17	Tyne Cot Memorial Belgium
Bennett G E	Pte	124	16th	27/07/16	Thiepval Memorial
Bennett H	Pte	1691	14th	02/08/16	Abbeville Com
Bennett H J	Pte	48310	14th	23/08/18	Adanac Mil
Bennett J H	Pte	17829	14th	03/09/16	Thiepval Memorial
Bennett J P	L/Cpl	325	15th	04/06/16	Faubourg D'Amiens
Bennett J W	Pte	1334	14th	30/07/16	Thiepval Memorial
Bennett P	Pte	18076	14th	07/09/16	Corbie Com Ext
Bennett S E	Pte	35232	16th	20/04/18	Tannay British Cem
Bennion P	Pte	14538	16th	09/10/17	Tyne Cot Memorial Belgium
Bennitt E G	L/Cpl	326	15th	04/06/16	Arras Memorial
Benson A	L/Cpl	1438	16th	16/04/17	Arras Memorial
Benson W	Pte	859	14th	23/07/16	Caterpillar Valley
Benton W E	Pte	783	16th	02/09/16	Guillemont Rd
Benwell W F	Pte	1649	14th	23/07/16	Heilly Station
Berry E B	L/Sgt	2030	15th	03/09/16	Thiepval Memorial
Berry F L	L/Cpl	1127	14th	11/09/16	La Neuville Br
Berry G E	Pte	1229	15th	23/07/16	Thiepval Memorial
Berry J	Pte	260428	16th	13/10/18	Romeries Com Cem Ext
Bertin B J	Pte	32521	14th	26/12/17	Etaples Mil
Best W	Pte	1647	14th	20/08/16	Quinton Church Cem UK
Bethell D	Pte	1210	16th	03/09/16	Thiepval Memorial
Betty W G	Pte	35975	15th	30/08/18	Vaulx Hill Cem
Bevan H J	Pte	16/1551	16th	28/08/16	Thiepval Memorial
Beynon T H	Pte	32748	15th	04/10/17	Tyne Cot Memorial Belgium
Bibb A	Pte	1052	16th	10/05/17	Arras Memorial

Bick L L	Pte	27653	16th	13/03/17	Cambrin Mil
Biddle F	Pte	18122	16th	03/09/16	Thiepval Memorial
Bigden A G M	Pte	33000	16th	06/10/17	Tyne Cot Memorial Belgium
Billett J H	Pte	29893	14th	31/10/17	Tyne Cot Memorial Belgium
Billingley C H	Pte	14/1684	14th	23/07/16	Thiepval Memorial
Billson C F	Sgt	7756	16th	03/09/16	Thiepval Memorial
Birch C P	Cpl	788	16th	24/07/16	Thiepval Memorial
Birch H	Pte	17021	14th	15/09/16	Thiepval Memorial
Birch J C	Pte	513	14th	31/07/16	Heilly Station
Bird A	Pte	14/1584	14th	03/09/16	Thiepval Memorial
Bird G	L/Cpl	3570	15th	02/07/17	Rc clincourt Mil Cem
Bird H R A	Cpl	97	15th	29/08/16	Dive Copse Br
Bird J A	Pte	8244	15th	26/10/17	Tyne Cot Memorial Belgium
Bishop S S	Pte	32514	14th	03/10/17	Tyne Cot Memorial Belgium
Blackham C	Pte	513	16th	26/07/16	Thiepval Memorial
Blake L	Pte	1633	15th	02/07/17	Duisans Br
Blakeman W	Cpl	34225	15th	12/04/18	Ploegsteert Memorial Belgium
Blakemore R M	Pte	342	15th	01/08/16	Heilly Station
Blanch J	Pte	16/1447	14th	22/07/16	Thiepval Memorial
Blick R A	Pte	330860	15th	26/10/17	Tyne Cot Memorial Belgium
Blight C	Pte	35830	14th	28/09/18	Vis-en-Artois Memorial
Bliss F H	Pte	156	14th	23/07/16	Thiepval Memorial
Blood J V	Pte	20510	14th	26/10/17	Tyne Cot Memorial Belgium
Blore B	Pte	245163	16th	04/09/18	Euston Road
Blower J	Pte	28525	14th	26/10/17	Boulogne Eastern Cem
Blundell A S	Sgt	1824	15th	03/09/16	Delville Wood
Boden T G	Sgt	531	16th	09/10/17	Tyne Cot Memorial Belgium
Bodman A	Pte	23258	16th	27/05/17	Aubigny Com Cem
Boland S	Pte	1123	15th	23/07/16	Thiepval Memorial
Bolton A	Cpl	3/2954	15th	24/09/16	Thiepval Memorial
Bolton R J	Pte	25269	14th	14/04/18	Ploegsteert Memorial Belgium
Bond C	Pte	24858	15th	26/10/17	Tyne Cot Memorial Belgium
Bond H	Pte	32876	16th	09/10/17	Tyne Cot Memorial Belgium
Boot J H	Pte	201728	16th	23/08/18	Adanac Mil
Bosley A	Pte	528	16th	24/08/18	Adanac Mil
Boss N	Pte	14/1752	15th	22/09/16	Bronfay Farm Mil Cem
Boswell A	Pte	50209	16th	21/08/18	Vis-en-Artois Memorial
Bott S G	Sgt	1516	14th	18/05/17	Aubigny Com Cem
Bott T W	Pte	15/1395	16th	09/10/17	Tyne Cot Memorial Belgium
Bough W	Pte	21096	14th	14/04/18	Ploegsteert Memorial Belgium
Bourne A	Pte	2135	16th	09/10/17	Godewaersvelde Br
Bowen A	Pte	27789	16th	09/10/17	Tyne Cot Memorial Belgium
Bowen A S	Pte	50587	14th	29/05/18	Thiennes British Cem
Bowen R B	Pte	330024	15th	13/04/18	Ploegsteert Memorial Belgium
Bowmer J	Pte	1505	14th	23/07/16	Caterpillar Valley
Bowyer A J A	Pte	1784	15th	20/11/17	Pennfields Churchyard UK
Box F	Pte	20166	14th	26/10/17	Tyne Cot Memorial Belgium
Box F	Pte	28660	15th	15/07/17	Roclincourt Mil Cem
Boyd C F	Pte	863	14th	23/07/16	Caterpillar Valley
Boyd W	Pte	34089	14th	05/06/18	Etaples Mil
Boyes E C	Pte	18757	15th	27/10/17	Menin Road South Belgium
Brace A S	Pte	43658	14th	27/09/18	Vis-en-Artois Memorial
Bradbury W	Pte	849	15th	26/04/17	Gouy-Servins Com
Bradfield M D	Pte	36461	16th	04/09/18	Bac du Sud Br Cem
Bradford B A	Pte	52253	16th	02/09/18	Vaulx Hill Cem
Bradley C A	Pte	1164	15th	04/06/16	Arras Memorial
Bradley H	Pte	22769	16th	09/10/17	Tyne Cot Memorial Belgium
Brain C	Pte	18749	15th	27/12/16	Bethune Town Cem
Brain H J	Sgt	9257	14th	08/10/18	Rocquigney-Equancourt Rd Br
Brain J C	Cpl	7971	14th	13/04/18	Ploegsteert Memorial Belgium
Braithwaite E	2nd Lt		14th	23/07/16	Caterpillar Valley
Brampton C C	Pte	123	16th	26/09/16	Thiepval Memorial
Branch W	Pte	28518	14th	24/06/17	Orchard Dump Cem
Brandham G	Pte	30171	14th	04/10/17	Tyne Cot Memorial Belgium
Brassington A	Pte	29613	15th	27/08/18	Mory-Abbey Mil Cem
Brassington H W	Pte	255	15th	03/09/16	Delville Wood
Brettell F B	L/Cpl	362	14th	16/04/16	Etaples Mil
Bridge J R	Cpl	1374	15th	09/05/17	Arras Memorial
Bridge V	Pte	30221	14th	03/09/16	Thiepval Memorial
Bridger A W J	Pte	33210	15th	26/10/17	Tyne Cot Memorial Belgium
Bridgewater F H	Pte	16/1938	14th	23/07/16	Thiepval Memorial
Brierley C W	Pte	32747	15th	26/10/17	Tyne Cot Memorial Belgium
Briggs T	Pte	52252	16th	01/09/18	Favreuil Br
Brinkworth A R	2nd Lt		14th	07/09/16	Peronne Rd Cem, Maricourt
Bristow C H	Pte	579	15th	07/05/16	Faubourg D'Amiens
Britt E G	Pte	1434	14th	11/06/16	Faubourg D'Amiens
Brittain G	Pte	16731	15th	03/09/16	Thiepval Memorial
Brittain H A	Pte	16760	14th	03/06/17	Orchard Dump Cem
Britton A S	Pte	1568	15th	23/07/16	Caterpillar Valley
Brodie A	L/Cpl	16181	14th	30/07/16	Thiepval Memorial
Bromiley H	Pte	202405	14th	08/07/18	Tannay British Cem
Bromley W L	Pte	10914	14th	23/10/17	Hinckley Cem UK
Bromwich E J	Pte	312	15th	04/06/16	Faubourg D'Amiens
Bromwich F	Pte	22391	15th	08/05/17	Orchard Dump Cem
Bromwich J G	Pte	14531	16th	29/07/16	St Sever Cem, Rouen
Bromwich L F	L/Cpl	308	15th	04/06/16	Faubourg D'Amiens
Brookes A D	Pte	120	16th	15/01/16	Citadel New Mil
Brookes C	Pte	13474	16th	10/05/17	Orchard Dump Cem
Brookes V J	L/Cpl	349	15th	02/06/16	Faubourg D'Amiens
Brookfield P W	Pte	585	15th	31/07/16	Delville Wood
Brooks P J	Pte	36354	14th	27/09/18	Gouzeaucourt New Br
Broomfield P T	Cpl	831	15th	15/12/15	Cerisy-Gailly Mil
Broughton E W	Pte	871	14th	23/07/16	Caterpillar Valley
Broughton H	Pte	30298	14th	24/04/17	La Chaudiere Mil
Brown A	Pte	21261	14th	27/02/17	Hazebrouck Com
Brown A H	Pte	17721	15th	03/09/16	Thiepval Memorial
Brown C E	Pte	48277	16th	23/08/18	Adanac Mil
Brown E	Pte	15/1325	14th	23/07/16	Caterpillar Valley
Brown E	L/Cpl	1093	14th	23/07/16	Thiepval Memorial
Brown E	Pte	12492	15th	29/06/18	Aire Com
Brown F	Pte	20612	15th	17/10/18	Cologne Southern, Germany
Brown F A	Pte	50591	14th	29/06/18	Tannay British Cem
Brown F H	Sgt	579	14th	30/07/16	Serre Road Cem No.2
Brown G h	Pte	28448	14th	09/03/17	Brown's Rd Mil, Festubert
Brown H A	Pte	939	15th	23/05/16	Arras Memorial
Brown H S	Pte	33211	15th	26/10/17	Tyne Cot Memorial Belgium
Brown H W	Pte	50223	16th	23/08/18	Adanac Mil
Brown J	Pte	34740	16th	28/10/17	Tyne Cot Memorial Belgium
Brown R	Pte	33723	14th	05/05/18	Aire Com
Brown W T	Pte	35835	16th	20/10/18	Romeries Com Cem Ext
Browning J H	Pte	22206	16th	14/05/17	Orchard Dump Cem
Bruce H	Pte	17745	14th	03/09/16	Thiepval Memorial
Bruce T H	Pte	29986	14th	26/10/17	Tyne Cot Memorial Belgium
Bryant C G	Pte	351	15th	23/07/16	Thiepval Memorial
Bryers W	Pte	34495	15th	15/04/18	Aire Com
Bryson G L U	Captain		14th	30/07/16	Thiepval Memorial
Buckland T H	Pte	14/1323	15th	30/07/16	Thiepval Memorial
Buckle C L	Pte	38600	14th	20/10/18	St Aubert British Cem
Buckley C R	Pte	1399	14th	23/07/16	Caterpillar Valley
Buckley H	L/Cpl	8240	16th	03/09/16	Thiepval Memorial
Buckley W F	L/Sgt	1066	15th	04/06/16	Faubourg D'Amiens
Buffey F W	L/Cpl	18767	15th	24/04/17	Barlin Com Cem
Bugby W J	Pte	28458	14th	07/05/17	Orchard Dump Cem
Bulley A J	Pte	18707	15th	02/07/17	Roclincourt Mil Cem
Bullivant F R	L/Cpl	32592	14th	10/05/18	Tannay British Cem
Burgess F	Pte	28046	14th	26/10/17	Tyne Cot Memorial Belgium
Burgess R H	Pte	185	15th	03/09/16	Thiepval Memorial
Burlison R R	Pte	518	16th	25/12/15	Citadel New Mil
Burn J E	Pte	261	15th	09/05/17	Arras Memorial
Burnell A W A	Pte	35838	14th	30/08/18	Vis-en-Artois Memorial
Burness W H	Pte	22194	14th	26/10/17	Tyne Cot Memorial Belgium
Burnett A	Pte	11411	15th	27/09/18	Gouzeaucourt New Br
Burnett W C	Pte	16/1818	15th	10/10/17	Tyne Cot Memorial Belgium
Burns J	Pte	33793	15th	14/04/18	Ploegsteert Memorial Belgium
Burnside J B	L/Cpl	356	14th	30/12/15	Carnoy Mil
Burnside W D	L/Cpl	361	14th	23/07/16	Caterpillar Valley
Burrows A R	Pte	50443	14th	27/09/18	Vis-en-Artois Memorial
Burrows J	Pte	1930	14th	20/05/18	Aire Com
Burt C H	Pte	15/1409	14th	23/07/16	Caterpillar Valley
Burt D	Pte	35248	16th	23/08/18	Vis-en-Artois Memorial
Burt H T	L/Sgt	235150	16th	23/08/18	Adanac Mil
Burton E	Pte	16/1660	16th	06/10/17	Tyne Cot Memorial Belgium
Burton E C	Pte	1079	16th	27/07/16	Thiepval Memorial
Burton F	Pte	27678	16th	21/09/16	Grove Town
Burton G H	Pte	18203	16th	10/10/17	Tyne Cot Memorial Belgium
Burton J	Pte	330602	14th	15/09/18	Metz-en-Couture Com Br Ext
Burton J	Pte	17101	14th	30/07/16	Thiepval Memorial
Burton W	Pte	32973	16th	09/10/17	Tyne Cot Memorial Belgium
Busby W	Pte	34969	14th	26/10/17	Tyne Cot Memorial Belgium
Butcher A W	Pte	32887	16th	09/10/17	Tyne Cot Memorial Belgium
Butcher E L	Pte	32518	14th	05/10/17	Tyne Cot Memorial Belgium
Butcher H	Pte	18595	15th	04/06/17	Etaples Mil
Butler A C	Pte	21166	14th	26/10/17	Tyne Cot Memorial Belgium
Butler F W	Pte	27657	14th	27/09/18	Neuville-Bourjonval Br Cem
Butler L S L	Pte	592	14th	21/07/16	Thiepval Memorial
Butler R W	Pte	35839	14th	20/09/18	Metz-en-Couture Com Br Ext
Butler T A	Pte	512	16th	30/07/16	Dantzig Alley Br
Buttery H G	2nd Lt		16th	27/09/18	Gouzeaucourt New Br
Byrd F	Pte	17416	14th	30/07/16	Thiepval Memorial
Bywater A H	Pte	16/1575	16th	16/06/16	Faubourg D'Amiens
Bywater L A	Pte	16/1590	16th	03/04/16	Faubourg D'Amiens
Callis J	Pte	32525	14th	04/10/17	Tyne Cot Memorial Belgium
Candler F J	L/Cpl	50595	14th	27/09/18	Vis-en-Artois Memorial
Cann E H	Pte	32526	16th	09/10/17	Menin Road South Belgium
Capers C C A	Pte	202344	15th	26/10/17	Tyne Cot Memorial Belgium
Capon A E	Pte	35250	16th	27/09/18	Vis-en-Artois Memorial
Carless A	Pte	550	16th	03/09/16	Thiepval Memorial
Carpenter W J	Pte	1759	15th	16/09/16	Netley Mil Cem UK
Carr H	Pte	34068	16th	31/05/18	Thiennes British Cem
Carr H	Pte	15/1379	16th	03/09/16	Thiepval Memorial
Carr R G	Pte	38775	14th	28/08/18	Mory-Abbey Mil Cem
Carter E	Pte	1303	14th	21/07/16	Serre Road Cem No.2
Carter F	Pte	1619	15th	28/08/16	Dive Copse Br
Carter J	Pte	1263	16th	02/09/18	Bailleul Rd East Cem
Carter W E	Pte	34132	15th	21/11/17	St Sever Cem Ext, Rouen
Carterw W	Pte	14/1695	16th	01/08/16	Heilly Station
Cartwright H	Pte	23429	14th	05/10/17	Godewaersvelde Br
Caseley J D	Pte	16/1465	16th	27/07/16	Thiepval Memorial
Castle R L	Pte	59	14th	21/07/16	St Pierre Cem, Amiens
Castle W E	Pte	1169	16th	25/12/15	Citadel New Mil
Cattle F	Pte	38718	15th	28/06/18	Merville Com Cem Ext
Chable R	Pte	32604	16th	09/10/17	Tyne Cot Memorial Belgium
Chalcroft W	Pte	32615	14th	04/10/17	Tyne Cot Memorial Belgium
Challen R F	Pte	33213	15th	15/04/18	Aire Com
Challis G	Pte	18599	14th	08/07/18	Tannay British Cem
Chamberlain J	Pte	1187	14th	23/07/16	Caterpillar Valley
Chance A S	Pte	28952	16th	29/09/18	Grevillers Br
Chance F E	Pte	267315	16th	27/09/18	Vis-en-Artois Memorial
Chance W G	Pte	35252	16th	20/10/18	Viesly Com Cem
Chandler E R	Pte	585	14th	23/07/16	Thiepval Memorial
Chaney W G	L/Cpl	33880	14th	08/07/18	Tannay British Cem
Chantler R	Pte	32732	15th	04/10/17	Tyne Cot Memorial Belgium
Chapman A	Cpl	14896	15th	09/05/17	Arras Memorial
Chapman J	L/Cpl	32883	16th	09/10/17	Tyne Cot Memorial Belgium
Charter S	Pte	30194	14th	27/12/16	Gorre Br & Indian
Chasey H	Pte	18748	15th	09/05/17	Arras Memorial
Chattock C A	Pte	704	15th	04/06/16	Arras Memorial
Chatwin A J	Pte	946	16th	31/08/16	Thiepval Memorial
Chatwin G F	Pte	678	14th	26/10/17	Tyne Cot Memorial Belgium
Checketts H W	Cpl	873	14th	03/09/16	Thiepval Memorial
Cheetham F	Pte	16/1709	15th	21/04/17	Boulogne Eastern Cem
Cherry W	Pte	1403	14th	23/07/16	Thiepval Memorial
Cherry W H	Pte	34957	14th	26/10/17	Tyne Cot Memorial Belgium
Child P H	2nd Lt		16th	23/08/18	Vis-en-Artois Memorial
Child W H	L/Cpl	601	14th	23/07/16	Thiepval Memorial
Chirgwin J C	Cpl	17031	15th	15/07/17	Roclincourt Mil Cem
Chopping R B	Pte	163	15th	28/08/16	Thiepval Memorial
Choularton J	Pte	16771	14th	03/09/16	Thiepval Memorial
Christie R L	L/Cpl	604	14th	30/07/16	Caterpillar Valley
Church A P	Pte	18567	15th	22/12/16	Brown's Rd Mil, Festubert
Churchill A E	Pte	1336	14th	23/07/16	Caterpillar Valley
Clackett A	Pte	14/1610	15th	04/06/16	Faubourg D'Amiens
Clague W E	Pte	291	16th	27/07/16	Thiepval Memorial
Clancy F	Pte	23558	16th	27/10/17	Tyne Cot Memorial Belgium
Clapham P T	Pte	20691	14th	22/09/18	St Venant Com Cem
Clare F C	Pte	868	14th	30/07/16	Delville Wood
Clare S	Pte	29532	15th	27/09/18	Vis-en-Artois Memorial
Claridge W	Pte	48261	16th	20/10/18	Vis-en-Artois Memorial
Clark C P	Pte	164	15th	03/09/16	Thiepval Memorial
Clarke A	Pte	1432	14th	01/08/16	Thiepval Memorial
Clarke F W	Pte	27228	15th	13/04/18	Ploegsteert Memorial Belgium
Clarke G H B	Pte	48282	16th	23/08/18	Adanac Mil
Clarke H	Pte	16829	14th	03/09/16	London Cem
Clarke H R	Pte	1333	16th	03/08/16	St Sever Cem, Rouen
Clarke P	Pte	17907	14th	10/06/17	Orchard Dump Cem
Clarke W H	Cpl	168	15th	03/07/17	Roclincourt Mil Cem
Clarke W J	Pte	28662	15th	26/10/17	Tyne Cot Memorial Belgium
Clarkson F R	Pte	34470	14th	29/06/18	Tannay British Cem
Cleaver A	Pte	35255	16th	29/06/18	Tannay British Cem
Cleaver A E	Pte	18877	15th	26/10/17	Tyne Cot Memorial Belgium
Cleaver T	CSM	945	14th	09/05/17	Villers Station Cem
Clement H	Captain		14th	10/10/17	Tyne Cot Memorial Belgium
Clement H G	Cpl	548	16th	09/10/17	Tyne Cot Memorial Belgium
Clements C	Sgt	102	14th	23/07/16	Thiepval Memorial
Clements G	Pte	22421	14th	27/06/17	Orchard Dump Cem
Clements H	Pte	1831	15th	30/07/16	Witton Cem B'ham
Clews J H S	L/Cpl	170	15th	04/06/16	Faubourg D'Amiens
Clifford J R	Pte	28601	15th	26/08/18	Vis-en-Artois Memorial
Climer H	Pte	16989	14th	27/06/17	Orchard Dump Cem
Clow A T	Pte	17816	14th	30/07/16	Thiepval Memorial
Clow J F	Pte	32523	14th	26/10/17	Hooge Crater Belgium
Cockerill H	Pte	15/1582	14th	23/07/16	Thiepval Memorial
Codling R E	Pte	27706	14th	14/04/18	Ploegsteert Memorial Belgium
Coffen N R	Pte	50603	14th	05/10/18	Grevillers Br
Cogbill E	Pte	16/1679	14th	23/07/16	Thiepval Memorial
Coggane M	L/Cpl	33908	16th	27/09/18	Vis-en-Artois Memorial
Coldicott A C	Captain		15th	14/08/18	Cologne Southern, Germany
Coldrick H	Pte	15/1600	16th	06/10/17	Tyne Cot Memorial Belgium
Cole A J	Pte	8976	15th	28/07/16	Thiepval Memorial
Cole F W	Pte	43452	16th	14/10/18	Romeries Com Cem Ext
Cole H S	Pte	1300	14th	30/07/16	Delville Wood
Cole P B	Pte	35966	15th	11/08/18	Aire Com
Coleing G	Pte	540	16th	27/09/16	Grove Town
Coleman F G	Pte	15/1619	14th	25/12/16	Brown's Rd Mil, Festubert
Coley H	Pte	16/1734	15th	05/10/17	Tyne Cot Memorial Belgium
Coley H B	Pte	296	16th	25/12/15	Chipilly Com
Coley W	Pte	1150	14th	14/04/18	Ploegsteert Memorial Belgium
Collett A	Pte	16326	14th	05/09/16	La Neuville Br
Collier W C	Pte	202908	16th	09/10/17	Hooge Crater Belgium
Collins A	Pte	16200	15th	09/05/17	Arras Memorial
Collins A	Pte	17406	15th	26/10/17	Tyne Cot Memorial Belgium
Collins F B	Pte	22001	14th	26/10/17	Tyne Cot Memorial Belgium
Collins J	Pte	1265	14th	04/06/16	Faubourg D'Amiens
Collins J H	Pte	1562	15th	30/08/16	Thiepval Memorial
Connell F	Pte	18765	15th	09/05/17	Orchard Dump Cem
Connolly J N	Pte	16/1852	14th	07/05/17	Arras Memorial
Constable G F	Pte	32601	14th	27/10/17	Tyne Cot Memorial Belgium
Conyers J	Pte	129	16th	02/07/17	Roclincourt Mil Cem
Cook E	Pte	30245	14th	26/10/17	Tyne Cot Memorial Belgium
Cook O	Pte	202995	16th	27/10/17	Tyne Cot Memorial Belgium
Cook W H	Pte	19206	15th	04/10/17	Tyne Cot Memorial Belgium
Cook W J	L/Cpl	6	16th	06/10/17	Tyne Cot Memorial Belgium
Cooke F C	Pte	28530	14th	23/08/18	Adanac Mil
Cooke H W	Pte	131	16th	24/06/16	Etaples Mil
Cooling A T	Pte	34946	15th	28/06/18	Ploegsteert Memorial Belgium
Cooney J	Pte	35967	15th	27/06/18	Aire Com
Cooper A S	L/Cpl	16/1647	14th	23/07/16	Thiepval Memorial
Cooper D P	Pte	194	15th	04/06/16	Faubourg D'Amiens
Cooper F P	2nd Lt		16th	26/09/16	Thiepval Memorial
Cooper F W	Pte	34133	15th	26/10/17	Tyne Cot Memorial Belgium
Cooper H	Pte	130	16th	31/08/16	Thiepval Memorial
Cooper H A	Pte	31	15th	03/09/16	Delville Wood
Cooper J	Pte	1163	15th	24/07/16	Heilly Station
Cooper J H	Cpl	12140	14th	13/04/18	Ploegsteert Memorial Belgium
Cooper J W	Pte	30302	14th	09/10/17	Lijssenthoek Mil Belgium
Cooper J W	L/Cpl	35846	14th	23/08/18	Adanac Mil
Cooper L S	L/Cpl	1241	14th	07/05/17	Arras Memorial
Cooper T	Pte	32728	15th	25/10/17	Tyne Cot Memorial Belgium
Cooper T	Pte	29839	15th	24/08/18	Vis-en-Artois Memorial
Cope E A	Pte	30246	14th	08/05/17	Arras Memorial
Cope T	Pte	267595	16th	27/06/18	Aire Com
Corless H L	Pte	36073	15th	24/08/18	Vis-en-Artois Memorial
Cornaby A	Pte	699	15th	30/08/15	Lodge Hill Cem B'ham
Cornish J A	Sgt	542	16th	27/07/16	Thiepval Memorial
Corns I	Pte	330207	15th	27/09/18	Vis-en-Artois Memorial
Cosgrove T	Pte	30476	14th	01/11/17	Wimereux Com Cem
Coslett T C	Pte	50	14th	23/07/16	Thiepval Memorial
Cotterill G T	Pte	36075	15th	27/09/18	Neuville-Bourjonval Br Cem
Cottrell C	Sgt	933	15th	23/05/16	Arras Memorial
Couch H J	Sgt	599	14th	30/07/16	Thiepval Memorial
Couldwell H	Pte	33771	14th	27/09/18	Gouzeaucourt New Br
Couling F J	L/Sgt	16/543	14th	07/05/17	Orchard Dump Cem
Coulthard H D	Sgt	870	14th	03/09/16	Delville Wood
Cowles F J	L/Cpl	848	15th	12/06/17	Smethwick Old Churchyard UK
Cox A J	Pte	1268	14th	30/07/16	Thiepval Memorial
Cox A S	Pte	36471	16th	09/11/18	Les Baraques Mil
Cox B	Cpl	28374	14th	27/10/17	Hooge Crater Belgium
Cox C	Pte	16/1846	15th	23/07/16	Caterpillar Valley
Cox C H	Pte	370	15th	27/10/17	Lijssenthoek Mil Belgium
Cox F A	Pte	50411	14th	08/07/18	Merville Com Cem Ext
Cox F J	Pte	15/1661	15th	23/07/16	Thiepval Memorial
Cox F W	L/Sgt	58	14th	30/07/16	Thiepval Memorial
Cox H	Sgt	709	15th	03/09/16	Thiepval Memorial
Coxall P	Pte	245156	16th	02/09/18	Bailleul Rd East Cem
Crabb J	Pte	11889	15th	24/05/17	Duisans Br
Craddock W H	Pte	1318	15th	03/09/16	Thiepval Memorial
Crake F W	Pte	32449	14th	03/10/17	Lijssenthoek Mil Belgium
Crane G	Pte	15/1457	14th	28/07/16	Caudry Old Com
Craner G F	Pte	16/294	15th	03/10/16	Abbeville Com Ext
Crates H	Pte	16/1509	14th	21/07/16	Thiepval Memorial
Craven J A	Cpl	15/1657	15th	29/05/18	Tannay British Cem
Creasey W	CSM	807	16th	14/04/17	Arras Memorial
Crees F	Pte	30070	16th	11/05/17	Orchard Dump Cem
Crennell G	Pte	196	15th	03/09/16	Thiepval Memorial
Cresswell	Pte	24075	15th	28/06/18	Ploegsteert Memorial Belgium
Cresswell E F	Pte	35260	16th	27/09/18	Sunken Rd Cem, Villars-Plouich
Crisp C H	Pte	8508	14th	03/09/16	Thiepval Memorial
Crisp E G	2nd Lt		15th	16/12/15	Suzanne Com Cem
Crisp F G	2nd Lt		16th	09/10/17	Tyne Cot Memorial Belgium
Crome J L	L/Cpl	645	15th	04/06/16	Arras Memorial
Cross E K L	Pte	23128	14th	04/10/17	Godewaersvelde Br
Cross F W	Pte	50613	14th	25/08/18	Adanac Mil
Cross H	Pte	795	16th	16/05/16	Faubourg D'Amiens
Cross H C	Pte	1220	14th	21/07/16	Thiepval Memorial
Cross V	Pte	431	15th	27/08/16	Thiepval Memorial
Crossley T H	Pte	17398	15th	29/08/16	Thiepval Memorial
Crosswell J T	Pte	242390	16th	02/10/18	Mont Huon Mil Cem
Crowe J J	Pte	34433	14th	14/04/18	Ploegsteert Memorial Belgium
Crump T	Pte	27771	16th	21/08/18	Vis-en-Artois Memorial
Cubbison W J	Pte	36074	15th	28/06/18	Thiennes British Cem
Culley A	Pte	35262	16th	23/08/18	Adanac Mil
Curtis C E	Sgt	34592	15th	27/09/18	Gouzeaucourt New Br
Curtis C W	Pte	21120	16th	08/10/17	Hooge Crater Belgium
Curtis K S	2nd Lt		14th	26/10/17	Tyne Cot Memorial Belgium
Curtis W G	Pte	64	14th	23/07/16	Thiepval Memorial
Cutler S	Pte	37878	14th	27/09/18	Gouzeaucourt New Br
Daft A H	Pte	50208	16th	20/04/18	Tannay British Cem
Dain J L	Pte	882	14th	04/07/16	Ste Marie Cem, Le Harve

Dale A E	Pte	30174	14th	03/09/16	Delville Wood
Dance L B	L/Cpl	16/1780	15th	03/09/16	Delville Wood
Dance L W	Pte	18	16th	03/09/16	Thiepval Memorial
Dangerfield J H	Pte	32848	15th	10/10/17	Tyne Cot Memorial Belgium
Danvers C	2nd Lt		15th	09/04/17	Arras Memorial
Darby D B	Pte	16/1940	16th	27/10/17	Tyne Cot Memorial Belgium
Dark E W	Pte	48400	16th	21/08/18	Adanac Mil
Darlington W	Pte	36081	15th	28/06/18	Merville Com Cem Ext
Darlow C J	Pte	18129	16th	03/09/16	Thiepval Memorial
Datson C	Pte	21310	14th	09/02/17	Bethune Town Cem
Davey R	Pte	36104	14th	08/07/18	Tannay British Cem
Davies A J	Pte	24863	16th	27/09/18	Vis-en-Artois Memorial
Davies F J	Pte	35264	16th	27/09/18	Fifteen Ravine Br
Davies H R	Pte	1069	15th	18/09/16	Awsworth Churchyard UK
Davies J	Pte	27909	15th	15/04/18	Etaples Mil
Davies J W	Pte	17520	14th	30/07/16	Thiepval Memorial
Davies N H	Pte	32752	15th	04/10/17	Tyne Cot Memorial Belgium
Davies W	Pte	27821	14th	27/09/18	Gouzeaucourt New Br
Davies W E	Cpl	309	16th	26/09/16	Thiepval Memorial
Davies W H	Cpl	8769	14th	14/04/18	Ploegsteert Memorial Belgium
Davis A D	Pte	27682	16th	12/05/17	Aubigny Com Cem
Davis A E	Pte	1445	15th	12/04/18	Ploegsteert Memorial Belgium
Davis A T	Pte	14/1599	14th	18/03/16	Caberet Rouge
Davis A T	Pte	30069	16th	26/09/16	Thiepval Memorial
Davis C E	2nd Lt		14th	15/09/18	Mont Huon Mil Cem
Davis J	Pte	23561	15th	09/05/17	Orchard Dump Cem
Davis J T	Pte	3647	15th	09/05/17	Arras Memorial
Davis P H	2nd Lt		14th	26/10/17	Bedford House Enc 2
Daw E W	Pte	24348	14th	26/10/17	Tyne Cot Memorial Belgium
Dawkins T	Pte	378	15th	01/06/16	Arras Memorial
Daws C	Pte	13466	16th	06/10/17	Tyne Cot Memorial Belgium
Dawson R	Pte	14/1471	15th	03/09/16	Thiepval Memorial
Day T	Pte	17442	14th	26/10/17	Tyne Cot Memorial Belgium
Deacon F	L/Cpl	968	15th	09/05/17	Arras Memorial
Dean C C	Pte	1769	16th	15/09/16	La Neuville Br
Dean R W	Sgt	313	16th	02/09/16	Thiepval Memorial
Dean W	Pte	34597	15th	28/06/18	Merville Com Cem Ext
Dean W J	Pte	16/1705	14th	03/09/16	Thiepval Memorial
Dear C J	Pte	26937	15th	05/05/17	Arras Memorial
Deeley A J	Pte	1237	15th	09/05/17	Arras Memorial
Deeming J	Pte	268338	16th	29/09/18	Vis-en-Artois Memorial
Delamy T	Pte	15/1670	14th	12/06/16	Faubourg D'Amiens
Denchfield H J	Pte	911	15th	23/05/16	Arras Memorial
Dent H	Pte	36082	16th	20/10/18	Belle Vue Br Cem
Dent W H	Pte	1251	14th	27/09/18	Vis-en-Artois Memorial
Denton A	Pte	22376	16th	08/04/17	Lodge Hill Cem B'ham
Denton F	Pte	263010	16th	27/05/18	Thiennes British Cem
Derrick A	Pte	35266	16th	27/09/18	Vis-en-Artois Memorial
Derry J J	Pte	20465	16th	15/06/18	Tannay British Cem
Derry W P	Pte	552	16th	25/06/18	Aire Com
Devereux G A F	Pte	17960	14th	03/09/16	Bronfay Farm Mil Cem
Devey T G	Pte	1277	14th	23/07/16	Thiepval Memorial
Dewar N S	Cpl	34649	15th	12/04/18	Ploegsteert Memorial Belgium
Dewberry J P	L/Cpl	331	14th	21/07/16	Thiepval Memorial
Dexter C	Pte	1629	16th	26/09/16	Thiepval Memorial
Deykin C J	Pte	328	14th	23/07/16	Caterpillar Valley
Dickinson C	Pte	13410	16th	19/11/17	Etaples Mil
Dicks B T	Pte	28658	15th	26/10/17	Hooge Crater Belgium
Dingley J	Pte	16855	15th	03/09/16	Corbie Com Ext
Dingley P G	Pte	1037	14th	23/07/16	Caterpillar Valley
Dipper W A	Pte	34971	14th	26/10/17	Tyne Cot Memorial Belgium
Disney H	Pte	52214	16th	22/09/18	Mont Huon Mil Cem
Dixon J	L/Cpl	555	16th	09/10/17	Tyne Cot Memorial Belgium
Doble H W	L/Cpl	14/1747	15th	03/09/16	Thiepval Memorial
Dobson W	Pte	1256	14th	30/07/16	Thiepval Memorial
Docker W E	Pte	14/1639	14th	23/07/16	Caterpillar Valley
Dockerill J	Cpl	30250	14th	12/09/16	Thiepval Memorial
Dodd A H	Pte	27721	14th	01/12/16	Brown's Rd Mil, Festubert
Dodgson T C	Pte	12286	15th	03/09/16	Thiepval Memorial
Dolman P A	Pte	50623	14th	23/08/18	Adanac Mil
Dolphin D	CSM	21242	16th	19/05/17	Aubigny Com Cem
Doughty J	Pte	16/1600	16th	27/07/16	Thiepval Memorial
Douglas A W	2nd Lt		14th	03/09/16	Corbie Com Ext
Dowler A	Pte	16/1771	16th	03/09/16	Delville Wood
Dowler A G	Pte	376	15th	04/06/16	Faubourg D'Amiens
Dowler A R	L/Cpl	876	14th	23/07/16	Caterpillar Valley
Dowler F	Cpl	613	14th	03/09/16	Guillemont Rd
Dowling G A	Pte	34115	14th	31/10/17	Lijssenthoek Mil Belgium
Dowling R	Pte	875	14th	30/07/16	London Cem
Downey A T	Pte	808	16th	03/09/16	Thiepval Memorial
Downing E	Pte	1267	15th	01/08/16	St Sever Cem, Rouen
Doyle F C	L/Cpl	539	15th	25/07/16	Dantzig Alley Br
Doyle W J	Pte	260281	16th	11/11/17	Tyne Cot Memorial Belgium
Drake R J	L/Cpl	30307	14th	26/10/17	Tyne Cot Memorial Belgium
Drake W	Pte	30415	14th	14/04/18	Ploegsteert Memorial Belgium
Draycott F E	Pte	50232	16th	27/05/18	Thiennes British Cem
Dreyheller W E	Pte	551	14th	14/04/18	Ploegsteert Memorial Belgium
Drinkwater W	Pte	1468	14th	23/07/16	Caterpillar Valley
Driscoll H C	Pte	240470	15th	09/10/17	Godewaersvelde Br
Druce H	Pte	18478	14th	04/10/17	Tyne Cot Memorial Belgium
Drury F G	Pte	18754	15th	24/09/16	Guards Cem
Duce W	Pte	28076	16th	30/09/18	Grevillers Br
Duckett E C A	Pte	19076	15th	09/10/17	Godewaersvelde Br
Duckett T F	Pte	18101	15th	26/10/17	Tyne Cot Memorial Belgium
Duffill F H	Pte	14/1568	14th	23/07/16	Thiepval Memorial
Dumbell W	Pte	36522	14th	26/09/18	Grevillers Br
Dunbar J T	L/Sgt	17719	16th	26/11/16	Hastings Cem UK
Duncan C	Pte	12393	15th	03/09/16	Thiepval Memorial
Dunkley H	Pte	16711	14th	30/07/16	Caterpillar Valley
Dunning L D	Pte	35856	16th	23/08/18	Adanac Mil
Durnell J O	Pte	16/1580	15th	04/09/16	Corbie Com Ext
Dury S	L/Cpl	483	15th	22/09/16	Flatiron Copse
Dutton F	Pte	17654	15th	09/05/17	Arras Memorial
Dwane J W	Pte	14/1575	14th	23/07/16	Thiepval Memorial
Dyson W	Pte	1314	15th	28/06/18	Ploegsteert Memorial Belgium
Eacott H W T	Pte	34958	14th	26/10/17	Tyne Cot Memorial Belgium
Eastman A	Pte	50242	16th	26/05/18	Thiennes British Cem
Ebourne L E	Pte	552	14th	23/07/16	Delville Wood
Eden G	Pte	17802	14th	30/07/16	Caterpillar Valley
Eden-Hurlstone	Pte	14/1742	15th	03/09/16	Thiepval Memorial
Edge P R F	L/Sgt	189	15th	22/12/16	Brown's Rd Mil, Festubert
Edinger W M V	2nd Lt		14th	23/08/18	Adanac Mil
Edmonds J H	Pte	15151	14th	08/01/18	Lodge Hill Cem B'ham
Edson A S	Pte	382	15th	03/09/16	Thiepval Memorial
Edwards A	Pte	19060	15th	02/07/17	Aubigny Com Cem
Edwards A J	Pte	20	16th	09/10/17	Tyne Cot Memorial Belgium
Edwards A J	2nd Lt		16th	27/09/18	Gouzeaucourt New Br
Edwards F J	L/Cpl	19393	15th	09/05/17	Douai Com
Edwards G	Pte	21987	16th	11/10/17	Menin Road South Belgium
Edwards H L	Pte	17694	14th	03/09/16	Thiepval Memorial
Edwards H M	CSM	565	16th	20/04/17	La Chaudiere Mil
Edwards P C	Major		15th	27/09/18	Lebucquiere Com
Elcock E	Pte	205732	15th	13/04/18	Ploegsteert Memorial Belgium
Eldridge C	Pte	35859	14th	31/08/18	St Sever Cem Ext, Rouen
Elliot A L	Pte	21	16th	10/05/17	Arras Memorial
Elliott H	Cpl	223	14th	16/06/16	Faubourg D'Amiens
Ellis E W	Pte	203696	15th	21/04/18	Le Grand Hasard Mil
Elmer T	L/Cpl	30309	14th	17/10/16	Bethune Town Cem
Elmore J H	Pte	16/1945	15th	09/05/17	Arras Memorial
Elsey C	Pte	36544	14th	17/09/18	Vis-en-Artois Memorial
Emanuel G	Pte	32835	16th	02/08/18	Aire Com
Emery W F	Pte	50626	14th	27/09/18	Gouzeaucourt New Br
Emptage C E	Pte	33192	15th	26/10/17	Tyne Cot Memorial Belgium
England A H	Pte	28514	14th	07/05/17	Arras Memorial
England F	Pte	34128	15th	28/06/18	Tannay British Cem
Ensor A	Pte	26223	16th	23/08/18	Vis-en-Artois Memorial
Essex H	Pte	1587	15th	19/04/16	Habarcq Com
Essex T	Pte	28615	15th	24/08/18	Ovillers Mil Cem
Eustace H	Pte	17751	15th	26/10/17	Tyne Cot Memorial Belgium
Evans C	L/Cpl	240531	16th	27/09/18	Vis-en-Artois Memorial
Evans G H	Pte	14/1532	14th	30/07/16	Serre Road Cem No.2
Evans H J	Pte	201774	15th	09/05/17	Arras Memorial
Evans H T R	2nd Lt		15th	09/05/17	Orchard Dump Cem
Evans J H	Pte	503	15th	11/09/18	Mont Huon Mil Cem
Evans P M	Pte	222	14th	25/11/16	Sutton Coldfield Cem UK
Evans W	Pte	16082	14th	10/06/17	Orchard Dump Cem
Evans W	Pte	649	15th	08/05/17	Arras Memorial
Evenden W	Pte	29900	16th	11/11/17	Tyne Cot Memorial Belgium
Everill J	Pte	28478	14th	08/11/17	Lijssenthoek Mil Belgium
Ewings W	Pte	1285	16th	10/05/17	Arras Memorial
Eyre H P	L/Cpl	1157	14th	30/07/16	Thiepval Memorial
Facer A	Pte	826	16th	21/12/15	Carnoy Mil
Fair R	Pte	32532	14th	26/10/17	Tyne Cot Memorial Belgium
Fairbairn J	Pte	34119	14th	13/04/18	Ploegsteert Memorial Belgium
Fairclough W	Cpl	46	14th	03/09/16	Delville Wood
Farley W	2nd Lt		15th	15/06/16	Faubourg D'Amiens
Farmer A E	Pte	16881	14th	25/06/17	Arras Memorial
Farndon A J	Pte	145	16th	28/07/16	Dernancourt Com
Farnell A B	Pte	149	14th	23/07/16	Thiepval Memorial
Farnell A C	L/Cpl	150	14th	23/07/16	Thiepval Memorial
Farr F H	L/Sgt	30253	14th	11/09/16	La Neuville Br
Farrar L	Pte	33927	16th	07/02/18	Giavera Br, Italy
Faulkner W J H	Pte	26617	15th	28/06/18	Ploegsteert Memorial Belgium
Faulks J G	Pte	15/1416	14th	23/07/16	Thiepval Memorial
Fawke J E	Pte	14/1730	16th	14/04/17	La Chaudiere Mil
Fear A C	Cpl	34221	16th	01/09/18	Favreuil Br
Fellows H J	Pte	1117	14th	22/07/16	Thiepval Memorial
Felton J H	Pte	1430	14th	26/05/16	Avesnes le Comte Com Ext
Fencott R	Pte	16/1400	15th	04/06/16	Faubourg D'Amiens
Fennell J L	Pte	16347	14th	13/04/18	Ploegsteert Memorial Belgium
Fenney J	Pte	29609	16th	27/09/18	Vis-en-Artois Memorial
Fermor C	Pte	22387	14th	04/10/17	Tyne Cot Cem Belgium
Field F A	Pte	147	14th	23/07/16	Thiepval Memorial
Field J	Pte	231	14th	23/07/16	Thiepval Memorial
Fielding W E	Pte	19316	15th	26/10/17	Tyne Cot Memorial Belgium
Finch H C	Pte	32932	16th	09/10/17	Tyne Cot Memorial Belgium
Finch W	Pte	14/1546	14th	23/07/16	Thiepval Memorial
Findon F L	Pte	68	16th	26/09/16	Thiepval Memorial
Findon R	Sgt	233	14th	23/07/16	Thiepval Memorial
Fisher G E	Pte	154	15th	04/09/16	La Neuville Br
Fisher H B	L/Cpl	393	15th	10/05/16	Habarcq Com
Fitchew H	Pte	16/1599	15th	23/07/16	Thiepval Memorial
Fitter R H	Pte	16/1596	16th	22/09/16	Grove Town
Fitzpatrick T	Pte	32803	15th	25/10/17	Tyne Cot Memorial Belgium
Flannigan F D	Pte	33218	15th	26/10/17	Tyne Cot Memorial Belgium
Flavell D C	Pte	242262	15th	26/10/17	Tyne Cot Memorial Belgium
Flavell H S	Pte	1186	15th	23/07/16	Thiepval Memorial
Fletcher G W	Pte	5215	16th	01/09/18	Favreuil Br
Fletcher J E	L/Cpl	478	15th	04/06/16	Faubourg D'Amiens
Fletcher J W	Pte	16301	14th	24/10/17	Tyne Cot Memorial Belgium
Fletcher R V	Pte	646	14th	11/06/16	Faubourg D'Amiens
Floyd A H	Pte	1644	16th	26/04/18	Aval Wood Mil Cem
Flynn H A	Pte	1439	14th	05/08/16	St Sever Cem, Rouen
Ford A J	Pte	21336	14th	26/10/17	Tyne Cot Memorial Belgium
Ford C	Pte	22364	16th	27/09/18	Vis-en-Artois Memorial
Ford E	Pte	30166	14th	03/09/16	Delville Wood
Ford H	Cpl	4617	16th	27/09/18	Vis-en-Artois Memorial
Ford J F	Pte	1064	15th	29/05/16	Abbeville Com
Fortin E O	Pte	571	16th	25/05/16	Faubourg D'Amiens
Foster A	Pte	32843	15th	14/04/18	Ploegsteert Memorial Belgium
Foster A	Pte	27679	16th	23/10/18	Delsaux Farm
Foster F	Pte	966	15th	23/05/17	Faubourg D'Amiens
Foster H	Pte	16/2005	15th	05/05/17	Arras Memorial
Foulks A	Pte	37848	15th	27/09/18	Vis-en-Artois Memorial
Fox A A	L/Cpl	17614	14th	27/09/18	Fifteen Ravine Br
Foy R	Cpl	32607	15th	03/10/17	Tyne Cot Memorial Belgium
France H G	Pte	921	15th	24/05/16	Habarcq Com
Francis A	Pte	238048	16th	23/08/18	Adanac Mil
Franklin A	L/Cpl	8548	15th	28/08/16	Thiepval Memorial
Franklin A W	Pte	15/1497	15th	04/06/16	Faubourg D'Amiens
Franklin F C	Pte	14/1745	14th	30/10/20	Yardley Cem B'ham
Franklin H E	Pte	43277	14th	26/10/17	Tyne Cot Memorial Belgium
Freeman S	Pte	19581	15th	09/05/17	Arras Memorial
Freeth E	Pte	28594	15th	21/04/17	Arras Memorial
Freman G	Pte	1247	15th	03/09/16	Delville Wood
French A G	2nd Lt		15th	23/05/17	Arras Memorial
French A W	Pte	23458	16th	14/05/17	Arras Memorial
French J	Pte	15057	15th	26/10/17	Tyne Cot Memorial Belgium
French W A	Pte	40651	15th	28/06/18	Merville Com Cem Ext
Friend D F	Pte	18270	15th	25/05/17	Duisans Br
Froggatt G E	Pte	1441	14th	23/07/16	Thiepval Memorial
Frost J	Pte	18052	14th	09/05/17	Aubigny Com Cem
Fry F C	Pte	260238	16th	27/09/18	Fifteen Ravine Br
Fry H	Pte	36038	16th	23/08/18	Adanac Mil
Fuidge J C	Pte	30135	15th	24/09/16	Guards Cem
Fuller T C	Pte	43669	14th	17/09/18	Metz-en-Couture Com Br Ext
Gabriel H M	Pte	1155	14th	30/07/16	Thiepval Memorial
Gale V	Pte	28471	14th	08/05/17	Arras Memorial
Galtress G E	Pte	32756	15th	25/10/17	Tyne Cot Memorial Belgium
Gamble L E	Pte	34106	14th	26/10/17	Hooge Crater Belgium
Gandy J	Pte	325163	15th	24/08/18	Ovillers Mil Cem
Gardner A J	Pte	15/1593	16th	20/04/17	La Chaudiere Mil
Gardner J	Pte	27691	14th	21/05/17	Bois-Carre Br Cem
Gardner W	Pte	9656	14th	11/09/16	Thiepval Memorial
Garner E	Pte	16/1496	14th	30/07/16	Thiepval Memorial
Garner G	Pte	17393	14th	02/10/17	Tyne Cot Memorial Belgium
Garner P A	Pte	7	14th	23/07/16	Thiepval Memorial
Garratt H W	Pte	896	14th	23/07/16	Thiepval Memorial
Garrett D	Pte	22414	16th	23/12/17	Mont Huon Mil Cem
Gasser F J	L/Cpl	27641	16th	29/09/18	Vis-en-Artois Memorial
Genders T A	Pte	28537	16th	30/04/17	Bruay Com Cem Ext
George A L	2nd Lt		15th	14/04/18	Tannay British Cem
George J J	Pte	18049	14th	11/11/17	Tyne Cot Memorial Belgium
George J W	Pte	30311	14th	03/09/16	Thiepval Memorial
Georgeson G F	Pte	36041	16th	01/09/18	Favreuil Br
German W L	Pte	329	16th	09/10/17	Tyne Cot Memorial Belgium
Ghent J E	Pte	20478	15th	28/06/18	Ploegsteert Memorial Belgium
Gibbon C	Pte	1336	15th	04/06/16	Faubourg D'Amiens
Gibbon E	Pte	21134	16th	03/09/16	Thiepval Memorial
Gibbons H	Pte	705	15th	30/08/16	Thiepval Memorial
Gibbs E L	L/Cpl	34768	16th	05/08/18	Longuenesse Souvenir Cem
Gibbs H S	Pte	1231	16th	27/07/17	A.I.F. Burial Ground
Gibbs W	Pte	16/1359	16th	23/01/16	Citadel New Mil
Gibson A	Pte	996	15th	29/08/16	Thiepval Memorial
Gilbert G	Pte	389	15th	04/06/16	Faubourg D'Amiens
Gilks A	Cpl	17611	15th	07/03/17	Longuenesse Souvenir Cem
Gilks F	Pte	21922	14th	13/04/18	Ploegsteert Memorial Belgium
Gill F W	Pte	330744	15th	10/10/17	Voormezeele Enc 1 & 2 Belg.
Gillmore D H	L/Cpl	18893	16th	12/05/17	Barlin Com Cem
Gilroy W	Pte	28441	14th	26/08/18	Mory-Abbey Mil Cem
Gittins C R	Pte	536	15th	04/06/16	Faubourg D'Amiens
Given S J	Sgt	906	14th	11/09/16	Serre Road Cem No.2
Glover L F	Pte	615	14th	01/08/16	Heilly Station
Glover W	Pte	22433	16th	17/10/17	Etaples Mil
Glydon R	Pte	1191	14th	23/07/16	Thiepval Memorial
Glynn T N	Pte	22749	16th	09/10/17	Tyne Cot Memorial Belgium
Godderidge J W	Pte	23716	16th	09/10/17	Tyne Cot Memorial Belgium
Godfrey H	Pte	16/1673	15th	09/05/17	Arras Memorial
Godfrey R C	Pte	18401	15th	09/09/16	St Sever Cem, Rouen
Godwin A J	Pte	21350	15th	28/07/17	Roclincourt Mil Cem
Golding T	Pte	12009	16th	09/10/17	Tyne Cot Cem Belgium
Goldsmith F T	Pte	28400	14th	27/06/17	Orchard Dump Cem
Goodall H	L/Cpl	246	15th	03/09/16	Thiepval Memorial
Goodby H	Sgt	578	16th	14/04/17	La Chaudiere Mil
Goodchild W	Sgt	402	14th	06/05/17	Orchard Dump Cem
Gopsill B G	Pte	11	15th	16/12/16	Huddersfield Cem UK
Gorman G F	2nd Lt		14th	30/07/16	Thiepval Memorial
Gossage T	Pte	242395	15th	26/10/17	Hooge Crater Belgium
Gossage W W	Pte	1200	15th	04/06/16	Faubourg D'Amiens
Goswell T E	Pte	32538	15th	26/10/17	Hooge Crater Belgium
Gough F	Pte	15/1583	15th	03/09/16	Thiepval Memorial
Gough R I	Captain		15th	14/10/16	St Sever Cem, Rouen
Graham T	Pte	48270	16th	23/08/18	Vis-en-Artois Memorial
Grainger W H	Pte	18045	14th	13/04/18	Ploegsteert Memorial Belgium
Graley J	Pte	18172	14th	03/09/16	Thiepval Memorial
Granger V H F	Pte	33159	15th	27/09/18	Gouzeaucourt New Br
Grant J W	Pte	35284	16th	23/08/18	Gommecourt Br
Gratton W L	Pte	1420	15th	23/07/16	Heilly Station
Gray A P	Pte	36421	14th	27/09/18	Gouzeaucourt New Br
Gray V L J	Pte	241787	15th	09/05/17	Arras Memorial
Grazier F C	Pte	1136	15th	09/05/17	Orchard Dump Cem
Greasley D J	Cpl	870	15th	15/12/15	Cerisy-Gailly Mil
Greaves E J	Pte	28473	14th	26/10/17	Tyne Cot Memorial Belgium
Greaves R J	Sgt	14/1683	15th	23/07/16	Thiepval Memorial
Greaves W F G	Pte	14/1252	15th	04/06/16	Faubourg D'Amiens
Green A	Pte	16883	15th	03/09/16	Thiepval Memorial
Green A	L/Cpl	1552	15th	03/07/17	Roclincourt Mil Cem
Green A H	Pte	28531	16th	09/10/17	Hooge Crater Belgium
Green A J	L/Cpl	16/1667	15th	26/10/17	Tyne Cot Memorial Belgium
Green A P	Pte	205	14th	23/07/16	Thiepval Memorial
Green H	Pte	1205	16th	24/07/16	Thiepval Memorial
Green J	Pte	1165	14th	22/07/16	Thiepval Memorial
Green J	Pte	27983	14th	04/10/17	Tyne Cot Memorial Belgium
Green N F	Pte	606	14th	23/07/16	Thiepval Memorial
Green R C	Pte	32456	14th	26/10/17	Tyne Cot Memorial Belgium
Greenfield C R	Pte	23654	16th	21/08/18	Adanac Mil
Greenhalgh H	Pte	14/1663	16th	03/09/16	Thiepval Memorial
Greenhouse J	Pte	28062	14th	08/05/17	Arras Memorial
Greenlees H	Pte	1085	15th	04/06/16	Faubourg D'Amiens
Greenwood F	Pte	30312	14th	20/05/18	Morbecque British Cem
Greenwood H S	2nd Lt		14th	23/07/16	Caterpillar Valley
Greenwood J L	Pte	27663	16th	10/05/17	Arras Memorial
Grew W E	2nd Lt		16th	07/10/17	Tyne Cot Memorial Belgium
Griffin J W	Pte	34190	15th	26/10/17	Hooge Crater Belgium
Griffin T E	Pte	22678	16th	14/03/17	Cambrin Mil
Griffin W G	L/Cpl	16/1572	16th	18/10/17	Courtrai Com, Belgium
Griffiths F T	Pte	236	15th	25/10/14	Witton Cem B'ham
Griffiths G J	Pte	15/1528	15th	23/07/16	Thiepval Memorial
Griffiths T	Pte	36543	14th	27/09/18	Fifteen Ravine Br
Griffiths W A	Pte	48264	16th	08/10/18	Cardiff Cem UK
Grimes A S	L/Cpl	834	16th	03/09/16	Thiepval Memorial
Grimes L C	Pte	609	14th	30/07/16	Thiepval Memorial
Gripton T L	Pte	15/1614	16th	10/10/17	Tyne Cot Memorial Belgium
Groom E	L/Cpl	17930	15th	29/07/17	Duisans Br
Grosvenor C	Pte	16797	15th	18/04/17	Boulogne Eastern Cem
Grove F W	Sgt	331	16th	01/01/16	Citadel New Mil
Groves A E	Pte	22562	16th	12/05/17	Caberet Rouge
Groves J W	L/Cpl	200491	16th	06/09/18	Euston Road
Grunsell G A	Cpl	396	15th	13/06/16	Faubourg D'Amiens
Guest W	L/Sgt	30086	16th	26/08/16	Orchard Dump Cem
Gulliver A	Pte	21122	16th	06/10/17	Tyne Cot Memorial Belgium
Gunter W E J	Pte	18298	14th	04/10/17	Tyne Cot Memorial Belgium
Gurden E E	Pte	20308	16th	13/05/17	Aubigny Com Cem
Gurney G T	L/Cpl	1617	15th	27/09/18	Gouzeaucourt New Br
Hackett A	Pte	1202	14th	08/12/15	Carnoy Mil
Haden W	Pte	1541	14th	13/05/16	Faubourg D'Amiens
Haggett T	Pte	27666	16th	15/04/17	La Chaudiere Mil
Haigh H	Pte	656	14th	08/05/17	Arras Memorial
Haines A C	Pte	32991	15th	26/10/17	Tyne Cot Memorial Belgium
Hale C W	L/Cpl	586	16th	25/07/16	Thiepval Memorial
Halford A	Pte	882	16th	03/09/16	Thiepval Memorial
Halford S A	Pte	16433	14th	03/09/16	Thiepval Memorial
Hall E	Pte	17023	14th	08/05/17	Arras Memorial
Hall F H	L/Cpl	907	14th	23/07/16	Caterpillar Valley
Hall J	Pte	16978	14th	05/09/16	St Sever Cem, Rouen
Hall J W	Pte	43278	14th	25/05/18	Aire Com
Hall T	Pte	1159	14th	31/12/15	Carnoy Mil
Hall T	Pte	1172	15th	03/09/16	Dive Copse Br

Hall W	Pte	48428	16th	14/10/18	Romeries Com Cem Ext
Hall W G	Pte	28633	15th	26/10/17	Tyne Cot Memorial Belgium
Hallgarth A	Pte	15/1590	16th	03/09/16	Thiepval Memorial
Hambidge E	Pte	1558	15th	08/09/16	La Neuville Br
Hamilton D J	Pte	35714	16th	15/06/18	Tannay British Cem
Hamlet J D	Pte	260357	14th	26/10/17	Tyne Cot Memorial Belgium
Hammett R H	Pte	1833	16th	25/09/16	Newport (Christ'ch) Cem UK
Hammond A D	Pte	18776	14th	13/04/18	Ploegsteert Memorial Belgium
Hammond A H	Pte	238051	14th	27/09/18	Gouzeaucourt New Br
Hammond B	Pte	30313	14th	25/12/16	Brown's Rd Mil, Festubert
Hancock F S	Pte	17055	15th	03/09/16	Thiepval Memorial
Hancox J F	Pte	25543	14th	14/04/18	Ploegsteert Memorial Belgium
Hancox J T	Pte	35968	15th	24/08/18	Vis-en-Artois Memorial
Hand H	Pte	1928	14th	30/08/16	Flatiron Copse
Handley J	Pte	1279	14th	26/07/16	Heilly Station
Hands G E J	Pte	22375	16th	30/06/17	Arras Memorial
Hands R	Pte	41	16th	27/04/16	Faubourg D'Amiens
Hanks G H	L/Cpl	85	15th	05/10/17	Tyne Cot Memorial Belgium
Hannigan D	Pte	34094	14th	28/10/17	Lijssenthoek Mil Belgium
Hanson T R	L/Cpl	380	14th	23/07/16	Caterpillar Valley
Hardiman J B	Pte	50652	14th	08/07/18	Tannay British Cem
Hardman F H	Pte	18312	15th	03/09/16	Thiepval Memorial
Hardman W J	Pte	242403	15th	27/10/17	Lijssenthoek Mil Belgium
Harker F	Pte	27360	14th	27/09/18	Fifteen Ravine Br
Harland A E	Pte	6	14th	23/07/16	Thiepval Memorial
Harling C	Pte	16762	15th	24/04/17	Arras Memorial
Harnett J H	Pte	32540	15th	16/10/18	Etaples Mil
Harnett W S	Pte	18729	15th	24/09/16	Guards Cem
Harper F	Pte	15081	16th	01/09/18	Favreuil Br
Harper H W	L/Sgt	17912	15th	21/04/17	La Chaudiere Mil
Harper J	Pte	23568	15th	09/05/17	Arras Memorial
Harris A G	Pte	37823	15th	13/04/18	Ploegsteert Memorial Belgium
Harris F	Sgt	32460	14th	15/09/18	Metz-en-Couture Com Br Ext
Harris F W	Pte	17397	15th	23/07/16	Thiepval Memorial
Harris G	L/Cpl	341	16th	16/04/17	La Chaudiere Mil
Harris J	Pte	30098	16th	03/09/16	Thiepval Memorial
Harris S G	L/Cpl	267938	16th	26/10/18	Mont Huon Mil Cem
Harris T H	Pte	14/1631	14th	23/07/16	Thiepval Memorial
Harris W G	L/Cpl	1884	15th	28/10/17	Lijssenthoek Mil Belgium
Harrison W	Pte	35984	15th	15/09/18	Serre Road Cem No.2
Harrison W E	Pte	15/1637	14th	04/02/17	Gorre Br & Indian
Harrop A R	Pte	22636	15th	27/09/18	Gouzeaucourt New Br
Hart H E	Pte	35983	15th	30/08/18	Vaulx Hill Cem
Hart T	Pte	203701	15th	14/04/18	Ploegsteert Memorial Belgium
Hartland H	Pte	37435	14th	08/07/18	Tannay British Cem
Hartland W	Cpl	1191	15th	31/10/17	Tyne Cot Memorial Belgium
Hartland W H	Pte	1109	15th	07/11/17	Bedford House Enc 4
Hartley R	Pte	11585	14th	25/10/17	Tyne Cot Memorial Belgium
Hartwell H G	Pte	244152	16th	25/04/18	Tannay British Cem
Harvey F	Pte	17450	16th	02/09/16	Thiepval Memorial
Harvey F W	Pte	17110	16th	13/10/18	Vis-en-Artois Memorial
Harvey W J	Pte	50655	14th	27/08/18	Vis-en-Artois Memorial
Harwell W	Pte	1650	14th	23/07/16	Caterpillar Valley
Harwood W	Pte	14/1630	14th	23/07/16	Thiepval Memorial
Hastings C J	L/Cpl	917	14th	30/07/16	Caterpillar Valley
Hastings E H	Pte	16/1711	16th	24/07/16	Thiepval Memorial
Hawcroft G	Pte	29907	14th	26/10/17	Tyne Cot Cem Belgium
Hawker P C	Pte	15/1636	14th	23/07/16	Thiepval Memorial
Hawkes A V	Pte	22438	15th	27/09/18	Gouzeaucourt New Br
Hawkes E W	Pte	400	15th	04/06/16	Faubourg D'Amiens
Hawkins G	Pte	15/1464	15th	03/09/16	Combles Com
Hawkins T	Pte	1620	15th	03/09/16	Delville Wood
Hawley G	Pte	245150	16th	02/09/18	Favreuil Br
Hawthorne H W	Cpl	235259	15th	04/07/18	Aire Com
Hayes J R	Pte	26642	15th	24/08/18	Adanac Mil
Haynes A	Pte	17294	15th	27/08/16	La Neuville Br
Haynes C	L/Cpl	408	14th	08/10/16	Mont Huon Mil Cem
Haynes E J	Pte	14/1651	14th	23/07/16	Thiepval Memorial
Haynes J H	Pte	18208	16th	02/07/17	Roclincourt Mil Cem
Haynes J W	Pte	30209	14th	14/04/18	Ploegsteert Memorial Belgium
Hayward F	Pte	32936	16th	09/10/17	Tyne Cot Memorial Belgium
Haywood S J	Pte	399	15th	04/06/16	Faubourg D'Amiens
Hazlewood J W	Pte	169	16th	09/10/17	Tyne Cot Memorial Belgium
Heafield H C	Pte	15/1597	14th	23/07/16	Thiepval Memorial
Heafield J E	Pte	15/1598	16th	23/08/18	Gommecourt Br
Hearn H	Pte	30175	14th	07/05/17	Arras Memorial
Heath A	Sgt	6843	14th	04/10/17	Delville Wood
Heath A H	Cpl	409	14th	23/07/16	Caterpillar Valley
Heath J	Pte	1594	14th	29/08/16	Corbie Com Ext
Heath W R	Pte	242	15th	03/09/16	Thiepval Memorial
Heathcote H H	Pte	30258	14th	24/09/16	Thiepval Memorial
Heathfield W	Pte	13406	14th	30/07/16	Thiepval Memorial
Heaven G F V	Captain		16th	25/01/16	Citadel New Mil
Hebbert J W	Cpl	112	14th	20/07/16	Dive Copse Br
Hedge H A	Pte	18995	15th	12/04/18	Ploegsteert Memorial Belgium
Hedley W	Cpl	32796	15th	28/10/17	Etaples Mil
Hemming G H	Pte	15/1395	16th	14/05/17	Arras Memorial
Hemming J	Pte	22776	15th	09/05/17	Arras Memorial
Hendra P	Pte	1766	15th	04/06/16	Arras Memorial
Henning W	Pte	18656	15th	09/05/17	Nine Elms Mil Cem
Henton C	Pte	16787	15th	09/09/16	Ste Marie Cem, Le Harve
Herbert L S	Pte	27668	16th	14/05/17	Roclincourt Valley Cem
Herbert R T	Pte	8013	14th	05/10/17	Tyne Cot Memorial Belgium
Herrick H D	Sgt	635	14th	23/07/16	Thiepval Memorial
Herriman G	L/Cpl	1136	14th	30/07/16	Thiepval Memorial
Herring J I	Pte	18073	14th	03/09/16	Thiepval Memorial
Hession C W	Pte	4475	15th	14/04/18	Ploegsteert Memorial Belgium
Hewett S H P	2nd Lt		14th	22/07/16	Thiepval Memorial
Hewitt A	Pte	1613	15th	04/06/16	Arras Memorial
Hewitt E J	Pte	2772	14th	27/02/17	Brown's Rd Mil, Festubert
Hewitt G A	Pte	977	15th	23/05/16	Faubourg D'Amiens
Hewitt W H	Cpl	413	14th	23/07/16	Caterpillar Valley
Hewson E S	Pte	30344	14th	03/09/16	Thiepval Memorial
Heywood W T	Cpl	36459	16th	02/09/18	Bailleul Rd East Cem
Hiatt J C	Pte	16331	15th	14/09/16	Boisguillaume Com Cem
Hibell A R	Pte	16/1445	14th	06/08/16	Niederzwehren Cem Germany
Hicklin L	L/Cpl	36399	16th	24/08/18	Adanac Mil
Hickman I	Pte	28569	15th	05/10/17	Tyne Cot Memorial Belgium
Hicks L	Pte	893	16th	10/04/16	Faubourg D'Amiens
Hildage P S	Pte	260421	16th	27/09/18	Vis-en-Artois Memorial
Hill A	Pte	2746	15th	09/05/17	Arras Memorial
Hill A B	2nd Lt		16th	27/09/18	Gouzeaucourt New Br
Hill E C	Cpl	371	14th	23/07/16	Thiepval Memorial
Hill F E	Pte	35296	14th	27/09/18	Vis-en-Artois Memorial
Hill G	Pte	19175	14th	04/10/17	Tyne Cot Memorial Belgium
Hill G	Pte	36472	16th	01/09/18	Favreuil Br
Hill JH	Pte	16/1712	16th	27/07/16	Thiepval Memorial
Hills R F	Pte	1096	15th	09/03/16	Caberet Rouge
Hilton D T	Pte	9857	14th	03/09/16	Thiepval Memorial
Hirons J	Pte	9056	15th	13/09/16	La Neuville Br
Hirons W T	Pte	16763	14th	14/04/18	Ploegsteert Memorial Belgium
Hitchings A C	L/Cpl	913	15th	23/07/16	Thiepval Memorial
Hitchman F P	L/Cpl	16/1812	15th	06/10/17	Godewaersvelde Br
Hobbs W H B	Pte	28570	15th	09/05/17	Arras Memorial
Hobson E C	2nd Lt		15th	20/05/17	Cologne Southern, Germany
Hodes F P	Lieut		14th	24/07/16	Warloy-Baillon Com Cem ext
Hodges P W	Pte	32865	16th	09/10/17	Tyne Cot Memorial Belgium
Hodgetts E H	Sgt	903	15th	27/09/18	Gouzeaucourt New Br
Hodgkins H	Pte	1636	16th	04/10/16	Smethwick (Uplands) Cem UK
Hodkinson H	Pte	36404	16th	23/08/18	Adanac Mil
Hodson P C	Pte	29908	16th	08/10/17	Tyne Cot Memorial Belgium
Holbrooke F T	Pte	1312	15th	18/04/16	Faubourg D'Amiens
Holden S N	Pte	693	14th	31/08/16	Flatiron Copse
Holdstock W	Sgt	32451	15th	26/10/17	Tyne Cot Memorial Belgium
Holland A	Pte	36411	16th	01/09/18	Favreuil Br
Hollick E	Pte	35982	15th	29/06/18	Ploegsteert Memorial Belgium
Hollins H	Pte	20633	16th	09/10/17	Tyne Cot Memorial Belgium
Hollis C A	Sgt	920	15th	28/06/18	Ploegsteert Memorial Belgium
Holme J E	Captain		16th	09/10/17	Tyne Cot Memorial Belgium
Holmes J F W	Pte	641	14th	31/08/16	La Neuville Br
Holt E	Pte	506	15th	03/09/16	Thiepval Memorial
Holt FL	Cpl	884	16th	26/09/16	Thiepval Memorial
Holt N	Pte	16397	15th	08/09/16	Thiepval Memorial
Holt S	Pte	1187	15th	04/06/16	Arras Memorial
Holtom J H	Pte	1189	15th	30/08/16	La Neuville Br
Homer B H	Pte	417	14th	23/07/16	Caterpillar Valley
Homer C J	Cpl	87	15th	15/06/16	Faubourg D'Amiens
Honeywill W R	Cpl	12373	15th	03/11/17	Boulogne Eastern Cem
Hooper A	Pte	34140	15th	26/10/17	Tyne Cot Memorial Belgium
Hooper H E	Pte	36042	16th	27/09/18	Vis-en-Artois Memorial
Hooper J	L/Cpl	32687	15th	26/10/17	Tyne Cot Memorial Belgium
Hooper L G	Pte	33798	15th	28/06/18	Ploegsteert Memorial Belgium
Hopkin F H	Pte	30316	14th	13/04/18	Aire Com
Hopkins A J	L/Cpl	3241	16th	16/04/17	Arras Memorial
Hopkins B P	Sgt	672	14th	11/09/16	St Sever Cem, Rouen
Hopkins H G	Pte	204	15th	15/06/16	Faubourg D'Amiens
Hopkins J S	Sgt	14/1570	14th	26/10/17	Tyne Cot Memorial Belgium
Hopkins J W	Pte	14/1568	15th	23/07/16	Thiepval Memorial
Hopkins W F	Pte	16087	15th	07/09/16	Corbie Com Ext
Horne R	Pte	27361	16th	02/09/18	Bailleul Rd East Cem
Horton A	Sgt	225	15th	21/12/15	Cerisy-Gailly Mil
Horton F H	Pte	24186	15th	30/06/18	Aire Com
Horton H F	Cpl	79	15th	03/09/16	Thiepval Memorial
Hough J	Pte	28378	15th	09/05/17	Arras Memorial
Houghton P	Pte	36536	14th	17/09/18	Vis-en-Artois Memorial
Hoult D G	Pte	33704	14th	14/04/18	Ploegsteert Memorial Belgium
Howard G	L/Cpl	330589	15th	26/10/17	Tyne Cot Memorial Belgium
Howard H L	Pte	32857	15th	26/10/17	Hooge Crater Belgium
Howe C F	Pte	599	16th	03/09/16	Thiepval Memorial
Howe J	Sgt	16003	14th	29/06/18	Tannay British Cem
Howell A	Pte	15/1635	15th	09/05/17	Arras Memorial
Howell D	Pte	113	14th	25/03/16	Caberet Rouge
Howells H H	Pte	32543	14th	05/10/17	Tyne Cot Memorial Belgium
Howes H E	Pte	897	15th	26/09/16	Thiepval Memorial
Howlett W R	Pte	28524	16th	28/06/17	Orchard Dump Cem
Hucker W T	Pte	33703	14th	12/04/18	Ploegsteert Memorial Belgium
Hudson C G	Pte	203491	15th	26/01/18	Giavera Br, Italy
Hudson L C	Pte	912	14th	04/06/16	Faubourg D'Amiens
Hudson W	Pte	17729	14th	26/10/17	Tyne Cot Memorial Belgium
Hughes A	Sgt	1156	16th	06/10/17	Tyne Cot Memorial Belgium
Hughes C H	L/Cpl	414	15th	04/06/16	Faubourg D'Amiens
Hughes C W	Captain		14th	01/10/18	Grevillers Br
Hughes FJ	Pte	16/1434	16th	09/11/16	Le Touret Mil
Hughes H	Pte	16350	15th	29/06/18	Aire Com
Hughes J M C	Lieut		16th	09/10/17	Tyne Cot Cem Belgium
Hughes W	Pte	32546	14th	05/10/17	Tyne Cot Memorial Belgium
Hughes W	Pte	38424	15th	28/06/18	Ploegsteert Memorial Belgium
Hughes W	Pte	36044	16th	23/08/18	Vis-en-Artois Memorial
Hulbert H H S	Pte	1292	14th	13/01/17	Bethune Town Cem
Humber W T	Pte	16159	14th	30/07/16	Thiepval Memorial
Humphries J	Pte	364	16th	21/09/16	Grove Town
Hundy W J	L/Cpl	1	15th	21/05/16	Faubourg D'Amiens
Hunter J F	Pte	29911	14th	06/07/18	Terlincthun British Cem
Huntley A W E	Pte	330222	14th	03/05/18	Les Baraques Mil
Huntley S	Pte	1672	16th	27/07/16	Thiepval Memorial
Hurley V H	Pte	15/1609	14th	23/07/16	Thiepval Memorial
Hurrell S	Pte	1350	14th	23/07/16	Thiepval Memorial
Hutchence F	Pte	12562	15th	09/05/17	Arras Memorial
Hutchinson H J	Pte	682	14th	30/07/16	London Cem
Hutton W	Sgt	34156	15th	27/09/18	Gouzeaucourt New Br
Hyde H W	2nd Lt		16th	20/05/16	Faubourg D'Amiens
Hyett A	Pte	33163	16th	23/08/18	Vis-en-Artois Memorial
Iddon R	Pte	29529	16th	20/10/18	Delsaux Farm
Iggulden W L	L/Cpl	952	15th	24/09/16	Thiepval Memorial
Illingworth C	L/Cpl	74	15th	03/09/16	Thiepval Memorial
Ince A	Pte	325054	16th	20/07/18	Tannay British Cem
Ingle D V	Pte	30199	14th	25/06/17	Arras Memorial
Ingram L	Pte	266513	15th	29/05/18	Aire Com
Ireland G	Pte	369	16th	29/06/17	Aubigny Com Cem
Ireland W S	Pte	43236	16th	10/02/18	Giavera Br, Italy
Ivens M E	CSM	607	16th	03/09/16	Thiepval Memorial
Izard F T	Pte	925	14th	04/10/17	Tyne Cot Cem Belgium
Izon E G	Captain		14th	27/09/18	Achiet le Grand Com Ext
Izzard R E	Pte	34031	15th	30/08/18	Vaulx Hill Cem
Jackman G	L/Cpl	17815	14th	12/04/18	Ploegsteert Memorial Belgium
Jackson A E	Sgt	14/1487	14th	27/09/18	Vis-en-Artois Memorial
Jackson A E	Pte	17668	14th	11/11/17	Tyne Cot Memorial Belgium
Jackson A G	Pte	505	15th	03/09/16	Delville Wood
Jackson C Y	L/Cpl	1034	14th	23/07/16	Thiepval Memorial
Jackson H	L/Cpl	1120	15th	30/07/16	St Sever Cem, Rouen
Jackson L	2nd Lt		14th	23/07/16	Thiepval Memorial
Jackson P T	Pte	168	14th	22/07/16	Thiepval Memorial
Jacob R G	L/Cpl	33242	16th	23/08/18	Adanac Mil
Jacobi W T	2nd Lt		14th	21/10/16	Norwood Cem UK
Jacobs I E	Pte	16/1508	15th	23/07/16	Caterpillar Valley
James A	Pte	201738	15th	26/10/17	Tyne Cot Memorial Belgium
James C H	L/Cpl	48288	16th	23/08/18	Vis-en-Artois Memorial
James H	Pte	200442	16th	09/10/17	Hooge Crater Belgium
James J	Pte	17116	14th	07/05/17	Orchard Dump Cem
James J M	Pte	171	16th	23/01/16	Citadel New Mil
James S W	Pte	35151	16th	02/09/18	Bailleul Rd East Cem
James T	Pte	16251	14th	03/06/17	Orchard Dump Cem
James W	Pte	34147	15th	26/10/17	Tyne Cot Memorial Belgium
James W H	Pte	36053	16th	21/08/18	Vis-en-Artois Memorial
Jarratt C A	Pte	15/1347	14th	10/06/17	Orchard Dump Cem
Jarrett F	Pte	48418	16th	23/08/18	Vis-en-Artois Memorial
Jarrett T	Pte	10018	14th	03/09/16	Thiepval Memorial
Jarvis E W	Sgt	523	15th	09/05/17	Arras Memorial
Jarvis H J	Pte	50463	14th	28/08/18	Vis-en-Artois Memorial
Jarvis J T	Sgt	16/1688	14th	03/09/16	Delville Wood
Jarvis W E	Cpl	51	16th	17/09/18	Canadian Cem 2
Jarvis W E	Cpl	51	16th	17/09/18	Haplincourt Com
Jeeves P	Pte	611	15th	22/07/16	Thiepval Memorial
Jeffery F	Pte	9956	14th	30/07/16	Thiepval Memorial
Jeffrey J W	Pte	22763	15th	26/10/17	Tyne Cot Memorial Belgium
Jeffs G O	Pte	17095	14th	30/07/16	Thiepval Memorial
Jeffs W E C	Pte	7273	16th	23/08/18	Vis-en-Artois Memorial
Jelfs G W	L/Cpl	1313	15th	04/06/16	Faubourg D'Amiens
Jenkins J R	Pte	631	14th	24/01/16	St Sever Cem, Rouen
Jenkinson A A	Pte	372	16th	27/07/16	Thiepval Memorial
Jenkinson T	Cpl	2795	16th	09/10/17	Tyne Cot Memorial Belgium
Jenks W I J	Pte	1626	16th	14/05/18	Aire Com
Jennings F	Pte	22515	15th	28/06/18	Ploegsteert Memorial Belgium
Jennings G H	L/Sgt	39766	16th	27/09/18	Vis-en-Artois Memorial
Jennings P D	Pte	375	16th	27/07/16	Thiepval Memorial
Jervis J S	Cpl	823	15th	25/07/16	Dantzig Alley Br
Jinks J	Pte	16722	14th	13/04/18	Ploegsteert Memorial Belgium
Jinks P G	Pte	1369	15th	04/06/16	Faubourg D'Amiens
Jinks W M	Pte	30178	14th	07/05/17	Orchard Dump Cem
Johnson A E	Pte	872	14th	30/07/16	Thiepval Memorial
Johnson C H	Sgt	222	15th	05/10/17	Tyne Cot Memorial Belgium
Johnson E E V	Pte	9137	14th	03/09/16	Thiepval Memorial
Johnson F	Pte	22693	16th	09/10/17	Tyne Cot Memorial Belgium
Johnson F C	Sgt	1041	15th	01/07/17	Roclincourt Mil Cem
Johnson F C	L/Cpl	26955	15th	12/04/18	Ploegsteert Memorial Belgium
Johnson M	Pte	15/1576	16th	03/09/16	Thiepval Memorial
Johnson S H	Pte	1176	16th	25/12/15	Citadel New Mil
Jolliffe L D	Pte	176	14th	23/07/16	Mericourt L'Abbe Com Ext
Jolly F W	Pte	1492	15th	11/08/16	St Sever Cem, Rouen
Jolly J	Sgt	28497	16th	23/08/18	Adanac Mil
Jones A	L/Cpl	174	14th	23/07/16	Serre Road Cem No.2
Jones A	Pte	16/1646	16th	26/09/16	Thiepval Memorial
Jones A E C	Pte	987	15th	03/09/16	Thiepval Memorial
Jones A V	Pte	1450	15th	24/09/16	Corbie Com Ext
Jones C J	Cpl	1134	14th	22/07/16	Delville Wood
Jones C V	L/Cpl	1135	14th	23/07/16	Thiepval Memorial
Jones E E	L/Cpl	174	16th	03/09/16	Thiepval Memorial
Jones E F	Pte	1757	16th	27/07/16	A.I.F. Burial Ground
Jones F	Pte	1572	14th	23/07/16	Caterpillar Valley
Jones F G	Pte	169	14th	23/07/16	Thiepval Memorial
Jones F W	Pte	1616	16th	03/02/18	Witton Cem B'ham
Jones G A	Cpl	615	16th	26/09/16	A.I.F. Burial Ground
Jones G F	Pte	1397	14th	26/04/17	Aubigny Com Cem
Jones G H	Pte	27714	14th	07/10/17	Godewaersvelde Br
Jones H F	Pte	28649	15th	26/10/17	Tyne Cot Memorial Belgium
Jones H W	Sgt	342	14th	03/09/16	Thiepval Memorial
Jones J B	L/Cpl	18117	16th	26/09/16	Thiepval Memorial
Jones J H	Pte	1577	15th	22/05/17	Faubourg D'Amiens
Jones J S	Sgt	177	16th	10/05/17	Arras Memorial
Jones J S	Pte	30075	16th	01/01/17	Gorre Br & Indian
Jones L W	Pte	1254	14th	23/07/16	Thiepval Memorial
Jones M	Lieut		14th	27/09/18	H.A.C. Cem
Jones N E	L/Cpl	831	14th	22/07/16	Thiepval Memorial
Jones R	Pte	2281	14th	14/04/18	Ploegsteert Memorial Belgium
Jones R	Pte	16/1627	16th	25/07/16	Thiepval Memorial
Jones R A	Major		15th	21/05/16	Faubourg D'Amiens
Jones S C	L/Cpl	917	16th	30/11/16	Handsworth Cem B'ham
Jones S F	Pte	619	16th	19/04/21	Handsworth Cem B'ham
Jones T E	Pte	22703	16th	09/10/17	Tyne Cot Memorial Belgium
Jones T J	Pte	22805	14th	09/10/17	Tyne Cot Memorial Belgium
Jones W	Pte	1379	14th	23/07/16	Thiepval Memorial
Jones W R	L/Cpl	109	14th	23/07/16	Caterpillar Valley
Jordan A L	Pte	1612	15th	20/05/16	Faubourg D'Amiens
Jordan L	Pte	16/2083	14th	23/07/16	Thiepval Memorial
Jordon J G	Pte	32938	16th	09/10/17	Tyne Cot Memorial Belgium
Jordon J V T	Pte	22558	16th	09/10/17	Tyne Cot Memorial Belgium
Joseph A E	2nd Lt		14th	10/05/17	Calais Southern
Joseph E	Sgt	336	14th	23/07/16	Thiepval Memorial
Joyce W	Pte	34476	15th	27/08/18	Achiet le Grand Com Ext
Jump G G	Pte	32703	15th	23/05/18	Aire Com
Kay A S	Pte	428	14th	23/07/16	Caterpillar Valley
Kefford L	Pte	25399	14th	23/04/18	Lille Southern Cem
Keighley J	Pte	621	16th	27/07/16	Thiepval Memorial
Kelly F	Pte	383	16th	16/04/17	Arras Memorial
Kelly R F A	Pte	20324	16th	11/05/17	Barlin Com Cem
Kemp E R	Pte	48369	15th	29/09/18	Grevillers Br
Kemp G	Pte	15281	14th	03/09/16	Thiepval Memorial
Kent S F	Pte	71	15th	30/08/16	Peronne Rd Cem, Maricourt
Kentell I F	Pte	18731	15th	26/09/16	Grove Town
Kenyon A A	Pte	17905	14th	30/07/16	Thiepval Memorial
Kightley S F	Pte	17427	14th	30/07/16	Thiepval Memorial
Killick W	Pte	32549	14th	29/04/18	Tannay British Cem
Kimsey W	Pte	34114	14th	24/10/17	Tyne Cot Memorial Belgium
King A S	Pte	14/1739	15th	04/06/16	Faubourg D'Amiens
King F	Pte	21154	14th	27/09/18	Gouzeaucourt New Br
King F	Pte	1321	16th	24/12/15	Corbie Com
King R	Pte	32825	15th	26/10/17	Tyne Cot Memorial Belgium
Kings E C	Pte	806	15th	23/07/16	Caterpillar Valley
Kingwell W D	Sgt	931	14th	23/03/16	Caberet Rouge
Kirby G F	Pte	1263	14th	23/07/16	Thiepval Memorial
Kirby J S W	Pte	24293	14th	27/09/18	Gouzeaucourt New Br
Kirby R H E	Pte	1111	14th	23/07/16	Thiepval Memorial
Kirkham J	Pte	36491	16th	28/09/18	Vis-en-Artois Memorial
Kisby C	Pte	30215	14th	24/10/17	Tyne Cot Memorial Belgium
Kitchen J M	CSM	1088	14th	16/12/15	Carnoy Mil
Kitely W B	Pte	16889	15th	03/09/16	Delville Wood
Knaggs G	Pte	32837	15th	26/10/17	Hooge Crater Belgium
Kneale F	Pte	30076	16th	03/09/16	Thiepval Memorial
Knibb J H	Pte	1130	16th	16/12/16	Leamington Cem UK
Knight A	Sgt	782	15th	23/07/16	Caterpillar Valley
Knight A J L	L/Cpl	919	16th	27/02/17	Caberet Rouge
Knight R	Pte	48405	16th	23/08/18	Vis-en-Artois Memorial
Knight W G	Pte	36107	14th	08/07/18	Tannay British Cem
Knowles F	L/Cpl	16/1392	16th	03/09/16	Thiepval Memorial
Knowles W E	Pte	35307	14th	29/05/18	Thiennes British Cem
Kyte H	Pte	306744	15th	24/08/18	Adanac Mil
Lafford F C	Pte	27801	16th	10/04/17	Arras Memorial
Lake H C	Pte	1219	14th	23/07/16	Caterpillar Valley

Lamb A F	Pte	22743	16th	19/09/18	Studley (St Mary) UK
Lambert B A	Cpl	57	16th	03/09/16	Thiepval Memorial
Lambert G W H	L/Cpl	33871	16th	29/06/18	Tannay British Cem
Lambert W W	Pte	30147	15th	14/05/17	Aubigny Com Cem
Lamble R G	Pte	943	15th	21/12/16	Bethune Town Cem
Lancaster G	Pte	28640	15th	09/05/17	Arras Memorial
Lander G	Pte	16/1539	16th	23/01/16	Citadel New Mil
Landon J R	Captain		15th	03/09/16	Thiepval Memorial
Lane F J J	Pte	18186	16th	27/09/18	Vis-en-Artois Memorial
Langford A	Pte	18426	14th	30/07/16	Thiepval Memorial
Langstone A H	Pte	16/1741	16th	03/09/16	Thiepval Memorial
Langwell W W	Sgt	631	16th	28/07/16	Heilly Station
Larkins J C	Lieut		15th	04/06/16	Faubourg D'Amiens
Law A	Pte	15/1378	14th	23/07/16	Thiepval Memorial
Lawley J W	Sgt	34227	16th	23/05/18	Tannay British Cem
Lawrence W A	Pte	6350	15th	28/08/16	Delville Wood
Lawson G	Pte	32551	14th	26/10/17	Tyne Cot Memorial Belgium
Lawson G W	Pte	25136	14th	23/08/18	Adanac Mil
Lawton H	Pte	34187	15th	24/08/18	Vis-en-Artois Memorial
Lay A T	Pte	4201	16th	03/09/16	Combles Com
Layton A F	Pte	260417	16th	29/09/18	Metz-en-Couture Com Br Ext
Lea C E	Pte	21121	16th	30/07/17	Arras Memorial
Leafe G E	Pte	20511	15th	09/05/17	Arras Memorial
Leake A E	Pte	15/1630	15th	26/07/16	Etaples Mil
Lebourne H	Pte	18768	15th	24/09/16	Guards Cem
Lediard G H	Pte	1754	14th	03/09/16	Thiepval Memorial
Lee H	Sgt	804	14th	30/04/18	Tannay British Cem
Lee J	Pte	753	16th	03/09/16	Flatiron Copse
Lee J	Pte	387	16th	26/09/16	Thiepval Memorial
Leeding T	Pte	33762	14th	05/05/18	Aire Com
Leeson E R	Pte	1109	14th	23/07/16	Thiepval Memorial
Leigh A G	L/Cpl	420	15th	04/06/16	Faubourg D'Amiens
Leith J	2nd Lt		14th	23/08/18	Adanac Mil
Lennane F	Pte	32733	15th	04/10/17	Tyne Cot Memorial Belgium
Leonard M	Pte	48419	16th	23/08/18	Vis-en-Artois Memorial
Lerrigo W G	Cpl	63	15th	03/09/16	Thiepval Memorial
Lester E S	Pte	18715	15th	09/04/17	Ecoivres Mil
Lewis A E	Pte	634	14th	26/10/17	Tyne Cot Memorial Belgium
Lewis B R	L/Cpl	421	15th	23/07/16	Thiepval Memorial
Lewis E	Pte	186	14th	23/07/16	Caterpillar Valley
Lewis I F	Pte	16/1791	16th	09/10/17	Tyne Cot Memorial Belgium
Leyland T	Pte	34487	15th	27/09/18	Gouzeaucourt New Br
Liddiard B	L/Sgt	931	16th	03/09/16	Delville Wood
Lilley F	Pte	30319	14th	24/09/16	Grove Town
Lilley L P	L/Cpl	30206	14th	25/06/17	Duisans Br
Liminton W E	L/Cpl	21271	14th	08/05/17	Orchard Dump Cem
Limmage G	Pte	30320	14th	14/04/18	Ploegsteert Memorial Belgium
Lincoln W	Pte	30218	14th	03/09/16	Thiepval Memorial
Lindley J	Pte	20368	15th	05/10/17	Outtersteene Com Ext Bailleul
Lister E	Pte	437	14th	23/07/16	Thiepval Memorial
Littleboy W E	Lieut		16th	09/10/17	Hooge Crater Belgium
Livesy R W	Pte	48391	16th	03/10/18	Grevillers Br
Lloyd J	Pte	30381	14th	20/04/18	Haverskerque Br
Lloyd W G	Pte	898	15th	07/03/16	Caberet Rouge
Loam G H	Pte	929	15th	30/08/16	Thiepval Memorial
Lock S V	Pte	260558	14th	26/10/17	Hooge Crater Belgium
Lockington A J	Pte	32861	16th	06/10/18	Mont Huon Mil Cem
Lockwood S A	Pte	16/1408	14th	23/07/16	Caterpillar Valley
Lockyer A H T	L/Cpl	43218	16th	23/08/18	Adanac Mil
Longmore C R	Pte	1223	14th	30/07/16	Thiepval Memorial
Lord F	Pte	15/1607	15th	03/09/16	Thiepval Memorial
Lord F W	Pte	1192	14th	30/07/16	Thiepval Memorial
Lord H C	Pte	16562	14th	03/09/16	Thiepval Memorial
Lovell F H B	Pte	15/1573	16th	27/07/16	Thiepval Memorial
Lovering G S	Pte	235177	16th	17/11/17	Lijssenthoek Mil Belgium
Lowe C E	L/Cpl	937	16th	08/10/17	Tyne Cot Cem Belgium
Lowe J	Pte	260297	16th	15/11/17	Buttes New Br Belgium
Lowe S M	Pte	33850	15th	09/10/17	Godewaersvelde Br
Lucas A	Pte	1413	14th	27/03/16	Faubourg D'Amiens
Lucas H E	Pte	48431	16th	27/09/18	Vis-en-Artois Memorial
Luck H J	Pte	16/1525	16th	25/01/19	Dunstable Cem UK
Ludlow J E	Pte	902	15th	04/06/16	Faubourg D'Amiens
Lunn W	Pte	37894	16th	23/08/18	Adanac Mil
Lunn W	Pte	32942	16th	09/10/17	Tyne Cot Memorial Belgium
Lunnon D	Pte	18507	14th	11/09/16	Corbie Com Ext
Lyon E	Pte	18302	15th	03/09/16	Thiepval Memorial
Lythgoe J W	2nd Lt		14th	23/07/16	Caterpillar Valley
Macauley A	L/Cpl	906	15th	23/07/16	Thiepval Memorial
Machin E	CSM	9243	15th	26/10/17	Tyne Cot Memorial Belgium
Macintosh J	2nd Lt		14th	23/07/16	Thiepval Memorial
Macklin F G	L/Cpl	10957	15th	28/08/16	Delville Wood
Maddocks J A	Lieut		15th	04/06/16	Faubourg D'Amiens
Madge W	Pte	23462	16th	20/03/17	Etaples Mil
Mahady F	Pte	14/1461	14th	30/07/16	Thiepval Memorial
Maley E	Pte	16/1681	15th	09/06/16	Faubourg D'Amiens
Malin F G	L/Sgt	654	16th	26/09/16	Thiepval Memorial
Malin J	Pte	18019	14th	11/09/16	Thiepval Memorial
Malin R	CSM	1030	14th	23/07/16	Thiepval Memorial
Manning H F V	Pte	645	16th	21/11/15	Radford Churchyard UK
Manning J	L/Cpl	16481	14th	30/07/16	Thiepval Memorial
Manning P H	Pte	27613	16th	27/09/18	Vis-en-Artois Memorial
Mansbridge A E	Pte	1563	15th	27/09/18	Gouzeaucourt New Br
Mansell C P	2nd Lt		16th	03/09/16	Thiepval Memorial
Mansfield H	L/Cpl	16500	14th	03/09/16	Thiepval Memorial
Manton A J	Pte	32904	16th	04/10/17	Tyne Cot Memorial Belgium
Margetts A V T	Cpl	50213	16th	23/08/18	Adanac Mil
Marks A F	Pte	34409	14th	26/10/17	Tyne Cot Memorial Belgium
Marley W	Pte	48322	15th	28/08/18	Vis-en-Artois Memorial
Marlow A E	Pte	15/1371	14th	23/07/16	Thiepval Memorial
Marlow H	Pte	34471	14th	16/04/18	Aire Com
Marsh G W	Pte	17293	14th	26/10/17	Tyne Cot Memorial Belgium
Marshall J H	Pte	17740	14th	07/05/17	Orchard Dump Cem
Marshall P	Sgt	638	16th	28/10/17	Bedford House Enc 2
Marshall T	L/Cpl	201899	15th	28/06/18	Ploegsteert Memorial Belgium
Marshall W P	Pte	35311	14th	14/04/18	Ploegsteert Memorial Belgium
Marshall W T	Pte	18018	16th	09/10/17	Hooge Crater Belgium
Martin A J S	Pte	50261	14th	27/09/18	Vis-en-Artois Memorial
Martin E	Pte	34874	16th	27/09/18	Fifteen Ravine Br
Martin F	Pte	32962	16th	27/10/17	Tyne Cot Memorial Belgium
Martin J A	Pte	28408	14th	18/05/17	Orchard Dump Cem
Martin M J	Captain		16th	09/05/17	Roclincourt Mil Cem
Martin W C	Pte	14/1720	14th	23/07/16	Caterpillar Valley
Masey A	Sgt	245148	16th	02/09/18	Bailleul Rd East Cem
Maskrey A V	Pte	1450	15th	24/09/16	Corbie Com Ext
Mason B	Pte	20420	15th	02/07/17	Arras Memorial
Maspero A F	L/Sgt	836	15th	23/05/16	Arras Memorial
Mathews H S	Captain		14th	23/07/16	Caterpillar Valley
Matthews F W	Pte	300117	16th	21/08/18	Gommecourt Br
Matthews W	Pte	48379	16th	23/08/18	Adanac Mil
Matthias A	Pte	32633	16th	23/08/18	Vis-en-Artois Memorial
May W F	Sgt	16630	14th	24/05/18	Aire Com
Maycock A E R	Pte	22748	16th	22/04/17	La Chaudiere Mil
Maycock G T	Sgt	16/1371	16th	26/09/16	Thiepval Memorial
Mayes G E	Pte	951	16th	01/08/16	Heilly Station
Mayhew F H	Pte	50237	16th	27/09/18	Gouzeaucourt New Br
Maylott A O H	Pte	16/922	15th	26/10/17	Tyne Cot Memorial Belgium
Mayrick T	Pte	17806	14th	28/09/16	Bidford Churchyard UK
McCrum J A C	Pte	1370	15th	23/07/16	Heilly Station
McDermid J	Pte	48336	15th	27/09/18	Vis-en-Artois Memorial
McDonald D	Pte	32673	15th	08/10/17	Godewaersvelde Br
McFarland E J	Pte	32820	16th	19/10/18	Romeries Com Cem Ext
McGown H	Pte	34121	14th	11/11/17	Tyne Cot Memorial Belgium
McGrath J N	Pte	34153	15th	14/12/17	St Pol Com Cem Ext
McGrevy J	Pte	32845	15th	20/10/17	Hooge Crater Belgium
McGuire P	Pte	330991	16th	11/05/18	Tannay British Cem
McKay D	Pte	35765	16th	27/09/18	Fifteen Ravine Br
McKey M C	Cpl	948	14th	11/10/17	Godewaersvelde Br
McLean W	Pte	33883	16th	29/06/18	Aire Com
Mcloughlin F	Pte	38273	16th	23/08/18	Lebucquiere Com
McMillan W	Sgt	88	15th	09/05/17	Arras Memorial
McQuay F	Pte	215	14th	30/07/16	Thiepval Memorial
McReynolds T A	Pte	32788	16th	09/10/17	Tyne Cot Memorial Belgium
McRill G H	Pte	26437	15th	27/09/18	Gouzeaucourt New Br
Meacham A E	Cpl	644	16th	09/10/17	Tyne Cot Memorial Belgium
Meadows W H	Pte	1349	15th	11/09/16	Mont Huon Mil Cem
Medcalf J J	Pte	1170	16th	27/07/16	A.I.F. Burial Ground
Medlock E	Cpl	30170	14th	12/09/16	Abbeville Com
Meese W H	Pte	50467	14th	10/05/18	Tannay British Cem
Meggs G	Pte	15/1666	16th	27/07/16	Thiepval Memorial
Mellor C W	Pte	69	16th	16/04/17	Arras Memorial
Mendham P W	Pte	30172	14th	03/09/16	Thiepval Memorial
Menzies E R	Pte	14639	16th	05/09/18	Brookwood Mil Cem UK
Mercer H N	Cpl	14/1491	14th	23/07/16	Thiepval Memorial
Meredith J	Cpl	253	15th	03/09/16	Thiepval Memorial
Merrick A S	Pte	949	14th	23/07/16	Thiepval Memorial
Merrick T	Pte	9238	14th	28/08/16	Thiepval Memorial
Meyler L J	Pte	59191	15th	27/09/18	Vis-en-Artois Memorial
Middleton J	Pte	89	15th	04/06/16	Faubourg D'Amiens
Middleton W	Pte	703	15th	25/07/16	Dantzig Alley Br
Mill H	Pte	1946	14th	30/08/16	Flatiron Copse
Millar D	Pte	16/948	14th	26/08/18	Vis-en-Artois Memorial
Miller A	Pte	258	15th	15/05/16	Erdington RC UK
Miller E	Pte	30149	15th	05/10/17	Hooge Crater Belgium
Millhouse T	Pte	36496	16th	27/09/18	Vis-en-Artois Memorial
Mills H	Pte	16/1946	14th	30/08/16	Thiepval Memorial
Mills H F	Pte	1147	14th	23/07/16	Thiepval Memorial
Mills J D	Pte	32631	16th	09/10/17	Tyne Cot Cem Belgium
Mills W H	Pte	22735	15th	26/10/17	Tyne Cot Memorial Belgium
Millward J H	Pte	1075	14th	30/07/16	Thiepval Memorial
Millward W F	Pte	189	16th	03/09/16	Thiepval Memorial
Milton C	Pte	30165	14th	07/05/17	Arras Memorial
Milton J	Pte	32764	15th	26/10/17	Tyne Cot Memorial Belgium
Minahan H C	Pte	16/1651	16th	27/07/16	Thiepval Memorial
Minchella M	L/Cpl	34209	16th	26/04/18	Tannay British Cem
Minton C	L/Cpl	66	16th	03/09/16	Thiepval Memorial
Mitchard E V	Pte	28572	15th	03/07/17	Roclincourt Mil Cem
Mitchell A	L/Cpl	2042	14th	28/08/18	Achiet le Grand Com Ext
Mitchell P J	Pte	238033	15th	12/04/18	Merville Com Cem Ext
Mockford J	L/Cpl	30124	15th	24/09/16	Guards Cem
Molesworth E	Pte	19486	15th	24/04/17	Arras Memorial
Momber H	Cpl	16/1500	14th	30/07/16	Thiepval Memorial
Montgomery A	Pte	21139	14th	26/10/17	Tyne Cot Memorial Belgium
Moon A	Pte	17033	14th	03/09/16	Thiepval Memorial
Moon F O W	Pte	34129	15th	26/10/17	Tyne Cot Memorial Belgium
Mooney N	Pte	32474	14th	02/05/18	Ploegsteert Memorial Belgium
Moorcroft H	Pte	32472	16th	09/10/17	Hooge Crater Belgium
Moore G A	2nd Lt		14th	02/05/18	Ploegsteert Memorial Belgium
Moore J	Pte	48247	16th	23/08/18	Vis-en-Artois Memorial
Moore W A	Pte	17915	16th	26/09/16	Corbie Com Ext
Moreton B	Pte	17713	16th	29/06/18	Aire Com
Morgan P S	RSM	856	16th	31/12/15	Corbie Com
Morgan V H	Pte	408	16th	03/09/16	Thiepval Memorial
Morgan W	Pte	17517	14th	13/04/18	Ploegsteert Memorial Belgium
Morgan W	Pte	32822	15th	26/10/17	Tyne Cot Memorial Belgium
Morley A	Pte	34477	15th	27/09/18	Vis-en-Artois Memorial
Morley E W	L/Cpl	40	14th	23/07/16	Thiepval Memorial
Morris A	Pte	16/1591	15th	22/03/16	Roclincourt Mil Cem
Morris A	Pte	650	16th	12/09/16	St Sever Cem, Rouen
Morris E	Pte	34148	15th	26/10/17	Tyne Cot Memorial Belgium
Morris J	Pte	1248	14th	03/08/16	St Sever Cem, Rouen
Morris P J	L/Cpl	256	15th	04/06/16	Faubourg D'Amiens
Morris R H	2nd Lt		15th	28/06/18	Tannay British Cem
Morris S	Pte	34951	14th	27/09/18	Vis-en-Artois Memorial
Morrison J W	2nd Lt		16th	30/12/16	Le Treport Mil
Morton W	Pte	30432	16th	05/10/17	Tyne Cot Memorial Belgium
Moston E	Pte	33896	16th	29/06/18	Tannay British Cem
Mould C V	Pte	533	15th	04/09/16	Corbie Com Ext
Mould E K	2nd Lt		16th	02/09/18	Bailleul Rd East Cem
Moulding A	Pte	14/1474	14th	30/07/16	Thiepval Memorial
Moulton E J	Pte	34110	14th	11/11/17	Tyne Cot Memorial Belgium
Mountney J	Pte	1307	14th	23/07/16	Caterpillar Valley
Mousley H G	Pte	166941	14th	03/09/16	Thiepval Memorial
Moy T W	Pte	32095	16th	09/10/17	Godewaersvelde Br
Mucklow C W	Pte	17942	14th	30/07/16	Thiepval Memorial
Muir L R	Pte	48378	16th	03/09/18	Vaulx Hill Cem
Mullis H	Cpl	7923	14th	03/09/16	Thiepval Memorial
Mulloy H	Pte	57277	16th	04/11/18	St Sever Cem Ext, Rouen
Mulroy J H	Pte	1361	15th	04/06/16	Arras Memorial
Mundy H G	Sgt	38653	16th	19/09/20	Witton Cem B'ham
Murphy A D	Pte	14/1638	14th	23/07/16	Thiepval Memorial
Murrell P C	Pte	32471	14th	04/10/17	Tyne Cot Memorial Belgium
Musselwhite S J	Pte	27384	15th	09/05/17	Arras Memorial
Mutlow P A	Pte	1433	15th	09/05/17	Arras Memorial
Nall T	Pte	17999	16th	03/09/16	Thiepval Memorial
Napper R H	Pte	48351	15th	26/08/18	Vis-en-Artois Memorial
Nash G H	Pte	30036	15th	15/04/18	Aire Com
Neale D	Pte	1218	14th	21/07/16	Mericourt L'Abbe Com Ext
Neate R	Pte	22220	16th	28/06/17	Arras Memorial
Negus P A	Pte	30269	14th	26/10/17	Tyne Cot Memorial Belgium
Neighbour H A	Pte	330524	15th	26/10/17	Tyne Cot Memorial Belgium
Nelson A	Sgt	1623	14th	30/07/16	Delville Wood
Newberry F W	Pte	15/192	14th	14/04/18	Ploegsteert Memorial Belgium
Newbury G	L/Cpl	52	15th	27/01/17	Longuenesse Souvenir Cem
Newman A	Pte	42137	14th	27/09/18	Fifteen Ravine Br
Newman J A	Pte	24638	14th	27/09/18	Vis-en-Artois Memorial
Newport C W	L/Cpl	34781	16th	23/08/18	Vis-en-Artois Memorial
Newsham R	Pte	32909	16th	11/10/17	Godewaersvelde Br
Newton C	Pte	34097	14th	27/01/18	Giavera Br, Italy
Newton G	Pte	8748	14th	26/10/17	Tyne Cot Memorial Belgium
Niblett A T	Pte	235170	14th	27/09/18	Vis-en-Artois Memorial
Nicholls H	Pte	260299	16th	11/11/17	Tyne Cot Memorial Belgium
Nicholls R A	Pte	16/73	15th	14/05/17	Etaples Mil
Nicholls R W	Pte	193	16th	03/09/16	Thiepval Memorial
Nichols T L	2nd Lt		15th	09/05/17	Orchard Dump Cem
Nicholson C H	Pte	48426	16th	24/09/18	Terlincthun British Cem
Nickless W J	Cpl	953	14th	23/07/16	Thiepval Memorial
Nickson S	Pte	44	14th	23/07/16	Thiepval Memorial
Nix J	Pte	1330	14th	23/07/16	Thiepval Memorial
Noak A	Pte	17530	14th	27/09/16	Thiepval Memorial
Noakes E C	Pte	18613	15th	09/10/17	Tyne Cot Memorial Belgium
Noden F W	L/Cpl	456	14th	23/07/16	Caterpillar Valley
Nokes B	Pte	34073	16th	14/02/19	Brandwood End Cem B'ham
Nokes G	Pte	16800	15th	27/09/18	Lebucquiere Com
Noon W	Pte	21691	15th	04/10/17	Tyne Cot Memorial Belgium
North C W	Pte	15430	15th	03/09/16	Delville Wood
North G H	Pte	25367	14th	13/04/18	Merville Com Cem Ext
North W J	Pte	45	14th	23/07/16	Thiepval Memorial
Northfield C	Pte	35171	14th	30/08/18	Vis-en-Artois Memorial
Norton H J	Pte	1070	14th	18/05/16	Faubourg D'Amiens
Norton T	Pte	932	16th	23/08/18	Adanac Mil
Nurden A	Pte	70	16th	27/07/16	Thiepval Memorial
Nurse J J	Pte	16/1736	14th	03/09/16	Delville Wood
O'Dowd B	Pte	21141	14th	18/05/17	Orchard Dump Cem
O'Dwyer A S	2nd Lt		14th	29/07/16	Thiepval Memorial
Offord W C	Pte	27241	16th	09/10/17	Tyne Cot Memorial Belgium
Ogburn H	Pte	14967	14th	30/07/16	Thiepval Memorial
Ogden A	Pte	32776	15th	26/10/17	Tyne Cot Memorial Belgium
O'Kane J	Pte	32634	16th	19/10/17	Godewaersvelde Br
Oldbury E J	Pte	46	15th	04/06/16	Faubourg D'Amiens
Oldham H H	Pte	35904	14th	28/09/18	Thilloy Road Cem
Olds G F	Pte	1133	15th	30/08/16	Thiepval Memorial
Oliver G	Pte	1665	14th	28/08/18	Mory-Abbey Mil Cem
Oliver H T	Pte	792	14th	03/09/16	Guillemont Rd
Olley W B	Pte	35797	14th	27/09/18	Gouzeaucourt New Br
Ollier E	Pte	42082	15th	27/09/18	Gouzeaucourt New Br
Onions W L	Pte	816	14th	23/07/16	Thiepval Memorial
Orange C B	Pte	18276	15th	09/04/17	Thelus Mil Cem
Orford R J	Pte	959	16th	27/07/16	Etaples Mil
Orme H	Pte	16/1912	16th	03/09/16	Thiepval Memorial
Orme J	Pte	20731	14th	04/06/17	Orchard Dump Cem
Osborne T J	Pte	203051	15th	25/04/18	Les Baraques Mil
Osbourn C E	Pte	50682	15th	26/08/18	Vis-en-Artois Memorial
Overton S	Pte	1741	15th	16/07/17	Duisans Br
Owen W	Pte	28412	14th	20/05/17	Arras Memorial
Oxford A	Cpl	16045	14th	23/08/18	Adanac Mil
Oxton S	Pte	33706	14th	13/04/18	Ploegsteert Memorial Belgium
Packer E G	L/Cpl	35323	14th	26/09/18	Neuville-Bourjonval Br Cem
Paddock R H	L/Cpl	419	16th	27/07/16	Thiepval Memorial
Paddy G F	Pte	28368	15th	09/05/17	Arras Memorial
Page A A	Pte	50695	15th	30/06/18	Aire Com
Page A E	Pte	30223	15th	27/09/18	Villers Hill British Cem
Page S	Cpl	176	15th	03/09/16	Thiepval Memorial
Palmer A	Pte	32562	14th	26/10/17	Tyne Cot Memorial Belgium
Palmer H J	Cpl	692	15th	03/09/16	Thiepval Memorial
Palmer T H	Pte	435	16th	26/09/16	Thiepval Memorial
Parfitt M	L/Cpl	201	16th	21/04/17	Barlin Com Cem
Parish C E	Pte	830	15th	23/07/16	Thiepval Memorial
Parker C W	Pte	30224	14th	03/09/16	Delville Wood
Parker E H	Pte	17070	14th	07/05/17	Arras Memorial
Parker F W	Cpl	557	15th	30/08/16	Thiepval Memorial
Parker L W	L/Cpl	1008	15th	04/06/16	Faubourg D'Amiens
Parker W E	2nd Lt		15th	09/05/17	Arras Memorial
Parkes F L	Pte	914	15th	23/07/16	Caterpillar Valley
Parkes H T	Pte	16/1592	14th	13/04/18	Ploegsteert Memorial Belgium
Parkin H	Pte	1327	16th	03/09/16	Thiepval Memorial
Parkinson N	Pte	34494	15th	27/09/18	Vis-en-Artois Memorial
Parry F A	Major		16th	27/09/18	Gouzeaucourt New Br
Parry W R	Pte	18145	15th	26/10/17	Tyne Cot Memorial Belgium
Parsons C W	Pte	22497	14th	09/02/17	St Sever Cem Ext, Rouen
Parsons H	L/Cpl	23434	15th	13/04/18	Ploegsteert Memorial Belgium
Parsons S	Pte	32767	15th	26/10/17	Tyne Cot Memorial Belgium
Partridge H	Pte	14/1503	16th	01/07/17	Duisans Br
Paskin G E	Pte	441	15th	09/01/16	Cerisy-Gailly Mil
Patch F R	L/Cpl	150	15th	04/06/16	Faubourg D'Amiens
Patterson R H	Pte	1166	16th	10/04/16	Faubourg D'Amiens
Pay R	Pte	33783	15th	14/04/18	Ploegsteert Memorial Belgium
Payne J	Pte	417	16th	27/07/16	Thiepval Memorial
Payne P O	L/Cpl	33913	16th	28/05/18	Thiennes British Cem
Payne W	Pte	3985	14th	03/09/16	Thiepval Memorial
Payton F E	Pte	433	15th	10/06/16	Habarcq Com
Payton R S	Lieut		14th	22/07/16	Thiepval Memorial
Peach H	Pte	470	14th	23/07/16	Thiepval Memorial
Peakman H E	L/Cpl	1118	15th	04/06/16	Faubourg D'Amiens
Pearce G	Pte	330529	14th	24/05/18	Wandsworth Cem UK
Pearce H W	Pte	15/1487	14th	21/07/16	Thiepval Memorial
Pearse H	Pte	434	16th	26/09/16	Thiepval Memorial
Pearson A W	Pte	904	14th	03/09/16	Thiepval Memorial
Pearson F G	2nd Lt		16th	20/10/18	Viesly Com Cem
Pearson R	Pte	201203	15th	16/04/18	Aire Com
Pearson S	Pte	882	15th	24/09/16	Guards Cem
Peel E	Pte	19255	15th	05/10/17	Tyne Cot Memorial Belgium
Peevor H E	Pte	668	16th	27/07/16	Thiepval Memorial
Pegg T	Pte	17497	14th	03/09/16	Thiepval Memorial
Pegrum F W	Pte	961	16th	15/03/16	Caberet Rouge
Pelling W A	Pte	28463	14th	10/11/17	Etaples Mil
Penn E	Pte	16221	15th	26/06/17	Niederzwehren Cem Germany
Penn F	Pte	1624	15th	14/04/18	Ploegsteert Memorial Belgium
Penn W J	Pte	34276	14th	27/08/18	Mory-Abbey Mil Cem
Penny H	Pte	18725	15th	09/05/17	Arras Memorial
Percival P J	Pte	22787	15th	09/05/17	Arras Memorial
Perkes R	Pte	16785	14th	07/07/17	Orchard Dump Cem
Perkins C	Pte	1420	14th	11/09/16	Erdington Churchyard UK
Perkins F	Pte	1150	14th	08/10/16	Lodge Hill Cem B'ham
Perkins H	Pte	418	16th	27/07/16	Dernancourt Com
Perks F	Pte	17581	15th	25/04/17	Lapugnoy Mil
Perring G C	Sgt	48210	14th	08/07/18	Tannay British Cem
Perrow W W	Pte	32734	15th	28/10/17	Lijssenthoek Mil Belgium
Perry C	Pte	1259	15th	07/09/16	Dive Copse Br

Perry G T	Pte	961	15th	06/01/16	Cerisy-Gailly Mil
Perry P H	L/Sgt	15/1401	14th	23/07/16	Thiepval Memorial
Peters F T	Pte	50689	15th	27/09/18	Gouzeaucourt New Br
Phelps W H	Pte	17550	14th	30/07/16	Caterpillar Valley
Phillips A H	Sgt	14/1628	14th	03/09/16	Thiepval Memorial
Phillips J J	Sgt	679	16th	14/11/15	Gwyddelwern Ch'yard UK
Phillips R H	2nd Lt		15th	25/09/16	Guards Cem
Phillips T H	CSM	38	15th	23/07/16	Caterpillar Valley
Phillips W D	2nd Lt		15th	28/09/18	Grevillers Br
Philp P	Pte	34782	16th	05/11/17	Tyne Cot Memorial Belgium
Pickersgill S T	Pte	48285	16th	13/10/18	Belle Vue Br Cem
Piggott P	Pte	33922	16th	28/05/18	Aire Com
Pilch W F	Sgt	814	15th	03/09/16	Thiepval Memorial
Pilgrim A C	Pte	18314	14th	04/10/18	Mont Huon Mil Cem
Pilley T E	Pte	26950	15th	14/04/18	Tannay British Cem
Pillinger F	Pte	28682	16th	24/08/18	Adanac Mil
Pinchin W H	Pte	125	14th	23/07/16	Thiepval Memorial
Pink S P	Pte	35993	16th	18/10/18	Vis-en-Artois Memorial
Pitt W	Pte	8286	15th	26/10/17	Tyne Cot Memorial Belgium
Pittman S	Pte	18690	15th	09/05/17	Arras Memorial
Pitts A	Pte	3689	14th	16/01/19	Lodge Hill Cem B'ham
Plant C	Pte	3361	15th	26/10/17	Tyne Cot Memorial Belgium
Plant H	2nd Lt		14th	20/12/16	Bethune Town Cem
Platt S W	Pte	126	14th	23/07/16	Caterpillar Valley
Plowman L D	Pte	18688	15th	12/04/18	Merville Com Cem Ext
Pocock C A	2nd Lt		14th	08/05/17	Orchard Dump Cem
Pollard F J	Pte	32912	16th	13/04/18	St Venant-Robecq Rd Br Cem
Pollard W F	Pte	50690	15th	28/06/18	Merville Com Cem Ext
Poole A	Pte	17742	15th	30/08/16	Thiepval Memorial
Poole F	Pte	20895	14th	24/04/17	La Chaudiere Mil
Poole F G	Pte	27398	14th	27/09/18	Gouzeaucourt New Br
Poole H	L/Cpl	10132	16th	14/05/17	Roclincourt Valley Cem
Poole J R	2nd Lt		14th	30/07/16	Thiepval Memorial
Poole L A	Pte	35910	14th	27/09/18	Gouzeaucourt New Br
Poole S	Pte	18862	16th	09/10/17	Tyne Cot Memorial Belgium
Pope H	Pte	30270	14th	03/09/16	Thiepval Memorial
Poplett W H	Pte	30152	15th	30/08/18	Vaulx Hill Cem
Portch R D	Pte	32555	14th	14/10/17	Abbeville Com Ext
Porter A W	Pte	242606	16th	04/07/18	Aire Com
Porter J	Pte	19115	15th	24/04/17	Arras Memorial
Porter R P R	Pte	50422	14th	03/02/20	St Stephens-by-Saltash UK
Posnette H L	Pte	431	16th	01/08/16	Heilly Station
Potter C W	Pte	969	16th	27/06/16	Dernancourt Com
Potter F	Pte	16/1643	16th	16/04/17	Arras Memorial
Potts T	Pte	35994	16th	23/08/18	Vis-en-Artois Memorial
Poulten E E	Pte	32913	16th	09/10/17	Tyne Cot Memorial Belgium
Poulton G	Pte	33845	15th	14/04/18	Ploegsteert Memorial Belgium
Powell C	Pte	3630	16th	03/09/16	Thiepval Memorial
Powell C W	Pte	23433	15th	15/04/18	Etaples Mil
Powell E	Pte	22718	15th	08/05/17	Orchard Dump Cem
Powell E	Pte	8940	16th	03/09/16	Thiepval Memorial
Powell J	Cpl	27290	14th	26/10/17	Tyne Cot Memorial Belgium
Powell J	Pte	36528	14th	27/09/18	Vis-en-Artois Memorial
Powell W	Pte	16/1398	14th	23/07/16	Thiepval Memorial
Powell W A	Pte	1001	14th	23/07/16	Thiepval Memorial
Power B C	L/Cpl	296	14th	23/07/16	Thiepval Memorial
Poynter W F	Pte	36502	16th	27/09/18	Vis-en-Artois Memorial
Pratt S	Pte	12636	15th	09/05/17	Arras Memorial
Preece A	Pte	17748	15th	07/09/16	St Pierre Cem, Amiens
Prescott T P	Pte	119	14th	23/07/16	Thiepval Memorial
Preston W A	L/Cpl	131	14th	23/07/16	Thiepval Memorial
Pretty W H	Pte	35329	14th	14/04/18	Aire Com
Price F L	L/Cpl	979	16th	03/09/16	Thiepval Memorial
Price J	Sgt	16/962	14th	01/09/16	La Neuville Br
Price J E C	Pte	295	14th	23/07/16	Caterpillar Valley
Price J W	Pte	967	14th	03/09/16	Guillemont Rd
Pridmore H A	Pte	22532	14th	27/09/18	Vis-en-Artois Memorial
Priest H	Pte	1048	15th	04/06/16	Arras Memorial
Pritchard F	L/Cpl	21959	14th	18/05/17	Orchard Dump Cem
Probert H E	Pte	17015	16th	27/05/17	Roclincourt Valley Cem
Proud A E	Pte	1201	14th	30/07/16	Caterpillar Valley
Pryer A O	Pte	23418	14th	05/05/17	Roclincourt Mil Cem
Puddick W F	Pte	20725	16th	01/09/18	Favreuil Br
Pugh H R	Pte	700	15th	19/04/18	Aire Com
Purdew H J W	Pte	18658	15th	12/05/17	Aubigny Com Cem Ext
Quarton P B D	Pte	16819	14th	03/09/16	Thiepval Memorial
Quinn W E	Pte	25390	14th	28/08/18	Vis-en-Artois Memorial
Rab S H	L/Cpl	140	15th	27/09/18	Lebucquiere Com
Radburn B	Pte	16550	15th	09/05/17	Arras Memorial
Rafferty E P	Pte	38252	14th	27/09/18	Vis-en-Artois Memorial
Rainbow F G	Pte	692	16th	27/10/17	Tyne Cot Memorial Belgium
Ramsbottom G	Pte	35788	16th	27/09/18	Vis-en-Artois Memorial
Randall W	Pte	33181	15th	20/10/18	Vis-en-Artois Memorial
Randle A	Pte	52217	16th	01/09/18	Favreuil Br
Randle G	Pte	18136	16th	31/08/16	Peronne Rd Cem, Maricourt
Randle J E	Pte	991	16th	27/07/16	Thiepval Memorial
Randle J T	Pte	992	16th	16/10/18	Caudry Br Cem
Ranford W H	Pte	43687	14th	27/09/18	Gouzeaucourt New Br
Rann L C	Pte	35331	14th	13/04/18	Ploegsteert Memorial Belgium
Ravenscroft J S	Pte	36527	14th	27/09/18	Gouzeaucourt New Br
Ray W F	L/Cpl	1394	16th	29/09/16	Grevillers Br
Raymond A S	Pte	30226	14th	03/09/16	Thiepval Memorial
Rayner C E	Pte	32812	15th	25/10/17	Tyne Cot Memorial Belgium
Read W	Pte	241862	16th	23/08/16	Adanac Mil
Reader C E	L/Cpl	32481	14th	27/09/18	Gouzeaucourt New Br
Reardon W	L/Cpl	34154	15th	27/09/18	Vis-en-Artois Memorial
Redhead F	Pte	19498	15th	04/03/17	Brown's Rd Mil, Festubert
Reed F A	Pte	30227	14th	24/04/17	Arras Memorial
Reed H G	Pte	23463	16th	22/04/17	Barlin Com Cem
Rees T	Pte	28630	15th	09/05/17	Arras Memorial
Reeve L F	Sgt	973	15th	14/04/18	Ploegsteert Memorial Belgium
Reeve V C	Pte	173	15th	15/06/16	Faubourg D'Amiens
Reeve W H	Pte	24882	16th	22/04/18	Morbecque British Cem
Reeves A G	Pte	18625	15th	06/02/18	Giavera Br, Italy
Reeves H A	L/Cpl	1159	16th	27/07/16	Thiepval Memorial
Regester E	Pte	43219	16th	30/09/18	Grevillers Br
Reid A	Pte	235131	15th	13/04/18	Ploegsteert Memorial Belgium
Reid J	Pte	34435	14th	01/06/18	Les Baraques Mil
Reid J	L/Cpl	1511	14th	11/05/17	Etaples Mil
Reynolds E R	Pte	22695	16th	09/10/17	Tyne Cot Memorial Belgium
Rhodes C	Pte	50701	15th	28/06/18	Thiennes British Cem
Rhodes J P	Pte	39085	14th	08/07/18	Tannay British Cem
Richards D	Pte	1218	14th	03/09/16	Guillemont Rd
Richards T H	Pte	972	14th	20/09/18	Canadian Cem 2
Richards T H	Pte	972	14th	20/09/18	Haplincourt Com
Richardson G	Pte	263019	16th	20/10/18	Viesly Com Cem
Richardson R	Pte	143	15th	03/07/18	Etaples Mil
Richardson W	Pte	20854	14th	07/05/17	Arras Memorial
Rickards R	Pte	29919	16th	07/10/17	Tyne Cot Memorial Belgium
Ricketts W	Pte	14/1405	14th	23/07/16	Thiepval Memorial
Riddell H	Cpl	682	16th	05/10/17	Tyne Cot Memorial Belgium
Rideout H S	Pte	18623	15th	11/04/17	Lapugnoy Mil
Rider F	Cpl	833	14th	03/09/16	Thiepval Memorial
Ridgway A	Pte	34098	14th	27/10/17	Lijssenthoek Mil Belgium
Ridley R G	Pte	35332	14th	13/04/18	Ploegsteert Memorial Belgium
Rigg L	Sgt	48298	14th	27/09/18	Gouzeaucourt New Br
Righton H G	Sgt	48245	16th	21/08/18	Queens Cemetery
Riley T	Pte	976	14th	23/07/16	Thiepval Memorial
Ring P	Pte	202724	15th	09/05/17	Arras Memorial
Risley S A	Pte	14/1626	15th	25/10/17	Tyne Cot Memorial Belgium
Robbie D	Pte	32589	16th	11/10/17	Godewaersvelde Br
Robbins T H	Pte	28477	14th	27/02/18	Giavera Br, Italy
Robert C T	Cpl	50423	14th	08/07/18	Aire Com
Roberts E	L/Cpl	30526	15th	27/09/18	Vis-en-Artois Memorial
Roberts G A	Pte	1501	14th	23/07/16	Caterpillar Valley
Roberts S H	Pte	458	15th	22/09/16	Flatiron Copse
Roberts W L	Pte	172	15th	30/07/16	Heilly Station
Robertson J	Pte	34124	14th	26/10/17	Hooge Crater Belgium
Robins B T	Pte	28505	16th	05/10/17	Tyne Cot Cem Belgium
Robinson A E	L/Cpl	989	16th	26/09/16	Thiepval Memorial
Robinson A J	Pte	17537	14th	30/07/16	Thiepval Memorial
Robinson G T	Pte	35995	16th	27/09/18	Gouzeaucourt New Br
Robinson H G	Pte	350143	16th	28/09/18	Grevillers Br
Robinson J	L/Cpl	1173	14th	27/09/16	Sutton Coldfield Cem UK
Robinson J R	Pte	16/894	15th	23/07/16	Thiepval Memorial
Robinson V A	Pte	34962	14th	26/10/17	Hooge Crater Belgium
Robotham W H	Pte	1449	15th	28/08/18	Lodge Hill Cem B'ham
Rockingham T	Pte	28588	15th	30/06/18	Ploegsteert Memorial Belgium
Roe F H	Pte	9	14th	30/07/16	Thiepval Memorial
Rogers C A	Pte	17301	16th	03/09/16	Corbie Com Ext
Rogers F R	L/Cpl	1203	14th	23/07/16	Thiepval Memorial
Rolinson J	Pte	30067	16th	26/09/16	Thiepval Memorial
Roper A M	Cpl	146	15th	30/07/16	Thiepval Memorial
Rose F	Pte	28051	16th	02/09/18	Bailleul Rd East Cem
Rose G	2nd Lt		15th	28/06/18	Thiennes British Cem
Rose J W	Sgt	483	14th	03/09/16	Thiepval Memorial
Rose N	Pte	30092	16th	03/09/16	Thiepval Memorial
Rosenbaum S	Pte	444	16th	03/09/16	Thiepval Memorial
Rosenthal L M	Pte	484	14th	23/07/16	Thiepval Memorial
Rouse R	Pte	17046	15th	07/05/18	Tannay British Cem
Routledge E W	Pte	16/1270	16th	25/01/16	Citadel New Mil
Row C E	Pte	202044	15th	05/05/17	Arras Memorial
Rowan W J	Pte	14/1414	14th	23/07/16	Thiepval Memorial
Rowbury B H	Pte	26571	15th	30/08/18	Vaulx Hill Cem
Rowcroft G A	Sgt	33	14th	23/07/16	Thiepval Memorial
Rowland R E B	2nd Lt		16th	27/07/16	Thiepval Memorial
Rowlands T S	Pte	16/1944	14th	23/07/16	Thiepval Memorial
Ruane M	Pte	48407	16th	27/08/18	Mont Huon Mil Cem
Rudd O	L/Cpl	486	14th	23/07/16	Caterpillar Valley
Rudell E A	2nd Lt		16th	27/09/18	Neuville-Bourjonval Br Cem
Rudhall N	Pte	16/1350	16th	28/07/16	Corbie Com Ext
Rushton T	Pte	34109	14th	11/11/17	Tyne Cot Memorial Belgium
Russell J	Pte	14/1659	15th	12/05/16	St Hilaire Cem
Russell L	Pte	9114	14th	13/04/18	Ploegsteert Memorial Belgium
Russell R	Pte	23133	16th	21/08/18	Adanac Mil
Russell W G	Sgt	993	14th	26/10/17	Tyne Cot Memorial Belgium
Rycroft L C	Pte	14/1714	15th	09/05/17	Arras Memorial
Ryley J R	Sgt	817	15th	30/06/18	Aire Com
Rymer H	Cpl	32684	15th	04/10/17	Tyne Cot Memorial Belgium
Sabin H	L/Cpl	703	14th	04/08/16	Etaples Mil
Sabin T E	Pte	36113	14th	27/09/18	Vis-en-Artois Memorial
Sackett F H	Pte	1416	14th	20/09/16	Mont Huon Mil Cem
Sadler F J	L/Cpl	785	15th	03/09/16	Thiepval Memorial
Sadler J J	Pte	982	15th	23/05/17	Arras Memorial
Sadler W	Pte	715	16th	26/09/16	Thiepval Memorial
Sainsbury W J	Pte	26939	15th	14/04/18	Morbecque British Cem
Sale H R	Pte	14/1702	15th	04/06/16	Faubourg D'Amiens
Salisbury C R	2nd Lt		14th	07/05/17	Orchard Dump Cem
Salmon R G	Pte	1011	16th	10/04/16	Faubourg D'Amiens
Salt A	Pte	16680	15th	03/09/16	Thiepval Memorial
Salt G G	L/Cpl	1271	14th	03/09/16	Thiepval Memorial
Sanders F	Pte	20094	14th	26/10/17	Tyne Cot Memorial Belgium
Sanders G E	Lieut		16th	09/10/17	Tyne Cot Memorial Belgium
Sanders H S	Lieut		16th	21/08/18	Adanac Mil
Sanders J M	Pte	133	15th	03/09/16	Delville Wood
Sanders J W	Cpl	1147	15th	24/04/17	Arras Memorial
Sanders T F P	Pte	272	14th	20/04/16	Habarcq Com
Sanders W R	Pte	456	16th	31/07/16	Heilly Station
Sangster F C	Lieut		16th	06/09/16	Corbie Com Ext
Sansome H V	2nd Lt		14th	26/10/17	Hooge Crater Belgium
Saunders F	Pte	1493	16th	11/10/17	St Sever Cem Ext, Rouen
Saunders J	Pte	17735	15th	29/08/16	Thiepval Memorial
Saunders J E	Pte	1446	14th	29/05/18	Thiennes British Cem
Saunter H C	L/Cpl	21149	14th	27/09/18	Gouzeaucourt New Br
Savage J	Pte	203242	15th	27/09/18	Gouzeaucourt New Br
Sayer L	Captain		16th	23/08/18	Shrine Cem
Scarborough R	Pte	714	14th	24/09/16	Flatiron Copse
Scarff A E	Pte	33708	14th	14/04/18	Ploegsteert Memorial Belgium
Scott A F	Pte	704	16th	06/08/16	St Sever Cem, Rouen
Scott C R	Pte	50416	15th	30/08/18	Vaulx Hill Cem
Scott J A	Pte	29719	16th	10/08/18	Les Baraques Mil
Scott R W	Pte	274	14th	03/09/16	Guillemont Rd
Scott W	Pte	448	16th	27/07/16	Thiepval Memorial
Scrivens G E	Sgt	16/1446	15th	11/06/16	Aubigny Com Cem Ext
Seabrook F G	Pte	32490	14th	23/05/18	Merville Com Cem Ext
Searston T H	Pte	52238	16th	19/09/18	St Sever Cem Ext, Rouen
Sellars F	L/Cpl	30228	14th	11/09/16	Thiepval Memorial
Seniscall W	Pte	52233	16th	27/09/18	Fifteen Ravine Br
Sephton R	Pte	36500	16th	03/09/18	Vaulx Hill Cem
Severn E C	Pte	14/1613	14th	03/09/16	Thiepval Memorial
Severs C V	Sgt	1480	14th	24/01/21	Harborne Churchyard UK
Sewall J K	Pte	32643	16th	09/10/17	Tyne Cot Memorial Belgium
Seymour S H	Pte	35340	14th	14/04/18	Ploegsteert Memorial Belgium
Sharlott H W	Pte	16986	15th	02/10/18	St Sever Cem Ext, Rouen
Sharp F	Pte	32768	15th	04/10/17	Tyne Cot Memorial Belgium
Sharples W A	Pte	18155	14th	03/09/16	Thiepval Memorial
Sharps E W S	Pte	35342	14th	14/04/18	Ploegsteert Memorial Belgium
Sharratt A E	Pte	1501	16th	31/03/16	St Sever Cem, Rouen
Sharratt R	Pte	15238	16th	27/07/16	London Cem
Sharrocks W A	Pte	32769	15th	04/10/17	Hooge Crater Belgium
Shattock G H	Pte	21356	14th	08/05/17	Arras Memorial
Shaw E C	Pte	43222	15th	27/09/18	Fifteen Ravine Br
Shaw H	Pte	26929	15th	26/10/17	Tyne Cot Memorial Belgium
Sheldon G W A	Pte	1255	14th	23/07/16	Thiepval Memorial
Sheppard E F	Pte	34812	15th	27/09/18	Gouzeaucourt New Br
Shergold C H	Pte	1258	15th	25/05/16	Aubigny Com Cem Ext
Shergold C J	Pte	50710	15th	17/06/18	Thiennes British Cem
Sherwood J M	L/Cpl	151841	15th	06/02/17	Brown's Rd Mil, Festubert
Shilton G J J	Pte	17955	16th	07/10/17	Tyne Cot Memorial Belgium
Shine E	2nd Lt		16th	20/10/18	Viesly Com Cem
Shingleton J	Pte	1220	15th	04/06/16	Faubourg D'Amiens
Shinton G H	Cpl	34964	14th	23/08/18	Adanac Mil
Shore J H	Pte	35343	14th	14/04/18	Ploegsteert Memorial Belgium
Short E	Pte	330147	15th	07/11/17	Tyne Cot Memorial Belgium
Short W	Pte	48268	14th	23/08/18	Vis-en-Artois Memorial
Shorter S F	Pte	209	16th	28/07/16	Heilly Station
Shough P C	Sgt	789	14th	23/07/16	Thiepval Memorial
Shrimpton H E	Pte	24879	16th	09/10/17	Tyne Cot Memorial Belgium
Shutt H	Pte	203792	14th	14/04/18	Ploegsteert Memorial Belgium
Sice W C	Pte	1338	14th	03/09/16	Thiepval Memorial
Silk B W	Pte	15/1415	14th	23/07/16	Thiepval Memorial
Silk E G	Pte	80	14th	20/09/18	Canadian Cem 2
Silk E G	Pte	80	14th	20/09/18	Haplincourt Com
Simkins A	Pte	1194	15th	05/02/17	Witton Cem B'ham
Simmonds F	Pte	32710	15th	26/10/17	Tyne Cot Memorial Belgium
Simmons E	Pte	14/1527	14th	23/07/16	Thiepval Memorial
Simmons H	Pte	17704	14th	06/09/16	Corbie Com Ext
Simmons J A	Sgt	214	14th	23/07/16	Caterpillar Valley
Simmons W J H	Pte	50712	15th	27/09/18	Gouzeaucourt New Br
Sims H	Pte	32640	16th	08/10/17	Tyne Cot Memorial Belgium
Simpson J	Pte	32985	16th	09/10/17	Hooge Crater Belgium
Simpson J C	Pte	48330	15th	27/09/18	Vis-en-Artois Memorial
Simpson W	Pte	30229	14th	03/09/16	Thiepval Memorial
Sinclair W	Pte	30331	14th	03/09/16	Thiepval Memorial
Singleton E	Pte	696	16th	13/01/17	Yardley Cem B'ham
Skelsey F	Sgt	289	14th	03/09/16	Thiepval Memorial
Skidmore F A	L/Cpl	15/1459	14th	03/09/16	Delville Wood
Skillern W	Pte	30078	16th	03/09/16	Thiepval Memorial
Skinner H	Pte	37817	15th	28/06/18	Ploegsteert Memorial Belgium
Skinner H N	Pte	27635	16th	03/06/18	Tannay British Cem
Skinner J	Pte	33009	16th	07/10/17	Godewaersvelde Br
Skinner W	Pte	14/1711	15th	03/09/16	Thiepval Memorial
Skipton W	Pte	9225	16th	01/09/16	Thiepval Memorial
Slater W E	Pte	52219	16th	01/09/18	Favreuil Br
Sloper E	Pte	32850	15th	25/10/17	Tyne Cot Memorial Belgium
Smallwood J	Pte	712	14th	21/07/16	Thiepval Memorial
Smith A	Pte	371	14th	09/05/17	Arras Memorial
Smith A	Pte	32568	14th	14/04/18	Merville Com Cem Ext
Smith A	Pte	17832	15th	29/08/16	Thiepval Memorial
Smith A B	Pte	17637	14th	03/09/16	Thiepval Memorial
Smith A E	Sgt	12763	15th	26/10/17	Tyne Cot Memorial Belgium
Smith A O	Pte	254	14th	23/07/16	Thiepval Memorial
Smith A W	Pte	14/1444	14th	23/07/16	Thiepval Memorial
Smith A W J	Cpl	48271	16th	03/09/18	Vaulx Hill Cem
Smith B	Pte	460	15th	04/06/16	Faubourg D'Amiens
Smith C	Pte	598	15th	31/07/16	Thiepval Memorial
Smith C A S	Pte	16/1555	16th	27/07/16	Thiepval Memorial
Smith C E	Pte	708	14th	23/07/16	Thiepval Memorial
Smith D	Pte	1387	14th	23/07/16	Thiepval Memorial
Smith E	Pte	18635	15th	23/11/16	Brown's Rd Mil, Festubert
Smith E A	2nd Lt		14th	23/07/16	Caterpillar Valley
Smith E R	Pte	26947	15th	22/10/16	Brown's Rd Mil, Festubert
Smith F	Pte	201095	14th	03/09/19	Yardley Cem B'ham
Smith F	Pte	21119	15th	26/10/17	Tyne Cot Memorial Belgium
Smith G	Pte	891	15th	03/09/16	Thiepval Memorial
Smith G	Pte	21136	16th	13/10/17	Godewaersvelde Br
Smith G A	L/Cpl	18679	15th	26/10/17	Tyne Cot Memorial Belgium
Smith G E	Pte	17368	15th	30/07/16	Thiepval Memorial
Smith G H	Pte	18068	14th	03/09/16	Delville Wood
Smith H	Pte	22752	16th	14/10/17	Boisguillaume Com Ext
Smith H	Pte	21686	16th	06/10/17	Tyne Cot Memorial Belgium
Smith H W	Cpl	19741	16th	23/08/18	Adanac Mil
Smith J A	Pte	17071	14th	08/05/17	Arras Memorial
Smith J B	Sgt	1764	14th	03/09/16	Thiepval Memorial
Smith J B	Pte	21	14th	23/07/16	Thiepval Memorial
Smith J B	2nd Lt		14th	19/08/17	Duisans Br
Smith J H	Pte	30236	14th	03/09/16	Thiepval Memorial
Smith J W	Pte	30288	14th	03/09/16	Thiepval Memorial
Smith R	Cpl	32503	16th	09/10/17	Tyne Cot Memorial Belgium
Smith R H	Pte	50717	15th	28/06/18	Ploegsteert Memorial Belgium
Smith S	Pte	144	14th	17/03/16	Caberet Rouge
Smith S	Pte	1103	15th	04/06/16	Faubourg D'Amiens
Smith S F	Pte	235227	14th	27/09/18	Vis-en-Artois Memorial
Smith T C	Pte	178	15th	02/07/16	Lodge Hill Cem B'ham
Smith T H	Pte	201199	15th	04/10/17	Tyne Cot Memorial Belgium
Smith V S	L/Cpl	235132	15th	26/10/17	Tyne Cot Memorial Belgium
Smith W	Pte	35351	14th	13/04/18	Merville Com Cem Ext
Smith W	Pte	24120	15th	27/09/18	Vis-en-Artois Memorial
Smith W G	Pte	987	14th	23/07/16	Thiepval Memorial
Smith W H	Pte	42742	14th	29/10/18	St Aubert British Cem
Smith W H	Pte	17415	14th	30/07/16	Thiepval Memorial
Smith W J	Sgt	28048	14th	07/05/17	Arras Memorial
Smout A H	L/Cpl	1278	16th	10/05/17	Arras Memorial
Snape G	Pte	1096	16th	27/07/16	Thiepval Memorial
Sneddon T	L/Cpl	33855	16th	27/09/18	Vis-en-Artois Memorial
Snell E C	Pte	26933	15th	26/10/17	Tyne Cot Memorial Belgium
Snewing A E	Pte	908	15th	18/04/16	Faubourg D'Amiens
Solomon W J C	Pte	1341	16th	11/10/17	Godewaersvelde Br
Sommers J P	Pte	16462	15th	26/02/17	Longuenesse Souvenir Cem
Souls F E E	Cpl	27636	16th	24/08/18	Adanac Mil
Southgate P T	Pte	34297	15th	29/06/18	Aire Com
Sowerby W	Pte	25721	14th	05/07/18	Ploegsteert Memorial Belgium
Spall H	Pte	331344	14th	15/09/18	Grevillers Br
Spare F V	Pte	6435	15th	30/06/17	Arras Memorial
Sparrow A W	Pte	20572	15th	09/05/17	Arras Memorial
Spearman W	Pte	761	14th	04/03/19	Brandwood End Cem B'ham
Spencer C A	Pte	28618	15th	22/04/17	Arras Memorial
Spencer S H	Pte	32821	15th	04/10/17	Aeroplane Cem. Belgium
Spraggitt G	Pte	330794	15th	07/10/17	Godewaersvelde Br
Spring A H	Pte	12341	15th	21/10/16	Brown's Rd Mil, Festubert
Spurr H	Pte	22766	16th	10/05/17	Orchard Dump Cem
Stacey H	Pte	1788	15th	14/03/17	Brown's Rd Mil, Festubert
Stainton H	Pte	16/1693	15th	04/06/16	Faubourg D'Amiens
Stait H E	Pte	890	15th	26/09/16	Thiepval Memorial
Stallard H	Pte	18376	15th	27/10/17	Lijssenthoek Mil Belgium
Standing S P	Pte	15/1307	15th	29/08/16	Thiepval Memorial
Stanford A	Pte	16/1864	14th	23/07/16	Caterpillar Valley
Stanford J H	Pte	132	15th	28/08/16	Thiepval Memorial

Stanley C	Pte	17985	14th	28/08/16	Thiepval Memorial
Stanley J	Pte	11677	14th	23/08/18	Adanac Mil
Stanley J A	Captain		15th	27/09/18	Lebucquiere Com
Stanley J R	Pte	17897	16th	06/03/17	Cambrin Mil
Stanley W B	Pte	23305	15th	12/10/17	Lijssenthoek Mil Belgium
Stanton F B	Pte	1186	16th	27/07/16	Thiepval Memorial
Stanton T	L/Cpl	752	16th	27/07/16	Thiepval Memorial
Stanworth G	Pte	36018	14th	27/09/18	Gouzeaucourt New Br
Staples W A	CQMS	851	16th	31/05/19	Wymondham Cem UK
Starkey E H	Pte	447	16th	27/09/18	Vis-en-Artois Memorial
Starmer W W	Pte	32875	16th	09/10/17	Tyne Cot Memorial Belgium
Statham E	Pte	482	15th	03/09/16	Thiepval Memorial
Statham J	Pte	10699	15th	28/06/18	Ploegsteert Memorial Belgium
Steadman A J	Pte	705	15th	05/10/17	Tyne Cot Memorial Belgium
Steel C	Pte	1057	16th	27/07/16	Thiepval Memorial
Steele H	Pte	210	16th	02/09/16	Thiepval Memorial
Steer H W	L/Cpl	32744	15th	06/10/17	Godewaersvelde Br
Stephens A	Pte	18132	16th	10/09/16	St Pierre Cem, Amiens
Stephens F W	Pte	240050	15th	09/05/17	Arras Memorial
Stephens L R	Pte	202040	15th	26/10/17	Tyne Cot Cem Belgium
Stevenson A	Pte	1007	16th	03/08/16	Corbie Com Ext
Stevenson T E	Pte	30289	14th	26/10/17	Tyne Cot Memorial Belgium
Stimpson A	Pte	32918	16th	09/10/17	Hooge Crater Belgium
Stockton R H	L/Cpl	14818	14th	22/06/17	Orchard Dump Cem
Stokes A	Pte	14471	14th	04/10/17	Tyne Cot Memorial Belgium
Stokes A W	Pte	14/1689	14th	03/09/16	Thiepval Memorial
Stokes J	Pte	15006	14th	03/09/16	Thiepval Memorial
Stokes W D	Pte	16/1407	14th	23/07/16	Thiepval Memorial
Stone G	Pte	33230	16th	20/10/18	Romeries Com Cem Ext
Stone J	Pte	17700	14th	03/09/16	Delville Wood
Storer E	Pte	28438	14th	07/05/17	Arras Memorial
Storey W E	Pte	30279	14th	08/05/17	Arras Memorial
Stratford W E	Pte	16999	14th	13/09/16	Thiepval Memorial
Streater J W	2nd Lt		15th	22/07/18	Les Baraques Mil
Stretton C H	Pte	30335	14th	09/11/17	Lijssenthoek Mil Belgium
Stringer W	Pte	21352	15th	14/04/18	Ploegsteert Memorial Belgium
Strong G H	Pte	267080	15th	02/02/18	Giavera Br, Italy
Stuart R	Pte	29593	14th	27/09/18	Vis-en-Artois Memorial
Stubbs W E	Pte	996	14th	23/07/16	Thiepval Memorial
Stych F J	Pte	446	16th	10/10/16	Brandwood End Cem B'ham
Styles A E	Pte	10155	14th	30/07/16	Thiepval Memorial
Styles E L	Pte	463	16th	27/07/16	Thiepval Memorial
Styles F	Pte	14/1756	14th	28/07/16	Heilly Station
Styles G R	L/Cpl	450	16th	03/09/16	Delville Wood
Suffolk T	Pte	23997	15th	26/10/17	Hooge Crater Belgium
Summers W F	Pte	19	14th	23/07/16	Thiepval Memorial
Suter F W	L/Cpl	10030	14th	26/10/17	Tyne Cot Memorial Belgium
Sutton A	Pte	50726	15th	28/06/18	Ploegsteert Memorial Belgium
Sutton A L	Pte	27697	14th	13/10/16	Brown's Rd Mil, Festubert
Sutton A M	Pte	32486	14th	26/10/17	Tyne Cot Memorial Belgium
Sutton J L	Pte	28646	15th	05/10/17	Tyne Cot Memorial Belgium
Swadling E	Pte	30155	15th	03/09/16	Thiepval Memorial
Swadling R F	Pte	16452	15th	08/10/17	Godewaersvelde Br
Swann L W	Cpl	701	16th	09/10/17	Tyne Cot Memorial Belgium
Swann S	Pte	16/1548	16th	27/07/16	Thiepval Memorial
Swarsbrick D	L/Cpl	1002	16th	27/07/16	Thiepval Memorial
Swede J A	Pte	48423	16th	25/08/18	Terlincthun British Cem
Swift W	Pte	36401	16th	27/09/18	Vis-en-Artois Memorial
Sylvester S	Pte	35971	16th	18/10/18	Vis-en-Artois Memorial
Symonds F G	Pte	18200	16th	19/09/16	Thiepval Memorial
Talbot H	Pte	7306	16th	09/10/17	Tyne Cot Memorial Belgium
Tams T	Pte	16/1793	16th	03/09/16	Delville Wood
Tasker E	Pte	16/1405	14th	23/07/16	Thiepval Memorial
Tasker F P	2nd Lt		16th	06/10/17	Lijssenthoek Mil Belgium
Tatlow A H	Captain		15th	04/06/16	Faubourg D'Amiens
Taunton R	Pte	1351	14th	23/07/16	Thiepval Memorial
Taylor A V	Pte	21992	15th	05/10/17	Tyne Cot Memorial Belgium
Taylor E	Pte	531	15th	03/09/16	Thiepval Memorial
Taylor F	Cpl	869	15th	28/06/18	Merville Com Cem Ext
Taylor F C	Pte	17946	16th	07/10/17	Ypres Resevoir Cem Belgium
Taylor H	Pte	35777	16th	20/10/18	Belle Vue Br Cem
Taylor H E	Pte	470	16th	25/12/15	Citadel New Mil
Taylor J	Pte	32772	15th	06/10/17	Tyne Cot Memorial Belgium
Taylor P W	Pte	18639	15th	12/04/17	Barlin Com Cem
Taylor R A	Pte	1247	14th	23/07/16	Lebucquiere Com
Taylor S A	L/Cpl	10395	14th	27/09/18	Gouzeaucourt New Br
Taylor T H	RSM	6317	14th	01/05/18	Aire Com
Taylor W	Pte	15/1291	14th	13/04/18	Ploegsteert Memorial Belgium
Taylor W	Pte	16/2069	16th	16/04/17	Canadian Cem 2
Taylor W	Pte	1606	14th	23/08/18	Adanac Mil
Taylor W A	L/Cpl	27698	14th	31/03/17	Ecoivres Mil
Taylor W H	Pte	16/1962	14th	30/07/16	Thiepval Memorial
Taylor W T	Pte	43328	15th	31/10/18	St Sever Cem Ext, Rouen
Teasdale E G	Pte	201805	16th	17/03/18	Giavera Br, Italy
Tedman W	Cpl	32502	14th	10/11/17	Boisguillaume Com Ext
Tedstone R R	L/Cpl	746	14th	23/07/16	Thiepval Memorial
Tennant H	Pte	32491	14th	26/10/17	Tyne Cot Memorial Belgium
Terry H A	Pte	28459	14th	07/05/17	Arras Memorial
Tetley H	Pte	468	16th	30/06/17	Arras Memorial
Tetstall C	Pte	18126	16th	03/09/16	Thiepval Memorial
Thacker P H	Pte	1498	15th	03/09/16	Delville Wood
Thackwell F	Pte	21020	14th	26/10/17	Tyne Cot Memorial Belgium
Thain W S	2nd Lt		15th	15/09/18	Mont Huon Mil Cem
Thayre A H	L/Cpl	33874	16th	27/09/18	Sunken Rd Cem, Villars-Plouich
Thexton J	Pte	22089	15th	08/05/17	Orchard Dump Cem
Thickett L	Pte	16/1684	15th	09/03/17	Arras Memorial
Thomas D E	Pte	48332	15th	29/09/18	Grevillers Br
Thomas F V	Pte	915	15th	23/07/16	Caterpillar Valley
Thomas J	Pte	298	15th	28/07/16	Dantzig Alley Br
Thomas P G	Pte	23578	15th	09/05/17	Orchard Dump Cem
Thompson A	Sgt	997	15th	30/08/18	Vaulx Hill Cem
Thompson A C	Pte	28586	15th	26/10/17	Tyne Cot Memorial Belgium
Thompson A E	Pte	76	14th	23/07/16	Thiepval Memorial
Thompson C	Pte	34113	14th	26/10/17	Tyne Cot Memorial Belgium
Thompson H	Pte	797	14th	23/07/16	Thiepval Memorial
Thompson L H	Pte	1243	15th	07/06/16	Habarcq Com
Thompson R K	Pte	263022	16th	14/10/18	Romeries Com Cem Ext
Thompson V H	Pte	311	14th	23/07/16	Thiepval Memorial
Thompson W	Pte	28446	14th	07/05/17	Nine Elms Mil Cem
Thompson W	L/Cpl	1181	15th	04/06/16	Faubourg D'Amiens
Thorn F E	Pte	14/1443	14th	26/10/17	Hooge Crater Belgium
Thorne W	Pte	96	16th	25/09/16	Thiepval Memorial
Thornton G H	Pte	50249	16th	27/04/18	Tannay British Cem
Thurston A	Pte	17522	14th	30/07/16	Thiepval Memorial
Tiernay J T F	Pte	82	14th	23/07/16	Thiepval Memorial
Tilbury W G	Cpl	30336	14th	26/10/17	Tyne Cot Memorial Belgium
Timmins H	Cpl	851	15th	29/08/16	Thiepval Memorial
Timmins H C	Pte	7281	15th	28/08/16	Delville Wood
Tinknell F C	Pte	35358	14th	14/04/18	Ploegsteert Memorial Belgium
Tipper W	L/Cpl	36564	16th	30/09/18	Grevillers Br
Todd J	Pte	238011	16th	07/10/17	Tyne Cot Memorial Belgium
Todd W	Pte	1354	16th	27/07/16	Thiepval Memorial
Tomkins F	Sgt	461	15th	08/08/16	St Sever Cem, Rouen
Toney C W	Pte	24823	15th	28/06/18	Merville Com Cem Ext
Toney J S	Pte	15/1544	14th	23/07/16	Thiepval Memorial
Tonge J T	Pte	36524	14th	28/09/18	H.A.C. Cem
Tongue C E	Pte	299	15th	04/06/16	Faubourg D'Amiens
Tongue F	Pte	14/1551	14th	23/07/16	Thiepval Memorial
Tonkin F	Pte	23266	16th	23/08/18	Adanac Mil
Tonks A	Pte	22775	15th	08/05/17	Arras Memorial
Tonks E C	Pte	462	15th	04/06/16	Arras Memorial
Tonks L A S	Pte	35930	15th	17/09/18	Vis-en-Artois Memorial
Tonks W H	L/Cpl	4072	14th	20/05/17	Etaples Mil
Toon A G	Pte	16/1470	15th	21/04/18	Le Grand Hasard Mil
Tovey P	Pte	28422	14th	27/09/18	Vis-en-Artois Memorial
Towell A C D	Pte	241067	15th	25/06/17	Nine Elms Mil Cem
Townley F L	2nd Lt		14th	26/10/17	Tyne Cot Memorial Belgium
Toye L	Pte	267389	14th	01/09/18	St Sever Cem Ext, Rouen
Tranter A	Sgt	312	14th	21/07/16	Thiepval Memorial
Tranter A S	Pte	22215	15th	06/05/17	Arras Memorial
Treadway H L	2nd Lt		15th	09/05/17	Arras Memorial
Treble W H	Pte	27734	14th	03/12/16	Brown's Rd Mil, Festubert
Treglown R C	Pte	1000	14th	23/07/16	Thiepval Memorial
Tremethick A	Pte	35932	15th	17/09/18	Gouzeaucourt New Br
Trenouth J H	Pte	33776	15th	28/06/18	Merville Com Cem Ext
Trevis A	Pte	35771	16th	27/09/18	Vis-en-Artois Memorial
Trickett A	Pte	26204	14th	28/08/18	Mory-Abbey Mil Cem
Trickett C	Pte	17534	14th	08/05/17	Arras Memorial
Trill G E	Pte	35809	16th	20/10/18	Belle Vue Br Cem
Trinder A C	Pte	18644	15th	12/04/18	Ploegsteert Memorial Belgium
Troman C G	Pte	83	14th	23/07/16	Caterpillar Valley
Troman H	Pte	17307	15th	03/09/16	Thiepval Memorial
Trowman A	Pte	999	14th	04/08/16	Thiepval Memorial
Trueman W	Pte	28450	14th	26/10/17	Hooge Crater Belgium
Truscott P I	Pte	1655	15th	05/06/16	St Pol Com Cem Ext
Tudor A E	Pte	466	16th	25/12/15	Chipilly Com
Tuffley D W	Sgt	1181	14th	21/12/18	Sutton Coldfield Cem UK
Tulley W T	Pte	260380	16th	27/09/18	Vis-en-Artois Memorial
Tunaley E H	L/Sgt	738	15th	31/07/16	Thiepval Memorial
Tuppen T	Pte	32921	16th	09/10/17	Tyne Cot Memorial Belgium
Turley D E	Pte	1459	14th	31/07/16	Ste Marie Cem, Le Harve
Turner A	Pte	203718	14th	14/04/18	Ploegsteert Memorial Belgium
Turner A L H	Pte	16/1557	14th	28/11/16	Gorre Br & Indian
Turner B	Captain		14th	08/05/17	Orchard Dump Cem
Turner G H	2nd Lt		15th	14/06/16	Le Treport Mil
Turner J P	Captain		14th	26/10/17	Tyne Cot Memorial Belgium
Turner W O	Pte	32725	15th	05/10/17	Tyne Cot Memorial Belgium
Turvey H	Pte	1674	15th	28/08/16	Delville Wood
Tustin J	L/Cpl	36116	14th	30/09/18	Grevillers Br
Tustin S A	Pte	313	14th	06/08/16	Yardley Cem B'ham
Tutty F	Pte	235153	16th	20/10/18	Viesly Com Cem
Twissell A	Pte	2067	16th	14/05/17	Orchard Dump Cem
Twittey G	Pte	14716	14th	24/01/17	Brown's Rd Mil, Festubert
Tye R S	Pte	245149	16th	02/09/18	Bailleul Rd East Cem
Tye S C	Pte	1160	16th	03/09/16	Thiepval Memorial
Tyler E	Pte	32492	14th	04/10/17	Tyne Cot Memorial Belgium
Tyrer C	2nd Lt		15th	24/07/16	Heilly Station
Tyrer E W	Pte	1126	15th	29/08/16	Thiepval Memorial
Tyson H J	Pte	48388	16th	24/09/18	St Sever Cem Ext, Rouen
Upton W T	Pte	15/1621	16th	09/10/17	Hooge Crater Belgium
Urpeth W	L/Cpl	32591	16th	23/08/18	Adanac Mil
Vallis N A J	Pte	28439	14th	28/10/17	Lijssenthoek Mil Belgium
Vaughan L	Pte	295	15th	04/06/16	Faubourg D'Amiens
Verney T	Pte	21277	14th	26/10/17	Hooge Crater Belgium
Vickerstaff E L	Pte	129	15th	28/07/16	Thiepval Memorial
Vince H L	Pte	32719	15th	04/10/17	Tyne Cot Memorial Belgium
Vince W L	Captain		14th	08/05/17	Orchard Dump Cem
Vincent E A	Pte	23724	16th	10/05/17	Arras Memorial
Vincent L	Pte	28602	16th	14/11/16	Mont Huon Mil Cem
Vint S A	Pte	94	14th	23/07/16	Thiepval Memorial
Virr S	Sgt	1144	14th	08/05/17	Orchard Dump Cem
Vivash E A	Pte	35927	15th	27/09/18	Vis-en-Artois Memorial
Voise G H	Pte	723	16th	06/10/17	Tyne Cot Memorial Belgium
Voyce W C	Pte	1170	15th	04/06/16	Faubourg D'Amiens
Waddup W	Pte	18467	14th	30/07/16	Thiepval Memorial
Wakefield O T	L/Cpl	1024	16th	27/07/16	Thiepval Memorial
Wakelin H S	Pte	719	14th	19/05/15	Yardley Cem B'ham
Wakeling M	L/Sgt	748	16th	23/08/18	Adanac Mil
Walby W	Pte	48375	16th	27/09/18	Vis-en-Artois Memorial
Waldron E J	Pte	28621	15th	26/10/17	Tyne Cot Memorial Belgium
Wales B W	L/Cpl	1025	14th	23/07/16	Thiepval Memorial
Walker A	Pte	1113	16th	27/07/16	Thiepval Memorial
Walker E A	Cpl	14/1862	14th	23/07/16	Thiepval Memorial
Walker E S	Pte	9507	14th	08/11/17	Tyne Cot Memorial Belgium
Walker H J	Pte	179	15th	04/09/16	St Pierre Cem, Amiens
Walker H W	Pte	1086	15th	23/07/16	Dantzig Alley Br
Walker J A	Pte	32773	15th	01/09/18	Bury Cem UK
Walker O J	Pte	25120	14th	14/04/18	Ploegsteert Memorial Belgium
Walker T	Pte	32586	14th	26/10/17	Tyne Cot Memorial Belgium
Walker W	Pte	36408	16th	01/09/18	Favreuil Br
Walker W S	L/Cpl	281	15th	04/06/16	Faubourg D'Amiens
Walkley V N	Pte	14/1509	14th	23/07/16	Thiepval Memorial
Wall S	Pte	33235	16th	27/09/18	Vis-en-Artois Memorial
Wallis H J	Pte	32569	14th	26/10/17	Tyne Cot Memorial Belgium
Wallis T	Pte	34415	14th	26/10/17	Tyne Cot Memorial Belgium
Walsh H F	Pte	16/1263	16th	31/01/15	Citadel New Mil
Walters G E	Pte	727	16th	03/09/16	Thiepval Memorial
Walters W	Sgt	14/1540	14th	03/09/16	Thiepval Memorial
Waltho A	Pte	23161	14th	07/05/17	Arras Memorial
Ward A C	Pte	41088	15th	27/09/18	Gouzeaucourt New Br
Ward H	Pte	16/1733	16th	06/10/17	Tyne Cot Memorial Belgium
Ward J P G	Pte	16/1925	16th	26/09/16	Thiepval Memorial
Ward W A	Pte	23495	14th	14/04/18	Ploegsteert Memorial Belgium
Warder A C	L/Cpl	240742	15th	30/10/17	Lijssenthoek Mil Belgium
Wark H	Pte	33882	16th	12/11/17	Menin Road South Belgium
Warnell W T	Pte	32652	15th	26/10/17	Tyne Cot Memorial Belgium
Warner W R	L/Cpl	749	16th	27/07/16	Thiepval Memorial
Warwood F G	Pte	727	14th	30/07/16	Thiepval Memorial
Waterhouse F	Pte	16/1906	15th	26/10/17	Tyne Cot Memorial Belgium
Waters J W	Pte	38291	16th	05/09/18	Euston Road
Watkin W B	Pte	21918	16th	09/10/17	Tyne Cot Memorial Belgium
Watkins E W	Pte	17741	14th	30/07/16	Thiepval Memorial
Watson G	Cpl	28931	14th	08/07/18	Tannay British Cem
Watson J S	L/Cpl	259	14th	23/07/16	Thiepval Memorial
Watson W	Pte	21055	14th	08/05/17	Arras Memorial
Watts G R E	Cpl	30233	14th	03/09/16	Thiepval Memorial
Watts M H	Pte	32548	14th	26/10/17	Tyne Cot Memorial Belgium
Watts T G	Sgt	20964	16th	30/07/17	Arras Memorial
Weatherall P	Pte	27446	15th	22/07/18	Thiennes British Cem
Weatherhead J	Sgt	1086	14th	23/07/16	Serre Road Cem No.2
Webb A	Pte	32965	16th	08/10/17	Tyne Cot Memorial Belgium
Webb G A	Pte	17683	14th	30/07/16	Thiepval Memorial
Webb J	Pte	20734	14th	04/06/17	Orchard Dump Cem
Webb S I	Sgt	15449	14th	03/09/16	Thiepval Memorial
Webber G L	Pte	260446	14th	27/09/18	Gouzeaucourt New Br
Webster W H	L/Cpl	657	15th	30/08/16	Thiepval Memorial
Weeks H G	Pte	18744	15th	24/09/16	Guards Cem
Welch A	Pte	9752	15th	21/04/17	Arras Memorial
Welch V C H	Pte	18742	15th	24/09/16	Guards Cem
Wells C J	Pte	33206	15th	26/10/17	Tyne Cot Memorial Belgium
Wells J T	L/Cpl	33746	14th	27/09/18	Gouzeaucourt New Br
West I	Pte	36557	16th	27/09/18	Vis-en-Artois Memorial
Weston A H	L/Cpl	34288	15th	28/08/18	Mory-Abbey Mil Cem
Westwood W A	Pte	30087	14th	27/09/18	Vis-en-Artois Memorial
Whateley W	Pte	33720	14th	27/02/18	Giavera Br, Italy
Wheeler E	Sgt	7839	14th	28/09/18	Thilloy Road Cem
Wheeler F H	Pte	1197	16th	27/07/16	Thiepval Memorial
Wheeler H	Pte	22202	16th	10/05/17	Arras Memorial
Whiley W	Pte	14/1462	14th	30/07/16	Thiepval Memorial
Whiston A W	Pte	601	15th	02/09/16	Thiepval Memorial
Whitbread B	2nd Lt		14th	23/07/16	Caterpillar Valley
Whitbrook E J	Pte	14/1635	14th	23/07/16	Thiepval Memorial
Whitcombe B	L/Cpl	785	14th	03/09/16	Thiepval Memorial
White C R	Sgt	935	15th	23/07/16	Thiepval Memorial
White C S	Pte	16/1801	16th	09/10/17	Tyne Cot Memorial Belgium
White D A P T	2nd Lt		15th	23/11/17	Etaples Mil
White F	Pte	27194	14th	23/05/18	Merville Com Cem Ext
White F	Pte	30158	15th	03/09/16	Thiepval Memorial
White H	Pte	32716	15th	05/10/17	Hooge Crater Belgium
White H J	Pte	21340	16th	16/04/17	Arras Memorial
White J R	Pte	30349	14th	01/10/17	Tyne Cot Memorial Belgium
White J W	L/Cpl	967	15th	04/06/16	Faubourg D'Amiens
White R T	Pte	34965	14th	26/10/17	Tyne Cot Memorial Belgium
White T C	Pte	1261	16th	27/07/16	Thiepval Memorial
Whitehead D	Pte	32649	15th	26/10/17	Hooge Crater Belgium
Whitehouse E	Pte	989	15th	23/07/16	Caterpillar Valley
Whitehouse J	Pte	1035	16th	27/07/16	Thiepval Memorial
Whitehouse W	Pte	665	14th	22/07/16	Heilly Station
Whitehouse W	Pte	241723	15th	13/04/18	Ploegsteert Memorial Belgium
Whiteman T	L/Cpl	15720	15th	03/09/16	Thiepval Memorial
Whittaker N E	Pte	1426	14th	26/07/16	Heilly Station
Whittet F	Pte	30337	14th	03/09/16	Thiepval Memorial
Whittingham A	Pte	243	16th	25/09/16	Thiepval Memorial
Whittle J	Pte	581	15th	09/03/16	Corbie Com Ext
Wickens A E	Pte	50409	14th	27/09/18	Vis-en-Artois Memorial
Wicks H J	Pte	16694	14th	30/07/16	Thiepval Memorial
Wilcox A	Pte	28509	16th	08/08/17	Brandwood End Cem B'ham
Wilcox C	Pte	1614	15th	26/10/16	Boisguillaume Com Cem
Wilcox D	Pte	17370	15th	09/05/17	Arras Memorial
Wilcox L C	Pte	15/1367	14th	23/07/16	Caterpillar Valley
Wileman E	Pte	16845	15th	09/05/17	Arras Memorial
Wilford G T	Pte	33943	16th	01/09/18	Favreuil Br
Wilkes C	Cpl	11791	15th	02/10/18	Grevillers Br
Wilkes C H	Pte	30089	16th	03/09/16	Thiepval Memorial
Wilkins A	Pte	3046	16th	11/05/17	Orchard Dump Cem
Wilkins A	Pte	34790	16th	11/11/17	Tyne Cot Memorial Belgium
Wilkins G S	Pte	17677	14th	03/09/16	Thiepval Memorial
Wilkins W F	Pte	16/1579	15th	04/06/16	Arras Memorial
Wilkinson F	Pte	32717	15th	04/10/17	Bedford House Enc 4
Wilkinson W E	Pte	232	16th	10/05/17	Arras Memorial
Willcock R C	Cpl	285	14th	23/07/16	Thiepval Memorial
Willday C T	Pte	1124	15th	21/07/16	Dantzig Alley Br
Willetts G	Pte	24787	14th	29/09/18	Fifteen Ravine Br
Willetts G J	Pte	43703	14th	27/09/18	Vis-en-Artois Memorial
Williams A H	Pte	17730	14th	30/07/16	Thiepval Memorial
Williams A J	Pte	1329	14th	23/07/16	Thiepval Memorial
Williams C	Pte	21264	14th	07/11/17	Tyne Cot Memorial Belgium
Williams E	L/Cpl	9219	14th	26/10/17	Tyne Cot Memorial Belgium
Williams E	Sgt	281	14th	23/07/16	Caterpillar Valley
Williams F	Pte	238012	16th	23/08/18	Gommecourt Br
Williams G W	Pte	43714	14th	27/09/18	Gouzeaucourt New Br
Williams H C	Pte	1240	14th	20/01/18	Padua Main Cem Italy
Williams I B	Pte	470	15th	23/07/16	Thiepval Memorial
Williams J	Pte	36117	14th	27/09/18	Fifteen Ravine Br
Williams J	Pte	28379	15th	09/05/17	Arras Memorial
Williams J A	Pte	19288	14th	22/10/17	Tyne Cot Memorial Belgium
Williams L F	Pte	469	15th	04/06/16	Faubourg D'Amiens
Williams T	Pte	14/1402	14th	23/07/16	Thiepval Memorial
Williams W	Pte	34131	15th	26/10/17	Tyne Cot Memorial Belgium
Williams W I	Pte	35949	15th	29/08/18	Vis-en-Artois Memorial
Williamson D	L/Cpl	33856	16th	27/09/18	Fifteen Ravine Br
Willis P W	Pte	1474	14th	29/05/18	Thiennes British Cem
Wills G	Cpl	1034	16th	27/07/16	Thiepval Memorial
Wilsdon F G	Pte	17395	14th	03/09/16	Thiepval Memorial
Wilson A E	Lieut		14th	03/12/18	Brandwood End Cem B'ham
Wilson E	Pte	32831	15th	28/10/17	Lijssenthoek Mil Belgium
Wilson T	Pte	12095	15th	05/05/17	Lillers Com Cem
Wimbush A	L/Sgt	481	16th	03/09/16	Thiepval Memorial
Wimbush S E	L/Cpl	10651	15th	30/08/16	Thiepval Memorial
Winbury A C	Pte	15/1662	14th	13/04/18	Ploegsteert Memorial Belgium
Winclip J	Pte	15956	14th	26/10/17	Tyne Cot Memorial Belgium
Windred W	Pte	17638	14th	13/04/18	Merville Com Cem Ext
Windridge A	Pte	36554	16th	27/09/18	Vis-en-Artois Memorial
Windridge H	Pte	15/288	14th	23/07/16	Caterpillar Valley
Wines J E	Pte	28369	16th	29/06/18	Tannay British Cem
Wint J W	Pte	52234	16th	03/09/18	Vaulx Hill Cem
Wiseman J E	Pte	28581	15th	27/09/18	Vis-en-Artois Memorial
Witcomb R A	Pte	1020	14th	23/07/16	Caterpillar Valley
Wood A	Pte	16918	15th	29/08/16	Thiepval Memorial
Wood A V	Pte	1305	14th	23/07/16	Thiepval Memorial
Wood G	Pte	16755	14th	08/05/17	Orchard Dump Cem
Wood G	L/Cpl	17594	15th	30/06/17	Arras Memorial
Wood G E	Pte	1524	15th	20/05/16	Faubourg D'Amiens
Wood H	Pte	16/1783	15th	09/05/17	Arras Memorial
Wood H F	Pte	16/1690	15th	29/09/18	Grevillers Br
Wood J C	Pte	36023	14th	09/07/18	Tannay British Cem
Wood L J	2nd Lt		14th	04/10/17	Tyne Cot Memorial Belgium
Wood S	Pte	30378	14th	03/09/16	Thiepval Memorial

Name	Rank	Number	Bn	Date	Cemetery/Memorial
Wood T E	Sgt	751	15th	23/07/16	Thiepval Memorial
Wood T L E	Sgt	292	15th	08/07/16	Abbeville Com
Woodall W B	Pte	35760	15th	27/09/18	Gouzeaucourt New Br
Woodcock A	Pte	32979	15th	26/10/17	Tyne Cot Memorial Belgium
Woodcock F A	Pte	286	14th	03/02/18	Brandwood End Cem B'ham
Woodings E	Pte	23288	15th	04/10/17	Tyne Cot Cem Belgium
Woods R	Pte	16964	15th	30/08/18	Mory-Abbey Mil Cem
Woods W	Pte	28357	15th	26/10/17	Menin Road South Belgium
Woodward H	L/Cpl	723	14th	06/06/17	Boldmere Churchyard UK
Wookey E	Pte	1502	14th	23/07/16	Caterpillar Valley
Wooliscroft W	Pte	33205	15th	27/09/18	Neuville-Bourjonval Br Cem
Woollaston N	Pte	16/1171	15th	07/11/17	Tyne Cot Memorial Belgium
Woolley F W	Sgt	1240	16th	27/05/18	Aire Com
Worley J	Pte	34392	16th	09/08/18	Les Baraques Mil
Worrall F	Pte	28583	15th	10/04/17	Lapugnoy Mil
Worsfold A W	Pte	35952	15th	29/06/18	Bleue-Maison Mil Cem
Worth C	Pte	28040	14th	26/10/17	Tyne Cot Memorial Belgium
Wray E	L/Cpl	487	16th	03/09/16	Thiepval Memorial
Wright A	Pte	288	14th	23/07/16	Caterpillar Valley
Wright A	Cpl	32582	14th	04/10/17	Tyne Cot Memorial Belgium
Wright E	Pte	17489	14th	03/09/16	Thiepval Memorial
Wright E J	Pte	231	16th	26/11/18	Smethwick Old Churchyard UK
Wright H	Pte	592	15th	23/04/17	Lapugnoy Mil
Wright R	Pte	188	15th	03/09/16	Thiepval Memorial
Wright R A	Sgt	15/662	14th	13/04/18	Merville Com Cem Ext
Wright S	Pte	24455	16th	24/08/18	Adanac Mil
Wright T H	Pte	35786	16th	27/09/18	Vis-en-Artois Memorial
Wright W H P	Pte	724	16th	27/07/16	Thiepval Memorial
Wyatt E L	Pte	1696	15th	03/09/16	Thiepval Memorial
Wyatt F J	Pte	14/1693	14th	23/07/16	Thiepval Memorial
Wykes A	Pte	17908	16th	23/04/17	La Chaudiere Mil
Wyness J T W	Pte	23238	14th	24/10/17	Tyne Cot Memorial Belgium
Yard W	Pte	1562	15th	06/06/16	Aubigny Com Cem Ext
Yardley E G	L/Cpl	9623	16th	25/08/17	Orchard Dump Cem
Yardley W E	Pte	28595	15th	04/10/17	Tyne Cot Memorial Belgium
Yates A B	Pte	117	15th	09/05/17	Arras Memorial
Yates F H	Cpl	116	15th	03/09/16	Thiepval Memorial
Yates P W	L/Cpl	28052	14th	23/05/18	Tannay British Cem
Yeandle H W	Cpl	664	14th	20/05/17	Arras Memorial
Young G J	Pte	32741	15th	04/10/17	Tyne Cot Memorial Belgium
Young H A	Pte	34416	14th	26/10/17	Tyne Cot Cem Belgium
Young H J	Pte	6473	15th	26/10/17	Hooge Crater Belgium
Young H L	Pte	34203	14th	26/10/17	Tyne Cot Memorial Belgium
Young R J	Pte	32988	16th	24/06/18	Aire Com
Young S	L/Cpl	114	15th	30/06/17	Orchard Dump Cem

Acknowledgements

First, I must thank my wife Yvonne and my children, Thomas, James and Louise for their support and understanding during the many long hours they spent on their own whilst I was either out doing research, sat at the computer typing or visiting France.

Over the five year period that I have been researching the Birmingham Pals, relatives of the men and various postcard collectors have allowed me to make copies of their photographs and postcards. Unfortunately, too many came to light concerning the period of training at Sutton Park and Moseley; thus, I could not use them all. In regards to this I must thank Dave Vaux, Steve Farrant and Dave Seeney for allowing me to copy their collections. The large photograph of the soldier in uniform that is depicted on the front cover is reputed to be a Private of the 3rd Birmingham Battalion; in fact his face crops up in other group photographs and I am indebted to Chris Coogan for allowing me to reproduce it.

I am also indebted to the Imperial War Museum for allowing me to spend several days at the Department of Photographs and giving me permission to publish those that I selected. For the meticulous research and collating Royal Warwickshire casualties from the newspapers of the day and for sifting through the *London Gazette* awards, I must thank Rob Williams. Which brings me to the courteous way I was always treated either by telephone or letter from the staff of the Commonwealth War Graves Commission, regarding burial places of those men that died.

Even though I visited the PRO, I used the battalion war diaries held at the Royal Regiment of Fusiliers Museum (Royal Warwickshire) at St John's House, Warwick CV4 4NF. Telephone 01926 491653. I must thank Brigadier J K Chater for allowing me access to material that helped enhance this book, especially the diary of Sergeant Arthur Cooper of the 1st Birmingham Battalion. It goes without saying that the museum attendant Mr Gordon Hutchings and his predecessor, Alf, gave me all the help possible.

Fortunately I live within a few miles of Birmingham City centre, and therefore I had the excellent facilities of the Birmingham Reference Library close at hand and I would like to thank Patrick Baird and Peter Drake and the staff of Birmingham Library Services for the help over the last few years.

Two of those who helped me have now passed away. The first was Mike Minton, he put me in the right direction with advice at the start of this project. The second was former Private Ted Francis of the 3rd Birmingham Battalion.

Over the past few years I have made several trips to the former battlefields in France and walked the ground where the Birmingham Pals served. I must thank the following for their help in getting me there and being good companions whilst there: Michael Harrison, Ray Fortey, Lol Langley, Tony and Dave Chinn.

The following list of names are relatives of former members of the battalions and those that gave me information, advice and guidance. The names are in no particular order, they are copied from my notebook. I thank you all:

David Griffiths (owner of the H V Drinkwater Diary); Dave Buxton (for his research done at the Public Record Office); John Blakemore; Steve Allen; Mrs Jacot de Boinod; Mr Mrs Bentley; Mr Jones; Peter Lawrence; 'Nocker' White (the old salty sea dog); David Bicknell; John Leatherland; Mr Hall; Ray Westlake; Bill Jinks; David Cross (Birmingham Police Museum); Fred Vickerstaff; Dennis Hurley; Les Philips; Gwyneth Pearman; Dr John Bourne (Senior Lecturer, Modern History Department, B'ham University); Dr Bob Bushaway (Director of Research Support and Industrial Liaison and an associate member of the History Department, B'ham University); Gordon Bayliss; Greg Neville; Miss F E Hopkins; Terry Norman (author: *The Hell They Called High Wood*); John Sharpe; Howard Stanley; Irene Ducker; Mr T B Wright; Mrs Abbott; Mr Gannaway; Brian Roberts; Miss Eileen Hart; Clive Hereward; Mrs C M Creswell; Colin Smith; Frank Hatwell; Mr Hastilow; Mr C A Sale; Mr F Woolley; Mrs Peggy Carter; Miss Rose Deakin; Mr Knight; Ken Birrell; Mrs Bobby Dixon; Dorothy Holder; Mrs Cope; Roni Wilkinson (Pen & Sword) and his assistant 'Hooray Henry'; Nigel Cave; Ray Frankel (this book would have been finished years ago if he had not kept dragging me off down the pub); Gordon Rea (Chairman of the Birmingham Branch of the Western Front Association) and all the other Birmingham WFA members who have give me their support and encouragement. If there is any person who I have omitted please forgive me.

Dr Carl Chinn is a very busy man, apart from being the Community Historian at Birmingham University, he is a popular broadcaster on local radio, hosting a Sunday dinner-time 'Chinn-wag' talk show on BBC Radio WM. He writes a weekly column in the *Birmingham Evening Mail* and he regularly give talks on local history at various venues around the city. Carl is an ardent champion of Birmingham and its people, and he believes that history belongs to everyone. I would like to thank Carl for the time he spared me out of his very busy schedule to look through some of my early work and also write the Foreword to this book.

Finally we must not forget the men who made this book possible, the non-manual workers of Birmingham, the Birmingham Pals. A former CO of the 1st Birmingham Battalion, Colonel G W Lewis said this after the war:

'The loss of many valuable lives is to be deplored. Their bodies lie in foreign soil; but they are not forgotten; they still live in the thoughts and hearts of their comrades, and their heroic deeds, their courage in the midst of terrible dangers, and their cheerful endurance of almost unbearable hardships will ever be remembered with pride by their fellow citizens, and will serve as an example and incentive to future generations.'

As one of those of that 'future generation' Colonel Lewis refers to in the above, it has been my privilege to record this history as a tribute to their memory.

Terry Carter
August 1997

Below: Taken sometime during the early part of 1915, a party of men from the 1st Birmingham Battalion (14th Royal Warwicks). Seen, taking a break after a session of trench digging near Westwood Coppice, Sutton Park, are several employees of the Birmingham Reference Library. *From Left to right:* Possibly William Howe (No.922, from Holliday Road, Handsworth, wounded 23 July 1916); Bernard Eckett (No.1156, discharged as unfit on account of war service, February 1917); Frederick Patrick (No.3, from Reservoir Avenue, wounded 22 July 1916); *Standing:* George Dyer (No.874, from Warren Road, Washwood Heath, wounded April 1917); *Sitting:* Henry Checketts (No.873, from Oldfield Road, Balsall Heath, killed 3 September 1916); unidentified sergeant; unidentified; Thomas Riley (No.976, killed 23 July 1916); Frank Izard (No.925, from Ashton, killed 4 October 1917); Percy Garner (No.7, died of wounds 23 July 1916). Checketts, Riley, Izard and Garner are commemorated on a Memorial Tablet that can be seen on the first floor of Birmingham City Library, Chamberlain Square.

Terence Edwin Carter

Terry Carter was born in Birmingham in 1953 and grew up in the Lea Village, Tile Cross and Chelmsley Wood areas of the city. After leaving Sheldon Heath Comprehensive in 1969 with an 'O' level education (he did not get any, he just got the education) he started an engineering apprenticeship with British Leyland at Morris Commercial, Adderley Park. He transferred to the Transmissions plant at Drews Lane in 1971. After spending eight years as a Toolsetter he changed career and moved to Alcan Plate (aluminium manufacturers), Kitts Green and become a Foundry Technician responsible for the spectrographic analysis of the many grades of aluminium that the foundry produced: 'I did not know much about aluminium, but I knew that photo copy machine inside out!' In 1994 he returned to engineering and got a job at Land Rover, Solihull, where he is now a machine operator in East Works. Terry married Yvonne in 1979 and they have three children, Thomas, James and Louise and they live in Castle Bromwich.

Terry is a member of the Western Front Association and also a member of the Birmingham branch of the WFA (monthly meetings held in Sutton Coldfield).

'I have always had an interest in local history, but my interest in the First World War started in 1971 when I bought and read The First Day On The Somme, by Martin Middlebrook. My first visit to the former battlefields was not made until October 1991. Accompanied by my brother Chris, my son Tom and chauffeured around the Somme by Ian Ward (now Councillor for Shard End), we spent a few days at Ovillers la Boisselle. Our very first stop, and my own very first visit to a Commonwealth War Graves Cemetery, occurred at London Cemetery opposite High Wood. Then, wandering down the lane a little in the direction of Longueval I stopped next to a ploughed field on my left.

'Unknown to me at the time, I was standing on Black Road and the ploughed field I was gazing over was once No Man's Land and somewhere not far off underneath the soil were probably the remains of many Birmingham Pals.

'On returning home, I picked up a book from my local library, The Hell They Called High Wood, by Terry Norman. In it, I read about the Birmingham City Battalions' attempt to take Wood Lane. At the time I had only a general interest in the First World War, but having never heard of these Birmingham Battalions (I had one grandfather in the Artillery and the other in the Ox and Bucks) I decided to learn and collect as much information about them as I could. The end result, this book.'